The War in Their Minds

The War in Their Minds

German Soldiers and Their Violent Pasts in West Germany

Svenja Goltermann

Translated by Philip Schmitz

University of Michigan Press
Ann Arbor

English translation copyright © by the University of Michigan 2017
Originally published in German as *Die Gesellschaft der Überlebenden: Deutsche Kriegsheimkehrer und ihre Gewalterfahrungen im Zweiten Weltkrieg*
By Svenja Goltermann
© 2009 by Deutsche Verlags-Anstalt, a division of Verlagsgruppe Random House GmbH, München, Germany

2020   2019   2018   2017   4   3   2   1

A CIP catalog record for this book is available from the British Library

Library of Congress Cataloging-in-Publication Data

Names: Goltermann, Svenja, author. | Schmitz, Philip (Translator), translator.
Title: The war in their minds : German soldiers and their violent pasts in West Germany / Svenja Goltermann ; translated by Philip Schmitz.
Other titles: Gesellschaft der èUberlebenden.
English Description: Ann Arbor : University of Michigan Press, 2017. | Series: Social history, popular culture, and politics in Germany | Includes bibliographical references and index.
Identifiers: LCCN 2016031014 | ISBN 9780472118977 (hardcover : alk. paper) | ISBN 9780472122516 (e-book)
Subjects: LCSH: Veterans—Germany—Psychology. | Veterans—Mental health—Germany—History—20th century. | World War, 1939–1945–Veterans–Germany. | World War, 1939–1945—Psychological aspects. | War neuroses—Germany. | Post-traumatic stress disorder—Germany.
Classification: LCC D810.V42 G4413 2017 | DDC 305.9/0697094309045--dc23
LC record available at https://lccn.loc.gov/2016031014

Geisteswissenschaften International—Translation funding for Humanities and Social Sciences from Germany. A joint initiative of the Fritz Thyssen Foundation, the German Federal Foreign Office, the collecting society VG WORT and the German Publishers & Booksellers Association.

Contents

Acknowledgments

This book has been in the making for a long time. When fifteen years ago I first started to analyze the psychiatric patient records of Wehrmacht soldiers who had returned home after the war, I found myself confronted with narratives of violence so intense that they caused me to doubt for the first weeks whether a book should and could be derived from them. That a book did finally result from my thinking about those remarkable documents and the many stories and relationships contained within and connected to them, is owed to the collegial support, the intellectual curiosity, and stimulating critique of many friends and colleagues. My thanks go in particular to Alon Confino, Ute Daniel, Ute Frevert, Christian Geulen, Michael Geyer, Neil Gregor, Ulrich Herbert, Doris Kaufmann, Robert G. Moeller, Annelie Ramsbrock, and Hans-Ulrich Wehler.

This transformation of the German original into an American book owes its success particularly to Kathleen Canning, but also to Geoff Eley, and the editorial board of the series "Social History, Popular Culture, and Politics in Germany." I am very grateful to Philipp Schmitz who has with immense care and expertise crafted a splendid translation of the German text. LeAnn Fields, Christopher Dreyer, and Mary Hashman from the University of Michigan Press have assisted the translation and production of the book with an uncommon dedication, that has earned them my thanks. My gratitude goes in equal measure to the DVA publishing house in Germany, especially to Gesche Wendebourg for her graciously agreeing to the production of a translation and her managing of all related legal matters. In Zurich, Cécile Stehrenberger, Brigitta Bernet, Lucia Herrmann, Jonathan Pärli, Bettina Zangerl, and Gesine Hübner have unfatiguingly assisted me with the review of the translation. Lastly, Peter-Tim Fritz has demonstrated equal tirelessness and great care in compiling the index. My sincere gratitude goes to them all for their work.

It would be remiss of me if I did not also thank the University of Zurich for the financial support of the translation. Finally, I owe special thanks to the people of the Geisteswissenschaften International program: Their funding may have initiated the translation of the German book into English, but it was their patience and flexibility that finally allowed the project to come to fruition.

Introduction

When in the spring of 1949 Hans H. proceeded to recount aspects of his life until then, he had experienced months—actually a few years—of grueling inner distress.[1] But over recent days everything had become more extreme. For several nights running he could not sleep. He was thirty-eight years old, and his life seemed ruined.

He had once been very successful, an ambitious young man. Future achievements had already been clear in secondary school, although he left before the final year. Serving with the police was more attractive to him. And this would actually result in a career. Hans H. described its individual stations in a brief, handwritten CV. His look backward was frank, almost mundane. He was promoted to police sergeant in 1932. After the dissolution of the *Landespolizei* and the introduction of universal military service in 1935, he was accepted into the air force as a noncommissioned officer. His reference to a further promotion to staff sergeant the following year was similarly brief—the period involved was clearly of minor importance to him—for Hans H. was looking for new, different challenges, and had found them.

The Spanish Civil War offered the first opportunity. He immediately volunteered for and entered the Condor Legion, and fought in Spain for two years. Even ten years later, Hans H. was openly proud of having been allowed to serve on General von Richthofen's staff. But his actual career leap took place following his return. "Because new police troop units had been established in the meantime," he was "offered the possibility of becoming a police officer with the prospect of promotion"—that is how he explained it. Hans H. seized the offered opportunity. (He noted in passing that when he returned from Spain he was convinced "that the police were more important and that the Wehrmacht represented a danger to the *Volk*.") In any case, in November 1939 he requested a discharge from the Wehrmacht in order to join the *Schutzpolizei*. His initiative would pay off. As early as eight months later, Hans H. could not only celebrate his promotion to police lieutenant but also take advantage of good exam results. Having meanwhile risen to the rank of an SS second lieutenant (*Untersturmführer*) and moved up into the SS's officer corps, he was "immediately" made a member of the "instructional staff," henceforth serving as an officer for instruction and training at various police officer schools. By January 1942, this appears to have no longer sufficed. What now attracted Hans H. especially was clearly the war, and in particular direct action on the front, for which he volunteered. He went to southern Russia as a platoon leader in a reserve police battalion.

Hans H.'s reports about the following years until the end of the war were also not extensive. Primarily, he summarized his honors: being named a first lieutenant in the police and company chief in a police regiment in February 1942; his nearly simultaneous promotion to SS first lieutenant (*Obersturmführer*); and a range of war-related distinctions. Thus, everything leaves a well-ordered impression, with only a mention of having consumed a great deal of alcohol during the war sounding a somewhat jarring note. But beyond that, Hans H. offered no details—at least concerning the war itself—just as he only recounted one experience in detail, namely, an injury from a grenade fragment, in January 1944. This was the only event he mentioned that gave any indication of the war's destructive force. The incident put an abrupt end to his participation. Hans H. was taken to a military hospital and was only able to leave months later. Four years after the end of the war, the pain was still nearly unbearable and takes up a relatively large amount of space in his narrative. It even led to "attacks of raving madness," with large quantities of morphine only offering temporary relief. At several points, he had actually entertained "thoughts of suicide." The injury to his left leg had indeed been substantial, and after two months the doctors saw no alternative but to amputate.

Hans H. used a prosthesis thereafter. But he didn't complain about this, at least not loudly. In his CV, he instead pointed to maintaining both his professional status and social situation after the injury. Late in the summer of 1944, his wife became pregnant for the first time, and in December 1944 his career further advanced through his appointment as an SS captain (*Hauptsturmführer*). "Based on exceptional conduct in the face of the enemy," as it was put at the time, he was then promoted to police captain and transferred to the *Schutzpolizei* in Dresden. This was a highly responsible position. But the period he had to fulfill his duties was limited—only a few months later, the German Reich surrendered. A few weeks beforehand, Hans H. found himself once again in a military hospital, this time in Bavaria. As he explained it, he was placed there just in time "to escape being taken prisoner by Soviet troops, which would have meant a certain death."

Hans H. was therefore a lucky man. The American occupation authorities not only did not make him a POW but even approved his release to the British zone, which he entered "without interference." Nevertheless, his account makes clear that he then went through difficult times. He felt burdened and restless. He put it as follows to his doctor, whom he first visited four years after the war: he was in a state of "morbid tension" and felt "responsible for all of Germany's plight." In addition, he was tormented by the thought of incriminating himself again "through passivity." He himself had "remained silent as an SS man," but "he did not wish to be silent any longer." He added that people should "no longer cry." Indeed, "Everyone should laugh and be happy."

If we follow Hans H.'s narrative, by the spring of 1949 he was firmly convinced he had long stopped having any reason to be happy. He had suffered—more specifically since traveling to the British zone, where he had, in fact, been promptly arrested and placed in an internment camp for Nazi functionaries and suspected war criminals. He remained incarcerated there for five months and was, as he explained, "much tormented" during "many nighttime interrogations." Ultimately, he was "released as an amputee"—albeit with "a file entry that he was not to resume any kind of activity" or he would be handed over to the "Russians" because of "his SS involvement in Russia." As a result, although he was now a free man, he was unable to regain his footing and was going through hard times. He had to struggle in his career, his marriage, and the denazification procedure. Particularly his marriage of just under six years came under significant stress. Here Hans H. even spoke of ever-deepening "hate." Apparently his wife "constantly harped on his situation," repeating, for example, "that he wasn't an officer anymore and should go out and make some money, etc." He had been trying to resume his career with the police force for four years, and had been rejected everywhere. All that remained was a job as a night watchman, but that had been temporary. Consequently, things were tough financially. His last job had paid so little that he could hardly take care of "the bare necessities" a family needed. And for some weeks now he had again been completely without an income. In Hans H.'s view, there was only one hope left. He clung to the idea of somehow or other returning to police service. He tied this to a higher mission: in the end, he explained, he wanted to help "build the kind of police force that would allow us to be forearmed against the East— once the occupation powers have withdrawn—where the Wehrmacht is being rebuilt in the guise of the police." Here, Hans H. clearly faced one problem: his return to police service was fundamentally tied to his denazification proceedings. When he entered the psychiatric clinic, these proceeding were still ongoing. But as the former SS captain explained to his doctor after only a few days of treatment, he had been willing to fight. He had taken it up to the "highest denazification court," "pushed through" his case, and presented evidence "that he had not entered the SS voluntarily." Shortly afterward, it turned out that Hans H. had convinced the court. He had received "exoneration by the denazification court." As the doctor reports, his mood was now transformed. There was a "colossal upswing," with the doctor noting further that "not the slightest psychiatric abnormality" could be observed. The psychiatrist came to this conclusion after learning from Hans H. that he had not only been offered a new job but had received a request "to submit a new application to the police authorities." Hans H. applied immediately and was already able to resume his police work the following month. From now on, he felt "fully able to bear stress," which indeed seemed the case from a medical perspective. For Hans H., who gave outsiders the impression of being "full of drive and joyful initiative," the war and its crimes seemed to have left no further traces.

· · ·

When World War II ended in Europe in the spring of 1945, people in this "destroyed continent" surveyed the results of an escalation of violence and annihilation that the Nazi regime had endowed with unique dimensions.[2] Roughly fifty million human beings had been killed in a war the German side had unleashed in September 1939. More than half of them had been civilians.[3] The figure was twenty-five million for the Soviet Union alone. In Poland, the number of deaths was around six million, circa three million of them constituting more than half of Europe's murdered Jews. In Eastern Europe, the Germans had conducted a barbaric war of extermination. The crimes committed primarily there but also elsewhere in Europe, mostly against Jews, were historically unparalleled in this form.[4]

The way people dealt after 1945 with this massive violence and the memory of the crimes is a question that is no longer discussed solely with regard to German society.[5] But as the debate in Germany on "a politics of the past" (*Vergangenheitspolitik*) has shown, Germans continue to find themselves in an especially precarious situation when they speak of their own victims and the suffering they themselves endured. Recently, this has repeatedly become clear when Germans cast their eye on the Allied bombing campaign, on the flight and expulsion of ethnic Germans from the east, and on German prisoners of war returning from the Soviet Union.[6] There is considerable—often justified[7]—suspicion that in taking up these subjects the Germans are promoting a form of self-victimization that relativizes Nazi crimes and even relegates them to the background.[8] One of the more outspoken forms this criticism has taken is the argument that German society is in danger of promoting a "rhetoric of victimization," an intensely selective memory of the war—one from which the victims of Nazism are effectively excluded. According to this critique, this process that can already be observed in the years immediately after the war and well into the 1960s.[9]

As it happens, not much would seem to speak in favor of approaching the recent focus on Germany's own victims as the breaking of some postwar taboo. Even in postwar German public memory, stress was placed on German victimhood. The way this was done took different ideological forms in East and West and bore the imprint of the Cold War.[10] For example, in the countless East German ceremonies held in memory of the bombing of Dresden and its civilian victims, "Western imperialists" were held responsible.[11] Conversely, there was a noticeable tendency in West Germany to hold the "Soviet terror" mainly responsible for the suffering of refugees and expellees from the east, as well as that of German veterans returning from the Soviet camps.[12] Finally, on both sides there were official pronouncements describing German civilians and soldiers as victims of Hitler and his "criminal" elite, who had begun a destructive war that was then lost "by everyone."[13] As early as 1946, we find East Germany's party leadership offering returned veterans the opportunity to demonstrate their inner resistance to that criminal war by embracing the new regime.[14] In the course of forming alliances in the West, the highest Allied representatives offered West German returnees similar bridges.[15]

These political efforts to create "new citizens"[16] clearly demonstrate the kind of memory of the Nazi war and its mass murder that was considered politically useful and socially necessary. But this obscures the question of whether and to which extent personal suffering resulting from the war was publically perceived and acknowledged. The ways in which the horrors of war and the Holocaust were present in highly personal memories and private imagination during Germany's postwar years also remains unclear. At least in the outwardly accessible history of postwar West German society, a reflex-like "normalization" of life circumstances emerges. For a long time, many Germans and historians were thus left with the impression that society had actually not been enduringly shaken by the war, and that the violent deeds and crimes on the German side had been eradicated from individual memory. Among other things, the prompt demand for entertainment and amusement seemed to speak for this, as did the great speed with which society drove forward reconstruction and increased prosperity.[17] In any event, if we extend our view to other Western European countries, the same phenomenon is evident there as well. In Italy,

France, and England, too, the rubble had hardly been pushed aside before droves of people started lining up at movie houses. Driven by what was truly a "wave of hope and enthusiasm for reconstruction," material damage in these countries as well was put aside with a speed that remains astonishing.[18] Nevertheless, despite these ubiquitous efforts to resume "normal" everyday life, recent historiography broadly assumes that in all the societies that had been caught up in the war, its extreme violence and the Nazi horror left abiding immaterial rubble—damage that endured beyond reconstruction.[19]

This assumption is also the starting point for the present book, with its focus on former Wehrmacht soldiers in postwar West German society. Their experience of the war had in no sense been consistent, and the severity and length of imprisonment endured by former German POWs also varied widely.[20] At the end of 1945 and the start of 1946, the number of POWs stood at roughly two million. After Germany surrendered, it jumped to around eleven million, more than two-thirds of whom were prisoners of the Western powers, while the remainder was held in the east, mainly by the Soviets. By the start of 1947, however, most of the POWs in the Western prison camps had been released, with most of the approximately two million remaining soldiers in both East and West returning to civilian life by the end of 1949. Around thirty thousand war prisoners remained in the Soviet Union, the last of whom would be released in 1956.[21]

As will be explained in the following chapters, the "normal" lives of a great many such returnees was more precarious than the prevalent impression of postwar West German society would suggest.[22] After the intensification of extreme violence in the 1940s, there was indeed talk of a "shock of events" that rendered people incapable of "seriously concerning themselves with war and death."[23] Nevertheless, what one would probably have to say is that the "normality" of West German society was precisely *not* characterized by a successful "repression" of the recent war or genocide. Rather—this is my first basic argument—both death and the dead were repeatedly present in the mental worlds and personal memories of a substantial portion of this postwar society. Its striving for reconstruction and renewed social security was permeated by deep-seated horror and tormented nightmares, contradicting the oft-confirmed sobriety of West Germany in the postwar period.

Little is known so far about this hidden underside of the "normalization" on the surface and a purportedly unscathed return to middle-class life. Yet this holds true for all the postwar societies after 1945.[24] It seems that for years, the question of how the violence of war permeated personal lives could hardly be asked, even after the war had ended. It will become clear that this was no coincidence. In relevant historiography, it is only recently, although with increasing frequency, that assertions have begun to circulate that these societies were traumatized after 1945, an assumption increasingly also made with respect to the returning soldiers.[25] But that assumption suggests knowledge about the significance of war, violence, and death for this war generation's behavior, and about the ways such experiences were individually processed, without specifically demonstrating the causal relationship between them. In actuality, the present presumption that those who participated in the war were traumatized is itself the product of a phenomenon that would first require an explanation. More precisely, the emergence of the trauma concept in scientific discourse and its establishment in society call for their own historicization, which is the second basic task of the present book.[26]

Work by historians of science has meanwhile offered sufficient support to this position. In different ways, a number of studies on the formation, transformation, and disappearance of psychiatric diagnoses have confirmed that such specialized interpretive models have their historical locus.[27] After World War II, mental trauma was an extremely marginal interpretive category in Europe, while over the course of the past two decades it has become a key concept throughout the so-called Western world.[28] But in the concept's nothing less than inflationary current usage, its historicity is hardly present—nor has it ever been, throughout its steadily progressing career. If we follow the psychiatrist Richard McNally, this blind spot reflects the presence of a widely ramified and decidedly multilayered "trauma industry."[29] Developed in the "laboratories" of Western industrial nations, it has been reaping steadily growing earnings since the 1980s.[30] It is also conceivable that in the case of human behavior, the natural sciences are accorded the sort of unlimited interpretive competence simply no longer enjoyed by the social sciences or humanities. The recent frequent recourse in historical memory studies to neuroscientific findings speaks for this possibility.[31] But when prevailing medical-scientific categories are transferred back to historical phenomena, we are not far removed from a concept of seamless progress.[32] This concept seems to be at play, for instance, when the American Psychiatric Association's official recognition of the diagnosis of post-traumatic stress disorder (PTSD) (developed in the wake of the Vietnam War) is taken as sufficient proof for the correctness of one's own historical argument.[33] Here, ideas about the reality of horror, violence, and brutality are generated as if they were already known quantities. This also applies to the impact of the events on the subsequent lives of those involved, which one purportedly already knows.[34]

These objections are not meant to diminish the historiographical importance of research on trauma. Through an acknowledgment of the concept of trauma, whether in its psychoanalytic or neurobiological variant, new paths have been opened to contemplating the effects of violence. In this respect, the more recent studies of postwar West German society can be understood as part of a more general tendency to question the decades-long assumption that many European countries regained their "normality" without much upheaval. In the process, attention has been focused for the first time on the possibility that the experience of violence has an enduring presence in the private lives of those who experienced it.[35] All told, in recent years we can observe an ever-greater awareness of an increasing number of violent and catastrophic historical phenomena, which have been subjected to historical study.[36] This development doubtless can be traced to a whole range of factors that cannot be treated here in detail. Still, a strong argument can be made that the category of trauma has become an important, key steering element for our historical imaginations—one that has altered our perception of the past and its long-term consequences for the lives of individuals and, specifically, their suffering.

Their various positive effects notwithstanding, there is still good reason to turn away from conceptions of trauma as a descriptive and analytic instrument applied to historical events and processes. "Retrospective historical diagnoses of PTSD constitute a psychiatric version of the Whig interpretation of history," argues Richard McNally, who urgently appeals for approaching the persons concerned in terms of their perception and interpretation of the events, not our own, if we wish to understand how they really reacted to them.[37] Based on her observations in Russia, historian Catherine Merridale argues similarly. Among most practicing Russian doctors and in broad segments of the general population, she identifies a continued distaste for assuming psychological disturbances resulting from the experience of mass death. At one point, she states: "They cannot picture it, this trauma, and they do not understand its privileged place in the Western understanding of violence and its consequences." In part, this resistance certainly results from mental illness continuing to be a taboo in Russia. But Merridale suspects another reason: "It is also possible that this particular diagnosis and its treatment are so alien to the Russian way of thinking about life, death, and individual need that notions of psychological trauma are genuinely irrelevant to Russian minds."[38]

Two observations by philosopher of science Ian Hacking may be helpful in this context. Psychiatry, Hacking explains, is not only a decidedly historical science but also a "science of memory."[39] It is characteristic for psychiatry to provide historically varying concepts of memory—also through the diagnoses of trauma and a range of terminological conventions pertaining to memory. At the same time, he argues that individuals capable of interpreting their behavior in a different way than before also develop a new awareness of themselves, see themselves in a different way, and even feel different as persons.[40] And this is precisely the reason the trauma concept, in its transmission of specific ideas of how memory functions and especially of the way it processes pain and harrowing events, is a problematic analytical instrument for historians.[41] To cite Allan Young: "Our sense of being a person is shaped not simply by our active memories . . . it is also a product of our conceptions of 'memory.'"[42]

Likewise appealing for a historicization of the view psychiatry takes of the mental processing of war and related horrors, this book takes a similar approach. In this respect, it will become clear that treating the production of psychiatric knowledge in postwar Germany as a simple extension of wartime psychiatric practice, one that sometimes seems very strange from our present perspective, is inadequate. Rather, we will see that this form of production was actually highly respected internationally as a basis for both diagnostic evaluation and therapeutic practice; and furthermore, that demands made by a private and public culture of memory played a role in the knowledge-production process. But above all—and this is my starting assumption—the process itself exerted great influence as the vehicle for interpretive models that defined both the private framework for processing experience and, in the public realm, the ways the results of the war were perceived and the rules for articulating the experience of suffering.

To this sense, the history of postwar German experience, together with that of the memory of the war, cannot be adequately understood without a history of the way psychiatry processed extreme experiences, which is my second central argument. We will therefore show how West Germany's intellectual horizon regarding the mental consequences of the war changed fundamentally in the two decades after it ended, in a way closely connected to prevailing psychiatric knowledge.[43] Here, the spectrum of scientifically and publicly recognized aftereffects of the war altered ways in which the war was spoken about. Although the fault lines between public and private memory shifted, they never fully dissolved.

The book will clarify this process in three steps. An opening part will focus on the degree and the ways in which a criminal war and the mass killings were a presence in the memories and personal milieu of former Wehrmacht soldiers. A second part will examine the manner in which psychiatry (and to an extent other medical disciplines) interpreted and tried to therapeutically treat the behavior of returned soldiers who were considered, for example, by close relations, to be noticeably or even alarmingly changed and in some cases actually mentally ill. The initial assumption of that period's psychiatric doctrine was something like unlimited human resilience. We will need to consider the conditions under which this position evolved to the point where psychiatry was willing to view enduring and even late-developing mental suffering as the result of extreme violence. In a third part, public memory will be analyzed in terms of the ways psychiatric explanatory models penetrated public narrative approaches to the effects of the war and—with special attention to the media— helped shape public perception of who should be recognized and acknowledged as a victim. The core period we examine extends from 1945 to 1970. We will therefore begin at a time when total military defeat and the collapse of the existing political system were unmistakably imminent. And we will finish at a time when an altered, differentiated perception view of the consequences of war and persecution had taken hold across a broad swath of the German public. During the two following decades, in West Germany at least, nothing would shake the widely held assumption that Nazi persecution had long-lasting psychological effects, while no such effects were associated with the experience of war itself.[44]

Specifically, the first part will explore the question of the manner in which the war and Nazi past were actually present in the personal memory of returned soldiers and thereby left their mark on the life of postwar society. In view of the many recent studies examining the impact of the Nazi crimes and wartime atrocities on German postwar society, such a focus requires a more detailed explanation. As already indicated, these studies are mainly concerned with the public construction of memory: they analyze discourses in the media, the symbolic politics of memory, and public memorial ceremonies and events. They all lay emphasis on Germany's highly selective memory of the war, which is to say, the predominance of narratives focusing on one's own suffering and victims.[45] In doing so, they corrected a picture that dominated historiography for a long time, namely, one of a nearly total suppression of the war. There can be no doubt that the lasting influence of Mitscherlich's theory of "the inability to mourn" can be seen here.[46] Ultimately, however, the studies themselves shared the view that the crimes committed by Germans from the beginning of the war played no significant role in memory, either personal or public.

There is undeniably much evidence supporting that impression. Even contemporary observers, mostly from abroad, confirmed a marked tendency among Germans to deny any responsibility for the mass exterminations, just as they seemed to have quickly forgotten the cause of their postwar hardship.[47] The denazification proceedings, during which outright competition in opportunism, denial, and refusal to recognize the truth erupted,[48] continue to this day to reinforce that suspicion and nourish the argument that in the slipstream of "self-victimization," Germans felt themselves free from the burden of remembering the past. This interpretation—in the meantime it has become nothing less than a kind of "national master narrative" for German history after 1945[49]—may be accurate in many cases. But as we suggested, drawing inferences from public to personal memory clearly falls short.[50] For a long time now, in fact, memory studies have been preoccupied with the problem of how the far more complex genesis and mutability of memory—and this on all levels—can be grasped.[51] For example, research on both narrative and memory emphasizes the importance of a group-centered "communicative memory" emerging between public memory culture and personal memory, say, in the realm of families and associations.[52] In this way, coexisting and diverging interpretations of the past, which lay claim to different discursive spaces, already have become recognizable in rudimentary form. At the same time, political parameters, moral imperatives, and even types of institutional logic have emerged as historically variable formative factors. These exerted stronger influence on the formation and possibilities for articulation of personal memory than the discourse of victimization described by historians would suggest.[53]

As a rule, accounts of putatively "purely personal" memory are available only in the form of family and veterans' narratives, mostly conveyed during interviews starting in the 1980s.[54] What could be repeatedly observed in these interviews was that "public" and "private" memory, official historical narratives and subjective interpretations, showed themselves to be closely interwoven. But at the same time, contradictory interpretations and divergences in the stories sometimes became evident. These indicated the presence, behind the accepted narrative conventions, of other personal memories of horrors associated with the war. Hence these forms of dealing with private war memories do not necessarily reflect the character of the personal memories in the postwar period. Likewise, they offer little insight into the way individuals during the immediate postwar period dealt with personal knowledge of crimes committed during the war. In this respect, it is precisely those first years following the total defeat that remain largely in the dark, just as most of the studies of postwar society focus on the 1950s and 1960s.[55]

Consequently, the following discussion will initially center on narrative transmissions of personal "memory fragments"[56] from the immediate postwar phase, and therefore on the past in the form it existed in the mind of returned German soldiers at that time. These narratives have been retained in a body of roughly 450 psychiatric records of men born between 1897 and 1929.[57] In terms of age, social origins and education, military rank, and length of service, the records cover a relatively broad spectrum of veterans. By no means had they returned only from the eastern front or Soviet POW camps; among former POWS who returned during the first years after the war, many had been deployed exclusively in the west. The majority of them had fought on both fronts. Both the course and the characteristics of the psychological changes that surfaced after returning from the war or interment varied widely. Importantly, the medical files offer no grounds for assuming that grave mental problems were evident only among those who had been in the Soviet camps. Rather, we gain the impression that a distinction needs to be made between returnees from the 1940s and those from the 1950s, with inner torment emerging far more openly in the former group. Some of them sought psychiatric counseling for their suffering of their own accord. Often, a man would be pressed into seeking help by close family members after they noticed marked changes. But usually it was a family doctor who referred them to a psychiatrist after reaching the limits of his own therapeutic or diagnostic abilities. In this respect, we have many indications—not least of all those offered by the psychiatric records themselves—that within the larger population of returnees treated by a doctor, those who saw psychiatrists represented only the tip of the iceberg.[58] The records, in any event, represent a previously barely tapped repository of the personal memories and confessions[59] of people who had considerable doubt whether they could be expressed in public. This applied to their private, family spheres as well.

For methodological reasons, it is best to limit a study of these memory fragments to the 1945–1949/50 period. For in a German society marked by general collapse, other rules concerning what could be said prevailed after the right to pension claims had been established. From that point onward applicants for war pensions pursued very specific goals in offering their accounts. The narratives about the war, and about the severity of the Soviet camps in particular, now followed entirely different patterns. This is especially noticeable in the practice of expert assessment, which played an increasingly large role after 1950.

But even in the medical records from the immediate postwar period, it is mostly mere fragments that revolve around the war. Since neither the doctors nor the bulk of the patients drew a causal connection between unusual behavior and the war, the war was not the focal point of their conversations. For this reason, it does not seem that the veterans being treated were particularly sensitive to the wartime events. Rather, the memory fragments emerging from these files appear to reveal a more widespread mental state palpable in each of the individual cases. One might say that the psychiatric files expose something like the interior side of an often painful and confusing legacy of the war. Beyond the individual medical history, they allow us to make statements about the deeper layers of memory, for instance, in the medium of dreams; about profound forms of disorientation and destroyed self-images; about the anxiety connected with a new beginning; and the alleged emotional "normalization" during the early years of Germany's economic miracle. Here, patterns for remembering the war can be identified in articulations of anxiety, disillusionment, and in coming to terms with oneself through an alter ego. Even when expressed only occasionally, their dreams, delusions, and hallucinations can claim the status of historical source material by virtue of being a component of perceived violence.

The cases we will consider in the following chapters will not be described and analyzed as if they were self-contained. The former soldiers' often erratic discourse—for example, frequent abrupt shifts of theme, followed by venting isolated thoughts related to the past as they were then perceiving it—would not allow such an approach. Nevertheless, a group of cases appear repeatedly in the first part and in relevant chapters of the second part of the book. In this manner, different aspects of each individual's personality will come to light.

Because of the specific nature of the source material, this analysis of memory fragments cannot claim to offer a direct view of wartime experiences. Rather, my intention is to provide insight into personal ways of processing the war. For this reason, the first part of the book should not be understood as a contribution to a history of the war but to the history of the way the horrors were imagined in postwar Germany. For memories are "constantly reconstructed in the present and under its specific conditions," even if, from this perspective as well, they can never be entirely separated from the past.[60] If we follow Reinhart Koselleck, this "present past, whose events have been incorporated and can be remembered" is also a central component of "experience"—in this case, the history of the German postwar experience.[61] This book will track that history. It tells of the way soldiers continued to lead their lives despite the mass exterminations, killing, and their knowledge of horrific crimes, but it also describes how they reacted to the defeat, to the complete discrediting of the previous political system, and often to the social degradation they experienced.

In general, families are considered to have been the place where personal experiences of war and life as a POW were worked through.[62] For this reason, my interest is also centered on the impact of the war on family life and on the inner tensions and burdens affecting family relations—not only between men and women but also between the generations. Here, forms of mutual perception and communication need to be examined closely in order to probe the possibilities and limits of what could be expressed in families when the emotional legacy of the war's violence and mass crimes was at stake. To what extent were the relatives of returned soldiers at all aware of such experiences? When did the former soldiers' behavior begin to seem strange and "abnormal"? How did the relatives interpret the behavior and torment they observed in the veterans? Irrespective of whether they showed understanding or not, many of the relatives stood helpless in front of these men and were often driven to seek professional advice.

In the second part of the book, the perspective shifts to psychiatry and focuses on prevailing postwar German psychiatric doctrine concerning the ability of the psyche to process intense stress, as well as on the origins and establishment of new psychiatric knowledge in this realm given the altered political conditions and moral challenges. Even in World War I, the state put psychiatry in charge of finding explanations for the origins of mental suffering in soldiers and developing ways to gain control of what was then the grave problem of "war neuroses." Psychiatrists viewed this as one of their basic tasks in World War II as well.[63] From the perspective of the psychiatric field, there existed a comprehensive body of knowledge about "human nature" and what psychiatry considered "normal" in terms of processing instances of extreme conditions. In the eyes of psychiatrists, it had stood the test of time. After the war veterans' entitlement to benefits was legally codified in West Germany in 1950, examining the causes for mentally related ailments of applicants continued to be reserved for psychiatrists. The core decision they were meant to reach was whether the suffering presented was to be recognized as related to the war.[64]

Until now, the manner in which postwar psychiatry interpreted supposed mental abnormalities and emotionally caused illness has been a topic largely unknown to historians. As a rule, historical studies of German psychiatric theory and practice ended with 1945.[65] Their significance for Nazi racial and population policies no doubt account for the continuing interest they generate.[66] As a result, our view of German psychiatry since the end of the war rests on a very small group of studies that originated primarily from a reparations context and revolved around the procedures for validating damage to mental health in victims of Nazi persecution. As those studies underscored, during the 1950s German psychiatrists declined to recognize mental suffering as the result of such persecution, because according to mainstream theory in the field the human ability to endure stress was nearly infinite. If we follow Christian Pross's influential thesis, the doctors and authorities engaged in nothing less than a "running battle with the victims" within the framework of the evaluation proceedings. In the meantime, however, occasional doubts have been raised about the sweeping nature of this claim.[67] Yet the studies agree in their interpretive thrust: generally, they recognize German psychiatric evaluation practice as essentially no more than a reflection of the profession's inadequate denazification, both culturally and in terms of personnel, and as a basic model for West Germany's "politics of the past."[68] In this regard, they underscore primarily two things: first, the relatively strong focus of the German psychiatrists on POWs who had returned from the Soviet Union, which is to say, on Germans as victims; and second, the fact that in other countries medical concern with the mental suffering of survivors began much earlier than in West Germany, where, the argument goes, doctors were still speaking in terms of hereditary illnesses, acknowledging only far later than their colleagues abroad the specific health damage caused by Nazi persecution.[69]

Nevertheless, a look at the actual situation in other countries does not necessarily support this assessment. Rather, there is considerable evidence that for the first decade and a half after the end of the war, in Western Europe, America, and Israel there was little public awareness of mental suffering by Holocaust victims.[70] To the extent we have sufficient information to judge, the disciplines of psychiatry (and psychoanalysis) as practiced there at the time create the same impression.[71] They, too, did not proceed on the assumption that the cause of long-term emotional abnormalities in veterans was to be found in the war.[72] Here again, the parallels with the position that took hold in German psychiatry starting in the wake of World War I is unmistakable.[73]

Against this backdrop, it seems inadequate to interpret psychiatric practice in Germany—which established a causal connection between lasting emotional change neither with the battlefront nor with Nazi persecution—as a reflection of the doctors' activities during the Nazi period alone, and their forms of assessment and treatment as a relic of that period. Granted, the continuity of personnel within the medical community beyond the political hiatus of 1945 is undeniable.[74] But we also need to recognize that the psychiatrists in question had either already been active during the period of World War I or had been trained in the 1920s. That is not a peripheral fact. The years of that earlier war marked the time when psychiatry developed the conviction that war itself did not represent the real cause of enduring mental suffering. It was the state of psychiatric knowledge that was prevalent at the time not only in Germany but throughout Europe.

The following chapters will therefore analyze German psychiatry during the "extended" postwar period as a field of knowledge with ties both to the psychiatric doctrine dominant in Germany since World War I and—to the degree possible—to international developments in the field. The shift here in interpretive models will not be understood as the result of an inevitable advance in medical-scientific reasoning. Rather, according to a new direction in the historiography of science, I will view these developments as the product of a dense network of interlinking forces, including professional logic and professional challenges, external definitions of problems, and political preconditions. Here as in general, scientific facts are generated within a force field where institutional interests, political demands, legal decisions, and moral considerations all have a decisive influence on which findings are finally recognized as valid knowledge.[75]

Naturally, exploring the professional psychiatric literature is not in itself enough to understand the shift in conceptual instruments and explanatory claims that led in the 1960s to a new way of seeing mental change in survivors of Nazi persecution as a result of experiencing excessive violence. For this reason, I will include the practice of medicine in my examination as well as strategies of professional legitimation against other, sometimes competing demands. In this respect, it was above all West Germany's general practitioners and internists, and the country's judicial and administrative systems (including the ministerial bureaucracy), that must be taken into consideration. We will consider the testing of psychiatric assumptions about "normal" human functioning, but also the aporias with which psychiatric experts saw themselves confronted in trying out their diagnostic instruments. As a first step, we will initially need to examine the challenges that the observable behavioral abnormalities and mental suffering of the returned veterans posed for these experts, in terms of both their research and their everyday activities as doctors. We will see that in practical terms psychiatric medical evaluations had to take provisional recourse to new diagnostic approaches in order to understand problems, which, contrary to expectations, did not promptly resolve in returnees from the Soviet camps. And we will need to consider the manner in which psychiatrists with their analyses and concepts often channeled, as it were, the way returnees and their families perceived their suffering. In other cases, the returnees insisted on a form of "knowledge" that contradicted the standard assumption of a "hereditary predisposition" being the cause of their mental problems. Here, the former soldiers were at the same time trying to prevent their entitlement to benefits, which had been filed based on alleged damage from the war, from being viewed as suspect as a matter of principle. Precisely in this framework it will become clear that in their diagnostic activities the psychiatric experts were to large extent participating in the production of a social reality that expressed itself in the recognition or denial of war-casualty status.[76]

We will, however, also need to explore the limits of psychiatry's definitional power—limits that emerge more clearly in the second half of the book's second main part. Here, I will describe the difficulties West German psychiatry faced in its need to evaluate the victims of Nazis persecution and their reparation claims, and will devote special attention to the "nonmedical" parties involved in the process: mainly lawyers, but also officials active in the ministries involved with West German reparations. These authorities were in a position to intervene in the evolving internal psychiatric controversy over a new understanding of the long-term mental effects of extreme violence through Nazi persecution. With their ideas concerning procedural technique and the legal system, these authorities had their own considerable impact on the transformation of psychiatric knowledge. To be specific, the professional validity of an expert psychiatric diagnosis was dependent on two different legal systems; within the care of war casualties on the one hand and the compensation rules for victims of Nazism on the other, these either privileged or excluded specific interpretations conveyed by professional psychiatric discourse on both juridical and political-moral grounds.

In this manner, the production of psychiatric knowledge in postwar West Germany was a historically complex process within which one ultimately had to come to terms with the accusation of Nazi infiltration and establish one's own claims to scientific validity within the framework of the international psychiatric community. For its part, the international professional community was involved in the federal German effort to clarify the mental consequences of Nazi persecution through so-called independent overseas physicians. The content, form, and social reach of psychiatric knowledge must therefore be defined as elements of complex power structures and negotiation processes.[77] It is only the interplay of these elements over time that allows us to explain the shift of professional discourse—and, in the public realm, the shift of ideational worlds and patterns of perception—regarding the effects of the war and persecution.

The third part of the book changes perspective again, turning now to the question of the public culture of memory regarding the Nazi war of extermination.[78] In this context, there has been highly insightful historical research on the role played in formulating a "politics of the past" by a wide range of political contexts, such as denazification, the amnesty movement, and the political rehabilitation of professional soldiers.[79] Historians have thus carefully worked out the strenuous efforts to obfuscate the biographical and institutional continuities with the Nazi *Volksgemeinschaft*, in order to gain a second chance in the new polity. But as suggested, this public effort to sever the ties to an often criminal or incriminating past cannot be interpreted as final proof that the return to what was perceived as normal middle-class life was enough to instill calm in, as it were, the internal management of memories. As a rule, research on the culture of memory assumes that the West German politics of self-exculpation regarding spoken and unspoken accusations about the past—in both the public and the personal sense—was tied to a very selective form of memory. As was mentioned at the outset, this selective memory, which centered on the victim status of non-Jewish Germans and their suffering, has been widely analyzed and interpreted as a moral refusal to accept responsibility for the mass crimes and to gain acknowledgement of one's own suffering.[80]

Yet such studies run the risk of understanding memory in a purely functional way. Moreover, in historical retrospect they presume a capacity for articulation in which the thematization of one's own complicity in or knowledge of the crime is elevated to a moral norm. After all, as Alon Confino has already suggested, the problems of one's own victim status and of responsibility are here considered as two diametrically opposing fields that cannot be correlated with one another.[81] However, the reasons for the different movements toward public memory and silencing in German postwar society require a more open approach and must be sought beyond the political expediency and self-exoneration of selective memory. Some more recent research devoted, for example, to the visual language of shocking images confirms this view, reading into them the broader repertoire of an iconography of horror, or else considering the "return of images" of the Holocaust in the course of the judicial processing of the crimes as an expression of imaginary memory's own productive power.[82] Characteristic of this work is the emphasis it places on the form and effect of the historically mutable imagination of violence—an area of inquiry that, I will argue, cannot be adequately approached in terms of the thematic frequency of guilt and expiation or the dramatic plots of different war films.[83]

In this respect, what must not be overlooked is the historicity of the categories for perceiving experiences of suffering. In order to track this dimension of public recognition or nonrecognition of oppressive memories of violence and persistent mental suffering, which has hitherto been excluded from the literature on cultures of memory, the third part of the book will examine how and why the horizon shifted for publicly addressing experiences of mental anguish. I will consider the effects that scientific-medical knowledge and its transformation brought about in public acknowledgment of such suffering, and in the rules for what could be spoken of within the framework of the general culture of memory. Starting with the premise that historical consciousness is shaped to a high degree by the media, I will focus essentially on media portrayals of the war and its effects on life in postwar society.[84] This will entail deciphering the grammar of popular assumptions and accepted forms of speech about the way human beings process mass murder and violence, as manifested in print media and film.

My aim is thus not to present a history of postwar West German media that focuses on their different technical possibilities and specific forms of influence—or on the media market and media-related policies of the time, which is to say, the state's efforts to control them.[85] Rather, I wish to identify the dominant interpretive patterns at work in the public space, which offer insight into the linguistically and visually mediated self-understanding of the mental consequences of experiencing violence.[86] The images themselves call for an analysis of the meanings ascribed to them at that specific historical moment. Without such an analysis, the impact of the images in postwar German society can hardly be understood.[87] For this reason, the first chapter of the last part of the book will examine the publicly negotiated ideas concerning the mental effects of war and imprisonment, which needed to be brought into line with plans for both self-normalization and social normalization in West Germany's reconstruction society, and with the expectations that the returned soldiers and society overall display a capacity to regenerate. Against that backdrop, the last part of the book will look at the "therapeutic discourse" under way in West Germany's public sphere in the late 1940s and 1950s. Even in respect to public acceptance of the veteran's suffering, a pronounced ambivalence is apparent. It repeatedly underscores that the limits of public recognition have always been drawn and altered in a specific political-moral context. Therefore, this research calls for more than tracking the penetration of contemporary medical-psychiatric viewpoints into the language of the media. We must also understand the media's "politics of memory," which were legitimized or indeed enabled by "sciences of memory" such as psychiatry.[88]

This linkage emerges even more sharply in the second chapter of the last part, which explores the interplay between the changes in the culture of memory beginning in the late 1950s, on the one hand, and the increasing exclusion of the so-called late returnees from the publically articulated concession of psychosomatic suffering, on the other. This acceptance would be increasingly accorded to the victims of Nazi persecution, thereby provoking an entire series of questions. What feedback effects can we observe between professional expertise and public moral sensibility? How did the emergence of new images of

Nazism's victims interact with the shift in West Germany's public perception of the perpetrators at the start of the 1960s and the establishment of new psychiatric knowledge regarding the long-term effects of extreme stress? What was the inner connection between the approval or denial of victim status and the problem of responsibility for the crimes committed? We will need to demonstrate that the changes in memory culture during the period cannot be explained in terms of either politics or generational shift alone. In the 1960s, the psychiatric differentiation between the mental effects of violence on victims of Nazism and on German soldiers solidified as an openly accepted cognitive model, thereby not only shifting the public limits on what could be expressed regarding the emotional effects of the war and Nazi persecution on the personal lives of those affected. Public memory of both the war and the postwar period was also shaped in a manner that would last decades and help determine social and political ideas about the processing mechanisms at play in West Germany at that time.

Moving in the area where the history of experience, the history of science, and the history of memory interface, this book draws on highly disparate sources. These include extensive material from the field of medicine, state documents, and a broad spectrum of print and visual media. Analyzing the psychiatric records represented a special methodological challenge. The great majority of these records are located in the Bodelschwingh Clinics (von Bodelschwinghsche Anstalten) in Bielefeld/Bethel, a far smaller number in Heidelberg's psychiatric and neurological clinic (Psychiatrische und Neurologische Klinik) and the medical care station for patients with nervous diseases (Fürsorgestelle für Nervöse) run by the Cologne health authorities. Systematic study of the records was only possible in Bethel, where the medical files of patients admitted from 1945 to 1960 were accessible. They add up to a rich and complex body of documents. Psychiatrists kept a written record of the sometimes extended conversations in which patients described their inner distress and symptoms. For their part, the patients prepared fragmentary accounts of their personal experiences during the war or internment, which they sometimes related to their suffering. The medical histories include impressions of family members concerning the former soldiers' lives until then and behavior since their return; relatives wrote letters that were intended to explain the behavioral changes to the psychiatrists; and in their therapeutic efforts, diagnoses, and official statements, the psychiatrists drew on all of that material, which they attempted to understand in the framework of their professional knowledge.

Thus, despite the richness of the accounts by relatives and the patients themselves, because the assessments, questions, and session notes the medical records contain were fundamentally determined by the professional interest of psychiatrists, they are first and foremost psychiatric output.[89] Nevertheless, since the files also include excerpts from the conversations with the psychiatrists, in addition to the patients' personal accounts, they emerge as a valuable, previously untapped, documentary source of personal memories of the war from the immediate postwar period.[90] In many cases, the medical records open a window onto "memory spaces" as a "partial illumination of the past"[91] that corresponds neither to psychiatric interpretation nor to prevalent narratives about the violence of the war. Instead, they allow us to view traces of suffering that was difficult to communicate. In a number of cases, it was articulated in dreams and hallucinations that can be read as a historical source for understanding spontaneous ways of processing the continued pressure of suffering. Because even if the material does not represent a "real" reproduction of experienced events, but rather fiction, it nonetheless attests to violence that was experienced. In that sense, it is subjectively "truthful" and hence, as suggested, illuminating for a history of West German experience and memory in the postwar period.

Since one of the book's broad aims is to argue for the need to conceptually broaden post-1945 history, render it plausible by incorporating the history of science, and advance it, I focus in part on the production of knowledge and therefore in the present context on the question of how new medical-scientific interpretive models are stabilized. To that end, I examined a large body of medical source material, including psychiatric literature consisting of journals, handbooks, and the patient medical files mentioned above. The material furnishes insight into the transformation of psychiatric knowledge, with the medical files illuminating the complicated interpretive process through which the medical community tried to arrive at a convincing explanation for the mental changes observed in the returned soldiers. In addition, the files allow us to reconstruct the way psychiatric interpretations and the everyday interpretations of the histories of personal suffering permeated one another, without merging entirely as a result. Particularly based on this source material, the professional medical analysis of suffering emerges as an interpretive effort that never reaches a final conclusion, although the individual stages can be reconstructed.

The examination of official West German documents, published legal judgments, and legal journals also proved productive in the analysis of the unfolding production of knowledge. Documents held by the German Ministry of Labor and Social Affairs and by the Ministry of Finance turned out especially valuable. The former ministry was responsible for the care of the war injured, the latter for questions regarding reparations to victims of Nazism.

Both these collections contain internal communications of the ministerial bureaucracy at the state and national level that participated in the negotiation over
which psychiatric knowledge on the mental processing of violence and extreme stress was to be officially validated, and, as a result, which war-, impris-
onment-, and persecution-related suffering would be recognized or not. In the
late 1950s, the West German government arranged "medical conferences" for
the purpose of clarifying questions regarding lasting damage to individuals
from Nazi persecution. The minutes of these conferences give us a sense of the
ways in which adjudication influenced the growing validity of an altered psychiatric approach. In conjunction with the travel reports of various officials,
these minutes further enable us to see the way intertwining international processes contributed to the production of new knowledge about the psychological effects of Nazi persecution. In respect to other countries—insight is possible into the situation in the United States and France, in England to a lesser
degree—but even more so to West Germany itself, it can be precisely documented that the shift in psychiatric knowledge was a negotiation process that
was simply determined by moral challenges and political expectations as well.

Finally, in order to analyze West Germany's postwar public narrative on
the personal effects of the war and on mental suffering, I examined both a
number of films, primarily feature films, from the period and local and national
newspapers. Above all, an analysis of the popular press clearly shows that
medical-scientific developments were the subject of media attention, which is
central to the transmission of scientific knowledge.[92] An accidentally discovered script of a 1960s radio broadcast about the psychological effects of Nazi
persecution completes the collection of source materials underpinning my
analysis of the medialization of the ways individuals processed the experience
of extreme violence during the Nazi war of annihilation and its consequences.
In addition, it proved advantageous to examine the printed annual reports and
statements of the Association of Returnees, and the minutes of the relevant
negotiations in the West German parliament on the topic of care for war casualties. In this fashion, it was possible to follow the debates over the long-term
consequences of the war and internment as a POW that occurred elsewhere in
society, and which developed over the course of the shift in psychiatric knowledge and the emergence of new perspectives on the imagination of the effects
of violence. Within this panorama, the limits of what could be articulated in the
public media emerge in sharper contour, without causing the ongoing struggle
for the acknowledgment of personal suffering to disappear.

In this manner, the following chapters connect three perspectives: the ir-
ritating presence of a destructive war and violent Nazi crime, as it surfaced in

personal memory fragments; the perspective of psychiatric knowledge production; and the negotiation of relevant rules for what could be discussed in public memory culture. Only by taking a synoptic view can we grasp how interpretations of the war emerged that repeatedly redefined social conceptualizations of its mentally destructive power and of the causes of human suffering. With respect to the historically determined perception and acknowledgment of the consequences of war and persecution, the book therefore makes a central contribution to understanding the history of experience of postwar West Germany, a history far more complex than a sweeping division into a society of perpetrators and victims would allow us to expect. We can assume that it was quite similar to the history of experience in other postwar societies. It demonstrates that this history is far more complex because of the knowledge order that obtained in West Germany about the ability to endure mental stress.

PART I

Remembering the War:
Private Fragments of Memory,
1945–1949

CHAPTER I

Linguistic Realms of War

Dreaming the War

It is only one sequence from many literary narratives about the postwar period, somewhere in Germany, in a bombed-out house, during the effort to rebuild it.[1] Elisabeth wanted simply to embellish the newly rebuilt space. She pulled a year's worth of glossy magazines from the rubble, tore out page after page, and pasted them onto the walls: "*Stukas over Warsaw. Troops on the March into Russia. Victory Parade before the Arc de Triomphe. German Tanks in Africa. U-boats in Skagerag.*"

Gustav, who had saved himself shortly before the end of the war along with some other fleeing soldiers and had thereby also avoided becoming a POW,[2] stormed in, "tore the still damp magazine pages from the wall, screamed something about the war and being fed up; Elisabeth cried because she didn't really understand what was going on; Maria came to her defense: after all, Elisabeth had only wanted to use the pasted paper against the draft."

But the paste had already stuck to the stones. It was no longer possible to remove the magazine pages entirely, so that "here a soldier's helmet" remained, "there the wheel of a utility vehicle, here a tank tread, there half a victory parade, here the wing of a Stuka, a patchy wall with set pieces from the war, the lowest-lying things above the highest, the Arc de Triomphe tilting over a cockpit, the old city of Warsaw beneath a U-boat, Berlin decorated with flags."

There were many dreams of a new beginning. These included the "dreams amid the debris" that city planners developed during the bombing campaigns, envisioning the destruction of historical city centers as a welcome basis for the implementation of new planning concepts.[3] As we know, not all of these dreams abruptly evaporated with the end of the war, although it did put an end to the Nazis' urban-planning euphoria. Much of that euphoria simply remained an idea on the drawing board. Yet, despite obvious efforts to underpin the spir-

27

itual and moral new start with new architectural visions, traces of this euphoria flowed into the reconstruction efforts, albeit in altered form. It constituted one element in shaping the new appearance of German cities, which continued to bear the mark of both the war and Nazism.[4]

The dreams of former soldiers were far less apparent amid the rubble of post-1945 German society. For the Allied photographers they were not decipherable in the faces of the war prisoners, just as the rich pictorial world of Germany's postwar press offers no access to the dreams of the photographed war prisoners and returnees.[5] No less than contemporary film and theater, publicly exhibited photography was an important element in the country's memory as produced by the media. Both the suffering of the returning soldiers, visualized in images of misery that circulated in the immediate postwar period, and the portraits of beaming, heroic surviving soldiers that predominated only a few years later, fostered a highly politicized vision of the hardships the soldiers had endured and of the moral fortitude that had putatively saved them.[6] Here, publicly available representations and the interpretations of these representations blended together, forming a narrative that even before the end of the 1940s created a drastically reduced memory of the Nazi war of annihilation and its consequences. Many have claimed that the soldier as perpetrator vanished from this memory. Moreover, all references to biographical ruptures—caused by the war, the "collapse" of the Nazi regime, or the shame of confronting its crimes—were also supposedly absent in this publicly articulated memory.[7]

At the end of 1949, Hannah Arendt took a nearly four-month trip through various West European cities, including some in Germany (letters indicate at least Bonn, Freiburg, Nuremberg, and Wiesbaden, along with Berlin). Upon her return, her impressions were fully in line with the observations above. In her subsequent essay in *Commentary* (October 1950) entitled "The Aftermath of Nazi Rule: Report from Germany," she indicated that "everywhere, one is struck by the absence of any reaction to what has happened." What Arendt observed was the prevalence of indifference and lack of feeling as the external symptom of "a deeply rooted, stubborn, and occasionally brutal refusal to face up to and comprehend what had actually taken place." Even when she made it clear that she was Jewish, Arendt encountered this fundamental mind-set. She thus perceived an entirely misplaced attempt to weigh "the suffering of the Germans against the suffering of others," which tacitly conveyed the view "that the balance of suffering was equal." Arendt's comparative observations left no doubt that in Germany "the nightmare of destruction and horror" was far less palpable than in other European countries.[8]

The Germans, she concluded, had embarked on a flight from reality, and hence from responsibility—an inclination that Germans shared with others in Western Europe in her view.[9]

Hannah Arendt's interpretation anticipated a position that historians of contemporary German history recognized, beginning in the 1990s, as German society's "discourse of victimization" in a form essentially analogous to Arendt's argument. In the meantime, it has been identified throughout public life up to the present day.[10] In some cases, the historians' findings are quite convincing.[11] Yet at the same time, the rediscovery of the "discourse of victimization" is so widespread and generalizing that one is occasionally inclined to perceive a pronounced political/moral incentive, namely, to prevent any doubts from arising as to the unique nature of Nazi crimes and thereby upsetting a specific historical image of the West German state. What is decisive in our context, however, is that the repeated interpretation of German public discourse as "victimization discourse" only prolongs a problem of public memory construction that was already present in the early postwar period. Public memory construction did not automatically provide insight into the horror, fears, and expectations that the returnees to defeated Germany brought along with them. For it was not least the "victimization discourse" itself—precisely because it brought German suffering to the foreground as a publicly recognized form of narration about the war—that also held contemporaries captive regarding their options for what could be said in public.[12]

So far, historians have paid little attention to the fact that in the attempt to process war experiences artistically, both early postwar literature and film at times pursued the goal of conveying a more differentiated sense of the fears and inner horror of the repatriated soldiers. The medium some writers and directors used to address the war's abominations, and beyond that as an interpretive vehicle for expressing an inner pain scarcely discussed in public, was the medium of dream—nightmares both by day and by night—and hallucinations. Published in 1949, Bruno Hampel's short story *The Business about the Corn* (*Das mit dem Mais*), is one example of this. For the repatriated soldier, whom the author allows to recount his own story, a cornfield is not merely a cornfield, because it awakens the memory of a person who suddenly stood before him between two rows of corn in the Ukraine—and whom he shot. It is not as if the narrator always sees the man before him. But as we read in the story,

> There is something that immediately conjures him up. Nothing else than that cursed corn! A couple of miserable corn stalks are enough, and he's immediately there. He and all the other things: the huge field—the green

ditch—the metallic rattle—the shooting on the right in front of me—the laughter of death, thirty-four times—the laughing voice of the lieutenant—the earth-brown pile—the shaved off stalks and the bloody corn cobs. All of that comes up, like a picture that's been pasted together. And straight through this image he's looking at me, smiling, with large very blue eyes and the smiling mouth of a child.[13]

Likewise, in his now famous film, *The Murderers Are among Us*, director Wolfgang Staudte depicts a surgeon named Mertens who has returned from the war. He falls into a hallucinatory state in which he undergoes a horrifying war experience, begging a captain to rescind his order to massacre civilians—men, women, children. Later in the film, we learn that the experience was based on an actual crime Mertens witnessed in the east.[14] There are numerous other examples, including the dreams of returned veteran Beckmann in Wolfgang Borchert's drama *Outside before the Door*.[15] Apparently, repatriated soldiers often dreamed about the war—at least, works such as the above from the immediate postwar period suggest this, all the more so since they occasionally portray an awareness, socially manifest as well as concealed, of returning soldiers' nightmares.[16] Seeing this simply as an early dramatic realization of the self-perception of German society in terms of victimhood—an interpretation recently applied to Borchert's play—certainly falls short.[17] Rather, we can presume that such films and literary texts captured a highly personal and precarious way of processing the most recent past.[18] The complexity and significance of what was involved here never received the close scrutiny it merits.

Naturally, we cannot conclude that all German veterans had nightmare recollections of the war. Such dreams are, however, described in the psychiatric records of some veterans. They provide rare access to a linguistic realm tied to the war, thereby bringing to light fragments of a very complex world of memories.[19] Granted, the dream images are generally only transmitted as fragments,[20] but the nature of their verbal rendition and the associative chains they set into motion still make the dreams recognizable as a medium for processing precarious experience, or else as a form of self-enactment. In addition, other narratives of the dreamers reveal important connections for interpreting the dreams, even when these accounts initially seem unrelated to them.[21] Yet resorting to a dream enables the narrator, however fleetingly, to render his own experience as less real.

In this manner, dreams of war do not serve as keys to the experience of war itself. Rather, they convey what has been experienced and what is imagined, combined in a fictional form,[22] within which the phantasmagoria of war were expressed in the postwar period. The dreams always represent distorted or hallucinatory images of the war that were nonetheless an integral part of postwar German reality.[23] While the meaning of many of these dreams may seem clear at first glance, that is in fact far from the case.[24] Much like "internal mental snapshots"[25] that present a detail from a relevant world of contemporary images, these dreams nevertheless allow us to expand the range of ways in which war-related violence was perceived, and to focus more closely on the array of emotions and behaviors that characterized the period.

In the stories they told their doctors, the former Wehrmacht soldiers doubtless did not portray their war dreams as overly important. In the interviews about their private lives and most intimate fantasies—interviews with a far greater thematic range—the war dreams were, in fact, the only dreams that were discussed, although they were never the center of attention. Details were rarely recounted. In a number of cases, the dreams were simply mentioned in passing, and at times it was not the returnees themselves who reported the dreams—instead, they had only been observed while dreaming.

Whether visible from the outside or recounted by those experiencing them, the dreams showed one thing: all of these returnees were troubled in one way or another. Of course, the dreams do not allow us to assess the extent to which their mental condition actually impaired their daily lives. Overall, many of them appear to have successfully begun to rebuild their civilian lives. By the same token, there may also have been reasons for the returnees' strikingly disturbed state of mind that remained completely unexpressed in the contents of the reported dreams. Perhaps some troubling events never even appeared in dreams. Nonetheless, the small number of dream fragments accessible to us reveal the enduring spell of the war. It was, if not drastically disturbing, at least unsettling for the Wehrmacht veterans, and was in any case something out of their control.

Reinhard K., for example, could not escape the war for years, even in his sleep, as his medical file indicates.[26] He had already attracted attention during his stay in a military hospital in 1942. Reinhard K. would wake up at night with a start, jump out of bed, shout, and issue orders. The chief staff doctor in charge, who observed and treated the soldier's nervous disorder for nearly two years in the psychiatric-neurological ward of the military hospital, described his daytime state as "shy, anxious, and depressed." But at night, when Reinhard K. was tormented by his dream, the lance corporal would assume command and was very clearly struggling to gain control of a situation that remained inaccessible to those observing him. The dreams left their mark on Reinhard K.

for days. "During the following days he appears shattered, derelict, and pale . . . and then suffers from nervous-spastic diarrhea for a week," the staff doctor reported. He was at a loss to identify an effective therapy and was unable to restore Reinhard K.'s fitness for duty. During a follow-up psychiatric examination, the former soldier added to his brief description of the dreams that he had "always dreamed of Russia." As the doctor in charge indicated earlier, Reinhard K. had served "in the east." By now he had been a civilian for months. Yet the dreams still clung to him in his sleep, as became clear the second night of his renewed stay in a psychiatric ward: he began to issue orders, thrashed about, and seemed to believe that he was still in Russia, at least for that night.

The temptation to read Reinhard K.'s dream as an anxiety dream is great. His shy, nervous, and anxious demeanor during the day and his reference to "Russia" could easily mislead us to make that assumption. Granted, the daytime anxiety that tormented him was indisputably evident. But did the fear really persist in the same way during the night? The reference to "Russia" is itself not self-explanatory. In the period between the attack on the Soviet Union in June 1941 and March 1942, when Reinhard K.'s treatment began, the war on the eastern front encompassed a broad range of experiences: the "blitzkrieg" and proclamations of victory; tens of thousands of dead and injured soldiers; the massacre of Jews at Babi Yar; the first Soviet counterattacks; and in some locations the start of exhausting trench warfare. Although the files do not allow us to reconstruct where Reinhard K. was deployed, he certainly experienced "stress and strain," *Strapazen*, as the staff doctor put it.[27] But only Reinhard K. knew exactly how much of it he imagined in his dreams and precisely which role he played in the events.

Daytime conduct and nocturnal dream-visions did not necessarily correspond with one another. In fact, the war could present itself in very different ways in dreams than in states of wakeful consciousness. Observations of horror could become overlaid and intersect with wishful fantasies. In the daytime and nighttime ways in which the war was perceived, awareness of the horror of war was not always equally sweeping and overpowering. This is evident in the case of Rudolf B., who began psychiatric treatment four years after the war.[28] When he was admitted to the hospital, this former professional soldier was twenty-eight years old, still unemployed, and barely capable of presenting a coherent narrative. His accounts, during which memories of the war sometimes erupted, were jumbled and disjointed. "It's terrible at night. The memory of being buried returns against my will. . . . Yes . . . ," he reported, his train of thought then breaking off before he added only, "Yes, terrible." Six years earlier, in the spring of 1943, Rudolf B., had been wounded by a bullet in his upper left arm. It becomes clear in another paragraph of the psychiatrist's interview protocol that he repeatedly experienced "the events surrounding his wounding" in his dreams. Long after his physical wounds had healed, he still contended anxiously with the war's destructive potential, which he had experienced on his own body. As the notes in this veteran's file show, his dreams attested to a restless and active memory that expressed itself in many ways, thereby exposing different layers of memory. After a few days, Rudolf. B. was observed asleep in bed as he issued military commands in a loud voice. In another dream, he later explained, he met his former comrades again and conversed with them.

The further course of the quite erratic initial interview, however, offers additional insight into the former soldier's repeatedly fractured dreamworld. Rudolf B. continued: "I can't help thinking about it, now it's gone. Am I imagining all this? Why all the victims? Everything for nothing. Betrayal, sabotage. I can't . . ." As the psychiatrist noted, a moment later Rudolf B. suddenly angrily raised his voice and shouted, "Is that possible? Everything in vain, yes, yes. Am I crazy or am I going crazy? (Poisoned?) No. (Human beings changed?) Human beings, human beings aren't worth anything. And I tell you, *Herr Doktor*, that's the way it was, we had the secret weapon. *Ach*, everything is, *ach*, you don't believe me anyway, *ach*, everything's so . . ." Several sentences later, he added that he had spoken with comrades and affirmed: "Those were the most beautiful times. Hitler made a lot of mistakes, but . . ." At this point, Rudolf B. faltered again, only to abruptly switch themes. Finally, after a few more sentences he ended the interview with the words, "Yes, yes, thou shalt not kill," and then he fell silent.

Rudolf B. was in a state of confused despair when he articulated these memory fragments. The knowledge of the mass killings that he carried around with him haunted him during the day like a nightmare. It was obviously impossible for him to assign meaning to this knowledge, or to his own acts of killing. Yet at virtually the same time, an old dream reemerged, the dream of the *Endsieg*, of final victory, even though it had been manifestly broken by the senselessness of mass death. Even four years after the end of the war, the dogged euphoric adherence of an obsessive fighter reverberated in Rudolf B.'s insistence on the existence of the wonder weapon, in his suspicions about sabotage, and in his half-protesting "but" that offered an exculpation of Hitler. Like many others—and if only because of a need to survive—he shared the belief in Hitler's ability to produce an *Endsieg*, upholding it even as the war entered its final phase.[29]

His controlled speech swallowed the remnants of his former emotional turmoil. Only a few days after his admission to the hospital, and now in a state of restored clarity of mind, Rudolf B. responded to the doctor's question regarding the source of his persistent brooding by simply referring to "the lost war, modern democracy." This answer clearly reveals his awareness of a postwar shift in the political and moral rules about what could be mentioned at that time as opposed to during the war years. In Germany, the *Endsieg* was propagated in ironclad fashion into the last weeks of the war; open misgivings about it were suppressed under threat of massive punishment; and the will to endure was constantly stoked. However, the total defeat of the Nazi regime, the revelation of the crimes the Germans had committed, and their humiliation by the Allies rendered the Germans' bitter clinging to faith in final victory taboo. A fantasy that had been openly cultivated for many years had suddenly become unmentionable.

What remained present, however, was the direct proximity of death during the war. In dreams as well as in conscious speech, the threat to one's own life through the war was present, and the dead bodies were appearing. The recurrent dreams of being wounded that tormented Rudolf B., for example,[30] attested not only to an experience that had—in the truest sense of the term—"gotten under one's skin,"[31] they also revived the mortal danger that one was exposed to in war and that one "had a brush with" when being wounded. In this sense, when it comes to the horror and violence of the war and mass death, the dreams are unmistakably characterized by what Koselleck has termed "testimonial character."[32]

A feeling of total vulnerability to death was mirrored in the dreams that continued to plague Hans S. in 1950.[33] Drawing upon the former soldier's descriptions, the doctor summarized the wartime situation to which Hans S.'s dreams referred as follows:

> During the collapse of the central front in the winter of 1941–1942, his unit, which was poorly equipped for the severe winter, became hopelessly surrounded after fierce fighting and heavy losses. During an attack by the Russians, he decided to end his life. He placed himself openly in the line of Russian machine-gun fire but was not hit, and he had come to view this as a decree of fate that nothing could happen to him in the war.

The additional testimony of Hans S. was not without its heroic undertones as he sought to demonstrate his invincibility to both his psychiatrist and himself. The doctor's transcript continues: "He explained that during the course of these battles he had broken through the ice of a river repeatedly and only could make it back to quarters after hours. His feet had already turned black, and he ended up in a field hospital." Although Hans S. escaped with his life, he could not shake off his sense of having coming close to death—especially the moment in the machine-gun fire clung to his memory. When the experience resurfaced in dreams, the images that played out were always associated with increased sensory stimulation, which kept the experience as deceptively and powerfully present, as if it were possible to live through it once again internally.

Finally, as we see at times, the dead themselves reappeared. In the dream narratives we have, the returning dead were always those on the German side. It would be pure speculation to conclude that the death of enemies had been banished from veterans' dreams, however. Even if we were to accept the natural assumption that the casualties the Germans had sustained had been considered more worth telling about than the casualties they had inflicted, that exceeds what our knowledge of the dreams permits us to conclude. All that can be seen is that dreams about the dead on the German side could be articulated, at least in a fragmentary way. But the dream reports were not concerned with the countless masses of German casualties, but rather with individual fallen Germans with whom the former soldiers had had an especially intense or powerful encounter. Dietmar F., a former noncommissioned officer in the Wehrmacht, indicated in August 1949 that he was still "affected by his grim experiences in battle and as a prisoner of war," and emphasized one dream experience in particular. As we read in the psychiatrist's notes, one evening he and a comrade had "to take fifteen dead soldiers to the cemetery. The horse bucked, forcing them to carry the dead men away on their shoulders."[34]

It is impossible to know whether the corpses in this dream represented the very epitome of the atrocity of war for Dietmar F. or whether they embodied a proxy for the manifold horrors of war. In any event, the dream report was an admission of how terrified Dietmar F. had been. They had been very close, these soldiers whose bodies he literally had to carry on his shoulders at the age of nineteen, and which continued to haunt him five years later when he relived "horrible scenes" at night. The insights into his daily life that we obtain from the psychiatric case notes nevertheless show an ongoing reality that strikes us as kaleidoscopic. For example, he was burdened because his father had favored his brother over him. On the other hand, Dietmar F. felt "entirely happy" as an apprentice gardener in his future vocation. Yet at night, when he woke up with a start from his dreams of the dead soldiers pressing against him, we read, he was "often bathed in sweat."

Dreams drew the dead into the living reality of the postwar years in a particular way. In dreams, the horror of the war solidified and became a presence, thus cutting off the escape route for those who actually or allegedly wished to flee from reality and moral responsibility, as Hannah Arendt observed everywhere in postwar Germany.[35] Dreams momentarily did away with the temporal distance from the war. This held true not only for dreams, such as those of Dietmar F., where the past played out again in the present of the dream. It also applied in those where the present as experienced in a dream became matted up with the past, so to speak. Rolf S.'s dream narrative of 1948 is an illustrative example.[36] By this time, five and a half years had passed since his last deployment as a railway engineer. He was conscripted into the Wehrmacht in 1941, but had already contracted tuberculosis of the lungs by the end of 1942. For the former army private, service in Russia and Poland was relatively brief. Despite his illness, he was not spared a year of imprisonment following the war's end. Years later, now in a psychiatric clinic, Rolf S. had a "mass of dreamlike experiences." Among other things, he mentioned "all kinds of war experiences" without specifying their nature. In contrast, he described dream images that did not belong to the past in considerable detail. But while Rolf S. had dreams based on the present, the atrocities and horror tormented him in these dreams as well. In the psychiatrist's notes we read that he "believed he was in the detention center for war criminals in Berlin; that he heard the cries of those who were being tortured and executed. When he heard the clatter of plates, he thought that it was the sound of torture, and that he would soon be executed himself." In the course of another dream, he observed Truman and Stalin. As he later explained, he saw them "negotiating over the fate of the war criminals."

After Rolf S. regained a clear waking consciousness, he did not find it difficult to restore inner detachment from these dream experiences. His medical file states that he did not ascribe "reality value" to the dreams. Although the events in his dreams appeared real, he was able to identify them as part of a dream—one that furthermore was not even tied to an actual event he had experienced in his own life. Yet the dreams of Rolf S. were recognizable as the product of a specific historical context and were characterized by a pronounced connection to reality. For example, there were the negotiations between the victorious powers—an expression of German defeat. Above all, Rolf S.'s dreams attested to a certain forcefulness with which the Allies pursued their program of political purging and legal prosecution of perpetrators during the early postwar years. It is certainly debatable whether the Allies actually leveled the charge of collective guilt in this period or, whether the Germans, as Norbert Frei has argued, reflexively anticipated this charge because of a "widespread feeling of personal complicity."[37] In any event, this dream clearly echoed the public confrontation with the crimes that Germans had committed. Rolf S.

dreamed of himself as a war criminal. It is impossible to determine whether this was a dream about the guilty or a dream of his own guilt. What is evident in Rolf S.'s case, however, is that the Allies' public shaming of Germans left distinct traces that surfaced in his dream. It attested to an indelible knowledge of criminal acts and unleashed—no later than then—fears that the time of reckoning for the murders had come.

The Echo of Fear

> *We saw how the Russian tanks approached us along with the infantry. I fired at the Russians with my machine pistol. For the first time I was shooting at people I saw directly before me. When danger is very close, you sometimes get unbelievably quiet. Fear shuts down, everything shuts down, and you see and feel the battle like an outsider.*[38]

It is a truism, writes Joanna Bourke, that among all the feelings that can arise in combat, fear is the most predominant.[39] Bourke bases her observation on the results of a medical survey conducted during World War II among men from two (otherwise unspecified) Allied infantry divisions. Only 7 percent of those surveyed maintained that they never felt fear. Three-quarters of them complained about shaky hands; 58 percent suffered from sweaty palms; and 38 percent tossed sleeplessly in bed at night.[40] The findings seem clear enough.

In actuality, we know very little about the extent of fear experienced by common soldiers and officers in the Wehrmacht. At the time, German military psychiatrists alleged that they were not encountering a problem with fear in German soldiers and officers,[41] and for the majority of historians the question of the prevalence of fear in "Hitler's army" was far from their minds.[42] Yet the problem of fear and anxiety is not entirely absent from historical studies of German society during the Nazis' war. The subject of fear is occasionally addressed. It is seen emerging in a range of contexts, in particular when it manifests as a crystallization of propaganda and experience, as an expression of suspicion about or actual knowledge of Nazi crimes, and finally as the resulting panic over an impending cataclysmic future. Reports from the security service itself offer indications. For example, reports filed in December 1942 mention signs of developing anxiety among the German population about future reprisals by the Jews if the war were not won.[43] Moreover, Allied bombing produced more than just the fear of the destructive potential of these weapons. The presumption that these attacks represented revenge for German wrongdoing unleashed anxiety about future retaliation.[44] Toward the end of the war, the German civilian population appears to have lived in a state of continuously escalating fear of Russian revenge. There can be no doubt that this spiral of anxiety reflected the success of Nazi propaganda.[45] There are, however, also clear indications that these fears were stoked by a sufficiently horrifying sense of the cruelty with which the war was waged in the east.[46] A wave of suicides, unlike any other in German history, offers a clear indication of the depth and scope of despair among the German population at the start of 1945. The numbers of suicide cases in the formerly German eastern regions and Soviet occupation zones reached tens of thousands. There are many plausible reasons for this. In the case of Nazi Party functionaries, fear of punishment at the hands of the Soviets or other victorious powers was likely the decisive factor in opting for suicide.[47] At the same time, a great many women took their own lives before the Red Army arrived, prompted by the idea—generated either by propaganda or by war stories—that they would endure unimaginable atrocities once the Soviets marched in.[48] In fact, these nightmarish fantasies became a brutal reality for well over one million women in eastern Germany.

German fears of retaliation were echoed by and found public reinforcement in Nazi propaganda, which instrumentalized them to steel the population's will to endure and maintain military discipline. However, other fears at the time met with only very limited resonance in the public space. The demise of Nazism did not by any means change this situation in every respect. Granted, the borders demarcating public space shifted as a result of the new political framework. Yet "public distaste for personal feelings and even more so for undisguised feelings" was "nearly unanimous," as Michael Geyer has noted for the 1950s.[49]

Nevertheless, traces of feelings of fear are detectable in the psychiatric files of the postwar years. Initially, this is not surprising. After all, symptoms of anxiety can also reflect specific psychiatric illnesses such as paranoia and schizophrenia. In fact, an awareness of the characteristics of particular illnesses is necessary. But this does not mean that the expressions of anxiety we find in these psychiatric sources refer only to a specific mental illness. Even in the case of diagnosed schizophrenia, which produces attacks of anxiety-filled paranoid ideation, the symptoms expose specific fears pointing to the experiential horizon from which they emerge. In the cases discussed here, this horizon unmistakably encompassed the lived reality and conceptual world of Nazism and the war.

The traces of anxiety are, to be sure, not easy to decipher, and the danger of mere imputation is substantial. This is evident in the few studies that have sought to uncover the anxiety German soldiers felt in the war. Such fears can hardly ever be truly established. Rather, readers are presented with a diffuse mix consisting of the author's own insight into Nazi policies of annihilation, the atrocity of the war in the east, and currently prevalent notions about the human capacity to endure stress.[50] But states of anxiety cannot be grasped through empathy. Such an approach glosses over the methodological dilemma that the presence of fear cannot be excluded even in situations where it is not recognizably expressed as such. Without a doubt, anxiety speaks many languages. For this reason, distorted interpretations involving ex post ascriptions can only be avoided when testimony is available, in which former soldiers articulated their fears themselves. Only then is it possible to understand fear as the reason for their abnormal behavior or as a driver of their actions. As it happens, the psychiatric files provide insight into situations in which the repatriated veterans expressed fears of all kinds, presupposing in a large majority of cases the experiential horizon of Nazism and war. However, anxiety always connects the past and the present,[51] as was evident in very specific ways during the transition from the war years to the postwar period. While it is true that the anxieties mentioned in the files cannot always be tied back to concrete experiences during the National Socialist war itself—in most cases that is not possible—as "conservatories of memory"[52] they nevertheless always tell something important about the past. Of course, these cases must always be examined in greater detail and within the concrete historical constellation in which they were expressed if one is to shed light on the wide range of anxieties that circulated in the postwar period and can be attributed to the distressing revival of deep memories of the war. In some cases, these anxiety states were generated by the war itself; in others they were not unleashed until Germany was defeated and occupied.

A review of the files quickly makes one thing clear: when the former soldiers spoke of their wartime anxiety, they were not usually describing situations involving open anxiety attacks. Rather, the reports suggest that anxiety was more often an externally invisible companion. The number of soldiers afflicted by it remained hidden. The degree of intensity the fear would achieve was not readily ascertainable from external appearances. Nor was it possible to predict with certainty when it would erupt. Sometimes it came on as insidiously as it was unsuspected. This was the experience of Gerhard K., who volunteered for the German air force in 1937.[53] During a stay in a clinic in 1947, he explained to a psychiatrist that he had flown many combat missions over France, Belgium, and Norway as a radio operator. He added that "his relationship with his superiors had always been good," thereby emphasizing that his behavior had never been cause for reprimand. But in 1940, we read, "a sense of anxiety" became noticeable "as soon as he boarded his aircraft." Afterward "it had bothered him a lot." Fear had crept up, and it had stayed with him. At the end of the same year, he was shot down over England. Something similar apparently took place with Willi M., who at some point during the war also began to struggle with anxiety.[54] His own account does not allow us to conclude that he had suffered from anxiety from the very start of his work for the Wehrmacht criminal police. Willi M. had been conscripted in 1943 at the age of forty-eight and served until shortly before the end of the war. But immediately before that time, he claimed to have suddenly and then repeatedly been subject to attacks of sheer panic, even though he was externally uninjured. As he attested in 1949, the train inspections that belonged to his daily duties became "increasingly more grueling and dangerous" toward the end of the war. One day, he collapsed. In the throes of what he perceived as a "nervous breakdown," he "simply went home, with blood pouring from his nose and mouth." At least in his perhaps merely retrospective interpretation, Willi M. "had simply not been able to stand the constant attacks in Osnabrück and the shelling of the trains."

Although others endured, that in itself does not indicate whether they wanted to endure or not. Perhaps they had given up hope, would have preferred to desert, and so on. Or perhaps they did want to endure (in the sense of a conscious desire) for the sake of their careers, for the sake of the Nazi cause, or similar reasons. Among them was Dietmar B., barely twenty years old at the end of the war.[55] In his interview with the attending physician in 1949, he did not initially mention having suffered from anxiety during the war. Yet when the veteran began to describe his persistent physical complaints—attacks of vertigo, sudden loss of consciousness, tingling in the fingers—he came to speak of the war. During the final two years, he served on the eastern front, where, near Leningrad at the end of 1943, he had "noticed an inner trembling and fluttering" for the first time. However, he denied that this had also been accompanied by "feeling anxious." Still, the physical complaints continued to bother him. Thus, the transcript of the admission interview states that the "symptoms" returned "especially after critical situations" such as military or bombing attacks. The following months saw episodes of restlessness and dizziness; on occasion he had blanched and collapsed. After entering the military hospital in 1944, he began to feel better. But later, back on the front, the "old symptoms" returned, as the record indicates. Only later, when a doctor asked him whether he had been afraid during the war, did Dietmar B. concede that it had "varied." Yet admitting fear was clearly difficult for him. He immediately underscored that he had been "the last person to run away in a retreat" even though he "had sometimes been afraid," as he again confessed at the end after this clarification.

Determination to persevere and fear were thus not mutually exclusive, just as these demeanors can hardly be interpreted as mirroring personal attitudes regarding the war. This is also the case for physical symptoms that seem easily interpretable as an expression of fear. That inference is not always correct, and fear is not always immediately recognizable in body language, as is often assumed.[56] Just as there is no physically obvious form of anxiety, the presence of fear does not necessarily presume particular behavioral manifestations. "Nobody noticed anything," recounted Werner P., for example, who was actually plagued by anxiety during the war.[57] His fears did not stem only from the war; rather he had struggled with various forms of anxiety for a long time. During the mid-1930s, when he was already more than twenty years old, Werner P. had suffered from persistent inhibitions and a tendency to cry easily. At the time, he had often prayed that nobody would see him "weak, soft, and ridiculous." He had even resolved that he would "rather die than cry." Werner P. had longed for the war, hoping, as he explained, that it would free him from his problems. Yet even his "glowing thoughts of the fatherland" could not fend off his anxiety. His interview transcript reports: "Great anxiety during the Polish campaign, much anxiety, frequent inner trembling. In France, of course, anxiety again." Werner P. described himself as an *Angsthase*, a "chicken." In the military, we read, he often prayed, "Lord, please let me persevere." He nonetheless tried, unsuccessfully, to achieve the rank of a noncommissioned officer. Werner P. saw himself as someone who had "always only wanted to avoid attracting attention," to always "remain . . . in the middle." On the other hand, he fully acknowledged his ambitions. It appears that his raw feelings of fear dominated only occasionally; usually his feelings were more fragmented, more ambivalent. This again became clear during the advance into Russia in 1941, when Werner P. had become "incapacitated," as the doctor put it. According to what he claimed in 1949, Werner P. had thought at the time: "I didn't care about anything; what's happening here is a scam, no one could stand this." Eight years later, he recalled failing to help a comrade. Pangs of conscience about abandoning the man continued to torment him for years. By his own account, Werner P. had saved his own neck. He soldiered on until his capture in the summer of 1944.

But the end of hostilities, which occurred for some when they were captured before May 8, 1945, and for others only through the German capitulation, hardly meant that the connection between fear and the war ceased to exist.

Feelings of anxiety could be triggered by internal or external stimuli, such as images or noises that momentarily revived the war. In other instances, fears reemerged without a recognizable cause. In such cases, anxiety became a linguistic realm of war.[58] Other cases suggest that anxiety scenarios developed in uncontrolled emotional states, which merged with lasting individual perceptions of the war and war-related anxieties. One thing surfaced here clearly: in the veterans' after-the-fact experiences, the war was characterized by deeply unsettling features.

Fears and anxieties were often diffuse and their origins difficult to decipher. This is revealed by the anxiety scenarios that Hermann M. experienced in the summer of 1945.[59] Upon returning home after a brief internment in an American POW camp, his father found Hermann M.'s behavior unremarkable, noting that he was "perhaps a little quiet." One night in July, however, he found his son lying outside in front of the front door, wearing only a shirt. After going inside again, "He became agitated, shouting loudly that his father should watch out—didn't he see that at least ten men were aiming at him?" Subsequently, his son continued to manifest these behaviors. Although he was usually quiet, he sometimes started "talking nonsense." Following the father's statements, the doctor noted that Hermann M. was apparently always "concerned with enemies who wanted to fire at him." Although Hermann's father had no idea why his son peered into every corner and crevice of the nearby stall, there was no doubt in his mind that Hermann was at times exhibiting "obvious signs of anxiety."

We can only identify scattered fragments of Hermann M.'s internal experiential world. In his initial interview with the psychiatrist, his responses were hesitant, scraps of words as in the following sequence: "(What did you see in the stall?) . . . a shadow . . . (What did it say?) . . . (Does the shadow speak?) . . . (nods his head affirmatively) (What does he say, then?) . . . Nazi dogs." At this point Hermann M. became silent. He offered no further clues to his fear, which continued over the following days. In response to the doctor's renewed effort to ascertain the causes of his fears, Hermann M. persisted in his silence and turned away. Only later did he hint that during his hallucinations he was driven by the fear of being killed. Hermann M. was tormented by a fear that his enemies wanted to shoot him; their voices plagued him. He was suffering from immense paranoia that manifested as hallucinatory voices announcing "they wanted to hang him, shoot him." Other times, he believed that "murderers" were at the door who "wanted to get him." The doctor could not determine precisely why his patient felt so threatened. Hermann M. had only mentioned one remark by the shadow that was stalking him: "Nazi dogs."

It remains unclear whether Hermann M. had already feared such animosity during the war or whether he was seized by it only in the postwar period. Perhaps he was exposed to hostility during a temporary, wartime assignment as a guard of "foreign workers," or when he himself was interned after the war for three months in a camp in Recklinghausen. But this is merely speculation. A precise time and place are impossible to ascertain. If we consider the different elements of his imagined, anxiety-filled scenarios, it becomes apparent that they represented a melding of wartime and postwar experiences. This was not unique, as the case of Rolf S. has already shown.[60] Rolf S.'s dreamworld was permeated with "all kinds of war experiences," but also encompassed postwar fantasies of his own execution as a war criminal. Similarly, his suddenly surfacing fears convey the impression of being a distorted echo of various layers of feelings from both the war and the postwar period. His symptoms began three years after the end of the war, which put his deployment on the eastern front five years behind him. But he nonetheless would ask, "Are the Russians here yet?" He felt persecuted, as his parents observed. He also repeatedly claimed that he had to fight for his relatives, and they reported that he once even called out, "Give us eggs, then we can fight for you." Now and then, he confessed that he was deeply afraid for his family, and he often spoke of "having to hang himself so that his family wouldn't have to suffer with him." His parents also often heard their son proclaim, "I have to fight, I have to fight." At other times, they observed that noises from passing trains or cars would startle Rolf S. He would suddenly "jump to his feet and look out the window," explaining to his parents that he was afraid "that the Russians were coming to get him."

In the postwar period such fear of persecution was common. Even for those individuals who sought out psychiatric treatment, we cannot view the paranoia exclusively as a symptom of a mental illness. In the postwar period, the fear of being followed, spied on, denounced, or taken away affected more than simply isolated individuals. Rather, a substantial number of cases make it clear that the anxieties at work, and the rumors accompanying them, had a realistic core.[61] In the cases we examined, what is especially striking is how strongly the Allied presence nourished the persecution anxieties. Often, as with Rolf S., they expressed themselves as a fear of the Russians. Günter B., as well, told his wife one day that he was concerned about being "transferred to the Russian zone," which was his explanation for "standing at the window and recording all of the cars that drove by."[62] Indeed, the presence of the occupying forces was generally the impetus that sparked or intensified paranoid anxieties. However, in the cases presented here there is a significant and telling difference. Many Germans experienced a panic-stricken fear of ultimately being unable to hide anything from the victorious powers. Sensing that further silence would only warrant more severe retribution for the crimes of the Nazi period, they turned themselves in to the American and British authorities.[63] No one surrendered to the Russians.

Apparently, there was enough knowledge of the crimes committed in the east to instill far greater fear of punishment by the Russians than any revenge that would be taken by the West. We are almost forced to make this assumption in the case of Herbert I., who additionally had his eye on the differing dispositions to impose punishment on the part of the individual Western powers.[64] As with the great majority of other repatriated soldiers whose fears of persecution focused on the Allied occupation forces, Herbert I.'s anxieties surfaced during the course of his denazification proceedings.[65] "Conflict in filling out the questionnaire," the doctor had entered in the patient's medical files under the rubric "present illness," additionally noting: "Fear of being handed over to the Russians. Patient traveled from the American to the English occupied zone, turned himself in voluntarily to the Secret Service, and was released after questioning there. Suicide attempt with a pocket knife." Herbert I., who had already procured a position as a pastor and had resumed living with his wife and child only a year after the war had ended, had seen no way out. The reaction of the British had not mitigated his fear of extradition. As he explained to the doctor, he was still oppressed by a "completely pathetic fear." Indeed the psychiatrist predicted that "if someone came to arrest him, he would make a pitiful figure. He would completely break down."

Herbert I. perceived his situation as entirely hopeless, although in his own eyes it was not his fault. "He had the misfortune," he explained, "to have belonged to an organization of very negative repute with the Allies." But he had recently done something he regretted deeply: "He had been, as he put it, so stupid as to have disclosed everything without having been asked, and also to have written it down in the questionnaire." He could already imagine the conclusions the Allies would draw from this: he would be falsely accused of a crime. In that respect, he was quite sure about that: "He hadn't broken any laws," he made clear to the doctor, "but who would even care?" He described his activities during the war as "the most harmless things one could imagine." Meanwhile, Herbert I. had not served as a pastor for the entire war. Born in Crimea, he later temporarily worked as an elementary school teacher in Rumania, and then as a pastor in Dobrudscha for a number of years. He spoke fluent Rumanian and Russian. In 1940 he began his service in the Wehrmacht, where he worked as an interpreter in the intelligence service until the end of the war.

In that capacity, Herbert I. asserted, he simply carried out orders, which was a recurring narrative in the postwar years. Regardless of the contents of the orders or the consequences they might have had, he saw himself as bearing no personal responsibility. In any event, he outwardly took the offensive with this position. At least, the doctor recorded his patient's explanations as follows: "He translated the interrogations or instructions for agents. He had been required to do so, and he was certain that he personally had harmed no one."

Although Herbert I. did not regard himself as guilty of any misdeed, his apprehensions and explanations make it perfectly clear he was very aware that the Wehrmacht had conducted no ordinary war in the east. He was familiar with the contents of interrogations; he transmitted agents' reports and relayed orders to them in their own languages. As an interpreter, he had ample insight: he was complicit. As long as his feeling of strength and superiority persisted during the war, internally consuming fears could be mostly kept at bay. But this changed after Germany was defeated, when German veterans saw themselves helplessly at the mercy of the occupation forces. In retrospect, memories of wartime events and actions became a source of anxiety, even if the anxiety was not necessarily accompanied by moral scruples concerning their own deeds. In any event, this anxiety did drive postwar fear of persecution. For Herbert I., the scale of the anxiety was so great that it dictated his actions. "His wife had long warned him against mentioning his work for the intelligence service at all," the psychiatrist noted. But as Herbert I. described it in his own words, it was "an internal demonic force" that drove him to talk about it. The doctor described it merely as "the fear that the information would come out."

In the postwar situation such fears could develop a dynamic entirely of their own. It often became difficult to distinguish which was the soldiers' greater source of anxiety: looking back at the past, or ahead to the future. For many people the anxieties they had experienced during the war merged with retrospective fears, acute fright, and the diffuse anxiety about life in general, echoing one another and shaping a broadly shared state of anxiety in the immediate postwar years. This is clearly evident in the case of Gustav N., who was admitted to a psychiatric hospital in January 1947, one day after his release from an internment camp.[66] Having attempted suicide shortly after his arrest by the Allied authorities in May 1945, he had already received different forms of psychiatric treatment for "depression" during his internment. Yet he was still tormented by "a deep-seated inner anxiety and restlessness," as the psychiatrist noted. Gustav N. had joined the Deutsche Arbeitsfront (German Labor Front, the Nazi trade union organization) in 1939 and had then briefly served as a soldier in the Volkssturm. Formed largely of those too young or old to serve in the Wehrmacht, this auxiliary force bolstered military efforts in the last phase of the war. The doctor's report on his admission interview reveals that Gustav N. "reproached himself in the harshest possible way . . . on account of his political activities from 1939 onward." Elaborating this point, his stammering only grew worse, revealing his profound fear of further retribution. He believed he would soon face another trial. He had "hurt many people," he stuttered, explaining that "because of my statement, my testimony . . . they were turned down for positions or lost their jobs . . . or even faced legal charges."

It is no longer possible to determine which position Gustav N. held with the German Labor Front. In conversation with his psychiatrist, he defined himself as a "[Nazi] party epicure" (a *Parteigenießer*) who had been able to live "lavishly" during the Nazi years. But it was difficult for an outsider to connect that with his newly kindled anxiety about the possibility of imminent arrest. As the doctor observed, Gustav N.'s entire manner was "driven and agitated," although no primary cause could be found for this general demeanor. The accounts he offered over the following days brought further anxieties to the fore, with some of them stemming from his time in an internment camp. Gustav N. was convinced that he was responsible for the arrest of his best friend. Gustav N. had been locked up in a cell together with a man he believed to be a member of the Secret Service—a story that he himself considered incomprehensible weeks later. But after several conversations with Gustav N., the man had stood up and declared "that was all he wanted to know from him, that he didn't require any further information, and then left the cell." Gustav N. suspected that the man was a Secret Service agent. In any event, his friend—Gustav N. believed—was arrested immediately thereafter. But an event from the war continued to preoccupy him as well, namely, his own escape. He was still struggling with it. At the time, fear had overwhelmed him, the same fear that he could not accept in others and that he could scarcely acknowledge in himself even now. The doctor's record of Gustav N.'s account states: "As the Russians advanced he had fled like a coward." On the eve of the Russians' arrival, he had belied his panic. Fully intending to flee, he had already arranged to receive orders from the responsible *Gauleiter* (regional party leader) to procure all sorts of goods in Lübeck for refugees from the east. Yet as soon as he had the necessary paperwork in his hands, he drove off. While he had demanded endurance and fortitude from others, he had tried to conceal his own plans to flee. "He would never forget how the workers in his street watched him drive off," he recalled, "and only the day before he had called on everyone to hold out—which is why all of his former friends are through with him!"

Many former soldiers were plagued by an immense unease in the postwar period. It is often difficult to distinguish which was more terrifying—to gaze back into the past or to look forward toward the future. At times it appears as if anxiety permeated every aspect of life, including the private sphere.[67] While still interned as a POW, Gustav N. had refused to see his son when he came to the camp's fence to visit him. Months later, after his release from the camp, we read in the interview notes, Gustav N. dreaded the reunion with his family, while they remained completely unaware of the misfortune he would cause for them. When his term of imprisonment came to an end, he by no means counted on being able to successfully rebuild a respectable existence. Much like many other repatriated German soldiers in those years, Gustav N. was trapped in a state of pervasive anxiety. These cases reveal just how deeply seated the veterans' fears were that they could not escape punishment for their actions under the Nazi regime. Innumerable soldiers came to recognize the burden of their previous actions only at the moment when the invasion of foreign troops was imminent and when Germany's defeat could no longer be prevented. "When the collapse came," we read in Gustav N.'s interview notes, "he erased his membership in the German Labor Front from his army ID." In fact, the fear that there would be no escape proved to be anything but a figment of the imagination in hundreds of thousands of cases. The fear of punishment was rampant in postwar Germany: even those whose denazification proceedings ended with a mild outcome continued to worry. A gnawing fear "that someone could turn the tables" had become entrenched.[68]

Facing Defeat and Ruin

> *At that time, we cultivated a berserk sense of humor. We heaped ridicule on death and danger, distorted things, and pushed all our thoughts into the realm of the grotesque. . . . But beneath this mask, a tragedy was unfolding, an inner disaster was taking its relentless course. I drifted into a neutral state of the soul. The final values broke down, the good, the noble, and the beautiful died. The spirits left me. The armor of numbness with which I steeled myself against horror, dread, fear, and madness, which allowed me to stop suffering and screaming out loud, crushed the gentle impulses within me, snapped off any sprout of hope, faith, and love for fellow human beings, and turned my heart to stone. I was perishing and made fun of myself.*[69]

When the unconditional surrender of May 8, 1945, sealed the complete collapse of the Nazi regime, the German populace experienced an enormous range of contradictory moods and emotions. Relief that the violence of war and the constant threat of death had come to an end mingled with distress and grief over the human, material, and nonmaterial losses. Countless numbers of Germans were marked by deep exhaustion paired with a longing, indeed a real hunger, for a more sheltered, unburdened life. Acceptance, even joy, but also rejection and fear confronted the occupiers, mixed with feelings of being helplessly at the mercy of outer forces because of the complete lack of clarity regarding Germany's future—and with it one's personal fate. What we are dealing with here comprises more than a just the coexistence of different feelings in different people for whom a number of factors were decisive, such as political convictions, the social situation, or even their initial experiences with occupying forces. Rather, what emerges from autobiographical reports and diaries are alternating streams of highly diverse, sometimes contradictory feelings, in a single individual.[70] Following total war, for most people in the now nonexistent German Reich total defeat in fact meant considerable insecurity. For some people in this situation, as accounts from memory inform us, virtually anything was conceivable. As an Austrian woman put it in reference to her own feelings, "Everything, literally *everything*, had become possible, even one's own destruction—and in view of what had taken place, that didn't seem unlikely."[71]

The simultaneity and interplay of the widely varying emotions was not simply a snapshot of the emotional panorama on May 8. Glimmers of hope and fearful premonitions followed one another in rapid succession, a phenomenon registered by foreign observers starting with the invasion and for weeks afterward.[72] It was, summarized a British reporter, as if the plot of a story "changed constantly so that advancing meant being constantly steered in different directions and facing fresh contradictions."[73]

For the occupiers, these contradictions were surprising and confusing. Even more confusing was the apparent absence of any consciousness of guilt. Every gesture that did not reveal deep distress, remorse, or guilt appeared grotesque given the atrocious nature of the crimes perpetrated on millions during Nazi rule. The Allied program of decreed confrontation, which put the revolting nature of the crimes before the Germans' very eyes, further increased the occupying forces' impression of a deeply inappropriate, evasive, and defiant behavior on the German side, causing the program to be scuttled after a short time.[74] Rather than grappling with the atrocities and accepting their responsibility as accessories to them, the Germans, it appeared, were insisting on their past ignorance and displaying detachment. Seemingly indifferent and full of self-pity, they were turning their backs on the past and resuming everyday life instead.[75]

The perception that a "society of perpetrators" had failed in its confrontation with Nazi mass crimes was not merely the conclusion resulting from the early observations but would influence the way postwar German society was perceived and described for a long time to come.[76] In light of their own dismay over the mass murder, for many people it seemed obvious to assume that the behavior of the German population at the time could reflect nothing other than an inappropriate stance toward the crimes that had been committed. Yet the violence the Germans themselves experienced—the horror of Nazi rule, the bombing attacks, the exertion of fleeing, sometimes as a result of violent expulsion—must surely also be considered as a reason that the population quickly immersed itself in daily life, and for the Germans' seemingly autistic concern for their own fate, their search for distraction, and their alleged silence about the mass death.[77] According to Richard Bessel, it was actually the "shock of the events" generated by the concentration and escalation of extreme violence in the 1940s that made it impossible for Germans "to concern themselves seriously with war and death." Within this perspective, the essential characteristic of Germany's postwar years was "life after death." Apparently, it consisted of a life in which death was no longer meant to be seen.[78]

This approach explains the often maintained postwar German silence regarding Nazi crimes in terms of a "shock of violence." It undermines prevailing morality-centered interpretive expectations and shifts the focus to the destructive force of the entire war. Pointedly formulated, the effects of violence also reveal themselves precisely where they have not recognizably surfaced. One could take such a perspective as a plea for recognizing the diversity of ways in which the violence of the war was processed. Until now, however, the way individuals coped with the experience of violence has not been further analyzed by historians. Perhaps this is not a coincidence. For the question of the shaping impact of violence becomes obsolete when that impact can be found everywhere, even in places where any traces of violence seemingly disappear.

One of these traces can be found in the mood of disillusionment so widespread in postwar Germany. Its reasons are frequently misunderstood: it was not exclusively a reaction to the occupiers or the denazification proceedings. Rather, it was also a reflection to violence and death. In the face of ruin, it represented a way of coming to terms with destruction and mass murder. Without a doubt, the disillusionment had highly disparate motivations. On the one hand, it stemmed from the total failure of Nazi promises—which became obvious to many whether at the front or at home, no later than by the last phase of the war.[79] On the other hand, it expressed an inner emptiness that sometimes seems to have formed during the war, an emptiness in which questions about the values that made a life worth sacrificing were no longer posed. The disillusionment not only involved the destruction of Nazi fantasies about the future, but also irrefutable insight into human failure and the annulment of everyday morality through the horror of war.[80] In addition, the expansion of the concentration camp system into the German interior, which proceeded at an ever faster pace and thus became more visible as the Third Reich began to disintegrate, erased all doubt as to the criminal nature of the regime.[81] When the Allies forced Germans to look the crimes in the eye, the result was a further devaluation of individual self-image, which even now continues to obstruct our view of the scope of personal disappointment over the vehemence of the wartime events.

On closer examination, it is difficult to tell with certainty whether the distance Germans across the board kept from Nazi politics and ideology during the first postwar years resulted from coercion or sweeping disillusionment, or whether it was the expression of a long-maintained oppositional stance. At least in the public sphere, almost nobody admitted to having championed Nazi ideas. Belief in Nazi ideals now seemed nothing less than an avowal of policies of annihilation, the "Nazi" a cipher for mass crimes. A few days after the capitulation, Ruth Andreas-Friedrich observed in her notebooks that "the certificate of good character rules the hour." She was aware that distinctions could be made between former party members. But she also knew that those who followed along with zealous Nazis felt the same urgent need to see their "Nazism attested away."[82]

This behavior is understandable against the backdrop of promptly ordered forced labor for former party members and their impending denazification.[83] An inclination toward self-deception concerning one's own former dreams that had been inextricably linked to the Nazi system is fully apparent here, and not only on the part of Nazi functionaries and activists. Completely ordinary fellow travelers also had difficulty admitting to themselves that their willingness to serve the system was actually tied to enthusiasm; retrospectively this had become disconcerting. One such person was Gustav B., who underwent psychiatric treatment for several weeks in September 1946.[84] Much like countless others, he had been a party member, joining in 1940, apparently from conviction rather than under any sort of pressure. As he explained it, "his patriotic orientation" had caused him to "believe . . . that the Nazi Party was capable of saving the fatherland." Gustav B. did not try to hide this idealism. Nevertheless, he did not hesitate to add that "after a short time" he "couldn't help discovering flaws and mistakes" in the party. He even thought that the deep shock that had seized him starting with the capitulation had basically been predictable for that reason: "All his hopes had been destroyed," recounted Gustav B., with which he explained his condition at the time to himself. As he saw it, he had had "a nervous breakdown."

Gustav B. left no doubt concerning the depth of this shock, whereby the reason he cited for it underscored the distance he had already achieved from Nazism. In speaking with the doctor, he further emphasized this distance by adding, we read in the notes, that this "nervous breakdown" had actually lasted a shorter time "than in '33"—when he had also suffered one. Gustav B.'s political views had been different then. In the early 1920s, he had initially been active in the German Communist Party and then in the Social Democratic Workers' Youth Movement (Sozialistische Arbeiterjugend), where, as he underscored, he had been "very active" and "idealistic" as well. The physician also recorded that "shortly before '33" he "again began to waver in his political position," because "in his party things weren't proceeding the way he had imagined they would as an idealist. That had weighed him down; he was inwardly torn." With the "upheaval," as Gustav B. put it, he had "completely collapsed." As he explained, he had "lost all support, all hope." Gustav B. did not explain how he positioned himself politically in the seven years between the Nazi accession to power and his own entry into the Nazi Party in 1940. But from the notes on his narrative, it becomes clear that his sense of confidence and his optimism had both been restored.

Gustav B.'s political orientation had moved from one political extreme to the other. Yet it was not his political involvement with the Communists and Social Democrats that he felt called upon to explain to himself and others, but rather his belief in the Nazi Party, which he expressed by becoming a member. As he portrayed it, his party membership amounted to a chapter of his life that held no special significance—a bagatelle from which only his family seemed to have suffered. For that, he reproached himself. He had "not provided for his family as he should have" and "should have stayed out of political life." Then everything could have taken its "normal course" after the capitulation. In any case, he had been able to begin working for the military government shortly after the defeat, but had been dismissed very quickly because of a denunciation. Gustav B. insisted he had done nothing wrong and indicated to the doctor that he could not find any plausible reasons why he was "shy, distrustful, very anxious" fourteen months after the end of the war. According to the psychiatrist's notes, the patient explained: "Earlier, he had been politically persecuted and had reason to be distrustful at the time; but it wasn't necessary to feel that way anymore, and nevertheless it had crept over him." Gustav B. presented himself to the doctor as an upstanding citizen. Nazism was a thing of the past, and he allegedly did not identify with the collapsed regime. What did weigh heavily on him, he claimed, was "especially the situation of the fatherland." Although it would appear that some aspects of Gustav B.'s self-representation were distorted, it also seems not to have been sheer masquerade. Rather, it reveals a need to ensure distance from the Nazi system for himself in such a way that his earlier enthusiasm could be enclosed in the past in order to reduce from afar its strength.

Nevertheless, as the case of Adolf W. from 1948 shows, even the memory of supporting the Nazi authorities in minor ways continued to be distressing and unpleasant for Germans, for devotion to the Führer had been expressed in trivial everyday matters, which people were reluctant to admit after the fact. This was the case of Adolf W.,[85] who entered psychiatric treatment in 1948 on the urging of his close relations, although his inner struggle is not immediately evident. It is only from the notes on his admission interview that we learn of his extreme anxiety and depression, and his sense of having no energy at all. Adolf W. had already been conscripted into the Wehrmacht in the spring of 1939. With the exception of one deployment in France, he spent the great majority of his time as part of the forces occupying Holland. When the war came to an end, he found it extremely difficult to gain a foothold in civilian life. According to information from his wife, he had never been a hands-on type anyway, showing instead an intermittent tendency toward "doom and gloom" (*Schwarzseherei*). She explained to the doctor, however, that there seemed to be particularly acute reason for his present condition. As the psychiatrist noted, she felt that Adolf W. was "very depressed about the course of the war."

This formulation pointed to more than depression resulting from a series of military defeats. It also circumscribed the concomitant end of his own delusions of military grandeur. But his despair over the "outcome and course of the war," which he reaffirmed in a later interview, comprised much more. His reference to the "war" was a way of referring to and processing not only military matters, but also Nazism and its crimes. This becomes clear in a short interview sequence in which Adolf W. attempts to explain to the doctor and himself the reason for his persistent and sporadically almost raving fear that others wished to harm him. "Well, I used to be *völkisch*," he responded to the psychiatrist's question. "We often dressed the shop window very beautifully for the commander. After the collapse, I believed the tables would be turned, and I'd be in for it."

What Adolf W. described here is a gesture of respect and affection. In his everyday life, he had made a demonstrative indication of support and his sense of belonging; he identified with the military might of the Nazi state. The files do not make clear whether this was limited to obeisance to the supreme ruler and an approval of his military megalomania, or whether his agreement with the Nazi ideology was more extensive. What does emerge clearly in any event is that Adolf W. was expecting the Allies to retaliate as a direct reaction to his behavior. Knowledge of the crimes would certainly have been sufficient grounds for such an expectation. Later we will see that Adolf W.'s delusional ideas and his family situation point to a conflicted relationship with Nazism.[86] For now, we can simply note that whatever differences he may have had regarding the regime's criminal policies, one thing emerged very clearly: in his own eyes he was not able simply to fend off the thought that in his *völkisch* zeal and veneration of the Führer he had condoned the crimes and become complicit. A gnawing insecurity had crept into his pronounced efforts to always "do the right thing," which the doctor in charge saw as stemming primarily from a "sensitive feeling for what's right and good form."

In the face of ruin and defeat, various ideological and patriotic illusions concerning the future Nazi state were shattered. But illusions about oneself had also been demolished, or had disintegrated beforehand. The violence of the war dismantled self-perceptions before the Third Reich fell amid total defeat. This is not about returning veterans who complained about the missing "thanks of the fatherland." (There is undeniably evidence of this disillusionment as well, as confirmed in scattered psychiatric files and letters to pension offices, but these stem from a later period.)[87] Rather, the reference here is to the sort of disappointment that gave rise to despair over oneself, disenchantment, and sometimes even shock at oneself during the war. The narratives involved here were not recounted in a rhetorical mode of victimization, as was often the case in later military memoirs, popular descriptions of the war, and public statements by former Wehrmacht members.[88] No tone of lamentation was struck here either in respect to fanatic generals or the fundamentally barbaric nature of the war. The burden lay with oneself. For it was one's own actions that became a burden over the course of the war, for some soldiers suddenly, for others gradually, and one could not readily exonerate oneself.

Drafted into the Wehrmacht in 1943 at the age of nineteen and trained to be a combat engineer, Gerd M., faced a moral dilemma from the start of his military service.[89] He was deployed in Italy. The war repulsed him. He told the doctor that although he had "a good relationship" with his comrades, "the entire environment and the way he was treated did not agree with him." Gerd M.

"did not like being a soldier." There is, in fact, little evidence that he tried to prove himself in this war. He remained a private during the entire period of service and never received any commendation. From a nurse in whom Gerd M. once confided, the psychiatrist in charge learned that "murdering" had "been difficult" for the former soldier. Killing was actually disgusting for Gerd M., and an agony, and he did not hide it. Yet he evidently could not gain a sense of moral superiority from his disgust. He had functioned as a soldier, and his horror at this apparently sat deep. His self-image had been broken. He had no sense of having maintained an intact personality in the war. This emerges from a short interview sequence with the psychiatrist in which Gerd M. explained: "Even as a soldier, his life often seemed senseless to him . . . his life was something indifferent to him." He had not, however, entertained thoughts "of ending it himself." Three years after the war, Gerd M. still had not truly succeeded in breaking through this feeling of emptiness. He had no "proper goal" in sight, and in the intervening years had been unable to find "meaning in the world."

Isolated expressions of such exhausting disillusionment are known from diaries kept by soldiers who experienced the inhumanity of the war in Russia.[90] In that context, such passages were the sum of a deep shock fed by two sources: First, the horror that seized so many, despite their ideological delusion, at the relentless barbaric aggression toward alleged "subhumans." And second, bitter insight into the extent violence had not only become a personal routine but actually a sinister form of entertainment, as opposed to the frequent state of "murderous waiting."[91]

The case of Ludwig D., however, shows that this was far from the only cause for shock at one's transformation during the war,[92] because the reality of the war was not only pitiless but incalculable. What continued to torment this former Wehrmacht soldier years later was a single nighttime episode. It was the reason he accused himself of being a "murderer." As Ludwig D. explained in the psychiatric clinic five years later, at the end of 1942 he had shot and killed a German lieutenant. It happened "by mistake, in fear and haste," we read in the case notes that record the event. Ludwig D. was on guard duty, and when the lieutenant suddenly emerged Ludwig D. had taken him for an enemy soldier. Allegedly, he called out to him twice but, as the doctor noted, "the lieutenant made a motion with his right hand as if he were reaching for his pistol." Ludwig D. had shot, "out of fear," he emphasized again, in order to "prevent the perceived attack."

Ludwig D. had been stationed in Poland and France and had participated in the "Russian campaign" and fought at Stalingrad. There can be no doubt whatsoever that he had seen many corpses during the war, and it is highly probable he had also killed people. But Ludwig D.'s accounts of the war circled without exception around the shooting of the German lieutenant, which he claimed to dream about every night. This incident was, he asserted as stubbornly as despairingly, the cause of his "imbalance" and "lasting torment." He believed that he had had no success whatsoever since then, even going so far as to embrace the idea that everyone was against him as of that day. If he told either his father or his fiancée about the events, he explained to the psychiatrist, he would expect only contempt.

Accordingly, Ludwig D. had always kept silent about the incident, not even reporting it on the night it happened. At the time, Ludwig D. was an officer cadet; if the incident had become known, his career as an officer would have been over—this was the argument he offered for his silence. Even though it temporarily allowed him to maintain the illusion of a military career in this way, he explained, the event during the night in question had nevertheless destroyed his previous self-image. Fear, cowardice, weakness, and negligence had determined his behavior. True, he had been tired and it was cold, but the "watch duty offense" he had committed was an inexcusable, discrediting deed. He recriminated himself for not "taking cover" and "then jumping out after calling a third time." "I had the advantage. He was exposed," the former soldier continued, underscoring not only the gravity of his offense but, above all, the baseness of his behavior, which had tormented him ever since. Before the catalog of military virtues, a catalog with which Ludwig D., given his keen aspirations to become an officer, had certainly identified strongly, he had failed. His martial, manly self had been thwarted. He stood before himself, so to speak, aghast and horrified.

A sense of failure in the face of general principles of ethics and values made many soldiers not only lastingly insecure about themselves. Beyond that, they came to see themselves as sinister. This war, too, was no "moral no-man's-land."[93] Loyalty, obedience, bravery, and a readiness to make sacrifices were certainly components of Germany's moral universe.[94] The Nazi leadership promoted them as social norms for strengthening the *Volksgemeinschaft* ("volk community"), and, within the Wehrmacht, additionally insisted on them as absolute preconditions for the effectiveness and comradely cohesion of the troops. Furthermore, these values signified an ideal of *Haltung* (inner attitude), to which countless soldiers were committed and which they often expressed through comradely solidarity.[95] But it was not merely the rigorous expectations of superiors and comrades about conduct and the threat of punishment that gave these values something like an inexorable character. Self-commitment also endowed them with a relentless quality that could be directed as much against oneself as against the enemy.

We see this in the case of Alfred J.[96] Four years after the end of the war, during his stay in the psychiatric hospital, he broke his own silence regarding a long-past wartime incident. We learn the following from the record of his narrative: During an alarm, a lieutenant rushed out of the mess hall and fired shots at random, thus accidentally wounding a petty officer. Although Alfred J. observed the entire incident, he kept quiet about it, supposedly on the lieutenant's order. Alfred J. had thereby obeyed the order, covered up the incident in comradely fashion, and protected the lieutenant. During the ensuing period, however, remaining silent became a crucial test of his inner strength. Keeping the incident secret made him uneasy. Nonetheless, he kept his word, even after the war, when he no longer needed to fear any unpleasantness from the lieutenant. Loyalty to the lieutenant doubtlessly also represented loyalty to himself to some degree, even though Alfred J. evidently felt morally unsure about his behavior in this matter. When he broke his silence, the struggle that had been simmering inside him surfaced. As the medical record states, he "could no longer endure" the silence; "it burdened his soul." Apparently, Alfred J.'s cooperation in the secret accord had increasingly become a tormenting source of shame.

After their return to Germany, Wehrmacht veterans did not always find it easy to shed wartime moral standards. In particular, gnawing guilt feelings resulting from transgressions against the moral demands associated with the ideal of comradeship were capable of remaining virulent long after the end of the war. Helmut G. was still suffering from such guilt feelings in 1949, as became clear during his stay in the psychiatric clinic.[97] He was nineteen when he was sent to the eastern front for the first time shortly before the capitulation. He was involved in a combat mission that lasted about three months. On May 9, 1945, his unit was dissolved, and like everyone else, as Helmut G. reported, he followed the order that "soldiers should fight their way through to the Elbe on their own to avoid becoming prisoners of the Russians." As he later indicated to the psychiatrist, his "experiences in combat . . . had already had an excessively strong effect on him," but what festered even more—if we are to take the feelings he reported at face value—were his experiences during the retreat, more precisely, his own lack of ability. Since he was a noncommissioned officer at the time, "An entire group of new, awkward recruits" attached themselves to him. But "since these people were either sixteen or over forty-five years old, they had not been able to brave the exhausting march, and for that reason he either lost them or left them behind." Helmut G. held out no hope as to the later fate of these men. "Corresponding to the circumstances," the doctor continued his paraphrase of Helmut G.'s account, the soldier "had to assume that they were either killed or taken prisoner by the Russians." Helmut G. had "reproached himself for this with extraordinary severity." "Even now" he bore "a strong sense of guilt."

In the face of defeat, Helmut G. had broken the "inviolable law of true comradeship" that continued to be glorified in public speeches commemorating veterans after the end of the war.[98] Clashing with the idealization of such comradeship in the postwar cult of the fallen—the image of German soldiers placing their lives on the line under the worst of circumstances to save their helpless companions from the enemy[99]—for Helmut G. such an act of heroic assistance had taken second place to the struggle for his own survival. Four years later, he was still lamenting the victims, and far removed from stylizing the Wehrmacht as a community of victims and the suffering, a process often discernible in various public statements by former Wehrmacht members,[100] Helmut G. was plagued by self-reproach. Within his own feelings, the horror of the war did not absolve him. He felt that he shared responsibility for the presumed death of the soldiers. In his own eyes, he was a perpetrator, and blamed himself.

The psychiatric files give the impression that self-reproach of this sort was no rarity among former soldiers. Sometimes the sense of guilt was tied to the death of a single close comrade; at other times it was associated with the many casualties of a battle, or with the hard fate endured by disabled German veterans.[101] We find expressions of shock and empathy, and talk of the inconceivable suffering of victims from one's own ranks. These were one focus of mourning by former Wehrmacht members, but above all they expressed feelings of responsibility for the deaths or severe mutilation of soldiers in the own ranks. This was not a specifically German phenomenon. Five years after the war's end, Irving N. Berlin, a psychiatrist at the University of California Medical School in San Francisco, emphasized a problem he saw as drastically underestimated or even denied among his colleagues, namely, the self-accusations of former soldiers who believed they shared responsibility s for the death of their comrades.[102] If we compare the American and German self-accusations, we see that in both cases veterans wrestled with a sense of having contributed to the death of others through negligence, cowardice, or recklessness and being thereby partially responsible for it.

Since the soldiers' hopes of surviving the war rested not least on their belief in mutual reliability and responsibility for one another, self-blame for the death of comrades is by no means surprising. In contrast, we rarely encounter explicit guilt feelings when it comes to the death of enemy soldiers. Their death tends to be seen as a logical consequence of a state of war that demanded obedience and the performance of one's duty,[103] and in which the threat to one's own existence made killing seem a form of action that followed the demands of reason.[104] It is well known that in postwar Germany similar arguments were applied with respect to Nazi war crimes and persecution. Yet, given the way the war was conducted against the partisans and the way the civilian population was treated in the east, it is likely that in the "total war" that the Wehrmacht conducted on the eastern front, at least some of the soldiers retained an awareness of the injustice being done.[105] In general, however, it will be difficult to find any open avowals of guilt in the sense of an acceptance of personal responsibility for these crimes.[106]

Nonetheless, statements by former Wehrmacht members during the postwar period suggest that the rigorous confrontation with the atrocities committed by the Nazis imposed on the Germans by the occupation forces did catalyze a deep sense of shame in many cases. In view of the mass murders, self-respect appears to have been difficult to maintain. Attempts to distance oneself from the events also illustrate this, as we can see in the case of Wilfried M., from the spring of 1946.[107] In one of the last interviews conducted before he was released from the clinic in Bethel, which was meant to check again on the patient's insight into his own illness, this former tank driver abruptly explained to his doctor, "You read so much about the whole concentration camp thing, the treatment there, and so on, but as a soldier no one even thought about that." He evaded a direct response to the psychiatrist's inquiry as to whether "political events" had "confused" him, and rather than conceding anything when the annoyed doctor told him to stop "tiptoeing," he peremptorily concluded as follows: "It's you who are bringing all that back to my mind. That's really not good. I realize that I shouldn't be thinking about all that stuff now, shouldn't be concerning myself with it."[108] Wilfried M. was quite obviously not only aware of the horrible nature of the crimes but was also burdened by the question of responsibility. Although the former tank driver argued that as a soldier he did not know what was happening, at the same time he revealed a need to somehow protect his self-image.

In view of the murderous Nazi past, living with oneself was evidently difficult for some former Wehrmacht members. But in many cases this could only be heard in quiet, dissonant tones. Even the "constant feeling of emptiness" that Reinhard G. described in 1950 in a kind of CV as being the dominant feeling he had experienced from day to day since the end of the war, expressed an awareness of crimes so hideous that afterward it was difficult to look oneself in the eye.[109] "If only mechanically, I fulfilled my previous duties in such a way that I could not reproach myself in that respect," the former officer indicated—while nevertheless considering himself in hindsight as a person he had never been, as if he were now genuinely disassociated from himself. "A human being recognizes that he was never a human being," he wrote as a person who by his own account had difficulty finding words for the feelings tormenting him. He had been a "dutiful, reliable officer"; now it all appeared to him simply an illusion, a belief held by outsiders who deluded themselves about him. He had certainly been ambitious, had reached the rank of captain, and had "always aimed high." He also believed he was an "idealist"—"all of that," he stated, had "collapsed." Reinhard G. did not wish to be the person he once was or seemed to have been. He had lost his self-confidence. As he explained elsewhere, after being on that "insane track," the only possible way out was "to begin over again from the bottom." What he had in mind, along with countless others at the time, was a transformation of the self. But constructing a new ego was difficult. Reinhard G. was not the only former soldier who foundered in the effort. As they experienced a recurrent "fearful anxiety that there is no escape any more, no way to get out," many others may have shared his thought: "If I had only been killed in the war, that would have been a decent end."

CHAPTER 2

Troubled Homecoming

Delusion and Reality

"In the beginning was the chaos!"[1]

The aftermath of the war was both unsettling and frightening. For the greater part of German society it was a challenge, because the immediate postwar reality offered hardly any orientation. After the first sigh of relief, irreconcilable perceptions, severe misfortunes, mass dislocation, and the pure fortuitousness of survival all produced a feeling of simply having escaped, without even an idea of how to live in the future with oneself and one's past.

The external signs of social destruction and dissolution were obvious, and they are widely known. Nevertheless, it is important to review some of the main aspects of the panorama. Millions of families were torn apart or destroyed; hundreds of thousands of German Jews and other people persecuted by the Nazi regime had been murdered. And then there were those who had died in the war or as a consequence of it.[2] More than five million German soldiers had perished in the course of this barbaric war, which had cost a total of roughly fifty-five million people their lives. During the bombing of German cities, half a million civilians had lost their lives. More than 1.7 million people had died during expulsions in the east or as they fled to the west, and hundreds of thousands of Wehrmacht soldiers had died in captivity, the great majority of them in the east, with the exact figure being impossible to ascertain. Estimates for the notorious so-called *Rheinwiesenlager* ("Rhine meadow camps") range from eight thousand to forty thousand soldiers.[3] The death rate in Russian POW camps was far higher, with roughly a third of the two to three million German POWs dying in these camps or in transit to them.[4] Over a million former soldiers were simply classified as missing—for the main part, their last known location was in the east.[5] Their families sometimes had to live for years with the burden of uncertainty as to whether the missing were dead or whether there was still hope that they would return.[6]

In addition to that, expulsion and mass flight severed social ties, terminated circumstances that had been familiar, and in many ways represented a literal step into the unknown. Among the 12.5 million persons who survived the journey into the remaining territory of postwar Germany, countless people worried when and where—or if—they would ever see their relatives who remained prisoners of war.[7] Their shelter was usually makeshift, a waypoint in any event, as was also the case for some nine million evacuees, many of whom were crowding back into their city after the bombing had ended.[8] Living conditions were a disaster, primarily in the cities. As long as entire districts remained nothing but rubble, living in ruins and derelict buildings was the norm for many people. Many others were jammed together in apartments that were far too small. Millions of so-called displaced persons, most of them forced laborers freed by the Allies, were trying to leave formerly German-occupied Europe in all directions for home, while around 1.5 million of them continued to live in camps inside of postwar Germany.[9] Millions of former German war prisoners—far more than half of the roughly eleven million soldiers who had been taken prisoner—were released by the end of 1946. They made their way to municipalities that were often completely overwhelmed and joined the struggle for living quarters, work, and food—a struggle that demanded a large amount of perseverance in every respect.[10]

In general, those who had made it through the war could feel anything but secure in Germany in the early postwar years. In fact most people faced a constant emergency situation—a day-to-day struggle over two or three years to secure continued existence for self and family. Often, ingenuity and violations of the prevailing moral and legal order were indispensable. After observing all sorts of people who no longer hesitated to search the streets of Berlin for food scraps in rubbish containers and garbage piles, Ruth Andreas-Friedrich wrote in September 1946, "Hardship, greed, and chaotic circumstances have broken through all human restraints."[11] As well, wide segments of the postwar German population were forced to participate in the scorned black market in order to survive. This applied less to people living in the countryside. Many farmers could even exchange their produce for other material goods. This led to various farmers being reproached for unethically enriching themselves through the need of others.[12] And indeed, the population was worse off in the cities, where hunger in particular was rampant. Food rations were extremely small, and, due to the collapse of the transportation system and enormous harvest losses, success in exchanging ration cards for food was by no means guaranteed. The situation was particularly drastic in the winter, especially during the so-called hunger winter of 1946/1947, when extreme cold paralyzed the supply system and further reduced already markedly reduced physical and mental stamina.[13]

A report by the English occupation authorities in the summer of 1947 presumably very accurately described the situation to which innumerable German women felt exposed after the end of the war as one of "daily crisis which at any moment may turn to disaster."[14] This perspective was by no means held only by women. The Allies' denazification policies made a major contribution here.[15] In retrospect, it is certainly true that the results of the procedures themselves clearly demonstrate that denazification had developed into what Lutz Niethammer has termed a "factory" for defining the great majority of those examined as fellow travelers (*Mitläufer*).[16] Nevertheless, neither the wave of arrests during the first months, which resulted in the internment of some 117,000 former party members in the American zone and 127,000—sometimes very arbitrarily—in the Soviet zone,[17] nor the outcome of the individual examinations before the civilian German denazification courts (*Spruchkammer*), introduced in the spring of 1946, were truly predictable for the suspects. The feverish search for exonerating documents is a clear indication of this. Many people succeeded in whitewashing their responsibility for past misdeeds with the help of denazification certificates, called *Persilscheine* in reference to a popular German detergent. But until the procedure was concluded, one's life hung in limbo. The verdict had existential importance for one's own subsistence and that of one's family. Only when the document had been issued were the classification of the charges and the sentence available. What lay in store for them: the denial of a pension claim, a long-term employment ban, a fine? Tens of thousands of Germans, especially those who had been in the Nazi civil service, could not know in advance. For millions of returning soldiers, even those who had not been Nazi Party members, it was likewise clear that searching for a job or training position was only possible after their denazification and political exoneration.[18] For many men, this meant a grueling, nerve-wracking period of waiting for a decision that was key for envisioning what kind of future lay ahead.

As of about 1948, most people in postwar Germany were increasingly feeling some relief. In particular, the currency reform improved the economic situation, and with it the ability to find work, food, and housing.[19] The "returnee amnesty" in the spring of 1948 led to a significant simplification of the denazification procedure.[20] Nonetheless, for soldiers repatriated after two or three years or even later, as was the case with many POWs who had been in Soviet camps, the return to Germany continued to be "a road to uncertainty."[21] At times, rumors and stories circulating during internment had already stoked fear before soldiers returned, and for some of them it was a source of anxiety to realize that they would have to demonstrate the ability to fend for themselves again after years of regimented activity. Many returnees encountered a world that seemed alien in many respects. It was difficult to find their way and gain a foothold. "We were robbed . . . of the old arrangements and still unsure of the new," as a returnee later remarked in retrospect.[22] It seems that for tens of thousands of veterans, the reduction of material and societal distress in postwar Germany did not bring an end to their sense of disorientation.

All told, we can designate the first postwar years as a gray zone of transition endured by most Germans and many "late returnees" in a kind of time lag. They confronted an as yet unfamiliar world that was initially very difficult to grasp. As a consequence of problems existing over many months and the intense stress associated with them, it was not uncommon during this phase for the initial impression of chaos gained during the fresh start to shift into a sense of being subjected to a permanent crisis. After a period of time, openness toward the Allied effort to rebuild a political-moral order often turned into deep skepticism, if not bitterness.[23] It appears that some segments of the German population came to perceive reality as both bizarre and crushing. For some people it was no longer easy to decide whether the past or the present was more absurd.[24]

In the psychiatric records, we find a number of cases that illustrate to what extent the inner compass guiding individual lives had lost its bearings. Remnants of stability in the form of family and communal "normality" were all the more important, but often only amounted to deceptive security.[25] States of inner disorientation were not uncommon. Even in cases where apparently no serious personal incrimination in the crimes of the Nazi system was present, after the returnees shifted loyalty away from the Reich and Führer, the future seemed threatening, reality hopeless.[26] Often it was simply a matter of complying with the concrete demands of the denazification procedure. Yet that challenge was enough to trigger such abrupt anxiety that the external appearance of inner stability noticeably fell apart.

Werner F. is a case in point.[27] When he was admitted to the psychiatric clinic in December 1947, he seemed a rather unremarkable case. At forty-four years of age, his posture was upright, the admitting doctor found his physical condition to be good, his facial expression was intelligent, and in his interviews the patient sounded very clear and well organized. The doctor found Werner F.'s "good demeanor" worthy of note; the patient did not "give one the impression of being sick." It was his wife who indicated that, after the "collapse," she had noticed a degree of disquiet and anxiety that was unusual for her husband.

For the past several months, she reported, he had been in a state of "constant anxiety and concern about the currency reform" because he believed it would mean "the downfall of his family." Furthermore, the doctor noted, Werner F.'s wife had remarked that "the questionnaire hung over him like a specter." She claimed that she had no clue as to why this should have been so. In the past, even though she had found her husband's "sense of justice and honor exaggerated," she had come to know him as always "very good and orderly." A few weeks before, however, his fear of being arrested "because of his earlier political orientation" gained the upper hand, and the former SS member reported himself to the British occupation authorities.

Taking that step amounted to an act of despair. Even his conviction that he would immediately be imprisoned no longer held him back. He presented himself at the British offices three times, but they only requested a résumé from him and otherwise showed no interest. From the psychiatrist's notes on the interviews with Werner F., it is difficult to determine whether it was his Nazi past or the present political-moral order that had become the greatest nightmare for him day to day. For about a year, his experiential world had included various hallucinations and delusions. When looking into a shop window, the doctor noted, he might suddenly see the SS runes. He felt watched and followed by the British occupiers. He thought his acquaintances were informers and spies who "acted on behalf of the Englishmen," as he put it. In the end, he could not even endure reading the papers, "because I always have the feeling that I'm the one they mean." He also shut off the radio "because they keep broadcasting innuendos" that were directed at him.

Werner F. did not say a word to the doctor about the crimes Germans had committed, but it seems he was finding it nearly impossible to bear up under the public confrontation with the crimes of the past. He only hinted that in the 1920s he had gone to his superior and filed a complaint against a colleague, underscoring that it had not entailed any consequences. Yet when he began to describe—in the very next sentence—his political stance during the Nazi period, he did not seem to be burdened by any deep sense of self-doubt. He even mentioned with pride his membership in "national associations," which, as he explained, only confirmed his love of truth. By mentioning that despite his Dutch citizenship, which he exchanged for German citizenship in 1932, he had always "had strong German sentiments" and had been "full of love for the fatherland," he seemed to be confirming his own probity. At the time of this retrospective look, Werner F. appears to have viewed his Nazi past as a passion rather than a burden.

The inner stability Werner F. had once found through commitment to the

Nazi regime still emanated from him. Consequently, it is not surprising that the occupiers' presence, a daily reminder of the collapse of the Nazi system, the mass crimes, and the failure of his personal track had a painfully anxious and disturbing effect. His hallucinations and delusions even indicate that his inner compass was, at least sporadically, still pointing to the Führer ideal. For weeks he even held the conviction that the Führer was still alive and had ordered him to be part of a series of experiments for which he had to be hypnotized. "That's why, in this state, I now have to live through the experience that the war is lost, that the English are in the country, and that there are borders between the occupied zones," he told the psychiatrist, adding the earnest declaration that he was gradually realizing that the war had in reality been won. Werner F. broke down in tears after these words. It was far from clear to him, as he openly confessed, what was "true" or "a dream" after all. He hoped that psychiatry would offer him relief by clarifying whether it was all "pathological" and he was "now truly insane."

Without a doubt his bewilderment was enormous. It apparently mirrored a difficulty that evidently many repatriated soldiers—and presumably civilians as well—could hardly cope with during the postwar years: facing up to the Nazi past while at the same time mastering the problems and demands of the present, and on top of that accepting them as a result of their own biographies. Many examples illustrate that it was anything but rare to be repeatedly overtaken by the horrors of the war and the revelation of the mass murder committed on those persecuted by the regime, while simultaneously experiencing the present as surreal or a kind of false reality. Rolf S. was one such case. In his dreams and hallucinations, he was tormented by all sorts of events from the war and postwar period, in particular the acts of the war criminals and their subsequent conviction and sentencing.[28] Two days before his release from the clinic, and fully awake, he explained to the doctor: "Everything that happened earlier, before I arrived here, seems like a dream to me. Sometimes it's as if I'm in another country." "In England or America," he replied to a question from the doctor, adding, when he was again asked why, that he had "seen so many people in English uniforms."

For some, confronting the military occupation of Germany was like entering a new, largely alien world with an entirely different set of coordinates. It was not difficult to localize the coordinates, but orienting oneself by them was still not necessarily conflict free. Even in the altered political situation, the old ordering concepts had not necessarily been overcome, as became evident in the tension between large parts of the population and the occupying forces, after an initial period of openness. The longer the social and material hardship lasted, the more difficult it became to acknowledge the moral superiority the victorious powers claimed for themselves, and their nearly exclusive authority in politically shaping postwar Germany. This evidently applied to Theodor M., who could not free his mind of "the present general misery," as he stated to a psychiatrist in 1947.[29] In the previous session, he explained that it was "the injustice now ruling the world" that weighed so heavily on him, a state of affairs he then immediately concretized: "Germany's enslavement" gave him no rest. The doctor commented in his report: "He repeatedly contemplates outwitting the Tommies at every possible turn."

It sounded as if Theodor M. were expressing a self-confident attitude toward the occupiers. Yet it was not a reflection of inner security at all. Rather, one gathers the impression from the psychiatric records that the ground was collapsing under his feet. "A single human life wouldn't matter" is the way he countered his wife one day when she reproached him for handling a kerosene lamp very carelessly. As she explained to the psychiatrist, that day her husband had received a letter from a former lieutenant that visibly shook him. Responding with silence to her question "whether something happened," in the evening he wrote back. During the day, he actually had been ruminating about the "events of the war," as we learn from a brief remark during his psychiatric interview, although the "misery" that weighed on him so greatly took up far more space in the physician's report. Theodor M. added regretfully that "his assets were not large enough to help everyone." As if he had to fend off the burden of the past that was befalling them before he could regain inner peace, he immediately added that "he had always liked helping everybody best of all."

It was as if an almost unbearable tension had built up between the Nazi past and present reality, which made it difficult and perhaps even impossible for some to regain their inner balance. Sometimes the feeling of uncertainty was reflected in stories that were quite removed from reality and distorted one's own past to the point of being unrecognizable. At the same time, the reality of the occupation was thoroughly recognizable in a persistently fluctuating inner perspective, without, however, necessarily creating a reassuring orientation. Thus, in an account given by Rudolf B. in 1949, it is still clear to see that up until the bitter end of the war, he maintained both his belief in the Führer— whom he was still defending—and his trust that Germany would achieve the *Endsieg*, the final victory.[30] At the same time, his encounter of mass death and his memory of his own killing tormented him. He could not find any meaning in them, especially since the war had been lost. In occupied Germany, he found himself in a world that, although in his eyes real, had become inverted in an apparently maniacal way. For instance, when the psychiatrist asked him if he felt persecuted, he promptly responded, "No, to the contrary. After all I was a soldier, but we are persecuted by our liberators."

Many people's inner world had been unmistakably shaken. It was nearly impossible to keep up with the changes in the external world. Much had been turned on its head. Germany's former enemies were now celebrating themselves as liberators. Meanwhile many Germans who had participated in the war had a sense that the public confrontation with Nazi-era crimes and the personal denazification proceedings were forcing them to once again take shelter from their enemies. Under such conditions, it is not surprising that a number of returnees sought refuge in a mental process of rendering the war unreal. But this by no means freed them from their own confusion and insecurity. Many former soldiers had the Nazi crimes virtually breathing down their neck. In an uncertain present, it is not implausible that some of them worked themselves into a paranoid state—a state that sometimes fueled the return of past horror within the framework of their own conceptual world.

Adolf W., the veteran mentioned above, exemplifies such a process.[31] Having once professed his allegiance to the Nazi system freely and without reservation, he found himself in various states of anxiety after 1948.[32] During one psychiatric session, he explained that he lived under the impression that "his mirror image was being held up to him" over the entire day.[33] Yet he added in a conciliatory tone, so to speak, "Recently, I've become aware that everything is actually an illusion, that the whole thing amounts to educational work on the people or peoples (*am Volk oder an den Völkern*)." And, indeed, he was suddenly no longer even sure whether "the entire war" had not been "just an illusion." After all, he explained, the war had started completely differently than World War I. It was also "very peculiar" that his "family members returned from the war very soon." Promptly, however, a knowledge of Nazi crimes committed filtered through his comments. When the doctor asked what all this meant, Adolf W. responded: "That good times are coming now, and everybody who's dishonorable and of no use is being eradicated, and I'm one of them."

It certainly can be argued that in the wake of Germany's total defeat and the abiding horror over the regime's colossal crimes, the "delusional world" of Nazi propaganda "was overtaken by reality in all its clarity and had collapsed."[34] It was only in the form of lunatic daydreams and hallucinations, it seems, that something of that world lived on, which gives us a sense of how deeply Nazi ideology had embedded itself in the perception and thoughts of many Germans. But this was not the only respect in which a piece of reality shimmered through in Adolf W.'s persecution mania. The crimes of the Nazi era really took place. And this former soldier, who at one point admitted to the psychiatrist that he was constantly afraid of retaliation, had been aware of the persecution and murder even before they had been discovered. His own son suffered from mild mental retardation, a condition associated with infantile cerebral palsy, and could have been euthanized as a result.[35]

For Adolf W., the war had taken on an unreal quality; it was as if he had shoved the past aside, only to become entangled in it once again somewhere else. Nevertheless, even in his confusion and tormenting paranoia he was fully aware that Nazism was over and the war lost. When he admitted—as the psychiatric records indicate—that the "course of the war and its outcome" rankled him, that he "revered the Führer," and that his son's illness had "weighed heavily on him," he was clearly speaking in retrospect. At present other rules prevailed, as he clearly knew, although he was repeatedly caught up in Nazi ways of speaking and interpreting the world. One day, on encountering a boy on the ward who suffered from cerebral palsy as did his own son, he became extremely agitated and immediately seized by the belief that the boy, as the psychiatrist noted, "had been sent specifically to suggest something to him." Another time, he interpreted a "Gypsy's song," "I Saw Four Leaves Falling," which he claimed to have heard a few days before, as implying that he himself was "no longer worth much." He further explained to the doctor: "He played it for my sake. It's really awful that healthy people sacrifice their time for me."

Contrary to the assumption that after the end of the horror an authentic "normality" ensued in a quasi-reflexive fashion, these cases create the impression that under the occupation people's inner compasses were oscillating between two irreconcilable poles. On the one hand, a number of people wished that the past were unreal. On the other, the encounter with the reality of occupation rule forced them to continuously deny their inclination to deceive themselves about their own past. The smallest matters produced disorientation, repeatedly casting the criminal war and the uncertain future in a threatening light.

The Other Self

"I need papers," said Hans. "Good grief!" exclaimed the doctor. "Good papers," he said, "there have to be papers here somewhere, from a dead person would be best. Please try." "You're crazy." "Not at all. I don't want to go to prison. I live here, have all sorts of things to take care of—to look after. Please help me." . . . The doctor pulled a paper from his bag, placed it under the candle, and said: "I believe this is what you need. Completely authentic." . . . "Completely unfit for military service for twenty-five years because of a serious lung ailment. Your name would be Erich Keller."[36]

In Germany's postwar years, clinging disillusionment and the never entirely successful process of rendering the past unreal led to what we can term a widespread doppelgänger phenomenon, in which individuals who wanted to secure their past while also wishing to be rid of it developed strategies centered around another self. This was most obvious in the case of those who obtained of false papers—including, as is well known, an entire series of former party officials and members of the SS and Gestapo. Some of these people chose flight abroad as an option, especially to South America. Here Eichmann was the most famous example. Having already adopted a false name and rank during his internment, he managed to escape to Argentina as Ricardo Klement in 1950.[37] Others remained in Germany, disappearing somewhere or other in order to build a new existence, such as former SA *Oberführer* Werner Blankenberg, who shared responsibility for the mass murder of ill and disabled persons.[38]

The exact number of people who believed such a change of identity to be the most promising way to rid themselves of their Nazi past is unclear. In December 1949, the Munich-based *Neue Zeitung* published an unofficial estimate of eighty thousand "illegals," as those who vanished after 1945 for political reasons came to be named,[39] but it is uncertain whether this figure is at all reliable. When the first amnesty law was debated and ultimately passed by the German Bundestag in 1949, governmental officials clearly voiced the hope that "many persons who . . . on account of their earlier ties to National Socialism" were staying "in federal territory under false names, with false papers, or without reporting in a proper way to the police," would now again have the opportunity to lead a "law-abiding life."[40] To that end, a clause was added at the last moment stipulating that the "illegals" would also be affected by the general amnesty and would enjoy impunity after revealing their true identities. By the deadline at the end of March 1950, only 214 persons had taken advantage of this opportunity, which in no way met the expectations tied to these legal efforts.[41] After the second amnesty law went to effect in 1954, the group widened by another 1,051 "illegals." Presumably, the far more expansive amnesty regulations were the decisive factor here. This second law even amnestied crimes of manslaughter.

Over the course of the postwar decades, increasing numbers of Nazi criminals who had gone into hiding would be discovered and finally even sentenced, for instance, Klaus Barbie, the so-called butcher of Lyons.[42] But the group of "illegals" was by no means limited to upper-echelon Nazis. Hierarchically less important state officials and members of its apparatus of violence as well as a great number of former Wehrmacht soldiers of various ranks nourished the same hope of totally or at least partially changing their identity with the help of false papers.[43] Not all of them, of course, bore the same degree of responsibility for the crimes, and we cannot even assume that they all had the same amount of knowledge about them. Yet the chaos of the new postwar beginning also encouraged the adoption of false identities even when the expected advantages would only be temporary. Obtaining false papers was rather easy. As a rule, if one presented oneself as a refugee at the Red Cross's tracing service, two witnesses were required to establish an identity.[44] In the black market or at a new job, a false identity could prove so strong an advantage that one could hope to secretly shed one's past as well. Although the majority of returnees wished to reestablish ties with their families and trusted networks, those who were homeless would often have seen the transition to new identities as freeing them for the new future. At the end of 1949, for example, in response to a *Frankfurter Hefte* survey ten avowed "illegals" expressed pride in not being estranged from themselves through their false identities, which was why most of them initially made no use of the amnesty program.[45]

During this time of transition, it was not only a question of the cases where a second identity was necessary or useful, but rather that the idea of a double self carried over into broader worlds of social imagination. In liberated Berlin, for example, one could observe how women set about showing the Soviets they were of kindred spirit by removing the swastika from Nazi flags and then using them as headscarves.[46] The understanding shown for invented identities was correspondingly great, with silence as to the possible reasons for them being ever more sympathetically preserved the longer the end of the war receded into the past. Likewise, in situations where new acquaintances were formed, one could note that personal histories whose authenticity could not be verified usually readily found credence, not least because in many cases the sheer fact of having endured often seemed like a miracle. This was exploited not only by alleged ex-comrades of missing soldiers who wished to profit from the ignorance of those who stayed behind.[47] We also find stories of double identities as explanatory factors in personal crises, as the case of Walter M. indicates.[48] In July 1946, he presented himself at the psychiatric clinic pursuing a request that appeared highly unusual: following a seemingly serious altercation, he needed a medical attestation of diminished accountability for his behavior at the time of the incident. The inference was that his behavior did not correspond to his "normal" self. Walter M. found himself under pressure: the military authorities would only refrain from arresting him, he explained, if he could present a statement from a "major institute" certifying that his misconduct resulted from a war injury.

It is therefore not surprising that in his account to the doctor Walter M.

devoted a great deal of space to the circumstances and consequences of the wound he received shortly before the war ended. In his handwritten résumé, he took rather unusual care in describing his last combat situation, where he incurred a head wound during a hail of grenades. He described the complaints he traced back to the head injury with the same meticulousness, even taking the doctor's further questions into account. In contrast, Walter M. at no point offered any really precise information on the event that had brought him into conflict with the military authorities. In the story he communicated to the doctor, his own behavior remained so obscure that the severity of the authorities is impossible to comprehend. In his initial interview, for example, Walter M. merely referred to "difficulties with a tenant," against whom he had initiated eviction proceedings, "after a long period of amicable effort." As a result, the tenant had reported him to the military authorities. It had been a defamation, he emphasized, that caused him to flee "in the dead of night." Months had passed since then. But although he believed the military authorities had abandoned their search for him, he did not think returning was in any way "advisable." He said nothing more about what he called the "kneejerk reaction" he had experienced. He had no explanation for it, but he was sure that "under normal circumstances he certainly would not have done that."

The matter was indeed delicate, although not entirely as dramatic as Walter M. depicted. At least, the general practitioner who had been treating him since his stay in a military hospital the previous summer and evidently enjoyed a special bond of trust with him, did not rate the situation as quite so dire. Thus, in a letter to the head physician at the psychiatric clinic, the GP underscored that "no reliable evidence" existed that occupation authorities intended to arrest Walter M. "Later inquiries" had shown that Walter M. had "made some sort of careless remarks" that the patient allegedly could "no longer [reproduce] precisely." But the GP's knowledge was apparently good enough to suggest that "these were probably political in nature and thereby led to the fear of arrest under discussion."

It may be that Walter M. markedly exaggerated the danger of being arrested. But even the GP, who suggests this interpretation, chose to request that his psychiatric colleague provide such a "expert opinion" to present to the military authorities if necessary. Presumably, he, too, was aware that Walter B. was not a clean slate. He had joined the Nazi Party in 1932, and apparently was an enthusiastic member until the end. He reported with unshaken pride on the commitment with which he had served as party speaker at an officers' assembly as late as the fall of 1944. At home, he could no longer adorn himself with that after the end of the war, as he bitterly experienced after his repatriation in

1945. When he returned, his wife and parents-in-law had "received and treated him like a stranger," the doctor commented in his report, before summarizing the rest of the patient's statement in this regard in the following words: "Left him standing in front of the house for 1½ hours without even offering him a drink of water. Was told he was a 'Nazi' and they wanted nothing more to do with him." The situation escalated on a second visit. When Walter M. appeared once again in order to collect some personal belongings, his father-in-law unceremoniously called the police. Allegedly, the returned soldier only escaped arrest through a "dramatic flight."

Walter M. was certainly exaggerating. Indeed, he seems to have been thoroughly bent on underscoring the injustice, trials, and suffering he felt he had endured. "First the wound, then Germany's collapse, the slander at home, the hunger in the army hospital and in the camp, the behavior of his wife"—ostensibly one continuous stretch of suffering as he portrayed it, from which he drew the conclusion that "it was simply too much." As with many others, he did not think of expending a word on the victims of the Nazi regime.[49] Yet as soon as conflict with the occupiers loomed, Walter M. believed he would be arrested. In such situations, the political baggage he carried seems to have weighed heavily on him. As soon as he was attacked and despised as a "Nazi" or found himself in trouble because of his political attitudes, he was clearly aware that he was in a risky, weak position. Expecting arrest, he thus left the place where he was living and went on the run the first time, staying with his father in a small town in Hessen before feeling it necessary to abscond from there as well and go underground. He had been forced to manage without ration cards ever since, hiring himself out for one sort of black market "deal" or another. As Walter M. very well knew, he could not escape this state of affairs simply by recounting stories about the injustice and suffering he had allegedly experienced. It could neither mitigate his Nazi past vis-à-vis the occupation authorities nor serve as a plausible explanation for his offensive political behavior. The additional reference to his head wound and the objectively verifiable piece of shrapnel remaining in his brain, did indeed, however, offer an avenue of escape from his precarious position. Accordingly, Walter M. explained to the psychiatrist that since incurring the head wound he frequently did things "against his better knowledge. He acted under a certain compulsion. He would decide not to say something, and then still say it. What he had gone through had been simply too much." In other words, he suggested that in a situation that was already difficult to bear, the injury could cause a short-term loss of control that distorted his "authentic" self.

This way of seeing things was fully compatible with the state of psychiatric knowledge of the time.[50] At least, the absence of unusual behavior on the patient's part at the clinic could not sufficiently neutralize the argument. The psychiatrist therefore issued an expert opinion cautiously confirming that Walter M.'s propensity for "impulsive and unconsidered actions" could be "credibly assumed" to stem from his wound. Consequently, Walter M. bore no responsibility for his political lapses. His "normal" self was not a source of any special concern. You might say that it had just been suspended for a brief moment.

No later than the beginning of the occupation, every repatriated soldier became aware of the extreme importance of official, bona fide documents of all sorts for identifying oneself to the Allies as a person not associated with the Nazis' terrible deeds. But imponderables certainly remained. Papers were not the occupiers' only source of information, as many Germans knew and—at least in the immediate wake of the total defeat—repeatedly feared. Clearly, during this period not all Germans believed themselves to be living in the comfortable "safety of silence."[51] Former Wehrmacht soldier Wilfried M. was unmistakably fearful. Since he had "risked a remark" and believed that the British were "observing him as especially suspect politically" anyway, it was making him very anxious to think that the Germans might "go somewhere and say this person's saying this and that, and that one's saying such and such." This reinforced his plans to disappear from Germany.[52] For his part, the above-discussed Gustav N. reacted immediately.[53] As soon as the "collapse," as he called it, took place, he almost reflexively erased the entry in his military service book that indicated his membership in the German Labor Front. Documents proved to the victors who you were—that was the hope he shared with many others who were working on transforming their identity by falsifying papers, destroying them, or by taking recourse to other written information about themselves.[54] But the desired sense of security was not forthcoming. Gustav N., for example, immediately developed strong scruples about the estrangement from his identity he had undertaken, an identity that had been transformed on paper faster than he was able to follow. Apparently disturbed by this doubling, Gustav N. turned for help to a comrade who tore up his Wehrmacht service papers. But the accounts Gustav N. offered during his stay at the psychiatric clinic in 1947 show that over the previous two years even this extreme measure had not helped him to convince himself entirely of an identity that outwardly seemed politically innocuous.

Since former Wehrmacht members stayed in psychiatric clinics for relatively short periods, the files do not tell us anything about how such an awareness of having doubled one's own self—it can be observed in a range of repatriated soldiers—changed over time. It is certainly questionable whether it ever completely disappeared.[55] It clearly emerges, however, that it would be inadequate to reduce the efforts to change one's biography, and thereby one's identity, to nothing more than an instrumental self-protective measure in the face of the Allies. There are two reasons for this. First, in the cases where the evident goal was to evade the political purge or at least to be treated leniently in the denazification proceedings, a mixture of calculation, anxious despondency, and genuine consternation over the Nazi mass crimes interacted in the construction of a self.[56] Second, the files also contain examples pointing to a need not so much for political as for personal rehabilitation, which had to be achieved not only in the eyes of others but also for oneself in the wake of violence and mass death. For many soldiers, this apparently did not necessarily occur automatically after they returned to civilian life, as the already mentioned case of Ludwig D. shows.[57] He suffered from a deep-seated fear that his acquaintances and family members would despise him. In the war, he had accidentally shot and killed a Wehrmacht lieutenant he knew well. He committed the offense while he was on guard duty and had been momentarily overcome by fear. During the war, he successfully covered up the deed. At home he lied, explaining that the lieutenant had died at Stalingrad. In this way, he evaded reproach for being afraid, for failure, and for unreliability. As an officer candidate with his eye on a military career, Ludwig D. very much wished to maintain before others as well as himself that such qualities were in no way associated with him. In his demeanor, he tried to continue embodying the fearless and daring person he still actually considered himself to be; in this respect, his intention to deceive and his need to reassure himself coincided. He pretended to be carefree and impressed others as "easygoing." But they had drawn an erroneous conclusion, as, Ludwig D. himself stated, explaining it during his later stay in the psychiatric clinic as follows. As the psychiatrist noted, Ludwig D. "projected a robust personality, drank, and carried on with girls." According to the former cadet's own interpretation, he behaved in this manner "in order to overcome his inner distress."

These constructions of a self that allegedly had incurred no damage by one's own behavior in the war were implemented in a performative process. It is much easier to see how the constructions of a different self were fabricated in the war stories repatriated soldiers repeatedly told. Such stories can be found in the returnees' medical records. As often was the case in postwar Germany, they tended not to speak concretely about German terror and violence and the suffering of victims. Nevertheless, the stories were clearly not the result of successful repression, but rather an expression of the soldier's marked disturbance over their own behavior during the war. The behavior was not easy to convey to or justify before those who had remained at home, especially in the context of civilian morality; it also appears that it was hard to justify to oneself. Rather, as in the case of Franz F., the stories read like efforts to foreground another self in order to render the tormenting memory of the past horrors at all bearable, and even perhaps to escape it.[58]

Three years after the war, Franz F. had not managed to rid himself of the experiences of the war. They dogged him even when he was asleep, and during the day he would repeatedly "catch himself being preoccupied with them," as he acknowledged to the psychiatrist. However, the notion of a split identity strengthened Franz F.'s hope of having a bearable life in the future, in spite of the acts of violence he had evidently committed but did not describe concretely. In his imagination, one part of his self—the more sensitive and now suppos-edly prevalent part—was freed from the atrocities and hence from responsibil-ity. At least, this was the idea that emerged in his accounts to the psychiatrist, to whom he one day explained, as the doctor noted, that "he actually has two natures in his chest or two souls; one proceeds recklessly, the other empathi-cally. If he were now facing many situations again, he would certainly be more considerate." Still, with regard to the past, he felt it important to emphasize that "all of this didn't torment him in the sense of an awareness of guilt. He was much too realistic for that; after all, he could always remind himself that he could have been killed in this war." He therefore believed that there had been a specific and unavoidable behavioral logic at work in the war, which had alien-ated him as a person at the time and which distorted him now.

This was doubtless a widespread argumentative pattern for many former soldiers, who could otherwise hardly explain that they participated in killing.[59] There is no mistaking how far this exercise in rationalizing one's own behavior was interwoven with the gnawing memory of past violence. It was the driver behind a persistent preoccupation with oneself that was an expression of his insecurity about his own identity. Personal identity had, as it were, slipped into a twilight state where a need was nourished to rediscover a remnant of support within oneself. This is especially striking in returnees such as Kurt T., who had not only been involved in the war as soldiers but had already joined the political-ideological battle earlier as committed Nazis.[60]

Kurt T. arrived at the psychiatric clinic in the spring of 1949. As we learn from a letter by the clinic administration, he and his family turned to the institu-tion "seeking help," because he had allegedly been "persecuted in the eastern zone on religious grounds." Kurt T. spent no more than a few weeks at his home in the East because he had only recently been released from a POW camp in Poland. He had been "severely shaken mentally" there, noted the directors of the clinic, who were willing to comply with the recommendation of the examining doctor and admit the ex-soldier for several weeks of psychiatric treatment. Even before starting the treatment, Kurt T., who had joined the SA in 1933 and the Nazi Party in 1937, composed a remarkable testimonial for the administration. It was a comprehensive, twelve-page "résumé" in which the veteran promised "to present the current reader of these lines a truthful insight" into his "person" and "the associated circumstances." This was, he announced, a "complete confession," thus emphasizing his seriousness about revealing his "real" self.

The "résumé" was unmistakably the product of a set of questions revolving around guilt and responsibility that were being posed so urgently in Germany's postwar period, and which play an important role in numerous other pieces of autobiographical and literary testimony by former soldiers.[61] The Nazi period occupied a great deal of space in Kurt T.'s account. His entry into the SA and his development there, his position in the party, and his position on the regime's policies, both before the war and after it began, after the mass crimes—all of this demanded an explanation. That much had become evident, even to him. His biographical self-presentation bore the mark of the distinct pressure he felt to justify his actions, either in the eyes of an imagined other or before himself, and to which he had yielded in writing his report.

The tendency toward a "narrative harmonization"[62] we find in many biographical accounts of the war generation is also evident in Kurt T.'s retrospective constructions of meaning: He had entered the SA, he alleged, only for the sake of "getting some sort of ground under my feet." Thus, his actual reason was the economic crisis, which had made it considerably more difficult to establish a household of his own with his wife. His intentions had been, he insisted, altogether honorable. After all, he did not wish to be only "a passive actor" in the "new construction of Germany," even telling himself: "If you do your share, you'll also win the right to a standard of living that will make it possible to found your own household." The account proceeded in this manner. Kurt T. did not hide his familiarity with the Nazi Party's program. He even emphasized that he had indeed found most of it reasonable. But then, he explained, much had turned out very differently. In fact, it seemed to him now that he had been deceived. Nonetheless, Kurt T. had remained in the SA, although he especially underscored his distance, presumably for that very reason. He had remained strong in his devotion to "positive Christianity," and he had even offered "resistance," to the extent he could. His entry into the party did not contradict this, because—and this was important for him—he had simply followed an "order" from the Führer. One could have the impression that Kurt T. had basically not been involved in what happened at all: he had no assignment in the SA and did not hold office in the party. This was important for him.

Kurt T.'s report had all the earmarks of being an act of self-denazification. It created the appearance that he had personally not really had anything to do with Nazism, aside from an initial belief—which seemed totally harmless to him—that the movement represented the answer to remaking Germany. But when faced with the experience of the war, that is, when it came to preventing himself from being personally associated with the atrocities and to denying any responsibility whatsoever, his ability failed him. This marks a distinction between Kurt T.'s "curriculum vitae" and the narratives of many other former German soldiers starting in the early 1950s.[63] Temporal proximity to the war is one possible reason for the difference. Furthermore, it must be taken into account that Kurt T. had spent the four previous years as a war prisoner in Poland. As a result, he had certainly not yet internalized the myth of the "clean" Wehrmacht soldier that was already being developed in West German public memory.[64] To be sure, in his report Kurt T. did idealize a soldierly life characterized by the "cultivation and devotion to true soldierly virtues." He, too, had been drawn to this aspect of the world of war; he made no secret of that. Yet the reality he then encountered had born little resemblance to it. Rather, what filters through in his report is the idea that daily life on the front was a kind of deformation and systematic instrumentalization of the common soldier by ruthless Wehrmacht commanders. This, too, was a widespread argumentative pattern in postwar Germany.[65] Nevertheless, Kurt T. evidently did not feel that this amounted to full exculpation, conceding, "I, too, initially unconsciously and then more consciously until the disastrous end, made myself in some way guilty, for which I will eventually have to answer before God."

In his "résumé," Kurt T. offered few hints of what he had experienced and participated in as a soldier. He left open the question as to the nature of what he termed his "actual capabilities," which had been "discovered quickly enough" for him to be "harnessed as a usable part of the great war machine." But, again, he did not try to hide that he had found himself in the midst of a criminal war. Apparently, he had been spared one atrocity or the other, albeit only by happenstance, as he was well aware. In his words: "Initially, I could only ascribe my not having been shaped into a methodical and deliberate mass murderer to the fact that I was the father of five children." Shortly before the end of the war, this protection lapsed, and Kurt T. was ordered into firing squad. Following orders, he shot and killed a deserter. That was "the only person," he insisted, at whom he "aimed his weapon on command and, thereby, been branded a onetime official murderer."

Until this execution, Kurt T. had somehow managed to preserve distance between his own person and the horrors of the war. But this deed had dissolved the distance. Even his assumption—which he underscored in the written exposition of his person—that had he refused to obey the order he "would have been placed in the same position without fail" did not restore the distance. Perhaps it was the "dying look" the soldier had allegedly cast at him that no longer permitted any distance. In any event, according to Kurt T. at that moment the conviction had taken hold that he as well would one day be condemned. Soon thereafter, his internment as a war prisoner began—first in Russia, then in Poland. He considered it "a necessary atonement," which was a widespread interpretation among German POWs in the east.[66] However, in the case of Kurt T. as well, the "atonement" was by no means for the murder of a German deserter alone, as shown by an "event" that he describes. During a hallucination that the veteran never entirely acknowledged as such, considering it a real experience instead, another theme surfaced that had apparently preoccupied him for a long time. When a voice sounded and announced that his body was "henceforth holy" and all his "sins" forgiven, the first question he raised was "And the Jews"?

Kurt T. saw this "event" as marking the day of his "rebirth"; it was an absolutely key element of his biographical self-construction, mirroring an intense urge for self-transformation. In his eyes, the incident represented a decisive turn in his life: it had not only relieved him in a lasting way but also shored up his self-assurance. For him, it was more than merely a sign that all his transgressions had been forgiven. He believed that he had become another person through the occurrence.

In many cases, it may well be that such self-presentations can also be interpreted as attempts to regain in part the power to define oneself. A good number of people felt that they had been robbed of this through their confrontation with the victors and Allied efforts to make Germans feel responsible for the crimes.[67] Still, in a large number of cases the impression is unavoidable that such insistence on another self expressed an ongoing, extremely precarious search for a new one. Frequently, what remained of this search was a persistent, vexing drivenness that entirely excluded experiencing peace and apparent certainty about oneself. This blind searching could produce paralyzing emptiness, but also result in an agitated rush to enter a new era that offered no security but merely held promise. Sometimes these emotional layers intertwined, complementing and even reflecting one another like mirror images. The process is epitomized in the written account that former officer Reinhard G. composed about himself.[68] Although it was his admission to the psychiatric clinic that occasioned the preparation of this text on his personal "development process," as he entitled the piece, it clearly had the character of an inner monologue that unfolded as he fabricated another self. He repeatedly emphasized what great "emptiness" he felt. "Pictures from some time or another" appeared "before his eyes," he explained, but it was "as if up until now nothing had left a trace behind." "The memories are present, but they tell me very little," he stated, once again illustrating the emptiness, which both frightened him and, above all, induced a state of extreme restlessness. "I feel like I never calm down," he indicated, then offering the following explanation: "Because this emptiness has become so clear to me, and the sense that I am rushing toward an abyss with open eyes."

Reinhard G. was manifestly wrestling with himself. His attempts to explain himself were markedly hasty. Over short intervals, he would repeatedly look for new descriptions that would accurately capture the way he perceived himself. His initial thought was "You are not the man you ought to be," followed immediately by the suspicion "that two people" lived inside of him. Only a few sentences later, he expressed the conviction that he was not the person who others had thought he was until then. "A person recognizes he was never a person" was a last effort for the time being to formulate the tormenting state that was "so difficult to express in words."

In his subsequent comments on his life, Reinhard G. vacillated between all these perspectives, while vigorously underscoring that he had never been the man he appeared to be in the past—particularly during the war. Supposedly, as the former officer now divulged, even as the war approached he had a sense of not belonging there. Evidently, the only way he could explain his promotion to captain in 1943 was as yet another instance where others had been mistaken about him. He had even viewed being slated for a general-staff career as "preposterous."[69] Reinhard G. did not succeed in developing a consistent picture of himself, however. Rather, whenever the new self he was designing lacked something he would have actually liked to retain, it seems that he would repeatedly become snarled in the way he imagined himself. For example, at various points he broke out of his propensity to denigrate his capabilities and represent his past actions as purely mechanical. It suddenly emerged that he had had genuine ideals during the Nazi period. They had only been shattered in the spring of 1945. And in spite of everything, he could not allow his stint as a *Pimpfenführer* (a Nazi scout leader) to pass without a brief expression of pride: "My boys loved and admired me, that much I can say." At another point, it becomes clear that he in fact did not wish his ability as an officer to be fully overlooked. In describing the great inner struggle he allegedly had to endure in this role, he added en passant and almost a little defiantly: "To say something positive for a change: I was respected and loved."

Here, Reinhard G.'s tone of voice became sentimental for a few moments. In the overall context of his self-presentation, it had a troublesome, dissonant effect. Although the former officer immediately tried to change that tone, it was not to be overheard. For a moment, it cut through his effort to distance himself from the war and his own Nazi past, illuminating all the more clearly the long road he still needed to travel in the process of distancing and transforming himself. In postwar civilian life, Reinhard G. indeed felt highly insecure. He did not find himself equal to taking up his old career as a teacher. He did not "feel like a human being," he explained, since all he was experiencing was this "emptiness." At this point, in spite of all his intention to order his life anew, his ability to reinvent himself came to a halt. To be sure, the need to sever his ties with Nazism, a need that in many cases was in a sense decreed, was a strong driver of the self-invention process in the postwar period. For many, however, the political upheaval represented a drastic biographical hiatus, all the more so because it was accompanied by significant social turmoil. This also affected Reinhard G., who confessed something remarkable to the psychiatrist only a few weeks after writing his "development process." The doctor noted: "He admits that many problems remain that he needs to confront. Basically, the only thing he loved heart and soul was being a soldier, and the teaching profession would require that he first blend in."

What emerges in all these cases is the search for a new inner identity in the transformational zone of the postwar period. This was, however, not only a compensatory expression of self-accusation or a consequence of the unavoidable concealment of one's Nazi biography. In addition, the echo of fear in which the violence and horror of the war reverberated, and the ongoing mental turmoil and personal disillusionment associated with the war and returning home, shook many a soldier's concept of self. In the postwar period, soldiers' self-image could no longer automatically serve as a foundation for continuity and internal structure. The idea of having remained true to oneself even under conditions marked by extreme danger and stress revealed itself in some as a refuge as they faced inner emptiness and troubled relationships with themselves. Inner repatriation itself was disturbed. In many cases, returning to loved ones and familiar places may have served as a kind of exterior framework and thereby helped in the inner reconstruction effort. For a long time after the end of the war, however, this, too, remained a precarious enterprise. For the new self-awareness that some felt could only be sustained by complete self-transformation, yet the structure in many cases offered only a deceptive footing. Too many of the expected social supports for life after the war lay in ruins. As many would discover, neither their return to the family, nor vocational prospects, nor ideals of masculinity guaranteed a quick recovery of social prestige and a sense of self-assurance.

CHAPTER 3

Social Rubble

Oh great God! Misery can be so awful! Sometimes when you walk along the streets, you think you can hardly bear to look at the sorrow. Amid the smart American uniforms, the well-nourished figures of our occupying powers, the first German soldiers surface, raggedly dressed and haggard, looking around timidly like sinners who have been caught. They slink down the streets. You want to look away when you see them because you feel ashamed at their shame, their destitute, sorrowful appearance. These are the resplendent, well-equipped victors Adolf Hitler sent to war years ago! They stagger along like walking ruins. Legless, armless, diseased, abandoned, and lost. A gray-bearded man stands leaning against a wall in a tattered soldier's coat. Arms crossed over his head, he cries to himself. People stream past him, remain standing, form a shy circle around him. He doesn't see them. Helpless, arms crossed over his head, he sobs like a small child. "Mama . . . mama . . ." "Are you hungry?" asks a woman and searches sheepishly in her shopping bag. "Perhaps you're ill . . . ?" He doesn't hear her. He cries. It is horrible when gray-bearded men cry. When they can't stop crying.[1]

At the start of the 1950s, sociologist Helmut Schelsky published the study *Changes in Present-Day German Families*. Based on 167 studies conducted on families in 1949 and 1950, his research results put a halt to all the Cassandra cries about the imminent disintegration of the "family" as an institution, which generally meant "marriage."[2] According to Schelsky,

> When one sees the extent to which even the modern family can counteract the effects on individual persons of a sudden and complete collapse of the state and economic order of the sort that occurred in Germany, and how the family has been ready and able to take on again general social functions of which it seems to have long been robbed by the modern state and economy, then viewing this institution as *the remaining stability in our social crisis* will appear justified.[3]

To put it bluntly, one of the most renowned German social scientists of the time was both heralding the end of a stormy debate on the "crisis" of the family and offering scientific legitimation to a sociopolitical development aimed at a substantial restoration of traditional gender roles and guiding images of the family.[4] Without a doubt, Schelsky was well aware that in the immediate postwar period most German families faced huge burdens due to the war's many consequences. In the midst of a collapsed political, social, and economic order, countless families were struggling for material existence, often in the absence of men who had been killed, had disappeared, or remained in POW camps. Hardship was the order of the day. For Schelsky, it was the earmark of a "typical social fate" during the war and its aftermath, as manifest in refugees and expellees, those rendered déclassé as a result of now being banned from certain professions, the seriously injured, late returnees from POW camps, war widows, and those whom the bombing had left homeless.[5]

In spite of the hardship, Schelsky saw the family not only as an important remaining source of social stability but also as a social unit whose cohesion was rendered all the stronger through shared survival and spouses' mutual understanding of the burdens they were enduring.[6] Along with that, he saw the function of the family for society as having shifted. It was no longer a kind of "unconscious basis of security," strengthening individuals and placing them in a position to invest their energy in fulfilling societal demands. Rather, the family now laid claim to this energy for itself (thus withdrawing it from the public sphere) to ensure its own cohesion, alleviate social distress, and thereby compensate for the "loss of general social support."[7]

A wide range of accentuations notwithstanding, his argument has basically been maintained across a broad spectrum of historical studies of Germany's postwar period. Today, however, we have a much clearer understanding that the "privatization of the war's consequences" represented a burden on families that would by no means be limited to the early postwar years. In fact, the burdens continued long after the Federal Republic had been established, and for many people extended over the course of their entire lives.[8] For example, in many families where the husband's ability to work was restricted by a war injury, an ongoing livelihood could only be ensured if the wife took a job.[9] In addition, these women often also had to care for their husbands, just as the physical pain of the war injured and the associated mental changes left their mark on family life in general. Here, the state offered little help, although it must be borne in mind that it did prevent extreme need by offering pensions to "war victims." Nevertheless, as Vera Neumann has shown, the government largely shunted war-related problems into the family sphere, thereby exploiting the family's potential to meet the challenge of socially reintegrating invalids and other repatriated soldiers.[10] In the meantime, it is a widely held assumption among historians that family members were confronted with more than just the temporary adjustment problems that even the media of the times were ascribing to the "very late returnees" from Soviet POW camps.[11] It is also widely claimed that "working through the recent past" (*Aufarbeitung*) and "processing" (*Verarbeitung*) of the entire "complexity of personally experienced and still existent burdens from the war" was something done within the family.[12] According to this view, therefore, the family was the arena in which the Nazi past and the horror of war—the killing and murdering, the threat of death, the loss and the pain—were overcome. Occasionally, the literature conveys the impression that the family was not only an unshakable enclave but also a unique, almost inexhaustible emotional storehouse. The claim is advanced that even for the immediate postwar years "the family again showed itself to be the only social place to which each member could return, despite all weaknesses and misdeeds, and count on receiving help."[13]

There is in fact a great deal of documentation, both from during the war and from POW camps, confirming that hundreds of thousands of former soldiers longed for and sought refuge in their families.[14] But it is just as clear that in many cases the thought of seeing one's family again, and that meant above all one's wife, was accompanied by anxiety about estrangement and sometimes the suspicion of unfaithfulness.[15] This intensified the longer the soldier had been interned as a POW. Reports about married women who had entered into new relationships during the early postwar years, and had found new life partners in the continued absence of their husbands, reached prisoners in camps even thousands of miles away through letters from friends and relatives.[16] We can assume that such bad tidings did not remain fully secret. Still, as a rule returning to one's family was associated with great hopes for the future, and many wives in postwar Germany saw the matter no differently. The family was a place of projection where one anticipated warmth and shelter, peace, understanding, and support—hence a return to "normal circumstances."[17]

The simple faith in the healing power of the family that we continue to find in the scholarly literature may have resulted from the same projection that cast the family as a last refuge at the time but was ultimately disappointed by the erosion of family happiness. In actual fact, the shattering of social relations did not spare the family. This was the case, for instance, when emotional estrangement in personal relationships, between men and women or between generations, could not be overcome; when repatriated soldiers found themselves deprived of their social status and lacked the support of a vocation to

fulfill their role in the family; or when physical injury stemming from the war
or internment became a personal or family burden.

After the men returned, tension and conflict between family members
were often not long in coming, as was the case with Kurt A.'s family.[18] Compared to countless other soldiers, he had not been separated from his family
for a long time. He had been called up by the Wehrmacht in January 1944 and
was released from a British POW camp only a few weeks after the German
surrender. It was difficult for him to bear this period of absence because he
was supposedly tormented by homesickness to an extraordinary degree. Consequently, he was very eager to return. When the moment arrived, his wife
clearly noticed his joy but, as the psychiatrist's report indicates, she also realized "it was a tormented joy." And even this did not last very long. She had
to "make room," she explained, for his "many worries," which in her eyes
were simply "nonsense." They included an anxious unrest she sensed in him,
as well as his fear that the British would come and imprison him again. She
only mentioned these things briefly; she found them incomprehensible, even
alienating. The situation was compounded by her husband's complaining
about the condition of the house and their remaining possessions, which also
seemed odd and absurd to her. Kurt A. likewise described his impressions on
returning home, leaving the doctor no doubt that he remained deeply disturbed by what he had found: the house he remembered as "once being so
beautiful" was not what he found, an experience shared by many returning
German soldiers. Parts of it had been demolished by a bomb. "No one was
seeing to its repair," noted the doctor after the initial interview with Kurt A.,
who also complained, appalled, that "he no longer had anything to wear.
Three Sunday suits were not enough." Confronted with the destruction of the
familiar life and world he longed for, coming home had turned into a burden
for him. Even at night, he no longer found peace. After "worrying so much
about home" in the POW camp, now, the psychiatrist recorded, "constant
worry about the house and its furnishings" robbed him of sleep.

Kurt A.'s family could not calm him down, let alone convince him to see
things differently. His wife apparently disagreed with him fundamentally. In
the end, she insisted, her husband had enough to wear, and damage to the house
was actually modest. Indeed, in her words it was "in excellent condition." She
evidently had a different idea of what constituted destruction and destitution.
She had survived the bombings along with her youngest son, dealt with the
collapse of everyday life, and managed to procure what was necessary for life
to go on. Mrs. A. was baffled by her husband's lamenting and faced it with a
certain impatience.

As we gather from the medical file, Kurt A.'s mental condition began to improve after a few days in the clinic. After a week, he showed self-confidence, readily conceding that the damage to the house was "actually not so bad." His only continuing lament was that he had a "good-hearted wife" who needed him and was waiting for him. Soon after, he was dismissed from the clinic. A year later, however, a spontaneous call on the family by the psychiatrist revealed that after Kurt A. returned from the clinic, family life had become a disaster. His wife now spoke of her husband in a bitter tone. She no longer described him as "having always been sensitive," a term she used a year earlier, but at best as "grouchy." From speaking with the couple, the psychiatrist also learned that Kurt A. had soon stopped helping with the family-owned inn. He complained about "young people" and preferred not speaking with them "because they're all so superficial." He didn't entirely trust his young son with the business, and he had begun to complain about the house again, along with other matters. All told, the doctor saw the situation as follows: "He finds fault with everything at home, sees everything in the darkest of terms, worries about things that are no cause for worry, and tyrannizes the family with his revolting pedantry."

A similar scenario played out in many postwar families.[19] The typical problems they faced are encapsulated in what we read about the family of Kurt A.[20] Expectations, held on all sides, that the husband would successfully take up his previous work were often disappointed. For Kurt A.'s family, his return was less a relief than a burden. New dependencies had formed, leading to an inversion of traditional roles. Kurt A. had lost his previous role as chief provider. The family could make do without his labor, as not only his wife but also his son self-confidently showed him every day. The displacement of competency had also shaken the hierarchy within the family; the distribution of power was under negotiation. As much as the son found himself exposed to the carping of the father, who considered him fully unqualified to help at the family inn, he could equally count on his mother to defend him against the denigrating attacks, and it was clear she, in turn, could count on her son's protection. When Kurt A. consented to enter the psychiatric clinic again—this involved the pretext that a medical report was required—where he then agreed to a further treatment, the son contacted the doctor one evening with the far-reaching request that his father no longer be granted leave for home visits, since "the situation was destroying his mother."

Nevertheless, Kurt A. ended up returning home after several days, having seemingly pulled himself together with great effort. When the doctor visited the family for a second time in the spring of 1947, the former patient initially seemed "unremarkable." After some time, however, he blurted out that he actually had great worries. They revolved around the same problems as during the previous two years: the condition of the house and, as the doctor learned from Kurt A.'s wife during his previous visit, "political things," meaning the denazification proceedings. She was tired of all her husband's worries, which she simply thought were a waste of time. On this occasion, Kurt A. only mentioned his concerns after she had left the room.[21]

Appalled by the external, visible rubble, the returnees largely passed over the preceding war in silence.[22] In many cases, family members apparently could not determine whether or in what way conflict and tension within the family were traceable to the war. For the most part, they did not interpret these conflicts as a result of the soldier's experiences in war. Later on, time spent in a POW camp, especially a Soviet camp, would be accorded a much larger role.[23] Yet the interview notes in medical records from the immediate postwar period show that the overwhelming number of families interpreted the reasons for the emergence of conflict and discord in widely differing ways. These different perspectives reflected the diversity of experiential worlds during the war. This is especially striking in a number of cases where sons, after they had returned from the war, could simply no longer stand the "drill sergeant" tones of their fathers, as Hubert B. explained to his doctor. For this reason, the former soldier had gone so far as to have his father admitted to a psychiatric clinic.[24] After coming home, Gerd M. was likewise offended, more than ever, by his father's behavior.[25] In the opinion of the community nurse, the father took things far too lightly compared to his conscientious son. Gerd M., who had disliked serving as a soldier during the war and had suffered greatly from the "murdering," could not confide in his father. Gerd M. began to brood, was increasingly unable to find meaning in life, and had difficulty reestablishing himself in civilian society, for which his father had shown almost no interest or understanding "Fathers often treat their sons who've returned from the war like small children," Gerd M. indicated to the doctor. But this did not amount to making a concession to his father, who supposedly believed he could continue to point the way for his son. Gerd M. bitterly reproached his father for demanding that he act against his convictions. He candidly told the doctor that since the war he could no longer bear it when his father behaved "like a sergeant."

When and how these different war experiences contributed to and sometimes even generated serious tensions within the family was not always apparent to family members. We see this in Herbert L.'s parents, who presented themselves at the clinic in the summer of 1947 for the purpose of having their son examined.[26] As the parents explained to the psychiatrist, they had felt baffled by their son's behavior for quite some time. They had already begun to notice the first changes in August 1944, they recalled, but initially did not attach any great importance to them. Nineteen years old at the time, Herbert, who had always been a "lively, happy boy," had been home on furlough before going to the front. He had been "calm and quiet," with "coldness and coolness" replacing the once "intimate relationship with his parents." During a later visit, they were taken aback by his "impoliteness, harshness, and reclusiveness," because, as they explained, he had still been writing "very nice letters" from Italy, where he was deployed. Following a short internment as a war prisoner, he returned home and was, they recalled, even more taciturn than before. If someone came to visit, he withdrew, and for some time he even had avoided contact with friends and comrades. Nevertheless, if we follow the parents' account, their son's life was soon back on its "proper" track. He began to study together with a friend from earlier days, and a short time thereafter even resumed secondary school. In the summer of 1946, as his parents reported, he again began to behave in an odd and incomprehensible way, complaining that his school friend had maligned him in the city and had labeled him a "criminal." When his parents expressed reservations, raising "logical objections" to his plan to sever ties with his friend, he reacted with sheer stubbornness. When his mother continued to intervene, he became verbally abusive toward her. To the parents' surprise, even his father's sternness failed to resolve the situation. Indeed, Herbert continued his verbal abuse, primarily directed at his mother, with increasing intensity. His performance in school declined, and motivating him to attend at all became extremely difficult. In addition, his behavior toward his peers was cool and sometimes rude, ultimately prompting his parents to seek psychiatric advice.

Although Herbert L.'s parents did not offer the doctor a particular explanation for their son's behavior, the way they presented their observations created a narrative thread with which they linked and weighted the events of the previous three years in a specific way. Herbert's own view of things was different. He, too, began by describing his behavior in general terms. He did not consider has actions unusual given the special circumstances of the times, especially the prevailing scarcity. After all, it did contribute to "changing the way people felt." As he responded to more detailed questions about individual situations, however, the spectrum of contexts he used to justify his behavior became more complex. Although they cannot be presented here at length, what emerges among other things is the way the war often continued its work of destruction in family relationships.

When Herbert L. visited his parents in August 1944, this became very obvious. When the psychiatrist asked him why he had become so taciturn, the former soldier replied, "When you go to war, you get peculiar feelings," and then added, "You don't know whether you'll ever get home again." Apparently, Herbert did not share these tormenting thoughts with his parents at the time. Whether it was because he was ashamed of his fear or did not want to burden them additionally must remain an unanswered question. In any event, his parents affirmed that he did not write alarming letters from the front lines, which had somewhat calmed their fears. Of "his" war they knew little. The world of the soldier's memories remained largely inaccessible to them, as did the manner in which Herbert still carried the horror and atrocities of the bygone war with him. He found no words that were capable of conveying to his parents the burden he bore. After the incident with his former schoolmate, who had allegedly labeled him "a criminal," this inability reemerged in his relationship to his family. As we learn from the psychiatrist's notes, Herbert explained to his parents that his friend's accusation had compromised his "honor." He had, therefore, not been able to stand for the denunciatory claim because others would have then exploited the opportunity "to exonerate themselves" and place all of the "blame" on him. As he explained to the doctor, he had not been able to forgive his parents for "making light of it all." When Herbert L. was asked exactly what his friend had circulated about him, he evaded the question but abruptly let the doctor know: "If you look at other people's past under a magnifying glass, there would be plenty to see. As far as that's concerned, I'm a shining light."

This kind of allusion to the atrocities of war and the crimes committed on the German side were not common within families.[27] Certainly, there were stories about the war. They were also mirrored in reports by family members. As an example, these offered relatively precise accounts of the harassment some men experienced during their tour of duty.[28] Wives and parents would speak of the "ordeals" suffered during the war and especially in Soviet prison camps, often underscoring in the same breath the extraordinary endurance of the men, who had "manfully" withstood the stress.[29] Mothers knew their sons' "favorite weapons";[30] wives and parents could name the military zones in which the men had fought. Above all, family members were in the know about injuries the soldiers sustained and the length of time they spent in military hospitals.

When family members interpreted the returned soldiers' seemingly altered behavior and described it to psychiatrists, they provided only sparse information about the veterans' war memories. In many cases, we gain the impression that family members who knew of the soldiers' war experiences through firsthand accounts did not consider them worth mentioning. In cases where the dreads of the war had been alluded to in family conversations, it was not uncommon for family members to immediately fall silent. For example, Rudolf R.'s mother reported to the doctor that her son had had a very "rough time" "with his superiors and comrades," who called him "either dumb or pig-headed."[31] Beginning in January 1945, her son had participated as a member of different military units in what she termed the "withdrawal chaos" in East Prussia, yet she offered no further information about his experiences. His furious and despairing outburst during an argument simply left her puzzled: "You have no idea how I've suffered! Just beat me to death!" he shouted at his family, and then broke out in tears. He made it unequivocally clear that his family could not understand the experiences he remembered. He provided no further words of explanation regarding the war. His mother did not pose any further questions. The war had been mentioned for just a moment, before vanishing once again into mutual speechlessness.

This course of events was not uncommon. The incapacity to speak about the war on the front and in the occupied zones revealed itself in many forms. On the side of the returnees, there were aggressive tones along with helpless crying and harsh rebuffs; on the side of those who had not fought, there was distancing, annoyed impatience, and self-sacrificing solicitude. Against the backdrop of their knowledge of the crimes committed and the horror they imagined, many family members may have shied away from asking detailed questions because of the threat of gaining certainty that a husband or son had participated in various forms of murder and pillage. In some families, verbal exchange probably faltered because of a "pact of silence" sought by many former soldiers who asked their wives not to pose further questions about the war.[32] Occasionally, the medical records even offer the impression that secret disappointment among civilians over Germany's defeat and political collapse contributed to many aspects of the war being passed over in silence. Sometimes silent reproach directed at her husband may have accompanied a wife's disappointment. In the case of Hans H. (mentioned in the introduction), his wife made no secret that she actually felt contempt for him.[33] She made it clear that, by losing his rank as an officer in the SS, he had forfeited her recognition. Not only had the war been lost, with the total military-political defeat this family had also lost its social status.

Many Germans experienced a loss of social status as a consequence of the denazification process, and its effect on family relationships should in fact not be underestimated. It is correct that historians have often pointed to the high degree of postwar continuity in various professions—particularly with respect to the Nazi elite—and the remarkable ease with which many pursued their careers after 1945. Yet from the perspective of countless people, in the immediate wake of the war matters initially looked different.[34] This was not only the case for those who had been interned for months or years in Allied camps because they had held leadership positions in the Nazi regime or had been active in organizations classified as "criminal": in 1946 that involved roughly 250,000 people. There are sufficient examples indicating that being released from a camp did not offset a loss of social status for these individuals. Many of them could expect major difficulties in resuming their careers.[35] For some, long-term professional prospects were blocked as a result of their former party-based careers.[36] But above all, many others who had not been interned for political reasons encountered the same situation. In particular, individuals who had worked in the Nazi civil service now faced the loss of privileged social and material security, as hundreds of thousands of them were dismissed as part of Allied efforts at political purging and reform. At the time, the people affected could not foresee that the great majority of them would be rehabilitated several years later.[37] This was especially true for former career soldiers. "Who's going to take a former officer?" a veteran bitterly complained, in 1948 in a letter to a comrade who had just returned from a POW camp, in an effort to prepare him for the situation in postwar Germany.[38] The writer himself had, as he revealed, been searching fruitlessly for a "suitable position" for a long time. He was in any case also well aware that constant switching between unemployment and casual labor was not something limited to former officers. He had much to report on the lack of success others had experienced in their attempts to find positions they considered appropriate for themselves. He was by no means alone in his fear of "soon being downright proletarianized," as he put it. Such fears were an important component of the deep sense of crisis and the social insecurity that took hold of and sometimes seriously frightened many Germans in the second half of the 1940s.[39]

The medical files clearly show that it wasn't only those who had formerly been in leading professions who were now affected by a deep fear of social descent and demise. Furthermore, it was not only men but also women who often found the loss of social status virtually unbearable.[40] The enervating stress of coping with economic need day after day was certainly one reason for this. But the psychiatric interview records also give the impression that for many people the truly oppressive burden was realizing full well that the social misery was intertwined with the Nazi past. The wife of Werner Z., for example, was fully aware of this connection. From her husband's account, we learn that after the end of the war she had already taken preventative action in his absence. Anticipating financial and social ruin and that everything would be taken away from them because he had been a Nazi, his wife had transferred all their property and furniture to her parents.[41] Shortly after Werner Z.'s return from the POW camp, she threw him out of the house, only reluctantly allowing him to return later on since he had neither work nor a place to live. Werner Z. was barred from resuming his career as a business economist because of the ongoing denazification proceedings. Later, his wife openly admitted to the doctor that she regretted having married Werner Z. during a furlough after knowing him only a short time. He, in turn, confided that he was convinced his wife, who came "from a modest background," had basically only wanted him for his title. It had obviously not bothered her at the time that he was a National Socialist. However, since the former system had been completely discredited and the political landscape of the postwar period was entirely different, it was no longer possible to shine with a Nazi husband.

This was something no one could fail to realize, and it was conveyed through many channels, especially through the denazification proceedings. Granted, their success of that process has often been called into doubt.[42] Yet the psychiatric records do suggest that the at least temporarily obstructed return to one's former profession, the pressure of having to do occasional and menial work, and the periods of unemployment, with all their material and social consequences, made the denazification experience an extremely painful turning point. In many cases, its biographical significance can barely be overestimated.[43] Despair-filled scenarios often unfolded. In the case of Egon M., even the anticipation that he would be dismissed from his job was enough to have this effect.[44] When he was admitted to the psychiatric clinic in September 1947, he explained to the doctor that he had received an "unfavorable" classification on his denazification certificate—classification IIIb.[45] We read in the files that this "totally destroyed him." He had been crying frequently ever since and could not cope with life any more. Egon M. confided to the doctor that he was "unbearably worried about his own and his family's future." It emerges from the doctor's record that the denazification decision reminded the former municipal engineering inspector in an unpleasant way that he, too, had joined the Nazi Party—"of necessity," as he claimed. In addition to that, the notification also generated existential anxiety in Egon M., who apparently once again held a position of responsibility in the building trade. Every day, his dismissal hovered over him, along with the bitter consequences it would have for him and his family.

In these situations, many former soldiers insisted on having always kept their distance from the Nazi regime. In countless cases, they may have been

deceiving themselves. It could have been a simple reaction to political expectations that they would distance themselves from Nazi policies; it may have been
an indication that shock over the crimes was finally setting in, and they did not
want to be identified with them. In the self-portrayals of the former soldiers
that are documented in the psychiatrists' files, an undertone of self-pity can
frequently be heard. Nevertheless, in many cases the social misery made a
noticeable contribution to doubts arising about the correctness of one's own
behavior in the Nazi period.[46] Karl D. is a good example. He had lost his position as a pharmacist; he and his family were now totally destitute. Not only was
he tormented by concerns about the future, but his worries brought self-
reproach in their wake.[47] He conceded, the interview record informs us, that
"many things should have been done differently. Because of his family, he
should not have affiliated himself politically." And as if he wished to reinforce
both his suffering and the lesson he drew from it, he underscored how much he
now worried "that the children could decline in social respects."[48]

Without doubt, this sort of reflection was highly self-centered. Nevertheless one gathers the impression that in this phase of bleak professional prospects and instability and the concomitant financial distress and social decline,
those affected remained imprisoned under an extended spell of the Nazi war,
where the past was a virtually incessant, grueling, and confusing challenge.
Amid the dismay over material loss and the shock of the social misery, the war
reverberated time and again. Flashbacks were unavoidable. For the above-
mentioned Hans H., dealing with the past became an inner test of endurance.[49]
His wife held it against him during a bitter quarrel that he had lost his officer's
status, and shouted that he needed to finally make some money. This not only
struck a blow to his sensitive self-confidence, but also stirred up tormented
memories. Hans H. faced the distressful accusation of having participated in
Nazi crimes. His past as an SS officer was a considerable burden for him. He
did not offer details, mentioning only that in 1942 he had been a platoon leader
in a reserve police battalion in southern Russia. Facing the burden of guilt, he
struggled to exonerate and even rehabilitate himself. As previously explained,
in this context the outcome of the denazification proceeding seemed to be of
special importance to him. In the end, as he told the doctor with undisguised
self-satisfaction, he managed to be reclassified in group V. The stubborn efforts
by this former SS man to be reinstated in his old position as a police captain
also reflected a desire to repair his damaged reputation. Only his reappoint-
ment would certify his personal integrity, so to speak. In his own eyes and the
eyes of others, it could be interpreted as the recognition now denied him publicly because of his career as a Nazi officer, and by his wife because he had lost

the social status of an officer. His experiences during the first four years after his return from a POW camp reinforced a sense of being discredited on a daily basis. "Rejection everywhere," noted the doctor. For a long time, Hans H. could not find any work other than being a night watchman, and that only temporarily. He was also unsatisfied with his present job as a salesman, especially since, as he complained, he earned so little that he was barely able to cover his family's "most necessary living expenses." When the denazification court's exoneration arrived, he was relieved. He was no longer tormented by fears, he now maintained; he believed that it heralded the end of occasional work, which had "in fact weighed heavily on him." Finally, after Hans H. had successfully applied for a position with the police, the former officer who had been deprived of his status seemed free of any heavy burden.

Such relief—euphoria, in the case of Hans H.—seems to have overcome an entire series of returnees once they had realistic prospects of returning to their jobs or finding regular work they considered suitable. This was the moment when hope for the future arose. Finally it had become possible to actually begin reconstructing a new life and put it in place. That was not only necessary for material reasons but was also the way, many people believed, to regain social standing and inner stability.[50] This expectation was not totally unrealistic. The economic development that began in the early 1950s and raised the standard of living in nearly all sectors of West German society would open new perspectives.[51] But the assumption that reentering working life would likewise automatically restore personal stability would often prove wrong, as seen in the case of Dietmar F.[52] His file from the year 1949 offers some information about his employment history. Having recently returned from a Russian POW camp, this still young man had decided to retrain as a gardener two years earlier. His stated goal was to open his own market garden. As the doctor noted when Dietmar F. was admitted to the clinic, he himself underscored that "it has all gone very well until now." After several interviews, the doctor chose a different formulation: "He is very happy in his occupation. Following his long internment, he simply still has difficulty integrating himself and finding his bearings in an orderly, civilized environment." Dietmar F. continued to labor under his "grave experiences during the war and imprisonment," we read further in the medical report from the patient's first interview. At night, terrible scenes tormented the former Wehrmacht soldier, scenes from which he would awaken bathed in sweat, for instance, when he dreamed of having to carry corpses away on his shoulders.

Although Dietmar F.'s new job, which he said gave him great pleasure, certainly sometimes cushioned his lasting shock from the war, his job did not

cancel it. In the difficulties he felt between himself and his father after his repatriation, his inner fragility expressed itself in another way: he felt that his
father "discounted him compared to his brother," as he put it. His father always
turned to his brother with any small request, he explained, and his efforts to
increase contact had failed to overcome the lack of intimacy in their relationship. As the returned son saw it, a "certain alienation" had been "hard to
bridge." Dietmar F. had become quieter since the war, and he felt that his father
was simply far more affectionate to his "more high-spirited brother."

It may well be that Dietmar F.'s father had always had a closer relationship with his younger son, or else that from the father's perspective his relationship with his older son was far different from what the latter described. The
files do not provide a clear answer, and Dietmar F. was the only person who
spoke with the doctor. It is certainly possible that the returnee misinterpreted
the behavior of the other family members. Even so, this makes his troubled
relationship with his father no less interesting. The feeling that the son articulated after his return from internment has all the earmarks of a sense of personal devaluation. This stands out in the files of many other former soldiers
who spoke of their relationship difficulties with their immediate environment.
With striking frequency, this feeling was associated with the war, although the
concrete backgrounds could vary widely.

What often emerged was primarily disillusionment over oneself, one example being the case of Ludwig D. One night he had accidentally shot and
killed a lieutenant who had also been a friend of his.[53] It had been a guard duty
violation resulting from fear, an emotion to which he was evidently not im-
mune, despite all his military ambitions. For years, he had not dared to tell
anyone. He anticipated only contempt from his father and a "phooey" from his
fiancée, he explained to the psychiatrist. All of this was projection, manifestly
fueled by his own sense of having failed back then, which Ludwig D. underscored in different ways during his interview with the doctor. The former soldier characterized himself as a "murderer," which is why he believed that he, in
contrast to other people, was not destined to experience any further happiness
in life. Viewing the last several years as proof, he felt that since that night he
had succeeded at nothing.

The disappointment with themselves that many veterans experienced
during the war continued to fester after the hostilities had stopped. This could
be overlaid with postwar failures, for instance, in resuming one's profession,
which were sometimes perceived as profound defeats. The case of Eberhard
L. serves as a good example.[54] After a suicide attempt in the summer of 1943,
the former Wehrmacht soldier was sent to an army psychiatric hospital,

where he received an early discharge from the service. Initially, he seemed to have had luck in his return to professional life. After returning home, he found a job with the company that had formerly trained him as a salesman. However, in the summer of 1946 he was dismissed. As Eberhard L. explained to the psychiatrist, the firm had reinstated more senior employees and disabled veterans instead.

Ever since, visiting the State Unemployment Office was a regular feature of his life. Although he detested the visits, there was no way around them, for the next job dismissal was never far away. Whether it entailed sorting mail for British army mail or working in a jam factory or in a warehouse for a household-goods factory, he struggled with every job. As a result, family tensions soon arose. He explained to the doctor that no one understood his aversion to the jobs. Instead, they reproached him, saying that there were "other people who were able to work those jobs, academics and officials who had once held very different positions." It hurt Eberhard L. that his relatives even accused him of being lazy. He said it was his sisters who had especially disappointed him most. Allegedly they had attacked him the most, probably because of their "fears about making ends meet," for which they held him responsible. Yet he showed understanding of the repeated attacks all the same, explaining to the doctor that his other family members had simply lost "confidence and faith that I'll manage to find something and that things will go on."

The returnee, who had just turned forty, tried to be forbearing. In point of fact, however, the accounts he provided during his stay at the clinic indicate that at the time he had no particular confidence in himself and his abilities. A sense of humiliation alternated with that of failure, with the two perspectives sometimes being coupled. Consequently, he conceded the possibility that he "had not been fully adequate" at his old job. He even mentioned to the doctor that he completely understood why he had been dismissed from the jam factory after only one and a half weeks. He agreed with his boss that he was "a person you couldn't do anything with." His memories of working as a messenger for a printing company were decidedly painful. He recounted that the job, which he had accepted at his family's insistence, entailed being a kind of "girl Friday." He was constantly required to be under way with a handcart, something he found very embarrassing. This was his hometown—with well-known places and familiar people lurking everywhere. "The high school I attended was across the street, and that bothered me," he stammered to the psychiatrist as an explanation for why one day he failed to make a delivery. He had recoiled from making this errand to avoid being directly confronted with the loss of the once-promising prospects his higher education had held out. Eberhard L. realized that he had collapsed along that track, not managing to fulfill even far-lower expectations over the last two years. Now he had been fired once again.

After this series of setbacks, Eberhard L. was struggling to "gain a foot-hold" again, as he put it after several weeks in the clinic. His "inability" seemed nothing less than "irreversible" to him, as the doctor summarized after a few days of observing him. During an additional interview about a week later, it abruptly became clear that failure at work was not the only thing gnawing at this patient. Rather, three years after the end of the war, he was still consumed by a sense that he had, in his words, "failed as a soldier." Eberhard L. started to cry as he said this. He had just looked back, the beginning of Nazi rule appearing gloriously in his mind. He had been present at the ceremony for the open-ing of the Reichstag on March 21, 1933. Confiding to the doctor, he burst out: "I was in Potsdam, too, watched everything, in the Garrison Church . . . expe-rienced everything very consciously. It made an impression on me; all of that it was a model for me." The files also show that even in the 1930s Eberhard L. thought of himself both professionally and privately as an insecure, sometimes anxious, not very resilient, and cautious individual. But with his enthusiasm for the regime's military power and in fact "everything military," he never sus-pected that after conscription he would fail at his duties. Yet he had already "broken down emotionally" during training when he had to do extra drill. After subsequently being deployed to the field troop in France, it wasn't long before he found himself in the psychiatric section of a military hospital. He was deeply disappointed in himself. "I should have been firmer, I should have en-dured it," he continued to reproach himself. At that time, the only work for which he was considered useful was in an armory office. He was, however, promoted to noncommissioned officer. When Eberhard L. began to talk about this, his voiced failed him midsentence. "Cries unrestrainedly," noted the psy-chiatrist. Eberhard L. continued to be bothered by the shame he felt in the face of comrades who "had participated in the French campaign," while he "only stayed at home." His inability to be a soldier in the same way as they became his personal wartime defeat.

In fact, various passages in the psychiatric files from the immediate postwar years show how narrowly self-esteem was tied to a sense of one's own ability to perform. Achievement was by no means only an ideal during the later period of West Germany's "economic miracle,"[55] and it was by no means limited to the world of work. The Nazis also propagated achievement, as long as its protagonists matched their biological racist view of the world.[56] Additionally, we must not forget that individual achievement took a central position as well in the bourgeois, predominantly male, ethos from the nineteenth century onward. Much of this continued to operate in West Germany's achievement-oriented, individualist society. As an orientation, it was now determining the way not only men but also women led their lives.[57] In many memoirs, personal and social reconstruction is presented as a history of achievement that entailed not only material accomplishment but primarily one's inner willingness to put forth the effort. After the most urgent needs had been met, such an inner stance may well have served many people as an incentive ultimately holding out the promise of a better future. A large section of society, however, also felt the burden this guiding image of achievement imposed. As indicated above, in postwar West Germany there were many examples of this. Among the most striking are the soldiers who returned from the war or prison camps with physical injuries. While their exact number will remain unknown, there were millions of them. The official statistics regarding the total number of war wounded who received benefits can only serve as a reference point. In March 1950, this was 1.44 million, with some 770,000 of them severely disabled, which is to say that the determined reduction of their ability to pursue gainful employment was 50 percent or more.[58] But the 1.44 million figure did not include all those whose injuries were assessed by the medical experts as amounting to less than a 30 percent loss of ability to pursue gainful employment. According to the official guidelines, this involved injuries such as simple facial disfigurations, loss of hearing in one ear, and light functional impediments following fractures.[59]

Overall, such assessments of the severity of an injury mirrored only to a very limited degree the extent to which disabled veterans felt restricted by their injuries and the amount of suffering they experienced. For example, from the perspective of the medical examiners who determined reduced earning capacity, it was considered especially weighty if an injured person was no longer able to pursue his profession in the same way as before. Therefore, for the physician responsible for establishing the reduced earning capacity, the loss of a hand, for example, did not always mean the same thing.[60] There is much to suggest that such logic failed to match the feelings of most repatriated soldiers. The personal burdens associated with the loss of physical integrity could not be measured in this way. Its significance often went far beyond professional life. Many former soldiers felt that the objective restrictions, and the even stronger subjective experience of them, affected nearly every aspect of their lives. This transformed and frequently also burdened family relationships.

The case of Helmut G. is only one of many examples.[61] Barely twenty years old in September 1943, he had been wounded by a shell in his upper right thigh. Without doubt, compared to countless other soldiers he still was lucky:

he had not lost his leg. He only had to cope with a fragment in his leg, although it was sometimes painful. Mostly, Helmut G. had been left with a slight limp. In the first weeks after returning to his parents' farm, it was not clear to anybody, perhaps not even to Helmut G. himself, how much the injured leg would bother him in the future. According to what Helmut G.'s father reported to the psychiatrist, the young man had actually been "very happy" during this period, which his son later confirmed.

But the veteran's mood and behavior soon changed. He became increasingly sullen. In the end, as his father observed, he withdrew into himself. Helmut G.'s initial palpable sense of relief at having survived the destructive war appeared to have dissipated. In many ways, daily civilian life seemed different from how he had previously known it. Because of the injury, the farmwork he once enjoyed was now more difficult, as he assured the doctor. Many of the tasks that needed to be done had become daily confrontations with the loss of his earlier capabilities, starting with simple jobs such as carrying heavy sacks of harvested potatoes, which caused lasting pain in his leg. On other occasions, the damage would manifest suddenly: a jolt from driving over a stone with a site dumper was more than enough. This incident drove him over the edge, so to speak. Since then, he acknowledged to the doctor, he had not been able to muster the will for daily work.

Helmut G. not only withdrew from work, but also turned his back on social life. In many ways the war had opened a gulf between him and other men from his hometown. "Earlier companions of the same age" had been "killed" or were "missing," he reported to the doctor. The experience of the war itself separated him from younger people. Above all, he apparently did not feel able to keep up with them because of his injury. It was "painful . . . no longer being able to keep pace with young people." He "just wasn't that capable any more. He couldn't dance with the others," Helmut G. explained in a later interview where he tried, one more time, to explain why he was "despondent." Reluctantly, he alluded that there was also another reason: "a relationship with a girl" had "broken up," as the medical report put it. The former soldier refused to speak about this in greater detail. The doctor was only able to discern one thing, which he interpreted as a positive development: Helmut G. appeared to "have recognized that this event is connected with his leg—with not being able to use his leg properly."

We find no additional indication in the medical file that the returnee was actually rejected on the basis of his minor injury, yet it is certainly possible. But the structure of the conflict could also have been different, as the family tensions reveal, although the war injury likewise contributed to the deterioration of family relations. Helmut G. admitted to the doctor that his mistrust mainly centered on his parents and his sister. He did not believe that they still saw him as a full-fledged human being because of his handicap. In any case, the doctor noted, Helmut G. felt that "they didn't approve of him anymore, no longer took him seriously." But that wasn't all. The medical file indicates that he immediately added: "That's the way it is: he couldn't work properly any more, and couldn't show himself on the dance floor any longer, so he was no longer drawn to it; he tried to dance but his leg would not let him do it."

That sounded like resignation, and, indeed, the war-wounded Helmut G. had in the meantime begun referring to himself as "unsociable." Yet his increasing reclusiveness reflected more than a broken sense of self-esteem. It was also a form of defense containing both grievance and rebellion. When, in one of his last interviews with the psychiatrist before his release, he expressed concern that things "wouldn't work" at home, both these dimensions were evident: "At home he was being treated like a sick little boy," the psychiatrist noted. "His sister was showing him the same kind of exaggerated affection as if he really were very ill! His parents, too, were not treating him the way they used to. He could not stomach it; that's when he became annoyed." Gestures of fondness had turned into gestures of humiliation. His parents did not realize this. According to the files, during the admission interview conducted with his father directly after Helmut's return, they had indeed suspected that he "was suffering mentally as a result of the wound." Still, his parents were helpless and could not come up with a plausible explanation for his increasing irritability and finally pronounced unfriendliness. After the former soldier's loss of his physical integrity, he and his family members had become uncertain of how to interpret the signals.

Finding new bridges of understanding in such cases was never easy, if it was possible at all. After some time, bitterness would quite often set in on both the side of the wounded individual and that of his family members.[62] One reason for this could be the emergence of physical or mental problems that rendered life even more difficult. Such problems were often not recognized as the consequences of a war injury. As a result, changes in behavior or mood were often not interpreted correctly. Even the advice received from a doctor did not necessarily help. While the doctor might make a diagnosis that did not necessarily mean that a connection was established between the illness and the injury sustained during the war or internment. Indeed, from the physicians' perspective, this connection was not always self-evident by any means, because, for example, "prevailing doctrine" considered the diagnosed physical illness—as was consistently the case with mental suffering—to be "constitutional."[63]

Nevertheless, even when the war injuries were fully acknowledged as such, it was often difficult for family members to gauge their full impact on a father, brother, husband, or son. Correspondingly, the ideas of how the future lives of injured returnees were to be structured sometimes diverged widely. A deep conflict in this respect smoldered, for example, between Walter W., who was injured during the war, and his father.[64] The reason for it was hinted at in the standardized questionnaire filled out by the referring doctor when a psychiatric admission was planned. The first entry under the rubric "What is the direct cause of the referral?" was "A question of vocational training." A letter from Walter W.'s father to the chief physician at the psychiatric clinic in April 1948, that is, two months after his son's admission, clarifies the problem and is worth citing at some length:

> As I already mentioned to you in person on March 1, 1948, my main concern is that my son should again become accustomed to regular work in some form. I have been struggling with him over this question since the first time he was wounded (the shattering of his calf bone) and his subsequent nearly one-year stay in a military hospital. Naturally, the loss of his right arm in 1943 has made the situation substantially worse. In response to my son's written declaration of a feud, I recently wrote to him in all seriousness that, based on almost six years of experience, I have no confidence in his willingness to work, and that I will consider him unsuited for engaging in an independent course of study until he can demonstrate through some simple activity that he again has both a will to work and a sense of duty.
>
> Naturally, it is very difficult for me as a layman to find an activity that is feasible for him based on his physical and mental capacities. . . . I remain hopeful, however, that through a correct assessment of my son's illness and your extensive medical and human experience you will help me to make my son a useful human being again who can then stand on his own feet once more and earn his own livelihood.

Walter W.'s father concluded by assuring the head doctor of his "readiness to cooperate," to the extent this was desired. The offer was certainly sincere, even though based on his knowledge of his son's medical assessment—as emerges from another passage in the letter—he believed himself to be in agreement with the psychiatrist in charge. Not a single passage in the file suggests he was mistaken here. He could be "sure" of himself—not only in view of the doctors' support for his concerns, but also in his stance toward his son, who had become increasingly strange, less accessible, and incomprehensible to him.

Walter W. had indeed once been much closer to his father, who was a former lieutenant general and whom he had actually emulated before serving as a soldier himself. "Military interests from a very young age," noted the medical report under the rubric for the patient's idiosyncrasies. When the psychiatrist asked him about his plans, Walter W. emphasized that he had "really wanted to become an active officer." "Probably," the returnee added, "my father's upbringing had made such an impression on me that I overlooked all my other aptitudes." The father, then, had been a guiding authority in his son's life. In his values and goal in life, the son had obviously felt in agreement with the lieutenant general. All of the medical reports indicate that there was no question of any "fight," as the father had termed it in his letter, between the two before October 1941. It had only developed over the following years, starting with the son's first war injury in the autumn of that year.

"Repeated disciplinary difficulties, was demoted," is the way the medical report described a series of events indicating that Walter W.'s attitude had changed. In the eyes of his father, the retired lieutenant general, Walter had been guilty of various "disgraceful actions," one, above all, that entailed a violation while he was on watch duty. Walter W. told the doctor that it led to a court-martial and a sentence of several months in jail, although the sentence was suspended because his father had intervened. What the former lieutenant general was not able to achieve, however, was to restore the harmony that had until recently characterized the relationship between father and son, who was an ambitious officer candidate, although relatively unsuccessful compared to his father. In the meantime, the son had been wounded a second time and lost his arm to a mine, which permanently changed his life. His life as planned until then had been ruined. What remained was a steady, pronounced awareness of his long-standing fascination with and devotion to everything military that he had shared with his father. His recollection of it was a mixture of a certain melancholy and a sense of meaninglessness. Walter W. confided to the doctor: "My entire futile life weighs on me; I can't get any closure on it. Time and again, you talk to somebody who reminds you of the earlier failings."

It might seem that Walter W. had not yet managed to reorient himself, to look forward, and to regain solid ground under his feet. But that was only partly the case, as he actually had a clear idea of how he wished to structure his life. Since the amputation of his arm, he had pursued a desire to study law. He had begun in the fall of 1944, but psychiatric treatment for what was diagnosed

as a "neurotic disorder" soon required a short interruption. Resuming his studies proved impossible because his father refused to support him. The way his
father saw it, Walter W. first had to take a "proper job" in order to prove that he
did not lack the "will to work" and a "sense of duty," as he very clearly put it
in the above-cited letter to the doctor. Meanwhile, Walter W. stuck firmly to his
goal of continuing his legal studies and refused to yield to his father's expectations and pressure.

Things continued in this way for three and a half years. In March 1948,
when the father met the psychiatrist to speak about his son for the first time,
there could be no question that Walter's constant presence at home—due to the
housing shortage and the economic situation, it was widespread in Germany
for grown children to be living with their parents well into the 1950s[65]—had
become a serious burden for his parents because of endless conflicts. He
scolded everyone loudly and was "dissatisfied with everything." As the father
explained to the doctor, his son was aware of his own behavior, but could do
nothing to alter it. The father reported that Walter W. occasionally even gave
free run to genuinely destructive rage. At the same time, he was incapable of
"being motivated to work." The maimed son was ruining "domestic peace,"
according to the father's verdict. In keeping with that, the doctor entered
"Pat[ient] no longer sustainable in family life" as the cause of clinic referral to
the clinic.

This father-son dispute bears similarities with some of the earlier-
mentioned cases in which the postwar intergenerational relationship was characterized by previously unknown authority conflicts. The differing experiential
worlds of the war left marks. Another manifestation of this was when values
and convictions that had previously been held in common were now no longer
shared in the same way. In any event, Walter W. would no longer accede to his
father's expectations regarding discipline and duty, although in a sense both
men still continued moving within the same "régime." Despite all the persistent
tension between father and son, during Walter W.'s stay in the psychiatric clinic
it became very clear that he wanted to prove something to his father. After a
lawyer presented him with the prospect of a job, Walter W. pursued the goal of
becoming "independent" both doggedly and with a certain euphoria. The impression of the psychiatrist observing Walter W. was that he wished above all
to earn a "passing grade" from the father, perhaps even "to boast somewhat."
The doctor believed it was not the job itself that spurred the war-disabled son
so much as the prospect of demonstrating to his father that he could "gain a
profession under his own steam." His father would presumably have called it
proving himself a "useful" person.

This case exemplifies that war-related disappointment in a veteran's self-image and the excessive demands on the families to which the veterans returned frequently produced insoluble tensions. Overall, in a broad spectrum of soldiers, we can observe that they felt a particular pressure and despair in dealing with the war and the countless dead. Yet the polyphony of narratives underscore that—as pointed out at the beginning of the book—the concept of "trauma" would actually offer a misleading answer as to causes and consequences. In the first place, the forms of remembering available here did not necessarily have to be the outcome of a specific event during the war. Above all, there is no "inevitable" reaction to the experience of extreme distress. The recall of horrible events, imagined or not, is "the event," and this is the only thing we can historically investigate.

Using this observation as a point of departure opens a new perspective on the perceptibility of a societal condition as accessible through memory fragments and specifically focused on personal crisis situations. In a complex way, this condition was characterized after the end of the war by distress that centered on combat and death, military defeat and vanished ideals, and left lasting marks on the lives of individuals. Among other things, this explains why the widespread and often remarked speechlessness in Germany's early postwar period should by no means be understood as simply a defense against guilt. Neither should the anxiety attacks that were often not understood by those experiencing them, and the observable feeling of emptiness, be exclusively interpreted as proof of a postwar German discourse of victimization. On the contrary, the examples presented in the previous chapters point to a difficult and painful process of searching, in which the frequent inability to speak about the horror in any way other than through dream narratives testifies not only to personal suffering but also to the suspicion or knowledge of one's own responsibility for the Nazi crimes.

The torment that reveals itself in such personal memory fragments after the war also encompasses a sense of disgrace. This could be paired with efforts to work through disappointed ideals of oneself just as well as the unfulfilled aspiration to find a place of acknowledgment for one's own experiences of wartime horror. In general, the cases presented here may paint a picture of self-doubt and instability not found in the external world of countless other survivors of the war who were able to organize their lives in one way or another. But the very point here is to understand that the external apathy we observe regarding the mass crimes, and the obliviousness toward one's own past, as formulated, for instance, in the denazification proceedings, were often simply lived expressions of virulent fears and anxieties in the shadows of the war. Reality represents a "space of memory" of its own. It comprises biographical disruption and both mental and political continuation patterns, which are often striking in the Nazi coloration of their language. There was a kind of transformation zone. For some, it already began during the war, for others at the very moment they faced total, irrevocable defeat, and for yet others it came after they were released from internment into an occupied Germany. In this personal reorientation process, with its open outcome, it was sometimes the view into the past, sometimes the view into the future that appeared more frightening. We certainly cannot draw direct conclusions regarding general societal conditions from the findings presented above. But we also cannot use the "normality" that was tangible on the surface to infer—as is common in the historiographical literature—an inner indifference on the part of the wartime generation. As the cases documented here show, many people were scarred by an inner unrest that was caused as much by their war experiences as by being forced to start anew, and was deeply anchored in a society defined by reconstruction.

PART II

The Production of Psychiatric
Knowledge: Professional
Transformations, 1945–1970

CHAPTER 4

"Prevailing Doctrine"

I consider "mental pain" in itself not at all a matter of fact but simply an interpretation (causal interpretation) of matters of fact that until now have not been precisely formulated: hence as something still hanging completely in the air and scientifically nonbinding—a fat word actually only taking the place of a spindly question mark.
—Friedrich Nietzsche, *On the Genealogy of Morals*[1]

Lessons of War

Two years after the end of the war, American psychiatrist Lothar B. Kalinowski undertook a journey to Europe, which focused primarily on Germany. Fourteen years earlier, he had fled the country—and the Nazis—because he was a "half Jew."[2] Much like many other psychiatrists, Kalinowski's trip was commissioned by the U.S. government. Where other colleagues such as Leo Alexander were delegated to find inculpatory material in preparation for the Nuremberg trials,[3] Kalinowski went to Germany as an "advisor to the American army."[4] The reason for his stay was not the trials, in which notable German scientists, including psychiatrists, served as prosecution witnesses relating to both the medical experiments on concentration camp inmates and the "euthanasia" program.[5] Rather, Kalinowski sought personal contact with German colleagues, among them Karl Jaspers and Karl Bonhoeffer, a very well known professor of psychiatry, in order to gain insight into the status of German scientific research. Kalinowski's main interest, however, was in exploring one particular phenomenon, which in his eyes was as remarkable as it was in need of explanation: the rate of psychiatric illness in Wehrmacht soldiers was extraordinarily low in comparison to the U.S. Army.[6]

Kalinowski made annual visits to Berlin starting in 1949.[7] Three years after his first stay in postwar Germany, he presented his findings: In his opinion, the apparently low level of psychiatric cases treated in the German army reflected a medical policy and practice that German psychiatrists had already established and systematically applied during the course of World War I: so-called traumatic neuroses were not viewed as effects of the war experience itself but were actually seen as caused by external factors. When it came to World War II, Kalinowski concluded that whenever therapeutic measures and government policies counteracted a flight into illness and thwarted unreasonable requests for state pensions, the rate of traumatic neurosis remained low. In his opinion, this could be confirmed by a look at the experience of other European countries in this area.[8] Furthermore, the psychiatric findings in both wartime and postwar Germany appeared to generally substantiate the assumption that there were almost no limits to the human capacity to cope with even the most horrifying experiences. In Kalinowski's opinion, this was indicated not only by the low rate of psychiatric hospitalization after the bombing of Freiburg, as documented by a German study; a Japanese colleague had also informed him that even after the atomic destruction of Hiroshima and Nagasaki, psychiatric symptoms among civilians were insignificant.[9]

In their basic direction, Kalinowski's observations are strikingly similar to those in an article published three years earlier in the first postwar issue of the German psychiatric journal *Der Nervenarzt*. The author of the article was none other than the above-mentioned Karl Bonhoeffer, who was now seventy-four years old and had been professor emeritus of psychiatry and neurology at Berlin's Charité hospital since 1938.[10] The article was entitled "A Comparison of Psychopathological Experiences from Both World Wars," and although Bonhoeffer conceded that the material had not yet been "sufficiently examined," the article provided an initial balance as far as Germany was concerned.[11] "To the extent that I have been informed through reports by military physicians with whom I am acquainted," he wrote, "it seems to me that the war has given no cause to make any fundamental corrections to the psychopathological experiences gained in the first war." In his view three things spoke for this. First, although the war had lasted longer and the "intensity of the emotional impact" had at times been stronger due to "heavier weaponry," and had been "especially oppressive during the final year of retreat," apparently there had been no "increase in actual psychoses" among the "troops." Second, according to Bonhoeffer the expectation of "grave impairment" above all among the civilian population and particularly in the cities had not materialized. As a result of the bombing, "direct symptoms of *Schreckneurose* [fright neurosis]" had indeed again often been described, but these had apparently been short term in nature. Bonhoeffer saw his views confirmed: during the bombing campaign the wish to escape into illness had been senseless. As to the so-called tremblers and shakers who had been so visible on German streets after World War I, the Berlin psychiatrist noted that they were not noticeable in that form in the aftermath of World War II. The psychiatric doctrine that prevailed at the end of World War I thus appeared to be the decisive factor to him: Because of the gradually growing "recognition by physicians and the public that a false presentation of symptoms" was at play, one had come to grips with the "hysterical responses" of these "psychopaths," at least in the form of trembling and shaking, as Bonhoeffer believed.[12]

Indeed, shortly after the beginning of World War I, German psychiatry found itself confronted with a phenomenon previously unknown on such a scale. More than a hundred thousand German soldiers were suffering at least intermittently from fugue states or paralysis, shivering, trembling, persistent vomiting, temporary deafness, mutism, or blindness. The same symptoms were observed in soldiers of other nations participating in the war.[13] Among German physicians, designations such as *Granaterschütterung*, *Granatfernwirkung*, *Granatexplosionslähmung*, and *Nervenschock* ("shell concussion," "indirect effects of a shell explosion," "shell-explosion paralysis," and "nerve shock," respectively) promptly began to circulate. Much like the English term "shell shock," these directly related the soldiers' symptoms to new destructive techniques of warfare while at the same time implying a somatic cause. In Germany, this expansion of the diagnostic arsenal proved to be an extraordinarily fleeting phenomenon. (In England, the term "shell shock" endured, even though its usage was officially forbidden by the War Ministry in 1917.)[14] How, then, did psychiatrists classify the problems, which—contrary to the assumption that the war would actually reduce nervous and mental diseases[15]—were spreading in an outright alarming way, and how could these phenomena be effectively countered?

During World War I, nearly all German psychiatrists were active in battlefield and home-front military hospitals. Because of a general-command directive, they were far more familiar than their British, French, and Italian colleagues with the problem of soldiers who were incapable of or unwilling to engage in combat.[16] During the first two years of the war, German psychiatrists were basically split into two camps. Many of them, most importantly the distinguished Berlin-based neurologist Hermann Oppenheim, insisted on the possibility of "traumatic neurosis," hence damage to the central nervous system, resulting from violent physical or emotional shock. This had been observed during the second half of the nineteenth century, particularly after train and factory accidents.[17] But even at the time under discussion, the concept of "traumatic neurosis" developed by Oppenheim had attracted controversy. We can identify three main arguments that were presented against it by his colleagues over the course of sometimes heated debates: One faction of his opponents argued that "traumatic neurosis" was not a disease in itself. The diagnosis was too broad and vague, and encompassed disorders that should have been classified as hysteria, neurasthenia, or even hypochondria. A second objection held that Oppenheim underestimated the importance of a hereditary predisposition in the emergence of these disorders, while still others argued that Oppenheim overlooked the possibility of simulation—a reproach that was highly explosive politically because since the introduction of statutory insurance in 1884 the provision of pensions for victims of occupational accidents had been under debate. In the so-called simulation controversy that reached its climax at the 1890 International Medical Congress in Berlin, this latter group of Oppenheim's opponents asserted that as a result of its vagueness the diagnosis of "traumatic neurosis" actually served as an incentive for simulation.[18] Not all critics went that far. Although many physicians shared the assumption that *Begehrungsvorstellung*, "compensation neurosis," was involved[19]—they did not generally believe that symptoms were being intentionally feigned, but instead to be a genuine illness sparked by prospects of a pension. Psychiatrist Alfred Hoche, a professor at Freiburg University since 1902, is an example of someone who took this position. Weakness of the "will" and "flight into illness" were among the main intellectual concepts in this effort to pin down the causes of the disturbances observed. With their distinct preference for a psychological or psychoanalytical etiology, these doctors tended to find a classification of "hysteria" far more plausible.[20]

"Hysteria" was thus the diagnosis that Karl Bonhoeffer, along with Robert Gaupp, director of the Tübingen psychiatric clinic, and many other colleagues offered in opposition to "traumatic neurosis" when they increasingly faced attacks of paralysis, trembling, and shaking on the part of soldiers in the winter of 1914. These doctors did not assume a physical basis for the symptoms, which they initially only suspected in persons who had been exposed to the fright of shell explosions. Considered from this perspective, the symptoms did not necessarily involve a disease, something that was indisputably manifest from a psychiatric viewpoint only when an organic cause could be assumed. And "hysteria" was no longer viewed as having an organic basis:[21] Since the beginning of the century, its status as a disorder in its own right had been increasingly disputed. Rather, "hysteria" was an "abnormal form of individual reaction," Gaupp argued in 1911 in the scientific journal *Zentralblatt für Psychoanalyse und Psychotherapie*, observing that "there are countless transitions leading from the normal person very gradually to the pronouncedly hysterical individual."[22] His colleague Bonhoeffer doubtless shared the general thrust of the argument, although he made the following distinction: in the aftermath of a traumatic experience, nearly every normal person could develop pathological responses. Yet hysteria was not only a psychological reaction; it also required a certain mental constitution or hereditary predisposition. For Bonhoeffer, the "will" appeared to be of central importance: only in a hysterically predisposed individual would the traumatic stimuli combine with a "will to illness" and develop serious, persistent neurotic conditions.[23] But this did not provide an adequate answer to the unavoidable question of how to distinguish between a normal reaction with hysterical symptoms and a truly "hysterical character." In many respects, further explanation was required.

From the perspective of the psychiatric experts, World War I soon proved to be of inestimable value for all these problems. It was an "experiment on an enormous scale in the question of the significance of exogenous damage for the development of mental disorders."[24] From a scientific point of view, it provided doctors with an amount "sample material" far beyond what was available during peacetime.[25] The prospect of better "deriving general principles from individual forms of reactions" seemed much more promising.[26]

Two years after the war began, in a convention organized jointly in Munich by the German Psychiatric Association and the Society of German Neurologists, the experts tried to draw initial conclusions. For the vast majority of psychiatrists present, one thing was already clear: the thesis of Hermann Oppenheim, who still insisted that countless soldiers were suffering from "traumatic neurosis," was no longer tenable. Numerous empirical observations and a large body of therapeutic experience spoke against this diagnosis and favored the view that the symptoms were wish-determined or even "functional in nature."[27] First, it was striking that among war prisoners and soldiers with serious physical injuries, which is to say, "those for whom the mental inducements for neurosis were absent," such symptoms were also very rare, as professor of psychiatry Oswald Bumke explained some years later in a very detailed article in a handbook. For these soldiers, the war was over. They were not afraid of having to return to the front, which seemed to be the decisive reason that the symptoms of war neurosis were absent. (After conducting his own examinations of war prisoners, Oppenheim, too, adopted the same opinion.)[28] Second, the symptoms often did not appear directly at the front but only after the soldiers were taken to the rear, for instance, during a stay at a military hospital. That confirmed suspicions that, consciously or unconsciously, the hysterical symptoms were being mimicked and adapted by those affected, some of whom had never been subject to shell explosions. Finally, the cures that had been achieved using only suggestion were a third reason. For example, medical hypnosis had shown highly impressive results: the technique had been used not only to resolve symptoms but also to achieve the opposite, namely, to revive symptoms that had since been eliminated.[29]

All of this argued for purely psychological causes. A few years later, Karl Bonhoeffer was able to encapsulate matters far more precisely than at the wartime conference of 1916. He presumed an inner conflict within the individual: "on the one hand the inescapable military compulsion and the war's menacing, death-bringing imperative, on the other the affirmation of life and the wish to be out of the fire, out of the danger zone." And further: "That war hysteria stems from this combination can be considered proven by the war."[30]

This psychiatric interpretation documents a new openness. German psychiatrists, the majority of whom were interested in processes that could be described scientifically, were in the meantime proving extremely receptive to the psychoanalytic explanation of war neuroses.[31] The parallels with psychoanalysis are unmistakable: Ernst Simmel, for example, stated that the war neurotic flees into illness; his "intellect is freed from decision, and the complex of emotions that is often born of the fear of death and a longing for life obtains redress." However, Simmel promptly added: "He was withdrawn from the front as a sick man; and at home in complete safety he reaps pity and hero worship."[32]

Simmel was not alone in his views. During the second half of the Great War at the latest, the assumption had taken hold that soldiers who showed persistent symptoms of shaking or paralysis, or fugue states, had "psychopathic" personalities. However, the concept of the psychopath as a "mentally abnormal" individual had lost the neutrality it possessed around the turn of the century.[33] It now designated types of character,[34] for instance, the person who was "weak willed"[35] or "neglectful of his duty,"[36] as well as the "excitable troublemakers and agitators."[37] On the other hand, in the broadly shared view of psychiatric and psychoanalytic professionals at the time, healthy individuals were characterized by their ability and readiness to bear the war's horrors. There was still no unanimous answer to the question of whether soldiers who were not capable of bearing those horrors suffered from an inherited or dispositionally determined "inferiority." Here as in other West European countries, elements from both fin de siècle doctrines of degeneration and eugenic theory informed the debate.[38] Toward the end of the Great War, one finding seemed to argue irrefutably in favor of "endogenous" factors, which is to say, those that were dispositionally determined. It demanded an explanation just as much as the appearance of the above-mentioned "tremblers." Namely, the great majority of soldiers endured severe physical and mental strain without developing any symptom whatsoever. To heighten the contrast: many went through the most stressful experiences conceivable without developing problems afterward, while others, as Oswald Bumke summarized, "collapsed for reasons far less serious." He thus concluded that the assertion made by various psychiatrists at the start of the war that "every participant in a campaign is capable of develop- ing hysteria" could "no longer be maintained."[39]

Nevertheless, it is by no means the case that psychiatric experts went as far as to completely discount war stress as a defining factor in mental reac- tions. Bonhoeffer vividly described so-called fright emotions, the sudden "mental shock" that can appear "when mortal danger and intense sensory impression suddenly manifest" and "sometimes lead to fainting." Other ex- amples showed that harrowing experiences could produce feelings of com- plete emptiness, a kind of "emotional paralysis," while intellectual mecha- nisms seemed to continue functioning concurrently.[40] Often, the psychiatrists argued, states of intense exhaustion as a result of long marches or hunger formed the basis for such mental responses. Nevertheless, as early as 1916, Bonhoeffer believed he could assert "with a degree of certainty" that the ef- fects of such states of depletion, which were unavoidable in wartime, were not extreme enough to produce serious mental illnesses such as psychosis. Rather, he indicated, the war showed that the "resilience of the healthy brain" could be "assessed as very high."[41] The only thing that could not be excluded were hallucinations from exhaustion.

The psychiatrists' willingness to accept the extraordinary mental strain and horror of war as a trigger for this type of mental state did not depend ex- clusively on whether they detected a condition of extreme physical exhaustion. There was an additional important criterion: the duration of the emotional changes. For Bonhoeffer the mental responses of a "healthy person" only "temporarily" resembled those of an individual with a "psychopathic constitu- tion." There was no doubt that in times of war "pathological forms of intoxica- tion, sudden absconding, affective crises, and fugue states" could be observed in soldiers who had been healthy until then. Yet, after a short time, these sol- diers were evidently able to gain control over the "disharmonies between affec- tive, volitional, and intellectual spheres" that are probably present "in every healthy person."[42] However, the psychiatrists viewed longer lasting or recur- rent mental afflictions that befell many soldiers when they were notified of having to return to the front—or others while they were in the trenches—as definite proof of "psychopathic inferiority."

The concept of psychiatric treatment near the front line (*frontnahe Psy- chiatrie*) therefore corresponded to the state of knowledge, as it had evolved, concerning the causes and course of soldiers' mental disturbances. It promised a therapeutic advantage over the treatment offered to soldiers in various military psychiatric hospitals throughout the Reich. The overflowing state of hospitals in the rear certainly drove such considerations, which first emerged in 1917.[43] While many a soldier, as Kurt Schneider expounded, "can completely recover and return to the trenches after a brief period in the tranquility of sick-quarters," once he had "reached a military hospital or even been sent home, the chances of fully restoring his fitness for combat were very slim." It was only under the "influence of friends, relatives, or one's own peaceful reflection," Schneider believed, that "'compensation neurosis' in the sense of a pension" could develop.[44] In other words, only in direct proximity to the front could one counteract the danger of soldiers developing a propensity to solidify their symptoms in the expectation of being discharged from service and evading the war.

As the Great War drew to a close, the concept of psychiatric treatment near the front lines was no longer implemented. Still, in the following period German psychiatrists largely considered its advantages to be one of the war's most important professional lessons, as did many of their British and French counterparts. Whether on the winning or losing side, it was viewed as a fact that sending psychologically unstable soldiers to army hospitals in their home countries had been a therapeutic error that caused the armed forces to lose many soldiers unnecessarily.[45] In the German psychiatric community, a large number of physicians saw this viewpoint all the more confirmed because after 1918 some of them, such as Robert Gaupp, saw "numerous neurotics quickly regain their health." Thus, cases where "simulation had been previously suspected" now seemed clearly proven correct.[46] In this way, as the war drew to a close, a discontent that psychiatrists had articulated while the war was still in full swing became even more widespread, namely, as doctors they were playing into the hands of the "war's terrible selection process" by ensuring that allegedly "inferior" men found care and protection in army hospitals at home, while the "healthy" men were dying on the front.[47]

When the next world war broke out at the end of the following decade, in contrast to 1914 psychiatrists were prepared for the phenomenon of "war hysteria" and its treatment. Building on findings from the Great War, which had gradually solidified into a guiding scientific paradigm since 1916, for example, Robert Gaupp—who exemplifies the majority of his colleagues—had no doubt that psychiatric insight from the earlier war had "proven correct" and "for this reason provides the *guidelines* for what we have to do *now*."[48]

On an organizational level, action had already been taken. Introduced during World War I, the practice of relying on the expertise of high-ranking scientists was now institutionalized through the appointment of consulting physicians and significantly expanded; this took place in the course of the establishment of the department of military psychiatry and psychology at the Academy of Military Medicine in Berlin in 1936. The number of consulting psychiatrists, mostly university professors or senior physicians with advanced academic qualifications, was increased. Once the war began, their area of activities was at least partly transferred to field hospitals at the front. As a rule, those with full professorships served as consulting psychiatrists in the reserve army, while younger senior physicians and specialists from the university clinics served in the regular army.[49] The network of psychiatrists was spread over the German Reich and the occupied territories—which consisted of seventeen military districts—in order to contribute their expertise and assist the "attending medical officers primarily with the treatment of psychopaths and war neurotics," as stipulated in military service regulation 21/230 of 1939.[50] The consultants' tasks included sharing their expertise to determine the adequate form of therapy for soldiers exhibiting mental symptoms. The treatment designated for those diagnosed as suffering from nervous exhaustion was different from that for those who appeared to have developed a "serious hysterical reaction" or even a psychosis; decisions regarding their future suitability for service in the war varied accordingly. The regulation left no doubt that the "consulting physicians" were to carefully assess the troops' mental condition and submit regular reports that would reflect their findings and be compiled by the office of the military medical inspector. For the broad majority of these psychiatrists, whose interests were mainly research oriented, the stipulated "acquisition of scientific material" was certainly the most attractive aspect of their duty.[51]

But the lessons from the Great War were not only influential at the institutional level. They also continued to determine diagnostic considerations, therapeutic provisions, and treatment regimens. In a scientific article published in 1940, Robert Gaupp, the long-standing director of the Tübingen University clinic, made reference to experience gained by German, English, and French colleagues in World War I to once again underscore that in the strict sense war was not the cause of mental disturbances. He emphasized that there were "*no specific war neuroses and war psychoses,*" but rather "psychopathically predisposed, namely, *anxious* and *temperamentally tender* natures" who "frequently succumb to the horror and abomination of modern war, younger men earlier and more readily than those who are older and more mature."[52] "Will," Gaupp insisted, was more decisive than "intellect and muscular strength"; above all, "biological health" was indispensable. Despite Gaupp's reference to an instinctive flight into "liberating illness," initiated primarily by "the frightened souls of unstable people," he did show a degree of understanding. Ultimately, he was himself aware that the war was an extreme situation: "For it is not the case that the physical-mental structure of every human being is geared to barrages, being buried through a shell burst, aerial bombs, and flamethrowers, and fully able to cope with this murderous process," he wrote, adding that "again and again that joking wartime expression will prove to be true: *better a coward for a minute than dead for lifetime.*" Gaupp went as far as to warn his colleagues against succumbing to an erroneous belief: there was "no discipline and training, however heroic," that could "entirely abolish . . . fear when a creature's life was threatened." For this reason, the psychiatrist anticipated another development: as soon as "the danger of horrific destruction of everything living" increased in a war, "there will be increasing numbers of human beings whose biological and often also moral strength is unable to cope with such destruction."[53]

Gaupp, who was seventy years old at that time and one of the most respected authorities in his field, impressed his ideas forcefully upon his younger colleagues. This, too, was one of the lessons of the Great War, during which the huge number of soldiers who developed mental disorders had taken psychiatrists by surprise. But that wasn't all. The profession had also learned, Gaupp recalled, "how great the elasticity of human nature" was. It could "pull itself together after hardship and gruesome experiences." There seemed to be ample evidence for a capacity to recover from "humanity's most horrific catastrophes" and overcome loss and death "*without lasting damage.*" Gaupp was convinced, however, that "*the insight of those who know*" was indispensable. Proper perception, proper treatment, and the proper personal approach, "strict but just, without scorn, but also without sentimental lenience," were called for if one was to "intervene *at the right time*" and thereby avoid "severe and offensive healing methods."[54]

Despite all the continuity of World War I psychiatric doctrine, this appeared to be a distancing from the aggressive and physically often extremely painful forms of shock therapy that psychiatrists had often used at the time. These treatments were aimed at convincing soldiers of their fighting strength by confronting them with a horror that exceeded their front-line experiences. In a large number of cases, the expectations of the psychiatrists had been fulfilled: the symptoms disappeared.[55] Yet the position of Robert Gaupp, who was already retired at this time and in his article from 1940 was instructing physicians from the outside, so to speak, serves as an indicator: during this first phase of World War II, German psychiatrists were in fact generally restrained when it came to aggressive treatment.

Four partly interconnected reasons for this come to mind. The first is political opportunism. To illustrate, Otto Wuth, who held a very influential position as a consulting psychiatrist to the army medical inspector's office (*Heeressanitätsinspekteur*), repeatedly made it unmistakably clear to his colleagues they were to abstain from rigorous therapeutic practices with soldiers and did not conceal his political motives. As he explained, he feared objections from the highest levels of government.[56] Wuth was clearly aware of the fact that the Nazi leadership had an ambivalent attitude toward "hard" therapies, although certainly without rejecting them completely.[57] A second reason is that the psychiatrists had come under increased pressure due to their competitive relationship with the psychotherapists at the Göring Institute. In cases of diagnosed neurosis, the latter adhered as a matter of principle to "softer" methods such as hypnosis, talk therapy, or even autogenic training.[58] In the air force, the psychotherapists had already succeeded in making the treatment of psychogenic reactions their exclusive domain.[59] The fact that Matthias Heinrich Göring, director of the German Institute for Psychotherapy, and Reich Marshal Hermann Göring, commander of the air force, were cousins probably did not hinder this development.[60] The voice of the psychotherapists at the Göring Institute also gained importance within the Wehrmacht's medical services. In May 1942, at the First Working Conference East of the consulting psychiatrists, to which a representative of the institute had been drafted, this was reflected in a jointly passed resolution concerning treatment of psychogenic responses.[61]

The circumstances called for prudence on the part of the psychiatrists. This was all the more the case because—and this is the third factor—a decree of the Wehrmacht's high command of December 6, 1940, had imposed at least formal limits on the therapeutic methods they used. According to the decree, major medical intervention could now only be undertaken with the patient's consent. It is known that not all the psychiatrists working in the army hospitals adhered to this.[62] Overall, however, the psychiatric experts were anything but entirely at liberty in their choice of therapies. For example, one of Friedrich Panse's psychiatric therapy plans was substantially curbed. Panse had previously been one of Bonhoeffer's assistants, had then joined the staff of "hereditary pathologist" Otmar Freiherr von Verschuer for a time, and ultimately served as a consultant for the Nazi "T4" euthanasia program.[63] In 1941, his request for permission to use direct galvanic current on patients (a procedure he developed in the Ensen reserve army hospital) without their permission was denied.[64] Once again, it was Otto Wuth who played a decisive role by submitting a negative assessment of so painful a method to the medical inspector's office. In a letter he argued that "hypnotic and suggestive treatments" had already proven fully adequate during World War I. A good year later, however, Wuth would give his consent to this method.[65]

Was this earlier expression of caution merely tactical and intended to obscure the fact that the psychiatrists had "eaten crow"?[66] Rather—and this is the fourth and perhaps most important point—it appears that at this time the physicians had no reason to assume that they would have to resort to this painful but often effective treatment of sick soldiers on a large scale. In their eyes, "war neuroses" were in fact not spreading as had been feared. After the attacks on Poland and France, the serious manifestations of shaking and paralysis known from World War I remained largely absent.[67] Likewise, at the above-mentioned First Working Conference East in 1942 it was still clear that very little had changed in this respect despite the brutal circumstances of the Russian campaign. Kurt Schneider was a military doctor during the Great War who had subsequently been active in the mental ward of an army hospital. Speaking in his capacity as a consulting psychiatrist, he reported that in the front hospitals they had indeed been seeing everything they had "come to know during the last war," but consistently only "isolated" cases.[68] At another point, he even emphasized that although there were many gunshot injuries to the brain, "problems with psychopaths" did not exist.[69]

Until then, the psychiatric experts had concurred in seeing the reason for the relatively low number of "psychopathic" cases in the way the war had unfolded. Unlike twenty-five years before, this war involved almost no grueling trench warfare. Naturally, after the planned blitzkrieg against Russia in the fall of 1941 had failed, this explanation was clearly inadequate. The rapid advance of German troops had been stopped, leading once again to the necessity of defensive static warfare on several sections of the front. The situation of these troops was in fact desperate, which was also clear to the doctors deployed there. The Wehrmacht had not only greatly underestimated the capability of Soviet army but was unprepared for the fierce Russian winter. There was soon a lack of technical equipment; hunger and the merciless cold began to drain both physical and mental energy.[70] The situation was reflected in the rate of illness. In December 1941, ninety thousand soldiers were immobilized by illness out of an army with a total strength of roughly 3.6 million men. By the spring of 1942, the figure had risen to half a million.[71] Under these circumstances, the number of diagnosed "psychopaths" increased as well.[72] Nonetheless, in the psychiatrists' view, the increase still seemed to stay within limits.[73]

For renowned psychiatrist Kurt Schneider, there was a self-evident, decisive reason for this restrained development: the therapeutic merits of "near front" psychiatric treatment, of which he and his colleagues had already been convinced in 1918. He left no doubts in this respect in the talk he delivered in May 1942 to the consulting psychiatrists, arguing emphatically for a systematic continuation of the "near front" approach. He never specifically pointed out the advantages of being able to recognize relevant symptoms early on, which he obviously considered self-evident.[74] He advocated the principle of not transporting diagnosed "psychopaths" home for treatment. Therapy was supposed to take place in a field hospital, from where soldiers would be sent back to the troops, fit to fight. The same held true for those with "psychogenic physical disorders." If it was brought home to them that only "the truly sick" were transported home in the hospital train, most would abandon "their symptoms without active treatment."[75]

In the course of arguing for a suitable resolution, Schneider underscored that his insights in this respect represented some of the "most important experiences" that he had gained "in the field army to date."[76] Indeed, he spoke before his audience with special authority, because although he held an extraordinarily high position as director of the clinical institute of the German Research Center for Psychiatry in Munich, in contrast to other full professors he had been sent to the front as a consulting psychiatrist. All of his efforts to counteract this decision were fruitless, and in 1942 he was actually sent to the eastern front.[77] Since Schneider was no champion of Nazism, it is not unlikely that he was being shunted aside in some way. The measure does not in any event reflect a paradox: political reservations about Nazism did not preclude advocating strict policies vis-à-vis the treatment of "psychopaths."[78]

As Schneider made clear in his talk, this treatment, however, required the ability to make a precise and differentiated diagnosis. Here he introduced a theme that would repeatedly occupy psychiatric experts during the period that followed. Three fundamental problems were suggested in Schneider's talk. The first of these was the difficulty of separating organic diseases from psychogenic responses. Since the start of 1940, doctors had been in a state of alarm: cardiac and circulatory problems, stomach and intestinal ailments, and rheumatic symptoms were occurring in soldiers with unusual frequency, and often a connection between the symptoms and the objective findings could not be identified. Apparently, many of these cases were psychosomatic illnesses, with a number of psychiatrists viewing them as equivalents to the "war neuroses" of World War I, a perspective not necessarily shared by internists.[79] The basic problem for the psychiatrists was that these cases threatened to escape them.

The same held true for soldiers whose war injuries took unusually long to heal, a phenomenon that seemed increasingly prevalent.[80] The psychiatrists spoke of "psychogenic overlays (*psychogene Überlagerungen*)," although recognizing them was anything but easy. In May 1942, Kurt Schneider was still warning that "psychopaths and abnormal perceptional reactions (*Psychopathen und Erlebnisreaktionen*)" were often disguised behind "physical symptoms." As a result, young, inexperienced doctors at the patient collection points were unable to recognize them. This was causing a "hole" to open up through which "psychopaths" were filtering back to the homeland.[81] It was impossible to stop the misdiagnoses. During the final year and a half of the war, however, the problem was evidently just the opposite, which made some of the consulting psychiatrists critical. In their view, neurological illnesses were now all too often being misdiagnosed as psychogenic reactions. In this context, Helmut Scharfetter, a consulting psychiatrist in Innsbruck, complained that a widespread propensity among younger doctors for "sniffing out simulation" had become noticeable.[82]

A second area that caused diagnostic difficulties was, according to Schneider, distinguishing between "abnormal perceptional reactions" (*abnorme Erlebnisreaktionen*) and "schizophrenic psychoses," which were considered hereditary "mental illnesses." One encountered the same problem, he observed, with the differential diagnosis of "symptomatic psychosis," that is, schizophrenia-like states that could emerge with brain injuries, for example.[83] It was the war, declared Schneider, that was contributing to a distortion of the picture. He cited two reasons for this. One of them certainly entailed the working conditions at the front. He mentioned this only in passing, but insisted on pointing to the "primitive examination conditions" that, as he underscored, prevailed even under the "the more favorable conditions in the military field hospitals." But he placed the weight of his arguments on another point: in his view, it had above all proven treacherous that the dreams of solders at the front were often unusually vivid, with "situations of fighting and danger" playing a "prominent role" in them. War experiences, he maintained, also figured prominently in all "abnormal states of disorientation." This could be seen occasionally after concussions, typhus, trench fever, and dysentery;[84] and finally, on the front war-related scenes unfolded in the course of acute schizophrenic episodes.[85] Schneider considered the resulting diagnostic difficulties so grave that he issued an unusual appeal "in any case to be very cautious" when it came to the diagnoses of colleagues who had observed the condition in its acute phase. Although Schneider was taking things very far, his impression stood firm: "too much schizophrenia" was being "diagnosed in the field"; the numbers seemed "remarkably high."[86]

Schneider was not the only one to reach this conclusion. Other consulting psychiatrists frequently voiced the same complaint.[87] They as well evidently did not believe there was a rise in the number of psychoses. A rise of that sort was irreconcilable with the prevailing state of psychiatric knowledge. Leading figures in the profession saw the Great War as having refuted the idea of specific "war psychoses." As they frequently put it, war was not a cause of mental illness. The affected soldiers had been ill since birth; the onset of the illness followed an "inner law."[88]

As Schneider indicated in his talk, however, identifying "psychopaths" posed difficulties of a third sort that also called for sound judgment. There had been broad consensus since the Great War that one needed to differentiate among various sorts of "psychopaths" according to their "psychopathic personalities." True, they generally manifested as "abnormal reactions," as Schneider asserted. Yet these, in turn—irrespective of whether they took the form of psychogenic physical disorders or anxiety, regular nightmares, fugue states, or pseudo-demented states—could not be classified according to a specific personality type, such as "asthenic failures," "sullen depressives," "querulous," "explosive," or "emotionally unstable." Indeed, even a "nonpsychopathic person" could "react abnormally," for instance, if his life were in extreme danger.[89] What the psychiatrist had in mind here were "acute fright reactions" (*akute Schreckreaktionen*) or "acute fright emotions," as they were called during World War I.[90] Schneider had no doubt that they had been widely experienced on the eastern front: fright at the slightest sound, persistent fear attack, or the fear of staying in the quarters alone. "Every soldier in the eastern campaign" had experienced a tinge of these things, "particularly when there was the danger of partisans." According to Schneider, there was a similar situation with nightmares: "fighting and danger" were such a strong presence in the minds of soldiers on the front that they often jumped up from their dreams, seized their weapons, and thereby occasionally even became "a serious danger to their surroundings."[91]

It seems in fact to have been mainly the consulting psychiatrists on the eastern front who diagnosed *Schreckreaktionen* with striking frequency, thereby handling the affected soldiers with great understanding.[92] In general there seems to have been little controversy among the psychiatrists over the stipulation that "acute fright reactions" were to be clearly differentiated from "psychopathology." However, it is questionable to what extent they adhered to the 1942 "guideline" indicating that with soldiers at the front it often took several days and sometimes several weeks of recovery in the field hospital before one could determine whether a case involved a "psychopathic personality" or rather an individual with a "healthy disposition." The decisive factor—one would have expected nothing else given the "prevailing doctrine"—was whether the "abnormal mental reaction" subsided of its own accord after a time.[93] Yet how much recuperation time did the soldiers actually receive under the ever-worsening conditions facing the Wehrmacht? We do not have a documented answer to that question. It is certain that the army doctors had increasingly less leeway to prescribe extended periods of rest for exhausted soldiers. The field hospitals had to care for a growing number of sick and wounded soldiers, and their capacity was limited. The pressure grew from all sides to return soldiers to their units, and it increased as the military situation worsened and the death toll mounted.

The soldiers whom the psychiatrists classified as "psychopaths" based on their persistent symptoms truly felt the growing pressure. Indeed, there had never been a lack of psychiatrists who considered the application of extreme measures justified to maintain military discipline. Thus, in the spring of 1942 Kurt Schneider acknowledged that in wartime it could be a fully correct decision "to have an otherwise worthy young man shot," since what counted was "preventing cowardice from becoming rampant by all available means and to maintain a high level of fighting strength." Under no circumstances were the "brave" to suffer from the "cowards."[94] Although his colleague Carl Schneider issued an appeal in 1944 "to make resistance to medical therapy and a lack of will to recover one's health during treatment a punishable offense" because it constituted an undermining of military morale, this nevertheless reflected that a shift in direction had taken place.[95] Its main effect was on the therapeutic treatment of soldiers whose physical afflictions had been classified as "psychogenic" and because of their duration were no longer evaluated as the result of stress overload alone. The change took on concrete dimensions late in 1942 and early 1943 with a new directive by Otto Wuth abolishing the physicians' previous obligation to obtain a soldier's consent before making use of Friedrich Panse's Galvanic current procedure. By all appearances, Wuth was reacting to a debate that had been rekindled a few months before among psychiatric experts concerning the need for this consent statement. This time it was to have a different outcome. "In numerous cases," Wuth now argued, this method "of restoring or improving fitness for service" was "imperative." He indicated that more simple "suggestive treatments," which he had continued to defend as fully satisfactory in his most recent denials of permission, now failed more frequently.[96]

The method of galvanic current treatment was soon instituted in various military districts. Out of a total of seventeen districts, we have evidence it was practiced in five, four of them lying in the so-called Old Reich.[97] This suggests that it was preferred in intractable cases, after a patient had been transported back to a reserve hospital at home following unsuccessful treatment in a field or military hospital. However, it is said that a growing number of special hospital wards at the front also adopted the method, so that over the course of 1943 it rose to become "the most important aversion procedure."[98] Possible concerns about the procedure—it was known to be extremely painful—had receded. The extraordinary effectiveness of the procedure had convinced the psychiatrists. Nearly every soldier who had developed "psychogenic physical impairments" now quickly seemed to abandon them; in many cases, apparently, a single application was sufficient. One report of success followed the next.[99] The assumption that the vast majority of the cases represented, in the words of Friedrich Panse, "avoidance responses" seemed to have been confirmed once again. In his experience, only "isolated cases" remained "therapy resistant" despite repeated use of the procedure.[100] In order to avoid "mental infection," beginning in May 1943 the "guidelines" provided for transfer to army hospital wards within sanatoriums and mental hospitals.[101] If the psychiatrists classified a soldier as *schlechtwillig*, "unwilling," a transfer to one of the so-called special field battalions could be applied for. Although the punitive nature of this measure was intentional, the battalions were still seen as giving the soldier an opportunity to acquit himself. If he failed here as well, starting in the summer of 1943 the "guidelines" even officially authorized transfer to a concentration camp.[102]

That was a hugely intimidating threat. Considering the very limited number of soldiers whom the psychiatrists viewed as completely inaccessible to therapy, it attests to the total doggedness with which the profession's leaders pushed to ensure that no soldiers at the front had a prospect of being sent home because of abnormal behavior or mentally driven physical disorders. We can assume that not every psychiatrist exhausted the full spectrum of officially approved preventative means; there are even indications that soldiers incapable of coping with what they were enduring were still occasionally dismissed from the army as unfit for service, the stricter guidelines notwithstanding.[103] As a rule, however, it seems that the profession's belief that it could come to grips with the phenomenon prevailed over any doubt that psychogenic impairments could be brought under control. This was the case despite the repeated emergence of insecurities that were themselves repeatedly manifest in a strained effort to arrive at a precise diagnosis. Yet in essence, the psychiatrists never wavered from their conviction that there was no causal relation between the war and long-term mental disturbances. The "responsibility" for such disturbances lay with those affected themselves, as Kurt Schneider again made unmistakably clear in 1944, when he once more declaimed against the concept of "neurosis." "The significance of recent psychopathology and psychotherapy," he argued, "lies precisely in having shown that neurosis involves something mental and not a *neurological* disorder." The term "neurosis" was thus misleading; it steered "those affected by it toward irresponsibility." In the end, the person had to realize "that he does not *have* a neurosis but *is* a neurosis."[104]

Within German psychiatry, this remained a prevalent conceptual figure as the war concluded. Ultimately, it was the basis for all the tried and tested therapies and measures, including transfer to a concentration camp. In the eyes of many, nearly any disciplinary measure could be justified through the basic assumption that even when "more primitive psychic mechanisms" were taken into account, "neurotics" could influence the "will" or "dispositional orientation" and were therefore able to play a role in the resolution of their psychogenic responses and symptomatic fixations.[105]

The possibility of self-deception in this context did not suggest itself to the psychiatrists. It is in fact entirely conceivable that the threat of being sent to the camps indeed had a drastic influence on the symptoms of soldiers who would then be declared fit for the front.[106] The experts sometimes already observed this effect after announcing a second painful "electrotherapy" treatment or when they threatened to transfer a soldier to the reserve army hospital in Ensen. They would, of course, see this as yet another demonstration of the correctness of their assumptions.[107] But the perpetuation of such firm belief in the efficacy of their methods may have had another source, one that is consistently overlooked. It was the collapse of well-regulated medical practice in the Wehrmacht during the last phase of the Russian campaign, when, more than ever, for a majority of German soldiers a loss of the ability to withstand the strain would be paid for with death. The mainly American but also British psychiatrists who held the military psychiatry of their German colleagues in high esteem did not take this into account. Much like Kalinowski (mentioned above), they measured the much higher rate of psychiatric cases in their own armies by the success record they observed among the Germans. It appears that in their interviews with the Allies, none of the German psychiatric experts were shy about offering a thoroughly self-confident explanation for the discrepancy. As Kurt Schneider put it, the reason was the doctors' united front against neuroses, a front they had formed right from the start, in contrast to the fractious debates between 1914 and 1916.[108] And Oswald Bumke flatly explained that a policy of keeping neurotics at the front whenever possible was the reason the German army coped so well with the problem they posed.[109] The common denominator is unmistakable. In essence, the German experts believed, the lessons drawn from World War I were correct. Under that premise, they now turned to postwar German society.

The Psychiatric Treatment of Repatriated German Soldiers, 1945–1953

In actuality, the war should have ended for German psychiatric experts with the capitulation in the spring of 1945. After all, according to the prevailing status of psychiatric knowledge, everything spoke against assuming any causal connection between the war and subsequent psychopathological problems. Still, a certain unease is evident in a good number of articles in the specialized journals through which representatives of German academia and, occasionally, institutional psychiatrists resumed their professional exchange.[110] For example, Walter von Baeyer, then head doctor at the Nuremburg mental hospital,[111] recalled that the "war hysteria" of the Great War was followed by "an epilogue, so to speak, during the postwar years in the form of those extraordinarily numerous compensation claims by former participants in the war."[112] Was it possible, then, to be sure that war veterans would not again allege that their mental suffering stemmed from the war and use this to justify claiming a disability pension, as could be observed on a large scale in clinical assessments during the 1920s?[113] Why should these "desires for securing one's livelihood and safety"—the actual cause of the suffering, as von Baeyer made clear[114]—not also come into play in this new postwar period, especially in view of the economic problems?

In the psychiatrist's interpretation, there was no reason to give the all-clear based on the results of a study conducted at the Nuremberg clinic on the development of abnormal perceptional responses (*abnorme Erlebnisreaktionen*) between 1928 and 1947 as reflected in clinic admissions. Granted, the number of "abnormal perceptual responses" continued to decline, but was that not perhaps deceptive? Not every "abnormal reaction" required stationary treatment, von Baeyer noted. In any event, most of those who appeared at the clinic presenting trembling and paralysis, demonstrations of pain, fugue states, or demonstrative suicide attempts shared a "performance-like" quality. What about the "quieter, less demonstrative, more intimate perception reactions"? Von Baeyer reminded his colleagues that they often developed into the kind of "organic neuroses" that were so difficult to distinguish from true internal illnesses, which explained why doctors often referred the patients to a clinic for internal medicine. There was a similar situation, he continued, with the majority of "simple neurasthenic cases," whether they involved intensified emotional irritability, forgetfulness, difficulty concentrating, or even the rapid exhaustion postwar Germans complained of with such remarkable frequency. It was above all the general practitioners and established neurologists, von Baeyer emphasized not without suspicion, who were concerning themselves with such cases. Although most of these cases also represented "forms of abnormal reaction" in his view, they were not presenting themselves as patients at the psychiatric clinic. In short, von Baeyer feared that the full extent of the "abnormal perceptional reactions" suffered in the general population was not being recognized.[115]

The psychiatric experts were forearmed. The experiences of the Weimar period were not the only reason that the absence of "hysterical demonstrations" gave rise to insecurity among them, however; it was also fueled by their horror at the unprecedented devastation accompanying this war. Against that backdrop, the apparently unremarkable behavior of postwar Germans seemed conspicuous, and the prevailing "silence" actually seemed slightly outlandish.[116] The doctors spoke of "stoicism," but more frequently registered impressions of "dullness"[117]—which immediately recalls Hannah Arendt's early postwar observations.[118] Psychiatrists tried to explain these reactions. Hans-Werner Janz formulated the core question as follows: could this "peculiar impoverishment of a personality's *genuine* experience, that is, an experience that shook what is essential to being human," in any way be termed "something healthy and natural"?[119]

Janz's answer was emphatically negative. And he was far from being the only one to convey a growing sense among psychiatrists that the dominant theories in their field about the "nature" of human beings and the "normality" of their mental capacity for processing experiences failed in the face of suffering on such a scale. But that didn't mean that the experts agreed on how to interpret these "frugal gestures," the "restrained conduct and, indeed, silence" they observed in Germans.[120] In the emerging debate, we find highly disparate assessments. From the perspective of cultural criticism, "technization and organized massification" had long ago set in motion a process of "steady emotional dedifferentiation." Others added—in complete concurrence with the prevailing cultural critique of modernity—that the "totalitarian form of government" had exacerbated that development even further.[121] According to this position, an "increasing loss of independence" and growing incapacity to make personal judgments had already been evident under the Nazi regime.[122] Janz argued that it had been a basic precondition for "self-abandonment" during the war, and he viewed postwar Germany's rampant "striving for self-preservation" as a continuation of the phenomenon. Indeed, Janz even claimed that this was accompanied by a profound alteration of personality structure, and he described what that meant in his eyes as follows: the reorganization had become the "pathogenic seed" of the resigned and sullen "attitude in Germany" that was observable far "beyond the medical sphere of influence" and determined by many "forms of fear."[123] Janz left no one in doubt that he deeply disapproved of this development.

For the most part, what is striking in the psychiatrists' observations is their dismay at behavior that seemed so odd. Jürg Zutt, acting director of the psychiatric clinic at Berlin's Charité hospital,[124] however, gave an initial all-clear signal in his report on the mental health of Berliners.[125] He started with the assertion that "despite justified fears," there was no sign of "illness." Here Zutt was addressing the concerns of the American occupation authorities. who in the winter of 1945–1946 had apparently asked him for an opinion on the matter.[126] He explained his position forthrightly—in view of the apparently omnipresent "silence," he clearly felt called upon to do so. In his eyes, the "impression of dullness" that was imposing itself on other observers was too superficial; rather, the silence was an "authentic expression of the fact . . . that a human being is surrendering to the unavoidable nature of a painful fate, accepting and bearing it." He did not share the opinion that this was a specifically German reaction. As an advocate of an anthropological psychiatry,[127] Zutt presumed a generally shared, essential human trait: "I believe," he concluded his remarks, "that the experience we are gaining here with Berliners can suggest something more general, namely, that 'in torment the human being becomes silent.' What we see here is nothing pathological, nor is it a case of a particular indifference or capacity for suffering. It is the silent face of suffering humanity."[128]

Deliberations of this sort were expressions of searching. They appeared in many forms as part of a general struggle to arrive at "a new image of the human being."[129] Yet this was still far from a revision of prevailing German psychiatric doctrine. After all, the psychiatric experts did see a certain need to review the principles that had been established based on experiences from the Great War. Walter von Baeyer nevertheless advised caution. He reminded readers, "We are still too close to the center of the upheaval; inner and outer distance is lacking,"[130] and suggested exercising restraint in the interpretation of the respective findings. His claim can be interpreted as a reference to the need for objectivity and scientific rigor. In the same vein, he emphasized that the generalizability of the findings had not yet been established. Von Baeyer emphasized that while local and numerically limited findings were certainly indispensable, taken in themselves they were of minor importance. Without "scrutiny on the broadest basis," it was impossible to speak of proof.[131]

From the way the psychiatrists presented, discussed, and mutually juxtaposed their findings in professional journals, it becomes clear that things were being measured by different standards. Suspicions concerning the proper interpretation and generalizability of the findings were constantly being directed at those studies in which psychiatrists argued, on the basis of their observations, that parts of the prevailing doctrine needed to be revised.[132] By contrast, whenever the psychiatric findings confirmed prevailing doctrine, it seemed that the burden of proof had already been met and the knowledge contributed had been verified.[133] In the psychiatric examinations that have been recorded this was the rule. On closer examination, this is not surprising. The perception and interpretation of the abnormal behavior and mental symptoms were—this is evident in nearly all the argumentation—fundamentally determined by the accepted school of thought and the associated underlying assumptions.

Thus, on the basis of "wartime and postwar" experiences that, according to Wilhelm Gerstacker, represented "a whole both historically and in terms of experience,"[134] the psychiatric experts saw their assumption completely confirmed that the "human organism had an astonishing capacity for equilibrium under extreme mental stress."[135] For example, in their view the bombings had demonstrated such a capacity. It was correct that psychiatrists had treated people with mental disturbances following bombing attacks, principally during the last phase of the war. But measured against the number of people living in the cities, the number of those affected was extremely small.[136] But above all, as Hans-Werner Janz emphasized, by and large the cases seemed to involve simple "fright reactions" that "generally resolved after several hours or at most days." As to the other cases with longer-term "psychogenic speech impairments and attacks," sometimes associated with paralysis, Janz had other explanations that corresponded to prevailing doctrine: for the majority of these patients, the "original fright syndrome" had become permanent by "secondary factors" such as "persistent anxiety," difficulties in the workplace, or family conflicts; two men with lasting tremor responses had already trembled for a time during the previous world war; and the psychomotor impairments suffered by a group of young people were to be understood, Janz explained, "against the background of developmental character anomalies."[137]

Nevertheless, the psychiatrists repeatedly confirmed to one another that such "massive psychogenic manifestations" had become rare. Thus, the word that had spread in the professional psychiatric circles concerning Wehrmacht soldiers was corroborated all the more strongly by the behavior of civilians. Despite "the worst possible horrors of war," despite "hardship and misery," the "classical clinical pictures of hysterical mechanisms" had nearly vanished.[138] "When life itself is at stake, there is no time to be ill," argued psychiatrist Kurt Beringer, who, like other colleagues of his, was convinced that these impairments were functional in character. He therefore further maintained that the reinterpretation of hysterical mechanisms that gained prevalence in the wake of the Great War, which is to say, their "strong decline in market value" and "loss of pathological significance," was now also now showing an effect in the civilian population. "We need only think of the revaluation of the tremblers," Beringer reminded his colleagues, and then recapitulated that although they had initially been considered "especially lamentable war victims," they were "then, following insight into the origin of the symptoms," treated in army mental hospitals with "brusque suggestive methods." Finally, they were "increasingly deprived of their pensions" and in this way "stripped of the notion of being the victims of war."[139]

There were hardly any psychiatrists in postwar Germany who did not share this view. Nevertheless, there could be no question—the psychiatrists also saw this—that emotional shock and mental suffering and anguish had taken place in postwar Germany. The psychiatrists themselves saw ample evidence of the strain, suffering, and anxiety throughout society. With respect to Berlin, Bonhoeffer outlined the situation vividly: "Complaints about memory loss and retention and the ability to concentrate are fairly widespread," with "exhaustion and affective disturbances" also being noticeable in public. "In the train stations one finds men and women sleeping at all times. There is a general lassitude, a reduced need to communicate, a propensity to explode over minor matters in the overfilled trains, sullen, emaciated, pale faces, unamiable and irritable behavior." Bonhoeffer's report continued in that vein; the symptoms he observed were virtually endless.[140]

The psychiatric experts were certain that they were dealing with a well-known phenomenon. The differences with the Great War were "only quantitative in nature"; in particular, the "intensified excitability" was "probably even more pronounced than at that time."[141] When it came to the cause, the doctors had no doubts. In essence, Jürg Zutt stated straightforwardly, the reasons lay in "states of physical exhaustion" caused by "hunger, physical exertion, and emaciation."[142] In view of the catastrophic nutritional situation and widespread hunger, above all in the cities—Bonhoeffer spoke of adults weighing between 35 and 40 kilograms (77–88 pounds)[143]—this was a plausible explanation.[144]

But also in cases where the situation was less drastic and people were aston-ished at the diagnosis, insisting they always had enough to eat, the doctors defended their argument. Against a background where mental abnormalities and tribulations appeared to represent a mass phenomenon, undernourishment and malnutrition were the only conceivable explanations that aligned with pre-vailing doctrine.[145]

This explanation was actually a source of hope for the psychiatrists. They believed that as soon as the physical exhaustion subsided, not only the physical but also the mental abnormalities and changes would vanish.[146] Manfred in der Beeck, psychiatrist at Lübecker Krankenanstalten Ost, for-mulated the expectations resulting from accepted doctrine as follows: "When the general nutritional situation" improved "in both qualitative and quantita-tive respects," then "the damages of endemic hunger as a *Volkskrankheit* [en-demic disease]" would be "quickly overcome." Hence a return of the affected people to their "physical and mental/emotional norm" was, in der Beeck and many of his colleagues believed, a question of "only a few months."[147] The psychiatrists repeatedly and emphatically insisted that the "effects on the mind" in themselves had not been the cause of the disease. "The findings are clear," underscored Zutt, who fully shared in der Beeck's position: "We must be careful not to erroneously view diseases that are surfacing right now as a consequence . . . of mental stresses."[148]

This remained the guiding principle for the psychiatric experts even when they confronted a growing number of repatriated soldiers whose "mental con-stitution" seemed clearly altered. Psychiatrist Walter von Baeyer spoke of striking "timidity about meeting and dealing with others" and of "difficulties in the family, in the professional sphere, in resuming old relationships and start-ing new ones within the social environment as a whole." Relying on the obser-vations of Hans Malten, an internist colleague, von Baeyer expressly stated that in the case of the former Wehrmacht soldiers, this was not an extraordinary finding.[149] As early as 1946, Malten observed and described a series of "func-tional mental disturbances" in the returnees that he termed "banal nervous symptoms . . . , difficulty thinking, absentmindedness, amnesic states, memory deficit ('forgetfulness'), and sometimes sleeplessness or impotence. All of this overlaid with a depressive fatigue that renders any beginning difficult,"[150] as Malten wrote in this initial report. Overall, he observed a "far-reaching, indi-vidually very diverse complex of symptoms." In his opinion the key factor was the "regular presence of the same basic features." His conclusion, soon there-after widely echoed by the German psychiatric profession, was that the phe-nomenon involved a "returnees neurosis."[151]

What Malten meant above all was a response of disappointment and a mental inability to cope with the reality of the *Zusammenbruchsgesellschaft*, that is, with a society defined by "the collapse." For the internist and many of his psychiatric colleagues, the soldiers' overblown expectations for their return home, idealized mental images formed during internment, played an essential role. "Instead of the longed-for happiness of being home," many former soldiers found only the "distress and sorrow of those who had been bombed out or expelled," the "loss of livelihood," and the death of relatives.[152] While the doctors found that the emerging "mental crisis" was characterized by a "lack of initiative in securing one's livelihood," a "loner-like lack of participation," and a "sometimes unthoughtful irritability," they nevertheless traced the crisis back to a very different source than disappointments such as those above. Malten asserted that the mental abnormalities were "mainly due to physical causes."[153] In other words, the broadly shared assumption among physicians was that physical injury, protein deficiency edema, and circulation problems were of huge importance as a "somatic substratum." The actual cause for all of this seemed to be the grave undernourishment and malnutrition suffered during internment. The internists spoke of "hunger disease," "lipophil dystrophy" (*Mangelfettsucht*), and "dystrophy."[154] The internists had acquired experience in this area as well, both in the Wehrmacht and in experiments on Soviet war prisoners—experience they promptly transferred to civil society after the war.[155]

In the professional literature, the initial discussion was of war prisoners in general, with little differentiation between the duration or place of imprisonment—two factors that were associated with widely varying living conditions and experiences.[156] When Malten declared that "never before in modern times have such masses of human beings been subjected to such a life of deprivation for such a long period,"[157] he was referring to "prisoners of all categories, the concentration camp inmates, the labor camps, and prisoner of war camps," and he was far from alone in his approach. We do not necessarily have to read this as an attempt to place the suffering of German returnees from the Soviet POW camps on the same level as concentration camp victims.[158] In view of the in part dire nutritional situation in many postwar societies (POW camps included), it makes sense that the image of hunger would predominate. It is important to note that the moral proviso that it was out of the question to "mention regular incarceration as a war prisoner in the same breath as political imprisonment and especially as the concentration camps" had already been formulated by the psychiatric profession in the early postwar period. "The difference in situation is so evident that nothing needs to be said about it," declared psychiatrist Heinrich Kranz, director of the sanatorium and mental asylum in Wiesloch.[159] A different perspective was involved here: "The only question we are concerned with is whether the experience of imprisonment in itself produced abnormal responses."[160]

Despite the "considerable adjustment difficulties" the psychiatrists observed among returnees, the connection between the two was for the most part not unequivocally given.[161] To the contrary, they began with the same assumption they had concerning civilians: that a stabilization of the nutritional situation would eliminate not only physical complaints and damage but the entire "complex of mental symptoms."[162] And, indeed, since the West German currency reform and the "defeat of the lean years," much seemed to confirm that in wide sectors of the population "mental deficits" had considerably declined.[163] Although the internists assumed that the organism needed some months to recover, many of them also signaled that the danger had passed. After examining roughly four thousand dystrophy files at the state insurance institution in Aachen, one specialist in internal medicine declared that lasting damage from having suffered dystrophy only occurred very rarely; when it came to mental changes it did not occur at all.[164] The assumption was supported by reports from sanatoriums for returnees, as we see in a letter from the health department of the Bavarian Ministry of the Interior dated May 4, 1949. According to the letter, the authorities had concluded that in Bavaria "true lipophil dystrophy" had emerged in at most 1 percent of returnees from the east. As a result they conveyed this information to the Bavarian State Chancellery and the Council of States in the American zone.[165] In 1949, one medical journal even indicated that the "substantial improvement in the returnees' nutritional condition over earlier periods has largely eliminated dystrophy as a research object from the clinics—one can only say 'thank God.'"[166] Yet the continued debate in both internal medicine and psychiatry would soon show that a big mistake had been made.

In the immediate postwar years, few if any German psychiatrists suspected as much, although some doubts were raised over the optimistic prognosis that an end of malnutrition would "normalize" the mental disposition of those affected. The objections came from various parties. Some psychiatrists considered it generally exaggerated to argue that hunger in a sense controlled mental behavior. For example, Johann Gottschick, who had spent the immediate postwar period in an American POW camp as a doctor, indicated that he could see no difference between descriptions of mental behavioral abnormalities among German soldiers imprisoned in Russia and those in the United States. Yet the latter group had only experienced short phases of hunger during which the grave physical symptoms that the prisoners in Russia had endured did not emerge. Therefore, other factors needed to be identified that would explain the prisoners' mental disposition.[167] Other psychiatrists asserted they had observed behavioral abnormalities among returnees from Russian POW camps that persisted after their diets had changed at home. In 1949, psychiatrist Willi Schmitz from Marburg summarized as follows: "In many cases the physical and mental damage of imprisonment is so substantial that a *restitutio ad integrum* requires a considerably longer period of time in both somatic and mental respects than one generally cares to assume."[168] This left only two interpretive possibilities open. Either the malnutrition in the POW camps had triggered a psychopathological development that, however, contained within itself an earlier source, that is, a specific hereditary predisposition; or one had to concede the possibility that the extreme conditions of imprisonment were able to perpetuate externally caused damage. But this exogenous explanation of pathological symptoms fundamentally contradicted prevailing psychiatric knowledge, according to which psychopathological manifestations without organic damage were to be attributed to endogenous causes.

Psychiatrist Walter Schulte was one of the first who tried to move his colleagues toward greater openness in this fundamental question.[169] In 1947, he had already raised objections to the stance taken by the German psychiatric profession, which almost unanimously opposed any new insight with respect to experience gained during World War I. "Isn't that rash?" he asked. Doesn't "elevating such negation to the level of dogma" mislead us into "lulling ourselves all too thoughtlessly with conceptual principles that have already become schematic?" And finally, in view of the "practical consequences" (here Schulte was making an explicit reference to the process of evaluating pension claims), could one speak of a "stabilization or stagnation of neurological-psychiatric experience since World War I"?[170]

Schulte, who at the time was still working at the University of Jena, was not trying to totally overthrow a doctrine that had defined psychiatric' evaluative practice since the Great War.[171] However, he argued that, all "recognition of the dominant endogenous factor" notwithstanding, he had seen individual cases of psychosis that did not justify denying "*every* causal influence" on development of the illness.[172] Nevertheless, he objected to generalizations. He expressly attributed hardly any role at all to "affective experiences" such as fright or "acute anxiety" in the formation of psychoses, but he did consider "those tormenting, gnawing pressure-effects, those chronic experiences of anxiety and isolation that are perceived as hopeless"—like solitary confinement—to be "psychogenetically significant."[173] It was his opinion, as well, that for "the majority of cases" the prevailing doctrine from World War I was best left intact, although some patients would "certainly be unjustly affected" by it.[174] Directing an unmistakably sharp remark at his colleagues, Schulte maintained that when it came to individual cases, "even the statistical studies" said little "about injuries associated with military service."[175] He therefore clearly formulated his position once more in closing: "The erstwhile evaluative schema has become overly rigid due to the effect of the alleged inexorability of the hereditary factor and statistical calculations"; it had to be relaxed and made receptive to considering the significance of exogenous factors.[176] Schulte indicated that scientific findings legitimating this shift of perspective had been published. They stemmed from most recent research on twins that had been conducted during the Nazi period.[177]

The experts' initial response to Schulte's foray ranged from reserved to completely dismissive.[178] Ernst Kröber, for example, after psychiatrically examining and treating a number of political prisoners from an Allied internment camp, insisted there was no cause to derive schizophrenia from exogenous factors. Repeatedly, there was an insistence that hereditary predisposition was the key factor, and this applied as well to cases of internment-related reactive-psychogenic states. There always appeared to be evidence of a hereditary predisposition in the patient's family or in his biography. Now as before, psychiatrists continued to recognize only one possible cause that "men who had previously been virtually normal" would reach the "limits of mental tolerance," namely, if hunger, maltreatment, forced abstinence, and similar experiences contributed physical factors. It was impossible to speak of mental reactions to imprisonment that had been caused exclusively by exogenous factors, Kröber declared apodictically.[179] Schulte's reflections would only be acknowledged as offering a point of departure at the end of the 1950s, when psychiatric evaluators sought ways to alter this aspect of prevailing psychiatric doctrine in the context of compensation claims submitted by the victims of Nazi persecution.[180]

Until that point, the "prevailing doctrine" proved extremely tenacious. It is entirely possible that this persistence stemmed at least in part from general societal and political attitudes that found their way into the scientific consensus. In any event, Kurt Schneider, doubtless one of the most influential postwar figures in the field, offered the following reflection on the countless civilians and military personnel whose "health had been damaged by the war": "It is unthinkable what would happen if everyone wanted to present a bill to the state. Participation in the general fate of a people (*das Gesamtschicksal eines Volkes*) cannot be legitimate grounds for awarding a pension."[181] In respect to both the legal and bureaucratic regulation of pension claims and the practice of psychiatric assessment, this idea would become very important.[182]

The transformation began slowly. Although the concept of a "prevailing doctrine" would seem to presume a self-contained, internally consistent conceptual edifice, scattered arguments in the professional psychiatric discussion proved to be remarkably elastic in spite of the stubborn self-perpetuation of the core perspective. Repeatedly, if in isolated form, intimations of a shift in interpretive and classificatory structure began to surface. Drawing on an entire network of conceptual strands, in its entirety this development paved the way for the eventual opening of psychiatric discourse in the late 1950s. In the midterm, the questioning of established psychiatric tenets adhered to the prevailing categories. Indeed, one can even observe that the very logic of the "prevailing doctrine" itself was no longer able to fully explain the symptoms seen in POWs in every case and created the impression that the available diagnostic arsenal was inadequate.

One example of this process is offered by Johann Gottschick, the above-mentioned psychiatrist from Göttingen, who had served as a doctor while a POW in the United States. He observed what seemed to him an extraordinarily high rate of psychosis, which was diagnosed as schizophrenia in the camp.[183] To Gottschick, for most of these "delusional and stuporous" individuals the diagnosis seemed questionable. Yet his doubts were not directed at the etiological understanding of schizophrenia as an endogenous disease that was rooted in an individual's "hereditary disposition" and developed as a kind of fate. However, he found "two circumstances" problematic in this context. First, his statistical calculations showed "that the select, highly resilient group of individuals from the Africa Corps more frequently showed symptoms of neuropsychiatric and especially psychotic illnesses during imprisonment than did the sample of soldiers from the western front in 1944–1945 who had not been specially selected."[184] The idea that an "inferior disposition" could be responsible for the mental disturbances thus seemed unfounded. Second, it occurred to Gottschick that the "psychotic" war prisoners could be divided into two groups. In the first, he explained, "the psychotic experiences of the patients" seemed "to have hardly any or at most a coincidental relationship with the imprisonment and all it entailed (camp life, the war situation, political events, etc.)." Here Gottschick did not doubt the presence of endogenous, "process-induced" psychosis. But in respect to the other group, in which the content of the depression, hallucinations, and paranoia was closely associated with the state of being a prisoner of war, he found the diagnosis inappropriate. Among his examples was the case of a thirty-three-year-old lieutenant who complained that "the Americans had devised a complicated system meant to destroy him: they berated him over the loudspeakers and tormented him with electrical current." On another day he reported feeling himself "pilloried as a war criminal through the headlights of passing American cars."[185] Gottschick suspected that these psychotic perceptions were reactive in origin, something suggested to him primarily by observing that the "mental symptoms" of "war prisoners who had remained healthy" consisted of very similar thoughts and ideas, simply not "to a psychotic degree." If, however, being a war prisoner was, as he assumed, the deciding factor for the "onset and symptomatology" in "these psychotics," then the diagnosis of schizophrenia based on hereditary disposition had to be wrong. But the psychiatrist did not have a term that would adequately explain the syndrome he had observed. Although he made an effort to move away from a diagnosis of schizophrenia—a diagnosis that was officially stipulated in one of the American POW camps—[186] he had to concede that "we did not achieve a satisfactory degree of success at that . . . because aside from the concept of schizophrenia there is currently no other alternative to explain genuine, nonorganic psychotic symptoms, especially delusion."[187]

As a result, there remained the need to formulate a plausible diagnostic concept within the framework of prevailing doctrine. All the more so because Gottschick suspected that in the absence of other explanatory principles, German institutional physicians probably tended "to view unclear psychoses that lacked a demonstrable organic background primarily as forms of schizophrenia."[188] The option the psychiatrist from Göttingen presented was to assign the mental symptoms he had observed to another diagnostic category, namely, psychogenic illnesses and neuroses. He argued that these especially severe "psychogenic and neurotic forms of psychosis" emerged as a specific pattern of symptoms that in his eyes simulated, so to speak, "endogenous," hereditary diseases.[189]

In this manner, the effort to comprehend the mental suffering of the war prisoners and returnees led to a process of diagnostic and etiological searching that unfolded cautiously but nevertheless revealed discontent with certain explanations found in prevailing psychiatric doctrine. Occasionally, psychiatrists who had been POWs even risked describing their own, highly disturbing experiences to their colleagues in order to explain the reservations they were beginning to have. As an example, Munster-based psychiatrist Cuno Peter, who had been a POW in Russia for nearly two and a half years,[190] recounted such self-observations. He believed that for a period of several weeks during the last third of his internment, he would have seemed "'not entirely normal,' even to a nonpsychiatrist." He had, he admitted, in fact become so tired of living—he referred to it as *taedium vitae*—that aside from taking in the "most crucial nourishment" he had blocked himself off from all the "feelings and impressions" that arose. "I had the distinct feeling," Cuno Peter continued, "it would take only the slightest push . . . , only one turn of the crank, or the throwing of *one* switch, for me to present, at least outwardly and completely unintentionally, of course, the clinical picture of a catatonic state very similar to schizophrenia."[191] He candidly admitted, "This gave rise to considerable reflection on the origins of catatonic symptoms, and has led to a fundamental revision of my previous views on the presumed mental life of stylites and the 'living statues' seen in institutions."[192]

The diagnostic search gained special momentum from the confrontation with the so-called late returnees from Soviet POW camps, those arriving in West Germany from about the start of 1949 onward. Initially, this may seem paradoxical: the doctors apparently did not immediately associate the sight of these returnees with the fact that the only recently still interned soldiers had contended with massive mental problems. On the contrary, as Gert Sedlmayr, head physician at the Ulm-Donau state returnees' camp, put it in a medical journal:[193] upon their arrival the "physical capacities and mental disposition" of the former soldiers made a "far more favorable" impression than was the case in those who had returned earlier, Indeed, the appearance of these men, whose nutritional condition was no longer cause for great concern, might even create the impression that they had "not experienced the same trials and deprivations as those who returned in 1947 and 1948."[194]

Nevertheless, speculation that these returnees from Russia represented a "result of natural selection," since only "those most fit for life" had remained "without profound damage," soon fell silent.[195] Complaints of mental and physical suffering began to emerge not long thereafter among the "late returnees" as well. Tachycardia, insomnia, and profuse sweating triggered by the slightest exertion, sometimes significantly reduced their general capabilities. And, much as was the case in the returnees from the immediate postwar years, they complained of a broader range of symptoms ranging from profound mood swings and excessive irritability, feelings of anxiety and inadequacy, to resignation, substantially impaired memory, and general listlessness.[196]

In view of the men's general external appearance, both the psychiatric experts and internists were now surprised to be confronted with such complaints, and in such high numbers. For both disciplines, finding plausible explanations represented a challenge. A strict separation of competencies was out of the question, since the physical and mental symptoms were frequently joined, sometimes apparently even interconnected "to the point of being inseparable."[197] Whereas internists often claimed to have satisfactory explanations for the returnees' mental symptoms from their perspective, the psychiatrists were remarkably reluctant to diagnose physical suffering that could not be directly traced to organic damage. What makes this striking is that psychiatrists had not always been so cautious in such cases. After all, during World War II they had been convinced that the soldiers' heart, stomach, and circulation problems were often merely another expression of the Great War's "war neuroses," which, they were likewise convinced, were purpose-oriented in nature.[198] Yet the physical and mental symptoms observed en masse among the late returnees did not seem plausibly explained as purpose-oriented responses, or expressions of wishes or a sense of failure. Psychiatrist Willi Schmitz stated this in unmistakable terms in his sharp critique of the concept of a "homecoming neurosis," which Hans Malten had proposed a few years earlier as a means of encompassing the symptoms. Schmitz considered that diagnosis mistaken, and not only in cases where the sole cause for a mental disorder was physical weakness due to long-term malnutrition. In actuality, psychiatry was already familiar with that phenomenon. Beyond that, he underscored, "We do not wish to see every reaction of a returnee to severe mental experiences and traumas designated as neuroses when we do not see the characteristic signs of neurotic processing."[199] Schmitz was not arguing that such "neurotic processing" was totally absent among the returnees. He saw the figure of Beckmann, the former POW from Russia in Wolfgang Borchert's "realistic drama" *The Man Outsider* as an excellent literary example.[200] But he believed it would be found only in a small segment of the released war prisoners, "most of whom had already exhibited personality structures with psychopathic traits and an inclination toward neurosis in their premorbid character disposition."[201]

It was undeniable: the tremendous emphasis that prevailing psychiatric doctrine placed on the hereditary factor in the development of neuroses made heredity seem highly unsuited as an explanation of the returnees' mental symptoms. But how to explain the mental changes and impairments that were being observed and appeared to be strikingly long term? Schmitz offered a warning that hinted at essential features of the path that would be taken in the future. He demanded, "We must never be satisfied with a diagnosis of a 'returnees' reaction' or indeed 'returnees' neurosis,' which is based more on the circumstances than on an objective examination, until we have achieved certainty that the possibility of organic changes to the central nervous system can definitely be excluded."[202]

From that point on, psychiatrists to a large extent shifted to interpreting the psychiatric abnormalities surfacing among late returnees from Soviet POW camps as accompanying symptoms or the aftereffects of organic damage. Here the diagnosis of dystrophy, which internal medicine had brought into play during the immediate postwar years, formed an important point of departure for further psychiatric reflection. On the one hand, recognition of dystrophy as the underlying pathology was fully consistent with prevailing psychiatric doctrine because it continued to imply that mental changes could be causally derived from previous organic damage, in this case caused by malnutrition. On the other hand, however, without violating the core of "accepted opinion," "dystrophy" offered psychiatrists a "bridge" for assigning exogenous factors greater weight than before, while still remaining within the framework of the core. To a much greater degree than before, not only the physical but also the mental stresses of internment would now be factored into the etiological explanation of the symptoms observed.

In this development, the importance of the professional medical debate among the internists can hardly be overestimated. Starting in 1949, they, too, focused increasingly on the potential long-term consequences of dystrophy, which, as the physicians now asserted after all, hardly a prisoner in the Soviet camps had been spared.[203] The internists attributed the often unexpectedly long periods of recovery from the organic damage to the extraordinarily heavy physical and mental stresses endured during internment. Possibly returnees' unending accounts of the grim conditions in the Soviet camps, including occasional accounts by their own medical colleagues, fueled the argument.[204] Above all, however, there was an additional factor: the near absence of raw physical symptoms among the late returnees. Instead, vague, poorly defined organic ailments and autonomic symptoms stood in the foreground.[205] In the mid-1950s, after some years of experience, cardiologist Max Hochrein, an authority in his field, observed that "we can only do justice to the medical problem posed by late returnees if we consistently remind ourselves that it involves a mind-body summation trauma (*Summationstrauma*)."[206] This represented more than just a major and heatedly debated step within internal medicine. It posed a challenge to medical research in general, which was now called upon to reconsider the significance of endogenous and exogenous factors for the emergence of physical and mental problems in a fundamental way.[207]

Psychiatric experts by no means set the pace in facing this challenge. Nevertheless, internist Hans Wilhelm Bansi[208] was certainly correct when he remarked at one of the central conventions of German psychiatrists in 1953 that it was "precisely on the side of the psychiatrists [that] the question of long-term damage and also the consequences of dystrophy" were being "earnestly discussed."[209] The debate among his psychiatric colleagues, however, revolved around one question in particular: the extent to which lasting organic brain damage was to be expected following serious dystrophy, which would, in turn, explain the neurological disorders and mental changes suffered by many returnees.[210]

The person mainly to be credited for this discussion was psychiatrist Walter Schulte, who tried to demonstrate on the basis of twelve cases that in some of the returnees the presence of dystrophy-related brain alterations had to be assumed. He argued that this was also the cause for fundamental abnormal personality changes that manifested primarily in "a morose, depressive mood and shattered sense of self-esteem," but also included reduced productivity and poor motivation.[211] After presenting his findings, the criticism Schulte experienced was only brief. Very soon thereafter he was able to present further findings in support of the relationship. Studies conducted by other psychiatrists now began to corroborate his claims. The ensuing professional discussions create the impression that interest gravitated toward studies of one sort: those in which doctors had been able to perform autopsies on patients who had died of dystrophy while they were still in the POW camps. Here the brain dissections revealed edematous swelling that had caused constriction.[212] By 1953, the finding of brain edema seemed solid enough for Schulte to state, "We now no longer need to delay ourselves . . . with the objections of this first stage [i.e., the opening phase of the debate two years earlier]. . . . The former thesis that even extreme cases of malnutrition are incapable of affecting the brain matter to the point where brain atrophies develop must in any event be corrected."[213]

The widespread professional recognition of these findings and the work behind it notwithstanding, a truly new problem soon emerged. It had not escaped Schulte that the fields of neurology and psychiatry now found themselves in the "somewhat uncomfortable situation" that "with growing use of the respective diagnostic methods, although probably also in the course of an actual increase, observations about brain atrophies are literally springing up like mushrooms."[214] The phenomenon was presumably also observable because mental changes in the returnees could be interpreted as the result of dystrophy-induced brain damage even when this was physiologically not (or no longer) demonstrable. Schulte himself thus stated: "Here, there are fluid transitions between demonstrable organic brain changes with depressive features and no less serious depressions that lack an encephalographically identifiable underlying organic brain disorder."[215]

Within a very short time, the problem became explosive. This cannot be adequately explained in terms of competition-based quarreling within the relevant disciplines, although such quarrels may well have existed. Far more important was the fact that the assessment practices used for granting war-related disability pensions was directly affected by the acceptance of this shift in perspective. First, organic brain changes, now certified as causally connected with dystrophy experienced as a war prisoner, had to be recognized as disabilities stemming from military service. Second, because of the organic linkage, the entire spectrum of mental changes considered to have resulted from dystrophy-induced damage now became part of the group of disorders recognized in principle as "pathological" in both psychiatric circles and in the practice of disability medicine. In other words, under these conditions the mental disorders met the criteria for recognition as war-related illness within the framework of the health care statutes.[216]

Walter Schulte made an effort to work against the "anxious reluctance to establish precedent-setting cases" that was evident in both medicine and the health care bureaucracy in the early 1950s. Yet he also left no doubt that he equally disapproved of "the edifying but scientifically imprecise" principle of *in dubio pro reo*.[217] He initially countered this by pointing out that "it must . . . be emphasized that measured against the countless numbers of serious dystrophy cases survived during the war and the postwar period, permanent cerebral damage is in fact a *relatively rare event*." He then stated more emphatically: "It would be a disservice to the cause if we were now to make the mistake of establishing a relationship between previous malnutrition and all manner of neurological and psychiatric symptoms with unclear etiology. And who is not of the opinion that he himself experienced malnutrition at some point! Only dystrophic damage of a truly great degree and duration can be considered here."[218] Accordingly, an agreement was reached that mental problems that had emerged following internment as a POW and could no longer be traced to an organic source after a maximum of two years must have subsided.

In this way, the interpretive conflict had been resolved in favor of "prevailing psychiatric doctrine." However, it would break out anew in connection with the question of disability pensions. It would become especially acute in the mid-1950s when the "very late returnees" from Soviet imprisonment sought medical advice. While it was generally accepted that there was no question as to their status as victims, psychiatrists were frequently completely unable to document organic damage to account for the mental suffering they expressed. During the following part of the decade, the late onset of symptoms, not only in returnees but especially in victims of Nazi persecution (their legal entitlement to compensation had only been established in 1953), would pose further fundamental challenges to the "prevailing doctrine."[219]

CHAPTER 5

Contentious Practices

Pension Claims under Suspicion

In the intensifying controversy over the validity of the "prevailing doctrine," a concern had arisen after the end of the war and had increased in importance as time went by. For most participants in the controversy, the large number of so-called war neurotics in post–World War I Germany served as a warning, and this irrespective of whether the doctors were internists or psychiatrists seeking new diagnostic approaches to the mental symptoms that seemed to emerge primarily in returnees with considerable frequency. Directly after the end of World War II, the occupying powers had entirely canceled the pension system for former soldiers with disabilities. Regulating such pensions was only resumed in the occupied zones in 1947; the regional regulations would be combined in the Federal Support Law (Bundesversorgungsgesetz; henceforth BVG) passed in December 1950.[1] With this legislation, the often-expressed fear that legally enforceable eligibility for benefits could force the psychiatrists' hand had become reality. The legal regulation of claims to war pensions had in fact produced a new need for clarity in the evaluation process—a need that could either lead to the confirmation of a previously defined norm or, under certain circumstances, force a deviation from that norm. In this manner, the production of psychiatric knowledge now faced an external factor that would influence the opposing positions within medical research itself.

At first, the question of how best to administratively and legally manage the diagnostic apparatus had seemed unproblematic. Based on a 1926 decision of the Reich Insurance Department, it seemed completely clear that a causal relationship between an accident—including a war injury—and a "neurosis" was to be negated. As a result, in such cases disability pension claims were denied on a large scale.[2] In that respect, the solution that had been found in the "dystrophy" question—which basically adhered to the idea that mental disturbances had physical causes—aligned with the definition of illness expressed in this decision. Kurt Schneider observed in 1946 that for postwar German psychiatry the concept of disease remained a purely ontological concept (a *Seinsbegriff*): "The mental disorders we consider 'pathological' are those determined by physical processes, their functional consequences, and local residues. In psychiatry, we therefore base the concept of disease exclusively on *pathological changes of the body*. . . . Under no circumstances do physical impairments that are *expressions of emotions*, for example, a psychogenic gait impairment following fright, qualify as pathological physical changes."[3] Within the German psychiatric profession, this disease concept was considered authoritative until the end of the 1950s. It therefore served as the basis for decisions regarding both pensions for veterans and compensation for victims of Nazism. It would be the marginal cases that sometimes arose in this context, and particularly the challenge that presented itself through the logic underlying the compensation for victims of Nazi persecution, that gradually contributed to a conceptual shift in the definition of "disease." Ultimately, the change built on Hemmo Müller-Suur's concept of "being ill without a disease," which took the position that mental changes that did not have physical causes could also be classified as disease.[4]

Initially, however, the psychiatric evaluation of disability-pension applications needed parameters that were administratively practicable. This was the purpose of the *Guidelines for Medical Evaluation (Anhaltspunkte für die medizinische Gutachtertätigkeit)* that were first issued in 1952. Physicians and government agencies were meant to use them as the basis for evaluating eligible "disabled veterans" and their stated health impairments. Albeit with some delay, the paragraphs pertaining to dystrophy in the various editions of the guidelines pointed to the growing importance of this diagnosis both in evaluation practice and in research. Beyond this, the guidelines mirrored an increasing opening of the diagnosis that included an expansion of both the causes held responsible for the disease and the damage attributed to it.

Published in 1958, the third edition made these changes evident for the first time. Other etiological factors had now been added to what was previously considered the only decisive factor, namely, undernutrition and malnutrition: for example, infectious diseases and "major stresses," long viewed by physicians as favorable conditions for the development of dystrophy. As well, for the first time the guidelines referred to "difficulties in the transition to everyday life," to work, family, and society in general, as potential consequences of dystrophy.[5] Seven years later, the relevant passage in the guidelines was amended again to read: "In connection with general physical and emotional stresses, and as a result of dystrophy, a pronounced *state of exhaustion* with autonomic and mental disturbances . . . can be observed in almost all returnees."[6] Neverthe-less, as we gather from the introductory paragraph of this edition, within the medical profession there seemed to be no consensus of any sort on whether this far more sweeping set of symptoms could in fact be appropriately designated as dystrophy; scientific unanimity, one could read, was lacking. The factor that favored the term "dystrophy" was that it had become "commonly accepted" and was "in general use."[7]

The diagnosis of dystrophy did not, however, become the master key that opened the door to general approval of permanent war-disability bene-fits, for the period of mental convalescence granted by the guidelines in 1958 was generally limited to two to three years, unless the dystrophy had caused permanent physical damage.[8] Consequently, if a number of years had passed since a soldier's internment, and no physical evidence could be found, it was very difficult to establish a causal relationship between a mental disorder and the dystrophy.

Likewise, in the search for a proper diagnosis of returnees from the Soviet Union, who indicated having suffered a case of dystrophy during their intern-ment, another basic problem now became acute. It had already worried psy-chiatrists before the institutionalization of the disability regulations and the diagnostic establishment of dystrophy. The unspoken and in a certain sense unavoidable question expressed in many patients' files was tied to the essential dependence of both patient and doctor on a common process of agreement as to what could be mentioned during anamnesis: were the former soldiers truly presenting their suffering in an appropriate form? Was their information actu-ally reliable, or did they tend to falsify past events or exaggerate their health impairments, say, in order to obtain a disability pension? A short time after the end of the war, Walter von Baeyer had warned his colleagues not to be fooled by an absence of explicit symptoms of illness. Possibly, he indicated, the "ab-normal perceptional responses" that appeared both frequently and prominently in "tremblers" and "shakers" after World War I were now simply more difficult to recognize than after the previous war—these fears have already been men-tioned above.[9] In fact, the patient files create the impression that the suspicion of deception on the patient's part, conscious or otherwise, was nothing less than a constitutive factor in nearly every psychiatric evaluation. At the same time, however, a diagnosis needed to be found; in most cases the sources of the suffering were probably not immediately apparent. The medical routine re-quired conducting an interview, undertaking an examination, and initiating treatment, whereby the interpretation of the outcomes depended on the particular reaction of each individual patient. This was also the case for returnees who arrived for treatment and appeared to be suffering from attacks of trembling.

One of these patients was Martin B.[10] As his wife explained, at the end of July 1945 he had been released from an American POW camp "due to a serious psychoneurosis." He had sought out a local doctor for treatment of pronounced "gait, speech, and cognitive impairment" and was soon referred to the psychiatric clinic. There, after an initial examination, the admitting physician noted only "tremor of the upper and lower extremities" and twitching of a facial nerve. Martin B.'s motor function was also abnormal. Despite stiffness in his left knee, Martin B.'s gait was rapid and abrupt. Although the patient stuttered and claimed he was unable to write, almost all other findings were normal. Under "general impression" the psychiatrist added a parenthetical note indicating that the veteran made a "very restless impression" during the conversation." When he was standing, he constantly shifted from one leg to another so that a "shudder" went "through his entire body"; he insisted that he could not help it. In addition, we read, the patient was literally racing, and could "only be made to slow down through strong restraint"—a "psychogenic gait impairment" that was very difficult to describe, as the doctor noted in his preliminary conclusion.

Although the symptoms presented and the initial findings indicated that the psychiatrist was dealing with a case of "war trembling," similar to those widely described in the wake of the Great War, it appears that questions remained that prevented him from making a definite diagnosis. The picture was meant to be clarified through the usual diagnostic procedures. The subsequent examinations and behavioral interpretations clearly followed prevailing doctrine concerning "war tremblers." Yet the patient's file also reveals the degree to which the apparently smooth picture formed by doctrine obscured the fact that finding a diagnosis was always the result of a negotiation process shaped by both the doctor and the behavior of the patient.

Hence, during Martin B.'s next visit the psychiatrist ascertained that the patient's intellectual capacity seemed "impaired at times," yet he remained mistrustful, indicating that the manner in which "the phenomenon presents itself" impressed him as "demonstrative." "He speaks too much about not being able to properly understand this and that for an organic impairment to be at work here." In addition, the doctor was able to attest that patient's concentration was excellent—"when he makes an effort." An "intelligence test" had reinforced that impression. Martin B. had completed number series "without mistakes or hesitation." Thus, in contrast to his insistence that he could not recall anything, his retentiveness appeared "excellent." It was similar with handwriting: Martin B. seemed to have difficulties with this skill, most notably maintaining that he needed an accompanying ABC to be able to write at all. A practice dictation proved this incorrect, however. He wrote down the dictated sentences quickly and hastily, although, as the psychiatrist noted, he did have to "'outsmart' his writing hand, so to speak." Much remained contradictory. In his likes and dislikes, Martin B.'s performance seemed weak in the doctor's opinion. For example, he expressed enthusiasm for the opera but could not name any operas by Verdi. The psychiatrist noted that the patient claimed to be "momentarily very confused, has not concerned himself with this material for months." The doctor became increasingly skeptical. Two days later, after Martin B. mentioned not being able to sleep for more than very brief periods, the doctor ordered the patient monitored at night to see whether "the information is reliable."

Strengthened in his suspicion that Martin B.'s attacks of trembling involved purely psychogenic symptoms, the psychiatrist gave his patient notice of his intention to use the "Panse method" of direct-current application. As discussed above, this had proven highly efficient in the treatment of "psychogenic somatic disorders" during the second half of World War II.[11] Applying the current, the doctor promised, would break through the "incipient automization" of the trembling. He immediately had to allay the patient's fears, assuring him that this method was only "externally similar to Panse" but "worked in a different way." For Martin B. had already heard about this extremely painful procedure during the war. He had been told that in the special field hospitals it was generally known as "ironing."

The treatment extended for more than five weeks. The psychiatrist interpreted a small improvement during the first days as a sign that his view of Martin B.'s disorder and his choice of method were both correct. This was soon followed by additional evidence. After the initial improvement decreased, "even stronger current" was applied despite the fact that current used even in the first session had already been experienced as "painful." What many psychiatrists had observed and recorded as a success during the war now set in. The doctor summarized it in a single sentence: "There are unmistakable signs of a desire to recover." Of course, the fear of pain may have simply led the patient to promise anything. In any event, after the following treatment, Martin B. did in fact keep his legs at rest. He no longer trembled.

This case appeared to confirm once again the medical experience gained during the two world wars: "will," in fact, seemed to be the decisive factor. "When he is lying on the treatment table, he makes sure that his legs don't twitch," the psychiatrist noted and then adjusted his approach accordingly, which included threats when no additional improvement followed. It was made clear to Martin B., we read in the notes from early October, that "if the trembling persists an electric shock treatment would need to be conducted." From previous conversations, he knew his patient was terrified of this. The present treatment regimen was retained and one further direct-current treatment followed, at a higher dosage, after which Martin B. showed "no psychogenic gait impairment whatsoever," as the psychiatrist reported with satisfaction. And yet his final assessment was that "all told" Martin B. was "hard to read as a patient." Despite the therapeutic success, his behavior seemed "somehow abnormal," as revealed in his efforts to interact "with the institution's psychopathological elements," his defiance of the house rules, and refusal to work as directed. When the psychiatrist made another attempt to warn him, Martin B. became "stubborn and inaccessible, entirely without insight and hostile." Even the threat that he would be discharged if he did not change his attitude was futile. Martin B again refused to work and was discharged. Two days later, a doctor from the clinic saw him on the street: the former soldier was walking "completely normally."

We can neither assume that Martin B. emerged from the described procedure entirely free of symptoms nor that the doctor was able to gain certainty as to whether his therapeutic efforts had truly been successful. What the case clearly points out is the doctor-patient negotiation process involved in therapeutic practice. Thus, even beyond the problem of pension claims, the process character of a diagnosis can be seen as a basic problem of medical procedure. In this respect, the conscientious use of medical examinations in keeping with prevailing doctrine was only of limited assistance. Hence, in order to clarify the diagnostic picture and come closer to the causes of their patients' suffering, psychiatrists drew whenever possible on information from people who knew the patients. That could have been a local doctor, and in some cases there were letters from pastors. Above all, however, doctors consulted relatives, whose information appears to have been extremely important for the anamnesis. Here, the psychiatrists' questions focused on several points: the "family history," which is to say, "hereditary diseases, abnormal personalities, suicide"; the patient's "own history," including early childhood development and elementary school, military service, marriage, and professional training; and finally information on previous illnesses and current abnormalities. In general, the questions were clearly aimed at gaining insight into patients' dispositions and character traits. While interpretive contexts were already outlined, relatives sometimes continued to contribute to formulating or confirming the diagnosis, through their information and intervention during the further course of treatment and occasionally even after a patient had been discharged.

In the case of twenty-six-year-old Ludwig D., who was brought to the clinic following a suicide attempt in 1947, the patient's father informed the psychiatrist in a first interview that his son had "been completely OK earlier," although as a child he had had a "somewhat vivid imagination."[12] The psychiatrist recorded other information from the father as well. Since the spring of 1945, his son seemed "entirely changed" to him. He was "very excitable, hot-tempered, and self-aggrandizing" and made "big scenes." His father's impression was that his son now "only felt comfortable when he was at the center of attention." He had made himself unpopular everywhere "through his harsh, bossy behavior." In particular, he had been "abusive" toward family members, berating his sisters everywhere, even though he could also behave more politely toward others. Finally, in his father's eyes the "suicide attempt" was "probably only feigned," "a way to scare people," he thought, because he was aware that his son's fiancée had broken off her engagement with Ludwig a few days before.

Since the physical exam showed "no abnormal physical findings aside from several scars from shrapnel and infantry bullets," as the notes conclude, the father's remarks represented important information for the doctor. They perceptibly influenced his first extended interview with Ludwig D.—all the more so because during a short preliminary conversation the patient had indicated that his relationship with his parents was all right and that he hadn't argued with his fiancée. Facing such completely different information, the psychiatrist probed further but, as he noted in the file, received no "useful answers" during this first consultation. Two days later during a subsequent meeting that Ludwig D. had requested, the patient's behavior also seemed "somewhat unnatural, exaggerated, forced." After an additional extended conversation, the psychiatrist noted a "preliminary diagnosis" of "endogenous depression? Reactive depression of a neurotic?" Or was the doctor dealing with—the following was handwritten—an "egocentric psychopathic underlying personality (with extreme fluctuations)"? How was he to assess the episode that Ludwig D. now recounted? "Do you really believe that a murderer will ever have good fortune in life? I don't," he interjected, seemingly abruptly during the conversation as an explanation of the growing nervousness and lack of balance he had been noticing in himself since May 1945. But above all it was to explain why he had always "sensed somehow" that nothing would come of the engagement. The psychiatrist did not understand. "Murderer?" he asked. "Yes, that's the way it is," Ludwig D. assured him before responding to a follow-up question by explaining that he had shot a lieutenant. It seemed to the psychiatrist that the story was told "in a laborious and verbose way," and at this point in the file he summarized the incident as "the killing of a German lieutenant that had occurred in fear and haste."

The psychiatrist found Ludwig D.'s behavior suspect. From further notes in the file we see that he was not even sure whether to believe the former soldier's account. He noted that Ludwig D. was "completely oriented, lucid. Memory, attentiveness, & perceptivity show no impairment." Nevertheless, the patient's "outbursts of despair" seemed "somehow not fully genuine." Offering him reassurance had been impossible—"But if a person dreams about it every night . . ." was his response to the doctor's efforts. When asked whether he was reproaching himself excessively, Ludwig D. had at first turned away and cried. Finally, he insisted that. whatever he touched, "it all goes wrong, every day." And everyone was against him "since that day, since that day, since that day," was the way the once so impassioned aspiring officer described the inner distress caused by the alleged deed committed one night years before.

From the psychiatrist's perspective, "prevailing doctrine" concerning the capacity of a physically healthy man to withstand and process even massive stress rendered it highly improbable that Ludwig D.'s behavior could be interpreted as the result of this wartime event alone. According to prevalent medical opinion, an impairment of that degree or, indeed, a personality change could not be triggered in that manner. As well, a letter from a doctor whom Ludwig D.'s father had consulted when he had difficulties with his son years before, and who now offered his assessment upon the psychiatrist's request, did not support such a connection. At the time it had emerged "that the son had always had all kinds of sensationally fabricated experiences," the doctor explained to his colleague, then enlightening him concerning the extremely complicated situation in the parental household. In his view, the young man could not "find a source of influence . . . that put him under the necessary pressure to integrate." The information supplied by Ludwig D.'s sister, who paid a visit to the clinic, likewise indicated that the veteran had always had a very difficult personality. She told the psychiatrist that Ludwig's "lack of self-control" had become much worse after his return from the POW camp in 1945: now "even trivial things violently upset him." On the other hand, she recalled that he "had already been very hotheaded as a child, extremely hot-tempered and boastful." Noting this information, the psychiatrist commented that Ludwig's earlier behavior "had always been very theatrical." In the eyes of his patient's sister, Ludwig had always been a person who "talked big" and simply understood how to play act—the written summary of the conversation makes this unmistakably clear. The doctor concluded with the following parenthetical comment: "The sister makes a calm, balanced, and insightful impression."

Without a doubt, even before Ludwig D.'s sister visited the clinic, the psychiatrist had already perceived Ludwig D.'s reaction to the event he described as exaggerated. The former soldier's efforts to explain himself and his behavior after his deed were largely unpersuasive. What was at play here, the doctor noted, was a "clutching" at an "exaggerated sense of guilt" and "self-lacerating forms of behavior." The psychiatrist tried to drive home that "according to generally accepted ethical principles his offense was entirely forgivable." As we learn in the notes from a week later, Ludwig D. had not spoken of his "experience with the lieutenant" since then. But the psychiatrist's distrust had far from abated. The patient's less remarkable behavior still seemed suspect, "inauthentic and contrived," as the doctor put it, and the next day he therefore once again warned the veteran: "Patient is told in unmistakable terms that based on his conduct he is considered a person who craves recognition and is inauthentic." In addition, he urged him to cooperate "in a reshaping of his intemperate and attention-seeking character."

Ludwig D. made only one more attempt to make the psychiatrist understand the story of the lieutenant, insisting that his description of the war experience was "true, entirely true." The doctor noted that the patient had requested the appointment "in a self-important manner." Ludwig D. explained that telling his family and acquaintances the lieutenant "had fallen at the gates of Stalingrad" had been a lie, at which point he broke off his remarks, and nothing more was subsequently said about the deed. From then on, the doctor observed, the patient had displayed no further "false forms of behavior." Consequently, soon nothing more seemed to stand in the way of his discharge. The patient showed himself to be "committed and eager to work," but at the same time modest in his requests. Above all, however, his statements about his illness seemed "very insightful and sensible." Nevertheless, doubts lingered, as the doctor still had the impression that Ludwig's "entire personality" did not stand behind the "the intentions and insights" he had expressed. Since the patient's behavior no longer seemed at all unusual, the psychiatrist could not corroborate his suspicions. He was simply left with a sense that Ludwig D., recently diagnosed as a "prestige-craving psychopath," was able "to adapt to the momentary situation" for the sake of "again leading his own life."

Three years later, the psychiatrist would again hear of Ludwig D., this time from a pastor who sent him a request for information because Ludwig D. was now planning to marry. Both families wished to know whether he could "have a real marriage" and "have healthy children." The pastor therefore posed the question as follows: "Has he had the illness from birth on, or is it the result of sexual confusion between the ages of fourteen and sixteen, or the effect of having received morphine for his war injury?" This example once again underscores that even in the community and in a veteran's circle of family and friends, a returnee's behavioral problems were not necessarily viewed as a consequence of the war. For those surrounding Ludwig D., the presence of physical injury was the only factor that rendered such a connection conceivable. The knowledge of experts offered a hope of certainty. The medical file contains no copy of a reply to the pastor. Whoever may have ultimately responded, we can be nearly certain that, to the extent his decision corresponded with the material in the file, he aligned it with "prevailing doctrine," and the doctor who had been treating the patient and attested no connection with the war injury.[13]

The judgment of colleagues was always taken very seriously. Still, this fact does not obscure that the explanation of observable symptoms often amounted to a diagnostic balancing act, which is to say, a normal feature of medical practice that was rendered especially "loaded" and complex through the preparation of pension claims. The concrete question of whether what was involved was a "military service-related" disability (*Wehrdienstbeschädigung*), also called a "war-related disability," demanded careful scrutiny by the doctor, since the cause of the symptoms—even a partial cause—had to be defined in the most precise terms possible. This is apparent in the psychiatric evaluation of applications for disability pensions even at the point where the basic premises of the discipline had changed, which is to say, when a conviction had already taken hold that the mental problems observable in countless returnees from Soviet POW camps were—at least for a limited period—traceable to having suffered "dystrophy" and the associated physical weakening if not impairment. Primarily in cases where former soldiers had not presented themselves for an examination immediately after their release in order to obtain a neurologist's assessment for a pension claim, physicians felt obliged to make doubly sure and furnish the most reliable reference points possible.

The case of Friedrich M., who was repatriated in 1950 after being interned for five and a half years as a POW in Russia, can serve as an example.[14] From the files we learn that his application for a pension was declined in 1953, which he subsequently appealed to the social court. To receive the necessary new medical evaluation, in 1956 his family doctor referred him to a neurologist who, however, reported that the ambulant examination "did not produce sufficient findings" to explain Friedrich M.'s complaints of right-sided headaches, cognitive performance, and anxiety. The neurologist suspected that the former war prisoner, who indicated he had been "considerably dystrophic" for a year and a half, potentially suffered from slight brain damage caused by the dystrophy. However, the neurologist explained that without a pneumoencephalogram, that is, an X-ray of the brain chamber after insufflation, an "exact" clarification was impossible. He suggested referral for observation in a specialized clinic. In any case, the invasive, painful, and highly risky procedure required stationary care.

Friedrich M. then spent nearly three months in the psychiatric clinic. On admission he answered the usual questions for the anamnesis. As far as could be told from what he said, there was no family history of neurological or mental illness, and in his case there was no indication of illness before his Wehrmacht service. All he reported for the period of the "French and Russian campaigns" was minor shrapnel wounds. Nonetheless, from the time he was taken prisoner onward, the psychiatrist summarized, "He no longer felt good." Friedrich M. explained that he went through a great deal during internment: hard labor, sickness, water in his legs and head, and malnutrition. As a former member of the special "Brandenburg Division," he was taken to an interrogation camp in Stalingrad, where he had "experienced frightful things during those frightful interrogations." Three years after returning home, the former soldier continued, he had stopped working because of his symptoms, which included stabbing headaches. Moreover, the former member of the special division had been suffering for years from "inner restlessness, a constant feeling of anxiety," and melancholy, seemingly without any cause.

Did the case therefore involve the "sequelae of dystrophy," as the psychiatrist recorded under the appropriate rubric as the grounds for Friedrich M.'s admission, in response to the expressly requested clarification from the referring physician and the patient? After the routine examinations produced no other obvious explanation of his suffering, and the psychiatrist was not under the impression that the veteran was prone to exaggeration, the doctor initiated the requested procedure in order to identify potential dystrophy-related brain damage. In the case of Friedrich M., however, imponderables remained. Contrary to hope, nothing unusual was revealed that might provide causal certainty in the form of visible damage: the pneumoencephalogram showed that the cavities within the brain (the ventricular system) were completely normal. A lumbar puncture and the removal of cerebrospinal fluid that had been ordered additionally also failed to reveal any abnormalities. Even though the psychiatrist's summarization continued to point out that the patient's "mental symptom complex" could be "that of an individual suffering from dystrophy," expectations of such an exact result, he informed his colleagues, "could not be confirmed by the examination." It therefore now seemed "certain" to the psychiatrist that "constitutional factors" played a "decisive role" in the emergence of Friedrich M.'s symptoms. In other words, he believed that the persistent autonomic symptoms had hereditary origins. Still, the psychiatrist made clear to the general practitioner that the dystrophy and intense mental stress endured as a POW could not be excluded, at least in terms of a potential "triggering factor."

Such cases point to a dilemma of which the attending psychiatrists were not always aware. On the one hand, in treatment and assessment a situation emerged in which a putatively certain diagnosis could only be made when the patient's behaviors fell into line with the medical measures taken. For this reason, the dispositional suspicion of being fooled could only be neutralized if the symptoms conformed to prevailing doctrine. On the other hand, when the symptoms claimed lay outside the realm of accepted long-term effects of dystrophy, psychiatrists were unable to provide the desired unequivocal diagnosis. Both cases clearly show that medical diagnostic ability was limited. Meanwhile, the legal incorporation of disability-pension entitlement in the so-called Federal Support Law (Bundesversorgungsgesetz) of 1950 required that physicians supply a reliable basis for determining claims. Freiburg University psychiatrist Clemens Faust emphasized this clearly before the West German Medical Advisory Board for Questions of Veterans' Disability Pensions (Sachverständigenbeirat für Fragen der Kriegsopferversorgung) in 1956. Referring to a Berlin colleague, he stated that "according to Schellworth the evaluator is prohibited from conducting experiments and presenting theoretical-scientific views that represent the sole opinion of an individual researcher. The contracting authority desires a representative scientific answer to the evaluation question that has been posed. 'Assessment does not mean *engaging in* science but *applying* of science.'"[15]

Thus, psychiatrists were directed to make their diagnostic criteria completely sound from the standpoint of pension-claim assessments, which amounted to normalizing the suspicion that had labeled problematic cases without physical findings as "neurotics" or "psychopaths" and steered them out of the pension system since the interwar period. As we have seen, this does not mean that attending psychiatrists frivolously ignored their doubts over the available repertoire of behavioral abnormalities. To the contrary, the standardized character of evaluations repeatedly led to self-induced rounds of testing that, in their effort to exclude new findings, pushed the limits of existing medical diagnosis. In the 1950s, the final fallback position in this searching process—a process that essentially unfolded on the basis of the "Guidelines for Medical Evaluation"—continued to involve a fundamental adherence to inherited disposition as the decisive factor for the denial of military disability compensation claims.

The case of Gustav K. allows us to closely follow the process of arriving at such determinations. Initially, the psychiatrist who examined the former POW several times during a five-week stay at a clinic in 1956 believed that the findings did not permit a clear decision.[16] Here, Gustav K. can stand as a paradigm for many cases in which illness resulting from what was termed "war damage" (*Kriegsbeschädigung*, henceforth WD) had already been recognized, but where the presence of military service-related disability was again reviewed after a number of years. It is difficult to ascertain the number of pension recipients who were affected by this. In any case, the experts, both psychiatrists and internists, who found themselves confronted with long-term physical and mental impairment, especially in returnees from Soviet POW camps, emphatically recommended restraint when it came to granting pensions and evaluating the degree of reduced earning capacity—even when injuries had been sustained during internment in the camps.[17] The premature determination of a high degree of reduced earning capacity actually tended to encourage "pension neuroses," noted internist Max Hochrein, who nevertheless made a very dedicated attempt to raise awareness among his colleagues about the complexity of suffering in the POW camps. Nevertheless, he underscored that "hardly any of those evaluated voluntarily give up support once it has been granted." The doctors also pointed out that in some cases it was the certification of reduced earnings capacity that gave rise to entrenched feelings of illness in the first place.[18] Caution therefore seemed appropriate. The causes of persistent problems were to be scrutinized with the greatest care.

As a consequence, this applied to the complaints that Gustav K. presented to a psychiatrist in the spring of 1956, eight years after being dismissed from a Soviet POW camp.[19] The doctor noted that the patient continued to suffer from "restlessness, hand tremor, and sleep disturbance"; he was easily upset, "nervous and driven," and experienced short-term "dizziness," and his ability to perform was increasingly failing. As he portrayed it, all of this and more had only taken hold in the camp. He had already received treatment, initially spending several weeks in a hospital in 1949, where the diagnosis had been "hunger dystrophy following Russ. POW internment." Two years later, the pension office approved his pension application, recognizing his "nervous-vegetative complaints" as "WD [war-related] illness." Although this was followed by several stays at health spas, no underwater massage or Kneipp cure provided lasting relief.

During the stationary treatment and observation of Gustav K., psychiatrists tried once more to get to the root of his suffering. The picture was unclear. A basic physical examination revealed somewhat elevated blood pressure in addition to pronounced neurological findings of autonomic instability. But there were no other findings that would have caused concern. The test for syphilis was negative (the test was carried out in psychiatric clinics in the case of many returnees). The pneumoencephalogram was "still in the normal range"; the extracted fluid showed no significant abnormality, with only a "modest protein elevation" evident. In his brief notes, the psychiatrist made it clear that he saw no solid basis for a diagnosis of dystrophic damage. Nevertheless, the psychiatrist hesitated, and this despite the behavior of his patient. Ten days before Gustav K. was to be released, the doctor noted: "Pt. raises the issue of his pension almost every day with his doctor. He is absolutely determined to see through his pension claims with the pension office, continuously demands medical certificates." While the psychiatrist had taken notice, he conceded as well that Gustav K. was "also in a somewhat desperate situation." Both the pension office and his health insurance had declined to cover the costs of his current stay in the clinic. Gustav K. was very concerned because his family had no money. All the same, the pension office had previously recognized the former soldier's afflictions as war-related illness. The psychiatrist himself thought that the patient's condition "was certainly the result of autonomic disregulation," but in his view it was impossible to clarify whether this could still be recognized as "WD suffering" without access to additional records.

When the pension office requested an official neurological assessment a few months later, the psychiatrist was forced to show his hand. His report was clearly formulated and concluded with the statement that "reduced earning capacity due to WD suffering is no longer present."[20] What had tipped the balance? In the assessment, the psychiatrist mainly recapitulated his file notes, which also included the results of a short ambulant examination that had been additionally conducted specifically for the purpose of preparing the pension assessment. It revealed no new physical or mental findings. But the doctor did write an unusually long comment on the mental findings, in which he solely referenced the final examination. The comment is quoted below:

> The content of his thoughts revolved exclusively around his complaints and their association with his internment as a prisoner of war. In this regard, the examinee was completely unreasonable, hardly allowed the examining physician the chance to speak, was often decidedly offensive, and then ill-tempered and irritable. When an effort was made to explain that he could not trace all his complaints to his internment as a POW, he

became very agitated, annoyed, and made offensive remarks. In his insults he no longer recognized himself. For example, he stated that he would fight for his rights, even if he had to take his case to the social-welfare court. He would stick to his guns, had already been cheated enough. The Reichsbund [Reich Association of War Disabled and War Veterans] would support him. The state he was in was completely and exclusively the result of his time as a war prisoner . . . If he wasn't granted a pension now, then he would try anything. But then he would also say that during his treatment here in Bethel he was forced to undergo air puncturing and fooled into believing that the examination was important for his pension claim. He would explain all of that. He would no longer let himself be given the runaround.[21]

Here Gustav K. had hit a sore spot for the psychiatrist and many other physicians. The former POW had not only made threats and charged the psychiatrist with underhandedly coercing his patients to undergo examination procedures—an accusation against which the doctor defended himself rigorously and copiously. Gustav K. had also vehemently made it clear that he set no store in a medical assessment that questioned the war-related origins of his suffering. To him, the connection was completely obvious, as was his demand to be acknowledged as a "war victim" and to receive a disability pension. For this reason, in his neurological assessment, the psychiatrist made the diagnosis of a "severe pension neurosis." As soon as the pension question came up for discussion, the patient became "completely unreasonable, incorrigible, and consumed by strong feelings of resentment."[22] The doctor made his suspicions very clear to the pension office: he was forced to assume that Gustav K. was not primarily concerned "with the alleviation of his symptoms but with the approval of his pension claim."[23] It was only with respect to the precise cause of Gustav K.'s vehement behavior that the psychiatrist conceded a certain degree of uncertainty. Was it due to the veteran's "idiosyncratic personality," or—and this was the second possibility he was considering—did it represent a "symptom of an incipient fundamental personality change . . . due to possible brain degeneration"? As the report shows, clarifying this question was actually of secondary importance for determining a connection between the symptoms and the war. In any event, the doctor considered it an "abnormal way of reacting"—sufficient grounds to conclude that the causes of the complaints Gustav K. described, and which were indeed verifiable, were "with great probability to be traced to a state of physical and mental malfunctioning due to hereditary disposition and age."[24]

The confirmed "probability" did not, of course, exclude the possibility of error. This was clear to the psychiatrist. In the evaluation, he in a sense acknowledged in passing the possibility that his decision was mistaken, yet his formulation left no doubt that he neither saw himself as responsible for this, nor viewed the psychiatric methods as a possible source of any such error. He declared that it was the veteran's "seriously neurotic and abnormal pension-centered attitude (*schwere rentenneurotische Fehlhaltung*)" "that made an objective assessment of the general condition very difficult."[25] He therefore left some aspects in abeyance—also, it seems, to avoid endangering acceptance of his final assessment by the pension officials. In his formulation, the "autonomic nervous complaints" that had previously been recognized as "WD suffering" were "probably" exacerbated by the dystrophy suffered years before. The doctor thereby asserted his view that the returnee's health problems basically involved a personality disorder or brain degeneration, but he was simultaneously conceding the correctness of the previous determination the pension office had made. Despite remaining uncertainties, the psychiatrist ultimately went so far as to confirm a process of change, and finalized his assessment: "The autonomic nervous system impairment which was recognized as WD illness is *no longer causing a significant reduction in earning capacity . . .* over the last several years it has completely resolved. It is certain that the present autonomic regulation problems are the result of other factors that are not connected with military service and internment as a prisoner of war."[26] In this context, the psychiatrist assigned great weight to the results of the pneumoencephalogram, although here as well he did not wish to speak in terms of unequivocality. It was no longer possible to identify ongoing consequences of dystrophy with the "necessary degree of probability," he stated toward the end of his assessment." Eight years after his release from the POW camp and after three rest cures, it was "improbable," the doctor emphasized, that a causal relationship with the period of internment was still present. Here he brought the prevailing status of psychiatric and general medical knowledge into play, and clearly signaled that he felt himself on the safe side with his interpretation of the findings. And he argued preemptively by citing the judgment of colleagues in the field of internal medicine. An internists' assessment that had been conducted the previous year had long since explained that the patient's "existing vegetative problems are dispositionally determined and seven years after his internment as a war prisoner [could] no longer be recognized as MSD [a military disability]."

Starting in the mid-1950s, one increasingly encounters this time-based argument that the absence of clear physical damage precludes interpreting a veteran's illness as related to the war. For the great majority of returnees, the period of internment, even in the Soviet camps, was now years in the past. And even when it came to the far smaller group of "very late returnees," most physicians now assumed that complications resulting from possible "dystrophies" subsided; they were considered a phenomenon from the late 1940s. Despite improved nutrition, soldiers in this group had not been spared hardship, sometimes of the most severe sort, as the doctors were aware. For this reason, some doctors in the mid-1950s appealed for very careful attention to be paid in disability assessments. What needed to be distinguished, they indicated, was the group to which a soldier belonged; especially in the case of the "very late returnees," one often had to assume that their complaints resulted from the completely "different atmosphere" they encountered when they came home. "A lack of training, professional disregard, and social decline that has often already taken place" were especially noticeable, which was appreciably confounded by the "equally unavoidable family difficulties."[27]

As indicated by the tenor of a medical conference held in 1956 in Bonn, for many physicians it was entirely conceivable that under these circumstances the generally accepted "two-year recovery limit" was inadequate. Internist Max Hochrein used a case study to draw his colleagues' attention to the severity of the provision and was very certain, based on his experience, that "it was insufficient in terms of the liver, the metabolism, and the psyche."[28] The situation was complex, however. In his experience, "mood swings and changes of character" were very frequent among the returnees, along with "intolerance and recklessness," and sometimes "a certain schizoid lack of empathy," but this did not exhaust his palette of observations.[29] The doctors had to answer the question of how long one could assume that a returnee was truly suffering from genuine "war-related" symptoms that justified a disability pension.

As we see in many medical files and neurological evaluations starting in the mid-1950s, in this regard skepticism among psychiatrists ran deep. Suspicion-tinged references to "tendencies toward pension neuroticism" and "claim neurosis" now increased markedly.[30] In the files, we encounter such assessments especially in cases where the former soldier seemed especially "complaining," went on about his maladies, presented vague problems that could not be physically localized, seemed particularly tenacious, and perhaps even showed irritation toward the doctor. Gustav K. was a prime example of this type of patient, even though tensions between doctor and patient did not always escalate in that way. From the perspective of many psychiatrists, such escalation was not by any means necessary to define a case as "pension neurosis." In 1957, Walter von Baeyer, the above-mentioned professor at the University of Heidelberg, warned that "just looking at them is no longer sufficient" and then went on to outline a "modern pension neurotic." He "complains quietly, humbly, factually, without dramatic scenes and obvious exaggeration. He hardly asserts himself any more but entrenches himself behind aid organizations, leaving the active fighting to verbally adept lawyers, sometimes even to an energetic wife."[31]

Von Baeyer was not the only one who shared this impression. Fear of the "modern pension neurotic" circulated across a broad front. The medical experts who published an official report on "neurosis" in 1960 under the aegis of the West German Ministry of Labor and Social Affairs cited von Baeyer directly.[32] The figure of the "pension neurotic" continued to be viewed as a serious danger and aggravation for every evaluator,[33] even by the younger colleagues (for example, Göttingen psychiatrist Ulrich Venzlaff) who, like von Baeyer, came forward in the late 1950s to overcome the rigidity of the prevailing doctrine of a healthy human being's unlimited mental resilience,[34] as it pertained to former victims of Nazi persecution. Venzlaff did little to hide his pique, depicting what he considered to be the classic representative of this neurotic category as follows: "If one has had no success in the pension proceedings, one at least tries to obtain coverage by glossy magazines and the boulevard press with a photo and headline portraying oneself as a victim of malicious evaluators or a miscarriage of justice, as a 'war invalid who has been mauled by the bureaucracy.'"[35] But Venzlaff, too, found that "pension neurotics" were anything but always strident, pushy, and coarse, and hence easily distinguishable. In his habilitation thesis of 1958, he urgently warned: "Through their sanctimony and skillful acting, they repeatedly dupe gullible doctors who gladly provide them with certifications that they then insist on using in the proceedings."[36] Venzlaff's actual interest, however, lay in establishing proof of "experientially determined personality change" (*erlebnisbedingter Persönlichkeitswandel*). Consequently, identifying "pension neurotics" seemed all the more important to him.

A number of times, Venzlaff emphasized that in addition to accidents, it was primarily war injuries that represented "a field particularly often chosen for neurotic conflict displacements." Money, he observed, was not even always a deciding factor; for employed men, pensions were often tiny. Rather, facing one's surroundings, it was something different to be considered ill not as a result of fate but to be officially recognized and certified by a pension decision as having parted with one's health in "service to the fatherland."[37] As Venzlaff explained, the background of "the desire for pensions" was in fact far broader, and the "pension neurotic" represented a mass phenomenon. That is, he understood this type of neurotic as the offspring of the *"constitutional social state"* that itself represented "an experimental situation of the first order." In his eyes, the emergence of the "pension neurotic" was not least a result of the twentieth century's political events and devastation, which had "shaken social conscience" in "broad swathes of the population" and, as Venzlaff feared, even shaken it irrevocably.[38] "Even the smallest regular monetary payment (which requires no exertion because it is an 'entitlement') sometimes has far greater psychological significance," he asserted, "than gainful activity, which, based on forty years of bad experiences, is seen in association with many precarious factors." Venzlaff then put it even more pointedly: "A pension has become *the magic word of our age*," but in the process, "Pension fraud has become the peccadillo of our times."[39]

The Dispute about Hereditability

Venzlaff was not far off the mark in suggesting that "the desire to receive a pension" was partly motivated by a former soldier's need for recognition of his "wartime accomplishments." What was at stake, however, was not only recognition of actual suffering but also confirmation that, contrary to what was implied by the denial of war-related illness, the disabilities were not hereditary in origin. The dispute over recognizing war-related illness actually centered around an implicit basic assumption of which not only psychiatrists but also patients and their families were aware: if a mental disability was deemed ineligible for such recognition, then the stigma of a problem grounded in hereditary disposition inevitably remained. For postwar German psychiatric practice, in cases of doubt this was the unstated and for everyone largely obligatory fallback option, and one that was repeatedly examined with care. Along with the former soldiers themselves, family members—as we will see, with the occasional exception of wives—presented the counterargument that only the war, and only the period of internment, could explain the abnormalities if they had not been present beforehand. For themselves and their families, they thereby defended a position that emphatically rejected the stain of hereditary disposition. Hence, this heritability dispute touched on the very foundations of "prevailing doctrine," but also concerned the general idea of mental health as it was understood in families.

Naturally, there were also cases that did not involve conflict between the psychiatrists and the families of returnees. This was the case with Hermann H., who presented himself at the psychiatric clinic in the summer of 1946 on his own initiative because of severe depression.[40] At the time, he had been relieved of his duties as a pastor because of his condition. He did not say much to the doctor about either his military service during the war, when he worked as a translator in a Wehrmacht intelligence unit, or his internment in a Russian POW camp. With respect to the latter, we only find a short remark in the notes on the intake interview: although he had been "rather poorly treated" in the camp, he had "calmly accepted" his imprisonment "without worry." After his release, he quickly resumed his pastoral duties but soon began having severe difficulty concentrating and developed what seemed an unusual aversion to performing his job. After his admission to the clinic, he impressed the psychiatrist as "burdened, slow, and somewhat inhibited," but not significantly changed. After five shock treatments, he assessed the patient as being "in order" once again. Despite the relatively short length of the treatment (two weeks), the psychiatrist was sure of his diagnosis. It was a case of "endogenous depression" and consequently hereditary, whereby he viewed the "strong family inclination in that direction" as an especially strong argument. Hermann H.'s wife found the diagnosis plausible, as we see in the letters she wrote eleven years later to the chaplain of the Bodelschwingh clinics asking for advice and help. Living with her husband had become unbearable because he would verbally abuse her in his "manic" phases, and had even stuck her. "Until 1945, he was a dear, good-hearted husband and father," she explained to the pastor, but there was a "family predisposition."[41] A year and a half later, she once again depicted the serious domestic conflicts as she sought advice on how to persuade her husband to spend some time in a psychiatric clinic. "It runs in his family," she repeated, stating more specifically that "there have been serious cases for four to five generations." Her husband did not deny this, although he was convinced he was healthy.[42]

Family problems (which appear very infrequently in the medical files) were not the only thing that convinced relatives that the illnesses of men who returned from the war and POW camps were "hereditary." For example, in 1948 a psychiatrist noted that the wife of above-mentioned Adolf W. had already reproached her husband before the outbreak of the war because in her eyes he was too "slack and gloomy and often let himself go."[43] When the veteran returned from a POW camp and began to make the same impression once again, even refusing to look after small tasks because they were "women's work," and ultimately felt he was being followed by the police and spied on by neighbors, his wife urged him to seek psychiatric treatment. The psychiatrist's notes indicated that she now saw his behavior overall in a different light. According to her newly formed explanation, he had obviously already been "ill" before the war. During his clinic stay, he embraced the idea that he was being confronted with his "mirror image" on a daily basis, that everything was merely "educational work on the people," and that the war was itself "only an illusion." The file indicates, however, that in his wife's eyes, such feelings did not fuel doubt but instead confirmed her suspicion that his illness was "dispositionally determined." After Adolf W. hanged himself in the summer of 1949, his wife contacted the psychiatrist on one additional occasion to obtain a neurological certificate. She was not interested in seeing whether "damage incurred during military service" might still be considered in her husband's case (a certificate to that effect would have entitled her to receive a small survivor's pension). Rather, what she wished to have certified by a psychiatrist was her husband's business incompetence, as this was her only option for freeing herself from the debt into which Adolf W. had plunged his family through reckless business dealings following the currency reform.

The files repeatedly suggest that wives tended to accept findings to the effect that their husbands suffered from "dispositionally determined" problems. Among other things, this relieved them of any responsibility for their husbands' behavior. However, a significant number of the returnees themselves objected to such findings. Parents, too, found it strikingly difficult to view and accept the afflictions of their sons—some of which emerged during the war, and some of them thereafter—as hereditary. Correspondingly, when the father of Wilhelm S., who could barely be induced to work and had inclined toward "dull brooding" since the war, wrote to the psychiatric clinic in 1948 to request that his son be admitted, he affirmed that "going back to my great grandparents, I cannot . . . find a single case of psychopathology among my ancestors."[44] He was fully convinced that for "people suffering from this kind of symptoms" the psychiatric institution he had contacted was very much an option. Yet he found it anything but plausible that his son was a "psychopath," as had been certified in 1944 on his discharge from the Wehrmacht—and this accompanied by "the statement that the illness was hereditary." Even at that time, we read in the files, Wilhelm S.'s parents had assumed that his problems had been "caused by military service and the front," so that in their opinion an application for "military disability" was justified. They had allowed themselves to be dissuaded from applying, however, as the attending psychiatrist at Hamburg hospital had explained the futility of doing so. Regardless of that, in 1944 Wilhelm S. had something else in mind, namely, to be deployed as a soldier again as quickly as possible, and had succeeded in convincing the psychiatrist.

After 1945, such a test of bravery, which generally neutralized the hereditary argument from the view of the young men and sometimes of their parents, was no longer available to the returnees. What we sometimes find are assertions to the effect that a soldier had "shown his mettle" during the war. Some people saw this as a convincing refutation of the doctors' claims that the symptoms were the result of hereditary illnesses. Endurance in war was irreconcilable with the supposed inferiority that clung to hereditary illness in the eyes of many. "I never felt better than then!" is the way Eduard S. put it, looking back at the war years in 1950 and bragging about having become both a lieutenant and battalion adjutant. He had been in Russia and participated in "fighting the partisans."[45]

Nevertheless, even when former soldiers had simply not stood up to the war's demands and, as was the case with Karl W., were no longer called upon for combat duty because of excessive "nervousness," the relatives sometimes emphatically resisted the hereditary argument.[46] This was also the case when a returnee showed pronounced symptoms of serious mental illness, and doubts concerning the diagnosis of its "hereditary" nature could express themselves in many different ways. When parents pressed for an early release of their son from the hospital, it was occasionally a clear reflection of such doubts. In the above-discussed case of Hermann M., who had been taken to the psychiatric clinic by his father in the summer of 1945, the behavior of both parents— referred to in the files at various points—points strongly in this direction.[47]

Here the parents did not call into question the psychiatrist's diagnosis that Hermann M. had suffered an initial schizophrenic episode. There could be no doubt that a few months after his return from the POW camp at Recklinghausen, Hermann M. had developed delusions that he was being shot by his enemies. Additional hallucinations became apparent in the clinic, for example, that a voice was pursuing him with cries of "Nazi dog." Some two months after his admission, Hermann M. left the clinic on his own initiative. Although his father did inform the doctor, he also explained "that a further stay was unnecessary, since his son was in fact now behaving in a totally 'normal' way." Only when the psychiatrist threatened that if Hermann M. did not return in a few days the public health officer would have the police institutionalize him in a secure psychiatric unit was the father willing to bring him back. Afterward, the psychiatrist noted, the patient's parents showed no further "insight" and once again pressed for Hermann to be discharged. Since there was no longer any evidence of hallucinations, the doctors yielded to the pressure several days later. After receiving a total of twenty-six shocks and with an "unfavorable prognosis," Hermann M. was, as the psychiatrist emphasized, "provisionally" discharged.

It appears that in the following years, Hermann M.'s parents did not bring him back to the clinic; we know this with certainty for the period up to 1949 because his medical file ends in that year with an attached neurological certificate from that year. It had been prepared at the request of the North Rhine-Westphalian social insurance board after his father had submitted an application for a military disability pension. For the father, it was unthinkable that his son's schizophrenia had not been caused by the war. He presented three points in support of his position; these were listed in the neurological certificate. First, there was an absence of any family history of mental illness. Second, he also considered the timing decisive: the psychosis emerged only a few weeks after his son's return from the POW camp. And third, the contents of the delusions were almost entirely related to the war.

The psychiatrists were accustomed to such arguments. In their evaluations, they often referred to such feelings by relatives and expressed, almost formulaically, an appreciation that it was virtually impossible to make the way "psychiatry handled" such cases comprehensible to them. "For they saw those concerned more or less in good health when they were conscripted and now, after all the burdens of the war, they get them back in a state of mental illness," commented the psychiatrist who evaluated Hermann M. And yet the doctor himself, in a follow-up examination conducted for the assessment in 1949, could attest that although the patient was meanwhile employed with light work in his father's firm, he continued to suffer from moderate delusions that consistently centered on the war. The patient spoke of "falsifications, persecution, threats, believes he is now a foreigner. He speaks of shipments, U-boats, about troops of his that came here etc.," the psychiatrist summarized, although he did not see the symptoms as "so very alarming" as in 1945. He did not, however, accept the reasons Hermann M.'s father cited about why his son's suffering stemmed from the war. According to all medical experience, he insisted, the "roots of this illness" lay in a "hereditary disposition," not in the effects of war. He then expressly added the following: "Finally, with respect to the delusions, we know that the delusional world of schizophrenics is frequently influenced by real experiences, even though it is not justified to conclude that the cause of the illness lies in such experiences." As late as 1956, Kurt Schneider (who had meanwhile become an eminent professor of psychiatry at the University of Heidelberg), compellingly formulated the same conviction: "Diagnosis examines the *how* (form), *not* the *what* (theme; content). When I ascertain [the delusion of] thought withdrawal, then this is important to me as a form of experience and a diagnostic indication. But *in terms of a diagnosis* it does not interest me whether the devil or a lover or a political leader [Führer] is withdrawing the thoughts."[48]

For Schneider, "authentic" diagnosis would have been at risk if physicians looked at such matters of content: "What is then seen is merely the biographical element or interpretable existence," he maintained, thus trying to take a swipe at both psychoanalysis and existential psychopathology, at least in their "more recent extreme aberrations."[49] Many of the returnees and their relatives had strong objections to such a stance; in view of an experience that was so strikingly destructive on many different levels, screening out biographical content did not make sense to everyone. For example, in 1948 the father of Martin M., who at the age of eighteen had been drafted into the Wehrmacht as a tank gunner—his "favorite weapon" at the time—wrote a letter to the psychiatrist treating his son, in which he bluntly stated, "It is simply preposterous to maintain that the war did not cause the illness to break out."[50] The year before, the evaluating psychiatrist had confirmed that the returnee suffered from hereditary schizophrenia. But because the illness had been misdiagnosed in an army surgical hospital, he carefully appealed for recognition of "exacerbating circumstances that included injury incurred during military service." Had that not been the case, the psychiatrist argued, and the soldier had received appropriate treatment, then he would not have been redeployed and subjected to "intense stress." Nevertheless, the state social insurance board denied the claim of disability incurred during military service. Martin M. appealed, and his father then wrote to the psychiatrist to request that the certificate be modified so that a positive determination could be obtained.

In his letter, Martin M.'s father, like many others, did not hide the indignation the board's negative decision had aroused; his sense of helplessness being evident as well. "A lost leg is easily verified, and also easy to get over compared to the loss of one's mind," he declared, openly struggling for the psychiatrist's help. He had informed himself and could offer some further suggestions: Another doctor had told him of two cases of neuritis that had produced aftereffects resembling the symptoms of schizophrenia. Couldn't it be neuritis that was actually involved? Perhaps this had been overlooked in his son's case. He had also learned of another case where a woman had died, and only her autopsy had offered perfect proof that the diagnosis of neuritis, which had previously been in question, was correct. Martin's father had become caught up in the idea of unrecognized neuritis, and he did not wish to be put off. He expressed himself forcefully: "If you basically leave the poor victims without any help, offering the crazy excuse that presently it's not provable in every case, then my poor head can't see any difference with the Third Reich's attitude toward the mentally ill." Surely, he suggested, "with such diseases the decision would have to be *in dubio pro*." The doctor, however, not only held fast to his earlier diagnosis of schizophrenia but was additionally convinced it was impossible to go further than recognizing the acute schizophrenic episode as an illness related to military service, in the sense of aggravating circumstances, as the evaluation recommended. He explained to Martin M.'s father in his reply that as a doctor his hands were tied. As much as he would like to help, "according to the present state of research" it would be unjustified to grant open-ended recognition for the further course of the illness.[51]

To the extent that diagnosed schizophrenia was involved, nothing fundamental would change in this respect during the 1960s and 1970s. Exceptions were extremely rare. In an essay published in 1950, Kurt Schneider admitted that only in very isolated cases, to the extent there was previous "serious, acute, and especially physical, injury," was it possible to concede war-related disability.[52] A principle was formulated here that we also find in evaluations, occasionally with direct reference to Schneider. For example, even when Walter Schulte, who was then working at the Bodelschwingh clinics in Bethel, conceded in an evaluation written in 1952 that "although we are currently open to the idea that certain external stress factors can also contribute to the manifestation of schizophrenia,"[53] such acknowledgment remained the exception. This was also reflected in his evaluations. Opposing both prevailing doctrine and accepted medical practice, Schulte repeatedly spoke out against the systematic rejection of disability pension claims based on the "hereditary nature" of a disease.[54] As early as 1947, he publicly acknowledged having seen cases of psychosis during the war where he did not think it justified to completely exclude the war as one of the causative factors.[55] However, as Schulte himself underscored in an evaluation, to the extent one could not claim that the stress had exceeded the "average [wartime] intensity and duration," then the possibility that the case was an exception was out of the question.[56] There was only one case where Schulte saw matters differently. Veteran Friedrich H. had been conscripted at age eighteen during the final phase of the war. Here, because of the general constellation, the psychiatrist considered it probable enough that the war had contributed to an early outbreak of schizophrenia.[57]

It sometimes seems that when confronted with the news that there was no causal connection between the war and the illnesses that had developed, the affected veterans and their families followed the evaluation process with Argus eyes, to the extent they could. Word spread of "exceptional cases" like that of Friedrich H; a letter in his medical file shows this in a paradigmatic way. It was written to the clinic's chief doctor in the summer of 1951 by the wife of another returnee. She had learned of Friedrich H.'s positive evaluation and believed that her husband's mental illness could also be recognized "as a result of the war."[58] Whether she was primarily motivated by a need to avoid the appearance that the defect was hereditary or by the prospect of a disability pension is, as so often, impossible to decide. Frequently the two issues were confounded.

This also applied to the family of the above-discussed Martin M. His father apparently did his best to inform himself as well as possible about the modalities through which his son could secure a pension. His effort to establish physical impairment—neuritis—certainly seems to reflect this. The father's letter makes clear that he obtained advice from various sources, gathering information from other physicians and the local government official responsible for disability cases in an effort to smooth the path to a pension. As an example, the concerned father professed that at the time no one was thinking about a pension, adding, however, "We want to have an entitlement to one if he has a relapse." His request to the psychiatrist "to do everything possible to make Martin's future more secure" was made in this spirit.[59]

The same urgent concern is revealed in one of the letters that former naval lieutenant Leopold F. wrote to a clinic psychiatrist five years after the end of the war.[60] "Even a very small pension is a life necessity for me," he explained, "since I cannot earn a single penny on my own, while amputees can still work and have their pensions, too." In this letter, he requested a house call for the specialist's examination that was required once again in connection with his appeal proceedings; he felt incapable of getting to the clinic himself.[61] Six years earlier, Leopold F., then twenty years old, had begun to complain about all sorts of physical problems, above all associated with his heart. According to his father, he had also become restless and begun to "find life tedious."[62] His parents assumed at the time that he had "begun to brood because of the death of brother," who had fallen in Italy. The doctors in the internal medicine unit of the army hospital could not find a cause for his "illness." The psychiatrist who was then called in pursued the idea of schizophrenia—a dubious diagnosis according to the psychiatric colleague in Bethel after treating the patient for about two months.

After his discharge from the hospital in the spring of 1945, Leopold F. at first seemed to be gaining a solid foothold and enrolled at the university. However, a year and a half later, as he recounted in 1950, his earlier problems began to torment him again. In the returnee's eyes, the connection between the two episodes of illness was obvious; in any event, there was only one way he could explain the reemergence of his symptoms: "The squadron doctor at the time . . . ruined my health forever by treating me with electrification because I was a malingerer (which was followed by a purely physical nervous breakdown that I have never been able to overcome)." Previously, he had only suffered from "a simple heart neurosis," which could have healed, he insisted, with a bit of rest.[63] In the former lieutenant's eyes, his "breakdown" had clearly been the doctor's fault. Above all, Leopold F. assumed the presence of physical damage—otherwise, he argued, the administration of twelve electric shocks and forty-eight insulin shocks would have produced improvement or a cure of the sort he saw in many patients at the Bethel clinic. Since this was not the case with him, a "purely psychic mental illness" (*seelisch-geistige Krankheit*) was out of the question. Incapable of working, without a pension, and lacking significant savings, the veteran urgently appealed for the psychiatrist's understanding and support; he was barely able to rein in his bitterness. In respect to the denial of his disability-pension claim he wrote:

> I have a right to life like any other person and have no intention of allowing myself to be written off by a government that currently no longer feels responsible for the malpractice of its doctors during the war. I was good enough for the war itself back then (and consequently for the people in the homeland who were sitting in their offices just like they are now), and as a war volunteer I carried out the heavy duties of a mine seeker. You can believe me, Herr Professor, that I would have wished to never again receive anything from this ungrateful entity that calls itself a state (and would also never have given it anything again) if I could earn one penny on my own, even as a street sweeper. That would be far, far better than to have been an officer, to have studied at the university, and still not be able to work.

Leopold F.'s efforts to obtain a disability pension also represented an attempt to save his personal honor: to receive recognition not only for his own "healthy" hereditary disposition but also for his deployment during the war, two factors that often seemed to go hand in hand. This offered something he could use to counter the feeling of a wasted life, an intention that stands out sharply in the former lieutenant's letters. He had already written to the psychiatrist the year before asking for help—indeed, clutching for him: "Because of my illness, my fiancée has left me on her parents' order," he explained at the time, urgently pleading: "For that reason alone I have to regain my health and be able to show that I can accomplish just as much as my comrades. In my youth, I always came in first, in the military as well; my comrades never achieved as much as I did. And now my life is finished, while x number of doctors continue to say: no physical findings."[64]

For many returnees, suffering from serious "mental illness" in the absence of an underlying physical problem was in itself incomprehensible; that they were usually denied a disability pension even more so. However, the dispute over "hereditability" did not flare up only when psychiatrists diagnosed what they viewed as a classical inherited disease such as schizophrenia. A far greater number of cases—we can only estimate how many—must have involved mental and physical afflictions where the time span considered normal for recovery had been exceeded. According to prevailing medical standards, the impairments could then no longer be seen in connection with previous injury. It was also possible, of course, that no recognizable physical damage had ever been present. As we have seen, the psychiatrists then usually made a diagnosis of "neurotic disorders" that they basically traced to the patient's "hereditary disposition."

The neurological evaluation of Leopold F. again demonstrates this in a paradigmatic way. The evaluating psychiatrist, who in 1950 was not at all convinced of the diagnosis of schizophrenia, therefore wanted to address the "remote possibility" of a "core neurosis." In the end, however, when it came to the question of linkage, he indicated that "in that event as well, matters are basically the same," even though it was well known that "neuroses [showed] a greater dependence on our conflict situations and mental and physical stress." Nevertheless, he saw the matter as follows: "If, however, as in this case, the disorders persist for more than six years, if they cannot be influenced by any psychotherapeutic treatment or even become increasingly pronounced, then the cause must be seen as lying in the personality of the affected individual, that is, in a deficiency of appropriate experiential processing." In the doctor's view, there was no choice. "It is unacceptable," he emphasized, "to now establish a causal relationship between these disorders and the effects of the war. Indeed, therapeutically that would be the most calamitous thing we could do, as it would simply contribute to a further entrenchment of the disorder." The psychiatrist thus adhered to his initially formulated decision that, as much as one was "convinced of the gravity of these mental disorders," "a connection of this illness to military service must be denied."[65] In other words, according to professional opinion the evaluation of Leopold F. clearly certified that the cause of his ongoing impairment was hereditary.

A great many returnees will have ended the "dispute over hereditability" at this point and not pursued it before higher administrative authorities. After all, it appears that a great many returnees were already weary of the evaluation process before it began. This emerges from the remarks of Heinz Meyeringh, a doctor who practiced in Schleswig-Holstein and conducted evaluations for the pension office there. At a convention of medical disability specialists held in

Bonn in November 1955, he explained to representatives of the Association of Returnees (Verband der Heimkehrer) that of eight "late returnees" who had been called in for an examination, only one had showed up at all; from the others he simply received responses to the effect that they "were fed up with examinations."[66]

Whether this ratio even came close to being representative can no longer be said. The most vocal group was doubtless made up of returnees who rebelled against the denials that the authorities issued in cases of ostensibly "dispositionally determined" illness—unless an exceptional decision had been reached based on a different rationale. In their indignation over this practice, the affected former soldiers sometimes turned to West Germany's political sphere. In a letter written in 1956 to the Ministry of Labor and Social Order, we thus find one returnee attacking, in particular, the authors of the "Guidelines for Medical Evaluation":

> Are the gentlemen blind and deaf that they did not notice long ago the misery they have inflicted through such nonsense and injustice? Do they never read the newspapers and realize how many disabled veterans threw away their lives because they were unable to bear the injustice of having their pensions revoked or denied on such ridiculous grounds? During the Third Reich, people were gassed and shot; today the bureaucracy (and who are those bureaucrats?!) cruelly drives people to throw away their own lives. Is one less reprehensible than the other? No! . . . Working alongside comrades who, like myself, have been damaged by these "guidelines," I will seize *every* opportunity to publicly denounce this injustice. Or can you explain why we are treated as second-class citizens vis-à-vis those who were persecuted by the Nazis?[67]

This embittered returnee, who very obviously lacked any awareness of the abomination of the Nazi mass crimes, was presumably alluding to the West German Federal Indemnification Law (Bundesentschädigungsgesetz) of 1953, which created a legal framework for compensation claims by individuals persecuted under Nazism—and which in one passage at least opened the possibility of cases of "hereditary illness" being granted pensions. (More on this in detail in the following chapter.)[68] At that time, the author of this letter would surely not have been able to cite medical evaluation practice that was markedly different for persecuted individuals than for disabled veterans. By far the greatest number of physicians involved were in any case concerned nearly exclusively with the physical and mental illnesses of returnees from the Soviet camps.[69] In fact, the Association of Returnees, War Prisoners, and Relatives of Missing Soldiers, which had been the umbrella organization for the local returnees' organizations since 1950, considered it to be one of its most important tasks to secure medical care for the veterans and to advance research on dystrophy and postdystrophic health problems. In 1955, the association's medical service comprised around two thousand volunteer doctors; they generated a certain amount of controversy among the doctors engaged full-time with governmental institutions in the evaluation of disability cases.[70] Founded in 1952, a "medical-scientific board" that the association financed held a number of conferences, with the proceedings published by the association and thus made publicly accessible, albeit sometimes with several years' delay.[71] Most of the talks were concerned with a range of physical injuries and ailments that usually fell within the field of internal medicine, or at least the internists claimed as much.

The situation was no different in the above-mentioned Medical Advisory Board for Questions of Disability Pensions, the expert commission of the Ministry for Labor and Social Order. When it came to the heritability controversy, this was anything but a trivial matter, as the transcripts of the convention reveal. The internists at the conference presented themselves as champions of a psychosomatically oriented approach that seemed to be finding increasing resonance in German postwar society. In doing so, they were sometimes extremely self-assured, although the approach was not unanimously accepted within their own ranks.[72] Psychiatrist Friedrich Panse had already been observing such a development since the early 1950s. Acknowledging the upsurge with noticeable annoyance in 1952, he wrote: "At present we are experiencing an alarming turn of attention to *psychosomatic contexts.*" In his judgment, the work of Siebeck, von Bergmann, and von Weizsäcker had already sufficiently curbed the "removal of the soul from the clinical perspective." "Today it seems," the psychiatrist thundered, "that we are experiencing nothing short of a rediscovery of this mental element within physical processes. Many have seized upon these concepts, and the pendulum of attention paid to mental phenomena has swung so far that many try to render nearly all physical phenomena understandable from a psychological standpoint as well."[73]

For Friedrich Panse, this view of things clearly went too far. Yet his main concern was the danger that the "psychosomaticists" could threaten psychiatry's status as the "guardian of this domain of mind-body symptomatology." According to his observations, the reproach become widespread that psychiatrists were "artificially separating indissolubly intertwined organic-functional processes and their mental consequences." Such assertions could already be found in evaluative practice, and wrongly so, as Panse lamented in defense of his own discipline. After all, since World War I the very focus of psychiatry had been on the mental causes of physical afflictions, and Oppenheim's purely somatic explanation for "traumatic neurosis" had been rejected. Indeed, over the course of the 1920s, a "reversal" was observable based on changes in the treatment of "war neurotics" after psychiatry had "taught how to properly gauge the scale and limitations of psychosomatic relationships."[74]

Doubtless Panse's intervention was not entirely incorrect. For a long time, there had been those in the field of psychiatry who assumed that "neurotic reactions" were psychogenetic. As shown above, the discipline now assumed that "disorders" of this sort consisted of "avoidance reactions" that in any case could not be causally traced to a specific event.[75] But this was precisely not the approach taken within postwar psychosomatic medicine, which spoke of a "physical-mental" connection, and in the case of returnees from the Soviet camps, especially the "very late returnees" during the final phase of repatriation, even of a "physical-mental summation trauma."[76] It seems that to a large extent the attraction of psychosomatic medicine for postwar society largely lay in this very approach.[77]

The reason for this was that the physicians, mostly internists, who leaned toward a psychosomatic viewpoint[78] placed the emerging health problems of former war prisoners in a distinctly different context. The personal, mental stresses individuals had endured during internment, as well as the sometimes painful experiences they underwent after returning to a completely altered life in their homeland, were considered in a very different way than was generally the case in medical circles (and not only in psychiatry), which resorted to the heredity argument.[79] In the view of internist Max Hochrein, for example, the social determinants of "illness" needed to be given distinctly more weight than "hereditary" factors or, say, "the inevitability of aging," as in "current procedure." This included, of course, an upward reevaluation of personal experiences and subjective perceptions. Accordingly, with a view to the frequent irritability, general hypersensitivity, dejection, and even simple ruthlessness apparently often manifest among the "late returnees," in 1956 Hochrein emphasized before the Medical Advisory Board that "it would be wrong to speak of neuroses in connection with such conditions, or in situations that the returnees had incorrectly processed in emotional terms. We must bear in mind that between a returnee's processing ability and the life circumstances he is expected to share at home a gap has opened that is hard to bridge."[80]

To the extent this involved conceding that the physical and mental health problems of the returnees were subsiding more slowly than usual in the "completely altered life atmosphere" of West Germany in the 1950s, it seems that a great many physicians were ready to concur. Fairly often, this concurrence expressed a degree of social criticism; references to the "pathology of our age" were symptomatic of this.[81] However, to view the circulatory system, the metabolism, and the psyche as "coordinated systems" that during internment were "burdened in an entirely similar way to the limit of physical-mental survival," and to see that as a causal explanation of subsequent symptoms,[82] demoted the hereditability thesis in a manner that was nearly inconceivable for many other physicians, especially within the field of psychiatry.

In his psychosomatic orientation, cardiologist Max Hochrein took the offensive here, as is clear from his presentation before the ministry's board of experts. In a highly skillful fashion, he injected what he termed a "case" into his argumentation to demonstrate both the hardship imposed when pensions were declined because an illness was supposedly "hereditary" and the mistaken nature of that diagnostic practice. Apparently taking aim primarily at psychiatry, he quoted extensively from a veteran's letter that had allegedly reached him only days before the conference. As the letter recounted, the soldier, then twenty years old, had been taken prisoner by the Russian army in August 1944.[83] He informed Hochrein that since his release in 1949, he had suffered from "health problems," mainly involving his heart. Acknowledgment of military disability "as the result of dystrophy" was initially granted, but then revoked two years later.[84] Although there had been no change in his symptoms, the returnee complained, the disability board had declared that his "vegetative dystonia" was the result of his "innate disposition." As we learn from the letter, the veteran had objected and filed appeals at various levels. Although this had resulted in additional medical examinations required for certification, as of 1956 he still had no disability pension. An internist had voiced the opinion that the veteran's neurological symptoms, for which there were no physical findings, could still involve "consequences of the war," but he recommended bringing in a neurologist. In the neurologist's opinion, however, the disorder derived, once again, from the veteran's "innate disposition." The returnee summarized the specialist's explanation as follows: "On the one hand, I am an overly emotional person with a fragile nervous system who ordinarily would not have survived internment as a POW. On the other, I am overly strong-willed type of person (disposition?), which saved my life. It was the divergence of these two innate dispositions, they say, that triggered my impaired state of health, and therefore this is not a case of war-related illness."

At this point Hochrein, an internist, refrained from making any comment and continued to allow the veteran to speak through the medium of the letter.

The soldier stated in unmistakable terms that he would refuse all further treatment by a neurologist, above all by a psychiatrist. After all, he was no "neurotic or malingerer," as stated in the evaluation. In addition, his family doctor had himself advised against further such treatment, recommending Kneipp hydrotherapy instead. For the former POW, the situation was clear:

> I still trace my present state of health back to the stress I endured during my imprisonment. Originally, I did not have a nervous system disorder. Before being taken prisoner, I was at the front for over a year and was lightly wounded. I was a gunner in an antitank company and was later a section chief and a reserve officer candidate. I believe that I would have hardly been deployed at the front for such tasks if I had a labile nervous system. My health problems only emerged in 1949, when I suffered from dystrophy for the fourth time, for which reason I assume that if I had already been predisposed to my current state of health in a pronounced way, then my illness would have emerged much earlier.

The question that the returnee hoped Hochrein would answer was clear: should he in fact defer to the psychiatrist's views?[85] Hochrein now was equally clear with the colleagues he was addressing:

> What sort of disability pension board, using formulations such as "innate disposition" and "conflicted character," would undertake to subject a young man—a man who began a five-year internment as a war prisoner in Russia at age twenty and unquestionably came away from it with considerable damage—to a situation in which he was robbed of compensation and consequently of treatment, and which now throws not only the competence of the medical judgment in question but also any effort to obtain a just evaluation in the first place?

In this way Hochrein clearly signaled he was ready to support the returnee's desire to have his illness acknowledged as "war related." This was a distinct critique of colleagues who in cases of long-term health problems without verifiable physical damage always resorted to "hereditary disposition" as the alleged actual cause, since such diffuse suffering could not be grasped using the usual approaches. When it came to the returnees from the Soviet camps, such an approach was clearly inadequate, as Hochrein underscored a number of times. As he had already emphasized at the beginning of his talk, "in its incomparability with analogous processes in civilian life, the fate of the late returnees" represented "something so new with respect to its mental-physical ramifications" that taking recourse as usual to "experience" was almost completely unproductive.[86]

Hochrein's colleague, Hans Wilhelm Bansi, likewise an internist, offered support in this point. Based on the observation that "it was above all the determination that we doctors make so liberally, namely, identifying phenomena as endogenous as opposed to exogenous or determined by fate and therefore not qualifying for disability pensions," which had led to lasting controversies between the different parties, he then pointed out the following to the medical evaluators: "Without . . . wishing to lose myself in an exaggerated concept of 'humanity,' I believe I must state that very many problems actually cannot be answered in the form in which we as physicians often choose, that is, by referring to so-called scientific knowledge even when such knowledge stands on a very weak footing."[87]

In fact, Bansi saw considerable need to clarify and revise the interpretation of a large range of illnesses that, in his view, were grounded far more often than widely maintained in the ordeal of imprisonment as a POW. "We need to keep the complete history in mind," he emphasized, thereby indicating that he, too, wished to see the complexity of physical and mental stress factors taken into account in evaluating the question of context. But as the internist knew well, this meant above all countering the widespread medical idea that the psyche simply did not come into play as a mediator between a preceding ordeal and subsequent health problems. At the above-mentioned experts' conference, Bansi therefore felt called on to state: "I agree with Herr Hochrein that we must not deny this *general trauma* nonprejudicial attention and recognition in the pathogenesis of illnesses that are strongly dependent on mental factors." He then added: "What is the meaning of 'determined by fate' or 'endogenous'? How high was the percentage of men who never came back? What good constitutions the returnees must have that they did not perish during internment like 80 percent of their fellows in misery."[88]

It is not difficult to imagine that this line of argument was well received by numerous returnees who continued to suffer from a range of mental and physical health problems for many months after repatriation and felt impaired in their daily and professional lives. In turn, before the board of experts the psychosomatically oriented physicians had a good sense of how to present, and even exploit, the fact they could expect backing from the returnees.[89] In fact, for many of the affected returnees the advantages of Hochrein's way of seeing things were indeed self-evident, even though internists such as he did not totally reject "hereditary disposition" as an explanatory basis for the problems requiring evaluation. In the understanding of "war and long-term internment" as a "summation trauma" from which functional disturbances could develop as the result of an "overload syndrome," the returnees saw a recognition of the ordeal they had experienced, in a form that had been absent in the psychiatric approach. Until then, hardly any attending physicians had gone as far as Hochrein, who demanded that "for men who were under thirty at the time of exposure and who could have been designated as healthy then, concepts such as 'dispositional' and 'hereditary' should be relinquished and a 'war-related' causal relationship be acknowledged, to the extent that an—otherwise undefined—'amount of overload' . . . was verifiable or there was credible evidence on record."[90]

Over the course of the talks and ensuing debates, two things became increasingly clear. First, the psychiatrists were experiencing growing professional competitive pressure from sectors within internal medicine. Second, among internists there was an ongoing effort to find an umbrella term that covered the virtually identical symptoms the returnees were presenting. The list was long and included persistent exhaustion, insomnia, irritability, and "palpitations." Ultimately, statements such as "I can't get anything done any more" and "I'm no longer worth anything" were some of the most common.[91] Some of the internal medicine experts were inclined toward a diagnosis of "vegetative dystonia," but others were opposed. Even Hochrein, who spoke out forcefully in favor of using the concept, had critically remarked at a medical congress for returnees in 1955 that "vegetative dystonia" was "at present almost a kind of stopgap diagnosis, i.e., a potpourri of vague health problems and unexplained pathogenic relationships."[92] Bansi voiced similar reservations. He, too, made use of the diagnosis but observed that it had in general become a "fashion." After all, he indicated, insurance board files showed that "vegetative dystonia" now represented "today's most frequently diagnosed syndrome by far."[93] Still, it also represented a mass phenomenon, continued Bansi, who had more than just German returnees in mind when he affirmed: "Across the entire world that has been overrun by war and persecution, and in which ten years after the end of hostilities war prisoners, deportees, concentration camp inmates, and those who suffered extreme malnutrition in labor camps are being treated or having the state of their health evaluated, the syndrome of general vegetative lability has revealed itself the most prominent one."[94]

At the conference of the Medical Advisory Board for Questions of Disability Pensions in 1956, which was especially instructive regarding the challenges posed to the entire medical profession by the psychosomatic perspective, many of those present may well have still agreed with Bansi's observation.

But among the internists as well it was a different question, namely, whether one should become involved with the diagnosis of "vegetative dystonia," when the proposed mode of usage was so patently influenced by the idea of assigning greater weight to the impact of stress from war and the POW camps and less to "hereditary" weaknesses. Renowned internist Gustav Bodechtel, a full professor at the University of Munich clinic, was not the only person to make it clear that such a diagnosis was forbidden across the board in his clinic.[95] The symptom complex did not represent anything new, he declared, and there was no justification "for speaking of vegetative dystonia among the returnees as something extraordinary." For Bodechtel, then, there was evidently no reason to move away from "hereditary disposition" as a decisive causative factor. In his eyes, it seems, this did not even require a medical explanation:

> Furthermore I do not believe that constitution changes. In this regard, I cite Goethe's old dictum "From my father I have my nature," and which he concludes with, "What, then, of the entire poor creature should be called 'original'?" I do not believe we are justified in doubting these old laws when what is at stake is judging transient phases that, naturally, strongly detract from life. But that they alter a person's constitution, I don't believe that.[96]

These apparently deep-seated tenets centering on the "dispositional" nature of many illnesses were also hard to shake within the field of internal medicine, as this contribution to the discussion demonstrates paradigmatically. Nevertheless, by the mid-1950s the hereditability controversy had clearly begun to gain momentum in many fields involving health problems and recognized diseases. We see this not only in West Germany, but also in other European countries, primarily in connection with the medical discovery of "late damage" (*Spätschäden*) inflicted by deportation and concentration camps.[97] In West Germany, the catalysts for this process had a different composition: representatives of psychosomatically oriented medicine supported returnees from the Soviet camps and their families in a broad social alliance with returnees' organizations and so-called *Heimkehrerärzte*—physicians engaged in examining and treating returnees. Nevertheless, there was only a partial overlap in what motivated the two factions in their efforts to increase acknowledgment of the psyche, as opposed to "disposition," as a causal factor in "late damage" stemming from captivity. This is reflected in the ideas concerning the granting of disability pensions, which in part diverge widely. Ultimately, even in the eyes of those who championed a stronger psychosomatic orientation, there was the danger that hastily recognizing military disability and, possibly, granting excessively generous pensions would literally cultivate "pension neuroses." In the medical debate over use of the concept of "vegetative dystonia," this objection was often repeated and taken seriously even by those who supported the concept, especially since the following problem could not be ignored: When did the symptoms observed actually involve long-term damage from the ordeal of the POW camps, and when did they result from the returnee's inability to adjust to a changed lifeworld after repatriation?

A compromise formula to which the doctors could agree appeared to lie in more precise observation of the individual case, which, it was maintained, became lost in the statistics but was actually the interesting matter from a scientific standpoint. Overall, we gain the impression that in the mid-1950s a constellation had emerged in which some of returnees from the Soviet camps could reckon that changes were forthcoming in the etiological approach to a wide range of health problems. It appeared that the change might even result in a new figuration of the diagnostic understanding of problems for which there was no definite physical explanation. The psychosomatically oriented internists in any event revealed themselves as very self-confident vis-à-vis their own as well as the other medical disciplines, especially psychiatry, which was unmistakably being challenged in the field of functional and consequently mental disorders. For despite all critique of the concept of "vegetative dystonia," some of it possibly even justified, the dilemma had not been solved, as internist Hochrein argued to his colleagues in his closing remarks before the medical experts' board. He voiced a disarmingly candid appeal: "But since we are specialists representing the most varied disciplines, we ought to be able to clarify one thing: What are we going to call what we all know, while refusing to give it a name?"[98]

At this point, the psychosomatically oriented doctors had clearly surged forward and hit a sore spot. For despite all critique from the camp of those maintaining the still dominant reading of protracted maladies that could only be explained mentally, there were a number of doctors, including some psychiatrists, who were in fact no longer so firmly convinced that established diagnostics, especially the argument of the hereditary origins of the illnesses observed, was really consistently on target. The change was not reflected in the relevant professional journals, but in the smaller circle of the Medical Advisory Board for Questions of Disability Pensions. Hamburg psychiatrist Hans Bürger-Prinz, for example, conceded that "God only knows why a genuine depression in a case of dystrophy" couldn't last for six years. And he added candidly that it "makes no sense to speak of neurotic fixation here, just as using the concept of 'neurosis' itself usually kills the problem the problem without explaining it."[99] A similarly critical position was expressed by Rüsken, chief medical officer for the Berlin pension disability office, who could lay claim to an overview of the majority of evaluations that had been processed for the last four years as psychiatric/neurological cases in his area. He, too, considered the diagnostic repertoire to be inadequate when it came to dealing with the "conspicuous mental behavior" of a great number of late returnees, which in his view was something that was impossible to overlook. As an introduction, he remarked, "All of you are certainly familiar with the peculiar mental behavior of these men, and with intensive questioning during the course of anamnesis the information they provide often leads to a gush of subjective maladies and pathogenic experiences and feelings." He then stated:

> The psychiatric classification, which in my view has not yet been satisfactorily completed, should by no means remain the most important measure. Neither the concept of a reactive depressive state or of neuroticizing forms of abnormal behavior, nor the assumption of the effect of a hereditary and now manifest psychopathic reaction shows us the path to effective therapeutic help.[100]

But neither Bürger-Prinz nor Rüsken could present an alternative. In fact neither of them appealed for a more generous approach to the disability pension claims. To the contrary, Rüsken expressed the suspicion that the medical examination procedure for disability claims, which was already resulting in "premature awareness of these manifold physical and mental symptoms," was responsible for "creating the state of mental decompensation in the first place or intensifying it in a threatening way." While Rüsken insisted that other measures were called for, his own suggestions remained extremely vague. Only the goal was clear to him: no effort was to be spared to help returnees regain their "productive capacity" and open a path for them "to become actively participating citizens." To follow Rüsken's thinking, this required "no great psychotherapy"—although he did request that his colleagues consider the "especially great vulnerability" of these returnees.[101]

In the mid-1950s, it is unlikely there were any physicians who did not realize what was being addressed with this reference to "vulnerability," and what expectations were being articulated of them. In the struggle over obtaining pension eligibility for a wide range of health problems, it had long since been clear that a great many returnees were refusing to be written off with a diagnosis of "hereditary disposition."[102] From the perspective of the returnees, even at the end of the decade nothing had changed regarding the reason for this revolt, as a letter from the State of Berlin pension office suggests. In this letter, the office's head physician informed the responsible officials in the Ministry of Labor and Social Order that because of pressure from the returnees' associations a discussion with doctors who examined the returnees had been necessary. The associations, he indicated, had harshly criticized "the excessive use of the term 'hereditary disposition'" in the medical evaluations undertaken by the government doctors. The "confidential discussion—among physicians only" led to the following decision: "With respect to the term 'hereditary disposition,' in this circle, it was argued that this designation should be avoided as much as possible. The formulation had probably been used somewhat schematically during the initial years of pension-related work and sometimes caused unease, particularly in nonmedical circles." This explanation to the ministry officials signaled a clear concession to the returnees on the part of the Berlin authorities.[103] Yet it actually marked anything but a turnaround, for although the term "hereditary disposition" had been dropped, the solution the Berlin authorities adopted was simply to replace it with references to "constitutional or endogenous (*konstitutionell/körpereigen*) factors."[104]

CHAPTER 6

The Moral Challenge, 1956–1970

"Personality Change" in Survivors of Nazi Persecution

The conflict over possible deviations from "prevailing doctrine" in psychiatric practice was not limited to Germany. Until well into the 1950s, German psychiatrists could assume that their basic assumptions were shared by experts elsewhere. In the United States, advocates of biological psychiatry included many proponents of the maxim that long-term mental disorders were only conceivable as a result of organic damage, a perspective shared with many of their colleagues in Israel[1] and throughout Western Europe.[2] It was not uncommon for even the former victims of Nazism to draw attention to the seemingly rare appearance of neurological and mental symptoms among Jewish survivors. As late as 1956, this was still pointed out in an article by H. H. Fleischhacker published in the London-based journal of the Association of Jewish Refugees. Fleischhacker saw this impression as largely confirmed by an early psychiatric study of refugees in Switzerland. He noted that among the Jewish survivors in the refugee camps the rate of suicides, endogenous depression, and exogenous, physically explainable psychoses was somewhat elevated, which, according to the author, was traceable to the "advanced age of the Jewish camp population and their sufferings in Theresienstadt, Belsen etc." In general, however, he stated: "Personality disorders and neuroses were very rare amongst Jews."[3] Another psychiatrist, Jacques Tas, who had himself been a concentration camp inmate, even maintained that he was able to observe a reduction of such disorders in the camps among those who had suffered from them before their deportation.[4] And in the standard German psychiatric handbook *Psychiatrie der Gegenwart*, Viktor Frankl, as well, indicated in 1961 that "neuroses in the narrower sense . . . were not observable in the concentration camps; neurotics healed there."[5]

Following liberation of the camps, this was a common finding among Allied doctors. What emerges from their reports is the far greater challenge of coping with the threat of starvation facing the survivors and with the rampant infectious disease among them, above all typhus and diarrhea.[6] Several years later, however, psychiatrists from formerly Nazi-occupied areas of Europe began to notice that the effects of internment had been underestimated. In Denmark, two state-sponsored follow-up studies of formerly interned resistance fighters indicated that years after repatriation a majority of them were still suffering from symptoms such as general fatigue, restlessness, irritability, difficulty concentrating, and memory loss, and in part from major vegetative disorders and underlying depression. In Copenhagen in 1954, French psychiatrists confronted doctors who had convened at the International Sociomedical Conference on the Pathology of Deportees and Interned Persons with nearly the same results: They spoke of a syndrome they termed "deportees' asthenia." Their Danish colleagues called it simply "concentration camp syndrome," or even more bluntly "hunger disease."[7]

Indeed, the medical experts from both countries considered hunger one of the most important causal factors—for the Danes it was clearly the most decisive one underlying the deportees' mental and physical problems, which sometimes emerged only many months after liberation but then apparently persisted. Paul Thygesen, director of the University of Copenhagen's neurological clinic, offered the following explanation for the emphasis on this point: the statistical processing of the results of the Danish and special psychiatric studies suggested "that the illegality as such, the life and danger of the resistance struggle, and the interrogations upon arrest [played] a secondary role—mental and physical torture notwithstanding . . . in sickliness overall." "Contrary to expectations," Thygesen added, "the mental stresses of the stay in the camp" itself probably had "no primary influence on the type of mental symptoms" characterizing "the persistent and sometimes progressive illness" they "had decided to name the *concentration camp syndrome*."[8]

There are unmistakable parallels between this line of argumentation and the manner in which the German psychiatrists and internists interpreted the stubborn mental and physical complaints of many returnees from the Soviet camps. In Germany as well, according to prevailing doctrine, the notion that mental upheaval resulting from the war and internment as a POW could be a sole cause of subsequent health problems was out of the question. A causal connection appeared plausible to the physicians only when physical damage was either currently present or had been so some time before. The hunger that countless soldiers suffered in Soviet POW camps offered a convincing explanation for those problems because, as the argument had it, malnutrition damaged the organism—in many cases weakening it in an enduring way and forming a basis for mental abnormalities even after demonstrable somatic findings had disappeared. This was the late damage of "hunger dystrophy" that the German doctors spoke of.[9]

When it came to the deported resistance fighters, the Danish psychiatrists identified precisely the same basic etiology. "Our present experimental and clinical knowledge tells us that all known and measurable functions of the organism are quantitatively and qualitatively compromised during 'hunger dystrophy,'" Thygesen stated in 1954. He also hinted that doctors had not recognized this right away and explained that after the food supply had normalized, the long-term nature of the regeneration process had been obscured by the "directly observable healthy appearance of those concerned.[10] Knud Hermann, professor of neurology and psychiatry and a member of the Danish Disabled Persons' Insurance Commission, went further, even speaking of diagnostic errors during the period: "Emotional instability can easily be confused with a propensity for hysteriform reaction," he conceded, although he then added that the error of judgment was often encouraged by the patients' attitude. Namely, for most of them it was nothing less than typical "to downplay their symptoms or actually hide them." And further: "The physical symptoms—asthenic and vegetative—often only surface with direct questioning because among other things many patients do not consider them to be truly pathological and see no connection with having endured a concentration camp."[11]

Regardless of whether German returnees or Danish resistance fighters were concerned, the same set of basic assumptions were at work among German and non-German psychiatrists. The key factor was tying the observed symptoms back to physical damage, something accomplished in both cases by a diagnosis of "hunger dystrophy." In France, the medical experts were more inclined to assume that a range of interacting physical and mental stress factors, similar to those described by Bansi's "summation trauma," explained the so-called neurasthenic symptoms of deportees.[12] Yet as the papers presented at the Copenhagen conference make clear, in all the countries involved the same problem had emerged. It wasn't only that the psychiatrists were obliged to justify themselves before their colleagues within the framework of prevailing doctrine. Because each national social insurance system was inclined to erect strict barriers against "pension neurotics," physicians were forced to attribute their patients' illnesses directly to the extreme, long-term stress of internment in unambiguous terms.[13] Special difficulties arose when mental or physical suffering had only emerged after a so-called latency period, that is, during an interval where no particular health problems had occurred.[14] In such cases, it was nearly impossible to convince the different national pension authorities of a causal relationship to the extreme stress and cruelty of the internment period.[15] It was in any case clear to the medical experts as well that such a precise demonstration of the causes of mental symptoms was nearly impossible. At the Copenhagen conference, their dilemma was evident in various ways. On the one hand, from the statistics in a study they began in 1951, Danish psychiatrists concluded that the degree of weight loss constituted "an approximately valid expression" of physical damage incurred by hunger.[16] As well, their suspicion that brain damage might explain the mental problems found support in information supplied by German researchers, who, the Danish physicians argued, had actually used radiographic examinations to show brain atrophies "in persons who had previously starved," which is to say, in returnees from Soviet POW camps.[17] On the other hand, however, the experts themselves were well aware that, as the Viennese internist Ludwig Popper put it, "the scientific assessment of effects that were complex and in addition lay fifteen years in the past" would necessarily be "incomplete."[18]

In a variety of ways, psychiatrists throughout postwar Europe found themselves in a similar situation. At the same time, they faced different moral challenges. Hence, in Denmark resistance fighters were at the center of what would eventually crystallize into a national myth.[19] Against that backdrop, the experts assembled in Copenhagen from Europe's various formerly Nazi-occupied countries indicated that they saw it as no less than a moral duty to disregard the strict standards of prevailing doctrine. Thygesen formulated the sentiment as follows: "We physicians and scientists—perhaps even formerly deported persons ourselves—are obliged to support the simple and ethical demand that our countries provide *decent economic conditions* to those who paid with ruined health and perhaps shortened lives for racial discrimination or participation in the resistance struggle."[20]

In this manner, German psychiatry found itself confronted with an expectation, primarily stemming from other countries, that it turn away from the basic tenets of the accepted German school of thought and recognize mental symptoms presented by those whom Nazi Germany had persecuted as, precisely, the long-term effects of Nazi terror. Corresponding to this expectation, starting in the mid-1950s when an important transition in the interpretation of mental disorders got under way in the West, applications for payments were submitted to the authorities of the different German states by patients whose mental health problems had been certified by doctors outside Germany as stemming from Nazi persecution and who were therefore entitled to compensation based on injury to their health.[21]

This problem complex was distinct from the question of entitlement to disability payments due to the effects of war, as regulated in the 1950 BVG (Federal War Victims Relief Act), which could be appealed before a social welfare court. Rather, in part because of Allied requirements, the need for new regulations for victims of the Nazi regime had arisen; the regulations were set forth provisionally in the federal law amendment of 1953 and then in permanent form in the BEG (Federal Law for the Compensation of the Victims of National Socialist Persecution) of 1956,[22] where the legal basis for compensation in the event of damage to health was formulated in section 28, subsection 1, with complaints being the responsibility of civil courts.

For the German psychiatrists and medical officials who were involved in the procedure as experts for assessing the causal connections in health disorders, this raised a twofold problem. Their initial assumption had to be that the scientific identification of a causal basis for mental damage had to hold up independently of prevailing legal criteria. As we have seen, when it came to granting pensions for war-related disability, the psychiatrists followed clear guidelines. According to the current status of medical knowledge, the mental reactions of former soldiers, whether diagnosed as "hysteria" or "neurosis," involved individual "wish determined" or "goal determined" reactions, but emphatically not health problems that deserved to be classified as diseases and traced directly to the war or internment as a POW. For this reason, granting a pension was strictly rejected. This had its counterpart in the rulings made by West Germany's social welfare courts, which continued to follow the 1926 decision of the Reich Insurance Agency.[23] On the basis of this medical-scientific and legal practice, it seemed sensible to the German psychiatrists to use the same prevailing principles in assessing the new compensation claims. At the same time, however, in evaluating the claims they saw themselves under pressure from their non-German colleagues to deviate from such a strict interpretation. Since these compensation cases were adjudicated in civil courts, such a development corresponded with the broader concept of causal connection used in damage cases under civil law. An additional factor was that the opening of medical interpretation that the non-German psychiatric colleagues were championing—a position their colleagues at home by no means consistently agreed with—was enjoying strong support from some German doctors who had already reflected on the possibility that prevailing doctrine was inadequate, especially in respect to long-term damage in the "returnees from the Soviet Union."[24] This was primarily the case for those psychiatrists who accepted the moral challenge posed by the compensation demands of victims of Nazism. This involved not only academics and university researchers but also the physicians who conducted examinations for the compensation authorities and who recognized both the possibility and the necessity of identifying a scientifically well-grounded deviation from the benchmarks of prevailing doctrine.

The result of this situation was to generate enormous pressure for clarification within the compensation authorities, who had to decide whether to recognize mental disorders as persecution-related illness on the basis of the psychiatric evaluations they were receiving from inside and outside Germany. What required clarification was both the validity of the current state of psychiatric knowledge and—in the medium term by no means unimportant—the handling of legal concepts and adjudication. With regard to the latter, since the mid-1950s two paragraphs were causing confusion and concern among officials and physicians: Paragraphs 3 and 4 of the second by-law of the federal amendment law of December 24, 1954, whose validity was then confirmed after passage of the BEG. The passages read as follows:

> *Section 3. Exacerbation of previous illness.* The exacerbation of a previous illness caused by violent National Socialist acts constitutes damage incurred through persecution corresponding to the extent of that exacerbation.

> If a previous illness has been worsened in a decisive manner, then it is to be considered damage incurred from persecution to the full extent.

> *Section 4. Hereditary illness.* Hereditary illness is to be considered caused by National Socialist acts in the sense of being their origin if such acts of violence constituted a substantial codeterminant of the illness.[25]

The potential for conflict contained in these clauses soon became manifest in communications between the German finance ministry, which was responsible for indemnification, and corresponding offices on the state level along with officials in the labor ministry who were responsible for war-disability pensions. The starting point here was a January 1957 inquiry by the reparations office in Hamburg to the higher-level office in the federal finance ministry regarding the interpretation of the concept of causation in the two clauses. Most likely, the underlying hope was to profit from the expertise of colleagues in the labor ministry's department for war-disability pensions. Their long-standing familiarity with matters pertaining to pension claims allowed one to expect that they would be well versed in the legal and medical ramifications.[26]

In fact, the labor ministry's department for war-disability pensions clarified a number of fine points having to do with the difficult complex of questions relating to causation. The central point was made at the start: "The causal concept is different in the natural sciences than in the field of disability-pension law." This in fact meant, the officials explained, that although a disease could often be traced to an entire complex of causes from a medical perspective, in terms of compensation law the concept of causation recognized only the factor considered primarily responsible as legally relevant within the entire nexus of causation. At this point, the officials in the labor ministry did not fail to point out the consequences this implied for the recognition of physical illness. If an evaluating physician considered hereditary disposition to be more important than exogenous damage, then, within such a legal framework, a causal connection between the health damage and the event that allegedly mandated compensation would have to be rejected. Only in cases where exogenous damage clearly predominated was it justified to speak of a "causal connection in the sense of origination."[27]

The German finance ministry forwarded this response to the reparations offices of the various regions, some of which not only reacted promptly but, much to the annoyance of the consulted authorities in the labor ministry, also emphasized the professional inappropriateness of the response. As an example, the doctors working for the reparation authorities in North Rhine Westphalia insisted that the definitions contained in the remarks of the labor ministry were completely irrelevant for federal reparations law. As the doctors had correctly recognized, the officials in the Ministry of Labor were relying exclusively on disability pension law, which, with respect to the causality question, was based on a different legal concept than was the BEG. This was the case because the BEG involved proceedings under civil law, while disability pension law fell into a different legal category, namely, social law (*Sozialrecht*), which followed the legal concepts and precedents set earlier by disability benefits courts during the Second Reich. The doctors' comments and corrections follow:

> In the BEG, the concept of causal connection between persecution and damage is understood more broadly than in disability pension and accident law. Within disability pension and accident law, the damaging event must occupy a paramount position within the range of causal conditions and have the characteristic of an essential contributing factor. In the BEG, it is sufficient that among the range of [causal] conditions the damaging event resulting from persecution is most likely *one* of the contributing causes.[28]

In this way, the doctors rejected the relevance of the medical reasoning underlying West German pension disability law to their own field of activity, namely, compensation. In their letter, they signaled clearly that they believed themselves to be on solid legal ground. They were also not impressed by the Superior State Social Court judgments confronting them in the communication from the Ministry of Labor. It had not escaped them that for its concept of bodily injury, the court had referred to the BVG. The doctors' position regarding these judgments was firm: "They do not have even a relative place within BEG law" and could not even "be applied in an analogous sense."[29]

Since the leeway for recognizing health damage as persecution-related illness depended on which legal concepts were considered valid, juridical precision was extraordinarily important for compensation procedures. The physicians who spoke up here were well aware of this, as were their colleagues in the labor ministry who had now been put in their place. At least their response seems to suggest this. The undersecretary who signed the letter, a certain Dr. Dierkes, readily conceded that the perspective was restricted to the disability pension law, while maintaining that the inquiries they received were concerned with the practice of the social welfare courts. But in the issue at hand Dierkes agreed. He was familiar, he indicated, with the differences in the legal concepts and believed that the definition from pension law could not be transferred "automatically." Consequently, he and his department could not be reproached for inadequate expertise, he insisted. Dierkes now pulled back by referring to political will. The German parliament's select committee on compensation questions, which had informed itself of the approach taken by the social-welfare courts in a meeting held on September 25, 1956, had "in part" taken the position "that it would be desirable" if applications made in the framework of the BEG, the BVG, and accident-insurance regulations were all decided "according to the same principles."[30] The advantage was obvious: one could expect that a mode of operation based on the more stringent criteria underlying accident and pension law would in any event lead to significant financial relief.

For their part, the North Rhine Westphalian doctors declined to be guided by such considerations. Rather, they insisted that the above-mentioned medical evaluation guidelines, which had been published by the German labor ministry's office for disability pensions, "did not apply in any way" for experts in compensation procedures.[31] The wider significance of this was hinted at in an opinion issued by the Lower Saxony reparation authority, which supported the position and additionally stated, "Under such circumstances, it is naturally questionable to use the fact sheet to continue drawing the attention of independent medical examiners abroad to the "Guidelines for Medical Evaluation in Disability Cases."[32]

In the opinion of the North Rhine Westphalian physicians, a departure from this practice—a development in which the judgment of medical experts from outside Germany had presumably played a role during recent years—was not only called for on legal grounds. If one followed the opinion of one's colleagues in North Rhine Westphalia, there was a medical-scientific rationale as well. Public medical officer Paul Didden commented that the "damage to body and health" that was to be assessed according to the BEG, could only be compared to the damage referred to in pension law (BVG) "to a very small extent." He thereby introduced a medical argument that he substantiated as follows:

> From a medical perspective, the damage that needs to be recorded under the BEG is so new and unparalleled, both in terms of its cause (the type, severity, and duration of the "exogenous" damage) and in terms of the effect of the damage that requires medical evaluation, that for this reason alone a more or less formal transfer of the otherwise usual legal guidelines governing disability and accident pensions is out of the question.[33]

This posture, which demanded nothing less of the field of compensation medicine than a correction of "prevailing doctrine," received support through an "expert opinion" that had been sent two months before to all the reparation authorities in West Germany's various states by a Professor Hans Strauss, independent medical examiner for the West German Consulate General in New York.[34] Strauss, a neurologist and psychiatrist who was himself a German-Jewish émigré from Nazi Germany to the United States, quickly came to the point: "The assessment of victims of National Socialist persecution with nonpsychotic mental symptoms is a highly topical problem." The difficulties arose "particularly in the evaluation of the causal relationship between the present disorders and the acts of persecution." In Strauss's experience, a huge and widening gap had opened in this question among those involved in the reparations procedure—a dire set of circumstances, he argued, for all those who "rightfully filed such claims" but because of the situation were forced to tolerate huge delays before matters could be clarified.[35]

Strauss expressed only limited appreciation of such differences. He was above all annoyed by the rigid adherence to "one principle or the other" that was developed on the basis of "entirely different facts." Having been educated and professionally active in Germany before being driven from the university system in 1934, Strauss knew German psychiatry extremely well, and he was referring to West Germany's prevailing theory of "neurosis." It had also made its way—with reference being made to Ernst Kretschmer, a professor of psychiatry at the University of Tübingen—into the so-called "Ammermüller-Wilden,"[36] a standard West German reference work for assessing health damage in reparations cases. Strauss quoted from the book: "The decisive fact is that emotions and experiences from the past, even when they are severe, do not in themselves produce long-term neurosis." The medical examiner in New York disagreed. He, too, was of the opinion that the development of these views had been justified with respect to "the hysterical compensation neuroses suffered by persons injured in war and accidents." Nevertheless, he maintained, the ideas did not automatically apply in the "entirely different" mental disorders suffered by the victims of persecution.[37]

Strauss's argumentation focused primarily on the "chronic reactive depression" he frequently observed among survivors. In this respect, he completely abandoned West Germany's prevailing doctrine. His impression was that in the group he had examined, lasting physical damage, for example, to the nervous system, could only rarely be identified as the cause of "abnormal mental behavior." Consequently, he also emphatically distanced himself from the consensus of opinion at the Copenhagen conference, describing it as "completely unproven."[38] Instead, Strauss asserted that the "decisive, persecution-induced factor is that these individuals were uprooted, a reality that exists for them as much today as on the day they were liberated."[39] For Strauss, who preferred the term *Entwurzelungsdepression* (depression resulting from being uprooted) to "neurosis," there was only one basic reason for the persistent nature of the mental suffering: the specific features of Nazi persecution itself, which he saw as lying primarily in the individuals' "complete *absence of rights*." "They were," he summarized, "the completely defenseless victims of any conceivable whim on the part of their often sadistic masters."[40]

Strauss presented his standpoint to both the reparation authorities and his psychiatrist colleagues with a great deal of clarity: it was by no means convincing to assume that compensatory ideas were the source of the kind of mental behavior manifest here. He himself did not exclude other factors. Indeed, "personality structure," in which "disposition" and previous environmental factors worked together, was "clearly very important." Above all, Strauss considered character and intelligence to be essential codeterminants. In addition, there were the "difficulties present *at the time*" in survivors' daily lives. Nevertheless, despite this concession Strauss insisted that "these individuals cannot be reproached and denied compensation because their personality structure and unfavorable external circumstances rendered them unable to surmount being uprooted by establishing firm, new roots."[41]

In arguing along these lines, Hans Strauss struck a sensitive nerve within the reparations office of the state of Schleswig-Holstein. An opinion on the matter that had been requested from the regional state health office prompted the federal finance ministry to take urgent action.[42] The information obtained from Dr. Hans Heigl, director of the state health office, copies of which had been sent to all the state reparations offices, seemed alarming in several respects. Heigl had found fault with the fact that ascertaining possible illness and reduced earnings capacity resulted from the medical examiner's "subjective mind-set," and the diagnosis itself was based only on "subjective, unproven information supplied by the applicant." He warned that on a practical level it was the medical examiners who determined the outcome of the claim along with the diagnosis and the amount of pension granted.[43] What he underscored as "especially questionable," however, was "including 'asocial character development' in persecution-induced damage." For Heigl, then, Strauss's approach was neither scientifically or ethically tenable. "If," he insisted, "medical examiners, especially those outside Germany, adopt the views maintained by Prof. Dr. Strauss, there will hardly be a single formerly persecuted person without the prospect of success in making one of the compensable symptom complexes into the object of an application."

While the officials in Schleswig Holstein still believed they could halt the foray of their colleague in New York through a German "counteropinion" and thereby avert the feared scenario,[44] neither the other state reparations offices nor the finance ministry viewed such a sweeping defensive position as sensible. An agreement was reached among them to clarify the contentious legal and medical questions in the framework of a conference, with the intention of formulating binding assessment-guidelines. Representatives with legal training, managing physicians of the chief compensation authorities, and selected medical evaluators from Germany were to be consulted to this end. As well, medical examiners from the United States could no longer be bypassed in this clarification process, which in any case was intended to standardize practices. Accordingly, the fulcrum for reconciling the conflicting positions was the so-called chief medical conference. It convened for the first time in Munich in April 1958, with officials from a broad range of federal West German ministries attending.[45] The conferences were held annually until 1970. At the first meeting, no one suspected the dimensions the problems under negotiation would ultimately assume.[46]

The contentious issues are recorded in the minutes of the different annual conferences, whereby the minutes sometimes deviate noticeably from the positions presented in the talks themselves. This reflects the searching process through which conference participants strove to establish a tenable and standardized policy for the practice of medical evaluation. Those in attendance were evidently well aware that it was a precarious process. In any event, at the initial meeting they agreed not to send the minutes to medical examiners outside Germany for the time being.[47] As it happens, opinions regarding how to interpret and diagnose the mental symptoms suffered by survivors clashed rather directly.

This was above all apparent in the controversy over the central concept of "neurosis." At the 1958 conference, Erich Kluge, an associate professor at the University of Mainz and psychiatrist who was assigned the keynote speech on the significance and assessment of depression and persistent psychogenic reaction in reparations-focused medical practice, had little sympathy with the far broader approach to the concept often taken in the United States: "Non-German and above all American assessors have designated highly differentiated symptoms as neurosis or psychoneurosis in a completely monotone fashion," he complained. To ascertain the diagnostic accuracy of preliminary assessments, he had examined sixty files for a state reparations office.[48] Fully in line with the German tradition, Kluge viewed "neurosis" simply as a psychogenic disorder based on the idea of being ill or the wish to be so, and which therefore did not mandate compensation. It seemed to him that the mental symptoms of the victims of Nazi Germany whose applications he had reviewed for the most part did not fall into this diagnostic category. In the vast majority of cases, a "tendentious 'neurotic' disorder" was not evident. He attributed 44 percent, or nearly half, of the cases to endogenous or constitutional causes and therefore did not consider them to be related to persecution.[49] An actual neurosis, in the sense of the prevailing German psychiatric opinion, was only present in 7 percent of the cases. In keeping with the above-discussed normative requirements, he was with few exceptions prepared to recognize persecution as a cause only when the long-term effects had resulted from physical damage. In this respect, Kluge primarily viewed the studies of "late damage" in repatriated Wehrmacht veterans from Soviet imprisonment as offering a way forward, whereby he was thinking specifically of hunger dystrophy, which, he indicated, had demonstrably even led to brain alterations.[50] In the end, Kluge saw the concept of "melancholia" as offering a diagnosis that would cover "chronic depression with organic features" in cases of persecution-related illness. "The organic, physical element" was already contained in the term itself, he observed.[51] Here, he had found a solution that conformed to prevailing opinion in that it interpreted mental damage as a result of an organic disorder, but did not attribute a regulative effect to the persecution itself in the form of an undifferentiated neurosis, as was the case in the American practice he criticized.[52] By falling back on a diagnosis of "melancholy," however, he also made clear that he did not consider the concept of neurosis normally used in Germany, which assumed what psychiatrists termed "compensatory illness," generally suitable under the altered circumstances. Kluge said this directly: "Following the destructive impact of the present situation in the word, we can no longer make do with rationalistic psychogenesis."[53]

Among the attendees of the first of these medical conferences, Kluge's position drew a mixed reaction. The main focus was on determining the survivors' status as victims. In their presentations, which were actually concerned with the legal content of the BEG, both the Hamburg physician Wolfgang Meywald, representing the city's reparations office, and medical officer Paul Didden of the North Rhine Westphalian reparation authority, suggested a broader position. Both men were convinced that the damage that had been inflicted on survivors was in no way comparable with that seen in veterans' disability pension cases.[54] Meywald based his argument mainly on the "inequality of positions" between the persecutors and those who were persecuted. The "personal starting situation" of the survivors, he maintained, was characterized by "one-sided displacement," in sharp contrast to the situation of soldiers. "Even the inferiority of an individual soldier or a fighting unit to a wartime enemy does not eliminate equality in terms of one's status as a person, which is fundamental to human existence," he commented, and then added: "Even the complete inequality of the means and recognition of the inadequacy or even impossibility of defense during military service does not annul moral equality. The persecuted person, however, is exclusively a victim."[55]

Didden, for his part, was hardly less outspoken in his insistence on this qualitative distinction, although he considered it from another angle. He argued that damage that came under the disability pension system was "as a rule independent of the personality of the party involved." This was only rarely the case with damage from persecution, where "the full scope of persecution as such" was the damaging factor, and this for one reason that Didden identified without euphemism: "It was the persecutor's intention to shatter and destroy the personality of the persecuted."[56] Did this in itself not raise the suspicion that the health damage involved here would differ from that found in normal disability pension cases? What they as doctors were seeing in this context, he commented, actually amounted to the results of a horrific "mass experiment" that was unparalleled in "all of human and medical history." The consequences were correspondingly unique. Didden emphasized that colleagues from abroad had also identified a pattern of symptoms unique to the Nazi persecution.[57] For him there was no doubt: what they were dealing with was first and foremost *"damage to the personality."*[58] The designation of "neurosis," all too often used in the absence of an adequate diagnosis and in misjudgment of what was new, was in Didden's eyes therefore misguided. In the future, he suggested, the concept of a "psychasthenic persecution syndrome," while still in need of greater precision, should cover the range of relevant symptoms.[59]

The conference minutes reflect the difficulty of reaching a consensus in these positions. The record therefore limits itself to stating that all the participants were in agreement that the concept of neurosis was "highly unfortunate" in the reparations context and should be avoided. But the attendees did not solve the problem of how to move forward. In the euphemistic language of the minutes, all the assessors "found it difficult to introduce a suitable concept that accurately expresses the matter."[60] Here, the ministers present were also voicing their pronounced mistrust of the assessors based outside Germany, who seemingly—as even the two assessors working in New York, Hans Strauss and a certain Dr. Riesenfeld, would assert soon thereafter—were inclined toward making accommodating assessments. In any event, the minutes of the convention, which was held in the summer of 1958, stated: "Certifications by attending physicians must be evaluated with the greatest caution, since they contain false representations. . . . The independent medical examiners who are trying to produce objective evaluations see themselves subjected to the greatest difficulties by their American colleagues."[61]

But the open formulation chosen in the conference transcript was also owed to the fact that if participants wished to retain definitional authority, they also had to take into account the recent efforts within German academic psychiatry to resolve the problem of mental-health damage from persecution. It was in any case possible to reach a common position regarding the inadequacy of the assessments from abroad, primarily because they lacked a precise case history as well as the psychiatric and neurological findings.[62] But as indicated in the debate that was unfolding at the same time in the professional literature, some German psychiatrists were now also insisting that when it came to restitution cases, "prevailing doctrine" and the evaluation guidelines had to be corrected.[63]

In this regard, a publication in 1958 by the above-mentioned psychiatrist Ulrich Venzlaff, an assistant physician at the Göttingen university clinic, was particularly noteworthy. Entitled *Psychoreactive Disorders Following Compensable Occurrences*, the study had been completed two years earlier, so that the author had in a sense anticipated an emerging trend.[64] Much like his colleagues in the main medical conference, Venzlaff made an effort not to shake "prevailing doctrine" to its foundations. Over the previous years at the Göttingen clinic, Venzlaff had been repeatedly charged with evaluating the compensation claims of survivors. Citing Kretschmer, Schneider, and Ewald, among others, he concurred with the explanation of purely mental, nonorganic disorders offered by prominent German psychiatrists. According to his interim conclusion, the essential preconditions for the emergence of such disorders were "abnormal character traits, experientially determined abnormal attitudes, unreasonable desires, and ungrounded anxieties."[65] However, he questioned the position that was being championed in German psychiatry (for instance by Kretschmer), namely, that the "endurance and capacity to withstand stress" of a physically healthy person of "normal" character was virtually unlimited.[66] Furthermore, in a departure from the prevalent natural-scientific orientation toward disease, which involved recognizing mental disorders as disease only when "pathological physical processes" could be demonstrated, Venzlaff actually spoke of the possibility of a "state of mental illness" (*seelisches Kranksein*), for instance, when a human being was overwhelmed by suffering.[67] For Venzlaff, when experience could not be successfully processed, when "the personality's ordering structure" had been "broken too profoundly," "when the contents and values upon which a life had been built" had been "*irrevocably destroyed*," "when human beings in their suffering and distress" had been "forced into years of isolation and no longer participated in communication with the community," "when the *phase of life* has expired during which the *personality can be shaped* and acquire new values and goals," then sometimes even incurable mental illness developed. It was precisely in such cases that he wished to dispense with use of the term "neurosis." In its stead, he suggested a diagnosis of "experientially determined personality change" (*erlebnisbedingter Persönlichkeitswandel*).[68]

Venzlaff made use of a broad spectrum of examples. It included refugees, above all older people who had been unable to overcome the loss of their raison d'être and their homeland. The psychiatrist spoke of an "*incurable disruption in the order of existence*" that they had suffered in realizing the irrevocability of their loss.[69] He indicated that a similar phenomenon could be observed among Nazi idealists who were subject to years of ostracism after the collapse.[70] But the true field of application lay in "events that were compensable" under the Additional Federal Compensation Act of 1953. Such events were constituted, on the one hand, through persecution itself and, on the other in a definite way through Venzlaff's interpretation of "experientially determined personality change."

In this framework as well, however, an individual chain of causation needed to be established. Venzlaff maintained he could demonstrate such a sequence, however. To this end, he presented a series of case histories chosen according to strict criteria so that potential objections could be rebuffed. This meant introducing only cases in which objective documents were available to attest that the mental symptoms that had existed ever since the persecution had ended and before there had been a legal basis for potential reparations. This was intended to disarm suspicions of "the desire to obtain a pension." In addition, Venzlaff offered the assurance that the individual's "life history, behavior, and character" displayed neither *abnormal character traits nor other neurotic conflict situations.*"[71]

In this manner, argued Venzlaff, mental suffering and its persecutory causes could be isolated. What then emerged he termed the "mental image of the ostracized person." This included a "permanent *sensitive timidity* and self-centeredness that could go as far as insecurity with *paranoid* features toward others," and "*emotionally charged memories* of humiliation and debasement" that robbed the environment of whatever innocence it might now possess, obtruding "in a *near compulsive* manner against all better insight." Finally, isolation generated a continuous confrontation with an "inner emptiness and an absence of meaning in existence" from which, in turn, an "*anxiety syndrome*" emerged. Venzlaff described it vividly: "An anxiety transformed through fear of torment, humiliation, and death into a *fear of life* (*Lebensangst*), a permanent inclination to be fearful that is repeatedly nourished by memories and awakened by a footfall on the stairs, or the doorbell ringing, but which is also felt as physically constricting and paralyzing." Such individuals, Venzlaff concluded, almost never regained their joy of life; they were all silent, inhibited, resigned. There was only one trait none of them had shown: "that demanding, tendentious attitude" which defined the "pension neurotic." And the Göttingen psychiatrist had safeguarded his position in another respect as well by excluding organic brain disorders in the clinic through differential diagnosis.[72] In light of the uniquely horrifying experiences the Nazi regime had created for countless people, he believed that everything seemed to favor interpreting the personality changes observed as a result of persecution-related events.

Venzlaff was well aware that proceeding with such care was absolutely crucial if his argument was to prevail. Only a few years before, the Bremen reparations office had reacted with something akin to panic when, acting as an evaluator on behalf of the Bremen regional court, he had diagnosed the case of one survivor as persecution-related neurosis.[73] The office had feared it would be inundated by pension claims if the psychiatrist's viewpoint were to become the standard. Commissioned by the same office, Ernst Kretschmer had written a supplementary evaluation rebutting Venzlaff's diagnosis while also charging him with misusing the concept of "sensitive neurosis," which Kretschmer himself had coined.[74] Although the court subsequently agreed with Venzlaff, the Bremen reparations office responded by distributing Kretschmer's counterevaluation to all the other state reparations offices as a guidepost.[75]

In the meantime, the debate on the interpretation of mental damage in survivors had taken a turn at the 1958 chief medical conference. An approach that continued to endorse without exception the restrictive theory of neurosis, as advocated by Kretschmer and most of his colleagues, no longer seemed tenable to those participating in the conference, even though they were undecided as to an appropriate designation for the mental disorders they were observing. In this open situation, Venzlaff's idea of "experientially determined personality change" promptly attracted the attention of the medical councils of the state reparations' offices. In the conference minutes that were specially prepared for non-German medical examiners, his just-published study was included in a list of articles on this controversial theme that had recently appeared in German professional journals.[76] This was intended as a handout for the medical examiners. The medical officials even explicitly referred to Venzlaff to clarify their standpoint to their foreign colleagues. Accordingly, the minutes cited his study, concerned as it was with general neuroses, including those in disability-pension cases, as follows:

> It is self-evident that in mental clinical pictures that are unrelated to accidents and can be traced instead to irrational desires, character abnormalities, or tension resulting from neurotic conflict, mandatory compensation must be strictly denied. Only in special cases . . . where mental disorders or characterogenically induced deviations are caused by serious physical illness or mental traumas that have the effect of key experiences and bear a causal connection to the accident, will the assumption of a causal relationship be permitted in one case or another after extensive consideration has been given to all circumstances. However, rather than having the effect of firmly establishing mental damage through a pension, such recognition should simply create the possibility of receiving medical help and compensation for mental suffering that has additionally developed from the damaging event.[77]

In spite of the assumption that, as the official communiqué put it, "the elements of persecution had a distinctive nature" and produced "distinctive mental damage," from the perspective of the chief reparation authorities of the various states, this clearly stated that only very few survivors were affected. For the authorities, these were exceptional cases. It was generally believed that the concept of "neurosis" adequately covered purely mental-reactive, non-physically based suffering. The German medical health officers assured the foreign medical examiners that in procedures that fell under the BEG as well, the same principle would be maintained that had been in place since the decision of the Reich Insurance Agency in 1926, namely, in cases of "neurosis" claims to compensation would be denied.[78]

The German medical officers and clinicians were therefore only prepared to proceed along a kind of double track. The traditional interpretation of long-term mental illness was given greater weight, as was usually the case in disability-pension law. At the same time, in reparations cases grounds of "experientially determined alteration of personality" were recognized as an exception, although a mere description of one's experiences during persecution was insufficient. "A punctilious personal biography, including above all professional development, family situation, etc." was to be recorded in the anamnesis, as was driven home to foreign colleagues in particular. In the case of former displaced persons, the fact was not to be neglected "that the persecution ended with liberation," and further that the difficulties emigrants experienced in their host countries were "no longer to be viewed as compensable events."[79] This amounted to a clear demarcation of borders, and while it had become difficult, proving a causal connection with persecution was still possible by using the concept of "experientially determined personality change." The door to a new interpretation of mental disorders had opened just a crack. In practice, the change had to prove itself, precisely because it involved something qualitatively new.

At the end of the 1950s, the officials in the German labor ministry quickly sensed the danger that the exception provision could be extended to Wehrmacht veterans. They therefore requested the Medical Advisory Board for Questions of War Victims' Disability Pensions to issue a report intended to take a binding position on the evaluation of "neurosis" in respect to both possible pension benefits and medical social services. The report was published in 1960.[80] The authors[81] confirmed that in rare cases "experientially reactive developments" could occur that were completely free of "wishful and goal-related tendencies "and would have to be defined "as adequate on the basis of the unusual extent of the damage suffered." The so-called "neurosis report" referred to Venzlaff, von Baeyer, Kolle, Kluge, and Strauss, who had spoken out for recognizing such long-term changes in cases of "overwhelmingly threatening experiences with serious injury of self-esteem" as occurred "under conditions of long-term fear of death and the most aggravated forms of violation in concentration and penal camps, especially in the case of Jews and prisoners of war who had been condemned to death." The report indicated, however, that those involved were for the most part former concentration camp inmates.[82] In general, the report served to prevent a sweeping interpretation of the exception that had been conceded. The Medical Advisory Board provided an unequivocal answer to the ministry's central question of whether a neurosis could "be viewed in causal relationship with the damaging effects of military service, the specific circumstances of war, or internment as a POW." The experts explained: "From the definition of neurosis as a disorder representing the outcome of an abnormal mental development that can be traced to childhood, the logical conclusion can be drawn that neuroses cannot stand in a causal connection with the damaging effects of military service, the specific circumstances of war, or internment as a POW."[83]

Soon, however, court intervention, public pressure (initially primarily Jewish pressure from abroad), and political considerations would endow Venzlaff s arguments regarding the victims of Nazism with growing validity, which meant that the problem of the feedback effect on disability pension cases remained. Ultimately, a moral question had been posed, and the answer would make a significant contribution to determining which psychiatric knowledge could be claimed valid for whom.

International Pressure and the Medical Revaluation of Suffering from Persecution

In all the previous attempts to explain the mental symptoms of the victims of Nazi persecution on the one hand, and of the returnees on the other, the question of the moral adequacy of the various definitional efforts had hardly ever been openly broached, and it certainly had not become a standard for medical evaluation practice. It can doubtless be argued that the strict application of a natural science-based perspective to both victims of Nazism and German war veterans reflected a tacit defense against German guilt.[84] But it is important to keep in mind that physicians from some other European countries unreservedly accepted the position of their German colleagues—for instance, when both Danish and French psychiatrists drew on German psychiatric findings regarding the "late damage" suffered by returnees from Soviet POW camps to explain mental disorders in deportees.[85] For this reason, there is much to suggest that the differentiation and hierarchization of these two groups, which in the middle term would be primarily inclined toward raising awareness of the health damage sustained by Jewish survivors, represented a process that only began in the late 1950s and unfolded only in Western Europe in this form.[86]

In West Germany, moral aspects and political considerations increasingly defined the interpretive and decisional framework in medical evaluation practice as it related to compensation proceedings. The growing influence of the survivors' attorneys and Jewish organizations played a central role here. In 1959, their criticism of the manner in which applications for health-damage compensation had been handled became so outspoken that, at the urging of the Conference on Jewish Material Claims against Germany (henceforth: Claims Conference) and the country's diplomatic missions, the German Foreign Office intervened and suggested to the state reparation offices that they send doctors to several reparations centers abroad.[87] Yet as would become clear only a few months later, in February 1960, public protest by relatively small Jewish groups who demonstrated against the certification process for health damage in victims of Nazism also did not fail to have an effect. A group of seemingly no more than two hundred mainly Polish Jews in New York City formed a Committee of Nazi Victims Deprived of Justice and Compensation by the German Medical Service, and sent a letter of protest to the West German general consulate in New York. They denounced the "long-distance diagnoses of hostile medical bureaucrats" and demanded, among other things, that in the future the consulate commission only medical evaluators who were characterized by "a human and sympathetic ear for persecuted persons."[88] Their discontent over the treatment of the applicants, who traced their health problems to Nazi persecution, was by no means directed exclusively at medical evaluation as it was practiced in Germany; their protest also extended to a large number of independent experts in their respective countries.[89]

Although representatives of both the Claims Conference and the United Restitution Organization (URO) appear to have been skeptical regarding this committee, and despite the fact that the assurances of German consulate general that the members of the committee could not be even "remotely compared" "with representatives of Jews in this country and the German Jewish émigré community,"[90] the Foreign Office once again became involved in the restitutions issue. Following swastika-scrawling in Cologne and many other West German anti-Semitic incidents the year before,[91] grappling with such reproaches could no longer be postponed. In the end, the theory that the incidents had been backed by the Sozialistische Einheitspartei Deutschlands (the ruling party in the German Democratic Republic) was not universally considered credible in the West; even providing some concrete evidence had not been successful in defusing the critical situation. West Germany's overall handling of its recent Nazi past was now on trial.[92] Accordingly, the procedure for recognizing persecution-related health damage had become an explosive foreign-policy issue. The Foreign Office was acutely aware of the young Federal Republic's still-precarious political status among the Western powers. It therefore urgently called upon its colleagues in the finance ministry to finally fund the assignment of authorized medical doctors to the primary centers where reparations claims were being handled so that the processing of the applications could be accelerated on location.[93] The Foreign Office argued as follows:

> Since compensation payments to date have had a very favorable effect on bilateral relations particularly in the United States, while on the other hand, particularly in the United States, the criticism that has now emerged could tarnish the favorable effect of the reparation payments, it must in my opinion be avoided at all costs that the dispatch of physicians fails for financial reasons. . . . Dispatching physicians would also have the positive effect of demonstrating that the Federal Republic is undertaking everything in its power to process reparations as quickly and appropriately as possible.[94]

Over the course of 1960, various German medical officials paid visits to Paris, London, Israel, and New York that extended over several weeks and sometimes even several months. Contrary to what they expected, however, the difficulties associated with granting reparations for medical reasons could not be resolved simply by instructing the foreign medical examiners how to fill out the evaluation form correctly, make a diagnosis that conformed to German standards, and handle the legal concepts of the BEG. Doubtless there were errors that resulted from a lack of knowledge and could be corrected through greater familiarity with German bureaucratic procedure. Nevertheless, in writing their evaluations, some of the foreign medical examiners seemed to be convinced that the victim status of the Holocaust survivors and their enormous suffering mandated granting pensions for their health problems in all cases, or at least supporting their compensation claims to the greatest possible extent. For many survivors, the granting of a pension was a measure of recognition of suffering as such; it stood for the acknowledgment of German guilt, and appeared to be a benchmark for Germany's overall willingness to make reparations.

As an example, the renowned Paris-based psychiatrist Eugène Minkowski—a Polish emigrant who was familiar with German medical practice from his period as a student in Munich—confronted visiting German medical officials over dinner, in the presence of embassy representatives, by stressing that "everything must be evaluated solely from a human standpoint. The state of the soul cannot be objectified in any case."[95] If we follow the German report, it appears that in preparing their evaluations French medical examiners chose a different route to express the same thing. "Almost as a rule," the French doctors made diagnoses of "psychasthenic persecutory syndrome" or "deportee asthenia," whereby the case histories did not take into account any periods beyond the persecution itself, and health complaints were associated with the period of persecution as if it were self-evident.[96] In addition, the French doctors allegedly conceded in a meeting that they frequently and intentionally followed the advice of older colleagues and specified an exaggerated degree of reduced earning capacity: the German reparation authorities would "in any case reduce the amount"—in fact, a reasonable assumption.[97]

Against this backdrop, the German delegation's impression could not be written off in a perfunctory manner: "There is a general effort to arrive at a reduced earning capacity of at least 25 percent," they indicated in their report to the compensation authorities.[98] The representatives of the Jewish deportees' association, with whom the German medical officials met for what were officially termed "negotiations," would have reinforced this perception through their own position. According to the minutes, the association heads stressed that they were speaking "exclusively for their members, that is, for former concentration camp inmates" and conveyed to the German physicians their belief "that in every applicant a priori the minimal conditions for §§ 28 ff. of the BEG should be considered as fulfilled."[99] In this group of victims, the deportees association therefore assumed that in every case there had been physical or health damage that mandated compensation, whereby granting a pension required a determination of an at least 25 percent reduction in earning capacity.[100] In the end, the German compensation physicians were presented with this in cold print: an article in the press directly called on all medical examiners who were recognized as evaluators by the German embassy to ignore the medical norms if necessary and proceed according to ethical principles in evaluating deportees.[101]

All this seemed like a very delicate matter. But following their second visit and intensive discussions lasting several weeks with more than thirty French doctors, the German medical officials were by and large optimistic. In their report to the various state compensation authorities, the delegation expressed clear respect for the examiners working in France. It had to be emphasized, they indicated at the beginning of the report, "that they are neither worse nor better than German physicians!" Many of them, they confirmed, had "good medical training and a great deal of knowledge."[102]

But this only signaled limited agreement. In professional terms, points of reference between the delegation from Germany and the French physicians did exist. The presence among the discussion partners of Rumanian and Polish Jews who had been trained in Germany was apparently meant to underscore that.[103] At the same time, the German delegation was aware it had not been able to have its way straight down the line. When the German medical officials nevertheless signaled the federal ministries that success had been achieved, the success lay in having explored what was doable, and that both sides had tried to arrive at a modus vivendi. The German physicians had at least come away with the impression that their French colleagues had shown professional interest and a desire "to seek ways of accommodating German adjudication practice in compensation procedures, despite the difficulties."[104] This was clearly a cautious way of phrasing it, and it was no coincidence that the delegation of medical officials used this formulation. They openly expressed that "the limits of receptiveness and willingness" had become clear. The physicians even went so far as to advise desisting from further "systematic schooling," which seemed to have "reached the limits of its potential for success." Instead, they recommended that conducting a "*concrete* review of the files" should be "managed 'from behind the desk,'" since this method was suitable for "avoiding anything that could convey the impression of pettiness, or of being a know-it-all or pedant." It was, therefore, clear to the delegates that they were treading on sensitive turf. But in light of the fact that the French doctors had "insistently requested" ongoing contact, the Germans seemed to believe that that they could continue along this track and, if necessary, intervene in a regulatory capacity.

Nevertheless, the German compensation authorities' sense of quick success, coupled with the impression of ultimately having kept the upper hand in medical questions to a large degree and in any case retaining bureaucratic control, had only emerged with respect to "other European countries."[105] Following their official travel, the German physicians for the moment appeared to once again believe they could evade the political-moral pressure being articulated in other countries. In any case, the ministry officials of the reparation authorities on both federal and state levels reacted with some displeasure that same year when the German embassy in London, imagining itself in pronounced political difficulties and acting under its own authority, relieved a medical examiner of his duties. Although the doctor was himself a Jewish emigrant, many compensation applicants had accused him of conducting a demeaning and insensitive evaluation practice and protested. Even though the medical examiner was no longer tenable from the embassy's perspective, the ministry officials in the reparation authority supported him, emphasizing that they valued him because of his extraordinary professional competence.[106]

In the United States, however, the German medical officials were much more cautious and adopted a significantly more conciliatory tone. Here, even more than in Europe, from a political perspective the entire matter seemed to resemble a balancing act. The German delegation felt that the public was observing their every step. They were acutely aware of the interest of the media, which in fact played a major role in defining the importance of the meeting and determining public expectations. This included the expectations that the application procedure for reparations would be fundamentally accelerated, that a large number of pending and contested applications could be clarified, and that the entire matter would "turn out favorably" for the survivors.[107] If one believed the information contained in the reparations supplement of *Aufbau*, the German-Jewish émigré newspaper in New York, the prospects were indeed favorable. In October 1960, one article reported that a German reparations physician, Dr. Sander, had commented on the "differences in medical views" and conceded "that the ideas of the American doctors have gradually exerted significant influence on German medicine, which is more conservative, so that today more and more German medical evaluators share the views of their American colleagues."[108]

It is impossible to verify whether Dr. Sander, director of the medical services in Hanover, actually made this remark. Both his discussion contributions and the presentations he gave at the chief medical conference that would be held in Hanover in 1962 do not suggest he would have greeted such an opening, let alone helped move the process forward. Yet the *Aufbau* article of 1960 indicated that German compensations medicine found itself in a defensive position in the United States. In the question of whether there was a causal connection between the health damage suffered by survivors and the fact that they had been persecuted, the representatives of German compensation medicine could only carry on by clearly conceding that in this field their American colleagues were a step ahead scientifically, and that Germany was prepared to follow suit. This was not only the expectation as it was more or less spelled out in the American press. Rather, a number of American psychiatrists apparently also made this clear to their German counterparts, firmly rejecting "any interference by the German doctors in their difficult-to-understand material."[109]

Although the German delegation did not encounter such a rough reception everywhere—at an initial meeting, representatives of the Claims Conference even expressed interest in extending the German doctors' activities to Chicago,

Los Angeles, and Montreal[110]—it quickly became obvious that the doctors would not reach a speedy, satisfactory agreement. In the view of the German consulate general in New York, success at the local level, where work on concrete cases fueled the hope that one was increasingly drawing closer to formulating uniform medical evaluation guidelines, had been able to calm the politically explosive situation somewhat. But the situation could not be considered stable, as the consulate was aware. The respective formulations chosen in various reports were only guardedly optimistic. For the German observers, the activities of the New York medical examiners at first primarily represented "valuable start-up assistance";[111] "useful" was the term they chose following the second visit in 1961.[112]

Particularly with respect to the psychiatric-neurological cases, which in the meanwhile accounted for some 30–40 percent of all cases according to an estimate by Dr. Staehr, a governmental health officer, in 1961,[113] it had basically been predictable that the physicians' delegation would not be able to fully come to grips with the conflict. Still, there were points of delicate rapprochement, even in the highly controversial realm of "neurosis," where the evaluating doctors in West Germany and the United States spoke "two completely different languages," as Staehr put it in a presentation he gave in the United States.[114] In Staehr's view, the work of Hans Strauss, an independent medical examiner in New York, on so-called "uprooting depression and experientially reactive disorders when persecution was suffered during youth," marked an important step. While Staehr emphasized that at least when it came to depressive symptoms they had "built a bridge . . . in the general dilemma," he nevertheless apparently considered it advisable not to recall the harsh protests against Strauss's stance by some German physicians. Instead, he asserted that "these concepts" had "long since been introduced into shared, cooperative work."[115] That was not all, Staehr tried to explain: in West Germany as well, in the meantime, research had accumulated "that concluded that neurosis theory as it was formulated in 1926 is outdated in its harsh application or is at least no longer supportable for the issues facing compensation medicine and the unusually serious persecution it confronts."[116] Staehr was concerned with "personality change" as observed by Venzlaff and others. But had this reading actually become accepted in German medicine as valid knowledge?

Staehr confronted his American public with a split in the German medical profession. However, he suggested that it had become irrelevant for the evaluation sector. The decisive, clarifying step had been taken in the so-called neurosis report. He put it this way in his talk: "The definitions of disease presented in the previously named scientific monographs for cases of long-term mental changes have now for the first time received—I would like to say—government recognition."[117] He continued in the same triumphant vein: "The general assessment makes clear that certain tendencies have emerged toward a softening of the strict concept of neurosis."[118] In Germany as well, he asserted, one had adopted the conviction that neuroses were not to be understood only as "wish determined" or "goal determined" reactions. Indeed, they could even claim the status of a disease in their own right. This was in any event the case, he continued, when "overwhelming threats" or "persistent fear of death and the gravest forms of abuse in concentration and penal camps" had been endured. In the course of his talk, Staehr explained this in greater detail. He also mentioned that in the neurosis report there was a sense that a diagnosis of so-called "adequate experientially reactive development" should only be made in "rare exceptions." Nevertheless, he mainly underscored positive aspects and progress. Especially in the case of young people, he noted, it had been possible also to view "a neurosis as a disease" and at least initiate treatment. And if the concept of "neurosis" were entirely circumvented, mental consequences could serve as the basis for reparations claims. Staehr thus appealed to the medical examiners "to speak of 'chronic-reactive uprooting depression, experientially determined personality change, experientially reactive sensitizations, or long-term reactions,'" rather than of "neurosis."[119] The German medical official assured his American colleagues that as a result of this different categorization it was possible to obtain justice for "persecuted individuals who were mentally seriously damaged and stranded in their life development." Staehr was optimistic: the new formulations contained in the neurosis report had, he asserted, brought previously opposing approaches to the concept of neurosis in West Germany and the United States closer together. In the future, he promised, it would be possible "to avoid some of the cautiousness and insecurity involved in determining long-term psychic damage."[120]

As explained above, however, in actual fact the neurosis report had only provided for an exception that was based on an assumption that even most Holocaust survivors had come through the experience without long-term psychic damage. This was formulated explicitly in the so-called blue brochure, where the "Göttingen Commission" explained the legal guidelines of the BEG for medical evaluation to doctors inside and outside of West Germany while also defining the status of medical knowledge considered valid in terms of the recognition of health damage.[121] For this reason alone, continued conflict with the German reparation authorities was, so to speak, preprogrammed. All the more so because the authorities, contrary to what Staehr had told the Americans, had by no means consistently changed over to using the new scientific findings of Venzlaff, von Baeyer, and others "as a basis for their decisions in most cases."[122] Thus, in their distance from these findings, a large number of clinical investigators very likely agreed with many, perhaps even the majority of, German psychiatrists.

What many medical officials and their psychiatric colleagues considered extremely problematical and scientifically untenable was the assertion, only a few years later, by a group of physicians—the best known among them included von Baeyer, Venzlaff, Helmut Paul, and Hans Joachim Herberg[123]—that in cases of mental suffering in survivors, entitlement to reparations should no longer be the exception but rather the rule. For example, in 1963 Ulrich Venzlaff wrote:

> These are no longer the "extreme cases" that prompted us years ago to view and evaluate the effects of stress from persecution in a light other than that of "prevailing doctrine." They are the "everyday cases," so to speak, those who did not survive persecution as derailed, human wreckage but who have been permanently marked and experienced a total impairment of their lives that the evaluation must also take into account.[124]

Walter von Baeyer likewise called for both the medical profession and compensation authorities to adopt a more generous approach to evaluations. Together with his associates Heinz Häfner and Karl Peter Kisker, he argued for skepticism when claimants had apparently experienced longer periods of symptom remission without health problems. In such cases, there was the possibility that "disruption and weaknesses in the person as a totality that were difficult to recognize and socially not disturbing or only mildly so" had existed for a long time, with which the subsequent "failure and abnormality" could be associated. Here, the psychiatrists emphasized, "decisions within the framework of compensation law" were to be made "in favor of the applicant." The three psychiatrists went even further: the same approach was to be taken "where it appeared that a sociogenesis or individual genesis of the disorder existed that was no longer directly linked to persecution." They justified this briefly, with one argument they considered sufficient: "There was hardly a single individual for whom the suffering and serious mental stress ended on the day of liberation."[125]

With this step, the concern was no longer limited to the debate over whether extreme stress endured through Nazi persecution was sufficient to cause long-term mental changes that were to be considered a disease. Rather, survivors' nervous disorders were also meant to be understood in their interaction with the circumstances they had been facing since the defeat of Nazism, and to be recognized as meriting compensation. Von Baeyer believed that the possible legal objections he foresaw could be countered with a medical argument: "If legislation does not recognize traumatizing circumstances that were at play *after* the persecution and beyond the individual, but were nevertheless a consequence of persecution, e.g. loss of relatives, as direct persecution-related health damage, then we could counter this by pointing out that persecution was directly related to a reduction of resistance."[126]

Similarities to the manner of argumentation during the late 1950s emerged. Then as well, uprooting or the difficulties of adapting to an alien world were cited as the direct results of persecution. Nevertheless, the talks that von Baeyer, Paul Matussek at the Max Planck Institute in Munich, and Wolfgang Jacob (an internist in Heidelberg) delivered in 1961 at the renowned rotating annual convention of the Southwest German Neurologists and Psychiatrists, held that year in Baden-Baden, suggested an altered perspective and a new concern. In essence, the new argument distanced itself from the prevailing assumption that "abnormality [lay] in the personality." This was to be replaced through the realization that since humans were "historical-social beings," mental damage was inflicted by society.[127] This also raised the question of responsibility. If one concurred with this shift of perspective, then responsibility no longer lay with the individual, as had been maintained for decades, but with society.

Thus, sociological elements had made their way into psychiatric perception and interpretation. Von Baeyer in particular did not hesitate to take direct recourse to the neighboring field.[128] Above all, psychiatrists Matussek and Jacob made it very clear to their audience that the new approach was tied to a critique of postwar West German society. Their assessment was severe, since now as before they saw the survivors' ongoing mental pain and suffering as caused to great degree by this society. "The camp inmates are in a sense still in the camps" is the way Matussek put it. In order to eliminate their psychic burden, "Society would have to look different than it actually does, namely, it would also have to be willing to internally accept what is probably the most terrible accusation in history."[129] The words of his colleague Jacob were no less harsh: "It seems to be the case that a human being who has been eliminated from a pathological social order will only find opportunities to thrive and develop once again within society when the society itself has changed, in others words, reoriented itself in a fundamentally new way." He further concluded: "The fate of human beings damaged in the concentration camps would then be an especially sensitive criterion for the unfolding of authentic societal change!"[130]

The presentations by members of this conference section, who all laid claim to breaking new scientific ground, sparked dissent within the German psychiatric profession. When set against previous and future controversies over the validity of "prevailing doctrine" as a basis for determining compensable mental suffering in the case of Holocaust survivors, this controversy stood out in one particular respect. Hermann Witter, a psychiatrist at the Saarland university clinic, broached the otherwise completely neglected problem of the relationship between "knowing" and "valuing."[131] Witter was convinced that despite his colleagues' assertions, when it came to the question of whether compensable psychoreactive disorders existed, there could be no talk of new scientific insights. Granted, "prevailing doctrine" was indeed based on medical findings that had been made during the course of World War I. Yet even then, Witter observed, the problem of causality and reduced earning capacity could not be solved with "categories of medical and empirical-psychological thinking." Strictly speaking, even if there had been efforts to establish "such regulation as "scientific knowledge," what "prevailing doctrine" involved was a "regulation of *assessment*." He now saw his colleagues proceeding in a similar manner: they were demanding a revision of "accepted opinion" on the basis of alleged new medical insight, while in his view it was not medical insight that had changed. The presence of victims of Nazism was merely causing what had previously been an exception to emerge more frequently, or even to become the rule, so that "the customary evaluative schema with all its simplifications" was no longer satisfactory. Witter insisted that "the need for revision" was basically fueled by the desire to have a different "regulation of assessment."

Witter did not wish his critique to be misunderstood. He expressly favored "a new evaluative schema for this group" and by no means considered a value judgment objectionable: "Just as conscientious doctors were previously allowed to deliver a value judgment against compensation for specific people, they should now be allowed to formulate one in favor of it." It was only that "knowing" and "valuing" needed to be strictly separated, and he reproached his colleagues for not adhering to that principle.[132] In any case, Witter did not leave it at that. He initiated a dispute about method, aiming his critique at "anthropological psychiatry," and therewith at Walter von Baeyer, who had increasingly adopted this perspective since the mid-1950s, as was clear from his writing on the recognition of mental disorders in survivors within the framework of the BEG.[133] Witter developed two points of criticism in particular. First, he faulted anthropological psychiatry, which he saw as methodologically concerned with "research, interpretation, and the interpretive reconstruction of *inner* life histories," for necessarily being inclined to "give the investigator's intuition and subjective interpretative capacity even greater leeway." But that wasn't all: "the very broad use of subjective interpretations" entailed the danger that the results of an investigation would be determined "more by the investigator than by what is being investigated."[134]

Second, Witter believed he saw another danger that had not been eliminated: "The aspiration to shift the *entirety* of human existence as a research object into the scientific categories of medicine and psychoanalysis" would, he explained, either have to "remain in a tentative realm"[135] or, apparently even worse in his opinion, become "a kind of weltanschauung through the intended totality of a comprehensive theory of human existence." For Witter, this meant that anthropological psychiatry had overstepped a border demarcating the competence of medicine as a discipline and was threatening, through "allegedly scientific arguments, to assert a claim to realms of intellectual and cultural life" rightfully the reserve of the "law, ethics, and religion." At this point, the psychiatrist returned to the question of the evaluation of compensation applications. Responsibility for such decisions lay in the hands of the courts alone, he insisted; no psychiatric expert should try to take on such a role. Witter made his position unmistakably clear:

> Whether and how experientially caused mental injury in the victims of National Socialist persecution should be subject to compensation benefits is primarily a question of ethical, legal, political, and perhaps also economic considerations—considerations that lie entirely beyond the scope of psychiatry. Whether lasting mental injury, which, particularly in victims of racial and political persecution that extended over years, will almost always be confirmed, is to be designated and evaluated as "health damage," and be compensated is a question of convention.[136]

A reaction to Witter's article was not long in coming. Having been personally attacked by his colleague in Saarbrücken, von Baeyer responded from Heidelberg together with his associates Heinz Häfner and Karl Peter Kisker.[137] His retort was openly irritated in tone and equally self-confident.[138] The three psychiatrists began by underscoring their expertise and suggested that Witter's text basically represented "a comment that stood in isolation in the literature" and could thus be ignored. It was in any event "empirically refuted" by the findings in a study of over five hundred certified persecuted persons that was on the verge of publication.[139] In the eyes of von Baeyer and his colleagues, Witter had simply revealed his professional weaknesses: "The great difficulties Witter has in objectively mastering psychiatric empiricism in the realm of experientially reactive long-term effects of extreme mental stress in persecuted persons . . . evidently have their source in insufficient methodological penetration and inadequate information about the studies already published in the professional literature."[140] The Heidelberg psychiatrists could have hardly stated more clearly that with their findings they claimed to represent a new "prevailing doctrine."

Von Baeyer, Häfner, and Kisker by no means agreed with Witter's argument regarding "regulation of assessment," even—and this may at first seem surprising—with respect to the now antiquated "prevailing doctrine." In fact, the three psychiatrists insisted that "its empirical-scientific substance" was to be taken seriously. It remained, they strongly emphasized, "a *scientific* maxim for judging individual cases" in medical evaluation. Yet von Baeyer and colleagues persisted in questioning the general validity of "prevailing doctrine," which in their eyes was "merely a law of large numbers and prevalent conditions." In fact, restoring "scientific dignity to 'prevailing' doctrine" was their stated goal. For only then "can we call into question Witter's assertion that there are no new psychiatric findings and no basis for its modification," they explained.[141] Von Baeyer, Häfner, and Kisker were therefore certain about one thing: only if they upheld the "scientific nature" of the old "prevailing doctrine" could they claim that their psychiatric insights in the realm of long-term mental damage represented scientific progress. They in no way agreed with the statement that "psychopathological knowledge never moves beyond a prescientific stage," as Witter was in their opinion suggesting. They commented, "In methodological guilelessness we would even saw off the branch on which all of us psychiatrists sit."[142]

Von Baeyer and his colleagues believed that the scientific basis of old "prevailing doctrine" had been proven by one particular fact: in the immediate aftermath of World War II, divergent scientific standpoints had already been formulated within its framework—and this even by psychiatric eminences such as Karl Bonhoeffer, who had contributed to the doctrine following his experiences in the Great War.[143] In 1947, Bonhoeffer had surmised that there might be "a limit to an individual's capacity for mental endurance" when an "excess of artificially induced, physically tormenting procedures that were demeaning to the personality" (he was referring to torture) were applied. He noted that he was familiar with cases of "short-term hallucination" resulting from such torment.[144] Von Baeyer, Häfner, and Kisker now reminded their readers that at the time Walter Schulte and Hans Werner Kranz had also concluded, based on their own psychiatric observations, that mental endurance was not absolute. What von Baeyer and his staff members were engaged in here was a kind of after-the-fact invention of a tradition. In the process, they simply screened out the fact that for more than a decade the German psychiatric profession, including von Baeyer, had by no means accepted this divergent approach, and that it was therefore completely irrelevant in terms of "prevailing doctrine."[145] Nevertheless, the psychiatrists constructed a quasi-necessary movement of scientific revision without needing to diametrically oppose established categories within their profession as Witter claimed.

However, it was probably by referencing international research that von Baeyer, Häfner, and Kisker most effectively underscored that the psychiatric findings presented in Baden-Baden with respect to persecution-related long-term mental damage stood for solid scientific method and scientific progress. The three associates emphasized that in the United States, the Netherlands, Germany, France, and Israel numerous researchers had begun to determine more precisely the proportion of survivors with "chronic, experientially reactive neurotic personality disorders (*Fehlhaltungen*)" and to empirically work out the conditions under which "significant long-term damage" emerged. Although the research projects involved were completely independent of one another, they had "led to remarkably consistent results."[146] Only those who had followed the debate closely could have known that this description of things passed over major interpretive differences regarding so-called long-term psychic damage.[147] In terms of research strategy, this was apparently beneficial. In another publication that also appeared in 1963, von Baeyer and his two colleagues even argued that "numerous studies of former camp inmates in various countries" had shown that there were "different forms of 'experientially determined personality change' as a long-term effect" of earlier intense stress.[148] Venzlaff expressed it more simply: "Everyone means and is describing the same thing."[149]

Without a doubt, these were rhetorical strategies. Such references to alleged international unity in the question of survivors' delayed or long-term mental damage unmistakably signaled to colleagues in Germany the direction that German psychiatry needed to take in order to avoid the reproach of international backwardness. The phalanx of countries von Baeyer and others cited to support the validity and importance of their scientific forays did not, of course, include any of the Communist states. The actual certifying authority was the non-German West, above all the United States. These countries embodied scientific progress, and it was the promise of association with the West that was, in the end, being held out to German psychiatry through a revision of "prevailing doctrine." And in actuality, recognition by the international scientific community would arrive only a few years later in the form of a signal that was important scientifically as well as in terms of articulating "politics of the past." The International Congress of Psychiatry, founded in Paris in 1950 as a reaction to the mental health devastation inflicted by World War II, appointed a German to an executive position for the first time. Twenty-one years after the demise of National Socialism, Walter von Baeyer was elected vice president at the congress's fourth session in Madrid in 1966.[150]

Divided Suffering: The Mental Anguish of Survivors of Nazi Persecution and of German Veterans as Part of an Expert Controversy

The acknowledgment (in terms of Germany's politics of the past) that Western colleagues extended to von Baeyer's position did not, however, settle the extent to which the new reading of "experientially determined personality change" should be used in the assessment of mental symptoms. The courts had an important say in the matter for procedures that fell under both German compensation law and the pension act. According to legal principles, in the context of mental suffering as elsewhere, similar matters needed to be treated in a similar fashion.[151] In reality, jurisdiction in the assessment of mental disorders took a somewhat different course in the field of compensation than in the field of war disability pensions.

It was already clear by the late 1950s that matters were moving in that direction. The differences were often explained using the argument that in compensation law, which fell under civil law, a different concept of causality was operative than in disability pension cases, which fell under social law.[152] Nevertheless, many questions remained controversial, not least because in medicine there could no longer be any question of consistent assessments of mental disorders, as was above all clear in compensation cases. In 1960, from a legal viewpoint the situation appeared as follows:

> In decisions regarding the degree of significance to attribute to mentally determined health problems and the question of whether and to what extent a legal connection exists between persecution and mental disorders, administrative lawyers and judges sometimes find themselves in a difficult position. This is not only because assessments are made differently in the different areas, but also because there are substantial differences in medical opinion on the pathological significance of such disorders and their causal relationship to external events.[153]

Adjudication practice reflected the dilemma in various ways. There will have been many judges who received a medical evaluation and copied it "blindly into the judgment"—as asserted by a critic at the end of the 1960s, who deplored the fact that so many compensation applications failed due to the medical argument that the health problems were caused by "hereditary" factors rather than persecution.[154] However, this apparently was not the case with a great many jurists. In light of the differing views within compensation-related medical practice, judges no longer necessarily considered physicians' assessments a reliable guidepost. In this muddied situation, they had to find ways of making decisions that potentially conflicted with the determination of a medical expert, decisions that—after due consideration of the facts presented— were adapted to their own adjudicative needs.

The demarcation between medical and legal realms called for by legal specialists was significant. For instance, the jurists invoked principles of tort law that recognized "that the question of causal connection should not be answered exclusively according to the viewpoint of medical experts but also independently in keeping with the legal premises that come into consideration in this matter."[155] A German Federal High Court (Bundesgerichtshof; henceforth BGH) ruling made in 1958 can also be cited. Precisely because physicians were guided not by a legal concept of causation but by one grounded in the natural sciences, the court had "to be aware that the question of a causal connection needed to be decided in keeping with legal principles on one's own responsibility—and, naturally, with due appreciation for medical knowledge." As the BGH argued, the object was to avoid the danger of "not correctly recognizing the problem relevant for *law*" because of a reliance on the scientific rationale of the medical experts.[156]

When it came to compensation, however, the lawyers did not wish to be misunderstood, as Berlin senior governmental councilor W. Brunn made clear in 1960: "It follows from the principles established in tort law that in compensation law persecution, as a culpable external event the effects of which are to be legally judged, must not remain unconsidered if it is accorded more than marginal significance alongside other causes." If one shared Brunn's thinking, and drew on a very recent ruling of the BGH (May 18, 1960) for support, this had concrete implications: if a doctor denied a causal relationship between a mental health problem and persecution by asserting that the basic precondition for such symptoms was located in the individual's personality structure and abnormal experiential processing, then, from the legal standpoint, that would by no means justify the rejection of a reparations claim. Rather, Brunn indicated, what had to be relevant for the reparation authorities and the courts was whether "the abnormal hereditary disposition had not instead 'first become active as an effective cause by being rendered manifest, set into effect, through the persecution.'" Furthermore, referring once again to the BGH judgment, Brunn insisted that according to the court's opinion a causal relationship was to be affirmed as long as it had not been ascertained "that the abnormal disposition would have also taken effect in the absence of persecution."[157]

The reversal of the burden of proof associated with this,[158] which demanded that doctors prove that "the hypothetical event would have occurred with certainty,"[159] allowed the legal profession to override the medical statements that pointed to hereditary factors as a sine qua non for the health problems that required explanation. In addition, in using the formulation "hereditarily determined illness in the actual sense of the term," the BGH ruling had created a concept that contrasted the very broad medical usage of "hereditarily determined illness" with a stricter legal definition. This definition restricted hereditary illness to cases where it was "*certain* that it is based on a pathological disposition that has become manifest."[160] This created a way to limit the debate over whether health damage was "constitutionally determined" to the rare "genuinely hereditary diseases."[161] In German psychiatry during the early 1960s, this was thought to include schizophrenia, although doctors meanwhile conceded that in cases where severe mental upheaval had been very recent, the external event could also be considered a catalyzing factor.[162] When conflicts emerged, the BEG could be cited, which eased the burden of proof through section 28 in conjunction with section 15 (2). Accordingly, persecution could be assumed to be the cause of health problems when the impairment had emerged in the persecuted individual during or directly after deportation.[163]

Finally, particularly in the case of "neuroses," the agnostic position taken by psychiatrists such as Hermann Witter or Kurt Schneider seemed useless to the legal profession in terms of adjudication. Judges were averse to an approach characterized by the assertion that medical opinion in the question of causal relationship was always based on a value judgment. They considered it their prerogative to make evaluation decisions and expected the medical experts to provide no more than a "clarification of the scientific context."[164] For this reason, it ultimately made more sense to follow the approach of a psychiatrist like von Baeyer, who insisted on use of his strictly "scientific methods and knowledge" and—knowing that adjudication was increasingly favoring the recognition of mental illness—openly acknowledged that "the 'general human dimension,' for instance, the moral obligation to offer reparations to persecuted persons," was self-evidently the "responsibility of the political, legislative, and judicial authorities."[165] In addition, for judges in compensation cases who had to decide whether a persecuted individual with a health impairment had possibly slipped into mental illness due to his attitude,[166] it was an advantage when medical experts claimed to be able to empirically determine the freedom of human will. Here, only "gnostics" like von Baeyer saw the task as resolvable. While they excluded the "degree of certainty claimed in scientific-mathematical knowledge," they asserted that it was possible to achieve "'approximate clarification' of psychopathological phenomena through psychological understanding, empathy, and constructive modeling." Here, the protagonists of this methodological extension in psychiatry began a triumphal march within jurisprudence that inversely lent legal weight to their shift of standpoint within the discipline of psychiatry.[167]

The need for the most consistent adjudication possible rendered part of the professional psychiatric controversy obsolete and was probably also the decisive reason behind the concluding regulation within the Final Federal Indemnification Law of 1965, which incorporated the so-called "concentration camp presumption" (KZ-Vermutung) as section 31 (2). This amounted to a special regulation for former concentration camp inmates because—in contrast to formerly ghettoized persons and those held in prisons—it favored them by presuming that if earning capacity was reduced by at least 25 percent, then the persecution-related amount of the reduced earning capacity equaled exactly this 25 percent. Proof was not required. Demonstrating a causal relationship with persecution continued to be necessary only for greater reductions of earning capacity.[168] The final law made clear that it was based on changes in the status of psychiatric knowledge, and it allowed former concentration camp inmates whose compensation claims had been denied to apply again.[169] Finally, in 1968 the BGH decided that recognition of experientially reactive suffering was no longer contingent upon compelling association with the experience of "especially serious and long-term" violence. This decision rendered obsolete the often controversial but previously unavoidable question of when it was possible to speak of a "constellation of extreme experience." At the same time, the BGH made clear that the effects of Nazi persecution that characterized the lives of survivors after 1945 qualified for reparations as persecution-related illnesses.[170]

These regulations tended to satisfy pressure from abroad, increasingly stemming primarily from American psychiatrists[171] and Jewish associations and their compensation attorneys. This did not mean the end of psychiatric rejections of applications for recognition of mental suffering or of protests over such decisions. One psychiatrist who would experience them on a massive scale was New York–based medical examiner Hans Strauss, who, as we have seen, was one of the first to call attention to chronic mental problems among survivors of Nazi persecution and had spoken up forcefully for recognizing their persecution as the source of their illnesses. As late as 1974, Jewish survivors whose cases he had evaluated contacted the West German general consulate with sharply worded accusations.[172]

With respect to returnees, for whom neither the BEG nor the BGH's decisions applied, various parties now considered whether the opening of "prevailing doctrine" could be transferred to disability law that was relevant in their cases. In 1959, in the context of a reorganization of the BVG, the Ministry for Displaced Persons, Refugees, and War Victims had approached the responsible office in the Ministry of Labor regarding an easing of the burden of proof for returnees. Apparently the request was first made by the Waldheim-Kameradschaftskreis (Waldheim Comrades' Circle), a group of former inmates in Soviet prison camps, which proposed formulating "a regulation for the BVG . . . that was similar to the BEG," so that "all health disorders that surfaced during imprisonment and internment and for a certain period thereafter are in principle considered the results of damage when not proven to the contrary." Senior state medical officer Dr. Goetz reacted defensively, arguing that "such a legal presumption would contradict the causal thinking underlying the care of disabled veterans."[173] He was evidently not the only official to resist the proposed easing of burden of proof, as it was incorporated into neither the first reorganization of West Germany's legal regulations concerning disabled veterans, which became effective in 1960, nor in any of the subsequent similar alterations.[174]

Other special provisions in the BEG that carried weight for the recognition of health impairment were likewise not incorporated into veterans' disability law. This was the case with the "concentration camp presumption." Despite all efforts made by the German Association of Returnees, no equivalent was created in the BVG for extreme forms of POW internment.[175] In addition, the Federal Social Court (Bundessozialgericht, henceforth BSG) continued to interpret the concept of "essential concurrent cause" more strictly than did the BGH, which evaluated this differently in the framework of the BEG, thereby facilitating the granting of compensation in cases of "hereditary illness." In veterans' disability cases, such recognition depended on whether the physicians actually went so far as to assert that the emergence of a disorder that was considered "hereditary" could be attributed at least 50 percent to the physical or mental stress of the war or internment.[176] The total number of differences between the two interpretive frameworks was actually substantially higher.[177]

The different legal systematics underlying the separate bodies of reparations law and disability pension law offered sufficient reason for the divergent development of policies pertaining to the recognition of mental problems in the victims of Nazism and among disabled veterans. As we have seen, this divergence, which continued during the 1960s, had in part already begun to take effect in the second half of the 1950s.[178] Attempts to make a transfer were in fact undertaken, however, with the BSG issuing a series of rulings in the late 1950s that gave greater weight to forms of mental reaction in assessing the presence of war-related damage.[179] And in its 1956 wording the BVG itself included a passage to that effect: in subsection 1 of a new section 30, it stipulated that in assessing reduced earning capacity—which in any case was to be judged according to "*physical* impairment in general professional life"—"the effects of accompanying mental symptoms and suffering" were to be considered.[180] The BSG went even further, in the process directly contradicting some tenets of the labor ministry. Thus, in an October 1958 decision, the court declared:

> Emphasis must not be placed exclusively on whether or not the type and degree of the accompanying mental symptoms are medically substantiated when a general standard is applied. Mental reactions inevitably always involve a subjective factor that therefore needs to be evaluated not only according to an average standard that is considered "normal," and hence in general terms, but also individually.[181]

The following year, in connection with a suicide, the BSG was even clearer: "There is no such thing as an 'average person' and therefore no such thing as an average standard," the judges stated, insisting again that a "human being can always only be legally judged according to his individual constitution." In disability pension law, they observed, that was not called into doubt to the extent it involved physical reactions. A person who suffered from heart problems as a result of military service was not judged on the basis that "according to a generalizing standard his heart was not so resilient." "In the field of mental illness, in principle the same must be upheld," the federal judges explained, reinforcing the point that in this area as well it was only a matter of "how this particular person could and should have reacted according to his personality structure."[182]

Such a revaluation of the individual and of subjective feelings in disability pension law, which had already had an impact on decisions of the BGH in reparations cases,[183] also offered an opportunity to curtail German psychiatry's "prevailing doctrine" in respect to returnees, which is to say, the unfailing validity it presumed with respect to the virtually unlimited resilience of the human psyche. In 1960, the Bavarian state social court therefore legally defined the BVG's central concept of "health damage" to the effect that "mentally caused, physically demonstrable functional disorder"—for instance, psychogenic paralysis—could itself constitute "a health disorder or health damage within the meaning of the disability law." In so doing, the court was rejecting the restrictive application of the concept still customary among leading physicians and psychiatrists active in the disability pension field, who continued to adhere to the old psychiatric definition, namely, that "disease" existed only in the physical realm and that purely mental disorders therefore had no "pathological value."[184] Doubtless this perspective was no longer universally held in Germany, and the court was bolstering the shift in perspective. Mentally caused, physically demonstrable functional disturbances could indeed be accorded such "pathological value," as long as they had "developed independently of 'conscious' volition," "and if the person affected" was "not in a position to overcome his mental abnormalities in the sense of self-correction."[185]

Compared to the concept of the "pension neurotic" that the practice of disability medicine used as an orientation point, and measured against the prevailing psychiatric principles applied in the assessment of returnees, this certainly represented an opening in terms of evaluating mentally caused symptoms, which the professional legal discussions had previously, as a rule, treated simplistically under the rubric of "neurosis."[186] Conversely, a consistently articulated principle continued to draw the line: "When 'neuroses' are essentially the result of wish-determined ideation, when the clinical picture involves wish reactions or compensation reactions (so-called genuine 'pension neuroses')," then, according to the rulings of the social court up to the highest level, a causal connection with experiences from war and imprisonment was "as a rule" to be rejected.[187] In spite of that, determinations were now only permitted on the basis of an individual examination, and the rulings provided that the medical experts were no longer to ignore the question of an individual's personal capacity to withstand stress.

Despite this tendency toward alignment in the treatment of "neuroses" within social and civil law, and despite the legal call for individual scrutiny, which included cases covered by the BVG, no truly deep-seated change in court decisions regarding returnees took place over the following years. This despite rulings by the highest social courts that corresponded to views held by some representatives of psychiatry. On the basis of their observation of the long-term mental symptoms of survivors of Nazi persecution, some of the psychiatrists spoke out in a general sense for the necessity of a more open psychiatric reading of mental disorders. Walter von Baeyer in any case raised the matter at an early point in the debate:

We . . . must not forget that damage that is similar in cause and structure to the persecution-related damage to be discussed here can also be encountered among war victims. . . . My personal opinion is that in cases of psychogenic disorders in war victims as well, a differentiated form of consideration and judgment should be called for, namely, a distinction between noncompensable neuroses that are based on a reaction pattern, and those certainly far less frequent mental disorders where compulsive attribution of meaning with its unavoidable consequences can be demonstrated in a biographically convincing manner.[188]

That was no concession to "war victims" in general, but only, as von Baeyer explicitly stated, to those who "had been forced to live without hope for years in prisoner of war camps, labor camps, and penal camps, under inhumane conditions."[189] The "late" and "very late" returnees from Soviet imprisonment were being referred to here. But in the public debate, even the psychiatrists who had begun to appeal for such an opening referred to this group only very rarely. Rather, they showed themselves concerned with underscoring that "those who were racially and politically persecuted started from a completely different position than the war and insurance neurotics,"[190] convincingly demonstrating the "unique and incomparable" aspect of the persecuted individuals' "experiential situation,"[191] and explaining to skeptics the completely "new element" one was encountering in the mental disorders of the persecuted.[192] For this reason, there was no lack of affirmations of prevailing doctrine being offered at the same time. For example, in 1963 we find Ulrich Venzlaff vehemently demanding that the valid proposition of the limitless resilience of the human soul was "be called into question under special circumstances." This had been confirmed by the evidence of the "pathological value of long-term or residual mental disorders" resulting from Nazi persecution. Yet at the same time, we find him insisting as well that "based on overwhelming medical experience it can hardly be doubted that experiencing an accident, participating in combat, or enduring terrorist threats (a bombing campaign, enemy occupation) for a limited time does not lead to lasting psychic changes."[193] Venzlaff continued to be convinced that after World War II "millions of people" had once again offered proof of this.[194]

Von Baeyer likewise differentiated between various groups, stating flatly that "trauma [did not] equal trauma, stress [did not] equal stress." Objecting to any schematism, he emphasized the broad range of possible reactions to even "serious loss, acute threat to life, physical torment, situations of chronic deprivation," and, for instance, the "radical reduction of economic and social status" as a result of war and flight.[195] Above all, he insisted on not losing sight of the different situations facing disabled German veterans and the victims of Nazi terror. According to von Baeyer, the development of persistent mental disorders, which were not to be equated with "neurosis" in the usual understanding of the term, depended on "the way" the individuals were "existentially affected." And in this point he saw grave differences: "In general," he explained, "at least for adults, offsetting options remain, because there are agencies to aid and rescue them; a community is maintained; no total deprivation of rights and dignity takes place; there is hope for better times, and not every last thing has become meaningless. For most of those affected by totalitarian persecution 'the way' they were traumatized is different. . . . This traumatization [is] designed . . . to destroy existential security completely because it is calculated to remove everything a person could hold onto, in which he could still find meaning and value."[196]

Thus, the psychiatrists who actually wanted to initiate a new professional approach to late sequelae or ongoing mental disorders only accommodated the need expressed by the legal profession to "finally [create] uniformity in the evaluation of the neurosis problem across all areas of the law" to a very limited extent.[197] In fact, it sometimes seemed they did not stint on words of warning. Ulrich Venzlaff, for instance, assured his legal colleagues that the traditionally strict medical and legal practice vis-à-vis psychiatrically based disability pension claims was called for not only on medical grounds but also for reasons of social responsibility. Invoking experience gained in both world wars and, in the same breath, a large body of expert reports on accidents, Venzlaff insisted that even in cases where it initially seemed as if someone had suffered "experientially acquired mental damage," ultimately "a goal-directed orientation of the will could not be overlooked." He explained that *"flight into illness"* was always the true backdrop of the complaints presented "to escape from a dangerous situation (example: war tremblers), to evade the demands of everyday life as a social insurance pensioner, to hide one's incompetence in life behind a guiltlessly suffered fate, or simply to gain material advantages from the fact of being insured." For such reasons, Venzlaff continued to have no doubts: "Without the rigorous rejection of claims due to such disorders on the legal basis of the September 24, 1926, ruling of the Reich Insurance Agency, we would have had to . . . reckon with an extremely serious upheaval of our social system, which is constructed on solidarity." In Venzlaff's view, therefore, the agency's decision needed to be "fundamentally affirmed even today," although he considered its formulation outdated.[198]

In actuality, in the early 1960s psychiatric opinions on the general question of how to evaluate exclusively mental disorders in disabled veterans or accident victims were often much more closely aligned than was apparent in the heated debate over reparations for survivors of Nazi persecution. As a result, in disability pension cases jurists usually found themselves in a different situation than in the reparations proceedings. In order to maintain their ability to make decisions, they needed to search for legal justifications and pay far less attention to the constant arguing among medical evaluators. In various cases, it was even becoming clear that legal experts who thought the BSG had gone too far in some pension decisions regarding "neurotics" were pressing for greater consideration of what was still deemed prevailing psychiatric doctrine in order to correct rulings they perceived as all too liberal. For example, Judge Günter Hennies of the Berlin state social court was critical of an August 1963 BSG judgment concerning disabled veterans. It implied, in his opinion, that it was easier to obtain a pension for "neurosis" within the framework of the Federal Law on War Pensions than under compensation law. This was because the BSG lacked a "clear indication that the damage suffered had to have reached an unusual level." Hennies reminded his readers that in its "neurosis" report the Medical Advisory Board of the labor ministry had required the identification of such a level of damage for recognizing pension eligibility. Adhering to this guideline was nothing short of imperative. Ultimately, he indicated, the courts responsible for social jurisprudence should not forget what the BGH had stipulated for receipt of reparations: "violent acts of extraordinary severity and duration—with an accumulation of experiences of fear and horror" that had affected the individual "in the deep layers of his personality." What was required, cited Hennies, was that a "fundamental restructuring of the personality" had taken place.[199]

This was meant to be the basic position of the disability pension physicians, as stipulated in the above-mentioned guidelines for medical evaluation in welfare administration. In some passages, the phrasing of the new 1965 edition creates the impression of having adopted the BSG's decisions. For example, explanations have been altered concerning the stipulation that when physical injury has occurred mental symptoms and suffering should also be taken into account in assessing reduced earning capacity. The new version specifically pointed out that the evaluators were legally required "to *devote special attention to* the impact of *the damage on the personality and the individual fate of the affected individual* (e.g., impairment of social functioning, reduction of a positive sense of life)."[200] The phrasing here was nearly legal. But in contrast to the BSG judges, the disability pension physicians did not extend the guidelines to cover "psychogenic reactions," which, they indicated firmly, "are not mental symptoms in this sense." At another point, however, they at least allowed for providing treatment for relief of an "abnormal mental attitude."[201] All told, the guidelines remained rather strict in respect to the recognition of purely mental disorders as war-related suffering. In the case of diagnosed "neuroses" there was only one exception: when the war coincided with a person's childhood and the "neurotic disorder" had already emerged at that time, then the evaluation guidelines did not entirely exclude the possibility of a causal relationship with the effects of war.[202] Otherwise such recognition was only provided for in cases of "experientially determined personality change." The new inclusion of this diagnosis into the disability pension catalog of "medical conditions" clearly demonstrated that assessment of states of mental suffering had begun to evolve. However, a brief explanatory paragraph reflected great caution: "After extreme, very protracted mental stress, in exceptional cases irreparable experientially determined personality change is possible. Diagnosing this requires especially careful professional medical examination."[203]

Various jurists may well have remained skeptical about the extent to which psychiatrists were actually in the position to consistently distinguish between different forms of "neurosis" in addition to "experientially determined personality change."[204] In the mid-1960s, the BSG judges finally agreed that "stringent standards" needed to be met to exclude the "suspicion of deceit," [205] and that it was "not permissible to award compensation or a pension for every abnormal mental attitude."[206] In 1965, five years after the publication of the so-called neurosis report to which he had substantially contributed, Friedrich Panse likewise intervened and expressed his support in this aspect of the medical-legal debate.[207] At a medical conference, he outlined the practical consequences of the diverging evaluative approaches in the United States and West Germany, in order to once again underscore the potential dangers of overly lenient evaluation practice. His above-mentioned American colleague, Lothar Kalinowski, served as his crown witness.[208] In 1950 Kalinowski had already critically pointed out that some 49 percent of all discharges from the American army were for mental reasons[209]—with dramatic consequences, as Panse now recalled. Not only had a majority of this 49 percent consisted of "war neurotics," he explained, but a portion of them were still being clinically treated in special psychiatric Veterans Health Administration (VA) hospitals—he had seen it himself in 1956. "How much misery is, in fact, contained in the fate of people who persevere in their subjective awareness of illness because of mistaken medical diagnosis," Kalinowski concluded, before once again praising a restrictive treatment strategy: "In West Germany, where until now the traditional guidelines in the assessment of neurosis have enjoyed general acceptance, not even 2 percent of pensioned, disabled veterans owe recognition of their pension entitlement to psychiatric and especially psychogenic disorders."

Contrary to what has been suggested in earlier historical studies, the regulations for German war victims were, broadly speaking, anything but generous, nor can it be sweepingly asserted that a stubborn attitude of refusal widely determined the treatment of reparations cases.[210] As we have seen, the very opposite was the case, at least when it came to compensation claims. Granted, there were doctors who pointed to similarities that emerged under certain conditions between imprisonment in a concentration camp and in a POW camp. As a result, delayed mental damage could in principle not be excluded following POW internment. However, this argumentation cannot be considered exclusively and hastily in the framework of an effort to equate the victim status of the two groups involved, that is, essentially to view disabled German veterans and the victims of Nazism as equal in terms of the suffering they endured and therefore to treat their entitlement vis-à-vis the state as equal. There were such voices as well.[211] Still, we need to keep in mind that such views were especially prevalent among the "reformers," who, more than their colleagues, had begun to free themselves from the "national confinement" of their profession. Walter von Baeyer and Ulrich Venzlaff, together with Hans-Joachim Herberg and Helmut Paul, come to mind most readily here, with Helmut Paul serving as a particularly good example. He was a member of the medical-scientific advisory board of the Association of Returnees and one of the very few German doctors who in the 1960s carried out studies of the mental consequences of POW internment.[212] At the same time, he was one of the only German doctors to try to inform the German medical community of the findings of research on health damage incurred through persecution, deportation, and concentration camp imprisonment that was being carried out by colleagues in Eastern Europe and elsewhere in Western Europe and was being reported for the most part at international medical conferences under the aegis of the International Federation of Resistance Fighters.[213] Despite all understandable attentiveness to a possible equation of suffering, such comparisons often caused no offense within the international scientific debate.[214] At an international conference organized in 1965 on the mental suffering of victims of persecution and survivors of the atomic bombing of Hiroshima, American psychiatrist Henry Krystal even spoke up on behalf of Ulrich Venzlaff when an American internist turned the discussion to German prisoners of war in the Soviet Union and skeptically addressed the opinion long prevalent among German doctors that all mentally caused symptoms subsided after several years.[215] "The view that all the veterans became well after a year or two is also familiar to us in our own Veterans

Administration, and is so much wishful thinking," declared Krystal before the plenum, adding, with a view to the German prisoners that "when we realize that the emotional after-effects are produced by the psychic reality of the people involved, we can anticipate aftereffect syndromes."[216]

This manner of argumentation was unquestionably aligned with the view of German psychiatrists who, like Venzlaff and von Baeyer, were speaking out for a methodological shift in their profession. In addition to that, von Baeyer and his colleagues Heinz Häfner and Karl Peter Kisker saw sufficient cause to trace a wide arc in comparing the experience of some POWs with, as they put it, "the tribulation of National Socialist persecution." At the beginning of their book entitled *Psychiatry of Persecuted Persons* (*Psychiatrie der Verfolgten*) they indicated that "particularly in the prison camps of the Soviet Union and those in Communist China and Korea, much took place that was entirely comparable to the horrors of the concentration camps, just as, on the other hand, numerous Polish, Russian, and other prisoners of war in German captivity during World War II were exposed to camp terror and mass annihilatory reactions that defied all customs and laws of war."[217] Here von Baeyer, Häfner, and Kisker were able to draw on a large body of literature that had meanwhile appeared inside and outside Germany. One study with shocking findings had just been published by Robert Jay Lifton: American soldiers who had been captured by the Communist Chinese in the Korean War had been subject to "brainwashing."[218] Von Baeyer and colleagues spoke in this context of "methods of terrorist indoctrination aimed at the political 'conversion' of prisoners" that was "virtually unparalleled under National Socialist terror."[219] However, if one looked back in the mid-1960s at the interest in the psychology and psychopathology of POW internment generated during World War I, the studies produced at that time seemed to have produced "relatively modest results."[220]

Hence, although the Heidelberg psychiatrists showed themselves convinced that living conditions in World War II POW camps were incomparably harsher than before, and that there were many references in the literature to "psychopathological deviations from the norm" during internment, they presented the findings that had been gathered up to that point only with caution. The picture seemed incomplete to them; there was a lack of scientific evidence. This applied above all to the question of the purely mental long-term effects that, as they themselves emphasized, played such a key role in the study of persecuted individuals they were presenting. In any case, in the view of these psychiatrists the chapter on POW internment in *Psychiatrie der Gegenwart* (*Contemporary Psychiatry*), one of the most important reference works in the profession, did not provide a satisfactory answer to the question involved. They concluded: "The question of *permanent* restructuring of the personality without a pathological correlation in the brain cannot . . . be clearly decided on the basis of the available psychiatric-neurological examinations of war prisoners." For this reason, their assessment remained that "even today, evaluation in the framework of welfare law is largely based on the traditional idea that permanent experientially reactive damage only appears in the form of purposive reactions or neuroses without pathological value in the meaning of welfare law."[221]

Theoretically, the extent to which the mental consequences of war would be identified in the future remained an open question. Yet it was not easy to recognize that discovering an answer to this question would generate a lively research interest in the psychiatric community. Ironically, in Germany it was the apologists for the old "prevailing doctrine" who opposed a possible acknowledgment of war-related mental problems in returnees and civilians by citing the unique nature of the concentration camp experience. In the controversy with the jurists, none other than Hermann Witter countered the social court judges by arguing that from a psychiatric perspective it was only possible to recognize a "special position" for "those reparations claims made in the framework of the BEG." He explained that the crucial point "from a medical-psychological perspective" was "the presence of not only short-term threats to health and life, but also long years of mental stress of the most extreme sort as a damaging factor." It was clear to everyone, he believed, that such "persistent mental stresses" should be evaluated entirely differently "than the experiences of fright and fear that are generally discussed in accident insurance, and also in veterans' disability cases." "In the case of victims of political and racial persecution, another consideration comes into play, namely, that the culpability of those inflicting the damage was exceptionally great."[222]

Accordingly, when the mental suffering of Wehrmacht veterans was under discussion or being evaluated, many psychiatrists and disability pension officials pointed out that the situation of individuals persecuted under Nazi terror was incomparably more hopeless and was not even remotely due to guilt on the part of those affected.[223] This would form the basis for the denial of claims within the framework of veterans' disability pensions. Toward the end of the 1960s, two young psychiatrists at the Bonn University Clinic judged evaluative practice to be so rigid they found it necessary to insist in an article that recognizing long-term mental damage in the case of deported civilians and prisoners of war could at least be justified "in especially grave cases."[224] In itself, their appeal shows how difficult it had become to circumvent the issue of equating the fate of German army veterans with that of survivors of Nazi persecution, if one wished to gain recognition of permanent mental change for former German soldiers as well. The argument of noncomparability of both the situation and stresses endured had quickly established itself as a useful instrument for rejecting claims made in the framework of veterans' disability pensions, whether on financial, moral, or medical grounds. Thus, in one case the two psychiatrists established the connection between a veteran's mental symptoms and the war by indicating that "all the factors were present that were used to explain the extreme mental stress endured by concentration camp inmates, such as uprooting, deprivation, the threat of annihilation, loss of homeland and family members, complete humiliation and loss of rights, etc." And in another case as well, that of a female returnee, they insisted on the presence of symptoms that were "virtually identical with those seen in individuals who have been "persecuted by the Nazis."[225] The office for disabled veterans' care refused to recognize such parallels. According to the authors' account, it denied the claim on the grounds that "in this case mental and physical stress comparable to that of a concentration camp cannot be assumed." In the end, the office indicated, in the Russian forced labor camps "no specific annihilation of human life had been planned," and "malnourishment and mistreatment" had been caused exclusively "by the inability of the custodial power . . . to procure sufficient food, shelter, etc. during those years."[226]

The protest of the two psychiatrists that the group of injured individuals they were concerned with represented "victims of the Third Reich, even though they may have worn uniforms," was inherently articulated from a highly defensive position because the political-moral question of recognizing Nazi crimes and their destructive force was always interwoven with the debate over mental suffering. The Bonn psychiatrists pointed out to the medical experts that "deliberating whether one individual or another contributed to his own fate would mean posing the question of guilt and expiation," and made an appeal that this problem, important as it was, should not be made a criterion for terming pension eligibility.[227]

We therefore see that the breakthrough in the question of acknowledging delayed or permanent mental consequences of stress—not only in an international context but also in the West German debate over the comparability of long-term mental damage among surviving camp inmates and POWs—was increasingly restricted to the victims of Nazism. The repatriated veterans, a group of national "victims" who dominated the debate over the consequences of the war within Germany during the 1950s, appeared to have increasingly moved to the background, whereas cases involving individuals formerly persecuted under the Nazi regime were gaining increasing attention and growing acknowledgment of these persons' continued mental suffering. This was a reflection of, among other things, the good publicity received by the attention focused on Nazi crimes, beginning with the Einsatz unit trials in Ulm in 1958, and continuing with the Frankfurt Auschwitz trials in 1963 and 1965. Presumably, however, the largely successful integration of the returnees into West Germany's "economic miracle" also played a role. In any event, from the mid-1960s onward nearly all debate surrounding the medically compensable pension claims of Wehrmacht veterans was absent from the professional journals. Above all, their mental symptoms raised no attention to speak of within the discipline, whereas the altered perception of symptoms in those who survived Nazi persecution yielded a new scientific perspective on the limits of human endurance. At the same time the facilitated recognition of such claims helped focus public attention on the extreme violence and dehumanization of persecution under the Nazi regime. For this reason, public opinion beyond the professional realm assumed ever greater importance in evaluating the moral challenge that had always played a concurrent role in the professional discussion of claim recognition.

PART III

Mental Suffering and Its Changing
Acknowledgment in West German
Media: Public Negotiations, 1945–1970

CHAPTER 7

Repatriated Wehrmacht Veterans
in the Public Eye

As the analysis of memory fragments in Part I of this book has suggested, postwar West Germany was marked by an acute private awareness of the war and the destruction it wreaked on the very core of an individual. Generally, however, this did not surface in public accounts. Neither the battle for a "clean Wehrmacht," of which one was inclined to assure oneself in the veterans' organizations, nor the burgeoning literature of soldierly nationalism in the memoirs of former Wehrmacht generals during the 1950s left any space for that awareness.[1] Often, the private dark side of memories of the war found expression only in tension or overload within the family or in personal situations marked by crisis and self-doubt. That those directly affected and their relatives sought recourse in psychiatric certainties may have reflected that reality. Thus, the personal memory fragments we find in the psychiatric files can often be understood as constituting a counternarrative to public memory. Nevertheless, a central assumption of this book is that professional psychiatric knowledge of the war's consequences played a pivotal role in mediatizing this private knowledge in the rules of what could be mentioned in public memory culture.

As we have seen in Part II, the professional knowledge was embedded in a broad context of expectation in which medical logic, the feasibility of claims by Wehrmacht veterans, and the moral challenge posed by Nazi crimes had to be reconciled. Yet private knowledge of the war and imprisonment in the Soviet POW camps was initially the most important challenge for psychiatrists. The discipline had great difficulties freeing itself from a basic assumption that was examined above, namely that mental illness as a result of extreme violence generally resulted from a person's hereditary weaknesses and not from the experience itself. In the end, psychiatry could only overcome this assumption entirely in the case of those persecuted by the Nazi regime.

In a certain sense, an initially small, then growing number of West German psychiatrists drew on the conceptual figure that Venzlaff articulated as "experientially determined personality change" to reenact scientifically an assumption about the destructive effects of such violence that had already been preformed as private knowledge—although initially only for the victims of Nazism, a group that on political-moral and legal grounds could not be dismissed. Without having to impute instrumental intentions to this process, implementing the new interpretive model, with its manifest general public repercussions, had a noticeable effect on public acknowledgment of the long-term suffering of Holocaust survivors. Thus, the realm of the mentionable in general memory culture changed over the course of this process. In part, what changed was the public memory of the Nazi war of extermination, although it did not necessarily provide for direct expression of former soldiers' private knowledge of the war. Rather, what developed was a secondary feedback effect in which the private knowledge on the mental effects of the war was reshaped by professional discourse and only made available in public memory within the boundaries set by that discourse. Hence, while the perils of internment played a constitutive role in the returnees' narratives from the 1950s, indeed the long-term mental impairments of the returnees themselves, especially those incurred through the devastation of the war, were screened out for decades.[2]

When we look at the media's representation of both the war and its impact on postwar West German life, it confirms that the public perception and recognition of the mental suffering incurred by Holocaust survivors and Wehrmacht veterans moved on separate tracks. If we focus on film, the first thing that becomes apparent is a striking difference between the so-called *Trümmerfilme* ("rubble films") made between 1946 and 1949, and the work produced during the following decade, which turned away from conditions in devastated postwar society to the war the soldiers fought on the eastern front.[3] In this later phase, the crimes committed on the German side were nearly completely absent, as were difficult questions concerning life after mass death and murder—a sharp contrast to the early postwar films, all abridgement notwithstanding.[4]

In the rules governing the thematic content of rubble films, the perception of postwar German society, and especially of the returnees, seemed to blaze a trail that could hardly be reconciled with prevailing psychiatric doctrine, which, as discussed above, ruled out in a general sense a causal relationship between the war and subsequent mental symptoms. In numerous film sequences, the public was shown images that suggested otherwise. However, the cinematic narratives in play are not immediately apparent. Rather, interpreting the mediatization of the mental states depicted in these films calls for a close reading of the image and text sequences along with a proper contextualization within the framework of the period's scientific and political rules of what was permissible to say.

The mental distress of Wehrmacht veterans is especially striking in two films made in 1946, Wolfgang Staudte's *Die Mörder sind unter uns* (*The Murderers Are among Us*) and Gerhard Lamprecht's *Irgendwo in Berlin* (*Somewhere in Berlin*).[5] In Staudte's film, the male protagonist is Hans Mertens, a former officer who has returned to a destroyed Berlin after 1945 and seems to be falling apart because of his frightful war memories. Over an extended period, the film offers various clues about Mertens's torment, before the viewer learns it primarily involves a mass shooting of children, women, and men in the east that has become a permanent nightmare for him. Among such hints we find the following scene during a game of chess: When Mertens—drunk as he so often is—surveys the chessboard, the expression in his eyes suddenly changes. "Doesn't it look like a battlefield"? he asks. When his female opponent makes her next move, he advises her against it because she would lose two pawns [in German pawns are called *Bauern*, which also means "peasants"]. She replies, however, that she is saving her king. Mertens then becomes very upset and exclaims, "The battle cry is 'Save the King'—pawns (peasants) can go to hell as long as the king stays safe." In a rage, he throws the chessboard to the floor, shouts, "I hate this game," and then moves to leave the room. When another woman tries to calm him down, saying, "It's only a game, a completely harmless game," he lowers his voice and answers her while putting on his coat and hat: "From a harmless game with tin soldiers, there's a short, dangerous path that leads to a harmless air gun, to a harmless small-caliber sport pistol, and from there"—standing in the doorway now, he turns and raises his serious face—"directly to a mass grave."

The film is full of such sequences. Mertens is constantly unnerved by seemingly negligible things such as ordinary exchanges of words, everyday events, or objects, for example, when he is asked whether he's ever thought about starting to work again, or when he simply casts a glance at a Christmas tree. Sometimes he freezes, aghast; at other times he flies into a rage or becomes suddenly aggressive. A doctor in civilian life, Mertens feels unable to work, as we learn in one such episode. It is as if he is "a very special surgeon, one who cannot see blood, who no longer wants to hear the crying and groaning of tormented fellow human beings, and who knows that curing humanity does not pay." Finally, in the last part of the film, Mertens freezes at the Christmas speech of his former captain, Brückner, before a decorated Christmas tree. His thoughts flash back to the east, and at that moment he cannot stave off the memory of a massacre that took place three years before. Images from Christmas Eve 1942 appear before his inner eye: children, women, and men who are herded together on Brückner's orders, whose Christmas speech that year said to line them up against a wall and shoot them.

Such chains of associations where the war is revived in the minds of returnees as a result of verbal and visual stimuli—often cinematically reinforced through dissolve shots—are probably not as frequent in any other West German rubble film as in Staudte's *The Murderers Are among Us*. They are also present, however, in Lamprecht's *Somewhere in Berlin*. In this film, it is the returnee Illner who becomes furious at the sight of his son Gustav's toy tank. For a brief moment, as he holds the toy in his hands in disbelief and horror, only his facial expression darkens. But when Gustav proudly declares, "This can really shoot," Illner loses self-control, throws the toy to the ground, stomps it to bits, and yells at his son, who watches for some seconds with a stunned and frightened expression etched on his face.

In their own way, these rubble films show that returning to the civilian world was difficult for former Wehrmacht soldiers, and that quite a few of them remained "prisoners of the war" for months after it had ended and they had been released from one POW camp or another. It was a war that continued to play out in the minds of individuals, and neither Lamprecht nor Staudte hesitated to depict the parallel worlds that emerged as extreme and profound mental illness. In *The Murderers Are among Us*, former Wehrmacht officer Mertens thus seems to lose consciousness without any external reason. In his hallucinatory states, he is completely cut off from the outside world and completely at the mercy of the tormenting world within. The entire process plays out when Mertens visits a doctor, who is a former colleague, in a clinic. While the man is still speaking, Mertens suddenly closes his eyes. "What's wrong?" asks the doctor. But Mertens is unresponsive. In the next film sequence, he is lying unconscious on a cot. Then, in the presence of a nurse and the doctor, who is about to leave the room, Mertens suddenly begins to move, still unconscious: his entire body is trembling. First we hear him stammering, then shouting, "Captain, Captain, can you take back the order? . . . Listen . . . the screaming." Mertens raises his upper body, still unconscious, his eyes wide open. "The children, what do the children have to do with it? And the women, the way they're screaming . . . I can't, I can't do that!" After his outburst, Mertens falls back on the cot, still completely unconscious. At some point during the day he will regain consciousness.

In Lamprecht's *Somewhere in Berlin*, Wehrmacht veteran Steidel, who has entirely gone to pieces, likewise continues to live in the world of war, albeit in a completely different way. He is not even aware of his surroundings. Initially, viewers might take the scene simply as a nightmare. A man lies on a sofa, sleeping. Suddenly he begins to breathe heavily; his sleep becomes restless. War images emerge, soldiers running, shells exploding, smoke and artillery fire—combat on the front is raging in the man's dream. Steidel finally awakens, startled from his sleep, and rises to an upright position. Shown in close-up, his face already gives the viewer an indication of the war's physical and mental effect on the man. His left eye is damaged, perhaps useless, and his right eye shows no life. It is as if this veteran is in a complete stupor. He is still in the war. Steidel stands up, mechanically buttons the jacket of the uniform he continues to wear, puts on the steel helmet that is lying on a table. Still acting as if he were absent, completely distracted, he takes a few steps and places himself in the open doorway to the balcony. He stands straight as a ramrod, clicks his heels together, offers a salute, the palm of his hand raised to his helmet. Over the course of the film, Steidel will reappear a number of times, his mental condition unchanged.

Such images are often mirrored in the memory fragments of Wehrmacht veterans who were treated in psychiatric clinics for their abnormal behavior.[6] The scenes suggest that the mental state of parts of postwar society, the returnees in particular, was extremely precarious. We find examples of this sort in nearly every rubble film, for example, in Josef von Baky's 1947 film *Und über uns der Himmel* (*And the Sky above Us*), as it happens the first German film made in the American occupation zone. Here one returnee, Werner, suffers from psychogenic blindness, while Walter, another returnee who is just as young, is unusually introverted and brooding. Not even his vivacious girlfriend Mizzi is able to build up his enthusiasm. When Mizzi criticizes him for his "bad mood," he flatly denies it and then offers the following explanation: "It's not that I'm in a bad mood. Look, Mizzi, I've come back, but I have the stupid feeling there's a bullet's still whizzing behind me, and it keeps on whizzing. That's an uncanny feeling, understand? And one day it'll get me."[7]

The layers of evidently widespread feelings that were processed in such films seem at first to contradict the basic psychiatric assumptions of the time. Many early postwar German films give the impression that explaining veterans' mental problems in terms of earlier war experiences is self-evident. But closer examination of these films presents a different picture. Even in the early postwar cinema, the majority of people appear to have endured the ravages of the war, including Nazi persecution, without any mental problems whatsoever.[8]

Figures such as Steidel, the deeply troubled veteran, are exceptions, and

Somewhere in Berlin itself suggests that discussing them in impartial terms was not exactly a given. The veteran's mother in any event speaks only reluctantly about him and his condition. The children call him the "crazy man," and sometimes people complain when he appears in the apartment window. *Somewhere in Berlin* does not attempt to offer an in-depth critique of such reactions, although the film certainly does make an effort to counter some prejudices. Steidel is not a man anyone needs to fear. Viewers are meant to understand that this veteran is suffering a tragic fate. But even Steidel's mother, who admits in a conversation that her life no longer has any meaning—in contrast to when her husband died in Flanders in 1914—does not have a socially acceptable way of interpreting this suffering. It is a problem the film does not wish to address. The mother recoils from spelling out the illness. Accordingly, when Illner comes to visit, she hesitates a moment before leading him into the living room, where he is about to encounter her son. "My son—I guess you know about it?" she asks quietly, as if confidentially. She then describes his odd behavior in two sentences, but offers no explanation. In the end the film leaves the question unanswered as to how Steidel's mental condition should be interpreted from a medical standpoint. When good-natured Herr Eckmann asks Steidel's mother, who has confided him in complete despair, what the doctors' opinion is and whether "there isn't some kind of a cure," she does not answer. Helpless and dejected, she shrugs her shoulders It seems the doctors have given her no reason to have hope.

In *The Murderers Are among Us* as well, we are offered no medical reading on Mertens's sudden mental absence and hallucinations that would imply any sort of contradiction to the etiological explanations prevailing in German psychiatry. Observing the hallucinations, the doctor does register that they revolve around "some sort of war experience," but his further reaction does not unambiguously indicate that he establishes a causal connection between the war and the symptoms. In response to a nurse's empathic observation that "it must have been something terrible," which seems to point to such a connection, the doctor's response is markedly sober: "War is always something terrible" he answers tersely, almost drily. "Of course, I still want to speak with him. Let me know when he's returned to his senses. I won't take all that long," he continues, and then immediately goes back to his daily business.

If we consider the expectations these early films articulated in terms of postwar society and the returnees from the war and the POW camps, it therefore becomes apparent that the underlying assumptions regarding how to "normalize" the situation closely paralleled prevailing psychiatric doctrine of the day. There seems to be scarcely a single rubble film that does not reflect the conviction that even under the most difficult conditions, reconstruction on a small scale can be achieved through determination and willpower. Indeed, a characteristic feature of these films is that the characters on the screen redress and overcome the destruction of war. In the films' confrontation with a mental illness, which in a number of cases appears to be a consequence of the war, the moral reconstruction message suggests that emotional recovery as well depends on the individual's effort and will. For this reason, despite the apparently everyday images of mental states of emergency, in this context as well the idea emerges that a "normal" human is able to withstand the gravest experiences. Here the cinematic idiom again fuses with the basic professional psychiatric assumption that, thanks to innate regenerative capacities, in the absence of physical symptoms such experiences did not lead to long-term or late-onset mental illness.

Essentially, that was the basic tenor of early postwar cinema. In the case of the psychogenically blind veteran in *And the Sky above Us*, the film makes it clear that the former soldier's recovery firmly rests on determination to truly defeat the malady. At the same time, the films emerging in Germany during this very early postwar period left no doubt that those who didn't put forth the effort to mobilize their own forces and cooperate in tackling all the challenges were not especially well tolerated. Still, empathy is not entirely absent, with loving women primarily playing the empathic role. "There are wounds that are invisible and take a lot of insight, patience, and love to heal," declares camp survivor Susanne Wallner, who has fallen in love with the down and out—and often unfriendly—Mertens in *The Murderers Are among Us*.[9] In *Somewhere in Berlin* as well, it is the wife of returnee Illner who displays empathy as she holds the clothing her husband wore when he arrived home, shortly before, from a POW camp. "These are all just rags," she says to herself, before turning to her husband's brother Kalle and remarking, "He's been through so much. We have to see how we can get him back on his feet again." Her brother-in-law gives her an encouraging smile and answers, "We can do it," once again signaling the same support he has repeatedly provided over the past years. The film points to his willingness to help. Illner's brother is a friendly, hands-on person who has already revived his craft business. In his conversation with Illner's wife as well, confidence is written all over his face.

The figure of Illner stands in sharp contrast to his brother Kalle. Illner's exhaustion immediately after his return was still understandable to his family, as was his weakness, which could basically be explained through the prolonged hunger he endured in the POW camp. He had lost a great deal of weight; his suit had become far too big for him; it had been a long time since he had enough to eat. In a society where malnutrition was commonplace, the image of the emaciated veterans returning from POW camps in both east and west was broadly familiar. When mental changes were seen, malnutrition often served as a plausible explanation in a large number of individuals. The medical prognosis was that in "normal" cases, with improved nutrition, the mental disorder would resolve,[10] an assumption also thematically present in these films. But as early postwar rubble films also suggested to viewers, empathy had its limits, indeed had to have limits.[11] In numerous variations, the films conveyed the expectation that when symptoms emerged was precisely when those who had returned from war and imprisonment had to pull themselves together. One was both capable of and obligated to overcome oneself, not only for the sake of others but also to reconstruct oneself emotionally.

Work, that is, actively proving oneself in the reconstruction effort, emerges as the central theme of these films—it holds out the promise of renewal and a future for German society, indeed something like the promise of a new collective identity. Work is also portrayed as a path to personal recovery, whereby the ability to work is in principle assumed in every person who has not been physically injured. The films convey the message that working is a question of willpower, and the mobilization of willpower separates "normal" from "abnormal" behavior. Thus, in *Somewhere in Berlin*, we thus find Kalle criticizing his brother for his lethargy after he has returned. In a despondent voice, Illner explains to his brother that he intends to stop rebuilding the bombed garages: "I don't have the strength any more. It's all too much for me. Am I supposed to start all over again, right from scratch? . . . A little more rubble doesn't matter." Then Kalle—who in this scene at first continues to repair a window—sharply takes Illner to task: "Is that so! And your boy? You're not thinking at all about him? He believed in you so strongly. What you call rubble he was guarding, the entire time, tirelessly. He told everyone that when you came back, you'd rebuild everything. And now you're bailing out on him? That really makes me furious!" In a later scene, Illner tries again to justify himself to his brother. Everything would be "much easier if a person weren't so busy with himself. Outside for all those years, always filthy, then the imprisonment." The returnee's voice is dejected, monotone, as he explains that the only way he had been able to stand it was by constantly thinking of home. In his mind, he had seen everything the way it looked when he had gone off to the front. But now, he observes, everything that was built with so much trouble has been destroyed, is "simply no longer there." "That's a huge blow," he summarizes, and this especially true when he thinks of his family, of "how everything will turn out."

Hopelessness and perplexity are the feelings that characterize the returnee. Yet his brother, Kalle, remains strict: "That's in your hands alone."

Kalle knows what he is talking about. Viewers only understand this later in the film, when he listens to his worried nephew, little Gustav, who seems very depressed and listless following a friend's death. Kalle has advice to give: having lost a son, he as well has had to overcome pain and suffering. Viewers learn that his search for meaning proved fruitless and all too painful. "It was only work that helped me move past everything," he confides to Gustav." "You've got to find a task in life. Otherwise you'll never come to terms with yourself." Yet Kalle is not the only one in the film to have moved on in this way. Gustav's father also ultimately regains his courage through work and—the end of the film allows no other conclusion—actually "recovers." When dozens of children gather before his garages as a regular "reconstruction troop" and offer their help, Illner finds that their resolve is infectious. Kalle came up with the plan, and it works. In the last scene, his previously disheartened, apathetic brother delivers a spirited, strong blow with a pickax.

Viewers are presented with a similar process in *The Murderers Are among Us*. The moment an embittered Mertens manages to surmount himself and no longer clings to his feeling of incapacity, things start looking up again. When suddenly confronted with a medical emergency in which a mother is about to lose her child, he intervenes and performs an operation. His completely changed, upbeat mood afterward makes it more than clear that by starting to work again, the path to both healing and renewed life has been taken. Mertens again feels happiness. He can even tell Susanne Wallner that he loves her.

These early postwar German films also acknowledged that not every returnee could be healed. Wehrmacht veteran Steidel is such a case; his mental condition remains unaltered throughout the film. The same is true for Walter, the young returnee in *And the Sky above Us*, who suffers from an abiding feeling of being pursued by a bullet and cannot gain a foothold. The unstable young man is not equal to the demands of a reconstruction society and takes his own life. Overall, however, German films from this period promoted the idea that success was possible, and a fixation on mental changes and complaints was to be avoided. Assisting the returnees were the understanding of friends and relatives—who confronted the returnees with the right mix of patience and strictness—as well as professional help from a doctor and better nourishment. Nevertheless, what mattered above all was one's own will. This sort of cinematic narrative "framing" was aligned with psychiatry's doctrinal viewpoint, namely, that long-term mental disorders in the aftermath of the war were no cause for fear and could even be prevented, as long as an innate disposition did not stand in the individual's way or the diagnosis was not "mental illness," which according to the status of psychiatric knowledge had hereditary causes and followed its own laws.

The image of the returnees' regenerative capacity as promulgated by the press in Germany's early postwar society largely corresponded to this cinematic narrative. Occasionally, reports did present the general state of the population in ways diametrically opposed to what was seen in many film scenes, with their largely unburdened, hands-on, and healthy men, women, and children. For example, in the fall of 1947, an article in the *Süddeutsche Zeitung* entitled "Memory Loss and Weak Nerves" claimed to have identified two prominent problems that were making themselves felt everywhere, in both family and public life, as the "nonbloody wounds of the war."[12] Whether in the street or the streetcar, standing in line, or dealing with the authorities, wherever one went one increasingly encountered glum, irritable, and in part extremely nervous people. But the newspaper, which had consulted an expert, then also sounded the all-clear: according to a supposedly "well-known Munich neurologist with a typical 'popular practice,'" "'genuine' mental illnesses" continued to be rare. Readers were informed that the great majority of his patients suffered from "nervous disorders" that resulted from the poor nutritional situation and the difficult living conditions. In the doctor's experience, it was above all women who were affected, although *Süddeutsche Zeitung* quoted him as saying that he also saw "very serious depressive conditions in patients facing unresolved, interminable denazification proceedings."

In the early postwar press, indications such as this—even when indirect, as with this mention of the denazification proceedings—that the Nazi past could perceptibly alter an individual's state of mind were very rare; this in contrast to the private memory fragments, which frequently provide points of reference.[13] As the expert attested, as a rule the mental impairments involved could be counteracted. The recommendations he offered as a neurologist included calming and reassurance, along with a receptive ear, together with "bolstering their mental resistance to the given circumstances," and if need be "psychotherapy." Nevertheless, implicit in the *Süddeutsche Zeitung* article were doubts concerning whether such changes in mental state, especially when the symptoms were dramatic, could still be understood as "normal" behavior. "An experienced old clergyman" the reporter cited in this context supposedly had spoken of "three types of human beings" who emerged from the war and misery, which he named in the following sequence: "The person who goes his way determinedly, despite the highest degree of mental and nervous stress; the group that, based on past and present experiences, rejects all values and lives only for the day; and those who are driven by the times into a morbid search for the mystical or occult."[14]

The basic thrust of the article, namely, that war and the postwar period exerted considerable pressures on the "mental strength" of ordinary people, was certainly not negated—indeed it was reinforced. Yet the sequence of "types of human beings" unmistakably expressed a declining valuation. Without the slightest hesitation, one could view it as expressing the conviction that there was something wrong with people who are thrown off track in a lasting way by the events and circumstances of life. In fact, looking through the press litera-ture of the period, we can easily gain the impression that early postwar society was virtually obsessed by this idea. At least in the late 1940s this was notice-able. There were, of course, many reports about the fate of disabled veterans and others who were gradually returning from the POW camps, although there was more coverage given to the fate of German refugees and expellees from the east. Most of the reports, in any event, initially focused on the question of how many soldiers were actually still being held as POWs and in which camps they were interned,[15] with information on the poor, sometimes horrific condi-tions gradually filtering in.[16] The focus on the Soviet camps and the pillorying attitude did not emerge until about three years after the end of the war and were related in part to the process of virulent political instrumentalization accompa-nying the onset of the Cold War.[17] Much of the journalistic reporting until that point, even if it pointed to the ordeal the returnees had suffered and the prob-lems and worries they faced, still brimmed with optimism about the coping abilities the veterans seemed to have, which allowed them to leave their experi-ences behind and return to civilian life with confidence and vigor. For example, in October 1947 *Stuttgarter Zeitung* suggested that the state of mind of the re-turnees in a southern German convalescent home had changed very quickly.[18] Although they had initially seemed "completely apathetic and despondent," many of those admitted to this home soon recovered their courage. Allegedly, this was ascribable to, among other things, the "maternal care of the institu-tion's director." But the report also spoke of a second, weightier cause, and no one who realized the large number of returnees who had passed through the convalescent home since it was founded in 1945 could deny that this was a reason for an outright report of success. Since the fall of 1945, some thirteen thousand to fourteen thousand returnees had spent time there, most of them disabled and in need of physical care. But that had been no reason for despair on the part of either the veterans or their relatives, the report suggested. "The zeal for work of the recovering comrades is infectious: most of them volun-

tarily ask to be assigned work as soon as possible," the author cheerfully reported. Presumably he was guided by information furnished by the administration of the convalescent home, which proclaimed that the life of the entire
operation revolved around "the *principle of work therapy*": it had resulted in
"the best of experiences" for them.[19]

Scores of German newspapers during this early postwar period conveyed
the same credo as the films: one could fight back against mental symptoms.
Granted, assistance from society, above all from doctors, the family, and the
authorities, was surely necessary; more than a few reports issued direct demands for such support.[20] Yet if it was in fact available, according to such reports one could assume that after some time an improvement of mood and
outlook occurred even in severely ill returnees, provided that they had the will
to recover and to work. This assumption literally saturates journalism during
the initial postwar years and can be found in quite a number of articles. For
example, returnees from Russia are heard speaking up against the background
of their experiences in POW camps to warn against letting oneself "sink" and
become "soft." In their eyes—and many psychiatrists shared their view—what
lay behind that process was nothing other than embarking on a "flight into illness." The returnees' report was clearly meant to be taken as a general warning.
After all, the problem was evident in everyday life, as a former lieutenant colo-
nel explained in 1946 in *Die Zeit*: "When a person has a positive inner attitude
toward work—regardless of who has employed him or the purpose of his
work—curiously, his physical strength lasts longer."[21] The increasingly alarming newspaper reports that began appearing in 1947 about the health of the
malnourished returnees from Russia[22] were not in themselves seen as conflicting with the idea that within three months the men could be helped "to fully
regain their physical and mental ability to work."[23] And descriptions of the
disabled Wehrmacht veterans' general attitude showed the expectations placed
on their willpower and coping capacity, especially once they had been nursed
back to physical health.[24] For instance, a full year after the end of the war, *Die
Zeit* reported: "It really is true that optimism and joy in life pulsate in the home
for wounded and severely wounded soldiers. Hardly any of them are disheartened, hardly any of them have a bleak view of the future. Each of them believes
he will again be able to do what is expected of him." The article presented a
breathtaking picture of the maimed soldiers' coping ability: Seeing men with
joint injuries and those who had lost their hands laughing and yelling on the
sports field left the reporter with the impression that the "gravity of the misfortune and the difficulty of the times" had been forgotten. The director of the
clinic had probably expressed a similar view when he attested that a state of

despair was only an initial, temporary phase. "They quarrel with God, feel helpless, inferior, degraded, and expelled from the circle of the healthy," he explained, then immediately offered the reassurance that "in most cases, experiencing the happy atmosphere that prevails here is in itself enough to revive their optimism. Those who lack the will, who must be compelled to see that we want the best for them, are few and far between."[25]

This account of things was certainly intended to counteract possible reservations toward disabled veterans.[26] And yet, as was the case after the Great War, it also unmistakably entailed a "discourse of surmounting and normalization,"[27] a discourse that in Germany's early postwar years largely portrayed a societal reality in which the long-lasting mental effects of war and imprisonment were absent. Either implicitly or explicitly, the various journalistic accounts made it clear that if the returnees' behavior clashed with this general image, the assumption of "unwillingness" could be made; as well, there was even a possibility that the individual's "mental health" was not intact. This often amounted to a stigma, as becomes very clear, for example, when journalists refer to the "brain injured." Although the loss of productive capacity and the often-observed "change of nature" could easily be attributed to physical damage, a good many of these former soldiers evidently lived with a sense of having to defend themselves against the suspicion of being "insane."[28]

In the public discourse of this period, the interpretive framework for longer-term mental disorders was narrow. Several interacting factors were at play here. One of them was a psychiatric doctrine that offered little interpretive leeway between recovery through willpower and permanent damage based on hereditary causes. Apparently, this perspective corresponded to widespread basic assumptions within the society regarding the mental resilience of "normal" people, even in war. Deep-seated reservations and resentment toward the mentally ill would sometimes erupt, which was compounded by the task of renewal and reconstruction that was assigned to the veterans. This demanded strength and the will to perform, not weakness and apathy that, as documented in various debates of the period concerning gender relations, triggered concern if not contempt.[29]

As this last point indicates, such a stance did not by any means exclude talking about both the consequences of the war and postwar hardship. The heated debates about allegedly rising criminality are another example of this.[30] Yet public discourse during the initial postwar years remained largely silent about the experience of violence in the war, especially the war of extermination on the eastern front. It is very rare to find evidence that a gap was perceived between public rules for what could be mentioned in this respect and the returnees' personal interpretations of their mental burdens and changes. However, an article by Rüdiger Proske and Walter Weymann-Weyhe in a 1948 issue of the *Frankfurter Hefte* does point to such a perception: "Few people have considered the forces and experiences that have shaped us. It is known that there is a 'problem of the thirty-year-olds.' But all too often, that marks the end of the matter," lamented the article's two authors, who then added the following, which was a virtual outcry: "Experiences have been burned into us, the experiences we had in the war." They were hardly being discussed, the authors observed, "or only in a hushed manner, in the dark, when people believe they will not be eavesdropped on"—the fear was too great, they added, that what had been experienced could "be confused with [traditional] war experiences, with the esprit of front solders, the generation of front soldiers, the Association of Front Soldiers, the Stahlhelm, the SA." At this point the authors interrupted their enumeration to remark that they were different from the previous "generation," which had experienced World War I. "Until now, no one has described what we saw, and it will be a while before one of us does it, because we have not yet really come to terms with it."[31]

Finding language capable of expressing and communicating the experiences of war was not easy. Nevertheless, the article unmistakably aimed at testifying to the intense inner struggle the horror they experienced was causing for many returnees; indeed, they were striving to make themselves heard so that their inner torment and strife would be perceived and understood. To achieve this, the authors confronted the readers unmercifully with horrific images: "We have heard the roaring of the mortally wounded, seen brains drip from spades, and have vomited," they recounted in one passage; and somewhat later: "Some of our enemies from the time, they as well, were not able to withstand the barbarism of war. Russians cut some of our men up on a buzz saw while they were still alive. French soldiers beat others to death in bestial fashion or let them starve. And Americans ordered yet others to lie unclothed for a full day on the ground so that they almost burned to death under Georgia's sun. Auschwitz and Buchenwald. There is no offsetting process here. Of course not. The weight is too uneven. But the facts are two parts of a single truth . . . : Hitler in us."[32]

Indeed, no "offsetting" was intended here—no leveling of crimes. According to Proske and Weymann-Weyhe, it was a question of conveying the painful insight that Nazism had been able to make a "system" out of the "worst that lies in all of us," and it involved the difficult, humiliating, indeed, self-lacerating admission to have believed in a set of ideals—the fatherland, "honor, fidelity, courage, obedience"—that amounted to upholding the "honor of executioners." In the eyes of the two authors, it was Nazism that cheated them of their ideals by perverting them. Doubtless, it can be argued that this perspective falls short.[33] Nevertheless, the authors' comments are striking in their effort at honesty, which is so clearly fueled by their discomfort with the hypocrisy and superficiality of the public discourse. The authors counter this with a confession that cannot be denied a certain unsparing quality toward themselves. They explain:

> It is no small thing to have been cheated of the ideals in which you have believed. Unless you become cynical, you do not simply mourn for them but cling to them, secretly, even now. And then, torn between past and present, it is not easy for you to come to terms with a reality that has now been tarnished and does not possess anything especially uplifting. It's not so easy to cope with, especially when you quite often meet people who callously say those ideals no longer exist. That is not true. It is a question of where the front lines are drawn.[34]

For many German veterans, returning home did not mean a new beginning, the piece in *Frankfurter Hefte* made this amply clear. Rather, the horror of the war and the knowledge of the scope of the annihilation permeated one another and continued to exert their effect in inner images and mental changes. In addition, there was the experience of mass internment in POW camps and of hunger that, as they put it, turned "human beings into animals." Overall, however, encounters with others varied so widely that the repugnant and the impressive stood side by side across the nationalities.[35] The message to readers was that none of this could be reduced to a simple denominator, not to mention that those concerned were limited in their ability to convey at home the degree of their ongoing personal distress, the blow to their self-image, and their struggle for orientation in the world. Illusions about being reunited and life at home were quickly shattered. Yet this was not all the authors noticed: they also believed that there was a political explanation for the attitude in Germany that they perceived as defensive.

> We had other images than they. *We* sought to process them and grope our way into the future. *They*, above all the politicians, sought to begin where the development had once been interrupted. They were afraid of our war experiences and did not know that for many of us our only experience lay in war. If we turned to politics, they were mistrustful, and if we deviated from the "line," *their* line, they all too easily said we were "inexperi-

enced," "dangerous," perhaps even, depending on their political stance, fascists and militarists, and tried to push us out as quickly as possible. But in the next round they said, "We have to win over the young people." We are not fascists or militarists, we are neither reactionaries nor stubborn. We are only different.[36]

The subtext of the rubble films notwithstanding, this article expressed a desire for recognition that was not met by the postwar German public in the immediate aftermath of total military and political defeat. Since it was known that the Wehrmacht participated in mass murder in the occupied eastern regions and in crimes against Russian soldiers in German POW camps,[37] such restraint is not surprising. On political-moral grounds alone, an empathic form of attentiveness and interest would have hardly been possible, perhaps not even conceivable.[38]

In 1949, when the press increasingly reflected the intensification of the Cold War, and a new enemy emerged that was the same as the old one, there was a significant change in this respect. The veterans' publicly articulated claim to recognition of their suffering would now focus one-dimensionally on returnees from camps in the Soviet Union.[39] As an example, this can be seen in a report published early in 1949 by the weekly newspaper *Die Zeit*. It was entitled "'Stacheldrahtkrankheit' der Gefangenen" ("Prisoners' 'Barbed Wire Disease'")[40] and the author, Walter Hemsing, had already spoken out a number of times as an expert on the mental condition of the POWs—a status he claimed not only by virtue of being a professional psychologist but also because of his own experiences as a POW in England and his activities in support of returnees. His talks and essays on the theme were highly similar and literally identical over broad stretches. Remarkably, in his contribution to *Die Zeit* one central statement was now absent. Due to his own experiences and in light of "numerous factual reports" on "mental phenomena behind barbed wire," he had previously always maintained that the situation facing POWs, while deviating "in details" from one country to another, nonetheless "essentially" resembled that in England.[41]

Instead, the *Zeit* article began by observing that "there are far more than three hundred thousand Germans remaining in Russian POW camps," thereby setting the stage for the subsequent remarks concerning the "mental shock of spending an extended period behind barbed wire," which had presumably not yet been overcome by an even greater number of soldiers.[42] The article confronted the reader with a harrowing depiction of the mental stresses in the camps, a picture that substantially exceeded what most papers had previously described. For example, it mentioned the prisoners' constant fear "of becoming mentally ill." In the camps, "schizophrenia-like symptoms" were hardly avoidable, and, Hemsing further observed, in many cases the situation was hardly different after the men had returned to Germany. The "spiritual-mental changes" in the returnees were frequently expressed not only in their "silence, caginess, reserve, and an outright need for distance," but also in "irritability, uncooperativeness, stubbornness, and pedantry." The veterans' changed behavior could be so pronounced that it merited description as pathological and sometimes resembled "the external symptoms of schizophrenia." Finally, Hemsing pointed out that "new serious forms of mental depression" were nothing short of preprogrammed for the POWs after their release, for at that point they stood in fear of responsibility and freedom. Furthermore, they anticipated the disappointment they were bound to experience upon the return they had dreamed of. The returnees were, in short, "not yet equal . . . to the demands of a life that was free yet one that also lacked illusions."[43]

Since this diagnosis of the mental suffering had, in a sense, medically certified the severity of the stress the POWs faced, it is initially surprising that assessments of the same tenor were lacking in the following period, especially since there was no dearth of reports on the abusive and demeaning treatment of German prisoners in the Soviet camps. On the contrary, news that the remaining POWs prisoners had been condemned as war criminals or ordinary convicts, who consequently faced up to twenty-five years in Soviet labor camps, intensified the public debate in Germany over the alleged hardship and perceived injustice in the camps.[44] Nonetheless, we rarely encounter passages addressing the prisoners' mental stress, and when we do, they use terminology that differs from Hemsing's in that it makes references to schizophrenia-like states and "neurosis." Supposedly, one returnee outlined the situation that he and other prisoners faced in the POW camps as follows: "Under constant, tormenting hunger, and the torture of only being able to lie down and sleep in alternating shifts due to the tiny cells, our nerves suffered to the extent that our will to live was almost extinguished, and for each of us a bullet would have meant mercy."[45]

Although such "factual reports" may have actually been fictional, their conceptual terminology nevertheless conveyed a discrepancy in the interpretation of states of mental suffering, if not even a simmering interpretive conflict between the returnees on the one hand and practitioners of prevailing psychiatric doctrine on the other. In postwar patient files, one also finds reference to "nerves." The term was used by both veterans and their relatives to address mental disorders[46] and was an everyday counterdesignation to the usual psychiatric classification of mental disorders as "dispositional," that is, hereditary. For this very reason, Hemsing himself ultimately rejected the existence of "barbed wire disease." "There is no pathological personality change that was caused exclusively by internment as a POW," he emphasized. It was only a case of "dispositional pathological conditions" that had been aggravated by imprisonment. Here as well, then, it was merely "hereditary disposition" that was "taking effect."[47]

In public perception, sharpened as it was by the hardening of the Cold War and the length of Soviet internment, the effects of having been a POW called for a different, socially accepted yet also medically sustainable explanatory model. Here returnees from Soviet POW camps benefited from an interpretation that was circulating in medical discussions and postulated a direct interaction between an individual's mental and physical condition. This "psychosomatic" approach and its understanding of the mind-body problem seemed to more closely address the concerns of families of returnees who were perceived as being disturbed (or others who had been through the war) than the prevailing biomedical explanations.[48] In the public debates of the early 1950s, it becomes increasingly evident that the concern of the "psychosomaticists" with directing attention to the mind-body connection also coincided with the political practicality of claiming victim status for German prisoners in the Soviet Union.

The leading representatives of psychosomatic medicine—among them Viktor von Weizsäcker, Alexander Mitscherlich, and internist Arthur Jores, professor (and intermittently rector) at the University of Hamburg—certainly did not intend such political expediency.[49] Rather, the growth of West German public interest in the psychosomatic approach during this postwar period was inseparably bound to the so-called Doctors' Trial that had taken place in Nuremberg before a U.S. military court in 1946–1947, as one of the "Subsequent Nuremberg Trials." The trial reports, which began emerging in October 1946, presented readers with "inhumane science," "medical mass murder," and a "crisis of humanity,"[50] and were quickly followed by an increasing number of supportive articles on psychosomatic medicine—flanked in Germany's transregional press by philosophically grounded arguments for stronger attentiveness to the unity of body and soul.[51] If we look at the country's major newspapers, it appears that representatives of the psychosomatic approach, competing as they did with prevailing traditional medicine,[52] were adept at using the media. After Alexander Mitscherlich (head of the German medical commission at the trials) and Fred Mielke published a brochure that was based on selected trial documents and entitled "The Dictate of Contempt for Mankind,"

Mitscherlich lamented to Karl Jaspers the "unfathomable indifference of our contemporaries."[53] Yet on the public stage, the picture was slightly different because it was the very horror over the crimes committed by the Nazi doctors tried and convicted at Nuremberg that lent psychosomatic medicine considerable momentum. "Holistic medicine" was now credited with taking the whole "human being" into account and, in contrast to traditional medicine practiced under Nazism, treating the patient with the appropriate respect and responsibility.[54] And it was above all psychiatry, which had been discredited far more than other branches of medicine because of its role in the Nazi euthanasia program,[55] that seemed to suffer from something approaching a general suspicion of being an unscrupulous, purely technocratic form of treatment that lacked a sense of personal responsibility.[56] When *Die Zeit* proclaimed a "crisis of psychiatry"[57] in 1951, it simply represented an expression of what had been evident in West Germany's major daily papers for a long time: it was an undisguised attempt to challenge the interpretive authority of traditional, scientific psychiatry in the field of mental illness.[58]

Even though the psychosomatic perspective initially did not apply to the returnees, by the early 1950s it became clear that it offered a gateway to a new assessment of their impairments—to the extent those affected had formerly been interned in Soviet camps. In many quarters, it was evidently believed that the incompatibility between the perceptible mental abnormalities of these German veterans and the prevailing rules for what was permissible to mention could be transformed into a gesture of recognition through a language of psychosomatics: a gesture that could abstain from attributing the returnees' long-term illnesses to hereditary disposition.

Nowhere was this shift clearer than in the diagnosis of "dystrophy," a condition that in 1953 suddenly became a topic in numerous local and national newspapers.[59] The articles regularly cited Kurt Gauger's above-noted book *Dystrophy as a Psychosomatic Symptom*, which had been published the previous year and addressed a broad audience.[60] With his reading of dystrophy, Gauger, who was billed as a doctor and psychotherapist, appears to have struck a nerve among the public. In any event, in professional medical circles the discussion of dystrophy was not entirely new. For some years, primarily internists but also psychiatrists had viewed this malnutrition-based disease as a plausible explanation for the reduced regenerative capacity of returnees. The doctors believed that their organs had sustained far greater damage than was initially apparent.[61] But in his interpretation Gauger went even further, as we see in the newspaper accounts. The press, we might say, "devoured" his characterization of dystrophy as a "physical-mental disease."[62] In the eyes of the public, Gauger had thereby corrected the fatal medical error of focusing exclusively on physically determined damage and the capacity for physical regeneration.[63]

Above all the local papers conveyed their discontent with both the medical establishment and the authorities responsible for veterans' care, who adhered to prevailing doctrine and refused to recognize mental illness as a result of hardship in the POW camps. The number of affected returnees had to be large, the press suggested, repeatedly pointing to the extraordinarily stubborn impairments with which these men had to struggle, even when objective findings were no longer present. Circulation problems for which there was no evidence were one such phenomenon, with which many ordinary people in the meantime were acquainted not only from hearsay; it represented a significant burden in their daily lives with the returnees.[64] It could also be widely read that the men were neglecting themselves, were extraordinarily irritable, completely isolated themselves, and tended to be "excessively egoistic." How many families fell apart as a result? The papers painted a thoroughly grim picture: the initial joy of being reunited was something that soon disappeared.[65]

The West German press reports accumulated to become a veritable collective sigh over the apparent difficulties of living together with the former POWs. The psychosomatic interpretation of dystrophy offered a touch of relief. At least in the local papers, the tenor was clear: finally, in Kurt Gauger an expert had emerged who could be cited to counter doctors when they refused to diagnose the suffering of returnees as a disease in the absence of physical injury. Yet these returnees were in fact ill, "probably far more ill than they themselves and their doctors assume," insisted one author whose article shared with others the character of an appeal—to finally realize and acknowledge the great significance of the mental dimension of human health, indeed, to recognize its close interaction with the physical dimension in the first place.[66]

While the local press occasionally created the impression that the pressure for recognition of this suffering was fed by the concrete distress of families' everyday lives, the more widely circulated national press rarely established a connection with the daily hardship that families were encountering. The primary focus of the national press was on social and moral order in a far broader sense since this was, the papers and journals indicated, endangered by the behavior of numerous returnees. Thus, *Der Spiegel* spoke of major "moral deviations and misconduct" in that group. Among late returnees, the magazine claimed, the crime rate was especially high; in the fall of 1949, late returnees made up 41 percent of the prison population in Lower Saxony, a number that spoke for itself.[67] *Der Spiegel* pointed out, however, that there was a previously unconsidered reason for the dramatically high number; namely, the returnees were "not criminals, but ill people." Once again, Kurt Gauger's recently published book served as a basis for the explanation.[68] For its part, *Die Zeit* also referred to the book in taking a similar perspective, which was even more pointed: "After reading the book, one cannot help asking whether the coarsening of morals, the denunciatory climate, the marital discord, and the inadequate ethical guidelines here in Germany might not be explained in terms of widespread dystrophy."[69]

It appears that in view of circumstances described as approaching the critical level, there was a strong propensity to embrace the psychosomatic reading of dystrophy. Two reasons for this come to mind. On the one hand, there was a need to free oneself of the suspicion of hereditability, as we observe on the private level in a very similar way.[70] Although the dystrophy diagnosis did encompass "pathological changes of the psyche," at heart the condition was still seen as caused by hunger, as the print media now made clear. Thus, the state of society, which was perceived as "nonnormal" in many respects, was manifestly not explainable in terms of the hereditary constitution of a broad section of the population. As well, it was certainly no coincidence that the print media emphasized that this was a "new disease." That it was "curable," as Gauger reassured based on his presupposition of its "simultaneous effect on body and soul," could be read as an additional confirmation of its exogenous causes. The language used also expressed this idea. The unusual and even highly abnormal behavior seen in many returnees could be understood as a "mental attitude" that remained "dystrophic" after the physical injuries had subsided.[71]

On the other hand, dystrophy seemed suitable for establishing a kind of political narrative in which the German returnees from the Soviet camps and, due to the extensive destruction visited on the entire society, ultimately all other Germans as well could be cast as victims of perfidious Soviet warfare that allegedly continued beyond May 1945.[72] Within this scenario, the Soviets used the starvation of POWs as a sort of weapon that cost the lives of thousands who were so debilitated that they were unable to ward off other diseases. In fact, there was no one who had been able to escape its destructive power. *Die Zeit*, targeting middle-class, educated readers, explained it as follows: "The survivors become dystrophic: physically, mentally, and spiritually broken, marked for years to come. They become submissive tools in the hands of the power that holds them prisoner. It has become apparent that in the POW camps between 1944 and 1949, a new, very effective weapon was being tested: the dystrophization (*Dystrophisierung*) of millions of people."[73]

It would be incorrect to assume that from this time on the press was flooded with reports on the emotional sequelae in returnees. Granted, the articles warning against underestimating such "mental damage" from internment did not abruptly break off. This appears to have been the general message emerging from the medical conventions that the veterans' organization had held since 1953. In any event, almost without exception the press found it worthwhile to continue reporting the statements of doctors on the mental effects of dystrophy.[74] Eventually, however, the wave of news items on the problem faded nearly as fast as it had arisen. This suggests that the primary reason the media publicized the mental problems of returnees from the Soviet camps at this particular time was the Cold War—spurred on by the Korean War[75] and continued delays by the Soviet government in releasing the last German POWs.

Two considerations support this assumption. First, the subject dropped completely out of sight at the end of 1955, presumably because of the successful conclusion of negotiations with the Soviet Union for the prisoners' repatriation. While some press voices continued to accuse the Soviets of despotic behavior in their treatment of the men and lambasted the purported injustice, overall completely different tones were now audible. For example, *Die Zeit* appealed for special patience in dealing with the former seventeen-year-olds, now nearly thirty, on their return. In the event that they went overboard in their need for entertainment and an exaggerated joy in consumption:

> They are physically completely healthy. Measured in calories, the final years in the camps were not that bad, and packages from home helped when the camp food was inadequate. These boys did not "suffer" for ten years; rather, they had been bored for ten years—and that can also be unbearable. Now they no longer want to be bored; they want to experience something . . . they want—*horribile dictu*—to have fun.[76]

The "late returnees" were "victims" but they were also felt to be "survivors" and "accustomed to getting down to it." Indeed, they actually represented a "select group of very capable men (*Lebenstüchtige*)" who, the papers promised, would vigorously help in the reconstruction of West German society after a phase of acclimatization to the "new order and new rules of the game."[77] We can doubtless interpret this stance, which is reflected throughout the media's staging of the return in 1955–1956, as a demonstration of triumph over the Soviet Union. However, if we expand our field of vision, and this is the second point, we see another aspect of these portrayals. No sooner had the newspapers focused attention on dystrophy and the serious mental consequences of internment as a POW than they launched another highly explosive debate centering on the problem of allegedly unjustified claims to pensions and, indeed, pensions that were being illegally drawn.[78]

In this context, which was examined by some papers in a more or less enlightening manner and by others in scandal-sheet style, there was no mention whatsoever of the possibility of extending recognition of mentally caused suffering. To the contrary, *Frankfurter Hefte*, for example, expressed the conviction that against the backdrop of economic hardship, expulsion from one's homeland, the general loss of a wide range of ties, "*striving for security in life*" had "increased extraordinarily." Accordingly, even simple broken bones now entailed a delayed restoration of physical functioning, since the patient's interest in a pension was greater than his interest in recovering.[79] For the same reason, the article indicated, complaints that emerged later on and were the result of common wear and tear had been wrongly associated with earlier damage. Even in the case of brain damage, the author insisted, many of the subsequent physical and mental disabilities had nothing to do with the "accident" itself. Rather, they were connected to "the general behavior of those affected," that is, to the "personality of the person involved." This was the factor, then, that determined whether the injured person let himself go to pieces, became defiant, claimed public care, or turned to a regular activity in which he found meaning and halted his "adverse change of nature." In the view of *Frankfurter Hefte*, one thing was clear: "For increasing numbers of people, the meaning of existence amounts to the highest possible pension."[80] Referring to a remark by Free Democratic Party chairman Thomas Dehler that infuriated the Reich Association of War Disabled and War Veterans in 1951, when he was West German justice minister, *Die Zeit* went as far as to claim that "a third of all pensions . . . involve a swindle and are wrongfully drawn." The crown witness for this was a psychiatrist who remained unnamed in the press. According to his statement, about one-fifth of all disability pension applicants examined in his clinic had "absolutely nothing" wrong with them.[81]

No matter how urgently it seemed desirable to show understanding for the difficulties of the returnees from Russia, the opinion quickly gained the upper hand that most of their suffering did not involve damage directly rooted in the events themselves and thus did not entitle then to a disability pension. The background of this debate is not difficult to decipher. The proportion of "social expenditures" in the federal budget seemed oppressively high, and even the number of young pensioners was trending higher.[82] An additional factor that may have contributed to the considerable irritation over social service costs was the extraordinarily high number of unemployed in the face of an almost insatiable need for workers that accompanied the economic boom. Irrespective of that, for the media the time had arrived to expose a good number of "true swindlers" and also to suggest that there was a much higher number of men who received payments on the basis of impairments "that they themselves have shaped in the dubious zone between consciousness and unconsciousness." "Neuroses" were at work here, explained *Die Zeit* in 1954—the weekly was striving for the proper medical terminology—"or more correctly and unambiguously . . . 'abnormal experiential reactions.'" The long article in question, paradigmatic for others, explained that recognizing the decisive role played by "the *personality of the affected person*, and not the *event* he encounters," in the shaping of the disorders was only one side of the coin. For grappling with "the question that was vital for social insurance" entailed the assessment of the conditions, whereby *Die Zeit* cited the "war neurotics" and "tremblers" of World War I. Although they suddenly recovered after the armistice, years later they had developed their familiar symptoms again, with the prospect of a pension tipping the balance. Therefore, *Die Zeit* argued, this was the point from which to begin, and in this case the liberal paper was not averse to drawing on psychiatric experience. In contrast to what had been suggested from a legal standpoint, in two cases the article cited a "disorder of the will to work" or a "disorder of 'willpower'" was out of the question. After all, a Viennese psychiatrist had recently reconfirmed what "every specialist and psychiatrist" had noticed "in two world wars": when it came to stress, the limits of mental tolerance were infinite.[83]

In order to pick up the trail leading to public recognition of mental disorders, we therefore cannot rely on isolated readings of press reports about the late returnees from Russian POW camps. Rather, we need to consider the media's own thematic logic. In this question, the attention of the media was perhaps more the result of political considerations than of the specialized professional discourse. Such discourse defined the boundaries within which statements about mental abnormalities could be made in the first place. Yet apart from that the press, to put it bluntly, seems to have tapped into the spectrum of specialized scientific interpretive possibilities according to its own political and moral needs. All told, public concern with mental damage suffered by returnees from the Russian camps, as can be derived from the press, was short lived, ending in 1955–1956 after about two years. The interest did not extend to other groups of returnees, nor was there any examination of the horror of war itself as a possible cause for long-term mental changes.

We find a similar picture in West German film production during the 1950s. Comparing it to the early rubble films, one is even justified in saying that in the interim the mental consequences of the war and POW camps had been almost completely dethematized. For example, viewers of Gerhard Lamprecht's *My Father's Horses* were confronted with a returnee released from a Russian camp in 1950 who seems not only gravely damaged physically but also mentally worn out.[84] Yet there are no dramatic images of either the general destruction or of mental torment, as had been the case in the late 1940s in Lamprecht's *Somewhere in Berlin*. Rather, the film shows the returnee, a young former Wehrmacht officer named Jürgen Godeysen, in the care of a hospital. The bed linen is white and envelops him, and just as we are not directly confronted with his physical suffering that, after all, is the reason for his imminent operation, we learn nothing about his inner world. No dreams are shown, no hallucinations pointing to terrible experiences in the war or the camps. The bedridden returnee is simply presented as completely unapproachable. He is serious, withdrawn, and hardly speaks. His initially spare, almost rough words suggest he lacks all joy in life and feels only cynicism.

Nevertheless, the film does not tell the story of a returnee's suffering. The figure of former first lieutenant Godeysen is not meant to convey the message that this was every veteran's fate. The doctor, after all, successfully stitches everyone together again, whether they "left their right leg in the Crimea or their left arm in Normandy," as the hospital custodian informs viewers. Only the first lieutenant stubbornly resists healing—a difficult case, then, and not necessarily typical. Viewers learn all this in relatively brief sequences. At one point, a narrator explains that Jürgen Godeysen had been "cheated out of his faith." Yet the film suggests that even his state of deepest despondency is a phase that might pass. The decisive element in this respect is the attentiveness, perseverance, and patience of his wife—a promise of healing that was ubiquitous in West Germany in the 1950s[85] and certainly needs to be interpreted in the context of public negotiations concerning the prevailing gender relations: *My Father's Horses* is one of countless examples of the "remasculinization" of German men being staged at this time. Using the diary of the despondent lieutenant's father, the young woman shows him that his father never gave up despite many a blow in life, and that raises Jürgen's morale. She reads to him from the diary for an entire night. In the morning, the returnee beams with confidence. He jokes with the doctor, who joins in his song of praise for women. There can now be no doubt that Jürgen Godeysen has regained his role as a strong man.[86]

While the framework plot of *My Father's Horses* still conveyed the idea that the former Wehrmacht soldiers, marked as they were through the events of recent years, might possibly have difficulties coping with the demands placed on them after returning home, most other West German films of the 1950s simply did not revolve around the problems of returnees. The so-called *Heimatfilm* genre left them out completely.[87] Yet even the films that focused in one way or another on the Nazi war took other directions.[88] For example, in the three-part hit film of 1954, *08/15*, directed by Paul May with a screenplay by Hans Hellmut Kirst, viewers were presented above all with the chicaneries of military training during the Third Reich, along with the despotism inflicted on soldiers by individual officers portrayed as deluded and profoundly misanthropic Nazis.[89] Despite all the humiliations, however, the soldiers honorably defend their fatherland. This point was not only brought home in *08/15*, which was essentially meant as a humorous critique of Wehrmacht regimentation. Many of the far more ambitious West German films made in the late 1950s left no doubts concerning the bravery of simple German soldiers. One of these films was Frank Wisbar's 1958 *Dogs, Do You Want to Live Forever?* (*Hunde, wollt ihr ewig leben?*), which was much praised in its time,[90] although not by the West German defense ministry.[91] This film makes no secret of the soldiers' miserable condition, which is primarily caused—herein lies the reproach—by a number of unscrupulous and deluded officers who demand senseless military sorties. Even the Führer, it is made clear, abandoned his soldiers by failing to supply them with necessary food and material, putting them at the mercy of the murderous Soviet winter and the barbaric battles in the East. *Dogs, Do You Want to Live Forever?* portrays this, as well as the growing awareness of the "betrayal" and the soldiers' complete disillusionment.

Nevertheless, this and similar films that attempted to depict the brutality of the war in the east, often at Stalingrad, suggested that as a rule soldiers did not collapse.[92] However, the films do consistently raise the possibility of adverse reactions. In *08/15*, it is the sensitive soldier Vierbein, a musician, who is rather frail compared to his comrades and nearly collapses during training. When he comes back to the barracks during the war, the faces of the passing young recruits turn into skulls. At one point, Vierbein says, "It's simply that a musician doesn't have the hands for canons, and if he does, then he no longer has the hands for music." In contrast to the other soldiers, he cannot cope with the war—and does not survive it. Without a doubt, the message to viewers was that war could sometimes push other men as well to the limit of their mental endurance. In *Dogs, Do You Want to Live Forever?* it is Staff Sergeant Kunowski who, to use the soldiers' jargon, "cracks up" for a moment. But it is not that he is mentally weak. Instead, we learn, "He's cracking up from hunger again," and we are also shown that he can still pull himself together. Contrary to the assumptions of the unpleasant Major Linkmann, the film demonstrates that were no "slackers" and "chickens" among the soldiers. In order to marshal an additional unit, Linkmann sends out his lieutenant, Wisse, to find those sorts of soldier by combing through the field hospital. But Wisse finds only soldiers who are indeed in a devastating condition, all of them seriously wounded. Yet there is an exception: Major Linkmann himself. One of the film's final scenes reveals that Linkmann, who strove to earn fame as a hero, is actually a coward. He is tracked down in a cellar where he is hiding, after once again sending his soldiers into a senseless battle. Linkmann's hands tremble. It is he who has become mentally disturbed. He is a "war trembler." When he ultimately betrays his own men and tries to defect to the enemy, he is shot by German soldiers, justifiably and, as it were, in keeping with the dictates of decency, as the film suggests.

In this manner, the Wehrmacht soldier was cinematically portrayed as the victim of false promises and irresponsible political leadership, and at the same time as very tough, with a capacity to endure suffering with great courage. These characteristics were without a doubt not specific to German soldiers in German cinema, but were rather typical of the genre. Furthermore, starting in the late 1940s the commercialization of the war had become an international phenomenon, with the figure of the heroic soldier a general international image, which could be found at the time in numerous war movies in and outside Germany.[93] In this way, the images were all the more effective in assuring West German viewers that a Wehrmacht soldier generally stood firm when facing the horrors of war—to the extent he was not weak or frail or, a final exception, almost a child. In the last scenes of Bernhard Wicki's multiple award-winning film *The Bridge* from 1959, we are shown how some German youths who were at first nothing short of obsessed with war are in the end emotionally unable to cope with its merciless violence. They scream, they cry—and they die.[94] But the grown men endure, as do the women, however exhausted they may be. Other films from the period show this as well. "Although you sometimes think you'll go crazy," concedes Maria Reiser after a bombing attack in Wisbar's *Night Fell on Gotenhafen*, the decisive fact is that no one actually did go "crazy," neither in the hail of bombs nor during the flight to the west, which for most people in this film ended in death.[95] Before the last group of "late returnees" was released from internment in Russia, the press had briefly voiced and virtually demanded public recognition of the resulting mental changes. But in the end, even the cinematic portrayals of the strain of the Russian POW camps that were likewise brought to the screen in the late 1950s were far from sufficient to sustain such acknowledgment.

An example of this is Werner P. Zibaso's film *The Doctor of Stalingrad*, which debuted in 1958 and doesn't even hint at the existence of mental suffer-ing.[96] The film does confirm the existence of former soldiers who were ill, but its main accusation is that they were bullied by the Soviet camp administrators who certified that they were healthy so they could be made to work. Neverthe-less, the damage involved is always physical, which underscores the repeatedly mentioned problem of inadequate supplies of medications, as illustrated in a short conversation between the camp doctor, Fritz Böhler, and his assistant, Dr. Sellnow. The latter firmly believes in vitamin injections, although not in "ther-apy for the soul," which in this case stands for the stopgap measure of dispens-ing placebos to sick prisoners: "Those swine won't come across with any-thing." The film does not hide the fact that illness occasionally became a means of increasing one's prospects of being dismissed from the camps, however. Such simulation is tolerated because it is intended to trick the prisoners' Rus-sian tormenters.

The quiet heroism and self-preservation strategies of the Wehrmacht sol-diers portrayed on the screen basically confirmed the press campaign against putative pension abuse. Whatever the war may have brought down on these men in terms of suffering, the topos of proving oneself, even in senseless bat-tles, was carried forward in a belief that such men could and should be able to cope with the emotional consequences of past events in peacetime. As they were represented to the public, the Wehrmacht soldiers, just like the returnees from the Soviet camps, were free of mental damage caused by extreme vio-lence. Meanwhile, as these films were arriving on the screen, the theme of lasting or delayed mental damage stemming directly from an experience itself and not tied to physical damage began to attract psychiatric attention. As has been shown above, however, psychiatry approached the phenomenon primar-ily, and increasingly, with a view to Holocaust survivors. This can only be un-derstood against the backdrop of evolving changes in the political-moral awareness of the Nazi crimes. Here, the establishment of changes in psychiat-ric knowledge beginning in the early 1960s played a role that can hardly be overestimated.

CHAPTER 8

The Reappearance of the Persecuted and the Rules Governing What Could Be Said in Public Memory Culture

During the first decade and a half after the collapse of the Nazi regime, a wide range of narratives regarding the war's horrors, stresses, and exertions circulated in public culture. Nevertheless, generally speaking explicit public recognition of long-term mental changes as a result of the war lasted only for an extremely short time. Following a spontaneous readiness to show understanding that viewers might have attributed to one "rubble film" or another, the print media brought the problematic issue to public attention only for a short time and in passing, in connection with addressing the situation of late returnees from the Soviet camps. The brevity of this recognition is remarkable because the national papers and periodicals contain many indications that interpreting personal states of mind with help of the arsenal of psychosomatics, psychotherapy, and sometimes psychoanalysis had become widespread. Hence, in the mid-1950s *Die Zeit* reported: "Psychosomatics and psychotherapy—presently these two catchwords very often replace conversation about the 'illumination of existence,' 'being,' and 'angst' at parties and women's coffee klatches."[1] Six years later, Hoimar von Ditfurth encapsulated this development in reviewing a new study on psychosomatics: "As a result of public taste and interests, all books with titles beginning in 'psycho-' are currently guaranteed a certain print run right from the start."[2]

As we can see, there was no lack of pointed remarks about the "psycho-" wave.[3] Yet the very same people making them were themselves strongly contributing to the spread of popular psychology. Staring in the late 1950s, major newspapers and magazines devoted increasing space to the topic. To an extent, they were simply continuing to tout a medical approach that viewed the sick as "human beings" and not as "scientific objects."[4] The field of biological medicine had been accused of this ever since the Nuremberg trials, when the press had widely held that its lack of compassion had contributed to the crimes committed by Nazi doctors.[5] Although debate about scientific medicine's lack of mercy slowly subsided, one cannot help thinking that the dispute over health policy in the early 1950s unfolded largely in its wake. In any event, after the so-called second social reform at the end of the decade, the print media argued forcefully in favor of the health insurance funds assuming the costs of major psychotherapy.[6] Many of those who insisted on the ideal of the "real doctor" were in the meantime speaking of the need to grant greater leeway to treatment methods located outside of standard medicine, in keeping with the rehumanization of medicine.[7] In 1960, when Alexander Mitscherlich spoke out in *Die Zeit* in favor of patient copayments for their medical treatment across the board, the fact that "express procedures during an office visit" did no justice to psychosomatic maladies was not the only reason he thought copayments unavoidable. He further maintained that a medical practice aimed "at the sick person himself and not only at the sick organism" demanded a "'different kind' of doctor, . . . greater flexibility in terms of time, and correspondingly better compensation." Further, according to Mitscherlich's train of thought, patient copayments created an opportunity for the societal therapy he considered necessary. The object was to dispense with a "concept of illness that has become doctrinaire," a concept that views illness as something "for which the weather, one's profession, or one's 'genotype' is responsible, but has nothing to do with the patient as a human being, one who experiences disappointment and anger and has hopes and fears." Mitscherlich was therefore convinced that patients themselves were involved in their illnesses and had to take personal responsibility. This needed to be reinforced. Yet, as Mitscherlich explained, a sense of responsibility could never, not even in the case of illness, be achieved without sacrifice, including economic sacrifice. In his eyes, however, this represented a "counterposition to that of the *welfare state*, with its "*standardized citizens*." Mitscherlich offered readers the following alternatives: either to be a "mature" human being or continue "to be reduced to a *pet of the state*."[8]

Presumably Mitscherlich's political argument found only limited resonance, inasmuch as it entailed unpopular financial contributions by insured people.[9] The notion of potential self-healing was better received. After all, the underlying concept of illness gave people "power over their illness" and rendered "fate a solvable task," in one blow.[10] According to Mitscherlich and other reports in the print media, addressing the task had become an urgent priority because a horrifying number of people seemed to be suffering from psychosomatic illnesses. Mitscherlich himself mentioned a figure of at least "50 percent of the mentally ill people" who visited general practitioners.[11] A few years before, *Stern* magazine had published the alarming information that a "Damocles sword of mental and physical collapse" was hovering over two million German children.[12] Based on expert opinions, the report explained that the children lacked "warm nests" because increasing numbers of mothers were working and putting their children in daycare. *Stern* showed the outcomes in a photo-essay with brief "life reports": juvenile delinquency including murder, underage sexual license, and suicide. In the end, the magazine explained, the mothers' work in the war effort had caused the problem of these "rockers."[13] The experts had informed the magazine that "the 'mental time-bombs' in the evacuation camps are exploding today."

While health care policy did not take into account the possibility of long-term or delayed mental disorders in German refugees, just as was the case with the returnees,[14] the apparent moral endangerment of allegedly neglected youth in the meantime did suggest a psychosomatic interpretation.[15] In the case of little children, readers learned in the *Stern* article, even serious illnesses could be predicted. The moral indignation informing these fears of illness centered on so-called latchkey children, who were viewed as proof of a cold, selfish, consumption-oriented reconstruction society where mothers preferred to get jobs and abandoned their children to their own devices.[16] An almost full-page photo in *Stern* showed one such neglected little boy, standing "lonely and abandoned" in a field of grass in a major city. Readers further learned: "From morning to evening the lifeless teddy bear is his only confidant in a bleak environment he helplessly faces on his own. For him, everything unknown spells danger. His body reacts with constant readiness to defend himself. His nerves are overtaxed. Heart damage is the result."[17]

To a growing degree, children, young people, and adults appeared to be suffering from mental illnesses. When people spoke of the causes, they referred to the "collapse of the old order," the decline of stabilizing traditions, the vanishing influence of the church, and the "radical realignment of social structures." All these developments had seemingly led to an alarming degree of "insecurity, isolation, and mental homelessness of human beings in the world."[18] According to *Die Zeit*, one could never pay enough attention to even the slightest signs of a mental disorder. Particularly in adults, its presence was often not so obvious, and the ties of the illness to its "environmentally determined causes" were not immediately apparent: "One sick person complains of insomnia or difficulty concentrating; another suffers from shyness and fear of contact; a third is plagued by inexplicable fears." This appeal and those of other media, which were directed at readers and especially doctors and politicians, were not difficult to decipher: they called for greater social sensitivity toward and understanding of mental suffering.[19]

In any event, when it came to the society's open-mindeness about the presence of psychosomatic illness, the situation seems to have been much less dire than the print media sometimes suggested. Not least, we see this—and the press noticed it as well—in the fact that the pharmaceutical industry skillfully turned the trend to its own ends, speedily flooding the market with new medications that promised more tranquility and composure, better sleep, and a greater capacity to work and concentrate.[20] On the other hand, the strong resistance to psychosomatic explanations within the medical profession and especially among psychiatrists is not to be overlooked.[21] Consequently, there is much to favor the argument that in the second half of the 1950s the media themselves were responsible in a very basic way, in the sense of "event-causing structures" (*ereignisbedingende Strukturen*) for Germany's unfolding wave of social psychosomatization.[22] Nevertheless, one group that had previously been perceived as highly endangered was excluded from this process, namely, the returnees. In striking contrast to the abundant, emotionalized reports about apparently mentally disturbed children, concrete references to the veterans are simply absent in the media.

This decoupling is by no means self-evident. One of the central reasons for it was that since the mid-1950s, images of perpetrators filtering back into the public sphere had literally blocked a media discussion of mental suffering among late returnees—especially since at the same time images of the victims of Nazism were surfacing that had basically been screened out of the public culture of memory beginning in the early occupation period.[23] In view of the journalistically and photographically disseminated images of horror, public avowals of "brave" soldiers who had fought in a "clean" manner appear to have slowly eroded. Although there is probably no German discussion of Nazi crimes from that period that, at least retrospectively, could not be criticized for falling short and being undifferentiated, we should not overlook that the second half of the 1950s was marked by the start of a journalistic and cultural confrontation with the Nazi period. While continuing to allow for the demarcation of a border against the perpetrators, it nevertheless increasingly damaged the consensus that had been reached about integration during previous years.[24] For example, over the span of only a few years, Anne Frank's story was brought to the attention of millions of readers and theatergoers, and countless photographs in newspapers, magazines, books, photo compilations, and exhibitions injected the horror of corpse heaps in death camps, the misery of the ghettos, and the war crimes in the Soviet Union into the pictorial memory of the West German public. The material was often skillfully laid out, with images of uniformed soldiers or SS men on one page, facing emaciated camp inmates on the other.[25]

Within this shifting field of public memory, late returnees from the Soviet camps could not entirely escape the suspicion of having been involved in the murders, as demonstrated by smaller trials conducted before the major turn in prosecution practice.[26] In addition to that, there was the East German campaign against the "blood judges," which raised the accusation that Nazi perpetrators had been covertly integrated into the judicial apparatus. The accusation was initially rejected as Communist propaganda but then ultimately taken up by the West German press after all.[27] Using scandal-filled exposés, it now pilloried the perpetrators' silent integration into West German society, where they would often continue to practice their former professions as doctors or lawyers.[28] Although the Allensbach Institute reported that in a 1958 survey 54 percent of Germans contacted were in favor of drawing a curtain on past events,[29] the media, which for a number of reasons had set about recalling the Nazi crimes to public memory, could count not only on indignation over the criminals by broad segments of society but even more so on widespread trepidation about the actual extent of the complicity that had occurred.[30]

This change in the culture of memory at the end of the 1950s cannot be overlooked if we wish to understand why the media excluded the late returnees—they had previously been treated with concern—from the general public acknowledgment of psychosomatic suffering that was now being extended to the victims of Nazi persecution, as they were increasingly making their way into public awareness. The 1961 trial of Adolf Eichmann in Jerusalem was extremely important in this respect. In contrast to the Nuremberg trials, the Eichmann trial was based on copious testimony from survivors.[31] A total of 111 witnesses were called to the stand. In his memoirs, the Israeli chief prosecutor, Gideon Hausner, indicated that his intent had been to offer "a living and vivid account of a gigantic human and national catastrophe." The events were no longer to remain the "fantastical, unbelievable ghost" of Nazi documentation; they were to be transmitted by human beings. This would put an end to the constant threat of derealization and, to use Hausner's words, "endow a phantom with the dimension of reality."[32] Hausner was therefore banking very specifically on the emotional effect of the witness testimony. Television reacted promptly: it was the first time a Nazi trial was broadcast, and in this case it included survivors. Although the American filmmaker Leo Horwitz recorded nearly the complete proceedings, TV stations across the world primarily requested footage of survivor testimony. It appears that the dramatic moment in which one witness, Yehiel Dinur Katzetnik, fainted after giving his account was, as far as we know, the most frequently transmitted trial episode.[33]

Hausner's strategy—it would be adopted by the prosecutors in the Frankfurt Auschwitz trials two years later[34]—was evidently largely successful. Attesting to inextinguishable suffering, the survivor/witnesses emotionalized a sensitized public; expectations that it would be ready to extend empathy were not often disappointed.[35] Peter Weiss's play *Die Ermittlung* (*The Investigation*), which has been staged hundreds of times since the mid-1950s was a result of this development. Relying on the same logic of emotionalization as the footage of the trials, it puts the figure of the survivor/witness on the stage. Although some West German reviews were harshly critical, and there were also efforts to discredit Weiss as a Communist, in general discussion of the play still conveyed the acknowledgment that the suffering of Holocaust survivors had to be directly addressed.[36] In the eyes of many, the moral reproach represented by the survivors themselves as witnesses had become irrefutable.

It was therefore no coincidence when at the end of May 1961, as the Eichmann trial was unfolding, German print media directed extraordinary public attention to an annual psychiatric congress that took place in Baden-Baden. In various articles, readers were now informed of the scientific discovery of "lasting mental damage" incurred by the survivors.[37] As we have seen, a number of psychiatrists who used the term "experientially determined personality change" had been struggling for several years to achieve intradisciplinary recognition of this finding.[38] *Süddeutsche Zeitung* now publicly declared that "prevailing doctrine" that had assumed that all exogenously based mental suffering would heal and leave no scars, had collapsed in that strict form. As the renowned newspaper informed its readers, the extraordinary long-term damage surfacing in former concentration camp inmates had nothing to do with a "pension neurotic" attitude. Instead, it was the "emotional trauma," as the exogenous events were now sometimes called, that had caused the "irreversible damage," whereby this apparently only manifested after the effects of hunger dystrophy had subsided. According to the report, the damage expressed itself in "anxiety dreams, nightmares, states of anxiety that mounted to crisis-like proportions, and mental hypersensitivity."[39] A comprehensive report in *Die Zeit* addressing this subject cited a Jewish merchant as follows: "The anxiety never leaves me. I physically feel how everything in me tenses up." Both he and his wife, the article explained, were now "sick," despite having suffered no permanent physical damage from their internment in the camp. The period of persecution had terrible aftereffects in the form of persistent mental suffering, and readers of *Die Zeit* could convince themselves by reading the man's harrowing account:

There are days when I feel so bad that I simply don't get up, or at least don't go outside because I'm paralyzed by unspeakable anxiety, and have to be afraid that my legs will fail me. . . . I no longer know any joy. What is there to be happy about? Who should I rejoice with? We've become lonely, the two of us. People rejected us, we can't find our way back to them, and they can't find their way to us. What we had before these tribulations has been lost forever. None of us can cope with things the way they are, and there's no longer a future for us.[40]

In this way, the print media made clear that for its victims the Nazi campaign of persecution and extermination was not part of the past. Rather, it continued to wreak destruction in the lives of the survivors every single day; no cranny of daily life seemed to be spared. For one person, even the jingling of a key chain could cause extreme panic,[41] while for others large groups of people could make their heart race or cause nausea; in a theater or a cinema or a place or worship some survivors could only sit in seats that would allow them to leave the premises immediately.[42] By quoting a few sentences from survivors, the media painted a picture of how one could imagine their lives more than fifteen years after liberation of the concentration camps. The various experts they consulted attested that there could be no doubt regarding the persistent torment, and that "horror scenes from everyday camp life" haunted former inmates "day and night."[43] *Die Zeit* reported that Paul Matussek of the Max Planck Institute for Psychiatry in Munich even believed that the former inmates were "in a certain sense still in the camps."[44]

Such formulations were highly media-effective. In light of the detailed information about the horror and humiliation in the concentration camps that was being reported at the time in connection with the trials, the survivors' present emotional torment could be imagined in terrible detail. As a result, in the broader West German debate about crimes during the Nazi regime, a cognitive model established itself in the media audience that increasingly assumed that mental consequences in those who survived Nazi persecution, particularly in the camps, was a given. On the one hand the professional breakthrough of the new diagnosis of "experientially determined personality change" played an important role in public media perception of the victims as individuals who had sustained permanent emotional damage. On the other hand, media descriptions of the horror in the concentration camps endowed what was now accepted as psychiatric knowledge—even against opponents in the field—with extraordinary moral authority.

This feedback relationship between professional expertise and public morality had another consequence. Such recognition of permanent consequences of Nazi persecution that were not ascribable to either heredity or other individual factors cast the blame for the suffering on German society as a whole. For the *Süddeutsche Zeitung*, Paul Matussek set the tone: "Society Stands Accused" was the title of its report on the psychiatric congress, which summarized the psychiatrist's judgment as follows: "In order to overcome the consequences of the degrading treatment former camp inmates suffered, society would have to be different. It would have to be willing to inwardly accept what is probably the most terrible accusation leveled in history"—an assessment the paper was now unmistakably endorsing.[45] The same tenor was evident in other papers as well: "Society, all of us, are tied in the most intimate way to the fate of the unfortunate individuals. Nothing will free us from this involvement," confirmed *Die Zeit*,[46] which elsewhere made the point more clearly using the words of the German-Jewish psychiatrist Erwin Straus, who had emigrated to the United States in 1933: "Since the camps came into existence, there have been those who were persecuted, that is, the inmates. The others, all of them, are persecutors."[47]

The media, which were creating the impression that they enjoyed the backing of the entire psychiatric profession, harshly castigated German society. The open reproach was that it neither acknowledged its own guilt nor felt any responsibility toward the survivors of the Nazi policy of extermination. Instead, as *Die Zeit* put it, "empathy" was limited mostly to "following the Eichmann trial and the inhumane actions of the camp henchmen with a mixture of curiosity and disgust." The paper continued:

> We take care of the matter over breakfast between coffee and bread and jam, and then turn to humdrum everyday life: the new washing machine we need to buy or our preparations for the next trip to the Mediterranean. But do we not owe yesterday's victims something more than merely ascertaining what bestial deeds humans are capable of? Are we not all somehow entangled in horrific guilt? And do we identify with that guilt?[48]

Although the German reporting of the Eichmann trial to some extent perpetuated the older "pattern of individualizing culpability," with Eichmann sometimes even being held personally responsible for the murder of all of European Jewry,[49] it is also unmistakable that in the early 1960s West Germany's major public media made a distinct effort to halt a presumed social tendency toward self-exculpation. When the Auschwitz trials opened, the new moral tone centering on accepting responsibility increased. In contrast to before, things did not stop with an admonishment to realize that everyone shared in the moral responsibility for Nazi crimes. Rather, what now expressly entered public consciousness was a sense that even the inconspicuous citizen next door could be a perpetrator. This notion may have been fueled by the rather unprepossessing figure of Eichmann the bureaucrat, along with an increasing awareness that the genocide of the Jews required broad-based cooperation. The director of the psychosomatic clinic at the University of Gießen, Horst Eberhard Richter, was one among many to point out that a number of those found guilty at the trials had "seemingly led upright bourgeois lives after 1945." There was no lack of examples of "relatively unobtrusive external conformity to the norms of postwar society." Richter elaborated, mentioning "well-ordered activity in often respectable professions, care for one's family, and no criminal offenses. Superiors and neighbors attest to the fact that the men were so well liked by those around them that people were in disbelief at their Nazi-era crimes that had only now become known."[50]

Richter's description exemplifies the more broadly present anxiety that was hinted at in the "renazification debate" of the 1950s but became much more intensely discussed during the major trials of the 1960s. It was now no longer limited merely to individuals but taken up a broad media public. It was no longer a question of the political scandal that former members of the SS, SA, and Nazi Party had been installed in high-ranking positions, including political office. The perceived problem was broader: it appeared that "completely normal people" (which applied only to men) were capable of committing the most horrendous crimes and were then effortlessly able to become "completely normal people" again.[51] This criminal profile not only required a different explanation than that of the pathological perpetrator of *Exzesstaten* (particularly brutal crimes) promulgated in the press during the late 1940s and early 1950s.[52] Beyond that, after receiving some reinforcement during the Auschwitz trials themselves,[53] it further intensified a concern that the perpetrators could be everywhere, as it were, among neighbors, friends, and close relatives.[54] For example, during the trials an interview by *Stern* magazine with Hamburg University psychiatry professor Hans Bürger-Prinz opened with the question: "There are many concentration camp murderers who have already been sentenced but lived among us for years as seemingly harmless types. Do you think it's possible that my nice barber from around the corner could at one time have taken pleasure in slaughtering defenseless camp inmates with his razor?"[55]

To a large extent, the reports were now also broadcast on television[56] and addressed the social integration of Nazi perpetrators in a serious tone. Coverage in glossy magazines, however, creates the impression of being bent on engaging readers not only through the covert fear that there could be murderers in their closest circle, but also through a secret joy in scandal. Yet in whatever way such reports played with the horror, they still contributed to and strengthened the idea that the murder and other crimes committed on the German side could not be shunted onto isolated "beasts." As *Stern* claimed in the title of its series on the defendants in the Auschwitz trials, the murderers were people "like you and me." They led normal lives, as exemplified in the case of Viktor Capesius, head of the pharmacy at Auschwitz beginning in 1943. Formerly, he had been an "amusing charmer who was dazzling in company, a fabulous dancer," and was even married to a "half-Jewess." Only a few years after the war, he was once again leading a bourgeois West German life as a successful, convivial businessman: "Everyone liked him." But the text accompanying a photo showing him with his three children in 1943 disabused readers: "Witnesses swore: 'A year later he sent business friends and acquaintances to the gas chambers.'"[57]

One can speculate in various ways about the effects of the Auschwitz trials on West German society.[58] For some Germans, perhaps, they actually triggered the "We're not like them" reflex. Writer Martin Walser was not the only one who feared this form of ongoing self-exculpation.[59] Others, such as journalist and former Wehrmacht soldier Horst Krüger, who attended the trials for several weeks, was plagued by multifarious questions and consumed by a painful "process of self-examination." A piece by Krüger, presented on the radio and published in the journal *Der Monat* while the trial was still under way, attests to this process in an impressive manner.[60] His *In the Labyrinth of Guilt* consisted of an interplay of voices emerging from a loudspeaker. They reported horrific events, depicted his inner world of perceptions and thoughts, and allowed readers and listeners to accompany him on a renewed first visit to the courtroom. Krüger had entered the room with some trepidation. As the piece made clear, in 1941 he had been charged with "conspiracy to commit high treason" and appeared before the notorious *Volksgerichtshof* in Berlin. Finding himself in the Frankfurt courtroom more than twenty years later, he was no longer sure that he himself would not have carried out the most horrible orders if he had been in a comparable situation.

> What would have happened if my marching orders had by chance not contained the word Smolensk but rather the unfamiliar, meaningless word Auschwitz? Naturally, I would have taken my wounded men there; natu-

rally, a soldier always obeys orders. I would have taken them to Auschwitz, and perhaps I would have delivered them to the camp doctor who is now testifying here as a witness: daily, one or two wounded men for the medical barracks in Auschwitz. After all, that's not so many. And after that? What other things would I have done? It would hardly have escaped me that it wasn't healing but killing that was being practiced here. What would I have done? Probably, I would have shut my eyes like everyone else and pretended for a while that I didn't notice anything. . . . I don't think I would have joined in the murdering, cremating, and sorting. That's a different dimension. But wouldn't I have tried to somehow get out it using one of the little tricks that every soldier knows? The depot or the orderly room or sick bay? I certainly wouldn't have been a hero. I would have dodged it and kept my mouth shut. But who can say how long I would have evaded it? Even killing can become a habit. When ten thousand people are killed every day, who's to say whether I wouldn't even have become used to that, after two years?[61]

The questions Krüger asked himself and, indirectly, his readers and listeners were unsettling in view of the Auschwitz trials, which held the former Wehrmacht member spellbound. He had wanted to be a spectator, he declared, but as he listened once again to the voice on the loudspeaker he sensed that "no one can remain a spectator here. Time limits have been suspended. The past has become present" was his comment on the inexorable pull that the trial testimony exerted on him. Much like a photomontage, images generated by what he heard and remembered images from the war merged in his mind. The "material stored in his own memory" could not help but come to the fore, he would later explain as he looked back at his experiences during the trial.[62] In *In the Labyrinth of Guilt* he formulated this as follows: "The film of life has been rewound and is lurching into motion once again. And why shouldn't the very next frame show me in a sea of uniforms, me in the campaign against the east, and what will I do in this frame? What will I be?"[63]

In the mid-1960s, Krüger thus confronted German society with questions that others were not publicly considering in this way, especially in respect to themselves. Of course, we cannot know how many Wehrmacht veterans went through a similar odyssey of images, fueled by the exhaustive coverage of the trials, perhaps even inwardly observing themselves as witnesses or perpetrators of a mass crime.[64] And despite all the knowledge we have about the interplay between the SS, the Wehrmacht, and the police in the context of the homicidal and genocidal policies in occupied Europe, it remains unclear how many soldiers actually participated.[65] Yet the eerie suspicion that one could basically encounter perpetrators anywhere not only repeatedly surfaced in the journalistic media but was also maintained by it. The suspicion even overcame Krüger when he arrived late for the proceedings and realized that the physiognomy of the defendants in the courtroom was no different from the others present in the courtroom. Recounting his futile attempt to orient himself, he explained, "I looked for the defendants in the room but I didn't see them. I looked for the witness stand but I didn't see it." "There are some 120 or 130 Germans sitting in the room, citizens of our country, West Germany, in the year 1964, but I can't distinguish between the prosecutors and the defendants."[66] It was only during a recess in the trial—a confusing and strangely unreal gathering of all parties in the foyer—that a journalist explained the situation to Krüger. It was an abrupt awakening for him:

> And then I understood for the first time that all of these friendly people who were in the courtroom just now, and whom I took for journalists and lawyers and spectators, they were the defendants, and that, naturally, they are indistinguishable from the rest of us. Twenty-two men were on trial here, eight were in prison, fourteen free on bail, and with very few exceptions all of them looked like everyone else, behaved like everyone else, were well-fed, well-dressed gentlemen who were well along in their years: academics, doctors, pharmacists, businesspeople, craftsmen, custodians, comfortable citizens of our new German society, free citizens who parked their cars in front of City Hall just like me and came to the proceedings. There's nothing to differentiate there.[67]

Nevertheless, Krüger kept searching for some characteristic features in the faces of the defendants that would betray them as perpetrators, and constantly found himself facing the same sobering and upsetting lack of distinguishability. Being able to confirm that Oswald Kaduk had "one of the few revolting faces," even if it triggered every conceivable idea of a "concentration camp thug," seemed almost less eerie to Krüger than discovering that Arthur Breitwieser, who stood accused of participating in the first trial gassings with Zyklon B in September 1941, was an interesting and intelligent man, "so convivial and composed that I would have hired him as an employee in an instant." Krüger articulated what clearly caused anguish in others as well: "In some way it has to oppress them, isolate them, make them lonely," he puzzled. And he was not alone in expecting the experts to provide an answer. He wondered what doctors, psychologists, psychiatrists had to say about how it was possible "to become such a civil and capable citizen again after Auschwitz."[68]

In an interview about the Auschwitz trials in the February 1964 edition of *Stern* magazine, Hans Bürger-Prinz had already offered some sobering remarks regarding that very phenomenon and the related question, posed by a journalist, of whether it was "normal": "Yes, I would consider that absolutely normal. That's the way people are—just like that, no different," he was quoted as saying. If one spoke in terms of "human" qualities, then one had to also include the "inhuman" qualities. Bürger-Prinz saw no reason to have any kind of illusions that the perpetrators incurred any kind of emotional damage through the atrocities they committed: "I've dealt with many men who . . . committed crimes during the Nazi era, but I recall only one where you would have noticed anything afterward. He was hung up about things."[69] As the journalist learned on behalf of his readers, the man in question had been a noncommissioned officer and participated in seventy-three mass shootings in Poland. The former soldier had—Bürger-Prinz let the interviewer's formulation stand—"cracked" under the experience. But the psychiatrist confirmed once again: "As I said, that was the only one I've seen who cracked."[70]

This psychiatric opinion therefore underscored that the indifference one registered in the faces of the mass murderers facing justice was no error, just as Wehrmacht veterans, with few exceptions, who participated in the most horrific events of a criminal war had emerged with no lasting mental damage. Here the broadening of the perpetrator profile and the dissemination of a psychiatric doctrine through the media reinforced each other. At least in the media, which accounted for a good portion of public memory discourse, the discussion of a possible victim status for former soldiers was thus more or less closed.

The conversation between the *Stern* reporter and psychiatrist Bürger-Prinz also typified the increasingly broadening concept of the perpetrator. Bürger-Prinz had spoken of "concentration camp butchers," members of mobile killing units, and soldiers more or less in the same breath. The journalist even provided the psychiatrist the opportunity to counter any speculations about mentally determined illness as a result of any actions during the war. As an example, readers were presented the (presumably hypothetical) case of a man who, they were informed, had applied for a disability pension some years earlier because he had developed stomach ulcers during the war. The man had explained the connection to the authorities in the following way: as a member of a mobile death squad, he had participated in shootings in the course of which he killed a two-year-old. He was now married and had a two-year-old himself.

"Whenever I see her, I have to think of the child I shot. That turns my stomach, and now I have ulcers." As the journalist presented this account, he described the man's conclusion as a "naive reaction," and the psychiatrist agreed. The man was exhibiting a "residual sensitive reaction," Bürger-Prinz declared, but the ulcers involved "neurosis." In his eyes, a true, causal relationship with the deed did not exist. This corresponded to prevailing psychiatric doctrine.[71] As Bürger-Prinz explained it to the public, "the thought of a disability pension" was "so preeminent" that the man "reacted in a totally naive way and claimed, 'I developed the stomach ulcer during the war, and therefore I'd like to have a pension.'" The Hamburger psychiatrist went so far as to assure the public: "Morality doesn't play any role at all for the man. He's not going to reproach himself for his entire life."[72]

Bürger-Prinz allowed no leeway here. It might be the case that after having horrific experiences a veteran would claim disability, but psychiatric experience had shown such claims were unjustified. Here the psychiatrist was in fact simply repeating what had long been undisputed in his profession: long-term mental illness was not to be expected in Wehrmacht soldiers after their return. Ever since the Eichmann trial, mass media reporting on the new psychiatric discovery of lasting damage incurred by victims of the Nazi regime had consistently mentioned this prevailing opinion. From the beginning, the media's urgent appeal to the public, through the voice of psychiatric experts, to finally accept responsibility for Nazi crimes and recognize that the long-term mental suffering of the survivors was caused by their persecution, had drawn a boundary between the survivors and the suffering of former soldiers and others affected by the war and their mental burdens. As a result, in 1961 Walter von Baeyer spoke out emphatically in *Die Zeit* for understanding

> the extent to which Nazi persecutors terrorized their victims and the ways in which the terror of that era differs from the mental stress caused by accidents, war injuries, the effects of aerial warfare, and similar matters. . . . Political terror is characterized by longer duration, incessant threat to life and limb, unforeseeability, and hopelessness. In contrast to those who were injured by bombs or fought on the front, the suffering of the victims of this absolute and merciless persecution was not limited to relatively isolated experiences of anxiety, dread, horror, physical injuries, and deprivation. For the duration of their horror, they were never returned to a sheltering haven of security, care, and good will. They were like hunted beasts, without hope of ever being received into an accepting community or caring institutions such as sickbays and hospitals; often they faced cer-

tain death. Add to this the total deprivation of their rights and dignity, and the denial of all respect; they were put on a level with undesirable vermin and subjected to discrimination that has never been more complete, systematic, and inhumane in world history.[73]

In the media campaign to gain societal acknowledgment of the mental destructiveness of Nazi German persecution and extermination policies, it initially seemed that the circle of people with long-term mental problems would not be limited to the "politically and racially persecuted of the period." As Walter von Baeyer speculated in *Die Zeit*, "emigrants and those expelled from their homeland" also suffered from "more or less tormenting 'feelings of isolation'"; even "a number of refugees from the Soviet zone" needed to be included. Here, the important concept was "uprooting," whereby the psychiatrists primarily had older people in mind. But *Die Zeit* only granted this broader psychiatric perspective a brief moment of attention, and additionally took a lengthy quote by psychiatrist Ulrich Venzlaff concerning older female German refugees out of its argumentative context so that it seemed he was actually referring to Holocaust survivors.[74]

In any case, media coverage of the intradisciplinary debate in psychiatry was only modestly distorted because the specialists' efforts to establish new knowledge about long-term mental damage actually did focus largely on Holocaust survivors. Ultimately, the argument repeatedly returned to the unprecedented nature of the horrors they had suffered. Therefore, the impact of the horrors on their mental health represented a case apart. In the end, it was not least this unique characteristic that created a framework within the discipline of psychiatry for the acceptance of a new diagnostic approach by those who adhered to the psychiatric doctrine—for which the evidence was still considered valid—of an unlimited human capacity to endure stress.[75] In the media, however, disputes such as the one mentioned above simply were not addressed. Rather, in relevant reports from the early 1960s it increasingly stood out that a sharp distinction was made between Wehrmacht veterans and surviving victims of Nazism, primarily those who had been interned in concentration camps. In the winter of 1963, the conservative *Frankfurter Allgemeine Zeitung* also informed its readers that people who had survived the Nazi prisons and camps had been "affected to the core of their personalities"; "physical and mental weakness" were their most common symptoms. Once again, Venzlaff was the psychiatrist who provided the background information. In a lecture, the article explained, he had allegedly indicated that "there had been no reason . . . for their torment at the time, as there perhaps had been for soldiers and the population of the bombarded cities." Now the article in *Frankfurter Allgemeine Zeitung* informed a broader audience as well that in contrast to the camp victims, "only a small percentage of the late returnees had been injured physically or mentally."[76]

Countless returnees saw things differently. As their spokesmen, representatives of the disabled veterans' associations formulated an extensive protest and conveyed it in various forums to West German politicians. But the Wehrmacht veterans' objections only partly found their way into the media. Granted, the veterans' struggle to have their disability pensions increased was met with a degree of understanding. When some twenty thousand returnees traveled to Bonn in the winter of 1963 to demonstrate in the capital against the government's austerity policies, they received detailed and predominantly sympathetic coverage in the national press. In December, *Süddeutsche Zeitung* wrote in support of the returnees that it was actually "macabre . . . that the loss of limbs has to be weighed in marks and pfennigs in order to guarantee the war wounded a minimum to live on." For some people, the news that neighboring countries (France, primarily) were supposedly providing their own disabled veterans better support elevated disability policies in Germany almost to the level of a scandal.[77]

Nevertheless, when it came to another aspect of the protest, the media showed considerably less sympathy. This involved the repeated demands by returnee associations that former war prisoners from the Soviet camps be granted the same easing of the burden of proof of injury that had been granted Holocaust survivors when it came to compensation.[78] At issue here was the sort of suffering that doctors largely considered to be "hereditary." The Association of Returnees protested the absence of any special recognition of extraordinary physical and mental stress endured by those former soldiers.[79] As a result, in 1963 and with the support of the social minister of Lower Saxony, Kurt Partzsch, and German secretary of state Walter Auerbach (both Social Democrats), the association submitted a request to the Bundesrat's committee for veterans' and returnees' affairs that a causal connection between present suffering and past internment be assumed as a matter of principle when "extreme living conditions" had been present. The federal government was asked to determine in legally binding form the POW camps where such conditions were to be assumed and determine "for which health issues it should be considered likely that a causal relationship was present."[80] The representatives at the state level did not go along with this, as we learn from association reports. Some representatives, the reports indicate, argued that "delayed effects following extreme living conditions" simply no longer existed, while others expressed doubt that eighteen years after the end of the war an individual could prove he had been in a specific camp.[81] As before,[82] the association had failed in its effort. Clearly annoyed, the head of the association explained the matter to the membership in a report:

> Recently, there has been no lack of attempts to establish differences in the consequences of the deprivation of liberty as it applies in the case of two major groups of individuals, namely, concentration camp inmates, whose hardship ended in 1945, and prisoners of war, whose hardship began in 1945. All international research and comparisons argue against this tendency. It would be desirable if in West Germany as well the human dimensions were to receive greater consideration than the political aspects in the evaluation of long-term damage caused by extreme living conditions.[83]

What may have been a scandal in the eyes of many returnees in the 1960s did not merit a headline in the eyes of the media. It was even less suitable for staging a political affair. During the ongoing Auschwitz trials and in the political and moral climate of the time, which the mass media were helping to create, it had apparently become unthinkable from a media standpoint to become a public advocate for the cause of the returnees and challenge the politic sphere over the equality of human beings when they are subjected to cruelty. A large segment of the media apparently wanted to know nothing of such comparisons. Once again, one has the impression that—following an apocalypse of violence—the question of acknowledging mentally caused long-term illness was being used to define who belonged to the victims and who was to be numbered among the perpetrators. Conversely, such a definition could not help affecting ideas about the extent of the violence suffered on each side and its impact on the lives of those involved. This appears likely because at least over the following two decades there seems to have been no public awareness that Wehrmacht soldiers could have been left with any enduring mental problems stemming from World War II. One might raise the objection that the diagnosis of post-traumatic stress disorder, developed in the wake of the Vietnam War, was only officially recognized by the American Psychiatric Association in 1980. Yet a look at illustrated German magazines shows that the mental effects of the Vietnam War were being addressed as early as second half of the 1960s, at least in American soldiers. For example, in late 1966 *Stern* published an article about an American lieutenant whose plane was shot down and was captured by the Vietnamese. The piece was entitled "The Anxiety Dreams Remain." The report was presented as a story of heroism, but readers learned that the lieutenant continued to suffer from anxiety dreams. He woke up at night bathed in sweat after reliving the savage deeds of his Vietnamese captors. Revealing and emphasizing the mental consequences virtually seems to have been a narrative mode for determining the real victims of the war.[84]

Clearly, the way the limits of soldiers' capacity of bearing mental stress were perceived was a selective process. Moral valuations and political requirements entered the equation and contributed to determining which of the available scientific explanations would be adopted by the media to interpret mental illness, and through which they conveyed specific ideas about each of the subjects at hand. The triumph of the notion of PTSD starting in the 1980s cannot be explained without taking such factors into account.[85] In the case of Germany, the feedback during the second half of the 1960s had the effect that the emotional sequelae of war were entirely discussable when it came to American troops in Vietnam, but could not be applied to war damage in German soldiers. Opposing such a transfer was the still dominant German psychiatric doctrine concerning the human capacity to endure the stress of war, in conjunction with the media's expanding image of the perpetrator as the trials of Nazi criminals progressed. At the same time, the acknowledgment that the (mainly) Jewish victims of Nazi persecution had a unique status, not only in terms of the Nazi war but also in the general framework of all crimes against humanity to date, emerged as a moral and political rule for what could be articulated in the West German media, which was also pressing for a decision in the professional debate that would favor compensation across the board.

As an example, this found expression in a two-part radio program, "Late Damage to the Psyche Following Political Persecution," that *Sender Freies Berlin* broadcasted in February 1965. It is no coincidence that the extensive manuscript of the broadcast is found in the archives of the German finance ministry, responsible as it was for reparations proceedings.[86] The previous year, the ministry had attempted to play down the quality and seriousness of a just-published anthology on the subject of delayed mental damage following political persecution.[87] A handwritten note by a senior official in the ministry in the margin of a letter indicates that in his eyes the book represented a danger: "Even now mental consequences are frequently overestimated in the assessment of health damage from N[ational] S[ocialist] persecution."[88] The psychiatrists under attack countered, however. In the two installments that ran for a total of two hours, they informed the station's listeners and the ministry, which received a copy of the broadcast manuscript, that people who had been persecuted by the Nazis, above all Jewish camp inmates, presented serious, persistent mental symptoms, because "the Nazi terror had caused experientially reactive damage to a previously unknown and unimaginable degree." The station went on to describe the resistance against this perception within the psychiatric establishment and the reparations administration, which for a long time had focused on "the unprecedented causes of fear and persecution" only with the greatest reluctance.[89]

Conflicts were thus already indicated at the start of the broadcast. The editor of the station's features section invited a range of experts from law, the psychiatric profession, the reparations administration, and politics to comment. The interviews are so skillfully arranged that in the end there could be no doubt that evaluators and judges who refused to recognize mental illness in victims of Nazi persecution were by and large taking a scientifically and morally untenable position. The radio station claimed that in the meantime such applications were generally approved if the evaluator simply "examined them thoroughly and reached his decision carefully and conscientiously."[90] Accordingly, there was no longer any question of a true debate over the new psychiatric insights. There were at best scattered evaluators who still refused to accept the new insight. Excerpts from the transcript of a purportedly typical medical examination and from an outrageous evaluation were read during the feature and testified forcefully to the absurdity of such a refusal. This absurdity had already been expressed by the distinguished psychoanalyst Kurt Eissler, a refugee from Austria of Jewish origin and now a naturalized U.S. citizen. In an article published in 1963, he asked a pointed question that the producer of the program passed along to listeners: "How many of one's children does one need to have murdered, while still remaining symptom free, if one's constitution is to be considered normal?"[91]

The broadcast on *Sender Freies Berlin* left no doubt as to who was discredited among German medical professionals and bureaucrats—particularly in the eyes of their international colleagues. In addition to that, it informed listeners that very early on there had been observations that registered "just how unprecedented the horror endured in the concentration camps had been."[92] Many interwoven case histories of persecuted individuals, mainly Jews, who lost close relatives in the camps, or endured horrific mortal fear there, or in the ghettos, or in hiding, and who continued to be tormented by images from that period, corroborated the impression, even if the accounts stemmed from later years.[93] This was a veritable *tour d'horizon* of the history of Nazi persecution. Psychiatric experts explained the mental impact that day-to-day discrimination and imprisonment in the camps had already had at the time. The survey emphasized that anyone who continued to deny that the mental complaints of survivors had been caused by persecution was simultaneously revealing his refusal to genuinely confront the Nazi past. Even at the start, the radio broadcast had made allusions to that extent. The narrator explained that the sluggish attitude shown by the disciplines involved in the reparations process corresponded to "the general picture of our belated examination of the past." In conclusion, he likewise made it unmistakably clear that the "belated elucidation" by medical science did, in the end, represent a path "for clarifying the relationship to our National Socialist past."[94] In this way, the radio station confronted its audience with a clear position: it was not absolutely necessary to create a seamless chain of evidence for the assertion of persecution-associated mental complaints, because there was a moral responsibility to help those who were still suffering from the persecution—indeed, "not merely whatever help is necessary, but as much help as possible." This was "far more important" in the eyes of the moderator than "dispensing with any remaining doubts in the new discovery of medical phenomena."[95]

From now on, there was an extraordinarily sharply divergence of perspectives in the media with respect to the suffering of Wehrmacht veterans and that of individuals who had been persecuted by the Nazis, primarily Jewish Holocaust survivors. They were viewed as two fundamentally different categories. This becomes very clear in two articles Der Spiegel published in 1969. One of them was concerned with the history of the POWs in Soviet camps. It documented great hardship and striking mental stress, the shock of being captured, the anguish of uncertainty, and above all the torment of starvation. Yet Der Spiegel also reminded readers that at 60 percent, the "death rate of the five million Red Army soldiers in Nazi custody" was far higher than the 35 percent of imprisoned Wehrmacht soldiers who perished in the hands of the Soviets. Above all, the magazine insisted, supported by historian Kurt W. Böhme's assessment, that the "theory that the Soviets had intended to subsequently liquidate the survivors of the battle of Stalingrad through aimless 'death marches' . . . was, on the whole and objectively examined,' not tenable." In the POW camps as well, the article continued, Germans soldiers had been fed "to the extent it was possible," and that meant no differently than the Russian civilians, who—because of the massive war damage and harvest losses—received as little to eat as the German soldiers who had laid their country to waste."[96]

In a newly forming "political correctness in memory culture,"[97] Der Spiegel left no misunderstanding as to who had been the aggressor in the war and who alone had been devoted to the goal of systematic extermination. Beyond this, the Spiegel pointed out unambiguously that the suffering of German POWs, including their mental symptoms, belonged entirely to the past. As Der Spiegel reported in a second article in 1969, the POWs' suffering was over and had long concluded, in stark contrast to the mental illnesses that still impaired the lives of many concentration camps survivors. The survivors' "camp fate" had marked them, frequently preventing them from achieving success in their professions, shattering their family lives, and encumbering their entire social existence. Although former camp inmates did not always discuss their mental problems with their doctors, as readers learned, *Der Spiegel* reported that psychiatrist Paul Matussek in Munich had developed special procedures for studying mental disturbances in former camp inmates. Based on his findings he was able to show that concentration camp survivors suffered far more frequently from contact disorders, delusional ideas, and anxiety dreams than they had indicated in their reparations proceedings or had been ascertained by evaluators. In general, it could be identified that roughly 88 percent of those Matussek interviewed still suffered from mental symptoms.[98]

Twenty-five years after the end of World War II and the liberation of the death camps, not everyone saw things this way. Yet it is unmistakable that a shift had occurred in mass media coverage during the 1960s as compared to the first postwar decade, and that this marked the start of a change in the public memory of the war and the Holocaust that was to unfold over many years. The transformation and establishment of new psychiatric knowledge, a process that would not have advanced as far without the political and moral pressure of the 1960s, played a distinct role. In the media, at least, the theme of the mental consequences of Nazi terror now occupied a fixed place. Long before the four-part American television series *Holocaust* was aired in West Germany in 1979, an event often described as a caesura in historical memory, the country had opened itself to both an awareness and the interpretation of the suffering of Holocaust survivors.[99] Television had also played its role, with West Germany's ZDF broadcasting what certainly was one of the most impressive documentaries on this theme in 1972. It was entitled *Mendel Schainfeld's Second Trip to Germany* and directed by Hans-Dieter Grabe.[100] In 1971, the year the documentary was filmed, Grabe accompanied the Polish-born Mendel Szajnfeld, a forty-nine-year-old Jew who now lived in Norway, on a trip by rail from Oslo to Munich. The travel had been necessary because the Munich reparations office refused to increase his meager pension, even though Norwegian doctors had meanwhile certified his almost complete disability stemming from torture in work and concentration camps. At the beginning of the film, the narrator informed viewers that Szajnfeld suffered "from insomnia, anxiety dreams, attacks of weakness, disturbances of equilibrium, depression, and head and back pain" and hoped that the authorities would attach credence to a German evaluator.

At the end of the film, we are offered no information as to the outcome of the proceeding; the recorded sequences of Szajnfeld's account are evidently meant to speak for themselves. He is the only person seen in the film, in his train compartment. The narrator rarely comments, the camera then capturing the landscape passing by outside the window. As a result, Szajnfeld is the sole focus of attention as he tells his story in German, the language he learned from his father and in the camps. His father had always spoken so highly of the Germans, of "German culture, German humanity, German justice." Szajnfeld cannot forget his father hammering it into his children: "Children, the Germans say 'Live and let live,'" he quotes the man, who continued to say it "until the last minute, so to speak." At this point, Szajnfeld has difficulty speaking. He did not have "the fortune to meet the good Germans," who were always spoken of at home, which was something he could not forget—and which he regrets, as he often emphasizes in the film. Yet there are other things he also cannot forget: "the concentration camps and the ghettos and the business with the bad people. I don't want to spell it out." Szajnfeld's response to a question by Grabe shows that he sometimes sees it all before his eyes—"Yes, unfortunately." Nevertheless, he tries "to be friendly and cordial to everyone," although he "can't always" manage. "I myself am convinced," he continues, "that I do what I can to . . . to be amusing, and, and in general I try to talk with people and so forth. But I can't always manage. Sometimes I have horrible periods. Of course, it's worst at night. What am I supposed to do? There's nothing you can do. I don't like speaking about these things."

Something Mendel Szajnfeld cannot do is to forget: the child simply taken from its mother and thrown away, the woman who wanted to be with her child and was beaten to death for that reason, just like his brother-in-law, who, when he had been selected, wanted to go to his child one more time. In the concentration camp, these things took place before his very eyes: every day he would see "five hundred, seven hundred people shot. That was an everyday thing." But the worst thing for him were the children's transports: "They screamed, and I saw them; unfortunately a person can't forget that. I've tried for so many years to get the picture out of my head. But it doesn't work. I don't like talking about this. But it was horrible, seeing the children."

Mendel Szajnfeld saw endless horrors, only a few of which he mentions. He lost his entire family. One night, he took bread from the body of a fellow "work comrade" who had died. It is not only something he cannot forget, but a source of tormenting guilt to this day, he confesses. That he was hungry, pitifully hungry, doesn't ease his conscience. "All I could think of was bread, bread, bread. To be full, just once. And then I took the dead man's bread. Unfortunately," he says and thinks that maybe he is now "being punished for it" by not being able to work. Now as before, Szajnfeld is tortured by many memories, and he indicates that he still often regrets, twenty-five years after he was liberated, not having been able to take his life after returning to the Polish village of his birth. Over the years, his illnesses have grown worse, but above all it is the emotional anguish of the memories that will not subside:

> Sometimes the war, the camp, and all that is with me in my own living room. When I'm really feeling joyless and don't want to live, in other words, when I'm depressed, I think the camp and Herr Goeth and, and all of that is right in my own living room. And sometimes I reach the point I think, oh God, you've really gone crazy, just let it go. . . . Sometimes I can forget things for a short time. But I don't always manage. That's bad, very bad. A person who can't work can't be happy. My father says so, too.

For Mendel Szajnfeld, the past is often his present. The sight of policemen is still a horror for him. If he sees a German shepherd, he runs. "And barbed wire?" Grabe asks. "Drives me crazy. Drives me crazy. Unfortunately. That's the bad thing," he replies. Then he sometimes thinks, "Well, what's a little wire. It's just wire, isn't it?" But for him it's something completely different. He can't bear it, so he knows very well he's "crazy." "Why shouldn't I be able to look at a piece of wire. But I can't handle it." Then, at one point Mendel Szajnfeld briefly acknowledges something, a brief remark that is easily overheard in spite of, or perhaps precisely because of, the many glimpses he has offered into his painful memories of inconceivable horror. It is a thought that runs entirely counter to the calls for remembrance that were emerging in West German society. At one point he had hoped that "some doctor" could help him "in that very way," namely, to "forget."

Conclusion

In the 1970s, hardly any doubt remained among the West German public that the survivors of Nazi persecution and extermination, especially Jewish Holocaust survivors, had been marked for life by profound mental suffering. In West Germany, a shift in perception concerning the impact of this massive crime against humanity had been initiated. As of this time, the shift could be observed throughout the Western world. In a book published in 2004, author Eva Hoffman, who lives in the United States and experienced this shift first and as a member of the so-called second generation, remarked that "the survivors of such events, we take it for granted, have been traumatized."[1] Hoffman recalls that in 1959 when she emigrated as a fourteen-year-old with her parents—Polish Jewish Holocaust survivors—from postwar Poland to Canada, the situation was still completely different. She suggests that during the first postwar decades neither the term "trauma" nor the concept itself existed in the general nonmedical vocabulary.[2] For Hoffman, the decisive factor was that, in keeping with prevailing medical doctrine, the medical profession rejected a causal relationship between the war and long-term mental suffering.[3] As she looks back, she continues to find it highly remarkable that even the psychiatrists who began to relate the mental symptoms they observed in survivors to the Holocaust were surprised at the discovery. As a child, she intermittently registered fear or despair in her parents. But she also knows that her parents did not perceive themselves at the time as "traumatized":

> The majority of the survivors [did not] think of themselves as "traumatized" or emotionally damaged in unusual ways. Even if the concept had been abroad early on, I doubt that many would have seen it as applying to them. My parents knew they had suffered terrible things, but so had others. They even knew that what they had gone through was much worse than their non-Jewish neighbors: but they did not know that pain could be parsed in different ways. I think this was true for most survivors. Most of

them were not psychologically savvy people. They did not come from a psychologically savvy generation, or from psychologically savvy subcultures. . . . Suffering is suffering, no matter how howlingly extreme. It is something you live with; take on; suffer. And so, many survivors, perhaps most, remained innocent of therapy, and suspicious of it.[4]

Here Hoffman confronts the reader with the basic problem inherent in retrospectively projecting "trauma" on the experience of people living in a time before the concept had gained general acceptance. As Hoffman makes clear, problematizing this projection is not tantamount to relativizing the survivors' suffering or denying the emotional consequences of the Holocaust. Nor does she express doubt of any sort that over recent decades therapeutic help was decisive in making unbearable torment bearable for many Holocaust survivors. Nevertheless, she believes that one must avoid forcing the subjective experiential worlds and lifeworlds of many victims of Nazism after 1945, or at an earlier point of emigration, into the straitjacket of a retrospective diagnostic ascription.[5] Hoffman explains this by drawing on personal experiences in her own family. After her parents died in the 1990s, she was able to read the psychiatric evaluations that were prepared during their reparations proceedings. Looking back, it seemed to her that the knowledge at her disposal as a family member was both less and, on the other hand, also greater than what the psychiatrists knew as professionals. There were both overlap and significant differences between the two kinds of knowledge:

I knew that my parents' sadness, although salient, was only a part of their temperamental texture: and that loss, although central, did not entirely define their lives. . . . To me, they were not "survivors"; they were only people who had undergone extremity and were now living another stage of their lives. Their very human condition did not appear to me as a condition, nor did it seem susceptible to being parsed into diagnostic categories.[6]

What Hoffman addresses here in regard to her own family is the danger of interpretive narrowing that arises anywhere the concept of trauma is applied retroactively. Peter Novick has already pointed out that strikingly false conclusions have resulted from this kind of back projection. According to Novick, for example, it is misleading to attribute the growing importance of the Holocaust in American culture since the 1990s to a putatively general traumatization of both Jews and non-Jews in the States through the Holocaust. He argues that we should not interpret the previous long years of silence about the subject as a form of "repression" in the sense of an inescapable reaction to the event. Rather, he indicates, much evidence suggests that "survivor's silence was a response to 'market considerations'" (hardly anyone was interested) as well as a result of frequently voiced calls for forgetting.[7] Novick explicitly affirms that for some American Jews (and possibly non-Jews as well) the Holocaust functioned as a traumatic event, yet he takes his argument a step further. To be "shocked, dismayed, or saddened"—the sorts of reactions recorded in the sources—is something different from being traumatized, and in any event "not for purposes of setting in train the inexorable progression of repression and the return of the repressed." Through an automatic ascription of "traumatization," other experiential worlds and ways of acting are co-opted and false conclusions drawn, in a circular argument. Novick encapsulates his position as follows: "It is simply assumed that the Holocaust *must* have been traumatic. And if it wasn't talked about, this *must* have been repression."[8]

To be sure, the meanwhile intensive examination of the personal memories of Holocaust survivors and the mental wounds inflicted on them has yielded numerous revealing studies that provide important insights into the many destructive consequences of this specific type of violence and the associated difficulties in communicating what took place.[9] It may be that precisely in this field an opportunity has once again presented itself to examine the problem of ex post ascriptions of trauma—in contrast to what is usually the case in the more recent uses of the concept for any other group of victims. What is at work here as well is what Novick suggests with respect to the position of the Holocaust in American discourse. It is possible that explaining things in terms of trauma has gone unchallenged because historians have not systematically concerned themselves with the changing perception of the suffering experienced.

It is only within the ranks of the psychiatric profession that some doctors have in the meantime begun to distance themselves from diagnosing PTSD in every case, because they believe it goes too far. Recently, psychiatrist Klaus Dörner intensified his criticism of the diagnosis.[10] In West Germany in the 1980s, he was one of the few physicians who did not preclude, in principle, the idea that Germans injured in the war may have incurred long-term mental damage.[11] Currently, his advice is that it is preferable to avoid the diagnosis of PTSD entirely, arguing that it has not been possible to separate the diagnosis from "political and historical valuations, the economic interests of those affected, and recently from the economic interests of the aid workers." Above all, the manner in which the diagnosis is being used has gone out of control "because of the nonspecificity of the syndrome (who would not be subject to involuntary memories after a catastrophe?), the nonspecificity of the traumata (new compensable traumata are constantly being invented), and the danger of monocausal appropriation of perception." Dörner ends in a deliberately provocative manner with the following advice to his colleagues: "At a time when, more than before, we all love the victims so very much, part of our medical professionalism lies in knowing that with too much love, too many entitlements, and too much pity we can fixate such patients on their role as victims, thus damaging and rendering them chronic. . . . 'The person who suffers a truly grave fate is as a rule strong enough to bear it.'"[12]

There are certainly good reasons to doubt that such warnings will end the history of post-traumatic stress disorder anytime soon.[13] In any event, such interventions do make clear that the scientific discussion of the "normal" human capacity to process extreme stress and its memory continues to be in flux. Only a significant amount of temporal distance will allow us to see clearly which challenges this continuing process of knowledge production is reacting to, and how it, in turn, may be transforming society's view of the way events are experienced, endured, and remembered. The trauma concepts that have become the dominant instrument in the Western world for interpreting the personal and societal processing of events perceived as threatening, and which meanwhile have also come to exert enormous influence on our historical imagination, have a history of their own. And this history, in turn, cannot be adequately understood without the history of the production of psychiatric knowledge.

For this reason, the present book has taken the path of systematic historicization, in order to reveal the circumstances in postwar West Germany under which medical-psychiatric interpretation changed with respect to the way human beings process violence, and thereby redefined the framework for processing experiences in the personal sphere as well as in public remembrance of war and genocide. As shown in the first part of the book, which analyzes personal memory fragments from the immediate postwar period, when it comes to German returnees, it is hardly possible to speak of repression of the war and Nazi crimes. Rather, for many Wehrmacht veterans this was a period where they unwillingly remained spellbound by the war. The war resurfaced in dreams and momentarily—for many it continued for years—cut off any escape from the past. Images or noises were also often enough to abruptly revive war memories. We can assume that in the immediate aftermath of the war countless returnees were driven by and trapped in the war's legacy, although the reasons that the war had become a burden to them doubtlessly varied greatly. This is even reflected in the forms in which the fear was articulated—forms so common one could almost conclude that anxiety was the general mood during the first postwar years, a distorted echo of a wide range of states of mind experienced during the war and the postwar period itself. Some former soldiers struggled with anxieties that had already plagued them during the war; for others the war only became a source of anxiety as defeat unmistakably loomed. For many, knowledge of the crimes committed was enough to produce the fear of being held to account. Confrontation with the occupiers, especially the denazification officials, contributed significantly in many cases. Following the total defeat, there was widespread fear of being exposed for providing even minor assistance to the Führer and Reich. It was often impossible to decide whether looking backward or into the future generated the greater fear. Both perspectives were also present in a widespread postwar disillusionment, which we can understand as an additional mode for processing the past. Here as well various factors were at play, because even before the total defeat, the violence of the war had dismantled idealized self-images. Some soldiers experienced their own fear as something unexpected and deeply dismaying, and hence as cowardice. Others grappled with the lost illusion of their own moral innocence. Assumptions about one's own person were sometimes badly shaken by the experience of having been able to kill. The complete collapse of the Nazi regime and the dissolution of dreams for the future that had been associated with it shook others to a degree that left them deeply bewildered. In fact, even some years after the end of the war, memory fragments described by various returnees point to belief in National Socialism as a source of enormous inner support. While this belief still radiated outward, it did not prevent that the same individual from being barely able to look himself in the eye because he was cognizant of the mass crimes that had been committed.

As a result, and contrary to outward appearances, postwar life for many Wehrmacht veterans was an inner ordeal, especially during the initial years as they struggled to regain their balance. This effort led to attempts to construct a different self, or even allegedly one's actual self, which would hopefully allow them to live their future lives with knowledge of the criminal war. Frequently, the goal of rewriting one's biography was to escape the political purge or get off lightly in the denazification proceedings, which is hardly surprising. Yet this sober calculation was not always the only driver. Despair over the life situation one faced along with one's family, and genuine consternation over the monstrosity of the mass murders were often additional motives.

Above all, however, the accounts of the war that reveal a desire to construct a "different" self express a need for personal rehabilitation. In the aftermath of war and mass murder, this did not develop of its own accord in many former soldiers, irrespective of the outcome of their political rehabilitation. The idea of two souls in one body, one of which came into effect only under the special conditions of war, was a construct that allowed the veterans to continue their lives despite the atrocities of the war. It was similar to the assertion that their allegedly true selves had often been misjudged during their military careers. Their quest for self-images they could live with was extraordinarily self-referential: the suffering of their enemies and victims was hardly mentioned. Nevertheless, the victims of Nazi crimes had a sort of secret presence, noticeably permeating the former soldiers' individual attempts to rationalize their behavior during the war. Their endeavor to divest themselves of the past repeatedly forced them to envisage their victims as well.

The evidence suggests that this situation did not entail general self-victimization or an attempt to equalize their own suffering with that of the Nazis' victims. Overall, coming to terms with the war was confusing and often humiliating for many soldiers for any number of reasons, but it was not characterized by a rhetoric of victimization. It appears that such a perspective on one's own role in a criminal war did not exist during that period. It was a consequence of such incommensurability in the biographical construction that the only communication, even with close family members, was silent. The political and moral rules governing what could be mentioned were in flux during the immediate postwar period. This made it difficult to communicate the reasons for the vexation, which was often experienced as a biographical hiatus. The material rubble of the war was mirrored in the social rubble of these former German soldiers, who inwardly knew more than they could say, even in their most intimate family circle. Often it was the women who established this silence, not only because they could not or did not wish to demand that the atrocities they themselves had experienced be heard, but also because they often did not realize that the past war was part of their present family relationships. Such silence and the inadequate efforts to raise the issues did not necessarily reflect a flight from the horror of the war or from complicity in the crimes. Rather, what manifested here was an alienation between men and women and between the generations. The veterans' disappointment over their previously held self-ideals and the total devaluation of their lives burdened the emotional condition of even those men who turned to their family circle or sought the help of neighbors to escape their own misery in the aftermath of the war. The mutual understanding required to cope with such difficulties reached its limits at the point where returning soldiers and their behavior seemed confusingly changed or did not meet the expectations of the time regarding a man's ability to endure stress over a longer period.

During the first postwar years, even close family members usually did not consider the war experience to be the decisive factor in such problems. In such cases of despairing and sometimes impatient perplexity, families turned to medical experts for professional advice.

As described in the second and main part of the book, in keeping with prevailing medical doctrine West German psychiatrists rejected the possibility that long-term mental abnormalities in repatriated veterans could be attributed to experiences during the war, or that the experiences could precipitate serious mental illness such as schizophrenia. This point of view was neither a product of Nazism nor limited to German psychiatry. Instead, it was based on professional conclusions that had already gained acceptance during World War I and had become established in other European countries as well. Contrary to the long-held, widespread assumption that this perspective represented a purely instrumental understanding of symptoms in terms of wartime requirements, a series of empirical observations and therapeutic experiences during the Great War had strengthened the view, long advocated by some psychiatrists, that mental disorders could not be caused by exogenous stress factors in the absence of organic damage. Even for a psychiatry mainly oriented toward biomedicine, which thereby opened itself to psychoanalytic approaches, the widespread symptoms of trembling, shaking, and paralysis associated with the war became scientifically explainable "functional suffering." Furthermore, since even under intense stress and hardship the majority of the soldiers did not develop symptoms in that direction, the notion of hereditary causes seemed plausible. Finally, based on what the war had taught them, in cases of severe mental illness leading psychiatrists believed they were in a position to conclude that the ability of the healthy brain to endure stress was extraordinarily high.

During World War II, psychiatrists built on this diagnostic and therapeutic approach, as manifest in the systematic practice of "forward psychiatry." This was intended to recognize mental disorders early and treat them on the spot, thereby preventing a soldier's "flight into illness," with its unconscious prospect of being discharged from military service. Despite all the diagnostic and therapeutic difficulties that psychiatrists faced during the course of the war, especially on the eastern front, in their understanding of their profession they continued to believe that psychogenic disorders were controllable. This produced frequent tension within the psychiatric ranks and repeatedly led to an adamant struggle for diagnostic differentiation and precision. Yet it changed nothing in terms of the basic conviction that the war did not come into question as a cause for the development of long-term mental disorders. All measures and therapies used were based on this conviction, and even the sharpest disciplinary actions ultimately only seemed to confirm it. Although psychiatrists differed in their choice of methods, at the end of World War II the correctness of conclusions drawn during World War I therefore seemed to have been borne out, with much support coming from non-German colleagues as well. There was worldwide agreement among numerous physicians and researchers that a healthy human being possessed a nearly limitless ability to withstand even the worst forms of hardship.

The same premise informed the approach German psychiatrists took toward returning Wehrmacht soldiers. However, because of their mental state, a great many of them posed a challenge to the attending physicians. These men were not alone in their suffering, however, and they initially received no special attention from the psychiatrists, for in postwar Germany postwar society doctors saw stress and suffering everywhere. Indeed, mental problems and disorders actually seemed to be a mass phenomenon. Above all, the evidently widespread uncommunicative apathy sparked a short-term professional debate over how to explain the phenomenon, although without calling for a revision of prevailing doctrine concerning the "normal" processing of extreme stress. This possibility was contradicted by expectations of "objectivity" and solid scientific evidence for postulating the general validity of new findings. A single observation of something that seemed unusual in a specific psychiatric treatment situation carried far too little weight to shake the foundations of that established doctrine. In addition, central assumptions of established doctrine determined to a large degree the interpretation of the behavioral abnormalities perceived in postwar society, so that we can speak of a stubborn self-perpetuation of the psychiatric approach. Accordingly, much of the mental suffering endured by the returnees was viewed as a kind of evasive reaction to the reality of a "collapsed society"; in other words, it was essentially something for which the affected individuals and their "hereditary disposition" could be held responsible. Initially, however, the state of physical depletion observable in broad segments of the German population often suggested that the mental problems were caused by physical exhaustion and pronounced malnutrition. This conclusion as well corresponded to the current state of psychiatric knowledge; such cases had been familiar since the Great War. It was also supported by colleagues in internal medicine, who introduced the concepts of "hunger disease" and "dystrophy" into the professional discussion mainly with reference to the returning war prisoners. From the standpoint of the medical profession, one could assume that the mental condition of the returnees, and of Germans in general, would "normalize" with an improvement in the food situation.

Thus, postwar Germany psychiatric knowledge modified itself only at an exceedingly slow pace. At first, isolated shifts in interpretation and classification structure suggested themselves for a highly disparate range of motives. Taken together, however, they prepared the ground for an opening of psychiatric discourse in the late 1950s. During the first postwar decade, the questioning of established psychiatric doctrine was carried out within its own categories. Dissatisfaction with the existing diagnostic arsenal sometimes developed as a result of the logic of prevailing doctrine itself because in many diagnoses it placed extraordinary weight on hereditary factors. Yet the search for new diagnostic tools and etiological theories was cautious. It first received a special impetus in 1949 when a new wave of POWs (the so-called late returnees) started arriving from Soviet camps. Although they did not seem to be in particularly alarming physical or mental condition when they arrived, after some time many of them presented doctors with a range of intractable problems. Physical complaints that were extremely difficult to pin down objectively and vegetative symptoms stood out and demanded explanations.

A broad segment of the German medical world now faced the challenge of fundamentally rethinking the significance of endogenous and exogenous factors for the emergence of physical and mental health problems. Psychiatrists were not the pacesetters in this development, but rather experts from internal medicine who were also addressing the late sequelae of interment in the Soviet camps and had introduced the concept of "physical-mental summation trauma." The psychiatrists were not yet willing to go that far. They increasingly adopted the dystrophy diagnosis from internal medicine, and this served as a starting point for further reflection. Recognition of dystrophy as a condition experienced in a POW camp as a result of inadequate nutrition was in fact fully compatible with prevailing psychiatric doctrine, which in no way disputed a causal relationship between mental problems and previous physical damage. Nevertheless the assumption of past dystrophy also offered the psychiatrists an opportunity to assign greater weight than before to exogenous factors in explaining mental changes. Recovery, they now began to suggest, was not only slowed by the enormous physical strain of imprisonment but by mental stress as well, which needed to receive greater consideration than before in etiological explanations. Yet from the standpoint of the psychiatric field, which had been concentrating on brain research, among other things, in previous years, another question seemed of far greater interest, namely, whether hunger-related changes in the brain could be detected that might explain the fundamental changes seen in many "late returnees." And in fact research that included examinations of the brains of dead patients pointed so strongly in this direction that by 1953 it was thought certain that extreme malnutrition could cause brain damage.

Although the psychiatrists had continued to argue within the framework of "prevailing doctrine," this shift of psychiatric knowledge nevertheless had a strong impact on the social reality of a specific group of returnees, for whom the prospect emerged that the veterans' pension administration would officially recognize their mental suffering as "war related" and they would be granted the official status of "war victims." Since the veterans' pension administration adhered to the concept of illness that was authoritative in West German psychiatry until the end of the 1950s, disorders that were strictly mental were not recognized as "pathological." Mental symptoms that were deemed to stem from dystrophy, and consequently from physical damage that had at one time been incurred, therefore fulfilled the criteria for being accepted as the result of hardship suffered during internment. But even in these cases, the evaluation of pension claims demanded administratively manageable answers to the question of how long a period of time was to be allowed during which one could speak of such "war related" mental damage in the absence of concrete, demonstrable physical findings. In the production of psychiatric knowledge, this caused external factors to come into play, which, along with the requirements of administrative action and the logic of legal decision-making, would exert an influence on what would be considered valid psychiatric knowledge.

For the returnees from the Soviet camps, the determination of what constituted a "normal" recovery period following extraordinary stress meant that in those cases where internment already lay a number of years back and there were no physical findings, mental problems could no longer be classified within the explanatory framework of dystrophy. Once again, as was the case for all other returnees as well, the illness was considered to be hereditary. Consequently, in the early 1950s the medical upgrading of dystrophy by no means led to an automatic attribution of the veterans' mental problems to Soviet imprisonment. In general, a close look at psychiatric practice during the period shows that the doctor's suspicion of being intentionally or unintentionally duped by the patient represented nothing short of a constitutive moment in medical evaluation. Here, something came into play that had been remarkably widespread among psychiatrists since World War I, namely, the fear of being fooled by the "factitious disorders," "war tremblers," or "pension neurotics." Supposedly such deceit stemmed from a striving for security and was frequently associated with an attempt to obtain a military disability pension.

Nevertheless, a diagnosis first had to be found; the cause of the suffering was rarely immediately apparent. Rather, a diagnosis was crafted in a complex negotiating process in which the psychiatrist's questions suggested an interpretive framework, but the patient's way of behaving and presenting his story also had an effect. Information from relatives and the assessment of other doctors had to be taken into account as well. In the cases analyzed above, a dilemma emerged for the evaluating doctors: the suspicion of deception could only be eliminated when the patient's behavior responded to the medical measures taken. If problems exceeding the accepted late sequelae of dystrophy persisted nonetheless, then it was impossible to gain certainty. Yet certainty was what the legal guidelines for pension claims demanded. Throughout the 1950s, when doubts arose, the clear fallback position was to assume hereditarily determined causes and to usher patients whose cases seemed problematic out of the pension system as "neurotics" and "psychopaths." Above all, starting in the mid-1950s the number of cases in which the suspicion of "pension neurotic tendencies" was present markedly increased.

The cases discussed in this book show that there were a large number returnees and their close relations who accepted the opinion of the experts without further ado, even when the veterans' mental problems were not attributed to the war or internment as a POW. Yet objections were raised as well, and in comparison to the quiet acquiescence they were very noticeable, especially since those affected often brought in the disabled veterans' associations and took legal measures. There can be no doubt that such protest occasionally resulted from a conviction that the war was the only true cause of the illness. However, avoiding a widely held stigma attached to long-term mental illness seems also to have played a role, especially when the problems were officially certified as hereditary. In any event, the reason for filing a war pension application occasionally reflected the desire to have one's "healthy" hereditary disposition certified by gaining official recognition of one's illness. In other words, it involved an attempt to save one's honor and was sometimes associated with a former soldier's need for acknowledgment of his effort in the war.

The importance of the "dispute over hereditability" can hardly be overestimated as a catalyst for the initiation of discourse about human processing of extreme hardship, all the more so because there was a faction within internal medicine that was receptive to psychosomatic approaches and was disputing psychiatry's interpretive authority in terms of mind-body processes. These advocates of psychosomatic explanations were pressing for stronger consideration of the social determinants of "illness" than was otherwise the case, not only in psychiatry but also in medicine in general, due to the recourse taken to the hereditability argument. The psychosomatic approach did, in fact, signal some basic methodological changes. Essentially, they involved placing greater emphasis on personal experiences and subjective forms of perception. For the returnees and a broad segment of West German society, this was read as recognition of the hardship they had endured. It is therefore not surprising that they often supported those who advocated the psychosomatic approach—and this in a broad social compact with the veterans' organizations. For the psychosomaticists, this meant having to prevail against a broad front of opponents throughout the medical profession and having to furnish a convincing diagnosis for a phenomenon that had previously remained unnamed in prevailing psychiatric doctrine.

In the mid-1950s, this dispute was not limited to the West German medical world but also played out in other European states where researchers struggled to explain the persistent mental problems they were observing in former resistance fighters and deported persons. In these groups of victims as well, such problems had not been anticipated. Striking parallels emerged not only in the basic medical-scientific assumptions of the various European countries; the way the previously unknown symptoms were interpreted was also sometimes remarkably similar, most notably when it came to the role ascribed to hunger in the development of long-term physical and mental disorders. In addition, we can identify core problems that confronted doctors in other countries to almost the same degree as in West Germany. These included the difficulty arriving at a precise causal classification of illness when it emerged following a phase in which no symptoms had been present. It was virtually impossible to present precise proof of the connection with the hardships and cruelties experienced, as the other national disability pension systems were also demanding. Apparently, they also shared the fear of "pension neurotics." Beginning in the mid-1950s, German compensation authorities were increasingly confronted with applications from abroad that demanded recognition of mental suffering in victims of Nazism. This not only posed a moral challenge for the German medical establishment but also confronted it with the question of how to reconcile such recognition with prevailing psychiatric doctrine.

Pressure from colleagues abroad played a major role in the development and establishment in Germany of new psychiatric knowledge on the mental effects of Nazi persecution and extermination policies. But in the end, an entire nexus of factors was decisive. For example, the professional debate about mental suffering was already under way to a degree, but it was decisively advanced by the need to evaluate the impairments of POWs from the Soviet camps. Here an etiological shift with respect to illnesses where physical causes could not be demonstrated was already in the air, so to speak. Furthermore, there was a considerable number of evaluating physicians working for the German reparation authorities who, in contrast to the majority of their colleagues, not only shared the non-German evaluators' sense of a need to deviate from Germany's prevailing psychiatric doctrine, but also saw the legal possibility of departing from restrictive reparations practice, at least in part. A decisive factor was that reparations fell under the purview of civil law and therefore required a less stringent demonstration of causal relationship than was the case for military disability pensions, which fell under social law and were therefore subject to a different legal framework. Thus, the pressure for clarification did not arise primarily in academia. It was the reparation authorities who, in their need to draft regulations, had to reach agreement among themselves regarding the validity of current psychiatric knowledge. A broad spectrum of players participated in the clarification process. Selected medical experts from German universities, leading physicians from the reparation authorities, jurists, senior officials from various federal ministries, doctors from outside Germany, the interested public (initially mostly Jewish interest groups), and even the Foreign Office took part in the complex, multiphase, and in part politically highly charged power and negotiation process through which a new form of psychiatric knowledge was established in Germany and its fields of application were defined.

If we take account of the extraordinarily long life of accepted medical theories, in Germany (as well as some other countries) a new reading of mental illness emerged in a remarkably brief span of time. Glancing sideways at other Western European countries for the sake of comparison, it appears that German psychiatrists—whose assumption of what Venzlaff termed "experientially determined personality change" requires no physical damage—even went a step further than many of their colleagues abroad, who for a long time continued to attribute late mental sequelae to previous brain damage. Still, the process in which these new perspectives gained acceptance was anything but smooth, with the concrete financial concerns of the various authorities playing a very important role. But different national traditions of medical research also stood in the way of quick agreement on common medical assumptions and on how to proceed. The framework of feasibility was explored in concrete exchanges between the medical representatives of the reparation authorities and the evaluators outside of Germany. A range of evidence suggests that the procedures were less complicated in Europe than in the exchanges with the United States, where the new psychiatric thinking also had to establish itself. This highlights the international exchange process without which the shift in the psychiatric approach to human processing of extreme stress cannot be understood. At the same time, however, the assertion of new knowledge was shaped by national discourse, its social reach influenced by specific lines of conflict. In West Germany, moral and political considerations contributed significantly to the setting of the parameters for both interpretation and action in the medical practice of reparations evaluation. The politically precarious status of the young West German state within the Western alliance doubtlessly played an important role. In furnishing a medical justification for the acknowledgment that mental disorders were the result of persecution, the political and moral argument was only indirectly conceded. It would, however, be openly avowed in the form of a social responsibility to compensate formerly persecuted individuals who had developed mental problems.

The acceptance of new psychiatric knowledge, which could be achieved only through the introduction of a new diagnosis, first had to overcome the resistance of a broad medical front. The reasons for this were not merely political. Psychiatrists who argued that the acceptance of compensable psychoreactive disturbances did not represent new scientific insight that called prevailing doctrine into question, but essentially involved only a new "valuation" of familiar phenomena. They were primarily defending the biomedical orientation from the growing influence of anthropological psychiatry, which employed other procedures. Behind the controversy, a tangible dispute over methods was unfolding, as these methods actually did produce different findings. Accordingly, the critics of "prevailing doctrine," who were speaking out in favor of methodological expansion, assigned far greater weight to the subjective perceptions of the person being evaluated. Since they viewed human "personality" as far more modifiable and socially determined, biographical events also informed their understanding of symptoms in a much different way. Accordingly, the critics of "prevailing doctrine" also favored a different concept of "illness" that, in contrast to before, was no longer defined exclusively in terms of physical malfunctioning but also in terms of a patient's subjective feeling of "being ill."

In the early 1960s, the prospects of gaining recognition of mental illness in formerly persecuted individuals, especially concentration camp survivors, began to improve. However, this did not require a methodological shift. Rather, it was jurisdiction involving several key changes in West Germany's Federal Indemnification Law and a number of benchmark judicial decisions that not only annulled compensation authority policies that had remained restrictive but also rendered the professional psychiatric controversy obsolete in many respects. Nevertheless, it cannot be said that this turned the recognition of mental illness into the prevailing interpretation, for example, in the framework of war pensions. Represented through their associations, the returnees claimed the same rights for themselves that were now accorded to Holocaust survivors. Indeed, there is evidence to suggest that the highest judicial authorities wanted to expand the concept of illness to include psychologically caused disorders. The judges argued that human individuality deserved greater attention and subjective feelings required more consideration—which furthermore reinforces the impression that a cross-disciplinary change in the basic assumptions regarding the general constitution of human beings was starting to emerge. Nevertheless, the higher courts did leave intact the possibility of a more restrictive practice when it came to recognizing mental illness in Wehrmacht veterans. This becomes clear from the social-court proceedings and, especially, the psychiatric evaluations. Among jurists as well as psychiatrists, there was a general consensus that strict measures were called for to avoid "wishful or compensation claim reactions" on the part of German veterans. In contrast to the heated discussion over reparations for Nazi victims, in this matter there was a greater consensus of opinion. Generally, the psychiatrists even agreed that in these cases the lessons from World War I regarding the human capacity to process war stress had once again been confirmed. Medical, moral, and legal arguments converged and produced a practice that, contrary to assumptions still commonly held today, by and large rejected a relationship between mental problems and experiences during the war and imprisonment in the case of returnees and other war victims.

The transformation of psychiatric knowledge had consequences for public memory discourse on World War II and the impact of Nazi extermination policies. In the media, the discussion basically unfolded in the framework of the available medical-scientific interpretations, so that assumptions about human endurance gained validity in public opinion. In the introduction of this book, I proposed the concept of the "politics of memory" to clarify how forms of scientific interpretation in this field have the effect of both enabling and limiting social perception of the personal consequences of violence and suffering. In this respect, psychiatry as well represents a "science of memory" that not only influences medical practice through its ideas about the human capacity to process violence but also, by virtue of its dissemination through mass media, defines the public rules for what can be discussed in that respect. This connection clearly emerged in the films and print media examined in Part III, whereby in individual cases both genre-typical particularities and political considerations contributed to a strengthening of the scientific positions taken.

It was shown that after the war long-term mental suffering in Wehrmacht veterans was openly recognized in the mass media only for a very short period during the mid-1950s. The "rubble films" of the immediate postwar years did take up the subject of their mental torment, with the returnees' dreams and hallucinations serving as the cinematic means used to portray their continued suffering from the horrors of the criminal war. Many spectators will certainly have interpreted this as an expression of a certain understanding of the personal condition of some returnees. Yet at the same time, the expectations these films articulated in terms of how society was supposed to "normalize" the suffering largely corresponded to the prevailing psychiatric doctrine of the era. Former soldiers who exhibited long-term behavioral changes due to mental suffering that affected their everyday lives had simply let themselves go—this was the moral message the rubble films conveyed. Faith in the human ability to surmount difficulties was readily apparent. This cinematic narrative corresponded to the message of postwar society's capacity for emotional regeneration that was being presented in the print media of the day. In both cinema and press, we also find consistent expression of the idea that the most reliable strategy for self-healing was the restoration of self-worth through work.

It was only in 1953, when the last of the remaining POWs returned from the Soviet Union, that there was a brief upswing in the local and national press in terms of acknowledging the mental impact of internment. On the one hand, it reflected the new public receptiveness to psychosomatic interpretative models, while on the other it emerged from considerations of political utility in the context of the Cold War. The diagnosis of "dystrophy" was an accepted way of referring to the mental disorders perceived among in this group of "late returnees." But after the final prisoners were repatriated in 1955–1956, the mental problems of veterans vanished nearly entirely from public attention. As of the late 1950s, nothing relating to these problems could be seen in films or read about in the national press. In keeping with the assumption that even the worst battle stress could be mastered through personal exertion, war films of the period portray hardly any mental suffering. Doubtless, in war films we need to take account of the generally heroic narratives of the genre itself. Yet in the case of the press, which continued to acknowledge psychosomatic approaches in other contexts, the quick disappearance of returnees from relevant discourse calls for another explanation.

This decoupling cannot be understood without the change in West German memory culture that slowly took hold when trials of accused Nazi perpetrators began once again in the late 1950s. In contrast to the Nuremberg trials of 1945–1946, it was no longer only the senior Nazi functionaries who now stood in the dock. The shifting image of the perpetrator had the effect of blocking discussion of possible mental suffering in Wehrmacht veterans, especially since the most horrific images of Holocaust victims were circulating and, ever since the Eichmann trial, the voices of survivors as witnesses were also heard in the media. Against this backdrop, the attention that West Germany was willing to devote to actual or putatively psychosomatically explainable illnesses—a readiness that the press had helped to generate for more than a decade—turned away from the returnees and was refocused, to great extent, on the victims of Nazism, who were now increasingly moving into public awareness. Accordingly, within the framework of the broader debate over Nazi crimes, major newspapers and periodicals began to publicize recent psychiatric research on the mental effects of Nazi persecution, thereby paving the way for the social anchoring of a new perception pattern that would increasingly view mental consequences in survivors of Nazi persecution, primarily camp survivors, as a given.

In similar fashion, the expansion of the perpetrator image, during which it entered public awareness that any "normal" person could have committed such crimes, and the media's propagation of the new psychiatric doctrine were also mutually reinforcing. Once the new research had been taken up by the media, it also strengthened the assumption that mental suffering was not to be anticipated even when the former Wehrmacht soldiers had participated in horrific crimes. The reports about the new psychiatric discovery of long-term mental damage in the victims of Nazism, which had been circulating in the mass media since the Eichmann trial, had always conveyed this argument. The media's urgent appeal to the public using the voice of psychiatric experts, to finally take responsibility for the crimes committed under the Nazi regime and thereby also to acknowledge that the persecution had caused the survivors' persistent mental suffering, more or less clearly delimited them from the publicly admissible illnesses of the former soldiers. In broad segments of the mass media, which played a crucial role in the development of public memory discourse, talk of possible victim status for the former soldiers was virtually put to an end. In addition, analysis of mass media coverage reveals a decidedly untypical absence of ambiguity. Here the professional debate among psychiatrists about the new diagnostic approach simply played no role. Rather, what became increasingly striking in the reports on mental illness during the early 1960s was a distinct demarcation between Holocaust survivors and regular groups that had been affected by the war. One even has the impression that the media conducted an outright offensive for societal recognition of the destructive mental impact of the Nazi persecution and extermination policies. A political and moral climate manifested itself here that presumably forced the formulation of an unequivocal position within the professional debates as well.

The media feedback process indicates that the double interpretation of the human reaction to extreme mental stress was not only a question of internal medical-scientific plausibility but also marked a central juncture within public culture of memory. Thus, the media no longer functioned as a public advocate for the returnees and their desire to sue the political sphere based on the equality of human beings when they faced cruel treatment and horrific experiences. In point of fact, the question of recognizing mental suffering was used as a public negotiation process to determine whom West German society was willing to identify and accept as victims. The pattern was confirmed by the start of reporting on the Vietnam War a short time later, where the narrative mode for establishing who were to be viewed as the true victims of the war was only established through reference to its mental consequences. How the upper limit was set for the mental endurance of stress was therefore a selective process. Moral valuations entered into the equation along with political exigencies, and both of these dimensions helped determine which of the respective medical-scientific interpretations would be reproduced by the media.

The analysis of the mass therefore allows us to see that along with the interpretation of mental suffering, a specific idea of the war and Nazi persecution was being transmitted as well. In the West German media of the 1960s—in comparison to the first postwar decade—an interpretative shift became noticeable that would ultimately change public memory of the war and the Holocaust for many years to come. The transformation and establishment of new psychiatric knowledge, which itself could not have progressed to the same extent without the political and moral pressure of the 1960s, played a noticeable role. Ideas about the extent of violence suffered or experienced by the respective groups involved and its impact on their lives could not remain unaffected by this. In any event, this suggests itself when we consider that at least for the next two decades, there was virtually no public expression of an awareness that World War II could have caused any sort of residual mental suffering in German veterans.

In the 1960s, there was a radical change in West Germany's public memory of the degree of violence perpetrated during the Nazi war of annihilation and its mental consequences. The former soldiers' private knowledge of the destructive effects of the violence they experienced and their mental suffering did not necessarily find expression in the public realm that had emerged for what could be discussed. Nevertheless the transformation of psychiatric knowledge did offer them the possibility of reading their divergent personal memories into the language of psychiatry.[14] For in general, the shift in psychiatric theory and practice that we have followed heralded new interpretive possibilities with respect to biographical processes and experiences that, despite official reservations, could not be denied to anyone on an individual basis. This corresponded to society's increasingly widespread sense that human beings were not to be understood in terms of fixed heredity but rather in terms of socially constituted individuality. Over the long term, this led to a new respect for subjective human experience, which demanded the acknowledgment of both the human sciences and the public. Some of the war's painfully present pasts could only find public expression in this context. In a second upswing that began in the 1990s, the long-contested transformation of psychiatric knowledge would also create the possibility of extending the claim of victim status to increasing numbers of groups both in the past and in the present.

Notes

INTRODUCTION

1. The case history laid out below is based especially on Hans H.'s vita, but also on information contained in interview notes with the doctor treating him. These are kept in the patient's medical records, compiled during his monthlong stay in the psychiatric and neurological section of the v. Bodelschwinghsche Anstalten Bethel (Hauptarchiv der von Bodelschwinghschen Anstalten Bethel [HBAB], Bestand Morija, 4944). The case will be discussed in greater detail in Part I, chapter 3 of this book. On grounds of privacy, the names of the men and women appearing in the psychiatric records have been altered. All other people mentioned in this book are referred to by their full names, to the extent the first names are known.

2. Instead of a wide range of individual studies see esp. Tony Judt, *Postwar: A History of Europe since 1945* (London, 2010), pp. 13–62 and pp. 803–831, citation p. 61; Bernd-A. Rusinek, ed., *Kriegsende 1945: Verbrechen, Katastrophen, Befreiungen in nationaler und internationaler Perspektive* (Göttingen, 2004); Ulrich Herbert and Axel Schildt, eds., *Kriegsende in Europa: Vom Beginn des deutschen Machtzerfalls bis zur Stabilisierung der Nachkriegsordnung 1944–1948* (Essen, 1998).

3. Mark Mazower, *Dark Continent: Europe's Twentieth Century* (London, 1998), pp. 215f.; if we include the period up to 1948 in our calculations, the number of persons killed and expelled in Europe was roughly ninety million.

4. Charles S. Maier, "Consigning the Twentieth Century to History: Alternative Narratives for the Modern Era," *American Historical Review* 105 (2002), pp. 807–831, claims that this involved a "Western narrative." A plea for a broader, comparative perspective on the twentieth century's different genocides and episodes of "ethnic cleansing" is offered by Mark Mazower, "Violence and the State in the Twentieth Century," *American Historical Review* 107 (2002), pp. 1158–1178. For a balanced comparison see Norman Naimark, *Fires of Hatred: Ethnic Cleansing in Twentieth-Century Europe* (Cambridge, 2001).

5. For an overview with a series of case studies, see Richard Ned Lebow, Wulf Kansteiner, and Claudio Fogu, eds., *The Politics of Memory in Postwar Europe* (Durham, NC, 2006); Norbert Frei and Volkhard Knigge, eds., *Verbrechen erinnern: Die Auseinandersetzung mit Holocaust und Völkermord* (Munich, 2002); Pieter Lagrou, *The Legacy of Nazi Occupation: Patriotic Memory and National Recovery in Western Europe, 1945–1965* (Cambridge, 2000); Henry Rousso, *The Vichy-Syndrome: History and*

Memory in France since 1944 (Cambridge, MA, 1991); Jan T. Gross, *Fear: Anti-Semitism in Poland after Auschwitz* (Princeton, NJ, 2006).

6. This debate was sparked above all by Winfried G. Sebald, *Luftkrieg und Literatur* (Frankfurt am Main, 2005; Günter Grass, *Im Krebsgang* (Göttingen, 2002); Jörg Friedrich, *Der Brand: Deutschland im Bombenkrieg 1940–1945*, 4th ed. (Berlin, 2002). For a critique see, among others, Robert G. Moeller, "Sinking Ships, the Lost Heimat and Broken Taboos: Günter Grass and the Politics of Memory in Contemporary Germany," *Contemporary European History* 12 (2003), pp. 1–35; Moeller, "Germans as Victims? Thoughts on a Post–Cold War History of World War II's Legacies," *History and Memory* 17 (2005), pp. 147–194.

7. Jörg Friedrich, for instance, suggests equating the Holocaust with the Allied bombing campaign using various formulations, as observed by various reviewers in Lothar Kettenacker, ed., *Ein Volk von Opfern? Die neue Debatte um den Bombenkrieg 1940–1945* (Reinbek, 2003). Further examples in Bill Niven, "Introduction: German Victimhood at the Turn of the Millennium," in Niven, ed., *Germans as Victims: Remembering the Past in Contemporary Germany* (New York, 2006), pp. 1–25, pp. 5ff.

8. See Niven, "Introduction," pp. 12f. Niven speaks of strategies for retroactive exculpation that, for example, consist of either pointing out that the bombs struck "normal citizens" or that Germans, Jews, and forced laborers all fell victim to the Allied bombardment. Niven indicates that this constitutes an after-the-fact victims' collective and eradicates essential distinctions. Examples for this are the books *Echolot* by Walter Kempowski and *Der Junge mit den blutigen Schuhen* by Dieter Fortes. For a pointed formulation of the dilemma posed by the accusation of exculpation see Reinhart Koselleck, "Die Diskontinuität der Erinnerung," *Deutsche Zeitschrift für Philosophie* 47 (1999), pp. 213–222, p. 216.

9. Among others, see Moeller, "Germans as Victims," pp. 150ff.

10. For a concise overview see Moeller, "Germans as Victims," pp. 153ff.; Christina Morina, *Legacies of Stalingrad: Remembering the Eastern Front in Germany since 1945* (Cambridge, 2011).

11. Among others, see Bill Niven, "The GDR and the Bombing of Dresden," in Niven, *Germans as Victims*, pp. 109–129; Sabine Behrenbeck, "Between Pain and Silence: Remembering the Victims of Violence in Germany after 1949," in Richard Bessel and Dirk Schumann, eds., *Life after Death: Approaches to a Cultural and Social History of Europe during the 1940s and 1950s* (Washington, DC, 2003), pp. 37–64, which examines the "memory strategies" at work in public celebrations in early West Germany and East Germany.

12. The differences in the refugee policies of the two states and agitation by the responsible associations are described in Pertti Ahonen, *After the Expulsion: West Germany and Eastern Europe, 1945–1990* (Oxford, 2003); and Philipp Ther, *Deutsche und polnische Vertriebene: Gesellschaft und Vertriebenenpolitik in der SBZ/DDR und in Polen 1945–1956* (Göttingen, 1998). On the returnees see Frank Biess, *Homecomings: Returning POWs and the Legacies of Defeat in Postwar Germany* (Princeton, NJ, 2006), with impressive examples of constructions of victimhood in both East and West Germany; Christina Morina, "Instructed Silence, Constructed Memory: The SED and the

Return of German Prisoners of War as 'War Criminals' from the Soviet Union to East Germany, 1950–1956," *Contemporary European History* 13 (2004), pp. 323–343.

13. Robert G. Moeller, *War Stories: The Search for a Usable Past in the Federal Republic of Germany* (Berkeley, CA, 2001), p. 3.

14. Frank Biess, "'Pioneers of a New Germany': Returning POWs from the Soviet Union and the Making of East German Citizens, 1945–1950," *Central European History* 32 (1999), pp. 143–180, pp. 147ff.; Jörg Echternkamp, "Arbeit am Mythos: Soldatengenerationen der Wehrmacht im Urteil der west- und ostdeutschen Nachkriegsgesellschaft," in Klaus Naumann, ed., *Nachkrieg in Deutschland* (Hamburg, 2001), pp. 421–443.

15. See Norbert Frei, *Adenauer's Germany and the Nazi Past: The Politics of Amnesty and Integration* (New York, 1997), pp. 147ff.

16. Biess, *Homecomings*, esp. chapters 4 and 5.

17. See, among others, Wolfgang Benz, "Postwar Society and National Socialism: Remembrance, Amnesia, Rejection," *Tel Aviver Jahrbuch für deutsche Geschichte* 19 (1990), pp. 1–12.

18. See details in Judt, *Postwar*, pp. 230ff. (here on going to the cinema, among other topics); on reconstruction: pp. 82ff.; the quotation on p. 89. On the distinctly more serious material damage in the Soviet Union, see pp. 166ff.

19. See, among others, Ian Buruma, *Year Zero: A History of 1945* (New York, 2013); Keith Lowe, *Europe in the Aftermath of World War II* (London, 2012); Mazower, *Dark Continent*, p. 222; Konrad H. Jarausch and Michael Geyer, *Zerbrochener Spiegel: Deutsche Geschichte im 20. Jh.* (Munich, 2003), pp. 16ff.; Richard Bessel, "'Leben nach dem Tod': Vom Zweiten Weltkrieg zur zweiten Nachkriegszeit," in Bernd Wegner, ed., *Wie Kriege enden: Wege zum Frieden von der Antike bis zur Gegenwart* (Paderborn, 2002), pp. 239–258; Klaus Naumann, introduction to Naumann, *Nachkrieg in Deutschland*, pp. 9–26, pp. 24f.

20. Especially relevant in this context: Christiane Wienand, *Returning Memories: Former Prisoners of War in Divided and Reunited Germany* (New York, 2015); Andreas Hilger, *Deutsche Kriegsgefangene in der Sowjetunion 1941–1956: Kriegsgefangenschaft, Lageralltag und Erinnerung* (Essen, 2000); Stefan Karner, *Im Archipel GUPVI: Kriegsgefangenschaft und Internierung in der Sowjetunion 1941–1956* (Munich, 1995); Matthias Reiß, *"Die Schwarzen waren unsere Freunde": Deutsche Kriegsgefangene in der amerikanischen Gesellschaft 1942–1946* (Paderborn, 2002).

21. The source of the figures is Rüdiger Overmans, "The Repatriation of Prisoners of War Once Hostilities Are Over: A Matter of Course?," in Bob Moore and Barbara Hately-Broad, eds., *Prisoners of War, Prisoners of Peace: Captivity, Homecoming and Memory in World War II* (Oxford, 2005), pp. 11–22, pp. 17f.; Arthur L. Smith, *Heimkehr aus dem Zweiten Weltkrieg: Die Entlassung der deutschen Kriegsgefangenen* (Stuttgart, 1985), p. 11. Further bibliographic references in chapter 2, "Troubled Homecoming."

22. On disabled veterans' policy and integration in West Germany see James M. Diehl, *The Thanks of the Fatherland: German Veterans after the Second World War* (Chapel Hill, NC, 1993).

23. Bessel, "Leben nach dem Tod," pp. 240f.

24. The few recent publications on this subject include Ralph LaRossa, *Of War and Men: World War II and the Lives of Fathers and Their Families* (Chicago, 2011); Alan Allport, *Demobbed: Coming Home after the Second World War* (New Haven 2010). On China: Neil J. Diamant, *Embattled Glory: Veterans, Military Families, and the Politics of Patriotism, 1949–2007* (Lanham, MD, 2009).

25. See, among others, Richard Bessel and Dirk Schumann, "Introduction: Violence, Normality, and the Construction of Postwar Europe," in Bessel and Schumann, *Life after Death*, pp. 1–13; Habbo Knoch, *Die Tat als Bild: Fotografien des Holocaust in der deutschen Erinnerungskultur* (Hamburg, 2001), pp. 18ff.

26. See Didier Fassin and Richard Rechtman, *The Empire of Trauma: An Inquiry into the Condition of Victimhood* (Princeton, NJ, 2009); Wulf Kansteiner, "Menschheitstrauma, Holocausttrauma, kulturelles Trauma: Eine kritische Genealogie der philosophischen, psychologischen und kulturwissenschaftlichen Traumaforschung seit 1945," in Friedrich Jaeger and Jörn Rüsen, eds., *Handbuch der Kulturwissenschaften*, vol. 3: *Themen und Tendenzen* (Stuttgart, 2004), pp. 109–138.

27. See, among others, Allan Young, *The Harmony of Illusions: Inventing Posttraumatic Stress Disorder* (Princeton, NJ, 1995); Ruth Leys, *Trauma: A Genealogy* (Chicago, 2000); Doris Kaufmann, "Neurasthenia in Wilhelmine Germany: Culture, Sexuality, and the Demands of Nature," in Marijke Gijswijt-Hofstra and Roy Porter, eds., *Cultures of Neurasthenia: From Beard to the First World War* (Amsterdam, 2001), pp. 161–176.

28. See, among others, Fassin and Rechtman, *The Empire of Trauma*; Kansteiner, "Menschheitstrauma"; Peter Fritzsche, "Volkstümliche Erinnerung und deutsche Identität nach dem Zweiten Weltkrieg," in Konrad H. Jarausch and Martin Sabrow, eds., *Verletztes Gedächtnis: Erinnerungskultur und Zeitgeschichte im Konflikt* (Frankfurt am Main, 2002), pp. 75–97; Andreas Huyssen, "Trauma and Memory: A New Imaginary of Temporality," in Jill Bennett and Rosanne Kennedy, eds., *World Memory: Personal Trajectories in Global Time* (New York, 2003), pp. 16–29; Richard McNally, *Remembering Trauma* (Cambridge, MA, 2003).

29. This is the pointed formulation of Carol Tavris, "Just Deal with It," *Times Literary Supplement*, August. 15, 2003, pp. 10–11, p. 10, in the review of McNally, *Remembering Trauma*.

30. In this context McNally, *Remembering Trauma*, p. 283, points out that many efforts to help people in other parts of the world with psychotherapy after wars have failed, among other reasons, "because the entire Western framework of diagnosis and psychotherapeutic treatment for trauma is utterly foreign to their cultures."

31. See, e.g., Johannes Fried, *Der Schleier der Erinnerung: Grundzüge einer historischen Memorik* (Munich, 2004); and Harald Welzer, *Das kommunikative Gedächtnis: Eine Theorie der Erinnerung* (Munich, 2002). With Lutz Raphael, we could understand this as a specific form of "scientification of the social." Lutz Raphael, "Die Verwissenschaftlichung des Sozialen als methodische und konzeptionelle Herausforderung für eine Sozialgeschichte des 20. Jahrhunderts," *Geschichte und Gesellschaft* 22 (1996), pp. 165–193, p. 166.

32. As a very insightful analysis in this context see Ralph Harrington, "On the

Tracks of Trauma: Railway Spine Reconsidered," *Journal of the Society for the Social History of Medicine* 16 (2003), pp. 209–223.

33. On the emergence and history of this diagnosis during the course of the Vietnam War, see, among others, Young, *Harmony of Illusions*; Leys, *Trauma*; McNally, *Remembering Trauma*; Paul Lerner and Mark P. Micale, "Trauma, Psychiatry, and History: A Conceptual and Historiographical Introduction," in Micale and Lerner, eds., *Traumatic Pasts: History, Psychiatry, and Trauma in the Modern Age, 1870–1930* (Cambridge, 2001), pp. 1–27, pp. 1ff., with additional bibliographic references.

34. Critical in this respect as well: Wulf Kansteiner, *In Pursuit of German Memory: History, Television, and Politics after Auschwitz* (Athens, OH, 2006), esp. p. 18.

35. See, among others, Alice Förster and Birgit Beck, "Post-traumatic Stress Disorder and World War II: Can a Psychiatric Concept Help Us Understand Postwar Society?," in Bessel and Schumann, *Life after Death*, pp. 15–38; Niels Birbaumer and Dieter Langewiesche, "Neuropsychologie und Historie—Versuch einer empirischen Annäherung. Posttraumatische Belastungsstörung (PTSD) und Soziopathie in Österreich nach 1945," *Geschichte und Gesellschaft* 32 (2006), pp. 153–175; Biess, *Homecomings*, pp. 70–94.

36. See Peter Gray and Kendrick Oliver, introduction to Gray and Oliver, eds., *The Memory of Catastrophe* (Manchester, 2004), pp. 1–18.

37. McNally, *Remembering Trauma*, p. 283.

38. Catherine Merridale, *Night of Stone: Death and Memory in Twentieth-Century Russia* (New York, 2000), p. 16.

39. On this concept see Hacking, *Multiple Persönlichkeit: Zur Geschichte der Seele in der Moderne* (Munich, 1996), chap. 14.

40. Hacking, *Multiple Persönlichkeit*, p. 93.

41. In contrast, see Förster and Beck, "Post-traumatic Stress Disorder."

42. Young, *Harmony of Illusions*, p. 4.

43. See Allan Young, "Suffering and the Origins of Traumatic Memory," *Daedalus* 125 (1996), pp. 245–260.

44. It is doubtless impossible to take into account all the audiences relevant to this discussion. As further explained below, I will limit myself here to the mass media and its public, drawing conclusions from medical practice and the spheres of pension and compensations law—areas of activity that created very concrete social realities.

45. From the broad range of studies of public memory in early postwar Germany and the Federal Republic, see, among others, Moeller, *War Stories*; Behrenbeck, "Between Pain and Silence"; Peter Reichel, *Erfundene Erinnerung: Weltkrieg und Judenmord in Film und Theater* (Vienna, 2004); Reichel, *Vergangenheitsbewältigung in Deutschland: Die Auseinandersetzung mit der NS-Diktatur von 1945 bis heute* (Munich, 2001).

46. Alexander and Margarete Mitscherlich, *Inability to Mourn: Principles of Collective Behavior*, trans. Beverley R. Placzek (original German ed., *Die Unfähigkeit zu trauern*, 1967) (New York, 1975), esp. pp. 23f. The Mitscherlichs argue that Hitler's death and the German defeat led to a narcissistic injury among the Germans, one result of which was an "inability to mourn" for those who were murdered (p. 24). See Tobias Freimüller, "Der Umgang mit der NS-Vergangenheit in der Bundesrepublik Deutsch-

land und die 'Unfähigkeit zu trauern'" in Françoise Lartillot, ed., *Die Unfähigkeit zu trauern* (Nantes, 2004), pp. 11–26. For a critique of the Mitscherlichs' thesis see esp. Moeller, *War Stories*, pp. 15f.; and Dagmar Barnouw, *Ansichten von Deutschland (1945): Krieg und Gewalt in der zeitgenössischen Photographie* (Basel, 1997), pp. 13f. For an explicit adoption of Mitscherlich's interpretation see Ernestine Schlant, *The Language of Silence: West German Literature and the Holocaust* (New York, 1999), pp. 13ff.

47. See Hannah Arendt, "The Aftermath of Nazi Rule: Report from Germany," *Commentary* 10 (1950), pp. 342–353, p. 343.

48. Ulrich Herbert, "Rückkehr in die 'Bürgerlichkeit'? NS-Eliten in der Bundesrepublik," in Bernd Weisbrod, ed., *Rechtsradikalismus in der politischen Kultur der Nachkriegszeit* (Hannover, 1995), pp. 157–173, citation p. 163. On the experience of denazification, see Part I of this book, where further bibliographical references are also provided.

49. A similar position is taken by Alon Confino and Peter Fritzsche, "Introduction: Noises of the Past," in Confino and Fritzsche, eds., *The Work of Memory: New Directions in the Study of German Society and Culture* (Urbana, IL, 2002), pp. 1–21, p. 10.

50. See also the critique of Alon Confino, "Narratives of Memory and Culture," in Confino, *Germany as a Culture of Remembrance: Promises and Limits of Writing History* (Chapel Hill, NC, 2006), pp. 188–213, pp. 200ff.; Confino, "Remembering the Second World War, 1945–1965: Narratives of Victimhood and Genocide," *Cultural Analysis: An Interdisciplinary Forum on Folklore and Popular Culture* 4 (2005), pp. 47–65.

51. Among the many studies of this topic, see Aleida Assmann's overview, *Erinnerungsräume: Formen und Wandlungen des kulturellen Gedächtnisses* (Munich, 1999).

52. Foundational for this distinction: Jan Assmann, *Das kulturelle Gedächtnis: Schrift, Erinnerung und politische Identität in frühen Hochkulturen* (Munich, 1999), pp. 15–48. For an overview with further bibliographic references, see Hans-Günter Hockerts, "Zugänge zur Zeitgeschichte. Primärerfahrung, Erinnerungskultur, Geschichtswissenschaft," in Jarausch and Sabrow, *Verletztes Gedächtnis*, pp. 39–73.

53. With respect to political-legal framing, Frei's *Adenauer's Germany* remains relevant.

54. On war narratives within the family, see Dorothee Wierling, "Nationalsozialismus und Krieg in den Lebens-Geschichten der ersten Nachkriegsgeneration der DDR," in Elisabeth Domansky and Harald Welzer, eds., *Eine offene Geschichte: Zur kommunikativen Tradierung der nationalsozialistischen Vergangenheit* (Tübingen, 1999), pp. 35–56; and Harald Welzer et al., *"Opa war kein Nazi": Nationalsozialismus und Holocaust im Familiengedächtnis* (Frankfurt am Main, 2002). See also the controversy in *WerkstattGeschichte* 30 (2001), with contributions by Harald Welzer, Alexander von Plato, and Dorothee Wierling, and the comprehensive work by Hans Joachim Schröder, *Die gestohlenen Jahre: Erzählgeschichte und Geschichtserzählung im Interview. Der Zweite Weltkrieg aus der Sicht ehemaliger Mannschaftssoldaten* (Tübingen, 1992). On the German World War II veterans' associations, see Jörg Echternkamp, "Mit dem Krieg seinen Frieden schließen—Wehrmacht und Weltkrieg in der Veteranenkultur

1945–1960," in Thomas Kühne, ed., *Von der Kriegskultur zur Friedenskultur?* (Hamburg, 2000), pp. 78–93; and Thomas Kühne, "Zwischen Vernichtungskrieg und Freizeitgesellschaft: Die Veteranenkultur der Bundesrepublik (1945–1995)," in Naumann, *Nachkrieg in Deutschland*, pp. 90–113.

55. As one of the few exceptions: Stefan-Ludwig Hoffmann, "Besiegte, Besatzer, Beobachter: Das Kriegsende im Tagebuch," in Daniel Fulda et al., eds., *Demokratie im Schatten der Gewalt: Geschichten des Privaten im deutschen Nachkrieg* (Göttingen, 2008). On the occasion of the sixtieth anniversary of the end of the war, a series of personal accounts were published that offered a look at subjective perceptions of this event from both the victor's and loser's perspective. See, among others, Gerhard Hirschfeld and Irina Renz, eds., *"Vormittags die ersten Amerikaner": Stimmen und Bilder vom Kriegsende 1945* (Stuttgart, 2005); Anonyma, *Eine Frau in Berlin: Tagebuchaufzeichnungen vom 20. April bis 22. Juni 1945* (Frankfurt am Main, 2003). Among the rare examinations of the immediate postwar period, see also Jörg Hillmann and John Zimmermann, eds., *Kriegsende 1945 in Deutschland* (Munich, 2002); and the work on the period's so-called rubble films and rubble literature discussed later in this book; see the references on this subject in Part I, "Remembering the War," section "Dreaming the War" and Part III, "Mental Suffering and Its Changing Acknowledgment in West German Media.", chapter "Repatriated Wehrmacht Veterans in the Public Eye". Also see the studies on the early debates about guilt and responsibility, in particular Jeffrey K. Olick, *In the House of the Hangman: The Agonies of German Defeat, 1943–1949* (Chicago, 2005); and Jan Friedmann and Jörg Später, "Britische und deutsche Kollektivschuld-Debatte," in Ulrich Herbert, ed., *Wandlungsprozesse in Westdeutschland: Belastung, Integration, Liberalisierung 1945–1980* (Göttingen, 2002), pp. 53–90. For an analysis of everyday life that includes personal narratives, see Paul Steege, *Black Market, Cold War: Everyday Life in Berlin, 1946–1949* (Cambridge, 2007); and Monica Black, *Death in Berlin: From Weimar to the Cold War* (Cambridge, 2010).

56. The term "memory fragments" is not meant to suggest that this involves grasping some sort of "authentic" memories; memories are always the product of perceptions and interpretations, which can also incorporate the memories of others. Rather, I have chosen the term because the (always) fragmentary quality of memory is especially pronounced in the sources analyzed in the first three chapters of this book. They often represent spontaneous and abrupt statements that emerged from the patients' chains of associations. The patients rarely spoke at length about the war in the medical records, which may sometimes reflect the doctors' failure to record such remarks.

57. I also evaluated some 250 additional medical records of women between 1945 and 1952. Scattered among these cases were female returnees—German Red Cross nurses who became POWs. We also have a large collection of files dealing with raped women who had to see psychiatrists on account of abortions. Another large group concerns female refugees. I do not consider these cases here or in the second part of the book that deals with psychiatric practice, because a causal connection between long-term mental suffering and previously experienced violence was not medically recognized at the time (see below), and a gender-specific interpretation on this level could not be identified.

58. For example, Hamburg physician Hans Kilian indicated at a convention that

between 1954 and 1956 he had examined twelve hundred returning soldiers. See Hans Kilian, *Das Wiedereinleben des Heimkehrers in Familie, Ehe und Beruf, in Die Sexualität des Heimkehrers: Vorträge gehalten auf dem 4: Kongreß der deutschen Gesellschaft für Sexualforschung in Erlangen* (Stuttgart, 1957), pp. 27–38, p. 32.

59. For a fleeting impression, see Biess, *Homecomings*, p. 70.

60. Assmann, *Erinnerungsräume*, p. 250.

61. Reinhart Koselleck, "'Space of Experience' and 'Horizon of Expectation': Two Historical Categories," in Koselleck, *Futures Past: On the Semantics of Historical Time*, trans. Keith Tribe (New York, 2004), pp. 255–275, p. 259. We there read further: "Within experience a rational reworking is included, together with unconscious modes of conduct which do not have to be present in awareness." Koselleck also presumes that there "is also an element of alien experience contained and preserved in experience conveyed by generations or institutions."

62. See, among others, Vera Neumann, *Nicht der Rede wert: Die Privatisierung der Kriegsfolgen in der frühen Bundesrepublik* (Münster, 1999); see further bibliographical references in chapter 3, "Social Rubble."

63. See Paul Lerner, *Hysterical Men: War, Psychiatry, and the Politics of Trauma in Germany, 1890–1930* (Ithaca, NY, 2003); Doris Kaufmann, "Science as Cultural Practice: Psychiatry in the First World War and Weimar Germany," *Journal of Contemporary History* 34 (1999), pp. 125–144; Ruth Kloocke et al., "Psychological Injury in the Two World Wars: Changing Concepts and Terms in German Psychiatry," *History of Psychiatry* 16 (2005), pp. 43–60. For further references see Part II, "The Production of Psychiatric Knowledge."

64. Officially stipulated for instance in *Anhaltspunkte für die ärztliche Gutachtertätigkeit im Versorgungswesen* (*Guidelines for Medical Practice in the Disability Pension Field*) issued by the German labor ministry, ed. Reichsbund der Kriegs- und Zivilbeschädigten, Sozialrentner und Hinterbliebenen (Bonn, 1952), p. 15. On the regulation of the care of physically disabled German veterans after 1945, see Neumann, *Nicht der Rede wert*; Diehl, *Thanks of the Fatherland*.

65. One of the few exceptions is a study that takes the perspective of the history of institutions by Sabine Hanrath, *Zwischen "Euthanasie" und Psychiatriereform: Anstaltspsychiatrie in Westfalen und Bandenburg. Ein deutsch-deutscher Vergleich (1945–1964)* (Paderborn, 2002). See also Cornelia Brink, *Grenzen der Anstalt: Psychiatrie und Gesellschaft in Deutschland 1860–1980* (Göttingen, 2010); Volker Roelcke, "Psychotherapy between Medicine, Psychoanalysis, and Politics: Concepts, Practices, and Institutions in Germany, c. 1945–1992," *Medical History* 48 (2004), pp. 473–492; Ruth Kloocke et al., "Psychisches Trauma in deutschsprachigen Lehrbüchern der Nachkriegszeit—die psychiatrische 'Lehrmeinung' zwischen 1945 und 2002," *Psychiatrische Praxis* 32 (2005), pp. 1–15. These studies offer an overview of the relevant textbooks published during this period and demonstrate the spectrum of diagnoses applied by doctors in connection with mental illness, for instance, "neurosis" and "hysteria." One anthology in particular advances into the 1960s: Hans-Werner Kersting, ed., *Psychiatriereform als Gesellschaftsreform: Die Hypothek des Nationalsozialismus und der Aufbruch der sechziger Jahre* (Paderborn, 2003).

66. Among the wide range of meanwhile highly differentiated studies, see Hans

Walter Schmuhl, *Grenzüberschreitungen: Das Kaiser-Wilhelm-Institut für Anthropologie, menschliche Erblehre und Eugenik 1927–1945* (Göttingen, 2005); Schmuhl, ed., *Rassenforschung an Kaiser-Wilhelm-Instituten vor und nach 1933* (Göttingen, 2003); Schmuhl, *Rassenhygiene, Nationalsozialismus, Euthanasie: Von der Verhütung zur Vernichtung "lebensunwerten Lebens," 1890–1945*, 2nd ed. (Göttingen, 1992); Doris Kaufmann, "Eugenische Utopie und wissenschaftliche Praxis im Nationalsozialismus: Zur Wissenschaftsgeschichte der Schizophrenieforschung," in Wolfgang Hardtwig, ed., *Utopie und politische Herrschaft im Zeitalter der Zwischenkriegszeit* (Munich, 2003), pp. 309–325; Volker Roelcke, "Psychiatrische Wissenschaft im Kontext nationalsozialistischer Politik und "Euthanasie," in Doris Kaufmann, ed., *Geschichte der Kaiser-Wilhelm-Gesellschaft im Nationalsozialismus: Bestandsaufnahme und Perspektiven der Forschung* (Göttingen, 2000), vol. 1, pp. 112–150; Kaufmann et al., "Psychiatrische Wissenschaft, 'Euthanasie' und der 'Neue Mensch': Zur Diskussion um anthropologische Prämissen und Wertsetzungen der Medizin im Nationalsozialismus," in Andreas Frewer and Clemens Eickhoff, eds., *"Euthanasie" und die aktuelle Sterbehilfe-Debatte: Die historischen Hintergründe medizinischer Ethik* (Frankfurt am Main, 2002), pp. 193–217.

67. Christian Pross, *Paying for the Past: The Struggle over Reparations for Surviving Victims of the Nazi Terror* (Baltimore, 1998). For a critique see esp. Hans-Günter Hockerts, "Wiedergutmachung in Deutschland: Eine historische Bilanz 1945–2000," *Vierteljahreshefte für Zeitgeschichte* 49 (2001), pp. 167–214, pp. 199f.; Constantin Goschler, *Schuld und Schulden: Die Politik der Wiedergutmachung für NS-Verfolgte seit 1945* (Göttingen, 2005), p. 18.

68. As an example, see Heiko Scharffenberg, *Sieg der Sparsamkeit: Die Wiedergutmachung nationalsozialistischen Unrechts in Schleswig-Holstein* (Bielefeld, 2004). For further bibliographic references, see chapter 6 in this volume. On denazification of the sciences and continuity within the German elites after 1945 see, among others, Tobias Freimüller, "Mediziner: Operation Volkskörper," in Norbert Frei, ed., *Hitlers Eliten nach 1945*, 5th ed. (Frankfurt am Main, 2012), pp. 13–65; Carola Sachse, "'Persilscheinkultur': Zum Umgang mit der NS-Vergangenheit in der Kaiser-Wilhelm- bzw. Max-Planck-Gesellschaft," in Bernd Weisbrod, ed., *Akademische Vergangenheitspolitik: Beiträge zur Wissenschaftskultur der Nachkriegszeit* (Göttingen, 2002), pp. 217–246; Mitchell G. Ash, "Verordnete Umbrüche—Konstruierte Kontinuitäten: Zur Entnazifizierung von Wissenschaftlern und Wissenschaften nach 1945," *Zeitschrift für Geschichtswissenschaft* 43 (1995), pp. 903–923.

69. See, among others, Constantin Goschler, "Zwei Wege der Wiedergutmachung? Der Umgang mit NS-Verfolgten in West- und Ostdeutschland im Vergleich," in Hans-Günter Hockerts and Christiane Kuller, eds., *Nach der Verfolgung: Wiedergutmachung nationalsozialistischen Unrechts in Deutschland?* (Göttingen, 2003), pp. 115–137, pp. 125f.

70. See, among others, Sabine Kittel, *"Places for the Displaced": Biographische Bewältigungsmuster von weiblichen jüdischen Konzentrationslager-Überlebenden in den USA* (Hildesheim, 2006), pp. 215ff.; Judt, *Postwar*, pp. 803ff.; Peter Novick, *Nach dem Holocaust: Der Umgang mit dem Massenmord* (Munich, 2003); Ido de Haan, "Paths of Normalization after the Persecution of the Jews: The Netherlands, France, and

West Germany in the 1950s," in Bessel and Schumann, *Life after Death*, pp. 65–92; Idith Zertal, *Nation und Tod: Der Holocaust in der israelischen Öffentlichkeit* (Göttingen, 2003).

71. For the Netherlands and France, see de Haan, "Paths of Normalization"; for the United States, Leys, *Trauma*, pp. 223ff. But see the essays in Annet Mooij and Jolande Withuis, eds., *The Politics of War Trauma: The Aftermath of World War II in Eleven European Countries* (Amsterdam, 2010).

72. Legendary in this respect is the story of Hiroshima pilot Claude Eatherly. After a suicide attempt in 1950 and several minor criminal infractions, he was diagnosed with schizophrenia and committed to a mental hospital. His delusions were treated with insulin shocks. See his illuminating correspondence with Günter Anders, in Anders, *Hiroshima ist überall* (Munich, 1982), pp. 191–360. On English and American postwar psychiatry, see Joanna Bourke, "Postwar Adjustment of British and American Servicemen after the War," in Bessel and Schumann, *Life after Death*, pp. 149–160, pp. 151ff. On Soviet psychiatry after World War II, see Merridale, *Night of Stone*, pp. 282ff.

73. See Part II, "The Production of Psychiatric Knowledge."

74. On continuities in the medical profession see, e.g., Geoffrey Cocks, *Psychotherapy in the Third Reich*, 2nd ed. (New Brunswick, NJ, 1997); and Franz-Werner Kersting, "Mediziner zwischen 'Drittem Reich' und Bundesrepublik: Die Anstaltsärzte des Provinzialverbandes Westfalen," in Kersting et al., eds., *Nach Hadamar: Zum Verhältnis von Psychiatrie und Gesellschaft im 20. Jahrhundert* (Paderborn, 1993), pp. 253–272.

75. Young, *Harmony of Illusions*, shows this for the establishment of "posttraumatic stress disorder." See also Bernd Gausemeier, *Natürliche Ordnungen und politische Allianzen: Biologische und biochemische Forschung an Kaiser-Wilhelm-Instituten 1933–1945* (Göttingen, 2005).

76. For a cursory overview of the role of experts in the fields of social welfare and the constitutional state since the late nineteenth century, see Raphael, "Verwissenschaftlichung," pp. 167ff.

77. For the complexity of such negotiation processes in the field of sociology, see Uta Gerhardt's impressive study *Denken der Demokratie: Die Soziologie im atlantischen Transfer des Besatzungsregimes: Vier Abhandlungen* (Stuttgart, 2007).

78. Here, the current study follows the broad understanding of "memory culture" as a "term for the totality of nonspecific public use of historical scholarship," as Hockerts, "Zugänge," p. 41, has formulated it.

79. See Frei, *Adenauer's Germany*; Bert-Oliver Manig, *Die Politik der Ehre: Die Rehabilitierung der Berufssoldaten in der frühen Bundesrepublik* (Göttingen, 2004).

80. Along with the above-mentioned literature see Robert G. Moeller, "Deutsche Opfer, Opfer der Deutschen—Kriegsgefangene, Vertriebene, NS-Verfolgte: Opferausgleich als Identitätspolitik," in Naumann, *Nachkrieg in Deutschland*, pp. 29–58. See also Frank Bajohr and Dieter Pohl, *Der Holocaust als offenes Geheimnis: Die Deutschen, die NS-Führung und die Alliierten* (Munich, 2006). The authors speak of a "strategy of offsetting" through which "one's own bad conscience, along with feelings of shame and guilt," is meant to be numbed (p. 78). Also Norbert Frei, *1945 und Wir: Das Dritte Reich im Bewusstsein der Deutschen* (Munich, 2005); Peter Reichel, *Politik mit der Erinnerung: Gedächtnisorte im Streit um die nationalsozialistische Vergangenheit* (Munich, 1995).

81. See Confino, "Remembering," p. 51.

82. Cornelia Brink, *Ikonen der Vernichtung: Öffentlicher Gebrauch von Fotografien aus nationalsozialistischen Konzentrationslagern nach 1945* (Berlin, 1998); Knoch, *Die Tat als Bild*.

83. See Moeller, *War Stories*; Ulrike Weckel, "The *Mitläufer* in Two German Postwar Films," *History and Memory* 15 (2003), pp. 64–93. See additional bibliographical references in Part III.

84. See Anton Kaes, *From Hitler to Heimat: The Return of History as Film* (Cambridge, MA, 1992), p. 196.

85. From the many works that have appeared within this expanding field, see esp. Christina von Hodenberg, *Konsens und Krise: Eine Geschichte der westdeutschen Medienöffentlichkeit 1945–1973* (Göttingen, 2006); and Habbo Knoch and Daniel Morat, eds., *Kommunikation als Beobachtung: Medienwandel und Gesellschaftsbilder 1880–1960* (Paderborn, 2003). Some of the essays in the latter anthology attempt to approach media-specific forms of impact through an analysis of contemporary debates.

86. On the meaning of the visual production of knowledge in the sense of a visual and, in general, sensory experience of reality, see the essays in Gerhard Paul, ed., *Visual History: Ein Studienbuch* (Göttingen, 2006), which also contains detailed bibliographic references.

87. See Kansteiner, *Pursuit of German Memory*, p. 22.

88. Ian Hacking, "Memoro-politics, Trauma and the Soul," *History of the Human Sciences* 7 (1994), pp. 29–52, p. 32; Hacking, *Multiple Persönlichkeit*, chap. 15.

89. See also Ulrike Hoffmann-Richter, "Das Verschwinden der Biographie in der Krankengeschichte: Eine biographische Skizze," *BIOS: Zeitschrift für Biographieforschung und Oral History* 8 (1995), pp. 204–221, p. 205.

90. Greg Eghigian, "Der Kalte Krieg im Kopf: Ein Fall von Schizophrenie und die Geschichte des Selbst in der sowjetischen Besatzungszone," *Historische Anthropologie* 11 (2003), pp. 101–122, shows how one can approach a post-1945 "cultural history of the self" through an analysis of medical records. Naturally, within the history of medicine these records have long been used as a source, mainly to fulfill the need for a "history from below." See, e.g., Karen Nolte, *Gelebte Hysterie: Erfahrung, Eigensinn und psychiatrische Diskurse im Anstaltsalltag um 1900* (Frankfurt am Main, 2003). This approach was already initiated in the mid-1980s by Roy Porter, "The Patient's View: Doing Medical History from Below," *Theory and Society* 14 (1985), pp. 175–198. Possibilities for a quantitative analysis of psychiatric records are considered in Marietta Meier et. al., *Zwang zur Ordnung: Psychiatrie im Kanton Zürich, 1870–1970* (Zurich, 2007), pp. 89ff.

91. Assmann, *Erinnerungsräume*, p. 408.

92. See, among others, Peter Weingart, *Die Wissenschaft der Öffentlichkeit: Essays zum Verhältnis von Wissenschaft, Medien und Öffentlichkeit* (Weilerswist, 2005), p. 11.

CHAPTER 1

1. The story is taken from Dieter Forte, *In der Erinnerung* (Frankfurt am Main, 2001), pp. 38f.; it has been abridged here. Italics are in original.

2. Forte, *In der Erinnerung*, pp. 26f.

3. See Werner Durth and Niels Gutschow, *Träume in Trümmern: Planungen zum Wiederaufbau zerstörter Städte im Westen Deutschlands 1940–1950*, vol. 1: *Konzepte*; vol. 2: *Städte* (Braunschweig, 1988); for an overview of the entire Nazi period: Werner Durth, "Architektur und Stadtplanung im Dritten Reich," in Michael Prinz and Rainer Zitelmann, eds., *Nationalsozialismus und Modernisierung*, 2nd ed. (Darmstadt, 1994), pp. 139–171, p. 166.

4. For an overview of the differing developments in West Germany and East Germany, see Werner Durth, "Kontraste und Parallelen: Architektur und Städtebau in West- und Ostdeutschland," in Axel Schildt and Arnold Sywottek, eds., *Modernisierung im Wiederaufbau: Die westdeutsche Gesellschaft der 50er Jahre* (Bonn, 1998), pp. 596–611; Klaus von Beyme et al., eds., *Neue Städte aus Ruinen: Städtebau der Nachkriegszeit* (Munich, 1992). For one of the best treatments of the subject see Gregor Thum, *Die fremde Stadt: Breslau 1945* (Berlin, 2003).

5. See Barnouw, *Ansichten von Deutschland*, esp. chap. 4, which is entitled "Was sie sahen: Alliierte Photographen in Deutschland"; Knoch, *Die Tat als Bild*, pp. 314–323.

6. See Frank Biess, "Vom Opfer zum Überlebenden des Totalitarismus: Westdeutsche Reaktionen auf die Rückkehr der Kriegsgefangenen aus der Sowjetunion, 1945–1955," in Günter Bischof and Rüdiger Overmans, eds., *Kriegsgefangenschaft im Zweiten Weltkrieg: Eine vergleichende Perspektive* (Ternitz, 1999), pp. 365–389.

7. One of many studies interpreting West German memory construction in this way is Moeller, *War Stories*.

8. Arendt, "Aftermath of Nazi Rule," citation p. 342.

9. Arendt, "Aftermath of Nazi Rule, p. 343.

10. Most pointedly: Moeller, *War Stories*. On the impact of this discourse of victimization on the historiographical debates about World War II, see, among others, Thomas Kühne, "Die Viktimisierungsfalle: Wehrmachtsverbrechen, Geschichtswissenschaft und symbolische Ordnung des Militärs," in Michael T. Greven and Oliver von Wrochem, eds., *Der Krieg in der Nachkriegszeit: Der Zweite Weltkrieg in Politik und Gesellschaft der Bundesrepublik* (Opladen, 2000), pp. 183–196. The debate over Friedrich, *Der Brand*, can also be understood in this context. The debate is summarized in Stephan Burgdorff and Christian Habbe, eds., *Als Feuer vom Himmel fiel: Der Bombenkrieg in Deutschland* (Munich, 2003). On the subject of victimhood in the German discussion of flight and expulsion, see, among others, Moeller, "Sinking Ships." For a broader overview: Niven, *Germans as Victims*, with additional bibliographic references.

11. A plausible example can be seen in the political debates in the early German Bundestag over compensation for the victims of the Nazi regime on the one hand, and the measures taken to reintegrate the returned POWs, expellees, and refugees on the other. See Moeller, "Deutsche Opfer," pp. 29–58.

12. Moeller, *War Stories*, p. 92, speaks accurately of "prisoners of public memory," although only in respect to the last German POWs to return from the Soviet camps, in 1955–1956.

13. Bruno Hampel, "Das mit dem Mais," in Thomas Friedrich, ed., *Aufräumungsarbeiten: Erzählungen aus Deutschland 1945–1948* (Berlin, 1983), pp. 10–15.

14. *Die Mörder sind unter uns*, film, 1946; screenplay Wolfgang Staudte, director

Wolfgang Staudte; see also Part III, "Mental Suffering and Its Changing Acknowledgment in West German Media," for greater detail.

15. Wolfgang Borchert, *Draußen vor der Tür* (1947) (Reinbek, 1983).

16. As an example, see the film *Irgendwo in Berlin*, which came to the screen in 1946. This is discussed in greater detail in Part III as well.

17. Peter Reichel, *Erfundene Erinnerung*, p. 49, sees Borchert's play as a "significant medium in the transformation of the German 'community of the Volk' (*Volksgemeinschaft*) into a community of victims (*Opfergemeinschaft*)" during the postwar period.

18. Suggestions in this respect can also be found in the analysis of the reception of Borchert's play by Ulrike Weckel, "Spielarten der Vergangenheitsbewältigung—Wolfgang Borcherts Heimkehrer und sein langer Weg durch die westdeutschen Medien," in Moshe Zuckermann, ed., *Medien—Politik—Geschichte* (Tel Aviver Jahrbuch für deutsche Geschichte, vol. 31) (Göttingen, 2003), pp. 125–161.

19. See Reinhart Koselleck, "Terror and Dream: Methodological Remarks on the Experience of Time during the Third Reich," in Koselleck, *Futures Past*, pp. 205–221.

20. See esp. Peter Burke, "Die Kulturgeschichte der Träume," in Burke, *Eleganz und Haltung* (Berlin, 1998), pp. 37–62, p. 43. Burke indicates that dreams are changed by being recorded in writing, which is at the same time the only possible way of gaining access to them. According to Koselleck, this is not necessarily a specific quality of dreams: "What 'really' happened already lies in the past, and what is reported no longer coincides with it" (p. 208).

21. For a historical analysis of dream notations, see the unpublished talk by Willibald Steinmetz, "Träumen im Zeitalter der Extreme," Bochum, 2000, p. 8.

22. See Koselleck, "Terror and Dream," pp. 208f.; Steinmetz, "Träumen," p. 1. Similarly already in Maurice Halbwachs, "Der Traum und die Erinnerungsbilder," in Halbwachs, *Das Gedächtnis und seine sozialen Bedingungen* (Frankfurt am Main, 1985), pp. 25–72, esp. pp. 26ff., who bases his discussion on Freud's *Interpretation of Dreams*.

23. Koselleck, "Terror and Dream," speaks of an "irresistible facticity of the fictive" (p. 209).

24. See Steinmetz, "Träumen," p. 7, and his critique of the dream collection in Charlotte Beradt, *Das Dritte Reich des Traums* (Frankfurt am Main, 1994), where the ambivalence and polyvalence of the dreams allegedly disappears because of editorial interference.

25. Koselleck, "Terror and Dream," p. 217.

26. Hauptarchiv der von Bodelschwinghschen Anstalten Bethel (HBAB), Bestand Morija, 3635.

27. See HBAB, Bestand Morija, 3635.

28. See HBAB, Bestand Morija, 4946. All further information and citations pertaining to this case have been taken from this source.

29. See, among others, Omer Bartov, *Hitler's Army: Soldiers, Nazis, and War in the Third Reich* (Oxford, 1991). Bartov argues that during the last two years of the war German soldiers on the eastern front never stopped believing in Hitler and final victory. On the contrary, they clung to it all the more firmly in their fear of the Russians and in their disinhibited struggle with the enemy (p. 169). And see the reflections of Michael Geyer

on the emergence of "catastrophic nationalism" in Germany: Michael Geyer, "End-kampf 1918 and 1945: German Nationalism, Annihilation, and Self-Destruction," in Alf Lüdtke and Bernd Weisbrod, eds., *No Man's Land of Violence: Extreme Wars in the 20th Century* (Göttingen, 2006), pp. 35–67.

30. See HBAB, Bestand Morija, 4946.

31. See Koselleck, "Terror and Dream," p. 210, who uses this term in a greatly expanded sense, however.

32. Koselleck, "Terror and Dream," p. 210.

33. HBAB, Bestand Morija, 5589.

34. HBAB, Bestand Morija, 5109.

35. See Arendt, "Aftermath of Nazi Rule."

36. HBAB, Bestand Morija, 4560.

37. Norbert Frei, "Von deutscher Erfindungskraft oder: Die Kollektivschuldthese in der Nachkriegszeit," in Gary Smith, ed., *Hannah Arendt Revisited: "Eichmann in Jerusalem" und die Folgen* (Frankfurt am Main, 2000), pp. 163–176, citation p. 165.

38. Carl Schüddekopf, *Krieg: Erzählungen aus dem Schweigen. Deutsche Soldaten über den Zweiten Weltkrieg* (Reinbek, 1998), Bruno Fichte's story: pp. 27–54; citation p. 42.

39. Joanna Bourke, "The Emotions in War: Fear and the British and American Military, 1914–1945," in *Historical Research* 74 (2001), pp. 314–330, p. 315.

40. Bourke, "The Emotions in War," p. 315. Bourke bases her discussion on findings referred to by M. Ralph Kaufman, "'Ill Health' as an Expression of Anxiety in a Combat Unit," *Psychosomatic Medicine* 9 (1947), p. 108. The survey he draws on was conducted among American soldiers fighting in the Pacific. Bourke herself does not indicate when, in which country, by whom, or how the survey was undertaken.

41. This is discussed in greater detail in the section "Lessons of War" in chapter 4.

42. An exception: Hans Joachim Schröder, "Töten und Todesangst im Krieg: Erinnerungsberichte über den Zweiten Weltkrieg," in Alf Lüdtke and Thomas Lindenberger, eds., *Physische Gewalt: Studien zur Geschichte der Neuzeit* (Frankfurt am Main, 1995), pp. 106–135; Schröder, *Die gestohlenen Jahre*, pp. 624–670.

43. See, among others, Bajohr and Pohl, *Der Holocaust*; Otto Kulka, "'Public Opinion' in Nazi Germany: The Final Solution," in Michael R. Marrus, ed., *The Nazi Holocaust: Historical Articles on the Destruction of European Jews*, vol. 5, 1: *Public Opinion and Relations to the Jews in Nazi Europe* (London, 1989), pp. 139–150, p. 149; Michael Geyer, "Das Stigma der Gewalt und das Problem der nationalen Identität," in Christian Jansen et al., eds., *Von der Aufgabe der Freiheit: Politische Verantwortung und bürgerliche Gesellschaft im 19. and 20. Jahrhundert* (Berlin, 1995), pp. 673–698, p. 683; Ian Kershaw, *Popular Opinion and Political Dissent in the Third Reich: Bavaria, 1933–1945* (Oxford, 1983), pp. 364ff.

44. In part, however, these fears were the result of deliberate propaganda generated by the Nazi leadership, which placed responsibility for the bombings on the Jews. See the examples in Peter Longerich, *"Davon haben wir nichts gewusst!" Die Deutschen und die Judenverfolgung 1933–1945* (Munich, 2006), pp. 284ff. In this context, the title of Gerd Ledig's book, *Vergeltung* ("Vengeance") (Frankfurt am Main, 1956), is misleading, because Ledig does not establish the connection between the bombardments

and the idea of vengeance. In the historical literature on the theme, there is generally greater emphasis on the German will to persevere that the attacks produced, than on the fear of them, which is rarely addressed. The two things were naturally not mutually exclusive. The clearest references to fear among the population can be found in Friedrich, *Der Brand*, pp. 493ff.

45. See, for example, Ian Kershaw, *Hitler*, 7th ed. (London, 1994), p. 182, and various examples in Otto Kulka and Eberhard Jäckel, eds., *Die Juden in den geheimen NS-Stimmungsberichten 1933–1945* (Düsseldorf, 2004). Frank Bajohr, "Hamburg—der Zerfall der 'Volksgemeinschaft,'" in Herbert and Schildt, eds., *Kriegsende in Europa*, pp. 318–336, points out that in the case of Hamburg at least, toward the end of the war the Nazis themselves realized that their propaganda about imminent Russian atrocities was not succeeding, since the populace was not under the assumption that the Russians would occupy the city (p. 325).

46. See Atina Grossmann, "A Question of Silence: The Rape of German Women by Occupation Soldiers," in Robert G. Moeller, ed., *West Germany under Construction: Politics, Society, and Culture in the Adenauer Era* (Ann Arbor, MI, 1997), pp. 33–52, pp. 39ff.; Regina Mühlhauser, "Vergewaltigungen in Deutschland 1945: Nationaler Opferdiskurs und individuelles Erinnern betroffener Frauen," in Naumann, *Nachkrieg in Deutschland*, pp. 384–408, pp. 394ff.

47. See Norman Naimark, *Die Russen in Deutschland: Die sowjetische Besatzungszone 1945–1949* (Berlin, 1999); Christian Goeschel, "Suicide at the End of the Third Reich," *Journal of Contemporary History* 41 (2006), pp. 152–173; and Ursula Baumann, *Vom Recht auf den eigenen Tod: Die Geschichte des Suizids vom 18. bis zum 20. Jahrhundert* (Weimar, 2001), pp. 376ff.. These studies make clear that the wave of suicides cannot be understood simply as a product of fear of revenge or despair at the fall of the Third Reich. In view of the enormous new stresses on the horizon, some people committed suicide due to a lack of courage or strength.

48. For example, see the description in Margret Boveri, *Tage des Überlebens: Berlin 1945* (Munich, 1970), pp. 108f.; Jan C. Behrends, "Freundschaft, Fremdheit, Gewalt: Ostdeutsche Sowjetunionbilder zwischen Propaganda und Erfahrung," in Gregor Thum, ed., *Traumland Osten: Deutsche Bilder vom östlichen Europa im 20. Jahrhundert* (Göttingen, 2006), pp. 157–177, pp. 158ff.

49. Michael Geyer, "Der Kalte Krieg, die Deutschen und die Angst: Die westdeutsche Opposition gegen Wiederbewaffnung und Kernwaffen," in Naumann, *Nachkrieg in Deutschland*, pp. 267–318, citation p. 290.

50. See, for example, Schröder, "Töten und Todesangst"; Schröder, *Die gestohlenen Jahre*; Thomas A. Kohut and Jürgen Reulecke, "'Sterben wie eine Ratte, die der Bauer ertappt': Letzte Briefe aus Stalingrad," in Jürgen Förster, ed., *Stalingrad: Ereignis—Wirkung—Symbol*, 2nd ed. (Munich, 1993), pp. 456–471. However, the latter argue that only minute interludes in everyday life at war were involved here. For a completely nonhistorical approach: Wolfgang Sofsky, *Traktat über die Gewalt*, 2nd ed. (Frankfurt am Main, 1996), pp. 65–82 (chap. 4: "Die Gewalt, die Angst und der Schmerz").

51. On the temporality of feelings see Ute Frevert, "Angst vor Gefühlen? Die Geschichtsmächtigkeit von Gefühlen im 20. Jahrhundert," in Paul Nolte et al., eds., *Perspektiven der Gesellschaftsgeschichte* (Munich, 2000), pp. 95–111, p. 102.

52. See Frevert, "Angst vor Gefühlen," p. 102. Frevert is not specifically referring to anxiety here but is arguing in general that feelings are "the actual curators of memory." The formulation is a citation of Aleida Assmann, "Funktionsgedächtnis und Speichergedächtnis—Zwei Modi der Erinnerung," in Kristin Platt and Mirhan Dabag, eds., *Generation und Gedächtnis: Erinnerungen und kollektive Identitäten* (Opladen, 1995), pp. 169–185, p. 179.

53. See HBAB, Bestand Morija, 4474.

54. See HBAB, Bestand Morija, 5009.

55. See HBAB, Bestand Morija, 5295.

56. But compare that to Luc Ciompi, *Die emotionalen Grundlagen des Denkens: Entwurf einer fraktalen Affektlogik* (Göttingen, 1997), p. 67, *passim*, who points to a far greater variability of expressive forms.

57. See HBAB, Bestand Morija, 5267.

58. See, for example, HBAB, Bestand Morija, 5054.

59. See HBAB, Bestand Morija, 3712.

60. For this and the following: HBAB, Bestand Morija, 4560. Compare the earlier description of Rolf S.'s dream sequences in Part I, "Remembering the War."

61. For examples see Anonyma, *Eine Frau in Berlin*, p. 212; Carl Schüddekopf, *Im Kessel: Erzählungen von Stalingrad* (Munich, 2002) (the example of Jakob Vogt), pp. 232–285, p. 282.

62. See HBAB, Bestand Morija, 4524. On this case in greater detail: Svenja Goltermann, "Languages of Memory: German POWs and Their Violent Pasts in Postwar West Germany," in Moore and Hately-Broad, *Prisoners of War*, pp. 165–173, pp. 170f.

63. See, for example, HBAB, Bestand Morija, 3885, 4473, and 4559; Heidelberg Psychiatric and Neurological Clinic, no. 47/163.

64. HBAB, Bestand Morija, 3885; also for all following information on this case.

65. See Svenja Goltermann, "Angst in der Nachkriegszeit: Entnazifizierung und persönliche Desorientierung," in Martin Sabrow, ed., *Zeiträume: Potsdamer Almanach 2006* (Berlin, 2007), pp. 29–37.

66. HBAB, Bestand Morija, 4189.

67. See below, chapter 3, "Social Rubble."

68. HBAB, Bestand Morija, 4559.

69. Willy Peter Reese, *"Mir selber seltsam fremd": Die Unmenschlichkeit des Krieges, Russland 1941–1944*, ed. Stefan Schmitz (Munich, 2003), p. 182.

70. On the basis of various autobiographical texts, Rolf Schörken, *Jugend 1945: Politisches Denken und Lebensgeschichte* (Frankfurt am Main, 1994), offers numerous examples of the simultaneity and sequentiality of such diverse feelings (see esp. pp. 27–50); see also Bernd Weisbrod, "Der 8. Mai in der deutschen Erinnerung," *WerkstattGeschichte* 13 (1996), S. 72–81. For an impressive personal account: Ruth Andreas-Friedrich, *Der Schattenmann: Tagebuchaufzeichnungen 1938–1948* (Berlin, 2000), pp. 295ff. Walter Kempowski, *Das Echolot: Abgesang '45. Ein kollektives Tagebuch* (Munich, 2005), has compiled a number of extremely varied expressions of feelings from this period.

71. Cited in Schörken, *Jugend 1945*, p. 29.

72. See Barnouw, *Ansichten von Deutschland*, which focuses particularly on the American and British perspectives.

73. The reporter was Alan Moorhead, cited in Barnouw, *Ansichten von Deutschland*, p. 83.

74. Knoch, *Die Tat als Bild.*

75. The most prominent expression of this perspective is Arendt's above-cited report of her trip through postwar Germany; her viewpoint is reflected in many recent studies, which often refer explicitly to her early observations.

76. Among the many studies pointing in this direction are Frei, *Adenauer's Germany*; Ralph Giordano, *Die zweite Schuld oder Von der Last ein Deutscher zu sein* (Hamburg, 1987).

77. See Bessel, "Leben nach dem Tod," pp. 240ff.

78. Bessel, "Leben nach dem Tod," p. 241, with citation.

79. See, among others, Bajohr, "Hamburg." The collection of Götz Aly, ed., *Volkes Stimme: Skepsis und Führervertrauen im Nationalsozialismus*, 2nd ed. (Frankfurt am Main, 2006), observes in various passages a shift of societal mood toward skepticism and anxiety with the start of the Russian campaign.

80. Impressive testimony in this respect is the above-mentioned diary of Willy Peter Reese, *Mir selber seltsam fremd.* On the brutalization of war on the eastern front see Bartov, *Hitler's Army.*

81. See, among others, Karin Orth, *Das System der nationalsozialistischen Konzentrationslager: Eine politische Organisationsgeschichte* (Hamburg, 1999), pp. 222ff.

82. See Andreas-Friedrich, *Der Schattenmann*, p. 324; her entry stems from May 17, 1945. She indicates that dozens of people showed up every day to ask her and her friends for such certificates.

83. See the section "The Echo of Fear" in this chapter.

84. HBAB, Bestand Morija, 4051. This case is also mentioned in chapter 3, "Social Rubble."

85. See HBAB, Bestand Morija, 4559. This case is also discussed below in chapter 2 in the section "Delusion and Reality."

86. See chapter 2, the section "Delusion and Reality."

87. See also chapter 5, "Contentious Practices."

88. See, among others, Thomas Kühne, "Kameradschaft—'das Beste im Leben eines Mannes': Die deutschen Soldaten des Zweiten Weltkriegs in erfahrungs- und geschlechtergeschichtlicher Perspektive," *Geschichte und Gesellschaft* 22 (1996), pp. 504–529, p. 529; Echternkamp, "Arbeit am Mythos," pp. 430ff.

89. See HBAB, Bestand Morija, 4466.

90. For this self-observation see esp. Reese's diary, *Mir selber seltsam fremd.*

91. See Reese, *Mir selber seltsam fremd*, p. 130.

92. See HBAB, Bestand Morija, 4387. See chapter 3, "Social Rubble."

93. This is the characterization of the war in Thomas Kühne, "Der Soldat," in Ute Frevert and Heinz Gerhard Haupt, eds., *Der Mensch im 20. Jahrhundert* (Frankfurt am Main, 1999), pp. 344–372, p. 356.

94. Until now this point has remained inadequately examined. See Claudia Koonz, *The Nazi Conscience* (Cambridge, MA, 2003).

95. For greater detail see Thomas Kühne, *Kameradschaft: Die deutschen Soldaten des nationalsozialistischen Krieges und das 20. Jahrhundert* (Göttingen, 2006); Kühne,

"Gruppenkohäsion und Kameradschaftsmythos in der Wehrmacht," in Rolf-Dieter Müller and Hans-Erich Volkmann, eds., *Die Wehrmacht: Mythos und Realität* (Munich, 1999), pp. 534–549.

96. See HBAB, Bestand Morija, 5054.

97. See HBAB, Bestand Morija, 5288.

98. See Kühne, *Kameradschaft*, which has the citation of the memorial speech for the fallen soldiers (p. 525).

99. See Kühne, *Kameradschaft*, p. 525.

100. See esp. Moeller, *War Stories*; Klaus Latzel, "Töten und Schweigen—Wehrmachtssoldaten, Opferdiskurs und die Perspektive des Leidens," in Peter Gleichmann and Thomas Kühne, eds., *Massenhaftes Töten: Kriege und Genozide im 20. Jh.* (Essen, 2004), pp. 320–338, pp. 331ff.; Kühne, "Zwischen Vernichtungskrieg und Freizeitgesellschaft," pp. 99ff.

101. See, among others, HBAB, Bestand Morija, 5242 and 7584.

102. Irving N. Berlin, "Guilt as an Etiologic Factor in War Neuroses," *Journal of Nervous and Mental Disease* 111 (1950), pp. 239–245. Berlin also refers briefly to the instrumentalization of guilt to keep soldiers ready for war (p. 240). In fact, the American psychiatrists did not see a direct causal relationship between such guilt feelings and the war any more than their German colleagues. Following the interpretation of American colleagues, Berlin cited three causes for such feelings: the soldiers' own death wishes; an unconscious and repressed hostility toward those who had died; and latent homosexuality.

103. See, among others, Kühne, *Viktimisierungsfalle*, pp. 183–196, p. 186.

104. Paradigmatic for this argumentation: HBAB, Bestand Morija, 4749 (the case Franz F.; see in chapter 2 the section "The Other Self").

105. See Klaus Jochen Arnold, *Die Wehrmacht und die Besatzungspolitik in den besetzten Gebieten der Sowjetunion: Kriegführung und Radikalisierung im "Unternehmen Barbarossa"* (Berlin, 2004); for powerful testimony from the war: Wilm Hosenfeld, *Ich versuche jeden zu retten: Das Leben eines deutschen Offiziers in Briefen und Tagebüchern* (Munich, 2005).

106. A rare exception: HBAB, Bestand Morija, 4333 (Werner N., see in chapter 2 the section "Delusion and Reality"); HBAB, Bestand Morija, 4949 (Kurt T., see in chapter 2 the section "The Other Self").

107. See HBAB, Bestand Morija, 3916.

108. See HBAB, Bestand Morija, 3916.

109. See HBAB, Bestand Morija, 5660. Case discussed below in chapter 2 in the section "The Other Self."

CHAPTER 2

1. Andreas-Friedrich, *Der Schattenmann*, p. 359 (entry of June 22, 1945).

2. The following figures from Hans-Ulrich Wehler, *Deutsche Gesellschaftsgeschichte*, vol. 4: *Vom Beginn des Ersten Weltkriegs bis zur Gründung der beiden deutschen Staaten 1914–1949*, 2nd ed. (Munich, 2003), pp. 942ff.

3. See Arthur L. Smith, *Die "vermisste Million": Zum Schicksal deutscher Kriegsgefangener nach dem Zweiten Weltkrieg* (Munich, 1992); Rüdiger Overmans, "Die Rheinwiesenlager 1945: 'Ein untergeordneter Eintrag im Leidensbuch der jüngeren Geschichte?,'" in Günter Bischof and Rüdiger Overmans, eds., *Kriegsgefangenschaft im Zweiten Weltkrieg: Eine vergleichende Perspektive* (Ternitz, 1999), pp. 233–264.

4. The precise number of German POWS in the Soviet Union is impossible to ascertain, as is the number of German soldiers who died there. The Soviet POW administration registered nearly 2.4 million German prisoners, with allegedly 356,687 deaths. See Hilger, *Deutsche Kriegsgefangene*, pp. 71, *passim*. Supposedly, however, the Soviets did not keep statistics about deaths in the POW camps until 1946. See Smith, *Die vermisste Million*, p. 78.

5. In 1952, the Landesarbeitsgemeinschaft für Kriegsgefangenenfragen estimated that 1,300,000 soldiers were missing. See Smith, *Die vermisste Million*, p. 81. James Bacque, *Der geplante Tod: Deutsche Kriegsgefangene in amerikanischen und französischen Lagern 1945–1946* (Frankfurt am Main, 1989), assumed that a million-odd missing German soldiers died in American imprisonment.

6. See Neil Gregor, "'Is He Still Alive, or Long since Dead?': Loss, Absence and Remembrance in Nuremberg, 1945–1956," *German History* 21 (2003), pp. 183–203.

7. See Smith, *Heimkehr*, pp. 16ff.

8. For an overview of the extent of destruction in Germany and throughout Europe, see Judt, *Postwar*; and Klaus J. Bade, *Europa in Bewegung: Migration vom späten 18. Jh. bis in die Gegenwart* (Munich, 2000), p. 299.

9. Mazower, *Dark Continent*, pp. 217f.

10. Upon their return, countless thousands of released POWs did not receive residency permits—the key to being able to search for an apartment and work—in the places where they wanted to live. This meant that they were forced to travel on after a short stay. What they needed was proof they had lived in a place before imprisonment or had close relatives there. Returning soldiers facing the greatest difficulties were those who had lost their previous dwellings because of the bombing and could not show any close relations at these places. Problems also emerged, for instance, when the returnees did not wish to return to a previous place of residence that was now in the Soviet zone but wished to establish new roots in the West, either alone or with their family. See Smith, *Heimkehr*, pp. 115ff.

11. Andreas-Friedrich, *Der Schattenmann*, p. 432 (entry for September 11, 1946).

12. There are many examples for this in the letter collection of the Bibliothek für Zeitgeschichte, Sterz Collection, postwar period 1945–1953 (among others, letters of December 22, 1945, March 24, 1946, and April 19, 1946).

13. See Günter J. Trittel, *Hunger und Politik: Die Ernährungskrise in der Bizone (1945–1949)* (Frankfurt am Main, 1990); Rainer Gries, *Die Rationen-Gesellschaft. Versorgungskampf und Vergleichsmentalität: Leipzig, München und Köln nach dem Kriege* (Münster, 1990); Robert G. Moeller, *Geschützte Mütter: Frauen und Familien in der westdeutschen Nachkriegspolitik* (Munich, 1997), pp. 23–68. For a short overview: Michael Wildt, *Vom kleinen Wohlstand: Eine Konsumgeschichte der fünfziger Jahre* (Frankfurt am Main, 1996), pp. 26ff.; also Malte Zierenberg, *Von Schiebern und*

Schwarzen Märkten: Zur Geschichte des Berliner Schwarzhandels im Übergang vom Zweiten Weltkrieg zur Nachkriegszeit (Göttingen, 2008).

14. Report prepared by Rita Ostermann, June 4, 1947, cited from Moeller, *Geschützte Mütter*, p. 30.

15. For an overview see Cornelia Rauh-Kühne, "Die Entnazifizierung und die deutsche Gesellschaft," *Archiv für Sozialgeschichte* 35 (1995), pp. 35–70.

16. See Lutz Niethammer, *Die Mitläuferfabrik: Die Entnazifizierung am Beispiel Bayerns* (Berlin, 1982).

17. The figures for the Soviet zone in Alexander von Plato and Almut Leh, *"Ein unglaublicher Frühling": Erfahrene Geschichte im Nachkriegsdeutschland 1945–1948* (Bonn, 1997), p. 97; for the American zone, see Wehler, *Deutsche Gesellschaftsgeschichte*, vol. 4, p. 957; this is also the source of the figures for the British and French zones, where the number of interned persons was distinctly lower—65,000 and 18,870 respectively.

18. See Smith, *Heimkehr*, pp. 129. Since the amnesty for young people in August 1946, this did not necessarily affect men born in 1919 and thereafter; in addition, the so-called Christmas amnesty benefited the physically injured.

19. But for many refugees in rural areas, the currency reform initially meant worsened conditions. When they could no longer receive payment in kind for the work they performed, many of them lost their jobs. See Rainer Schulze, *Unruhige Zeiten: Erlebnisberichte aus dem Landkreis Celle 1945–1949*, 2nd ed. (Munich, 1991).

20. Smith, *Heimkehr*, pp. 130f.

21. *Die Zeit*, July 22, 1948, cited from Smith, *Heimkehr*, p. 122.

22. *Zum politischen Bewusstsein ehemaliger Kriegsgefangener* (Frankfurt am Main, 1957), pp. 3, cited from Smith, *Heimkehr*, p. 33.

23. See among others, Judt, *Postwar*, p. 270.

24. Judt, *Postwar*, pp. 87ff., speaks of a more general "crisis in Europe" in 1947, with a view to Western and Central European countries where, he indicates, a state of disappointment over the ongoing lack of "normal economic conditions," hopelessness, and fear of the future prevailed. Following the initial reconstruction efforts, American observers spoke of a "profound exhaustion of physical plant and emotional vigor"—from the American perspective a dangerous development.

25. See below, chapter 3, "Social Rubble."

26. This also applied to the large number of "ethnic Germans" (*Volksdeutsche*). Doris L. Bergen, "The 'Volksdeutschen' of Eastern Europe, World War II, and the Holocaust: Constructed Ethnicity, Real Genocide," in Keith Bullivant, Geoffrey Giles, and Walter Pape, eds., *Germany and Eastern Europe: Cultural Identities and Cultural Differences* (Yearbook of European Studies 13) (Amsterdam, 1999), pp. 70–93.

27. HBAB, Bestand Morija, 4473, also the source of following information and citations.

28. HBAB, Bestand Morija, 4560. On his dreams see also the section "Dreaming the War" in chapter 1.

29. HBAB, Bestand Morija, 4185.

30. Following information on this case is from HBAB, Bestand Morija, 4946.

31. HBAB, Bestand Morija, 4559, which is also source of following information and citations.

32. See the interpretation of this case in the section "Facing Defeat and Ruin" in chapter 1.

33. In other cases, Wehrmacht veterans suffered from a feeling that the occupiers and sometimes their fellow Germans were looking askance at them. Many also had fantasies that their minds could be read by other people, and as a result they reported themselves to the occupying authorities. See, for instance, the case of a former SS member at the Psychiatric and Neurological Clinic in Heidelberg, no. 47/163.

34. Rolf Schörken, *Jugend 1945: Politisches Denken und Lebensgeschichte* (Frankfurt am Main, 2001), p. 51.

35. His son suffered from Little's Disease, a form of infantile cerebral palsy that causes motor impairment, HBAB, Bestand Morija, 4559.

36. Heinrich Böll, *Der Engel schwieg* (Munich, 1997), pp. 14, 221.

37. For a summarization, see Irmtrud Wojak, *Eichmanns Memoiren: Ein kritischer Essay* (Frankfurt am Main, 2001), pp. 19ff.

38. See Ernst Klee, *Was sie taten—was sie wurden: Ärzte, Juristen und andere Beteiligte am Kranken- oder Judenmord* (Frankfurt am Main, 1995), pp. 15ff.; with many other examples as well.

39. See Norbert Frei, "Identitätswechsel: Die 'Illegalen' in der Nachkriegszeit," in Helmut König et al., eds., *Vertuschte Vergangenheit: Der Fall Schwerte und die NS-Vergangenheit der deutschen Hochschulen* (Munich, 1997), pp. 207–222, p. 218.

40. This is the justification for the additional clauses to the bill of the amnesty law, cited from Frei, *Adenauer's Germany*, pp. 12f. On the course of the debate, see pp. 11ff.

41. See Frei, *Adenauer's Germany*, p. 23.

42. Klaus Barbie was, among other things, head of the Gestapo in Lyon, where he was responsible for countless deportations and executions and was known for his cruel methods. In the 1960s Barbie was discovered living in Bolivia under the name Klaus Altmann, although he was only extradited in 1983. See Hermann Weiß, *Biographisches Lexikon zum Dritten Reich* (Frankfurt am Main, 2002), p. 30.

43. See, for example, the essays by Michael Wildt, Klaus-Michael Mallmann, and Konrad Kwiet in Klaus-Michael Mallmann and Gerhard Paul, eds., *Karrieren der Gewalt: Nationalsozialistische Täterbiographien* (Darmstadt, 2004); Smith, *Heimkehr*, pp. 122f. One official spoke of two million former POWs who were living with false papers in the American and British zones and were active in the black market.

44. Adolf Eichmann's own false papers were obtained through the Italian Red Cross. See Wojak, *Eichmanns Memoiren*, pp. 20.

45. Karl Wilhelm Böttcher, "Menschen unter falschem Namen," *Frankfurter Hefte* 4 (1949), pp. 492–511, cited from Frei, "Identitätswechsel," pp. 215f., 222.

46. See Andreas-Friedrich, *Der Schattenmann*, p. 305 (entry of May 1, 1945).

47. Smith, *Heimkehr*, p. 123, points to an apparently widespread scam during the period. Returnees targeted the families of missing soldiers, presented false stories about their whereabouts, and asked for help in smuggling supplies to them or even having them released from a camp. The returnees thereby enriched themselves with food, clothes, money, etc.

48. HBAB, Bethelkanzlei, Patientenakten, 2593II, which is also the source of the following information and citations.

49. Moeller, *War Stories*.

50. See the discussion of psychiatric doctrine in Part II.

51. As formulated by Carl Schmitt (who wanted to withdraw into such silence after returning from the interrogations in Nuremburg) as cited in Dirk van Laak, *Gespräche in der Sicherheit des Schweigens: Carl Schmitt in der politischen Geistesgeschichte der frühen Bundesrepublik*, 2nd ed. (Berlin, 2002).

52. See HBAB, Bestand Morija, 3916.

53. HBAB, Bestand Morija, 4189. More on the case in chapter 1 in the section "The Echo of Fear."

54. See Valentin Groebner, *Der Schein der Person* (Munich, 2004).

55. The case of Schwerte/Schneider suggests that knowledge of this doubling never entirely disappeared—even if Hans Ernst Schneider, a former official in the SS *Ahnenerbe* (ancestral heritage) think tank, and the later president of Aachen Technical University, Hans Schwerte, wished to create another impression. Schwerte/Schneider countered the accusation that he had led a double life as follows: "I led one life, and then a new one." Nevertheless, at the age of eighty-five he decided to report himself and expose his identity. On the person of Schwerte/Schneider see the essays of Gjalt R. Zondergeld, Ludwig Jäger, and Klaus Weimar in Helmut König et al., eds., *Vertuschte Vergangenheit*, and Frei, "Identitätswechsel," which is also the source of the citation (p. 208).

56. This can also be observed among higher Nazi officials. We see this, for example, in Werner Best's behavior before his trial, which was a mixture of "calculation and despair," "cowering before authority," and "dominating self-pity." See Ulrich Herbert, *Best: Biographische Studien über Radikalismus, Weltanschauung und Vernunft 1903–1989*, 2nd ed. (Bonn, 2006), p. 425.

57. See HBAB, Bestand Morija, 4387. For more on the case, see also in chapter 1 the section "Facing Defeat and Ruin."

58. See HBAB, Bestand Morija, 4749.

59. See Thomas Kühne and Benjamin Ziemann, "Militärgeschichte in der Erweiterung. Konjunkturen, Interpretationen, Konzepte," in Kühne and Ziemann, eds., *Was ist Militärgeschichte?* (Paderborn, 2000), pp. 9–48, pp. 27ff.

60. See HBAB, Bestand Morija, 4949, also the source of the following information and citations.

61. See, among others, Ulrike Jureit, "Ein Traum in Braun: Über die Erfindung des Unpolitischen," in Christian Geulen and Karoline Tschuggnall, eds., *Aus einem deutschen Leben: Lesarten eines biographischen Interviews* (Tübingen, 2000), pp. 17–36, p. 22.

62. Jureit, "Ein Traum in Braun," p. 23.

63. Erhard Schütz, "Von Lageropfern und Helden der Flucht: Kriegsgefangenschaft Deutscher—Popularisierungsmuster in der Bundesrepublik," in Wolfgang Hardtwig and Erhard Schütz, eds., *Geschichte für Leser: Populäre Geschichtsschreibung in Deutschland im 20. Jahrhundert* (Stuttgart, 2005), pp. 181–204.

64. See, among others, Echternkamp, "Arbeit am Mythos."

65. Echternkamp, "Arbeit am Mythos." This argument was also presented in countless public calls for the release of German POWs from the Soviet Camps during the

postwar period. Paradigmatic in this respect: "Das deutsche Volk für seine Kriegsgefangenen, Kriegsvermissten, Kriegsverschleppten und Kriegsinternierten" [1949], in HBAB, 2/12-197, with the often-heard explanation that the Nuremberg trials showed who the guilty people were.

66. Various examples in material recounted in interviews in Hans Joachim Schröder, *Die gestohlenen Jahre.*

67. See Barnouw, *Ansichten von Deutschland*, pp. 13f.

68. See HBAB, Bestand Morija, 5660, which is also the source of following information and citations. See additional discussion in chapter 1 in the section "Facing Defeat and Ruin" and in chapter 3, "Social Rubble."

69. The plans for him to be channeled into a general staff career are not included in the written vita that Reinhard G. compiled. Rather, he referred to them during an interview with the consulting psychiatrist.

CHAPTER 3

1. Andreas-Friedrich, *Der Schattenmann*, p. 376 (entry for July 30, 1945).

2. In this regard, see also Dagmar Herzog, *Die Politisierung der Lust: Sexualität in der deutschen Geschichte des 20. Jahrhunderts* (Munich, 2005), pp. 108ff. and 127ff.; Sybille Buske, "'Fräulein Mutter' vor dem Richterstuhl: Der Wandel der öffentlichen Wahrnehmung und rechtlichen Stellung lediger Mütter in der Bundesrepublik 1948 bis 1970," *WerkstattGeschichte* 27 (2000), pp. 48–68; Elizabeth D. Heineman, *What Difference Does a Husband Make? Women and Marital Status in Nazi and Postwar Germany* (Berkeley, CA, 1999).

3. Helmut Schelsky, *Wandlungen der deutschen Familie in der Gegenwart: Darstellung und Interpretation einer empirisch-soziologischen Tatbestandsaufnahme* (Dortmund, 1953), p. 13.

4. See Moeller, *Geschützte Mütter*, pp. 188ff; Franka Schneider, "'Einigkeit im Unglück'? Berliner Eheberatungsstellen zwischen Ehekrise und Wiederaufbau," in Klus Naumann, *Nachkrieg in Deutschland*, pp. 206–226, pp. 206ff; Ute Frevert, *Frauen-Geschichte: Zwischen bürgerlicher Verbesserung und neuer Weiblichkeit* (Frankfurt am Main, 1986), pp. 253f.; Dagmar Herzog, *Sex after Fascism: Memory and Morality in Twentieth-Century Europe* (Princeton, NJ, 2007); Sybille Steinbacher, *Wie der Sex nach Deutschland kam: Der Kampf um Sittlichkeit und Anstand in der frühen Bundesrepublik* (Munich, 2011).

5. Schelsky, *Wandlungen*, esp. pp. 63–72, 87f.

6. Schelsky, *Wandlungen*, 87f.

7. See Schelsky, *Wandlungen*, p. 91.

8. See Neumann, *Nicht der Rede wert.*

9. In 1952, the official statistics for disabled West German Wehrmacht veterans showed 745,135 seriously injured (i.e., loss of ability to pursue gainful activity of 50 percent or higher). Disability pensions were generally insufficient to cover expenses—which was politically intentional. See Neumann, *Nicht der Rede wert*, pp. 144f., 158.

10. See Neumann, *Nicht der Rede wert*, p. 158, and Neumann, "Kampf um Anerken-

nung: Die westdeutsche Kriegsfolgengesellschaft im Spiegel der Versorgungsämter," in Naumann, *Nachkrieg in Deutschland*, pp. 364–383.

11. See Heineman, *Difference*, p. 116; Robert G. Moeller, "The Last Soldiers of the Great War and Tales of Family Reunions in the Federal Republic of Germany," *Signs* 24 (1998), pp. 129–145. At the time, *Spätestheimkehrer* (very late returnees) was the usual term applied to POWs who were released from the Soviet Union only after 1952–1953.

12. See Merith Niehuss, "Kontinuität und Wandel der Familie in den 50er Jahren," in Schildt and Sywottek, *Modernisierung im Wiederaufbau*, pp. 316–334, here p. 322; or Neumann, *Nicht der Rede wert*, p. 159.

13. See Wehler, *Deutsche Gesellschaftsgeschichte*, vol. 4, p. 961.

14. Numerous letters of this kind can be found, for example, in Anatoly Golovchansky et al., eds., *Ich will raus aus diesem Wahnsinn: Deutsche Briefe von der Ostfront 1941–1945. Aus sowjetischen Archiven* (Reinbek, 1993).

15. See Heineman, *Difference*; Ulrike Jureit, "Zwischen Ehe und Männerbund: Emotionale und sexuelle Beziehungsmuster im Zweiten Weltkrieg," *WerkstattGeschichte* 22 (1999), pp. 61–74.

16. A large number of such letters can be found in Bundesarchiv-Militararchiv Freiburg, B 205 v. 40 (Briefsammlung von Eugen Weller). Additionally see Hilger, *Deutsche Kriegsgefangene*, pp. 308f.

17. See, among others, Lutz Niethammer, "Privat-Wirtschaft. Erinnerungsfragmente einer anderen Umerziehung," in Niethammer, ed., *Hinterher merkt man, daß es richtig war, daß es schiefgegangen ist: Nachkriegserfahrungen im Ruhrgebiet* (Lebensgeschichte und Sozialkultur im Ruhrgebiet 1930 bis 1960, vol. 2) (Berlin, 1983), pp. 17–105, pp. 46ff.; Sibylle Meyer and Eva Schulze, "Als wir wieder zusammen waren, ging der Krieg im Kleinen weiter: Frauen, Männer und Familien im Berlin der 40er Jahre," in Lutz Niethammer, ed., *Wir kriegen jetzt andere Zeiten: Auf der Suche nach der Erfahrung des Volkes in nachfaschistischen Ländern* (Lebensgeschichte und Sozialkultur im Ruhrgebiet 1930 bis 1960, vol. 3) (Berlin, 1985), pp. 305–326, pp. 309ff.; Hanna Schissler, "'Normalization' as Project: Some Thoughts on Gender Relations in West Germany during the 1950s," in Schissler, ed., *The Miracle Years: A Cultural History in West Germany, 1949–1968* (Princeton, NJ, 2001), pp. 359–375.

18. See HBAB, Bestand Morija, 4099, which is also the source of the subsequent information and quotations pertaining to this case.

19. See, among others, Heinemann, *Difference*; Meyer and Schulze, "Als wir wieder zusammen waren"; Meyer and Schulze, *Von Liebe sprach damals keiner: Familienalltag in der Nachkriegszeit* (Munich, 1985); Moeller, *Geschützte Mütter*, pp. 55f.

20. The following continues to reference HBAB, Bestand Morija, 4099.

21. A document issued by the central office of the Evangelical Church in Germany indicates that this was an extremely widespread problem. However, even the denominational aid organizations were apparently not sufficiently prepared to meet it. In a letter of July 9, 1947, which the central office dispatched to, among others, the church governing boards at the state level and the chaplains in overseas POW camps, it drew attention to the inability of some church agencies to deal with returnees, making specific mention that the topics of the outlook for the future, marriage, and denazification were

essential points of reference for the provision of pastoral counseling to returnees. Landeskirchliches Archiv Bielefeld, C 11-04, vol. 1.

22. For a further example from the immediate postwar period, i.e., the fall of 1945, see HBAB, Bestand Morija, 3742.

23. See chapter 5.

24. See HBAB, Bestand Morija, 4710.

25. See HBAB, Bestand Morija, 4466. This case has already been mentioned in chapter 1, in the section "Facing Defeat and Ruin."

26. See HBAB, Bestand Morija, 4320.

27. As an example, see Welzer et al., *Opa war kein Nazi*; Sven-Oliver Muller's *Die deutschen Soldaten und ihre Feinde: Nationalismus in der kriegführenden Wehrmacht, 1941–1944* (Frankfurt am Main, 2007) contains a number of military mail service letters mentioning exceptions during the war.

28. See, for example, HBAB, Bestand Morija, 3959.

29. See, for example, HBAB, Bestand Morija, 5510.

30. See HBAB, Bestand Morija, 4329.

31. See HBAB, Bestand Morija, 3959.

32. This is also expressed in the poem "Künftige Heimkehr" ("Retuning Home in the Future"), written by Walter Bauer during his internment as a POW, in BA-MA Freiburg, B 205 v. 1368, pp. 48–49.

33. See HBAB, Bestand Morija, 4944; also see the presentation of this case in the introduction to this book.

34. See, among others, Norbert Frei, ed., *Hitlers Eliten nach 1945* (Munich, 2003); Wilfried Loth and Bernd-A. Rusinek, eds., *Verwandlungspolitik: NS-Eliten in der westdeutschen Nachkriegsgesellschaft* (Frankfurt am Main, 1998); Michael Wildt, *Generation des Unbedingten: Das Führungskorps des Reichssicherheitshauptamtes* (Hamburg, 2003), pp. 767ff. Legitimate skepticism toward taking a general approach to continuity research has been formulated by Ulrich Herbert, "Rückkehr in die Bürgerlichkeit? NS-Eliten in der Bundesrepublik," in Bernd Weisbrod, ed., *Rechtsradikalismus in der politischen Kultur der Bundesrepublik* (Hannover, 1995), pp. 157–173, pp. 159f. Herbert advocates a more differentiated approach, inasmuch as proximity—in the sense of concentric circles—and responsibility for the regime's policies of terror and annihilation are intended as criteria for evaluating membership in Nazi elites (citation on p. 159).

35. One of the few studies in which this is not overlooked is Hartmut Berghoff and Cornelia Rauh-Kühne, *Fritz K: Ein deutsches Leben im 20. Jahrhundert* (Munich, 2000), pp. 224ff.; see also Konrad Jarausch, *Die Umkehr: Deutsche Wandlungen 1945–1995* (Munich, 2004), pp. 66ff.; similarly in tenor, Herbert, "Rückkehr in die Bürgerlichkeit," p. 162.

36. Suggestions to this effect in Tim Schanetzky, "Unternehmer: Profiteure des Unrechts," in Frei, *Hitlers Eliten*, pp. 69–113, p. 84. Schanetzky argues that a lack of professional competence is what led to the end of the careers of those who had hoped to be successful in business based on their Nazi Party affiliation alone; Norbert Frei, "Hitlers Eliten nach 1945—eine Bilanz," in Frei, *Hitlers Eliten*, pp. 269–299, p. 280, points to the fact that at the time, "since everyone wanted to be at a distance from the regime," no

place was available for such individuals who had used party membership as a way to switch careers.

37. On passage of the "131-ers" law, which saw to the rehabilitation and pensioning of a large number of officials dismissed after the war, see Frei, *Vergangenheitspolitik*, pp. 69ff.

38. Letter to Johann de Boer, June 2, 1948, in Johann de Boer estate, private possession.

39. Letter to Johann de Boer, January 12, 1948, Johann de Boer estate. Fear of "proletarization" has been considered above all in the context of the period's perception of a problem integrating refugees and expellees. See also Paul Nolte, *Die Ordnung der deutschen Gesellschaft: Selbstentwurf und Selbstbeschreibung im 20. Jahrhundert* (Munich, 2000), pp. 227f.

40. The question of how women dealt with social decline in the postwar period has not yet been studied.

41. See HBAB, Bestand Morija, 4102.

42. See Rauh-Kühne, "Entnazifizierung," pp. 35–70.

43. Frei argues in this direction in *Hitlers Eliten*, p. 281.

44. See HBAB, Bestand Morija, 4410.

45. That was the group of those who were deemed "less incriminated." Generally, they could expect a fine.

46. There is a similar assessment by Frei in *Hitlers Eliten*, pp. 274f.

47. See HBAB, Bestand Morija, 4139.

48. Similar in tenor: HBAB, Bestand Morija, 4051 (case of Gustav B.; see chapter 1, the section "Facing Defeat and Ruin").

49. See HBAB, Bestand Morija, 4944, on the following see also pp. 140 as well as the accounts in the introduction.

50. In addition to the case of Hans H., see HBAB, Bestand Morija, 4095, and HBAB, Bestand Morija, 3885 (Herbert I.; see chapter 1, the section "The Echo of Fear").

51. As an example, see Werner Abelshauser, *Deutsche Wirtschaftsgeschichte seit 1945* (Munich, 2004), which contains additional bibliographical references.

52. See HBAB, Bestand Morija, 5109; on this case see also chapter 1, the section "Dreaming the War."

53. See HBAB, Bestand Morija, 4387. See detailed discussion in chapter 1 in the section "Facing Defeat and Ruin."

54. On the following case see HBAB, Bestand Morija, 4765.

55. Occasionally, this is still suggested, as in Neumann, *Nicht der Rede wert*, p. 76.

56. Again, see Wehler, *Deutsche Gesellschaftsgeschichte*, vol. 4, pp. 684ff.

57. See Wildt, *Vom kleinen Wohlstand*, pp. 209–227.

58. See Neumann, *Nicht der Rede wert*, pp. 144f. The figures stem from the various state ministries responsible for disabled veterans.

59. See table in Reichsbund der Kriegs- und Zivilbeschädigten, Sozialrentner und Hinterbliebenen, *Anhaltspunkte für die ärtzliche Gutachtertätigkeit*, pp. 31ff. The total number is also distorted because in many cases it was difficult to demonstrate war-

related damage, particularly in the case of internal diseases, but also when mental disorders were involved. See the more detailed discussion in Part II of this study.

60. Reichsbund der Kriegs- und Zivilbeschädigten, Sozialrentner und Hinterbliebenen, *Anhaltspunkte für die medizinische Gutachtertätigkeit*, p. 30.

61. For the following case see HBAB, Bestand Morija, 4109.

62. The *Müttergenesungswerk* (German maternal convalescence organization) cited the embitterment of many severely disabled veterans as one of the heavy burdens placed on the wives who were caring for them; see Neumann, *Nicht der Rede wert*, p. 123.

63. Many examples are presented in *Sammlungen von Entscheidungen aus dem Gebiete der Sozialversicherung und Versorgung* 42 (1953) and in following volumes (starting 1955 under the title *Sammlungen von Entscheidungen aus dem Gebiete der Sozialversicherung, Versorgung und Arbeitslosenversicherung*). On the problem of causal connection, see in chapter 5 the section "Pension Claims under Suspicion"; on the growing critique of the hereditability paradigm, see in chapter 5 the section "The Dispute about Hereditability."

64. For the following case see HBAB, Bestand Morija, 4540.

65. See Vera Neumann, "Kampf um Anerkennung. Die westdeutsche Kriegsfolgengesellschaft im Spiegel der Versorgungsämter," in Naumann, *Nachkrieg in Deutschland*, pp. 364–383, p. 375.

CHAPTER 4

1. Friedrich Nietzsche, "Zur Genealogie der Moral," in *Sämtliche Werke: Kritische Studienausgabe*, vol. 5, ed. Giorgio Colli and Mazzino Montinari, 3rd ed. (Munich, 1993), pp. 245–412, citation p. 376.

2. Kalinowski reached his final place of residence, the United States, in 1940. He had first emigrated to Rome, which he left in 1939, then moved to Paris, and finally to England. See Edward Shorter, *Geschichte der Psychiatrie* (Berlin, 1999), pp. 330f. On Kalinowski's trip to Germany, see also Ben Shephard, *A War of Nerves: Soldiers and Psychiatrists, 1914–1994* (London, 2000), pp. 299f.

3. See Hans-Walter Schmuhl, "Hirnforschung und Krankenmord: Das Kaiser-Wilhelm-Institut für Hirnforschung 1937–1945," *Vierteljahreshefte für Zeitgeschichte* 50 (2002), pp. 559–609. In addition to brain researcher Julius Hallervorden, Leo Alexander also interviewed psychiatrist Oswald Bumke; see Shephard, *A War of Nerves*, p. 309.

4. Lothar B. Kalinowski, in Ludwig J. Pongratz, ed., *Psychiatrie in Selbstdarstellungen* (Bern, 1977), pp. 147–164, p. 159.

5. See, among others, the anthology by Angelika Ebbinghaus and Klaus Dörner, eds., *Vernichten und Heilen: Der Nürnberger Ärzteprozeß und seine Folgen* (Berlin, 2001); in this volume above all Hans-Walter Schmuhl, "Die Patientenmorde," pp. 295–328.

6. See Lothar B. Kalinowski, "Problems of War Neuroses in the Light of Experiences in Other Countries," *American Journal of Psychiatry* 107 (1950), pp. 340–346, p.

340. Statistics concerning psychiatric treatment in the Wehrmacht are not available. Yet German psychiatric experts spoke of a fraction of "war neurotics" compared to World War I, and only scattered cases proved to be "therapy resistant" (see below). In contrast, American psychiatrists spoke of roughly a million cases of neuropsychiatric treatment of American soldiers; some 63 percent involved "psychoneurosis" (the figures can be found in Joachim Ernst Meyer, "Die abnormen Erlebnisreaktionen im Kriege bei Truppe und Zivilbevölkerung," in *Psychiatrie der Gegenwart*, vol. 3: *Soziale und angewandte Psychiatrie* [Berlin, 1961], pp. 574–619, p. 594). According to Shephard, *A War of Nerves*, pp. 326, circa 504,000 soldiers were suffering from mental health problems in American ground forces alone—enough to have made fifty divisions.

7. Kalinowski, in Pongratz, *Psychiatrie in Selbstdarstellungen*, p. 159.

8. Kalinowski, in Pongratz, *Psychiatrie in Selbstdarstellungen*, pp. 340ff.

9. Kalinowski, in Pongratz, *Psychiatrie in Selbstdarstellungen*, pp. 343f.

10. Klaus-Jürgen Neumärker, *Karl Bonhoeffer: Leben und Werk eines deutschen Psychiaters und Neurologen in seiner Zeit* (Berlin, 1990).

11. Karl Bonhoeffer, "Vergleichende psychopathologische Erfahrungen aus den beiden Weltkriegen," *Der Nervenarzt* 18 (1947), pp. 1–4, p. 2.

12. Bonhoeffer, "Vergleichende psychopathologische Erfahrungen," pp. 2–4.

13. On the psychiatric approach to so-called war neurotics or war hysterics in German-speaking Europe, see esp. Lerner, *Hysterical Men*; Kaufmann, "Science as Cultural Practice"; Kaufmann, "'Widerstandsfähige Gehirne' und 'kampfunlustige Seelen': Zur Mentalitäts- und Wissenschaftsgeschichte des Ersten Weltkriegs," in Michael Hagner, ed., *Ecce Cortex: Beiträge zur Geschichte des modernen Gehirns* (Göttingen, 1999), pp. 206–223; Hans-Georg Hofer, *Nervenschwäche und Krieg: Modernitätskritik und Krisenbewältigung in der österreichischen Psychiatrie (1880–1920)* (Vienna, 2004); Martin Lengwiler, *Zwischen Klinik und Kaserne: Die Geschichte der Militärpsychiatrie in Deutschland und in der Schweiz 1870–1914* (Zurich, 2000). On British and American psychiatry see esp. Shephard, *A War of Nerves*, pp. 21–169; Peter Leese, *Shell Shock: Traumatic Neurosis and the British Soldiers of the First World War* (London, 2002). On France: Gregory M. Thomas, *Treating the Trauma of the Great War: Soldiers, Civilians, and Psychiatry in France, 1918–1940* (Baton Rouge, LA, 2009); Marc Rodebush, "Battle of Nerves: Hysteria and Its Treatment in France during World War I," in Micale and Lerner, *Traumatic Pasts*, pp. 253–279; on Italy: Bruna Bianchi, "Psychiatrists, Soldiers, and Officers in Italy during the Great War," in Micale and Lerner, *Traumatic Pasts*, pp. 222–252; on Russia: Paul Wanke, *Russian/Soviet Military Psychiatry 1904–1945* (New York, 2004); on Finland: Ville Kivimäki, "Battled Nerves: Finnish Soldiers' War Experience, Trauma, and Military Psychiatry, 1941–44," PhD diss., University of Tampere, 2013.

14. Shephard, *A War of Nerves*, pp. 97ff.; Lerner, *Hysterical Men*, pp. 61ff.; Jay Winter, "Shell-Shock and the Cultural History of the Great War," *Journal of Contemporary History* 35 (2000), pp. 7–11.

15. Much like broad segments of the Wilhelminian bourgeoisie in general, psychiatrists themselves believed in the healing power of the war and that it would end the "nervous age." See in more detail Lerner, *Hysterical Men*, pp. 45ff. More broadly: Jeffrey Verhey, *The Spirit of 1914: Militarism, Myth, and Mobilization in Germany* (Cam-

bridge, 2000); Wolfgang J. Mommsen, ed., *Kultur und Krieg: Die Rolle der Intellektuellen, Künstler und Schriftsteller im Ersten Weltkrieg* (Munich, 1996).

16. Kaufmann points this out explicitly, "Widerstandsfähige Gehirne," pp. 213f. In the above-mentioned European countries, Kaufmann indicates, it was less common for soldiers to be examined for mental illnesses; instead they were "placed before military courts with far less ado." Contrary to their German counterparts, these courts did not take psychiatric evaluations under consideration, as emerges, for example, in British judgments. Shephard, *A War of Nerves*, p. 101, speaks of German military courts condemning 150 soldiers to death (48 of the sentences were carried out); the corresponding figure for Britain was 3,080 (of which 307 were carried out). In France there were around 2,000 death sentences and 700 actual executions.

17. In the 1860s, the London surgeon John Eric Erichsen was a pioneer in studying such accidents among railway men. He presumed very subtle injuries of the spinal cord due to the impact suffered during the accident. See, among others, Ralph Harrington, "The Railway Accident: Trains, Trauma, and Technological Crises in Nineteenth Century Britain," in Micale and Lerner, *Traumatic Pasts*, pp. 31–56.

18. For greater detail, see Lerner, *Hysterical Men*, pp. 27ff.; Lerner, "From Traumatic Neurosis to Male Hysteria: The Decline and Fall of Hermann Oppenheim, 1889–1919," in Micale and Lerner, *Traumatic Pasts*, pp. 140–171; Greg Eghigian, "The German Welfare State as a Discourse of Trauma," in Micale and Lerner, *Traumatic Pasts*, pp. 92–112.

19. See Lerner, *Hysterical Men*, p. 34. The word was coined in 1895 by Adolf Strumpel, an internist and neurologist in Leipzig.

20. See Lerner, *Hysterical Men*, pp. 36ff. On the debate in England, where protagonists of the "hysteria" diagnosis ultimately prevailed, see Shephard, *A War of Nerves*, p. 98.

21. On the interpretive shift in the diagnosis of hysteria see esp. Mark Micale, "On the Disappearance of Hysteria: The Clinical Deconstruction of a Diagnosis," *Isis* 84 (1993), pp. 496–526.

22. See Paul Lerner, "'Ein Sieg deutschen Willens': Wille und Gemeinschaft in der deutschen Kriegspsychiatrie," in Wolfgang U. Eckardt and Christoph Gradmann, eds., *Die Medizin und der Erste Weltkrieg* (Pfaffenweiler, 1996), pp. 85–107, p. 98. The same general thrust is found in Emil Kraepelin, who designated "hysteria" as "a personal type of reaction that cannot be clearly distinguished from the range of what is considered health." Citation in Kaufmann, "Widerstandsfähige Gehirne," p. 211; see also Kaufmann, "Science as Cultural Practice," pp. 130f.

23. See Lerner, "Traumatic Neurosis," p. 153.

24. Karl Bonhoeffer, "Erfahrungen aus dem Kriege über die Ätiologie psychopathologischer Zustände mit besonderer Berücksichtigung der Erschöpfung und Emotion," *Allgemeine Zeitschrift für Psychiatrie und psychisch-gerichtliche Medizin* 73 (1917), pp. 76–95, citation p. 77. Comments of this type can be found in great number; see the many examples presented in Lerner, *Hysterical Men*, pp. 43ff.

25. See Bonhoeffer, "Vergleichende psychopathologische Erfahrungen," p. 2. See also Kaufmann, "Science as Cultural Practice," p. 134.

26. See Bonhoeffer, "Vergleichende psychopathologische Erfahrungen," p. 78.

27. Shephard, *A War of Nerves*, p. 99, sees German psychiatry in this respect moving in the same direction as the French and the British, who already largely assumed that the symptoms of soldiers involved "functional disturbances."

28. See Lerner, *Hysterical Men*, p. 6.

29. On the debate see Oswald Bumke, "Kriegsneurosen: Allgemeine Ergebnisse," in Oswald Bumke and O. Foerster, eds., *Handbuch der Neurologie* (Berlin, 1924), pp. 54–71, citation p. 55. A concise summary of the arguments is in Kaufmann, "Science as Cultural Practice," pp. 134f.; in more detail: Lerner, *Hysterical Men*, pp. 67ff.

30. Thus Karl Bonhoeffer, in *Handbuch der medizinischen Erfahrungen im Weltkriege 1914/1918*, ed. Otto Schjerning, vol. 4: *Geistes- und Nervenkrankheiten*, ed. Karl Bonhoeffer (Leipzig, 1922). Citation from Kaufmann, "Widerstandsfähige Gehirne," p. 216. Bonhoeffer had already argued very similarly in 1916; see "Erfahrungen aus dem Kriege," p. 94.

31. See above all Kaufmann, "Widerstandsfähige Gehirne," p. 218; and Karl-Heinz Roth, "Die Modernisierung der Folter in beiden Weltkriegen: Der Konflikt der Psychotherapeuten und Schulpsychiater um die deutschen 'Kriegsneurotiker' 1915–1945," *1999* 3 (1987), pp. 8–75, pp. 17ff.

32. Ernst Simmel, *Kriegsneurosen und "psychisches Trauma"* (Leipzig, 1918), p. 31, cited in Roth, "Modernisierung der Folter," p. 21.

33. A short suggestion to this effect in Carl Schneider, "'Der Psychopath' in heutiger Sicht," *Fortschritte der Neurologie, Psychiatrie und ihrer Grenzgebiete* 26 (1958), pp. 1–9; and in Georg Berger, *Die Beratenden Psychiater des deutschen Heeres 1939 bis 1945* (Frankfurt am Main, 1998), pp. 135f. Nevertheless, some psychiatrists, for instance Robert Gaupp in 1940, argued that the concept of "psychopathic inferiority" was meant to be understood in a purely biological and not a moral sense. See Robert Gaupp, "Die psychischen und nervösen Erkrankungen des Heeres im Weltkrieg," *Der Deutsche Militärarzt* 5 (1940), pp. 358–368, citation p. 367.

34. Emil Kraepelin, who founded the theory of psychopathic personalities, classified such individuals as one of those who were "adrift," "bellicose," or "an enemy of society." See Schneider, "Der Psychopath," p. 2. In general, on the position of psychopathology within Kraepelin's theory of disease: Paul Hoff, *Emil Kraepelin und die Psychiatrie als klinische Wissenschaft* (Berlin, 1994), pp. 144ff.

35. Schneider, "Der Psychopath," p. 2.

36. See Hofer, *Nervenschwäche und Krieg*, pp. 351ff., p. 353.

37. See Kaufmann, "Widerstandsfähige Gehirne," p. 218.

38. See Lerner and Micale, "Trauma, Psychiatry, and History," p. 19; Hofer, *Nervenschwäche und Krieg*, pp. 350ff. On the concept of degeneration in pre-1914 psychiatry see Volker Roelcke, *Krankheit und Kulturkritik: Psychiatrische Gesellschaftsdeutungen im bürgerlichen Zeitalter (1790–1914)* (Frankfurt am Main, 1999), pp. 8off.; Paul Weindling, *Health, Race and German Politics between National Unification and Nazism, 1870–1935* (Cambridge, 1993).

39. See Bumke, "Kriegsneurosen," p. 57. Toward the beginning of World War II (1940), Robert Gaupp proposed greater caution, arguing that "whoever has himself experienced" how easy it is to retain a protective attitude longer than necessary, for example, with a once-painful joint injury, and then grown accustomed to it, would see "a

certain justification" in the view of Paul Julius Möbius and Alfred Hoche, namely, "that *every person is 'a little hysterical' or at least capable of hysteria*." It was not necessary, he insisted, to assume a "highly defective conscience with regard to one's health." Once one recognized the mechanism and had mustered sufficient "will to become healthy and work," it was usually easy to overcome the overprotectiveness. See Gaupp, "Psychischen und nervösen Erkrankungen," citation p. 366.

40. Bonhoeffer, "Erfahrungen aus dem Kriege," pp. 87ff. He himself doubted that during such states the intellect was completely intact. He saw clear indications—e.g., in both the professional literature and the soldiers' stories—of a simultaneous disturbance on the level of perception.

41. Bonhoeffer, "Erfahrungen aus dem Kriege," p. 95. In 1941 Bonhoeffer reflected over the manner in which this insight had altered the therapeutic treatment of psychosis. See Kaufmann, "Widerstandsfähige Gehirne," p. 217 n. 35.

42. Bonhoeffer, "Erfahrungen aus dem Kriege," p. 94.

43. See Peter Riedesser and Axel Verderber, eds., *"Maschinengewehre hinter der Front": Zur Geschichte der deutschen Militärpsychiatrie* (Frankfurt am Main, 1996), pp. 71ff.

44. Kurt Schneider, "Einige psychiatrische Erfahrungen als Truppenarzt," *Zeitschrift für die gesamte Neurologie und Psychiatrie* 39 (1918), pp. 307–314, p. 311. Similarly: Gaupp, "Psychischen und nervösen Erkrankungen," p. 367.

45. See Shephard, *A War of Nerves*, pp. 165f.

46. Gaupp, "Psychischen und nervösen Erkrankungen," p. 367; Max Nonne, "Therapeutische Erfahrungen an den Kriegsneurosen," in Bonhoeffer, *Geistes- und Nervenkrankheiten*, pp. 102–121. Further examples in Riedesser and Verderber, *Maschinengewehre hinter der Front*, pp. 80ff.

47. See Kaufmann, "Widerstandsfähige Gehirne," p. 219; there also the citation of Max Nonne. See also Karl Bonhoeffer, "Psychopathologische Erfahrungen und Lehren des Weltkriegs," *Münchener Medizinische Wochenschrift* 81 (1934), pp. 1212–1215, p. 1215. Such unease was also arising among psychoanalysts during the Great War, as we can infer from Roth, "Modernisierung der Folter," p. 21, but eugenic modes of thought are not yet apparent here. As a part of the eugenic discourse after the war, criticism was voiced over the "contra-selective" effects of modern medicine—and likewise over contemporary social policies—within the ranks of sociology and anthropology. On the development of eugenics as a field of knowledge see Doris Kaufmann, "Eugenik—Rassenhygiene—Humangenetik: Zur lebenswissenschaftlichen Neuordnung der Wirklichkeit in der ersten Hälfte des 20. Jahrhunderts," in Richard van Dülmen, ed., *Erfindung des Menschen: Schöpfungsträume und Körperbilder 1500–2000* (Vienna, 2000), pp. 347–365.

48. Gaupp, "Psychischen und nervösen Erkrankungen," p. 358. The fear that Bonhoeffer supposedly expressed in 1916, namely, that what seems "a secure area of scientific knowledge to us" would "be outmoded in perhaps thirty years at most," had not materialized, as Gaupp underscored with relief. References with the scientific-medical insight gained during the Great War can be seen everywhere in the professional literature of the 1930s and early 1940s. Some examples: Adolf Heidenhain, *Die Psychiatrie im Dienste der Wehrmacht* (Leipzig, 1938), pp. 17, 29, *passim*; F. W. A. Weber, "Wie

sollen wir uns in einem zukünftigen Kriege den Kriegsneurotikern stellen?" *Münchener Medizinische Wochenschrift* 86 (1939), pp. 1305–1306; Werner Villinger, "Psychiatrie und Wehrmacht," *Münchener Medizinische Wochenschrift* 88 (1941), pp. 432–443; Gustav Störring, "Die Verschiedenheiten der psychopathologischen Erfahrungen im Weltkriege und im jetzigen Krieg und ihre Ursachen," *Münchener Medizinische Wochenschrift* 89 (1942), pp. 25–30.

49. On the organization of the medical corps in the army and the tasks of the consulting doctors and psychiatrists, see Berger, *Die Beratenden Psychiater*, pp. 25–56. An official list from 1938 (Berger, p. 247) indicates twenty-one psychiatrists, with ten more in the "reserves"; Berger, p. 44, indicates that during the campaign against the Soviet Union the number would be increased to sixty.

50. Citation from Riedesser and Verderber, *Maschinengewehre hinter der Front*, p. 108. Also Berger, *Die Beratenden Psychiater*, pp. 41ff.

51. Berger, *Die Beratenden Psychiater*, pp. 41–43, pp. 80–83; Riedesser and Verderber, *Maschinengewehre hinter der Front*, p. 108. The additional tasks of consulting psychiatrists included, notably, producing evaluations for the military courts and providing professional advice concerning brain injuries. The doctors could also apply for research leave, although this was only granted when military-medical relevance was recognizable (see Berger, *Die Beratenden Psychiater*, p. 52).

52. Gaupp, "Psychischen und nervösen Erkrankungen," p. 367.

53. Gaupp, "Psychischen und nervösen Erkrankungen," pp. 367f.

54. Gaupp, "Psychischen und nervösen Erkrankungen," p. 368.

55. These procedures included, among others, the use of electric current for the so-called Kaufmann cure, which was named after a procedure used by the Austrian physician Fritz Kaufmann, who practiced in Ludwigsburg. During World War I, Gaupp referred to the painfulness of the treatment but praised Kaufmann's "humaneness" since the therapy speedily relieved symptoms. See esp. Lerner, *Hysterical Men*, pp. 102–113, p. 113.

56. It can be seen in various ways that Wuth's interventions did not by any means involve a deep sense of forbearance, for in contrast to some other colleagues, he spoke out clearly for treating "psychopaths" harshly before the military courts, for example, when the question of accountability had to be legally determined according to the provisions of section 51, subsections 1 and 2 of the criminal code. See Berger, *Die Beratenden Psychiater*, pp. 84ff.; Riedesser and Verderber, *Maschinengewehre hinter der Front*, pp. 130ff.

57. As a reason for this split Roth, "Modernisierung der Folter," p. 60, suggests a strong awareness of the embittered reactions of soldiers to psychiatric methods during World War I. For who would guarantee that this might not also contribute to destabilizing the Nazi regime? There was also, Roth indicates, a fear that worthy party members might be subject to the harsh methods.

58. Johannes Heinrich Schulz developed autogenic training in the 1920s. He was a member of the Göring Institute and a psychotherapist in the Luftwaffe. See Cocks, *Psychotherapy*, p. 227.

59. See esp. Cocks, *Psychotherapy*, pp. 310ff.; Roth, "Modernisierung der Folter," pp. 35ff.; Thomas Müller, "Zur Etablierung der Psychoanalyse in Berlin," in Müller,

ed., *Psychotherapie und Körperarbeit: Praktiken der Etablierung—das Beispiel Berlin* (Husum, 2004), pp. 53–95. Berger, *Die Beratenden Psychiater*, pp. 73f., points clearly to this competitive situation.

60. Berger, *Die Beratenden Psychiater*, p. 124 and Riedesser and Verderber, *Maschinengewehre hinter der Front*, p. 135, especially emphasize the familial tie.

61. On the presence and influence of Luftwaffe psychotherapists at this conference, see Roth, "Modernisierung der Folter," pp. 53ff.

62. Roth, "Modernisierung der Folter," p. 50ff.; Riedesser and Verderber, *Maschinengewehre hinter der Front*, pp. 128, 130.

63. In 1947 Panse was arrested and accused of being an accessory to murder and crimes against humanity before a court in Düsseldorf. He was found not guilty. In 1955, he was appointed to the chair in psychiatry at the University of Düsseldorf, where he then taught until 1967. See Uwe Heyll, "Friedrich Panse und die psychiatrische Erbforschung," in *Die Medizinische Akademie Düsseldorf im Nationalsozialismus* (Essen, 1997), pp. 318–340. Working for the West German labor ministry in 1960, Panse wrote the regulations for the conditions in which neuroses could emerge: central guidelines for the question of both pension claims on the basis of war-related suffering and compensation claims by victims of Nazism. See chapter 6, "The Moral Challenge, 1956–1970."

64. The procedure developed by Panse and his assistant Elsässer was a variation on the "Kaufmann cure." The altered treatment was meant to be used in therapy-resistant cases. In a communication to the army medical service inspector's office, Wuth described the therapy, known as "Pansing," as the most effective but also the most brutal available. See Roth, "Modernisierung der Folter," pp. 42ff.; Berger, *Die Beratenden Psychiater*, p. 116. As we will see below, during the second half of the war treatment with galvanic current then became fully established.

65. Riedesser and Verderber, *Maschinengewehre hinter der Front*, pp. 129.

66. This formulation in Riedesser and Verderber, *Maschinengewehre hinter der Front*, p. 144; it encapsulates a basic assumption informing the analysis of both Roth and Riedesser and Verderber.

67. Roth, "Modernisierung der Folter," pp. 33f.; Riedesser and Verderber, *Maschinengewehre hinter der Front*, pp. 116f.

68. Kurt Schneider, "Die Psychopathenfrage beim Feldheer," in *Bericht über die 1: Arbeitstagung Ost der beratenden Fachärzte am 18. und 19. Mai 1942 in der Militärmedizinischen Akademie Berlin* (no place or year), pp. 158–167, p. 160.

69. See Berger, *Die Beratenden Psychiater*, p. 104. Schneider asserted this in a comment made at the same conference; it is not contained in the printed report. The number of brain injuries and severe concussions, and especially the frequency of nerve damage caused by bullet wounds, clearly exceeded the diagnoses of psychopathic and psychogenic reactions. See Berger, pp. 100ff. Berger's findings are based on an evaluation of all the diaries and observational reports that had to be regularly submitted by the consulting psychiatrists to the army medical service inspector's office.

70. See the discussion on the "demodernization of the front" in Bartov, *Hitler's Army*, pp. 12–28.

71. Bartov, *Hitler's Army*, p. 31 (the information regarding the strength of the army

334 Notes to Pages 118–19

refers to the time of the attack on the Soviet Union in June 1941), also see p. 44. There is also a remark by Bartov to the extent that in January 1942 two-thirds of the casualties—totaling 214,000—were the result of illness or exposure to the cold, and not a consequence of enemy action.

72. In one of the above-noted reports to the medical-service inspector, Kurt Kolle, a consulting psychiatrist for the Wehrmacht's army group south, mentioned a strong rise in psychiatric-neurological cases between December 1941 and the end of July 1942, with approximately 40 percent of the seventeen hundred treated soldiers being diagnosed as "abnormal personalities"—equivalent to the diagnosis of "psychopath"—or as "abnormal reactions." See Berger, *Die Beratenden Psychiater*, pp. 127. Kurt Schneider, "Die Psychopathenfrage beim Feldheer," p. 159, only hinted that he assumed an increase in "psychopaths" during static warfare.

73. By and large, the psychiatrists did not speak of the suicide rates in the context of their observations on "psychogenic reactions." Although the number of suicides in the Wehrmacht—later calculated at some seven thousand by mid-1943—was already higher during the first half of the war than during all of World War I, from the psychiatrists' point of view this was presumably not a dramatic development for a million-man army. In any event, the Wehrmacht's medical services inspector referred to the number as being so small that it had no military significance. He calculated—apparently using somewhat lower numbers but including suicide attempts—a monthly rate of 0.02 per thousand in the reserves and 0.05 per thousand in active service. See Berger, *Die Beratenden Psychiater*, p. 166. On suicide in the Wehrmacht: Angelika Ebbinghaus, "Soldatenselbstmord im Urteil des Psychiaters Hans Bürger-Prinz," in Angelika Ebbinghaus and Karsten Linne, eds., *Kein abgeschlossenes Kapitel: Hamburg im "Dritten Reich"* (Hamburg, 1997), pp. 487–531; here also the suicide calculations (p. 518). See also Baumann, *Vom Recht*, pp. 357–368, here above all in respect to debates in the military and among psychiatrists concerning recognition of suicide as a military-service injury.

74. Schneider's colleague, Max Mikorey, a consulting psychiatrist with the First Army on the eastern front since the fall 1940, emphasized in his presentation at the "second working conference east" in the fall of 1942 the advantages of "early treatment in the military," because it could be decisive for the further course of "hysterical reactions." Max Mikorey, "Hysterische Reaktionen im Feldheer," in *Bericht über die 2. Arbeitstagung Ost der beratenden Fachärzte in der Militärmedizinischen Akademie Berlin* (Berlin, 1942–1943), p. 141.

75. Schneider, "Die Psychopathenfrage beim Feldheer," pp. 163 and 167.

76. In the resolution, which was passed after the second talk (by Carl Schneider), these points were reiterated. As the foreword to the report makes clear, the conference transcript was sent to all the consulting physicians and directing medical officers. See *Bericht über die 1. Arbeitstagung Ost*, p. 3; the resolution on p. 171.

77. See Berger, *Die Beratenden Psychiater*, pp. 286f. Although Schneider retained his director's position in Munich until 1945, he spent a total of five years on the eastern front. After the war he was awarded a chair at the University of Heidelberg, and was an influential figure in West German psychiatry into the 1960s.

78. Inversely, "soft" therapeutic methods hardly indicate political distance from Nazism, as we can see in the case of several employees at the Göring Institute.

79. This was clearly evident, for example, in the comments made by a staff doctor, a man named Büssow, and professor of psychiatry Friedrich Panse at the Second Working Conference East in the fall 1942; see *Bericht über die 2. Arbeitstagung Ost*, pp. 141f. Roth, "Modernisierung der Folter," pp. 36ff., likewise points to tensions between psychiatrists and internists. The Wehrmacht medical service commissioned the internists to find the most effective treatment for soldiers who had developed psychosomatic illnesses, which included, starting in 1941–1942, the "stomach battalions." Both Berger, *Die Beratenden Psychiater*, p. 113, and Cocks, *Psychotherapy*, p. 317, indicate that the so-classified soldiers were given special nutrition and were "medically monitored on a regular basis." The units involved were not sent to the front but performed guard duties in the rear. The "stomach battalions" were first deployed, for mainly disciplinary purposes, beginning in the summer of 1943. During the postwar period as well there were references to a change in form in war neuroses between World Wars I and II. As one example among many, see Gerhard Schmidt, "Gestaltwandel von Massenreaktionen auf Kriegs- und Nachkriegsüberlastung," *Fortschritte der Neurologie, Psychiatrie und ihrer Grenzgebiete* 22 (1954), pp. 125–129, where we read of "organ hypochondriacs" in contrast to "active, demonstrative presentations of illness during the Kaiserreich" (p. 126). See the following chapter.

80. At the Third Working Conference East in May 1943, professor of psychiatry Werner Villinger clearly addressed this problem, expressing open annoyance that in his view the neurologists were being inadequately consulted in such cases. *Bericht über die 3. Arbeitstagung Ost der Beratenden Fachärzte vom 24.–26. Mai 1943 in der Militärmedizinischen Akademie Berlin* (Berlin, 1943), p. 218.

81. Schneider, "Die Psychopathenfrage beim Feldheer," p. 158.

82. See Berger, *Die Beratenden Psychiater*, pp. 120ff.; citation of Scharfetter, p. 121. In this context, Scharfetter insisted that younger doctors had to be reminded of the "embarrassing possibility" of overlooking organic diseases. Berger draws on comments by Ernst Kretschmer and Heinrich von Kogerer as further examples of this urgent concern among consulting psychiatrists.

83. In contrast to schizophrenic psychosis, in which there is an assumption that the symptoms will inevitably manifest, irrespective of external events, symptomatic psychosis is directly associated with severe injury or illness; it emerges after a brief interval at the latest and subsides after several days or weeks.

84. Berger, *Die Beratenden Psychiater*, p. 162.

85. See Schneider, "Die Psychopathenfrage beim Feldheer," pp. 162f. Schneider added that the diagnosis was also made difficult because the "pictures" were "toxicologically blurred" due to injections and other medications. However, he noted that medication was necessary because the patients were "very disturbing for the sickbay" and had to be sedated (p. 163).

86. Schneider, "Die Psychopathenfrage beim Feldheer," pp. 162f.

87. According to Berger, *Die Beratenden Psychiater*, p. 157, in every other report the consulting psychiatrists expressed the criticism that schizophrenia was being diagnosed too frequently.

88. Bonhoeffer stated this explicitly again in 1934 "Psychopathologische Erfahrungen," p. 1212. Occasionally, psychiatrists would concede that "stresses" could play a

causal role in manic-depressive illness. Examples for this discussion in military psychiatry can be found in Berger, *Die Beratenden Psychiater*, pp. 156f. In any case, the
general principle followed was that soldiers diagnosed as "schizophrenic" were unfit
for military service and had to be discharged. Once the diagnosis was made, psychiatrists had no leeway, even if some of them regretted the sweeping nature of the rule.
Hence Berger, p. 161, informs us that Friedrich Meggendorfer, a professor in Erlangen
and, beginning in March 1944 a consulting psychiatrist in the reserves (military district
XIII), tried to circumvent discharging soldiers by diagnosing not schizophrenia but
rather a "schizoid reaction" when single episodes were involved. In February 1945, we
read, Hans Bürger-Prinz inquired of Maximinian de Crinis—who had replaced Wuth as
a consulting psychiatrist in the army medical service inspection—whether in fact "all
manic-depressive soldiers" were to be discharged; in the end, these soldiers constituted
"very precious human material." De Crinis categorically declined. Berger sees both
Meggendorfer and Bürger-Prinz as being motivated by purely military considerations,
although this does not seem to necessarily follow from his citations.

89. Schneider, "Die Psychopathenfrage beim Feldheer," p. 159.

90. During World War II, psychiatrists spoke of "fright reactions." As a general rule,
psychiatrists did not view these mental abnormalities, which were apparently diagnosed
primarily on the eastern front, as an expression of "inferiority." See Berger, *Die Beratenden Psychiater*, pp. 122ff.

91. Schneider, "Die Psychopathenfrage beim Feldheer," p. 160.

92. See Berger, *Die Beratenden Psychiater*, pp. 126f.

93. "Richtlinien für die Beurteilung psychogener Reaktionen," in *Bericht über die
1. Arbeitstagung Ost*, pp. 170f. Both the youngest soldiers—those between seventeen
and twenty—and the oldest were, however, accorded special status in this respect, the
former group because of "diminished capacity for resistance," the latter based on "exhaustion." *Bericht über die 1. Arbeitstagung Ost*, p. 173; this was reinforced in the
guidelines issued in late fall 1942 for assessing soldiers with mental/nervous abnormalities ("psychopaths") and reactions. See *Bericht über die 2. Arbeitstagung Ost*, p.
143.

94. Schneider, "Die Psychopathenfrage beim Feldheer," p. 166.

95. Carl Schneider, "Die strafrechtliche Verfolgung der Neurotiker," in *Bericht über
die 4. Arbeitstagung der Beratenden Ärzte vom 16. bis 18. Mai 1944 im SS-Lazarett
Hohenlychen* (no place or year), pp. 273–274, argued that this was above all called for
because such behavior led to imitation; citation p. 273.

96. See Riedesser and Verderber, *Maschinengewehre hinter der Front*, p. 146; and
Roth, "Modernisierung der Folter," p. 61.

97. Berger, *Die Beratenden Psychiater*, p. 118, names military districts IV, VII, XII,
IIXX, and XXI, associated with the following cities: Leipzig, Munich, Heidelberg,
Innsbruck, and Posen. Here Berger is more precise and cautious than Roth, "Modernisierung der Folter," p. 64, who asserts that most consulting psychiatrists adopted
treatment with galvanic current.

98. See Roth, "Modernisierung der Folter," pp. 63–65, citation p. 63. Information
on the frequency with which the method was applied would be purely speculative. For
the Ensen reserve hospital, we read that by the end of the war it had allegedly been used

on fourteen hundred treatment-resistant cases. See Günter Elsässer, "Erfahrungen an 1400 Kriegsneurosen (aus einem neurologisch-psychiatrischen Reserve-Lazarett des 2. Weltkriegs)," in *Soziale und angewandte Psychiatrie*, pp. 623–630.

99. Examples in Roth, "Modernisierung der Folter," pp. 63ff., and in Riedesser and Verderber, *Maschinengewehre hinter der Front*, pp. 148f. Other psychiatrists reported success using electric shock, with Werner Villinger recommending it in combination with subsequent hypnosis. This worked very well, he indicated, "even in therapeutically resistant cases." See *Bericht über die 3. Arbeitstagung Ost der Beratenden Fachärzte vom 24.–26. Mai 1943 in der Militärmedizinischen Akademie Berlin* (Berlin, 1943), p. 219.

100. Friedrich Panse, "Hysterie, Simulation, unter besonderer Berücksichtigung der psychogenen Überlagerung bei organischen Schädigungen," in *Bericht über die 3. Arbeitstagung Ost*, pp. 217–218, citation p. 217.

101. "Richtlinien. Hysterie, Simulation, unter besonderer Berücksichtigungder psychogenen Überlagerungen bei organischen Schädigungen (Ergänzung zu den Richtlinien in H. Dv. 209/2, Blatt 126)," in *Bericht über die 3. Arbeitstagung Ost*, p. 219. Max Mikorey had initially been a consulting psychiatrist in military district VII (Munich) beginning in the fall of 1940, and then served with the First Army on the eastern front. In 1942, he had already spoken out in favor of placing cases of severe, therapy-resistant "hysterical reaction" in public hospitals for the duration of the war. Oswald Bumke, a consulting psychiatrist in the same district, argued almost identically, while also advocating that "if possible, unsuitable people should not be recruited at all" as a matter of principle. See Max Mikorey, "Hysterische Reaktionen im Feldheer," in *Bericht über die Arbeitstagung Ost der beratenden Fachärzte in der Militärmedizinischen Akademie Berlin, Berlin 1942/1943*, p. 141; Oswald Bumke, "Hysterische Reaktionen im Ersatzheer," in *Bericht*, p. 142.

102. Guidelines for the evaluation of soldiers with mental/neurological abnormalities ("psychopaths") and mental/neurological reactions, version of July 21, 1943, referred to in Riedesser and Verderber, *Maschinengewehre hinter der Front*, pp. 155f.

103. This was the case with Wilhelm S., who was diagnosed as a "psychopath" in 1944 (HBAB, Bestand Morija, 3887); likewise, after the war Walter M. reported to the psychiatrist that his brother, a young officer, had been dismissed because of "nervous exhaustion" in 1944 (HBAB, Bestand Morija, 4523). In the case of lance corporal Reinhard K., the psychiatrists diagnosed "general neurasthenia and psychasthenia with nervous-spastic intestinal complaints" in 1944; Reinhard K. had already received psychiatric treatment for two years with no improvement in his nervous complaints and nightmares. The attending psychiatrist in the reserve hospital finally requested K.'s discharge by means of a "remote evaluation," in order to prevent that K. would again suffer "extreme mental states" at night, which would "immediately again require his commitment to a specialized military hospital or sanatorium." The discharge from the Wehrmacht was approved for one year. HBAB, Bestand Morija, 3635. On Reinhard K., see also in chapter 1 the section "Dreaming the War."

104. Kurt Schneider, "Neurosen vom Standpunkt der klinischen Psychiatrie," in *Bericht über die 4. Arbeitstagung*, pp. 270–271, citation p. 270.

105. At the fourth working conference, Carl Schneider concluded from such "re-

sponsibility of the neurotic for his neurosis" that "resistance to medical therapy" and an inadequate "will to recover" could and should be rendered punishable. He advocated that those involved should be sent to special field battalions by court order or remanded to a concentration camp for an indefinite period to improve their condition. See Carl Schneider, "Die strafrechtliche Verantwortung der Neurotiker," in *Bericht über die 4. Arbeitstagung*, pp. 273–274, citation p. 273.

106. In one study, the former head psychiatrist of the Alexandria, Egypt, military district, Bruno Lewin, made clear that one reason that needed to be considered for the striking rarity of psychogenic illnesses in German as opposed to British POWs was the German soldiers' fear "of being brought before a hereditary health court (*Erbgesundheitsgericht*) and being sterilized if you reported yourself suffering from nervous symptoms." This was evidently a result of later research he conducted as a psychiatrist. See Bruno Lewin, "Neurologisch-psychiatrische Untersuchungen und Beobachtungen an deutschen Kriegsgefangenen in Ägypten 1941–1947," *Psychiatrie, Neurologie und Medizinische Psychologie* 1 (1949), pp. 230–236, p. 231.

107. Still evident in Elsässer, "Erfahrungen an 1400 Kriegsneurosen."

108. See Shephard, *A War of Nerves*, p. 306.

109. See Shephard, *A War of Nerves*, p. 309.

110. Following the victory of the Allies, the publication of German professional medical journals was temporarily stopped. Although *Ärztliche Wochenschrift* was already relaunched by 1946, opportunities for professional communication were greatly reduced. The central psychiatric journal *Der Nervenarzt* would reappear in 1947; *Fortschritte der Neurologie, Psychiatrie und ihrer Grenzgebiete* would follow in 1949. That year, *Allgemeine Zeitschrift für Psychiatrie und ihre Grenzgebiete* would also be published again, but for the last time. In the Soviet zone, 1949 saw the launching of *Psychiatrie, Neurologie und Medizinische Psychologie*. Initially there was no strict demarcation between psychiatric research in West Germany and East Germany, as the editorial board of that journal makes clear: it included Gottfried Ewald, a professor in Göttingen, and Kurt Schneider, a professor in Heidelberg since 1945.

111. Born in 1904, Walter von Baeyer became one of the most prominent figures in German postwar psychiatry. During the war, he was a consulting psychiatrist and served as chief staff doctor. But his career during the Nazi period faced obstacles because his habilitation (academic teaching qualification process) was twice delayed through intervention of the National Socialist Students' Association, despite its approval by Ernst Rüdin and Oswald Bumke. The reason for this was an early-eighteenth-century Jewish-Christian marriage in his family. Von Baeyer would obtain his teaching qualification after the war under Friedrich Meggendorfer in Erlangen. As indicated above, during the war Meggendorfer had taken an extremely hard position toward therapeutically intractable "psychopaths." The biographical information on Walter von Baeyer is from "Walter Ritter von Baeyer," in Pongratz, *Psychiatrie in Selbstdarstellungen*, pp. 9–34, pp. 17ff. See below, chapter 6, "The Moral Challenge, 1956–1970," and Part III, "Mental Suffering and Its Changing Acknowledgement in West German Media."

112. Walter von Baeyer, "Zur Statistik und Form der abnormen Erlebnisreaktionen in der Gegenwart," *Der Nervenarzt* 19 (1948), pp. 402–408, citation p. 404. We also find

a reference to this in the talk given on December 3, 1947, by a psychiatrist named Steinkopff (chief physician at the Sudenburg neurological clinic) and entitled "Psychopathologie der Nachkriegszeit." A synopsis was published in *Das deutsche Gesundheitswesen* 3 (1948), pp. 379–380, p. 380.

113. On the politization of mental illnesses in postwar Germany after 1918 and the competing interpretations of mental suffering after the war between different political groups, see Jason Crouthamel, *The Great War and German Memory: Society, Politics and Psychological Trauma, 1914–1945* (Exeter, 2009).

114. See von Baeyer, "Zur Statistik."

115. See von Baeyer, "Zur Statistik."

116. One example is Jürg Zutt, "Über den seelischen Gesundheitszustand der Berliner Bevölkerung in den vergangenen Jahren und heute," *Ärztliche Wochenschrift* 1 (1946), pp. 248–250, citation p. 250.

117. Arendt, *Nachwirkungen*, p. 39, noted it was striking that wherever one went "there was no reaction to what had happened," and she was not speaking only of the crimes committed but equally of the "indifference" or "apathy" with which Germans, according to her impression, reacted to the destruction of their cities and the fates of the refugees.

118. See, for example, Baeyer, "Zur Statistik," p. 408; Zutt, "Gesundheitszustand," p. 250.

119. Hans-Werner Janz, "Psychopathologische Reaktionen der Kriegs- und Nachkriegszeit," *Fortschritte der Neurologie, Psychiatrie und ihrer Grenzgebiete* 17 (1949), pp. 264–293, citation p. 267.

120. Citations from Zutt, "Gesundheitszustand," p. 250.

121. Janz, "Psychopathologische Reaktionen," p. 266. Swiss psychiatrist Gustav Bally made a similar argument in "Zur Anthropologie der Kriegszeit," *Schweizer Archiv für Neurologie und Psychiatrie* 61 (1948), pp. 22–40.

122. Argued in detail in Janz, "Psychopathologische Reaktionen," pp. 266f.

123. Janz, "Psychopathologische Reaktionen," p. 267.

124. Jürg Zutt (1893–1980) was a student of Karl Bonhoeffer and had served as a chief staff physician under him. Between 1945 and 1949, he codirected the psychiatric division of Berlin's Charité hospital, together with Heinrich Roggenbau, likewise a Bonhoeffer student and a consulting army psychiatrist during the war. See Neumärker, *Karl Bonhoeffer*, p. 204.

125. Zutt, "Gesundheitszustand," p. 248.

126. Zutt, "Gesundheitszustand," n. 1.

127. Zutt gained his reputation as one of the most prominent representatives of anthropological psychiatry after moving to the Frankfurt Neurological Clinic, which he directed between 1950 and 1962. Walter von Baeyer likewise developed an affinity—as he explained, influenced by Zutt—for a phenomenological-anthropological approach and existential analysis, with a strong debt to Heidegger (*Being and Time*) and, later, Sartre. In the 1950s, this was reflected in the way von Baeyer interpreted psychotic and neurotic phenomena; see "Walter Ritter von Baeyer" in Pongratz, *Psychiatrie in Selbstdarstellungen*, p. 24; see also chapter 6, "The Moral Challenge, 1956–1970." After World War II, existential analysis and anthropology experienced a passing upsurge in

the field of philosophy as well. A history of science of philosophy after 1945 remains a desideratum.

128. Zutt, "Gesundheitszustand," p. 250. Zutt here is citing from Goethe's play *Torquato Tasso*.

129. Steinkopff, "Psychopathologie," p. 380.

130. Von Baeyer, "Statistik," p. 403.

131. Von Baeyer, "Statistik," p. 403; likewise Heinrich Kranz, "Zeitbedingte abnorme Erlebnisreaktionen: Versuch einer Übersicht," *Allgemeine Zeitschrift für Psychiatrie und ihre Grenzgebiete* 124 (1949), pp. 336–357, p. 337.

132. Walter Schulte, "Äußere Einflüsse auf neurologisch-psychiatrische Krankheiten, ein Vergleich mit den ersten Weltkriegserfahrungen," *Ärztliche Wochenschrift* 1 (1947), pp. 550–563, represents a rare exception here.

133. One good example, particularly in its differences with Schulte, is Ernst Kröber, "Über Haftpsychosen (Anlage- und exogene Faktoren bei der Entstehung von Haftreaktionen. Erfahrungen an Internierten)," *Der Nervenarzt* 19 (1948), pp. 408–413.

134. Wilhelm Gerstacker, "Vorüberlegungen zur allgemeinen Psychologie und Psychopathologie des Krieges," *Archiv für Psychiatrie und Nervenkrankheiten* 182 (1949), pp. 32–50, citation p. 32.

135. See, for example, Janz, "Psychopathologische Reaktionen," citation p. 265. This was also the conclusion of early postwar psychiatric studies concerning the effects of flight and expulsion on the mind, as shown in Volker Ackermann, "Das Schweigen der Flüchtlingskinder—psychische Folgen von Krieg, Flucht und Vertreibung bei den Deutschen nach 1945," *Geschichte und Gesellschaft* 30 (2004), pp. 434–464, pp. 452f.

136. See, among others, Kurt Beringer, "Über hysterische Reaktionen bei Fliegerangriffen," in Heinrich Kranz, ed., *Arbeiten zur Psychiatrie, Neurologie und ihren Grenzgebieten: Festschrift für Kurt Schneider* (Heidelberg, 1947), pp. 131–138; Janz, "Psychopathologische Reaktionen," p. 266; von Baeyer, "Statistik," p. 406. However, one psychiatrist, E. Henßge, "Reaktive psychische Erkrankungen der Nachkriegszeit," *Psychiatrie, Neurologie und Medizinische Psychologie* 1 (1949), pp. 133–137, emphasized that in his earlier Erfurt practice he saw few patients who had been completely bombed out. There were far more, to be sure, in his practice in Dresden, where, as his article indicates, he had been working since January 1, 1946. In Dresden, those who had become homeless because of the bombing amounted to 5.17 percent of his patients (sixty-two cases), the largest group among the twelve hundred he treated during the first seven months. The next largest group were those mourning battlefield casualties (eighteen cases).

137. Janz, "Psychopathologische Reaktionen," pp. 268f.

138. Beringer, "Über hysterische Reaktionen," p. 135; von Baeyer, "Statistik," p. 406.

139. See Beringer, "Über hysterische Reaktionen," pp. 135f., citation p. 136, as well as Bonhoeffer, "Vergleichende psychopathologische Erfahrungen," p. 3; Janz, "Psychopathologische Reaktionen," p. 277; Schulte, "Äußere Einflüsse," p. 265, and others.

140. See Bonhoeffer, "Vergleichende psychopathologische Erfahrungen," p. 4; similarly in Zutt, "Gesundheitszustand," p. 249; von Baeyer, "Statistik," p. 405; Schulte, "Äußere Einflüsse," p. 562; Manfred in der Beeck, "Psychische und charakterliche

Veränderungen bei Hungerzuständen (Beobachtungen in Gefangenschaft 1945/46 und Heimat 1947/48)," *Hippokrates* 20 (1949), pp. 44–47, pp. 46f.

141. Bonhoeffer, "Vergleichende psychopathologische Erfahrungen," p. 4.

142. Zutt, "Gesundheitszustand," p. 249.

143. Bonhoeffer, "Vergleichende Psychopathologische Erfahrungen," p. 4.

144. According to a report of September 20, 1946, in *Volksecho*, the weight loss averaged forty-one lbs.; see Plato and Leh, *Ein unglaublicher Frühling*, p. 36. In 1946, in the French zone, the officially stipulated number of daily calories per person that the distribution of ration cards was intended to provide (although it often fell short) was 900 calories. In the British Zone it was 1,050, in the Soviet Zone 1,083, and in the American Zone 1,330. See Plato and Leh, p. 35. On the food situation and malnutrition in postwar Germany, see also Willi A. Boelcke, *Der Schwarz-Markt 1945–1948: Vom Überleben nach dem Kriege* (Braunschweig, 1986), pp. 33–71; Wildt, *Vom kleinen Wohlstand*, pp. 26ff.

145. In der Beeck, "Psychische und charakterliche Veränderungen," p. 46, expressed his astonishment at the number of patients who showed surprise at this diagnosis and insisted they had had enough to eat.

146. Bonhoeffer, "Vergleichende Psychopathologische Erfahrungen," p. 4; Zutt, "Gesundheitszustand," p. 249.

147. In der Beeck, "Psychische und charakterliche Veränderungen," citation p. 47. In 1947, in der Beeck participated in the treatment of "abnormal experiential reactions" in Jewish refugees who had been on the *Exodus* ship. In the 1960s, together with Walter von Baeyer, Heinz Häfner, Walter Schulte, and others he was part of a group of reformers within psychiatry. See Franz-Werner Kersting, *Anstaltsärzte zwischen Kaiserreich und Bundesrepublik: Das Beispiel Westfalen* (Paderborn, 1996), pp. 357ff.; Kersting, "Vor Klee: Die Hypothek der NS-Medizinverbrechen als Reformimpuls," in Kersting, ed., *Psychiatriereform als Gesellschaftsreform: Die Hypothek des Nationalsozialismus und der Aufbruch der 60er Jahre* (Paderborn, 2003), pp. 63–80.

148. Zutt, "Gesundheitszustand," p. 250.

149. Von Baeyer, "Statistik," p. 407.

150. Hans Malten, "Heimkehrer," *Medizinische Klinik* 41 (1946), pp. 593–600, citation p. 597.

151. Malten, "Heimkehrer," p. 597; von Baeyer, "Statistik," p. 407.

152. Malten, "Heimkehrer," p. 598.

153. Malten, "Heimkehrer," pp. 593–599.

154. Von Baeyer, "Statistik," p. 407. The scientific term for this type of obesity was Lipophilic dystrophy. Contrary to what we read in Biess, "Opfer," p. 367, and in many newspapers dating from the early 1950s (see esp. *Der Spiegel*, October 7, 1953, pp. 26–27), the term "dystrophy" did not stem from the Russian, nor was the concept unknown in pre–World War II German medical literature. Research on dystrophy as a malnutrition-related, edematous condition was reported on after the Great War and had an established place in interwar lexicons. See, for example, *Klinisches Wörterbuch: Die Kunstausdrücke der Medizin*, founded by Otto Dornblüth, revised by Willibald Pschyrembel (Berlin, 1937), pp. 133f. After World War II, however, German doctors followed Russian nomenclature because the grounds for the release of countless POWs from Soviet

camps in 1946–1947 was in fact "dystrophy." Presumably the assertion that the term was first introduced by Russian doctors (as *Der Spiegel* indicated in 1953) has to be seen against the backdrop of the Cold War. See chapter 7, "Repatriated Wehrmacht Veterans in the Public Eye."

155. Ulrike Thoms, "Die 'Hunger-Generation' als Ernährungswissenschaftler 1933–1964 zwischen soziokulturellen Gemeinsamkeiten und der Instrumentalisierung von Erfahrung," in Matthias Middell et al., eds., *Verräumlichung, Vergleich, Generationalität: Dimensionen der Wissenschaftsgeschichte* (Leipzig, 2004), pp. 133–153, pp. 140ff.

156. In his talk before the Working Group for the Cultural Support of War Prisoners and Returnees on June 11, 1948, Dr. Walter Hemsing, for example, argued that based on his activities in support of returnees and "many factual reports" he knew that "the internment situation in other countries may deviate *in details* from that in England, but *in essence* it is similar." Hemsing had been a POW in a British camp for two years. Walter Hemsing, "Die seelische Situation des Kriegsgefangenen und die innere Gesundung des Heimkehrers," p. 1, in Bundesarchiv Koblenz, BA 150, 339 (vol. 1). More differentiated in Manfred in der Beeck, "Zur Psychologie der Kriegsgefangenschaft," *Der Nervenarzt* 19 (1948), pp. 136–140, p. 136.

157. Malten, "Heimkehrer," p. 593. We also find this agglomeration in, for instance, Gerstacker, "Vorüberlegungen," p. 38.

158. In a similar vein Biess, "Opfer," p. 368.

159. In this sense see, among others, Kranz, "Zeitbedingte abnorme Erlebnisreaktionen," p. 346.

160. Kranz, "Zeitbedingte abnorme Erlebnisreaktionen."

161. See Kranz, "Zeitbedingte abnorme Erlebnisreaktionen," pp. 346ff., citation p. 347.

162. See Malten, "Heimkehrer," pp. 24f., citation p. 25. In the case of "returnees' neurosis" the internist thus referred to a "tendency toward healing that is highly unusual for nervous disturbances" (p. 24). In predicting the same, von Baeyer, "Statistik," p. 407, explicitly referenced Malten's dictum.

163. See Schmidt, "Gestaltwandel," p. 128.

164. According to W. Marx, "Über Dystrophie-Dauerschäden," *Deutsche medizinische Rundschau* 3 (1949), pp. 1272–1274, the long-term damage primarily involved tuberculosis of the lungs, inner-ear hearing loss, and damage to the heart muscle. See also Hans Wilhelm Bansi, *Das Hungerödem* (Stuttgart, 1949).

165. Bundesarchiv Koblenz, B 150, 339 (folder 1).

166. Heinz Meyeringh, "Über Folgeerscheinungen der Dystrophie," *Ärztliche Wochenschrift* 5 (1950), pp. 889–893, citation p. 889.

167. See Johann Gottschick, "Neuropsychiatrische Erkrankungen bei deutschen Kriegsgefangenen in den USA im Lichte statistischer Betrachtungen," *Archiv für Psychiatrie und Nervenkrankheiten* 185 (1950), pp. 491–510, p. 491. Gottschick became a POW in August 1944.

168. Willi Schmitz, "Kriegsgefangenschaft und Heimkehr in ihren Beziehungen zu psychischen Krankheitsbildern," *Der Nervenarzt* 20 (1949), pp. 303–310, p. 303 (italics mine).

169. During the war, Schulte was initially an assistant doctor, then a chief doctor (1941), and finally a staff doctor (1942) in different field and reserve hospitals. Between 1947 and 1954 he was chief doctor at the von Bodelschwingh Clinics, then became director of the Gütersloh mental hospital, before being appointed director of Tübingen University's neurological clinic as Ernst Kretschmer's successor in 1960. These biographical details from Hauptarchiv Bethel, Bestand 2/33–470, and Walter Schulte, *Über das Problem der seelischen Entstehungsbedingungen von Krankheiten* (Stuttgart, 1966), p. 22.

170. Schulte, "Äußere Einflüsse," p. 550.

171. See chapter 5, the section "Pension Claims under Suspicion."

172. Schulte, "Äußere Einflüsse," p. 561.

173. Here, Schulte was agreeing with speculation by Bonhoeffer that in the case of torture victims—Bonhoeffer was thinking above all of concentration camp inmates—there might indeed be "limits of endurance" (Bonhoeffer, "Vergleichende psychopathologische Erfahrungen," p. 3). Much like his younger colleague Schulte, he encountered skepticism in this respect from fellow psychiatrists over many years.

174. Schulte, "Äußere Einflüsse," p. 561.

175. Schulte, "Äußere Einflüsse."

176. Schulte, "Äußere Einflüsse," p. 563.

177. See Schulte, "Äußere Einflüsse," p. 561. The psychiatrist added that according to the findings at hand, there was a "very broad presence of predisposition." "Every fifth person has to be viewed as having partial schizophrenic predispositions," he insisted. Was it so surprising, he adroitly asked, "that following the impact of war schizophrenic or schizophrenia-like psychoses were triggered here and there, provoked, accelerated in their manifestation, patho-plastically colored or, under circumstances, caused in the sense of significant partial causation?" (Schulte, p. 561). It is clear from the evaluations that Schulte prepared some time later in the Bodelschwingh Clinics that Hans Luxenburger's research in hereditary psychiatry and schizophrenia played a role in this argument. For greater detail, see Kaufmann, "Eugenische Utopie." On the problem of evaluative practice see in chapter 5 the section "Pension Claims under Suspicion."

178. Especially clearly formulated in Kröber, "Über Haftpsychosen," p. 413. Judging from the research overview that Swiss psychiatrist Manfred Bleuler published on the problem of schizophrenia in 1951, psychiatric researchers in other Western European countries, the Soviet Union, and the United States were by and large also far from connecting the emergence of schizophrenia with war stress, in the broadest sense. Thus, referring to recent research findings on the war and postwar periods, Bleuler speaks of a consensus: "All told . . . no fundamental causal reinterpretation could be ascribed to military service during peace or under conditions of war." Nevertheless, he observes, various authors presumed that military service has "catalyzing effect" because "short-term schizophrenic reactions during military service" had been observed. See Manfred Bleuler, "Forschungen und Begriffswandlungen in der Schizophrenielehre 1941–1950," *Fortschritte der Neurologie, Psychiatrie und ihrer Grenzgebiete* 19 (1951), pp. 385–452, p. 414.

179. See Kröber, "Über Haftpsychosen."

344   Notes to Pages 134–37

180. See chapter 6, "The Moral Challenge, 1956–1970."

181. Kurt Schneider, "Selbstmord als Dienstbeschädigung—Schizophrenie als Dienstbeschädigung," *Der Nervenarzt* 21 (1950), pp. 480–483, citation p. 480.

182. See in chapter 5 the section "Pension Claims under Suspicion."

183. For the following see Johann Gottschick, "Kriegsgefangenschaft und Psychosen," *Der Nervenarzt* 21 (1950), pp. 129–132.

184. Gottschick, "Kriegsgefangenschaft und Psychosen," p. 130.

185. Gottschick, "Kriegsgefangenschaft und Psychosen," p. 130.

186. Gottschick explained elsewhere that the diagnostic approaches taken by German and American doctors toward schizophrenia probably differed. He arrived at this presumption after comparing American statistics from 1923 with German statistics from 1935. According to the statistics, schizophrenia had been 33 percent more prevalent in the American civilian population, a difference that could not be explained by the passing of twelve years. See Gottschick, "Neuropsychiatrische Erkrankungen," pp. 500f.

187. Gottschick, "Kriegsgefangenschaft und Psychosen," p. 130.

188. Gottschick, "Neuropsychiatrische Erkrankungen," p. 501.

189. See Gottschick, "Neuropsychiatrische Erkrankungen," pp. 508f., citation p. 509.

190. Cuno Peter, "Psychologische und psychiatrisch-neurologische Beobachtungen und Erfahrungen aus 29monatiger Gefangenschaft," *Der Nervenarzt* 20 (1949), pp. 202–206.

191. Cuno Peter's descriptions appear to point not to states of so-called catatonic excitation but rather to catatonic stupor, in which the patients are withdrawn and frozen, so to speak.

192. Peter, "Beobachtungen und Erfahrungen," pp. 204.

193. See Gert Sedlmayr, "Wandlungen im Krankheitsbild der Ostheimkehrer," *Medizinische Klinik* 44 (1949), pp. 1223–1225, citation p. 1223. The minutes of the conference held by the Working Group for the Cultural Support of War Prisoners and Returnees at the German *Länderrat* of the American-occupied zone in June 1948 make clear that Sedlmayr conveyed as much to those present in this venue as well. See "Die Notstände der Heimkehrer. Bericht über die Tagung auf der Comburg bei Schwäb. Hall vom 9. bis. 12. Juni 1948," in Bundesarchiv Koblenz, B 150, 339 (folder 1).

194. "Die Notstände der Heimkehrer." After the arrival of more than eight thousand returnees from Russia at the Ulm-Donau returnees' camp in March 1949, Sedlmayr had the impression that in some 80 percent of the cases "their nutritional condition was moderate to sufficient, sometimes even good" ("Die Notstände der Heimkehrer"). By contrast, in the July 29, 1947, medical report on the returnees from Russia in the Ulm-Kienlesberg transit camp, we read that "approximately 95 percent of the returnees urgently require medical attention." See "Kurzer Erfahrungsbericht über Russlandheimkehrer," in BA-MA Freiburg B205/v. 699. The later improvement in the nutritional condition of returning soldiers / POWs was due to the supply situation, which had meanwhile stabilized in the Soviet Union. See Hilger, *Deutsche Kriegsgefangene*, pp. 135ff.

195. Sedlmayr, "Wandlungen," p. 1223.

196. Forcefully summarized in K. Franke, "Katamnese der Heimkehrer," *Deutsche*

medizinische Rundschau 3 (1949), p. 1278; see also Hans Kilian, "Zur Psychopathologie der Heimkehrer," *Deutsche medizinische Rundschau* 3 (1949), p. 1278.

197. Schmitz, "Kriegsgefangenschaft," p. 303.

198. See in this chapter the section "Lessons of War."

199. Schmitz, "Kriegsgefangenschaft," p. 303.

200. Schmitz, "Kriegsgefangenschaft," p. 304. Schmitz speaks of the play as presenting a particularly striking example of "psychasthenic failure" that culminates in Beckmann's suicide: "He is the typical example of the returnee who cannot follow the straight path into the new land of hardship after his protracted long suffering in the past. We always find him 'on the brink of failure,' until a final blow of fate frees him from this borderline situation and the neurotic structure of his character is clearly revealed in his failure."

201. Schmitz, "Kriegsgefangenschaft," p. 303.

202. Schmitz, "Kriegsgefangenschaft," p. 305.

203. See, for instance, Hilmar Haag, "Gefangenschaftsschäden," *Kriegsopferversorgung* 3 (1954), pp. 75–78, p. 76.

204. See, among others, Fritz Hansen, "Kriegsgefangenschaft als ärztliches Erlebnis," *Münchener Medizinische Wochenschrift* 93 (1951), pp. 538–541, 606–613, 690–696. On the public forms of relating the experience of being a POW in a Soviet camp, see Moeller, *War Stories*; Biess, *Homecomings*.

205. See, for instance, Manfred Baldermann, "Wesen und Beurteilung der Heimkehrerdystrophien," *Münchener Medizinische Wochenschrift* 93 (1951), pp. 118–123; Baldermann, "Die psychischen Grundlagen der Heimkehrerdystrophien und ihre Behandlung," *Münchener Medizinische Wochenschrift* 93 (1951), pp. 1285–1290. This development is confirmed from a psychiatric perspective in Heinz-Harro Rauschelbach, "Zur Klinik der Spätfolgezustände nach Hungerdystrophie," *Forschritte der Neurologie, Psychiatrie und ihrer Grenzgebiete* 22 (1954), pp. 214–226.

206. "Kreislaufstörungen beim Spätheimkehrer," a talk given by Max Hochrein at a conference organized by the Ärztlicher Sachverständigenbeirat für Fragen der Kriegsopferversorgung (Board of Medical Specialists in Questions of Veterans' Disability Pensions) 1956, p. 26, in BA Koblenz, B 149, 1955.

207. For examples, see the various discussion contributions at the conference sponsored by the Ärztlicher Sachverständigenbeirat für Fragen der Kriegsopferversorgung; additionally, see in chapter 5 the section "The Dispute about Hereditability."

208. Born in 1899, Wilhelm Bansi focused his research on the effects of hunger, starting as an assistant doctor under Hermann Zindek in Berlin. He was a consulting internist in the Wehrmacht, where he encountered the clinical symptoms of hunger, but also apparently gained a reputation through his determined struggle against soldiers who were thought to be feigning illness. See Thoms, "Die Hunger-Generation," pp. 140ff.

209. See Hans Wilhelm Bansi, "Spätschäden nach Dystrophie in der Sicht des internmedizinischen Gutachtens," a talk given at a conference organized by the Ärztlicher Sachverständigenbeirat für Fragen der Kriegsopferversorgung in 1956, p. 50, in BA Koblenz, B 149, 1955. Here, Bansi was referring to a remark he had made as a speaker

at the Nordwestdeutsche Gesellschaftder Psychiater (northwest German psychiatric society) in Lübeck.

210. See also the research overview by Rauschelbach, "Klinik."

211. See Walter Schulte, "Hirnorganische Dauerschäden nach Dystrophie: Wesensänderungen, Epilepsien und Apoplexien," *Medizinische Klinik* 46 (1951), pp. 1356–1359.

212. See, for example, G. Wilke, "Zur Frage der Hirnödeme bei Unterernährung," *Deutsche Medizinische Wochenschrift* 75, issue 5 (1950), pp. 172–176; Hansen, "Kriegsgefangenschaft." Special emphasis in Rauschelbach, "Klinik," p. 215; Clemens Faust, "Organische Hirnschäden nach Hungerdystrophie," *Fortschritte der Medizin* 21 (1953), pp. 71–72, and , "Hungerdystrophie als ausschließliche oder Teilursache von organischen Hirnschäden," talk given at a conference organized by the Ärztlicher Sachverständigenbeirat für Fragen der Kriegsopferversorgung in 1956, pp. 118–120, in BA Koblenz, B 149, 1955.

213. Walter Schulte, "Cerebrale Defektsyndrome nach schwerer Hungerdystrophie und Möglichkeiten ihrer Kompensierung mit dem Blick auf Heimkehrerdepression und forensische Komplikationen," *Der Nervenarzt* 24 (1953), pp. 415–419, citation p. 416.

214. Walter Schulte, "Gibt es eine Hirnversehrtheit infolge schwerer Dystrophien?," *Ärztliche Wochenschrift* 8 (1953), pp. 233–236, citation p. 233.

215. Schulte, "Hirnversehrtheit," p. 234.

216. See below, chapter 5, the section "Pension Claims under Suspicion."

217. Schulte, "Hirnversehrtheit," p. 233.

218. Schulte, "Hirnversehrtheit."

219. See below, chapter 6, "The Moral Challenge, 1956–1970."

CHAPTER 5

1. For details see Neumann, *Nicht der Rede wert*, pp. 132 ff.; Diehl, *Thanks of the Fatherland*, pp. 109ff.

2. Eghigian, "German Welfare State," pp. 108ff. For a thorough and more nuanced analysis, see Stephanie Neuner, *Politik und Psychiatrie: Die staatliche Versorgung psychisch Kriegsbeschädigter nach dem Ersten Weltkrieg in Deutschland, 1920–1939* (Göttingen, 2011). As Neuner reveals, psychiatric experts did not always have the last word in pension cases during the Weimar Republic, as officials were in some cases still willing to accept mental injuries as a result of war.

3. See Kurt Schneider, "Zum Krankheitsbegriff in der Psychiatrie," *Deutsche Medizinische Wochenschrift* 17 (1946), pp. 306–307, citation p. 306.

4. See Hemmo Müller-Suur, "Abgrenzung neurotischer Erkrankungen gegenüber der Norm," in *Handbuch für Neurosenlehre und Psychotherapie*, vol. 1 (Berlin, 1959), pp. 250–262.

5. See the sections on dystrophy in *Anhaltspunkte für die medizinische Gutachtertätigkeit*, 1952, p. 45; 1954, p. 78; 1958, pp. 120–122.

6. See *Anhaltspunkte für die medizinische Gutachtertätigkeit*, 1965, pp. 152–154, p. 153.

7. *Anhaltspunkte für die medizinische Gutachtertätigkeit*, 1965, p. 152.

8. See *Anhaltspunkte für die medizinische Gutachtertätigkeit*, 1958, p. 121.

9. See the discussion in the previous chapter.

10. HBAB, Bestand Morija, 3725; also the source of following information on this case.

11. See in chapter 4 the section "Lessons of War."

12. This case is discussed at various points in this book. See the sections "Facing Defeat and Ruin" in chapter 1 and "The Other Self" in chapter 2, and chapter 3, "Social Rubble."

13. This is suggested by many other cases where information about the causes of the diagnosed problem was obtained again later on.

14. HBAB, Bestand Morija, 9045; also the source of following information on this case.

15. Faust, "Hungerdystrophie," p. 134, in BA Koblenz, B 149, 1955. In Germany, Walter Schellworth, *Neurosenfrage, Ursachenbegriff und Rechtsprechung* (Stuttgart, 1953), was considered a standard work in the field of medical-assessment research.

16. HBAB, Bestand Morija, 9002.

17. Opting for this caution is evident in a wide range of talks held by internists and psychiatrists at the above-cited 1956 conference organized by the Ärztlicher Sachverständigenbeirat für Fragen der Kriegsopferversorgung; see, for example, Hochrein, "Kreislaufstörungen," pp. 45ff., Bansi, "Spätschäden," p. 72; Faust, "Hungerdystrophie," p. 135, all of which can be found in BA Koblenz, B 149, 1955.

18. Hochrein, "Kreislaufstörungen," pp. 45ff., citation p. 45 in BA Koblenz, B 149, 1955; Faust, "Hungerdystrophie," p. 135. Additionally, see the following chapter.

19. HBAB, Bestand Morija, 9002, also the source of following information on this case.

20. Neurological evaluation, August 17, 1956, p. 16, HBAB, Bestand Morija, 9002.

21. Neurological evaluation, August 17, 1956, p. 8.

22. Neurological evaluation, August 17, 1956, p. 12.

23. Neurological evaluation, August 17, 1956, p. 13; also source of following citations.

24. Neurological evaluation, August 17, 1956, p. 14.

25. Neurological evaluation, August 17, 1956, p. 14; also source of following citations.

26. Neurological evaluation, August 17, 1956, pp. 14f.

27. Hochrein, "Kreislaufstörungen," p. 28; Bansi, "Spätschäden," pp. 50ff. in BA Koblenz, B 149, 1955.

28. See Hochrein, "Kreislaufstörungen," p. 33 in BA Koblenz, B 149, 1955; also see the discussion in the following chapter.

29. Hochrein, "Kreislaufstörungen," p. 29.

30. See, for instance, the following cases: HBAB, Bestand Morija, 8879, 9039, 9079, 9112, 9163.

31. Walter von Baeyer, "Die Freiheitsfrage in der forensischen Psychiatrie mit besonderer Berücksichtigung der Entschädigungsneurosen," *Der Nervenarzt* 28 (1957), pp. 337–343, citation p. 342.

32. *Die "Neurose": Ihre Versorgungs- und sozialmedizinische Betreuung*, ed. Bundesminister für Arbeit und Soziales (Schriftenreihe des Bundesversorgungsblattes, vol. 1) (Bonn, 1960), p. 5.

33. See Ulrich Venzlaff, *Die psychoreaktiven Störungen nach entschädigungspflichtigen Ereignissen* (Göttingen, 1958).

34. See chapter 7, "Repatriated Wehrmacht Veterans in the Public Eye."

35. See Venzlaff, *Die psychoreaktiven Störungen*, p. 43.

36. Venzlaff, *Die psychoreaktiven Störungen*, p. 42.

37. Venzlaff, *Die psychoreaktiven Störungen*, p. 64.

38. Venzlaff, *Die psychoreaktiven Störungen*, p. 29f.

39. Venzlaff, *Die psychoreaktiven Störungen*, p. 30.

40. HBAB, Bestand Morija, 3937; also the source of the following information.

41. Letter of August 7, 1958, HBAB, Bestand Morija, 3937.

42. Letter of December 14, 1960, HBAB, Bestand Morija, 3937.

43. HBAB, Bestand Morija, 4559. For detailed information on this case, see also in chapter 1 the section "Facing Defeat and Ruin" and in chapter 2 the section "Delusion and Reality."

44. HBAB, Bestand Morija, 3887.

45. HBAB, Bestand Morija, 5510.

46. HBAB, Bestand Morija, 5764.

47. HBAB, Bestand Morija, 3712; also source of the following citations / information (see above). For a detailed discussion see also in chapter 1 the section "The Echo of Fear."

48. Kurt Schneider, "Kraepelin und die gegenwärtige Psychiatrie," *Fortschritte der Neurologie, Psychiatrie und ihrer Grenzgebiete* 24 (1956), pp. 1–7, citation p. 4.

49. Schneider, "Kraepelin." Emerging in the 1920s, existential analysis was tied to both the Swiss psychiatrist Ludwig Binswanger and Viktor von Weizsäcker; it would slowly become popular in West Germany during the second half of the 1950s. Walter von Baeyer, director of the Heidelberg University psychiatric clinic after Kurt Schneider, would himself become interested in this approach and in anthropological psychiatry in the late 1950s. See the earlier references in the section "The Psychiatric Treatment of Repatriated Soldiers, 1945–1953" in chapter 4.

50. HBAB, Bestand Morija 4329, letter of September 14, 1948.

51. HBAB, Bestand Morija 4329, letter of November 18, 1948.

52. Schneider, "Selbstmord," p. 482.

53. HBAB, Bestand Morija, 5764.

54. See the appreciative letter of a colleague, HBAB, Bestand Morija, 5007.

55. See the discussion above in chapter 4, the section "Lessons of War."

56. See medical opinion in HBAB, Bestand Morija, 5764. Similarly, for instance, HBAB, Bestand Morija, 5811, medical opinion from 1951.

57. See HBAB, Bestand Morija, 4379.

58. Letter of June 8, 1951, HBAB, Bestand Morija, 4379.

59. See HBAB, Bestand Morija, 4329, citations from letters of September 14 and November 7, 1948.

60. HBAB, Bestand Morija, 5644.

61. Letter of September 11, 1950, HBAB, Bestand Morija, 5644.

62. HBAB, Bestand Morija, 5644; also the source of following information and citations.

63. Letter of September 11, 1950, HBAB, Bestand Morija, 5644; also the source of following information and citations.

64. Letter of October 5, 1949, HBAB, Bestand Morija, 5644.

65. Neurological evaluation, October 25, 1950, pp. 10 and 12f., in HBAB, Bestand Morija, 5644.

66. "Minutes of the conference organized by Ärztlicher Sachverständigenbeirat für Fragen der Kriegsopferversorgung, November 7–9, 1955, at the West German labor ministry, Bonn-Duisdorf," p. 179, in BA Koblenz, B 149, 1954. At this conference, the Association of Returnees had one delegate present.

67. Letter of June 14, 1956, in BA Koblenz, B 149, 2353, vol. 1.

68. The passage in question was in sections 3 and 4 of the second executive order (Durchführungsverordnung) of the federal supplementary law of December 24, 1954, which remained in force even after passage of the BEG in 1956. For a detailed discussion, see in chapter 6 the section "'Personality Change' in Survivors of Nazi Persecution."

69. Precise numbers are hard to ascertain. Pross, Paying for the Past, p. 341, relies on the figures offered by internist Hans-Joachim Herberg in 1967. Here the number of processed applications due to bodily injury and health damage until December 31,1960, is given as only 176,897, that is, no more than 46 percent of the applications submitted. In 80,317 cases (45.5 percent of those handled), applications were approved. Information on the specific health problems and their classification by the doctors as persecution related or caused by "hereditary disposition" has not been furnished. In contrast, a decade earlier, on March 31, 1950, the figure for all pension-eligible disabled veterans had already reached 1,440,000; two years later, on January 31, 1952, the figure was 1,537,000, as Neumann indicates in Nicht der Rede wert, pp. 144f. According to the statistical data for 1950, 10 percent of these veterans were classified as suffering from "nervous and mental illnesses." This indicated not only problems that—even in the broadest sense—could be considered mentally based, but also included nerve damage from bullets and problems resulting from concussions. On the medical evaluation of persons persecuted by the Nazis and the establishment of a new interpretive model to address their needs, see the following chapter.

70. The 1953 report of the Association of Returnees contains a reference to the in part harsh criticism of the association's doctors by the official evaluators. Their main accusation was that the association's doctors produced evaluations that reflected a desire to "obtain a pension even if there is no basis for one." Such complaints are documented for Munich, Cologne, and Düsseldorf. Even as late as 1964, the association conference saw grounds to ask its directors to contact the minister for labor and social order with the request that the ministry officially urge the pension administrators to "pay greater attention and give more consideration than previously" to the evaluations of returnees' doctors. Archives of the Verband der Heimkehrer, Bonn: "Verband der Heimkehrer, Kriegsgefangenen und Vermißtenangehörigen Deutschlands e. V., Ein Rechenschaftsbericht," September 1951–September 1953 (Schriftenreihe des VdH, no. 7)

(Bonn, 1953), p. 86; "Wir bleiben uns treu: Ergebnisbericht über den 8. ordentlichen Verbandstag des Verbandes der Heimkehrer, Kriegsgefangenen und Vermißtenangehörigen Deutschlands e. V.," n.p. [1964], p. 25.

71. The results of the medical congresses of 1953, 1955, and 1957, for example, were published collectively in *Extreme Lebensverhältnisse und ihre Folgen* (Schriftenreihe des medizinisch-wissenschaftlichen Beirates des Verbandes der Heimkehrer Deutschlands e. V., vol. 7), ed. Verband der Heimkehrer, Kriegsgefangenen und Vermißtenangehörigen Deutschlands (Bad Godesberg, 1959). A multivolume handbook of medical experience pertaining to internment was published under the same title: Ernst G. Schenck and Wolfgang von Nathusius, eds., *Extreme Lebensverhältnisse und ihre Folgen* (Bad Godesberg, 1958f). The information on the medical service can be found in Christiane Winkler, "Männlichkeit und Gesundheit der deutschen Kriegsheimkehrer im Spiegel der Ärztekongresse des 'Verbands der Heimkehrer,'" in Martin Dinges, ed., *Männlichkeit und Gesundheit im historischen Wandel ca. 1800—ca. 2000* (Stuttgart, 2007).

72. See Anne Harrington, *Die Suche nach Ganzheit: Die Geschichte biologisch-psychologischer Ganzheitslehren: Vom Kaiserreich bis zur New-Age-Bewegung* (Reinbek, 2002), pp. 356ff.; see also chapter 7, "Repatriated Wehrmacht Veterans in the Public Eye."

73. Friedrich Panse, *Angst und Schreck in klinisch-psychologischer und sozialmedizinischer Sicht: Dargestellt an Hand von Erlebnisberichten aus dem Luftkrieg* (Stuttgart, 1952), p. 162.

74. See Panse, *Angst und Schreck*, pp. 162ff., citation pp. 162 and 164.

75. In this regard, see the first chapter in this part of the book.

76. Thus Hochrein, "Kreislaufstörungen." In BA Koblenz, B 149, 1955.

77. In this context, Harrington, *Suche nach Ganzheit*, pp. 356ff., underscores the "moral authority" granted to medical practice and science that focused on the "whole" patient, since its representatives, for example, Viktor von Weizsäcker, seemed untainted by Nazism.

78. Among the champions of psychosomatic medicine numbered, in particular, Kurt Gauger, who had already published in the area in the 1920s after studying psychology, philosophy, and pedagogy. Gauger first came into contact with psychotherapeutic practice in 1926. During the Nazi period, he served as deputy director of the Institute for Psychological Research and Psychotherapy, which had been founded by Matthias Göring in 1936. On Gauger's career, see esp. Cocks, *Psychotherapy*, p. 125ff., *passim*. His most important postwar publication was Kurt Gauger, *Die Dystrophie als psychosomatisches Krankheitsbild* (Munich, 1952).

79. See Hochrein, "Kreislaufstörungen," p. 26, in BA Koblenz, B 149, 1955; Hochrein "Diagnostik und Therapie der vegetativen Dystonie," in Schenck and Nathusius, *Extreme Lebensverhältnisse*, vol. 7, pp. 125–159, pp. 127f.

80. Hochrein, "Kreislaufstörungen," p. 29, in BA Koblenz, B 149, 1955.

81. See Hochrein, "Kreislaufstörungen," p. 28. Although Hochrein himself was somewhat skeptical regarding this tendency, he also considered it a "fact" that the "modern human being" was caught "in an especially dramatic test . . . because of the

climate of life he has created." The outcome of this climate is what has been provisionally termed "manager's" or "entrepreneur's" disease."

82. Hochrein, "Kreislaufstörungen," p. 33.

83. The following information and citations regarding this "case" stem from the letter presented by Hochrein in his talk, in Hochrein, "Kreislaufstörungen," pp. 34f., in BA Koblenz, B 149, 1955.

84. According to the letter, the pension office recognized reduced earning capacity of 70 percent for the first three months and 30 percent for the following one and a half years.

85. Hochrein, "Kreislaufstörungen," p. 35, BA Koblenz, B 149, 1955.

86. Hochrein, "Kreislaufstörungen," p. 27.

87. Bansi, "Spätschäden," p. 49, BA Koblenz, B 149, 1955.

88. Bansi, "Spätschäden,", pp. 61f., BA Koblenz, B 149, 1955.

89. Hochrein, "Kreislaufstörungen," in BA Koblenz, B 149, 1955, noted this not only by weaving the returnee's letter into his talk but also through references to the Association of Returnees. The association had indicated, he explained, "that 15 percent of late returnees (*Spätheimkehrer*) have indeed returned, but have not yet 'arrived home' because they cannot orient themselves in our daily life"—a piece of information that gave rise to much reflection, according to the internist. Before his audience, Hochrein emphasized clearly that he took the returnees' problems very seriously—all the more so by calling into question the significance of the percentage figures. As a reason, he offered the example of one former Wehrmacht soldier who, although "unassuming and quiet," had chosen a "lonely death" (p. 36).

90. Hochrein, "Kreislaufstörungen," pp. 47f.

91. See Hochrein, "Kreislaufstörungen," p. 37.

92. Hochrein, *Diagnostik*, p. 125.

93. In his talk Bansi, "Spätschäden," pp. 65f., in BA Koblenz, B 149, 1955, referred to a study by Hans Hoff that showed, he indicated, that of 71,967 sick patients registered in a neurological polyclinic, 28,314 had been referred with a diagnosis of "vegetative dystonia." Bansi did not furnish information on the period involved.

94. Bansi, "Spätschäden," p. 67. Here Bansi relied on recently published findings of the "Copenhagen conference," in which mainly non-German colleagues exchanged their latest observations about the delayed health consequences of deportation and imprisonment. In the context of the exchanged information, Bansi emphasized that "one very likely had to admit that in the case of deportees to the concentration camps the mental traumatization was even greater" than in the case of the German POWs (p. 68). For the conference talks see Max Michel, ed., *Gesundheitsschäden durch Verfolgung und Gefangenschaft und ihre Spätfolgen* (Frankfurt am Main, 1955). Discussed in more detail below.

95. Discussion remark of Prof. Gustav Bodechtel (Munich), in BA Koblenz, B 149, 1955; see also discussion remark of Prof. Hans Hoff (Frankfurt), BA Koblenz, B 149, 1955.

96. Discussion remark of Prof. Gustav Bodechtel (Munich), BA Koblenz, B 149, 1955.

97. In this regard, see the following chapter and the references listed there.

98. Concluding remark of Prof. Dr. Max Hochrein, BA Koblenz, B 149, 1955.

99. Discussion remark of Prof. Hans Bürger-Prinz (Hamburg), BA Koblenz, B 149, 1955.

100. Discussion remark of Prof. Rüsken (Berlin), BA Koblenz, B 149, 1955.

101. Rüsken (Berlin), BA Koblenz, B 149, 1955.

102. Even in the early 1950s, this perspective was noted by pension officials in many returnees. The concept of disposition had "fallen into discredit" among the disabled and their representatives, observed *Der Versorgungsbeamte* (*The Pension Official*), the central organ of the pension bureaucracy, which saw cause to defend the concept. See "Anlagebedingt," *Der Versorgungsbeamte* 3 (1952), pp. 85–87, citation p. 85.

103. It was the impression of a governmental medical director, Dubitscher (given name unknown), writing in *Der Versorgungsbeamte* in 1968, that house doctors made a similar concession, avoiding terms such as "simulation" and "neurosis" in their evaluations and limiting themselves simply to a description of subjective complaints. In this manner, they avoided taking a position on the question of reduced earning capacity. Dubitscher explained that patients had their own ideas about their illnesses, and general practitioners could simply not afford to deviate significantly from the patients' assessment of their "suffering"; otherwise the doctor would forfeit the medical service fee for the person involved, and possibly for his household. See Dubitscher, "Der behandelnde Arzt und der ärztliche Gutachter," *Der Versorgungsbeamte* 19 (1968), pp. 1–2.

104. Letter of August 10, 1959; chief physician of the Berlin state pension office to *Oberregierungsmedizinalrat* (senior governmental medical councilor) Ernst Goetz, Ministry of Labor and Social Order, in BA Koblenz, B 149, 2354.

CHAPTER 6

1. Leys, *Trauma*, pp. 223ff. By contrast, the psychoanalytically oriented American psychiatrists argued that the disposition toward "neurotic symptoms" that they occasionally observed in their patients after the end of the war was based on early childhood disturbances or experiences. See, among others, Paul Friedman, "Some Aspects of Concentration Camp Psychology," *American Journal of Psychiatry* 105 (1949), pp. 601–605, p. 603. On the penetration of psychoanalysis into American psychiatry starting in the late 1940s in general, see Shorter, *Geschichte der Psychiatrie*, pp. 261ff. Only a few years after the end of the war, Walter von Baeyer traveled to the United States to inform himself about American psychiatry. He conveyed his subsequent insights in a differentiated report largely dedicated to the range of analytic and therapeutic approaches he had observed. He made an attempt to weigh their advantages and disadvantages and to compare their differences and similarities to German psychiatry. See Walter von Baeyer, "Gegenwärtige Psychiatrie in den Vereinigten Staaten," *Der Nervenarzt* 21 (1950), pp. 2–9.

2. Shephard, *A War of Nerves*, pp. 327ff.; de Haan, "Paths of Normalization," pp. 65–92.

3. H. H. Fleischhacker, "Healing the Wounds," *AJR Information* 11 (1956), p. 6.

Lucie Adelsberger, herself a prisoner in the Birkenau death camp for two years, indicated that the inmates' "propensity to become ill" had already changed because "all energies" were focused on "enduring that miserable life." Hence the "incidence of disease" had been defined by serious infectious diseases, damage from hunger, exposure to cold and heat, and finally by injury from the enemy. All diseases of "civilization" such as rheumatism and other joint problems, neuralgia and stomach ulcers, allergic reactions and neuroses were hardly present at all. The "will to live" seemed to be one of the decisive factors. See Lucie Adelsberger, "Psychologische Beobachtungen im Konzentrationslager Auschwitz," *Schweizerische Zeitschrift für Psychologie* 6 (1947), pp. 124–131, pp. 127f.

4. See Jacques Tas, "Psychical Disorders among Inmates of Concentration Camps and Repatriates," *Psychiatric Quarterly* 25 (1951), pp. 679–690, pp. 683f. First published in 1946, Tas's report was mainly based on observations in Bergen-Belsen, where he had been active as a doctor-inmate.

5. Viktor E. Frankl, "Psychologie und Psychiatrie des Konzentrationslagers," in *Soziale und angewandte Psychiatrie*, pp. 743–759, citation p. 752.

6. See, among others, F. M. Lipscomb, "Medical Aspects of Belsen Concentration Camp," *Lancet*, September 8, 1945, pp. 313–315.

7. Paul Thygesen, "Allgemeines über die Spätfolgen," in Michel, *Gesundheitsschäden durch Verfolgung*, pp. 21–29; Knud Hermann, "Die psychischen Symptome des KZ-Syndroms," in Michel, *Gesundheitsschäden durch Verfolgung*, pp. 40–47; Knud Hermann, "Das Syndrom der Konzentrationslager: Zehn Jahre nach der Befreiung," in Michel, *Gesundheitsschäden durch Verfolgung*, pp. 59–72; Per Helweg-Larsen et al., "Die Hungerkrankheit in den deutschen Konzentrationslagern," in Michel, *Gesundheitsschäden durch Verfolgung*, pp. 148–171; René Targowla, "Die neuropsychischen Folgen der Deportation in den deutschen Konzentrationslagern. Syndrom der Asthenie der Deportierten," in Michel, *Gesundheitsschäden durch Verfolgung*, pp. 30–40.

8. Thygesen, "Allgemeines über die Spätfolgen," p. 24.

9. See in chapter 4 the section "The Psychiatric Treatment of Repatriated German Soldiers, 1945–1953," and in chapter 5 the section "Pension Claims under Suspicion."

10. Thygesen, "Allgemeines über die Spätfolgen," p. 25. Similarly Per Helweg-Larsen et al., "Die sozialen Folgeerscheinungen der Deportation," Michel, *Gesundheitsschäden durch Verfolgung*, pp. 256–267, p. 262.

11. Hermann, "Psychische Symptome," pp. 44f.

12. See Targowla, "Die neuropsychischen Folgen," p. 39. On "Summationstrauma" see also in chapter 4 the section "The Psychiatric Treatment of Repatriated German Soldiers, 1945–1953."

13. The reference to the national pension system was owed to the fact that the BEG had a so-called territorial principle as its basis, according to which only those formerly persecuted persons could claim reparations who lived in West Germany or "had their last place of residence or long-term domicile in areas" that had belonged to the German Reich on December 31, 1937. BEG, version of June 29, 1956, in *Bundesentschädigungsgesetze, Kommentar von Georg Blessin et al.*, 2nd ed. (Munich, 1957), pp. 5–76, citation pp. 6f. On regulation of the claims of those who had lived outside those stipulated areas see Hans Günter Hockerts, "Wiedergutmachung: Ein umstrittener Begriff

und ein weites Feld," in Hans Günter Hockerts and Christiane Kuller, eds., *Nach der Verfolgung: Wiedergutmachung nationalsozialistischen Unrechts in Deutschland?* (Göttingen, 2003), pp. 7–33, pp. 16ff.; Ulrich Herbert, "Nicht entschädigungsfähig? Die Wiedergutmachungsansprüche der Ausländer," in Ludolf Herbst and Constantin Goschler, eds., *Wiedergutmachung in der Bundesrepublik Deutschland* (Munich, 1989), pp. 273–302. In detail: Hans Günter Hockerts, Claudia Moisel, and Tobias Winstel, eds., *Grenzen der Wiedergutmachung: Die Entschädigung für NS-Verfolgte in West- und Osteuropa 1945–2000* (Göttingen, 2006). In fact, the widespread interpretation of mental and physical suffering in the various national pension systems as "pension neurosis" was an abiding theme at the Copenhagen conference. In Denmark, a decision had been reached that deportation to a German camp was equal to 15 percent invalid status. But this decision did not ensure steady pension payments, since assumptions of what was equivalent to "pension neuroticism" and "traumatic neurosis" informed it. In principle, then, there was an assumption that those affected underestimated their working capacity. For this reason, short-term pension payments and small one-time financial reparations were considered a sensible incentive for resuming work. See Thygesen, "Allgemeines über die Spätfolgen," p. 26; Targowla, "Die neuropsychischen Folgen," p. 31; Hermann, "Die psychischen Symptome," pp. 44f.; Max Michel, "Spätschäden und Summationsschäden," in Michel, *Gesundheitsschäden durch Verfolgung*, pp. 48–51. Now as before the problem of recognition of health damage to victims of Nazism within the various pension systems is in need of a detailed historical analysis.

14. See for instance, Paul Thygesen et al., "Die psychischen Symptome der Heimkehrer," in Michel, ed., *Gesundheitsschäden durch Verfolgung*, pp. 52–58, pp. 54f.; René Targowla, "Bericht zur Ausarbeitung einer neuen Rententabelle für ehemalige Verfolgte, Internierte und Deportierte," Michel, *Gesundheitsschäden durch Verfolgung*, pp. 274–280, p. 276. In the case of physical illnesses as well, for instance, tuberculosis that emerged many years later, medical examiners were reluctant to recognize a causal relationship with deportation, as one doctor at the Copenhagen conference made clear during the discussion; Targowla, p. 334.

15. This problem was in fact evident in all European countries after World War II. There are many indications of this in the proceedings of the international medical congress held in Bucharest in 1964. For Czechoslovakia see, for example, Frantisek Blaha, "Folgen des Krieges für die menschliche Gesundheit (Schlußbericht über das Forschungsproblem des Gesundheitsministeriums für die Jahre 1960–1963)," in *Ätio-Pathogenese und Therapie der Erschöpfung und Vorzeitigen Vergreisung (IV: Internationaler Medizinischer Kongreß, Bukarest, 22.–27. Juni 1964)*, 2 vols. (no place or date), pp. 121–198, pp. 140ff., *passim*; Frantisek Blaha, "Die Folgen des Krieges für die menschliche Gesundheit nach 20 Jahren," in *Ätio-Pathogenese und Therapie*, pp. 241–244; R. Bures, "Beurteilung der Folgen des Krieges und der faschistischen Verfolgung," in *Ätio-Pathogenese und Therapie*, pp. 199–240. For Belgium: W. Deveen, "Fachgutachten und Pensionen," in *Ätio-Pathogenese und Therapie*, pp. 579–581.

16. Hermann, "Syndrom," p. 62.

17. Eigel Hess Thysen and Jörn Hess Thaysen, "Medizinische Probleme bei früheren, in deutsche Konzentrationslager Deportierten," in Michel, *Gesundheitsschäden durch Verfolgung*, pp. 172–180, p. 180. With respect to the findings of German brain

research see in chapter 4 the section "The Psychiatric Treatment of Repatriated German Soldiers, 1945–1953."

18. Ludwig Popper, "Ärztliche Erfahrungen bei Untersuchungen nach dem Österreichischen Opferfürsorgegesetz," in Michel, *Gesundheitsschäden durch Verfolgung*, pp. 281–287, citation p. 287; similarly Bures, "Beurteilung," p. 580.

19. Lagrou, *Legacy of Nazi Occupation*.

20. Thygesen, "Allgemeines über die Spätfolgen," p. 29.

21. See, among others, Senator for the Interior to Minister of the Interior for Lower Saxony, Berlin, November 8, 1957, in BA Koblenz, B 126, 9903, vol. 1 (main medical conferences).

22. Hockerts, "Wiedergutmachung in Deutschland," offers a very good overview. Constantin Goschler, *Wiedergutmachung: Westdeutschland und die Verfolgten des Nationalsozialismus (1945–1954)* (Munich, 1992), has relevance for the early phase of planning and realization.

23. See chapter 4, the section "The Psychiatric Treatment of Repatriated German Soldiers, 1945–1953."

24. See, among others, Bansi, "Spätschäden," who, speaking of delayed damage resulting from dystrophy in his talk at the conference sponsored by the Ärztlicher Sachverständigenbeirat für Fragen der Kriegsopferversorgung in 1956, explicitly referred to several of the presentations at the Copenhagen conference; pp. 68ff., BA Koblenz, B 149, 1955.

25. Second by-law for enactment of the BEG, in *Bundesentschädigungsgesetze*, pp. 1239–1245, citation p. 1240.

26. The correspondence is in BA Koblenz B 126, 9838.

27. German Federal Minister of Labor to the German Federal Minister of Finance, April 26, 1957, in BA Koblenz, B 126, 9838.

28. Minister of the Interior for North Rhine-Westphalia, Section V, to the German Federal Minister of Finance, September 3, 1957, BA Koblenz, B 126, 9838.

29. Minister of the Interior for North Rhine-Westphalia, Section V, to the German Federal Minister of Finance, September 3, 1957, BA Koblenz, B 126, 9838.

30. German Federal Minister of Labor to German Federal Minister of Finance, September 23, 1957, BA Koblenz, B 126, 9838.

31. Minister of the Interior for North Rhine-Westphalia, Section V, to German Federal Minister of Finance, September 3, 1957, BA Koblenz, B 126, 9838.

32. Minister of the Interior for North Rhine-Westphalia, Section V, to German Federal Minister of Finance, September 3, 1957, BA Koblenz, B 126, 9838. The fact sheet in question was the *Merkblatt zum Gutachtenformular* (fact sheet for the evaluation form) that had likewise been prepared by the medical section of the Federal Ministry of Labor and provided evaluation guidelines for independent medical examiners abroad. The medical section indicated that the guidelines as well were losing importance due to differences between the BVG and the BEG.

33. Minister of the Interior for North Rhine-Westphalia, Section V, to German Federal Minister of Finance, September 3, 1957.

34. The so-called *Vertrauensärzte* were doctors who lived and practiced outside of Germany, and were appointed by the West German diplomatic missions in the countries

where they worked. They were responsible for evaluating the health-related compensation claims of Holocaust survivors and other victims of Nazism.

35. Hans Strauss, "Besonderheiten der nicht-psychotischen seelischen Störungen bei Opfern der nationalsozialistischen Verfolgung und ihre Bedeutung bei der Begutachtung" (transcript), p. 1, in BA Koblenz, B 126, 9903, vol. 1. Strauss's text was published at the same time in *Der Nervenarzt* 28 (1957), pp. 344–350.

36. Hermann Ammermüller and Hans Wilden, *Gesundheitliche Schäden in der Wiedergutmachung: ärztliche und rechtliche Beurteilung* (Stuttgart, 1953).

37. Strauss, "Besonderheiten," p. 3.

38. Strauss, "Besonderheiten," p. 5.

39. Strauss, "Besonderheiten," p. 8.

40. Strauss, "Besonderheiten," p. 5.

41. Strauss, "Besonderheiten," pp. 7f.

42. Minister of the Interior for Schleswig-Holstein to German Federal Minister of Finance, Section V, reparations, September 24, 1957, in BA Koblenz, B 126, 9903, vol. 1.

43. For this and following citations, see Ministerial Medical Doctor Heigl to the state reparations office of Schleswig-Holstein, September 9, 1957 (transcript), in BA Koblenz, B 126, 9903, vol. 1.

44. See Ministerial Medical Doctor Heigl to the state reparations office of Schleswig-Holstein, September 9, 1957 (transcript), in BA Koblenz, B 126, 9903, vol. 1. It was recommended that an evaluation from Dr. Ernst Kretschmer, a professor at the University of Tübingen, should be requested. He was known for adhering strictly to the scientific position that long-term mental disorders did not exist in the absence of physical damage.

45. Also in attendance were representatives of the federal ministries of finance and justice, and the Foreign Office. See transcript of the main medical conference, Munich, April 23–24, 1958, in BA Koblenz, B 126, 9903, vol. 1. A preliminary discussion of the conference and its themes was held in Göttingen on January 13–14, 1958. This led to the "Göttingen Commission," its basic purpose being to develop ideas for improving evaluations from abroad that were deemed unsatisfactory.

46. These conferences are documented in the files of the main medical conference, in BA Koblenz, B 126, 9903, vols. 1–3, B 126, 42530, and B 126, 42531.

47. As formulated in the minutes themselves, after being vetted the "transcripts or even simply excerpts would be forwarded to the *Vertrauensärzte* doctors abroad," if necessary. See transcript for the main medical conference, Munich, April 23 and 24, 1958, p. 16, in BA Koblenz, B 126, 9903, vol. 1.

48. See BA Koblenz, B 126, 9903, vol. 1. The talk by Erich Kluge is appended to the transcript as appendix IV, which contains the citation, p. 7. Kluge published the talk under the title "Über die Folgen schwerer Haftzeiten" ("On the Consequences of Harsh Periods of Imprisonment"), *Der Nervenarzt* 29 (1958), pp. 462–465.

49. Among disturbances with a "constitutional basis," Kluge included "vegetative dystonia," which he consequently also classified as not persecution related. The evaluators, he indicated, had been mistaken and "in addition strongly exaggerated the extent

of the damage." Transcript for the main medical conference, appendix IV, p. 4 (with a presentation of Kluge's diagnoses) and pp. 8f.

50. See transcript for the main medical conference, appendix IV, p. 7. Kluge particularly mentioned the studies of Wilke, who had found a brain edema during the autopsy of a former POW in the Soviet Union, and those of Faust, which had led to insight into the connection between changes in the brain and protein deficiency. In this regard, also see in chapter 4 the section "The Psychiatric Treatment of Repatriated German Soldiers, 1945–1953."

51. See transcript for the main medical conference, appendix IV, p. 7. Kluge was alluding to the Greek χολή (cholé), or "gall" in English. In the ancient doctrine of four humors, "melancholia" was associated with a surplus of black gall.

52. Foreign, above all American, evaluators were evidently paying no attention "to severe somatic injuries," complained Kluge. In his view, the question of causal relationship received far too little consideration by these colleagues. And if it was considered at all, then it was only in terms of psychological linkage. Transcript for the main medical conference, appendix IV, p. 6.

53. Transcript for the main medical conference, appendix IV, p. 9.

54. See transcript for the main medical conference, appendix I (Dr. Med. Meywald, "The Concept of Causation in the BEG"), pp. 8f., and appendix II (talk of Dr. Med. Didden), pp. 1ff.

55. Transcript, appendix I, pp. 8f.

56. See transcript, appendix II, p. 1.

57. See transcript, appendix II, p. 1. Didden was referring primarily to the findings of Danish researcher K. Hermann and his term "concentration camp syndrome," while at the same time clearly showing support for the perspective of Hans Strauss in New York.

58. See transcript, appendix II, p. 2 (also for citation).

59. See transcript, appendix II, pp. 2f.

60. Transcript of the main medical conference, Munich, April 23 and 24, 1958, p. 10, in BA Koblenz, B 126, 9903, vol. 1.

61. Exchange of views between independent examining doctors in the United States and doctors working for the compensation authorities (letter from the Federal Ministry of Labor and Social Order, September 15, 1958), in BA Koblenz, B 126, 9903.

62. See transcript of the main medical conference in Munich, April 23–24, 1958, p. 11, in BA Koblenz, B 126, 9903, vol. 1. The minutes of the first meeting of the "Göttingen Commission" in November 1958 reinforced this disapproval. The evaluations from abroad, the consensus went, were neither anamnestically nor diagnostically produced in a medically adequate manner for the final assessment. See transcript of the Göttingen Commission, Düsseldorf, November 6–7, 1958, p. 3, in BA Koblenz, B 126, 4253, vol. 1.

63. The debate was initiated in 1957 in Der Nervenarzt with an article by Walter von Baeyer, "Die Freiheitsfrage in der forensischen Psychiatrie mit besonderer Berücksichtigung der Entschädigungsneurosen" ("The Question of Freedom in Forensic Psychiatry with Special Consideration of Compensation Neuroses"), Der Nervenarzt 28 (1957),

pp. 337–343, followed by Strauss, "Besonderheiten"; Kurt Kolle, "Die Opfer der na- tionalsozialistischen Verfolgung in psychiatrischer Sicht," *Der Nervenarzt* 29 (1958), pp. 148–158; and Kluge, "Folgen." On this shift of perspective see also Pross, *Paying for the Past*, pp. 154ff.

64. Ulrich Venzlaff, *Die psychoreaktiven Störungen nach entschädigungspflichti- gen Ereignissen (die sogenannten Unfallneurosen)* (Berlin, 1958). In 1956, Venzlaff had successfully submitted this study as his "habilitation" thesis. On his positions, see also in chapter 5 the section "Pension Claims under Suspicion."

65. Venzlaff, *Die psychoreaktiven Störungen*, p. 69; elaborated in detail in the re- spective chapters on *Wunschreaktionen* (reactions based on the desire to obtain a pen- sion), "psychopathic reactions," and "neuroses in the actual sense" (pp. 28–67).

66. See Venzlaff, *Die psychoreaktiven Störungen*, p. 70.

67. See Venzlaff, *Die psychoreaktiven Störungen*, pp. 67ff., citation p. 69. As a pro- tagonist of the accepted psychiatric concept of illness, and a person who adhered to scientific principle, Venzlaff quoted Kurt Schneider, the former chair of psychiatry at the University of Heidelberg: "Disease itself exists only in the physical body, and we refer to abnormal mental phenomena as 'pathological' only when they can be traced to pathological physical processes." Schneider's definition stemmed from 1946 and still dominated the field of psychiatry. Venzlaff supplemented Schneider's definition with the concept of "being ill," which he defined—following Hemmo Müller-Suur—as "the distressful experience of adversity in the mental/emotional sphere."

68. See Venzlaff, *Die psychoreaktiven Störungen*, p. 74.

69. See Venzlaff, *Die psychoreaktiven Störungen*, pp. 75ff., citation p. 75.

70. Venzlaff, *Die psychoreaktiven Störungen*, p. 77.

71. See Venzlaff, *Die psychoreaktiven Störungen*, p. 82.

72. Venzlaff, *Die psychoreaktiven Störungen*, pp. 83f.

73. On this case see Pross, *Paying for the Past*, p. 156, who was the first to write on the subject.

74. This emerges from the court records for the session of October 24, 1955, in the context of the compensation lawsuit, here pp. 4 and 6, in BA Koblenz, BA 149, 2353.

75. Pross, *Paying for the Past*, p. 156. However, the labor ministry, which was re- sponsible for war disability pensions, reacted, presumably because in his evaluation Kretschmer had once again firmly stated that in the case of former soldiers as well, there was no war-related mental damage if no evidence of physical damage could be found. The labor ministry—the responsible party was *Regierungsmedizinalrat* (senior medical officer) Dr. Ernst Goetz—prepared an abridged version of the minutes of the compensa- tion proceedings, made two hundred copies, and mailed them to, among other places, the responsible authorities on the state level and the federal insurance agency for em- ployees. The abbreviated evaluation and distribution lists are contained in Goetz's letter of August 18, 1956, in BA Koblenz, B 149, 2353.

76. "Draft of the Minutes of the Main Medical Conference, April 23–24, 1958, for Independent Medical Examiners Abroad," p. 2 (appendix to the letter of Bavarian fi- nance ministry to Lower Saxon interior ministry, January 26, 1959), in BA Koblenz, B 126, 9903, vol. 2. The publications mentioned included only those by Strauss, von Baeyer, Kluge, and Kolle that had appeared in the *Nervenarzt* since 1957.

77. "Draft of the Minutes of the Main Medical Conference," p. 4.

78. "Draft of the Minutes of the Main Medical Conference," citation pp. 1 and 2.

79. "Draft of the Minutes of the Main Medical Conference," p. 3. On this problem see "Report on the Most Frequent Mistakes in the Trial Evaluations of the New Independent Medical Examiners in the Paris Embassy," in BA Koblenz, B 126, 42530, vol. 1. The report is based on a trip to Paris undertaken by two governmental medical advisers for the purpose of familiarizing the local independent medical examiners with the requirements of German evaluative practice. See "Report on the Official Visit to the German Embassy in Paris for Instruction and Selection of Independent Medical Examiners," in BA Koblenz, B 126, 42530, vol. 1.

80. Die "Neurose": Ihre Versorgungs- und Sozialmedizinische Beurteilung, hg. v. Bundesminister für Arbeit und Sozialordnung, in *Schriftenreihe des Bundesversorgungsblatts*, vol. 1 (Bonn, 1960).

81. The evaluation was signed by Prof. Dr. Sr. G. Bodechtel (director of the 2nd medical clinic of the University of Munich), Prof. Dr. F. Panse (director of the Düsseldorf psychiatric clinic), Prof. Dr. G. Störring (director of the Kiel psychiatric clinic), Oberregierungsmedizinalrat Dr. F. Dubitscher (governmental medical director, North Rhine state pension office), and Regierungsmedizinaldirektor Dr. Hirt (governmental medical director, Bavarian pension office). Bundesminister für Arbeit und Sozialordnung, "Die 'Neurose,'" p. 11.

82. Bundesminister für Arbeit und Sozialordnung, "Die 'Neurose,'" p. 5. Beyond this, Panse appealed for possible acknowledgment in cases involving severe deformation, particularly of the face, which permanently affected an individual's sense of self-esteem.

83. Bundesminister für Arbeit und Sozialordnung, "Die 'Neurose,'" p. 10.

84. Pross, *Paying for the Past*; Stefanie Baumann, "Opfer von Menschenversuchen als Sonderfall der Wiedergutmachung," in Hockerts, Moisel, and Winstel, *Grenzen der Wiedergutmachung*, pp. 147–194, pp. 154f.

85. In this regard, see the previous chapter.

86. See Svenja Goltermann, "Negotiating Victimhood in East and West Germany," in Withuis and Mooij, *Politics of War Trauma*, pp. 107–140. On postwar developments in Poland, see Gross, *Fear*; Adam Krzeminski, "Polen," in Frei and Knigge, *Verbrechen erinnern*, pp. 262–271.

87. This becomes clear in a communication from the Foreign Office to the Bavarian finance ministry, February 17, 1960, in BA Koblenz, B 126, 9856, vol. 1.

88. The letter's contents according to Pross, *Paying for the Past*, p. 133; here also the citations.

89. Further cases of protest are documented in BA Koblenz, B 126, 9856, and 47169 (France), and BA Koblenz, B 126, 42511 (England).

90. Pross, *Paying for the Past*, p. 133.

91. Summarized in Ulrich Brochhagen, *Nach Nürnberg: Vergangenheitsbewältigung und Westintegration in der Ära Adenauer* (Berlin, 1999), pp. 319ff. Based on the West German government's "white book" for 1960, Brochhagen speaks of 470 registered incidents by January 28, 1960 (p. 320).

92. Brochhagen, *Nach Nürnberg*, pp. 334ff.

93. West German Foreign Office to Bavarian Ministry of Finance, February 17, 1960, in BA Koblenz, B 126, 9856, vol. 1.

94. Express letter, West German Foreign Office to West German finance minister, to the attention of Undersecretary Blessin, August 2, 1960, in BA Koblenz, B 126, 9856, vol. 1.

95. "Official trip to Paris February 22, 1960–March 3, 1960," p. 13, BA Koblenz, B 126, 9856, vol. 1.

96. "Report on the Most Frequent Mistakes in the Trial Evaluations of the New Independent Medical Examiners in the Paris embassy," pp. 5f., BA Koblenz, B 126, 42530, vol. 1.

97. "Most Frequent Mistakes," p. 7.

98. "Most Frequent Mistakes," p. 7. During the second meeting of German and French doctors in Paris, some French doctors apparently expressed the view that "under certain circumstances of a *non*medical sort reduced earning capacity of 25 percent should *automatically* be attributed to persecution." See "Official trip to Paris February 22–March 3, 1960," p. 3, BA Koblenz, B 126, 9856, vol. 1.

99. "Official trip to Paris February 22, 1960–March 3, 1960," p. 13, BA Koblenz, B 126, 9856, vol. 1.

100. Third amendment to the BEG, in *Bundesentschädigungsgesetze*, pp. 15f.

101. "Translation from the French. 'Doctors, Problems, and Complexes' by I. Weinberg," in BA Koblenz, B 126, 9856, vol. 1.

102. "Official Trip to Paris February 22, 1960–March 3, 1960," p. 13, BA Koblenz, B 126, 9856, vol. 1.

103. "Official Trip to Paris," p. 14.

104. See "Official Trip to Paris," p. 14. for all following citations in this paragraph.

105. In the opinion of the West German medical officials who visited Israel in 1961, apparently for the purpose of establishing personal contact with the Israeli independent medical examiners and the medical board there, the trip itself did not raise any serious medical controversies with respect to the evaluations. Although the psychiatric evaluations were indeed addressed as a problem, the difficulties were due to the fact that "only a small number" of specialized psychiatric evaluators were available. As a result, "Many evaluations took a long time to prepare." The medical delegation had pronouncedly positive things to report about the Israeli medical board, which in their view made an effort "to check and evaluate the work of individual medical examiners on the whole." Value was placed, they reported, "on an exact and correct processing" of the applications. A comparable agency is not mentioned in the reports on other countries. Minutes of the main medical conference, May 23–24, 1962, in Hanover, pp. 7f., in BA Koblenz, B 126, 42531, vol. 5.

106. See BA Koblenz, B 126, 42511. The proceedings, which developed into litigation between the West German embassy in London, the independent medical examiner, the North Rhine-Westphalian compensations office, and the West German Foreign Office, extended over several years before being resolved in court in 1965, when the embassy's appeal for denial was declared unjustified. Thus, the German compensation authorities had prevailed. But the discussion of compensation officials at the 1962 main medical conference suggests that German embassies, with West Germany's political

standing abroad in mind, at times steered the commissioning of independent medical examiners, thereby exerting influence on evaluative practice. As an example, we read in the conference minutes: "In general the impression emerges that in their assessment of individual medical examiners the German diplomatic missions are more inclined to accommodate the wishes of the associations of persecuted people than the suggestions and objections of the compensation authorities. The Foreign Office is requested to inform the diplomatic missions of this and urge them to have greater regard than previously for the authorities' objective arguments for or against further using the services of an independent medical examiner." "Minutes of the main medical conference, May 23–24, 1962, in Hanover," pp. 6f. BA Koblenz, B 126, 42531, vol. 5.

107. "Report on the official trip to New York from October 4–November 7, 1960," pp. 7f., in BA Koblenz, B 126, 9856, vol. 1.

108. "Die Wiedergutmachung," October 14, 1960, p. 1, in BA Koblenz, B 126, 9856, vol. 1.

109. "Minutes of the main medical conference, May 23–24, 1962, in Hanover," p. 4., in BA Koblenz, B 126, 42531, vol. 5.

110. "Report on the official trip to New York," p. 10, in BA Koblenz, B 126, 9856, vol. 1.

111. Consulate General of Federal Republic of Germany to the Foreign Office, February 23, 1961, p. 1, in BA Koblenz, B 126, 9856, vol. 2.

112. "Transcript concerning the basic results of a discussion between representatives of the Conference on Jewish Material Claims against Germany, Inc. (Claims Conference) and the United Restitution Organization (URO) with representatives of some German consulates general and consulates in the USA, as well as with doctors sent to New York by the compensation authorities of [West German] states, May 12, 1961 in New York," p. 4, in BA Koblenz, B 126, 9856, vol. 1.

113. "Transcript concerning the Basic Results," pp. 4f.

114. "Neues zum Neurose-Begriff aus der Sicht des Entschädigungsmediziners," v. Reg. Med. Rat. Dr. Staehr, April 13, 1961, p. 1, in BA Koblenz, B 126, 9856, vol. 2.

115. "Neues zum Neurose-Begriff," p. 2. On the reactions of the compensation authorities to Strauss's work, see in this chapter the section "'Personality Change' in Survivors of Nazi Persecution."

116. "Neues zum Neurose-Begriff," p. 3.

117. "Neues zum Neurose-Begriff," p. 4. On the evaluation see the section "'Personality Change' in Survivors of Nazi Persecution" in this chapter.

118. "Neues zum Neurose-Begriff," p. 6.

119. "Neues zum Neurose-Begriff," p. 7.

120. "Neues zum Neurose-Begriff," p. 8.

121. "Erlebnisreaktive psychische Störungen durch und nach nationalsozialistischer Verfolgung" (ms. accompanying transcript of the Göttingen Commission, September 19, 1963, in Bad Salzdetfurth), in BA Koblenz, B 126, 42530, vol. 1.

122. "Neues zum Neurose-Begriff," p. 3, in BA Koblenz, B 126, 9856, vol. 2.

123. At the time *Regierungsmedizinalrat* Helmut Paul was in the West German health ministry; *Oberregierungsmedizinalrat* Hans-Joachim Herberg was an internist in Cologne's medical-pension inspectorate. Both men showed great interest in researching

"late damage" suffered by both German late returnees from the Soviet POW camps and survivors of Nazi persecution. On a number of occasions, Herberg served as a private evaluator for such persecuted individuals in compensation proceedings. In 1964, to the chagrin of the North Rhine-Westphalian interior ministry, he founded a documentation center for health damage following imprisonment and persecution in Cologne. While the various state compensation authorities seem to have denied the documentation center any substantive justification and refused financial support, the West German health ministry interceded supportively in various ways. See, among other sources, BA Koblenz, B 126, 61073. On the involvement of Herberg and Paul in compensation issues and the controversies about their activities, see also Pross, *Paying for the Past*, pp. 97ff., *passim*. With respect to compensation, it seems there were also efforts by the compensation offices to exclude Herberg as an evaluator when he opted for recognizing mental damage. This becomes clear when one examines a multivolume file of the Bielefeld pension office, where an applicant fought—as documented in many evaluations starting in 1979—for recognition of his mental problems as war-related illness. In 1990, the state social court ruled in favor of recognition following a long legal and evaluative dispute. Versorgungsamt Bielefeld, 143913, vols. 1 and 2; Handakte I a des Landesversorgungsamtes Nordrhein-Westfalen.

124. Ulrich Venzlaff, "Gutachten zur Frage des Zusammenwirkens erlebnisreaktiver, vegetativer und hormonaler Faktoren bei Verfolgungsschäden," in Helmut Paul and Hans-Joachim Herberg, eds., *Psychische Spätschäden nach politischer Verfolgung* (Basel, 1963), pp. 111–124, pp. 111f. See also Walter von Baeyer, "Erlebnisbedingte Verfolgungsschäden," *Der Nervenarzt* 32 (1961), pp. 534–538. In contrast to three years before, von Baeyer now emphasized findings that indicated that "chronic, possibly long-term and irreversible changes of experience and behavior" in survivors of Nazi persecution were "no rarity" (p. 535).

125. Walter von Baeyer et al., "Zur Frage des 'symptomfreien Intervalls' bei erlebnisreaktiven Störungen Verfolgter," in Paul and Herberg, eds., *Psychische Spätschäden*, pp. 125–153, p. 149.

126. Von Baeyer, "Erlebnisbedingte Verfolgungsschäden," pp. 535 and 538.

127. Paul Matussek, "Die Konzentrationslagerhaft als Belastungssituation," *Der Nervenarzt* 32 (1961), pp. 538–542, citation p. 539; von Baeyer, "Verfolgungsschäden," citation p. 538; Wolfgang Jacob, "Gesellschaftliche Voraussetzungen zur Überwindung der KZ-Schäden," *Der Nervenarzt* 32 (1961), pp. 542–545, esp. p. 543.

128. Von Baeyer, "Verfolgungsschäden," p. 538; this is a reference to Alfred Schütz. Clearly evident as well in Walter Mende, "Gutachterliche Probleme bei der Beurteilung erlebnisreaktiver Schädigungen," in Paul and Herberg, *Psychische Spätschäden*, pp. 281–292, pp. 283ff.

129. Matussek, "Konzentrationslagerhaft," p. 542.

130. Jacob, "Gesellschaftliche Voraussetzungen," p. 544.

131. Hermann Witter, "Erlebnisbedingte Schädigung durch Verfolgung," *Der Nervenarzt* 33 (1962), pp. 509–510, p. 509. A description of Witter's position can be found in Pross, *Paying for the Past*, p. 94 with a somewhat different emphasis.

132. Witter, "Erlebnisbedingte Schädigung durch Verfolgung," p. 509.

133. See the discussion in the section "The Psychiatric Treatment of Repatriated Ger-

man Soldiers, 1945–1953" in chapter 4. See Walter von Baeyer, "Der Begriff der Begegnung in der Psychiatrie,' *Der Nervenarzt* 26 (1955), pp. 369–376—considered an authoritative discussion from that period. But von Baeyer's turn to anthropological psychiatry is more clearly expressed in the 1960s than in the previous decade; see, for example, von Baeyer, "Verfolgungsschäden," p. 536. For a look at the circle of proponents of anthropological psychiatry, see Marion Grimm, *Alfred Storch (1888–1962): Daseinsanalyse und anthropologische Psychiatrie* (Gießen, 2004).

134. Witter, "Erlebnisbedingte Schädigung," p. 510.

135. Witter, "Erlebnisbedingte Schädigung," p. 510. Witter complained that in "phenomenological-anthropological diction with its emphasis on the provisory," this problem was often present.

136. Witter, "Erlebnisbedingte Schädigung," p. 510.

137. Walter von Baeyer et al., "'Wissenschaftliche Erkenntnis' oder 'menschliche Wertung' der erlebnisreaktiven Schäden Verfolgter?" *Der Nervenarzt* 34 (1963), pp. 120–123, p. 121.

138. Witter's assertion that the contributions to the Baden-Baden conference should be considered less an "exchange of scientific knowledge" than a "*demonstration* in current affairs" was doubtless one of several remarks that prompted the annoyance. See Witter, "Erlebnisbedingte Schädigung," p. 509; von Baeyer et al., "Wissenschaftliche Erkenntnis," p. 120.

139. See Walter von Baeyer et al., *Psychiatrie der Verfolgten: Psychopathologische und gutachtliche Erfahrungen an Opfern der nationalsozialistischen Verfolgung und vergleichbarer Extrembelastungen* (Berlin, 1964). The authors spoke of 700 compensation evaluations, of which they had statistically analyzed 535 (p. v).

140. Von Baeyer et al., "Wissenschaftliche Erkenntnis," p. 121.

141. Ibid., p. 122.

142. Ibid., p. 121.

143. Ibid., p. 122. See chapter 4, "'Prevailing Doctrine.'"

144. Bonhoeffer, "Vergleichende psychopathologische Erfahrungen," p. 3. Therefore, Bonhoeffer advocated it was "scientifically desirable" that "concentration camp inmates who experienced torture be interviewed with this in mind." But he still did not view the connection between the torture and psychotic states as proven. He wrote as follows: "Naturally, we must also keep in mind that toxic substances that removed inhibition and stimulated speech were also given, so that we must clarify the question of whether it was simply the excessive mental and physical torment that generated the hallucinations." He firmly separated these cases from "experiences of terror and exhaustion" that were part of the "general course of the war."

145. See in chapter 4 the section "The Psychiatric Treatment of Repatriated German Soldiers, 1945–1953."

146. Walter von Baeyer et al., "Wissenschaftliche Erkenntnis," p. 122.

147. Few German psychiatrists would have followed the scientific-medical debates about "late damage" suffered by survivors of Nazi persecution in other countries. An exception was Helmut Paul, "Internationale Erfahrungen mit psychischen Spätschäden," in Paul and Herberg, *Psychische Spätschäden*, pp. 37–84, who offered a differentiated portrait of the international research that also examined national differences.

148. Walter von Baeyer et al., "Zur Frage des 'symptomfreien Intervalles,'" p. 146. In their listing, the authors even included the work of the Danes, which, as already indicated, von Baeyer had elsewhere described as untenable since it was based on physical damage as a cause for the belated emergence of mental symptoms. See in this chapter the section "'Personality Change' in Survivors of Nazi Persecution."

149. Ulrich Venzlaff, "Erlebnishintergrund und Dynamik seelischer Verfolgungsschäden," pp. 95–109, citation p. 104. Of course, Venzlaff knew better: "The explanatory attempts span the entire spectrum, namely, from a largely 'somatic interpretation' based on central nervous damage caused by hunger dystrophy, which is supported by interesting findings"—Venzlaff's example was Leo Eitinger—"and extend to the other end, which is to say, a mainly psychoanalytic interpretive approach, through which this problem complex has been enriched, especially in the United States, through the work of Byschowski, Eissler, Engel, Hoppe, Krystal, and Niederland." Ulrich Venzlaff, "Die Begutachtung psychischer Störungen Verfolgter," *Rechtsprechung zum Wiedergutmachungsrecht* 17 (1966), pp. 196–200, citation p. 196.

150. Walter von Baeyer, "Walter Ritter von Baeyer," in Pongratz, *Psychiatrie in Selbstdarstellungen*, pp. 9–34, p. 29.

151. The problem is addressed, among others, in Ulrich Venzlaff, "Das Problem des mitwirkenden Verschuldens (BGB § 254) in der Neurosenbeurteilung," *Rechtsprechung zum Wiedergutmachungsrecht* 14 (1963), pp. 193–198, pp. 193f.

152. See in this chapter the section "'Personality Change' in Survivors of Nazi Persecution."

153. W. Brunn, "Die entschädigungsrechtliche Problematik psychischer Störungen," *Rechtsprechung zum Wiedergutmachungsrecht* 11 (1960), pp. 481–484, p. 481.

154. U. Kessler, "Kritisches zur Praxis der Entschädigungsverfahren," in Hans-Joachim Herberg, ed., *Spätschäden nach Extrembelastungen: Referate der II. Internationalen Medizinisch-Juristischen Konferenz in Düsseldorf 1969* (Herford, 1971), pp. 322–325, citation p. 325. At the conference, Kessler presented himself as an assistant to Bundestag delegate Martin Hirsch, for whom he was speaking.

155. Brunn, "Die entschädigungsrechtliche Problematik," p. 482.

156. Brunn, "Die entschädigungsrechtliche Problematik," p. 482. Brunn was referring to the BGH decision of June 10, 1958.

157. Brunn, "Die entschädigungsrechtliche Problematik," p. 482. Brunn based his stance on the following principle from the BGH decision: "If an illness caused by persecutory measures persists for a certain period after such persecution, for the sole reason that abnormal mental predisposition on the part of the injured person prevents recovery of his health, then the ongoing state of illness is not determined by predisposition but by persecution, when it is clear that the abnormal predisposition had taken effect (become manifest) as a result of the persecution, and it is not clear that it would also have taken effect without the persecution. These prerequisites are also to be viewed as having been fulfilled when they are probable." BGH decision of May 18, 1960, in *Rechtsprechung zum Wiedergutmachungsrecht* 11 (1960), pp. 453–456, here p. 453.

158. Already determined through a BGH decision of April 8, 1959. *Rechtsprechung zum Wiedergutmachungsrecht* 10 (1959), p. 333.

159. BGH decision of May 18, 1960. *Rechtsprechung zum Wiedergutmachungsrecht* 11 (1960), p. 455.

160. BGH decision of May 18, 1960. A second criterion was that the illness "would also have emerged inevitably . . . on the basis of this predisposition even without the persecution."

161. G. Hand, "Zur Definition der anlagebedingten Leiden im Sinne des § 4 der 2. DV-BEG," *Rechtsprechung zum Wiedergutmachungsrecht* 12 (1961), pp. 103–105, p. 104; Hand, "Zu den Begriffen: 'Anlage, wesentliche Mitverursachung, Manifestation und Krankheit,'" *Rechtsprechung zum Wiedergutmachungsrecht* 14 (1963), pp. 154–156. At the main medical conference of February 7, 1963, in Munich, this text formed a basis for discussing the consequences of the BGH decisions. In BA Koblenz, B 126, 42531, vol. 5. The legal definition of "predispositional illness" (*anlagebedingtes Leiden*) was relevant to the causality question in many forms of illness. For example, illnesses classified by doctors as "age related" could be excluded as "predispositionally determined." See Wolfgang Jacob, "Die entschädigungsrechtliche Beurteilung der Anlagebedingtheit innerer Erkrankungen nach den Gesichtspunkten naturwissenschaftlich-medizinischer Grundlagenforschung," in BA Koblenz, B 126, 42531, vol. 5. Ernst Goetz, "Das 'anlagebedingte Leiden' im Recht der Entschädigung für Opfer national-sozialistischer Verfolgung," *Rechtsprechung zum Wiedergutmachungsrecht* 12 (1961), pp. 246–248, criticized the BGH procedure of legally defining "predispositional illness as such" and thus giving it a meaning it did not possess medically.

162. See Ulrich Venzlaff, "Schizophrenie und Verfolgung," *Rechtsprechung zum Wiedergutmachungsrecht* 12 (1961), pp. 193–196. A few years later, Venzlaff evidently leaned toward a more open position but found no agreement at the main medical conferences. In any case, in their *Psychiatrie der Verfolgten* of 1964 von Baeyer, Häfner, and Kisker maintained that endogenous psychoses, although earlier viewed as "purely hereditary diseases," often resulted "from a web of different causal fields that is difficult to penetrate." "Psychiatric research on causes," they observed, was "more in flux than ever" (p. 110). Also in this sense Walter Schulte, *Über das Problem der seelischen Entstehungsbedingungen von Krankheiten* (Tübingen, 1966), pp. 1of.

163. *Bundesentschädigungsgesetze*, pp. 11, 15. In any case, the assumption of a linkage could also not be disproven. Consequently, showing that health disorders were purely "predispositional" became increasingly difficult in the legal framework outlined above.

164. Brunn, "Die entschädigungsrechtliche Problematik," p. 483 n. 24, maintained "considerable reservations . . . from a legal standpoint" regarding medical ideas that included value judgments.

165. Walter von Baeyer et al., "Wissenschaftliche Erkenntnis," p. 123.

166. According to section 254 of the West German code of civil law (Bürgerliches Gesetzbuch, BGB), in civil compensation proceedings so-called contributory negligence on the part of the claimant needed to be examined. See Venzlaff, "Das Problem des mitwirkenden Verschuldens"; critical of Venzlaff: Karl Heinz Heuer, "Mitwirkendes Verschulden bei Neurose-Schäden?," in *Rechtsprechung zum Wiedergutmachungsrecht* 15 (1964), pp. 429–432.

167. Adolf Pentz, judge at the Higher Regional Court in Frankfurt and an authority on neuroses, in *Rechtsprechung zum Wiedergutmachungsrecht* 17 (1966), pp. 49–54, citation p. 50. Pentz put it as follows: "If someone who is also an agnostic regarding compensation law . . . where the main concern is generally a state of freedom or non-freedom, believes it is impossible to answer this question not only in the specific case at hand but in principle, he will be an unsuitable appraiser. A judge would not be able to follow his findings, since they could already be influenced by his basic viewpoint; he may have forgone a meticulous personality analysis because in his view the real facts cannot be researched. Just as in criminal law gnosticism seems to be prevailing, the civil judge will grant gnosticism the advantage in the realm of neuroses." Pentz also designated it as "legally erroneous" "to commission an evaluator who denies a priori any pathological significance to the symptoms requiring evaluation in the absence of physical damage" (p. 51).

168. The Final Federal Indemnification Law designated a minimum period of one year in a camp. See *Bundesentschädigungsgesetz*, 14th ed. (Munich, 1966), p. 23.

169. Section 31 (2) specified retroactive applicability of the regulation starting October 1, 1953. Section 171 as well, which regulated the award of a hardship settlement, was expanded in response to changes in the status of medical knowledge. Paragraph 2a specified—albeit only starting on September 18, 1965—that such a settlement would also be granted "when the probability of a causal connection between damage to body and health and the persecution cannot be determined only because of uncertainty in medical science with respect to the cause of the illness." *Bundesentschädigungsgesetz*, pp. 23 and 115, here also citation.

170. Eberhard Schubert, "Die derzeitige höchstrichterliche Rechtsprechung zum Neurosen-Problem im Wiedergutmachungsrecht, im Versorgungsrecht und in der gesetzlichen Unfallversicherung," *Rechtsprechung zum Wiedergutmachungsrecht* 19 (1968), pp. 481–490, p. 485.

171. Beginning in the early 1960s, these psychiatrists included primarily William Niederland and Kurt Eissler. See Kurt Eissler, "Die Ermordung von wie vielen seiner Kinder muss ein Mensch symptomfrei ertragen können, um eine normale Konstitution zu haben?," *Psyche* 17 (1963), pp. 241–291, and a collection of evaluations published a good two decades later: William Niederland, *Folgen der Verfolgten: Das Überlebenden-Syndrom Seelenmord* (Frankfurt am Main, 1980). Sometimes illuminating: Wenda Focke, *William G. Niederland: Psychiater der Verfolgten. Seine Zeit—sein Leben—sein Werk. Ein Porträt* (Würzburg, 1992).

172. Those who signed the complaint accused Strauss of being hostile to Jewish refugees, claiming that "they felt 'so rudely treated' during the examination that he seemed more like a 'tormentor' in the concentration camps than a well-meaning medical expert." See Pross, *Paying for the Past*, p. 101.

173. Communication of Goetz (subsection V b) to subsection V a, February 17, 1959, in BA Koblenz, BA 149, 2353, vol. 2. At the fourth conference of the Association of Returnees in June 1957, the attendees had already unanimously accepted the proposal that the association should urge the government authorities to set forth identical requirements in respect to demonstrating causation for disabled Wehrmacht veterans to those that applied to victims of Nazi persecutions. Only those who had suffered physical in-

jury were being referred to here. In any case, the association argued that in these cases as well, the veterans were frequently being denied recognition of their illnesses because it was allegedly predispositional in nature, whereas predispositional illness in the persecuted *was* recognized. The association insisted that this violated the "principle of equality of all citizens." Archiv des Verbandes der Heimkehrer, Bonn, ed., "Beschlüsse des 4. ordentlichen Verbandstages des Verbandes der Heimkehrer, Kriegsgefangenen und Vermißtenangehörigen Deutschlands e. V." (no place [1957]), p. 9.

174. See "Gesetz zur Änderung und Ergänzung des Kriegsopferrechts (Erstes Neuordnungsgesetz) vom Juni 27, 1960," *Bundesgesetzblatt* 1, no. 32 (1960), pp. 453ff.; *Gesetz über die Versorgung der Opfer des Krieges (Bundesversorgungsgesetz)* (Munich, 1965); Reichsbund der Kriegs- und Zivilbeschädigten, Sozialrentner und Hinterbliebenen e. V., ed., *Bundesversorgungsgesetz in der Fassung des Dritten Gesetzes zur Änderung und Ergänzung des Kriegsopferrechts* (Bonn, 1967).

175. In the run-up to the second BVG reorganization act, which took effect in 1964, the Association of Returnees circulated the following proposed formulation: "To the extent that an internment as a prisoner of war . . . was associated with extreme circumstances, the probability of a causal relationship is to be assumed." The object was for legal regulation to determine "in which POW camps and for what period of time extreme circumstances are to be assumed." In the experts' discussion in the Bundesrat's Committee for Labor and Social Policy, individual state delegates apparently argued that belated consequences of extreme circumstances simply no longer existed; and that after such a long time it was in any case impossible for individuals to prove they had been in specific camps at specific times. The proposal of the returnees' association did not prevail. Archiv des Verbandes der Heimkehrer, Bonn: "Wir bleiben uns treu: Ergebnisbericht," pp. 28–30, citation p. 29.

176. The BEG did not require the approximate equivalence of factors. In compensation cases, as explained above, the minimum share doctors had to attribute to persecution as an "exogenous factor" in the emergence of the illness was one-fourth. See Heinz-Harro Rauschelbach, "Unterschiede und Gemeinsamkeiten in der Begutachtung nach dem Bundesentschädigungs- und Bundesversorgungsgesetz," *Der Medizinische Sachverständige* 65 (1969), pp. 248–251.

177. For example, so-called determining exacerbations were measured in different ways. In a reparations case, if a doctor concluded that a preexisting illness had been aggravated in a "determining" manner, then the health damage was considered to be persecution related to the fullest extent. In a similar case, according to the BVG, recognition of the entire illness as "war related" was not possible; reduced earning capacity could only be attributed to the "degree of exacerbation." Rauschelbach, "Unterschiede und Gemeinsamkeiten," p. 249; further examples in Schubert, "Die derzeitige höchstrichterliche Rechtsprechung."

178. See in this chapter the section "'Personality Change' in Survivors of Nazi Persecution."

179. See for instance. BSG, decision of October 29, 1958, in Hermann Breithaupt, ed., *Sammlung von Entscheidungen der Sozialversicherung, Versorgung und Arbeitslosenversicherung* 48 (1959), pp. 152–154; BSG, decision of July 28, 1959, in Breithaupt, *Sammlung von Entscheidungen der Sozialversicherung, Versorgung und Ar-*

beitslosenversicherung 48 (1959), pp. 1108–1110; BSG, decision of November 11, 1959, in Breithaupt, ed., *Sammlung von Entscheidungen der Sozialversicherung, Versorgung und Arbeitslosenversicherung* 49 (1960), pp. 146–149.

180. Law on the Supply of Victims of War, Federal Pensions Act as amended June 6, 1956, Federal Law Gazette 1 (1956), p. 475. Neumann, *Nicht der Rede wert*, p. 158, mistakenly believes the phrase was only added in 1960 to the Restructuring Act. The section of the 1956 Act can be found there in the text.

181. BSG, decision of October 29, 1958, *Sammlung von Entscheidungen der Sozialversicherung* 48 (1959), p. 153. The *Anhaltspunkte für die ärztliche Gutachtertätigkeit im Versorgungswesen* (Bonn, 1958), p. 28, stipulated that the standard of judgment had to be a damaged person with a "normal mental reactive state." The revised edition (Bonn, 1965), p. 23, did not contain this passage.

182. BSG, decision of November 11, 1959, in *Sammlung von Entscheidungen der Sozialversicherung* 49 (1960), p. 148.

183. References to BGH decisions are repeatedly found in decisions of the BSG, for example, in the decision of October 29, 1958, *Sammlung von Entscheidungen der Sozialversicherung* 48 (1959), p. 153.

184. Decision of the Bavarian state social court, November 14, 1960, *Sammlung von Entscheidungen der Sozialversicherung* 50 (1961), pp. 151–155, 151, 153. In respect to the medical concept of disease the court referred to the standard work by Georg Schöneberg, ed., *Die ärztliche Beurteilung Beschädigter*, 2nd ed. (Darmstadt, 1955).

185. Decision of the Bavarian state social court, November 14, 1960, in *Sammlung von Entscheidungen der Sozialversicherung* 50 (1961), p. 153; likewise: Decision of the state social court of Rhineland-Palatinate, May 12, 1964, *Sammlung von Entscheidungen der Sozialversicherung* 53 (1964), pp. 687–690, p. 689.

186. See, for example, Eberhard Schubert, "Die Neurose: Ihr Wesen und ihre Bedeutung in der Sozialversicherung," *Die Sozialgerichtsbarkeit* 10 (1963), pp. 321–327; Max Kerschbaumer, "Die Neurose in der Unfallversicherung und Kriegsopferversorgung," *Der Medizinische Sachverständige* 61 (1965), pp. 134–142, esp. pp. 135f., here with a reference to a "conceptual definition considered adequate until now for legal usage, according to which neurosis is to be understood as an abnormal mental attitude or abnormal development expressed in mental, physical, or mental and physical suffering that lacks an objective basis."

187. See, for example, decision of the Federal Social Court, August 20, 1963, cited from Günter Hennies, "Kriegsopferversorgung," *Der Medizinische Sachverständige* 60 (1964), pp. 71–72, citation p. 71.

188. Walter von Baeyer, "Erlebnisreaktive Störungen und ihre Bedeutung für die Begutachtung," *Deutsche Medizinische Wochenschrift* 83 (1958), pp. 2317–2322, citation p. 2319.

189. Von Baeyer, "Erlebnisreaktive Störungen," p. 2319.

190. Ulrich Venzlaff, "Grundsätzliche Betrachtungen über die Begutachtung erlebnisbedingter seelischer Störungen nach rassischer und politischer Verfolgung," *Rechtsprechung zum Wiedergutmachungsrecht* 10 (1959), pp. 289–292.

191. Venzlaff, "Erlebnishintergrund," p. 97.

192. Von Baeyer et al., *Psychiatrie der Verfolgten*, p. iii.

193. Venzlaff, "Erlebnishintergrund," p. 95.

194. Venzlaff, "Grundsätzliche Betrachtungen," citation pp. 289 and 290.

195. Von Baeyer, "Verfolgungsschäden," p. 536. "Individual, biographical significance" varied, von Baeyer indicated.

196. Von Baeyer, "Verfolgungsschäden," pp. 536.

197. A. Köhler, "Die Neurose: Ihr Wesen und ihre Bedeutung in der Sozialversicherung," *Der Medizinische Sachverständige* 60 (1964), p. 165, cites Eberhard Schubert (Schubert was a judge on the Federal Social Court). In this sense, see also Günter Hennies, "Zum Neurose-Problem. BGH-Beschluß vom 13. Juli 1963," *Der Medizinische Sachverständige* 60 (1964), pp. 119–120, p. 120.

198. Venzlaff, "Grundsätzliche Betrachtungen," citation pp. 289f.

199. Hennies, "Neurose-Problem," p. 120.

200. *Anhaltspunkte für die ärztliche Gutachtertätigkeit im Versorgungswesen* (Bonn, 1965), p. 23.

201. In order to counteract doctors' fears that awarding pensions would simply reinforce "neurotics'" sense of being ill, the Federal Social Court ruled in a decision of April 7, 1964, that "measures to retain, improve, and restore earning capacity" were to receive precedence over pensions. See passages from the decision in Günter Hennies, "Neurose und Leistungen aus der Rentenversicherung," *Der Medizinische Sachverständige* 55 (1964), pp. 169–175, p. 171. Citing his medical experience, Hennies himself underscored that "to the extent it is possible and promising, medical help should be provided first and as soon as possible; then, if necessary, vocational advice and assistance in finding work, but never a pension! . . . The neurotic is never helped with a pension; rather, healing is made more difficult if not rendered fully impossible" (p. 172).

202. Hennies, "Neurose und Leistungen," p. 124. Possibly, this regulation had greater impact on the evaluation of former child refugees than on the applications of the men who shortly before the end of the war, at an age of sixteen or seventeen, had become members of the Volkssturm.

203. Hennies, "Neurose und Leistungen," p. 124.

204. See, for instance, Karl Leonhard, "Lassen sich in der Begutachtung von Neurosen keine schärferen Gesichtspunkte gewinnen?," *Der Medizinische Sachverständige* 62 (1966), pp. 201–210.

205. Citation from Hennies, "Neurose," p. 171.

206. Köhler, "Die Neurose," p. 165, citing Eberhard Schubert.

207. See Friedrich Panse, "Der Krankheitswert der Neurose," *Der Medizinische Sachverständige* 61 (1965), pp. 114–120.

208. See in chapter 4 the section "Lessons of War."

209. Panse, "Der Krankheitswert der Neurose," p. 119, added that 38 percent of recruits were weeded out beforehand due to neuropsychiatric symptoms, which underlined the significance of the high dismissal rate.

210. See esp. Pross, *Paying for the Past.*

211. See Winkler, *Männlichkeit*; Biess, *Homecomings*; Moeller, *War Stories.*

212. In the late 1950s, Helmut Paul initially devoted himself exclusively to late (mental) consequences following dystrophy; see, for instance "Die Psyche des Hungernden

und des Dystrophikers," in Schenck and Nathusius, eds., *Extreme Lebensverhältnisse und ihre Folgen*, vol. 5 (1961), pp. 5–127. In 1962, he then began a research project financed by the Association of Returnees that considered the mental consequences on all returning soldiers (including those who had not been captured). The study was only published in 1986, three years after Helmut Paul's death, when two doctors at the Zwiefalten psychiatric hospital, commissioned by the Foundation of Returnees, revised the "preliminary rough draft." In respect to "mental disorders," Paul evidently concluded that these were more frequent among former soldiers who had not been POWs than among the others. This corresponded to the thrust of his concluding findings that "isolated hardships such as long imprisonment, dystrophy, and different sorts of brain damage can lead to diminished performance capacity," whereas, to Paul's surprise, "especially severe hardship consisting of a combination of several of these factors" could actually lead to improved capacity. As a possible explanation, Paul suggested that particularly damaged individuals either died early or were released from the POW camps early, while only the "most capable and intelligent" could actually survive long, hard years of captivity. And after release, he observed, these individuals were "able to integrate into the meanwhile altered circumstances in the homeland." See Helmut A. Paul, "Einflüsse extremer Belastungen auf die psychischen und psychosozialen Verhältnisse ehemaliger Kriegsgefangener," in *Extreme Lebensverhältnisse als Risikofaktoren*, vol. 8 (Stuttgart, 1986), pp. 37ff. and p. 89, *passim*.

213. See, for instance, Helmut Paul, "Erforschung der Spätfolgen von Gefangenschaft und Deportierung," *Ärztliche Praxis* 13 (1961), pp. 1565–1566. According to Pross, *Paying for the Past*, pp. 99f., few German doctors, among them Venzlaff and Kluge, dared to appear at congresses of the International Federation of Resistance Fighters.

214. That does not mean that there weren't also many attempts within the scientific debate to elucidate differentiated mental stress for the individual groups of victims, survivors, and veterans whereby it was entirely not the case that a distinction was drawn only between German POWs and the victims of Nazism. For example, it was occasionally claimed, as indicated above, that resistance fighters withstood Nazi terror better, even in the camps, than those who were suffering "racial" persecution. Meanwhile, others conjectured that persecution and internment in a camp had affected German Jews more severely that Polish or Russian Jews since the latter had always known nothing other than a life of isolation and persecution. See, for example, the contribution by the psychiatrist and psychoanalyst Robert Gronner in Henry Krystal, ed., *Massive Psychic Trauma* (New York, 1968), pp. 197.

215. See Krystal, *Massive Psychic Trauma*, pp. 194f. (statement by Wulf Grobin).

216. Krystal, *Massive Psychic Trauma*, pp. 195 (statement by Henry Krystal).

217. Von Baeyer et al., *Psychiatrie der Verfolgten*, p. 41.

218. Robert Jay Lifton, *Thought Reform and the Psychology of Totalitarianism: A Study of Brainwashing in China* (New York, 1961).

219. Von Baeyer et al., *Psychiatrie der Verfolgten*, p. 43.

220. Von Baeyer et al., *Psychiatrie der Verfolgten*, p. 41.

221. Von Baeyer et al., *Psychiatrie der Verfolgten*, pp. 46f. The authors referred to

Hans H. Kornhuber, "Psychologie und Psychiatrie der Kriegsgefangenschaft," in *Soziale und angewandte Psychiatrie*, pp. 631–742.

222. Hermann Witter, "Zur Kausalität bei sogenannten Neurosen," *Der Medizinische Sachverständige* 61 (1965), pp. 143–148, p. 147.

223. See, for instance, Kolle, "Opfer," p. 152; Kluge, "Folgen," p. 463; and the argument of an evaluator in Versorgungsamt Bielefeld, 143913, vols. 1 and 2; Hand Act I, State Pension Office of North Rhine-Westphalia.

224. See Eberhard Lungershausen and H. Matiar-Vahar, "Erlebnisreaktive psychische Dauerschädigungen nach Kriegsgefangenschaft und Deportation," *Der Nervenarzt* 39 (1968), pp. 123–126, citation p. 123.

225. Lungershausen and Matiar-Vahar, "Erlebnisreaktive psychische Dauerschädigungen," p. 124.

226. Lungershausen and Matiar-Vahar, "Erlebnisreaktive psychische Dauerschädigungen," p. 124.

227. Lungershausen and Matiar-Vahar, "Erlebnisreaktive psychische Dauerschädigungen," p. 125.

CHAPTER 7

1. See, for example, Birgit Schwelling, *Heimkehr—Erinnerung—Integration: Der Verband der Heimkehrer, die ehemaligen Kriegsgefangenen und die westdeutsche Nachkriegsgesellschaft* (Paderborn, 2010); Manig, *Politik der Ehre*; Kühne, "Zwischen Vernichtungskrieg und Freizeitgesellschaft"; Jay Lockenour, *Soldiers as Citizens: Former Wehrmacht Officers in the Federal Republic of Germany, 1945–1955* (Lincoln, NE, 2001).

2. See Albrecht Lehmann, *Gefangenschaft und Heimkehr: Deutsche Kriegsgefangene in der Sowjetunion* (Munich, 1986); the articles in Anette Kaminsky, ed., *Heimkehr 1948: Geschichte und Schicksale deutscher Kriegsgefangener* (Munich, 1998); and Hilger, *Deutsche Kriegsgefangene*.

3. Andreas Etges, "Der Deutungswandel des Zweiten Weltkriegs in US-amerikanischen Filmen am Beispiel von 'The Best Years of Our Lives' und 'Saving Private Ryan,'" in Bernhard Chiari et al., eds., *Krieg und Militär im Film des 20. Jahrhunderts* (Munich, 2003), pp. 163–178, basically points to a similar shift in the United States. The 1946 film *The Best Years of our Lives* depicted the extraordinary adaptive challenges of a physically and emotionally wounded veteran in the immediate postwar era, thereby representing a period during which World War II was not recalled exclusively as a "good war"; a few years later this theme had been left out of films and replaced by portrayals of heroes.

4. On the "rubble films," see, among others, Robert R. Shandley, *Rubble Films: German Cinema in the Shadow of the Third Reich* (Philadelphia, 2001); Weckel, "The *Mitläufer*"; Thomas Brandlmeier, "Von Hitler zu Adenauer: Deutsche Trümmerfilme," in Hilmar Hoffmann and Walter Schobert, eds., *Zwischen Gestern und Morgen: Westdeutscher Nachkriegsfilm 1946–1962* (Frankfurt am Main, 1989), pp. 33–59. With a

view to war prisoners and returning soldiers in postwar films of the 1950s: Moeller, *War Stories*, pp. 123ff. In general on the history of German postwar films see esp. Reichel, *Erfundene Erinnerung*; Frank Stern, "Film in the 1950s: Passing Images of Guilt and Responsibility," in Hanna Schissler, ed., *The Miracle Years: A Cultural History of West Germany, 1949–1968* (Princeton, NJ, 2001), pp. 266–280; Heide Fehrenbach, *Cinema in Democratizing Germany: Reconstructing National Identity after Hitler* (Chapel Hill, NC, 1995); Irmgard Wilharm, *Bewegte Spuren: Studien zur Zeitgeschichte im Film* (Hannover, 2006), esp. pp. 95ff.

5. *Die Mörder sind unter uns*, film, 1946, written and directed by Wolfgang Staudte; *Irgendwo in Berlin*, film, 1946, written and directed by Gerhard Lamprecht.

6. Brandlmeier, "Von Hitler zu Adenauer," p. 34, is thus mistaken in asserting that the rubble films had little to do with everyday life in postwar Germany.

7. *Und über uns der Himmel*, screenplay: Gerhard Grindel, director: Josef von Baky, produced in 1947. Numbering among these films is also *Liebe 47*, which is based on Wolfgang Borchert's *Draußen vor der Tür* (screenplay: Wolfgang Liebeneiner, director: Wolfgang Liebeneiner, produced 1949). Here we see former noncommissioned officer Beck, a returnee from Russia, who nearly breaks under his sense of guilt about the death of eleven soldiers. His nightmares are haunted by the relatives of the soldiers. For an analysis of the different performances of Borchert's play in radio, stage, and film versions see Weckel, "Spielarten."

8. Exemplary for this is the second protagonist in *Die Mörder sind unter uns*, Susanne Wallner (Hildegard Knef), who returns to Berlin from a concentration camp and finds Mertens in her bomb-damaged apartment. Instead of throwing him out, she arranges matters with him. In contrast to Mertens, Wallner is a roll-up-your-sleeves, forward-looking type who immediately goes back to work. See Ulrike Weckel, "Die Mörder sind unter uns oder: Vom Verschwinden der Opfer," *WerkstattGeschichte* 25 (2000), pp. 105–115.

9. For reflections on the screening out of the new order of relations between the sexes, Weckel, "Die Mörder, pp. 107ff. On changes in the depiction of gender roles in German films of the early postwar years see Massimo Perinelli, *Liebe 47—Gesellschaft 49. Geschlechterverhältnisse in der deutschen Nachkriegszeit: Eine Analyse des Films "Liebe 47"* (Münster, 1999).

10. This is discussed in greater detail in chapter 4 in the section "The Psychiatric Treatment of Repatriated German Soldiers, 1945–1953."

11. The film *Ballad of Berlin* (*Berliner Ballade*, 1948; screenplay by Günter Neumann, directed by Robert A. Stemmle), a satire that should be considered one of the later rubble films, portrays a society that no longer pays any attention to the returnees, or if it does, then it is in the form of annoyance. It is the "ballad" of the returnee Otto Normalverbraucher ("Otto Normal Consumer"), who dreams of for once eating to the point of complete satiation; the story looks back from the year 2048. When the Wehrmacht veteran arrives on the scene, the narrator of the film comments on the presumed reaction of spectators in 1948 in a voice that is meant to reproduce the irritated, bored, and weary mood of the day: "Oh, dear, another movie about returning veterans," the audience will have said, because in those days such images were everywhere. Later scenes emphasize the ignorance and snideness with which an already prospering society confronts the veterans.

12. "Gedächtnisschwund und schwache Nerven: Psychische Folgen des Zusammenbruchs—Was sagt der Nervenarzt?," *Süddeutsche Zeitung*, September 30, 1947, p. 3. Even more frequently, we find generally formulated complaints that the visible rubble of the buildings only demonstrated part of the war damage, since "strength of mind" had also been destroyed. See, for instance, "Stunde der Prüfung," *Die Zeit*, February 28, 1946, p. 1. In an article entitled "Überwindung seelischer Depression" ("Overcoming Mental Depression"), a local Bremen paper, the *Weser-Kurier*, September 11, 1948, p. 4, commented that "present-day mental hardship" cried out for a remedy "that could bring lasting healing to all the unhappy people who have lost their mental balance." To this end, the article indicated, a Society for Practical Psychology had formed in Bremen, which would feature a number of "enlightening lectures" by pastors and doctors. This apparently had been received with much public interest.

13. See the numerous examples in Part I of this book, above all in chapter 1 the section "The Echo of Fear" in chapter 2 the section "Delusion and Reality"; and see chapter 3 "Social Rubble."

14. "Gedächtnisschwund und schwache Nerven" *Süddeutsche Zeitung*, September 30, 1947, p. 3.

15. As could be read, for example, in *Stuttgarter Zeitung*, August 9, 1947, p. 3, at this time the first figures from the interior ministry became available concerning the "preliminary results of the official registration of war prisoners and missing persons from the former Wehrmacht in Württemberg-Baden." Other examples: "Deutsche Kriegsgefangene in Rußland," *Frankfurter Hefte* 2 (1947), pp. 331–332; *Weser-Kurier*, October 2, 1948, p. 2. The form of reporting clearly reflects the fact that the main concern was achieving some initial clarity about how many soldiers were actually still living and could therefore be expected as returnees. See above all Gregor, "Is He Still Alive"; and Kühne, "Zwischen Vernichtungskrieg und Freizeitgesellschaft," p. 91, with examples for a meeting of German veterans in 1952.

16. As very early discussions of German POWs' experiences in French and in Russian camps, see respectively "Deutsche Kriegsgefangene," *Stuttgarter Zeitung*, October 31, 31, 1945, p. 1 and "Die Heimkehrer berichten: Erlebnisse aus russischen Kriegsgefangenen-Lagern," *Die Zeit*, August 29, 1946, p. 2. On the amplifying role of both churches, see Biess, *Homecomings*, pp. 56ff. See also Michael Borchard, *Die deutschen Kriegsgefangenen in der Sowjetunion: Zur politischen Bedeutung der Kriegsgefangenenfrage 1949–1955* (Düsseldorf, 2000).

17. This shift is often overlooked. Early efforts to limit oneself to objective data and facts such as the tasks assigned to the POWs in the Soviet camps are often striking. There were presumably various reasons for the marked change of tone, including the escalating Cold War and the amnesty process that was about to begin in West Germany, together with the obviously worse condition of German returnees who had been in the Soviet Union as compared to those in the West. An additional factor would have been the near complete release of the latter group from the POW camps by 1948–1949.

18. See "Erholungsbedürftige Heimkehrer finden gute Unterkunft," *Stuttgarter Zeitung*, December 10, 1947.

19. "Erholungsbedürftige Heimkehrer finden gute Unterkunft."

20. The appeal was mainly directed at families and the authorities. See "Ehen in der Krise," *Weser-Kurier*, October 13, 1945, p. 3; "Kriegsgefangene in ärztlicher Behand-

lung," *Stuttgarter Zeitung*, November 19, 1947; "Heimkehrer ohne Heimkehr," *Die Zeit*, July 22, 1948; "Heimkehrer ohne Heim," *Die Zeit*, September 30, 1948, p. 1. See also, among others, Franka Schneider, "'Einigkeit im Unglück'? Berliner Eheberatungsstellen zwischen Ehekrise und Wiederaufbau," in Naumann, *Nachkrieg in Deutschland*, pp. 206–226.

21. "Die Heimkehrer berichten," *Die Zeit*, August 29, 1946, p. 2.

22. Typical in this respect: "Mehr Kalorien für Russlandheimkehrer," *Stuttgarter Zeitung*, August 9, 1947; "Kriegsgefangene in ärztlicher Behandlung," *Stuttgarter Zeitung*, November 19, 1947.

23. "Ein Heimkehrer-Sanatorium in Adelheide," *Weser-Kurier*, April 2, 1949 (a typical article).

24. In actuality, during the first postwar years the disabled veterans appear to have received special attention in the newspaper columns. A year after the end of the war, *Die Zeit* commented that one had a special duty toward these men because they had "sacrificed their best, namely their health"—a demonstration, the article concluded, of "the ultimate fulfillment of duty." See "Kriegsbeschädigte," *Die Zeit*, May 16, 1946, p. 7. On the disabled Wehrmacht veterans as a model: "Ist der Amputierte ein Krüppel? Der Appell eines Kriegsverletzten," *Weser-Kurier*, August 14, 1946, p. 3.

25. "Das Tor der guten Hoffnung: Besuch im Hospital der Kriegsversehrten," *Die Zeit*, July 11, 1946, p. 2. Two later articles are distinctly less optimistic: "Die Sorge für die Kriegsbeschädigten," *Frankfurter Hefte* 5 (1950), pp. 124–125; "Versehrtsein als Schicksal," *Frankfurter Hefte* 8 (1953), pp. 751–756.

26. This intention is clear in, for instance, "Ist der Amputierte ein Krüppel? Der Appell eines Kriegsverletzten," *Weser-Kurier*, August 14, 1946, p. 3. A similar tendency could also be observed after World War I, once a sufficient workforce became available after demobilization. At the time, the German labor ministry tried to intervene with the help of a "law for the employment of the seriously disabled" enacted on April 6, 1920. In firms with twenty-five employees or more, 2 percent of the jobs were to be set aside for officially recognized severely disabled men. Following the end of World War II, passage of the "law concerning the gravely disabled" on June 16, 1953, again established a nationwide legal remedy in West Germany. In firms with more than seven employees, 6 percent were to be assigned to such persons; in government agencies the figure was set at 10 percent. For every nonoccupied, mandatory position, a compensation fee of 50 DM was to be remitted. See Deborah Cohen, *The War Come Home: Disabled Veterans in Britain and Germany, 1914–1939* (Berkeley, CA, 2001), p. 157; Neumann, *Nicht der Rede wert*, pp. 146 f; Uta Krukowska, *Kriegsversehrte: Allgemeine Lebensbedingungen und medizinische Versorgung deutscher Versehrter nach dem Zweiten Weltkrieg in der britischen Besatzungszone Deutschlands—dargestellt am Beispiel der Stadt Hamburg* (Hamburg, 2006), pp. 109ff.

27. Sabine Kienitz, "Körper-Beschädigungen: Kriegsinvalidität und Männlichkeitskonstruktionen in der Weimarer Republik," in Karen Hagemann and Stefanie Schüler-Springorum, eds., *Heimat-Front: Militär und Geschlechterverhältnisse im Zeitalter der Weltkriege* (Frankfurt am Main, 2002), pp. 188–207, esp. pp. 198ff. Beate Fieseler, "Der Kriegsinvalide in sowjetischen Spielfilmen der Kriegs- und Nachkriegszeit (1944 bis 1964)," in Bernhard Chiari et al., eds., *Krieg und Militär im Film des 20. Jahrhun-*

derts (Munich, 2003), pp. 199–222, makes similar observations in respect to the public representation of the war disabled in the Soviet Union.

28. See "Versehrtsein als Schicksal," p. 753. As an example of an explicit delimitation of amputees from the brain damaged, written in a clearly stigmatizing tenor, see "Ist der Amputierte ein Krüppel?"

29. We can observe this above all in debates on the sexual order and the "crisis of marriage." See, among others, Schneider, "Einigkeit im Unglück," p. 214; Uta Poiger, "Krise der Männlichkeit: Remaskulinisierung in beiden deutschen Staaten," in Naumann, *Nachkrieg in Deutschland*, pp. 227–263, pp. 228f.

30. Detlef Briesen and Klaus Weinhauer, eds., *Jugend, Delinquenz und gesellschaftlicher Wandel: Bundesrepublik Deutschland und USA nach dem Zweiten Weltkrieg* (Essen, 2006); Imanuel Baumann, *Dem Verbrechen auf der Spur: Eine Geschichte der Kriminologie und Kriminalpolitik in Deutschland, 1880 bis 1980* (Göttingen, 2006).

31. Rüdiger Proske and Walter Weymann-Weyhe, "Wir aus dem Kriege: Der Weg der jüngeren Generation," *Frankfurter Hefte* 3 (1948), pp. 792–803, citation p. 792.

32. Proske and Weymann-Weyhe, "Wir aus dem Kriege," pp. 793f. Here the authors referred to a book by Max Picard, *Hitler in uns selbst* (Zurich, 1946).

33. Proske and Weymann-Weyhe, "Wir aus dem Kriege," p. 794.

34. Proske and Weymann-Weyhe, "Wir aus dem Kriege," p. 794.

35. Proske and Weymann-Weyhe, "Wir aus dem Kriege," pp. 795f., citation p. 796.

36. Proske and Weymann-Weyhe, "Wir aus dem Kriege," p. 797.

37. See in detail, Jörg Echternkamp, "Wut auf die Wehrmacht? Vom Bild der deutschen Soldaten in der unmittelbaren Nachkriegszeit," in Rolf-Dieter Müller und Hans-Erich Volkmann, eds., *Die Wehrmacht: Mythos und Realität* (Munich, 1999), pp. 1058–1080, esp. pp. 1060ff.

38. What also comes to mind in this context is the political and moral mission of the press, which at times had "antimilitarism" on its banner. See Echternkamp, "Wut auf die Wehrmacht," p. 1060.

39. See Biess, *Homecomings*; Moeller, *War Stories*; Borchard, *Die deutschen Kriegsgefangenen in der Sowjetunion: Zur politischen Beinterpretation der Kriegsgefangenenfrage 1949–1955* (Düsseldorf, 2000).

40. "'Stacheldrahtkrankheit' der Gefangenen," *Die Zeit*, January 20, 1949, p. 10.

41. Walter Hemsing, "Die seelische Situation der Kriegsgefangenen und die innere Gesundung des Heimkehrers," talk delivered at the conference of the Association for the Cultural Support of War Prisoners and Returnees, Schwäbisch Hall, June 31, 1948, in BA Koblenz, B 150, 339 (vol. 1). In the same direction: Walter Hemsing, "Seelische Not hinter Stacheldraht," *Caritas* 49 (1948), pp. 6–10, pp. 6f.

42. "Stacheldrahtkrankheit der Gefangenen," *Die Zeit*, January 20, 1949, p. 10.

43. "Stacheldrahtkrankheit der Gefangenen." On the basis of official reports on postwar living conditions in Germany by the British occupation authorities in 1945, Diehl, *Thanks of the Fatherland*, p. 69, indicates there were reports of returnees who returned to their POW camps after finding their houses destroyed or their close relatives no longer alive.

44. One example is the three-part series in *Die Zeit*, "Was sie in Sowjetrußland erlebten: Berichte deutscher Kriegsgefangener," August 24, 1950, p. 9; August 31, 1950,

p. 9; September 7, 1950, p. 9. The three installments can be translated as follows: "Old Tyranny and New Injustice"; "The Imperative of the Headcount"; and "The Secret of the Eastern Mentality."

45. "Was sie in Sowjetrußland erlebten," part 1, *Die Zeit*, August 24, 1950. "Seelen-qual in Kriegsgefangenschaft" ("Mental Torment during POW Internment") was, in turn, the title of an article in *Weser-Kurier*, October 18, 1949, p. 2; but the article did not address the question of whether the POWs were holding up mentally during their long imprisonment in the camps. Rather, the term "mental torment (*Seelenqual*) was meant to designate the extent of injustice meted out to the POWs who continued to be held in camps east of West Germany. The article left no doubt that in this question support from the United States was certain: Word was out in "Washington circles," readers were in-formed, that Soviet policies toward the POWs constituted "unjustified torment inflicted on German men, which cast scorn on all humanity."

46. This was especially the case for the patient files from the first five postwar years. To choose two cases discussed above: in HBAB, Bestand Morija, 3959, Rudolf R.'s mother speaks in 1946 of her son's "nervous breakdown" after his return from a POW camp; in HBAB, Bestand Morija, 4946, Rudolf B. declares in 1949 that since being wounded his "nerves" have been on edge. In the course of his psychiatric treatment, he decides to apply for a larger war pension since he is convinced that his "nervous break-down" is a result of injury incurred as a soldier. In this second case, the doctor's official diagnosis is "psychopathic reaction."

47. "'Stacheldrahtkrankheit' der Gefangenen."

48. It seems that in West Germany the period was characterized by a growing stream of people who were consulting "miracle doctors" and "practicing healers," including many certified doctors whose methods were similar to those of the miracle doctors. This tendency was perceived as alarming, but also as a symptom of an age that had a strong need to view sick people in a nontraditional way. No warning was, however, issued about psychosomatic research. Rather it was considered to be one of the more promis-ing approaches. See "Ein Psychologe zum Fall Gröning," *Süddeutsche Zeitung*, July 16, 1949, and the discussion in chapter 5, the section "The Dispute about Hereditability."

49. See in general Harrington, *Suche nach Ganzheit*; Martin Dehli, *Leben als Kon-flikt: Zur Biografie Alexander Mitscherlichs* (Göttingen, 2007); Tobias Freimüller, *Al-exander Mitscherlich: Gesellschaftsdiagnosen und Psychoanalyse nach Hitler* (Göt-tingen, 2007). Idealizing: Günter Goldbach, *Der ganze Mensch im Blickfeld: Aus der Geschichte der psychosomatischen Medizin in Deutschland* (Baden-Baden, 2006).

50. See, for example: "Medizinischer Massenmord," *Süddeutsche Zeitung*, Decem-ber 12, 1946, p. 1; "Das ärztliche Experiment," *Süddeutsche Zeitung*, December 12, 1946, p. 2; "Sühne für ungezählte Verbrechen," *Süddeutsche Zeitung*, December 21, 1946, p. 2; "Unmenschliche Wissenschaft," *Weser-Kurier*, October 30, 1946, p. 2; "Sterilisierung als Waffe: Erschütternde Zeugenaussagen im Nürnberger Ärzteprozeß," *Weser-Kurier*, December 18, 1946, p. 2; "Krise der Humanität," in *Die Zeit*, February 13 1947, p. 3.

51. See, among others, "Vom Arzt, vom Kranken und von der Gesundheit: Gedan-ken zum Nürnberger Ärzteprozeß," *Süddeutsche Zeitung*, March 8, 1947, p. 5; Hedwig Conrad-Martius, "Wie hängen Leib und Seele zusammen," *Süddeutsche Zeitung*, Sep-tember 4, 1948, p. 5.

52. With reference to the postwar period, see also in chapter 4 the section "The Psychiatric Treatment of Repatriated German Soldiers, 1945–1953" and in chapter 5 the section "The Dispute about Hereditability." See Ackermann, "Das Schweigen der Flüchtlingskinder," p. 440, explicitly referring to Mitscherlich, who "in 1947 recommended his science as a key to Germany's 'renewal' and even to the 'happiness' of its youth."

53. Citation from Jürgen Peter, "Unmittelbare Reaktionen auf den Prozeß," in Ebbinghaus and Dörner, *Vernichten und Heilen*, pp. 452–475, p. 459; Alexander Mitscherlich and Fred Mielke, *Das Diktat der Menschenverachtung: Der Nürnberger Ärzteprozeß und seine Quellen* (Heidelberg, 1947). As Peter shows, Mitscherlich's assessment at the time was pronouncedly contradictory: elsewhere he expressed strong satisfaction that the publication "received much attention within the country and abroad." In Mitscherlich's autobiography (*Ein Leben für die Psychoanalyse: Anmerkungen zu meiner Zeit* [Frankfurt am Main, 1984]) the only assessment is negative (see Peter, pp. 458f., citation p. 458).

54. See, for example, "Vom Arzt, vom Kranken und von der Gesundheit: Gedanken zum Nürnberger Ärzteprozeß," *Süddeutsche Zeitung*, March 8, 1947, p. 5, here primarily with respect to Mitscherlich's writings.

55. Both over the course of the Nuremberg doctors' trials as well as during subsequent proceedings against Nazi doctors, there were news reports that the murders of the sick included "old, infirm, and convalescent individuals without any 'assessment of their condition,'" as *Der Spiegel* reported in 1950, for example. This was presumably the reason that the dismay in West German society was especially great. "Listen mit roten Kreuzen," *Der Spiegel*, May 18, 1950, pp. 8–9, citation p. 8. Still a standard work on Nazi euthanasia: Schmuhl, *Rassenhygiene*. Instead of a large number of individual studies, see also the broader-based overview by Winfried Süß, *Der "Volkskörper" im Krieg: Gesundheitspolitik, Gesundheitsverhältnisse und Krankenmord im nationalsozialistischen Deutschland, 1939–1945* (Munich, 2003), with extensive bibliographical references. An obvious reason why details of the euthanasia program caused such indignation was that the program was directed at "defective" people from ordinary, "Aryan" German families.

56. See, among others, "Zehntausende in den Gaskammern von Grafeneck: 'Grauenhaft sachliches' Prozeßmaterial im Rittersaal—Euthanasie-Befehl und ärztliches Gewissen," *Süddeutsche Zeitung*, July 2, 1949. Also illuminating in this context: the report on the trial of a psychiatrist who was suspected of having arranged to have his wife committed to a psychiatric hospital on three occasions in order to free himself of her. The case caused a public furor and vividly illustrated the tense relationship to the field of psychiatry; one letter to the editor referred to a complete disappearance of the "relationship of trust" to the field of psychiatry. See the reporting in *Die Zeit* starting in November 1950; esp. a letter to the editor of January 4, 1951. On the Corten case in greater detail: Cornelia Brink, "Zwangseinweisungen in die Psychiatrie," in Herbert, *Wandlungsprozesse*, pp. 467–507, pp. 469ff.; Thorsten Noack, "Über Kaninchen und Giftschlangen—Psychiatrie und Öffentlichkeit in der frühen Bundesrepublik," in Heiner Fangerau and Karen Nolte, eds., *"Moderne" Anstaltspsychiatrie im 19. und 20. Jahrhundert: Legitimation und Kritik* (Stuttgart, 2006), pp. 311–340.

57. See "Immer neue Methoden der Psychoanalyse," *Die Zeit*, January 11, 1951, p.

11; for a description of caprice in psychiatric institutions: "'Ich war im Irrenhaus': Nachhaltige Eindrücke und der Protest eines geistig Normalen," *Frankfurter Allgemeine Zeitung*, November 2, 1949, p. 10.

58. See, for example, "Krankheit bedeutet häufig Krise: Über die psychosomatische Medizin—Eine Wissenschaft am Anfang," *Die Zeit*, May 5, 1949; "Über den Sinn der Krankheit: Umschaltung der Medizin vom Patienten auf den Menschen—Thesen aus der Hamburger Rektoratsrede von Arthur Jores," *Die Zeit*, November 23, 1950, p. 4.

59. See, for example, "Heimkehrer, die keine sind," *Die Zeit*, May 14, 1953; "Dystrophie: Die Krankheit der Heimkehrer," *Der Spiegel*, October 7, 1953, pp. 26–27; Hauptstaatsarchiv (HStA) Stuttgart EA/8002, Bü 13: "Die Heimkehrer-Krankheit. Das Schreckgespenst der Dystrophie," in *Badische Rundschau*, November 21–22, 1953; HStA Stuttgart EA/8002, Bü 14: "Die Heimkehrer-Krankheit. Stoffwechselentgleisung und Kontaktschwierigkeiten hängen zusammen," *Deutsche Zeitung*, October 28, 1953, p. 12; "Wie geht es unseren Kriegsgefangenen? Erste Ärztetagung des Heimkehrerverbandes—Späte Schäden schwer zu heilen," *Stuttgarter Zeitung*, April 20, 1953, p. 6; "Heimkehrer in seelischer Not. Reihenuntersuchungen nach Jahren notwendig," *Deutsches Volksblatt*, December 16, 1953, p. 3. Also see the discussion of dystrophy in chapter 4, the section "The Psychiatric Treatment of Repatriated German Soldiers, 1945–1953."

60. Gauger, *Dystrophie*. On Gauger as an individual see the discussion in in chapter 5, "The Dispute about Hereditability." Gauger's book was also embraced and recommended by the West German Lutheran church. The chancery, which was primarily concerned with the effect of dystrophic illness (in the form of mental injury as well) on marriage, in a letter of November 4, 1953, to all West German Lutheran churches explicitly pointed out the book. Landeskirchliches Archiv Bielefeld, C 11-04, vol. 4.

61. For greater detail, see in chapter 4 the section "The Psychiatric Treatment of Repatriated German Soldiers, 1945–1953."

62. "Dystrophie: Die Krankheit der Heimkehrer," p. 26.

63. "Die Heimkehrer-Krankheit: Stoffwechselentgleisung und Kontaktschwierigkeiten hängen zusammen," *Deutsche Zeitung*, October 28, 1953, p. 12 (HStA Stuttgart, EA/8002, Bü 149).

64. See, among others, "Die Heimkehrer-Krankheit."

65. Two examples are "Heimkehrer, die keine sind," *Die Zeit*, May 14, 1953, p. 6, and "Heimkehrer in seelischer Not: Reihenuntersuchungen nach Jahren notwendig," *Deutsches Volksblatt*, December 16, 1953 (HStA Stuttgart, EA 8002/Bü 13). See also Moeller, "Last Soldiers."

66. See, for example, "Die Heimkehrer-Krankheit," p. 12, here also citation.

67. "Dystrophie: Die Krankheit der Heimkehrer," p. 26.

68. "Dystrophie: Die Krankheit der Heimkehrer."

69. "Heimkehrer, die keine sind," p. 6.

70. See especially the chapters in Part II of the current study, in particular chapter 5, the section "The Dispute about Hereditability."

71. "Dystrophie: Die Krankheit der Heimkehrer," pp. 26f.

72. Above all Moeller, *War Stories*, and Biess, *Homecomings*, emphasize such a rhetoric of victimization.

73. "Heimkehrer, die keine sind," *Die Zeit*, May 14, 1953, p. 6, and "Dystrophie: Die Krankheit der Heimkehrer," *Der Spiegel* of October 7, 1953. Citing Gauger, the author spoke of a "systematic dystrophization entailing millions of people" (p. 27).

74. Two examples: "Wie geht es unseren Kriegsgefangenen? Erste Ärztetagung des Heimkehrerverbandes—Späte Schäden schwer zu heilen," *Stuttgarter Zeitung*, April 20, 1953; and "Die Folgen der Dystrophie. Ärzte fordern ein Forschungsinstitut für die Gesundheitsschäden der Heimkehrer," *Schwäbisches Tageblatt*, October 23, 1953, p. 3 (both in HStA Stuttgart, EA/8002, Bü 14).

75. A short outline of the way the Korean War accelerated West Germany's alliance with and integration into the West is found in Bernd Stöver, *Der Kalte Krieg* (Munich, 2007), pp. 35ff.

76. "Viele sagen: Heimkehren ist schwerer als Weggehen," *Die Zeit*, December 15, 1955, p. 3.

77. Especially succinct: "Der Freiheit entwöhnt: Heimkehrer brauchen zur Umstellung viel Zeit und Geduld," *Deutsche Zeitung*, December 17, 1955, p. 3 (HStA Stuttgart, EA/8002, Bü 13). Many other examples in Moeller, *War Stories*, pp. 88ff. and Frank Biess, "Männer des Wiederaufbaus, Wiederaufbau der Männer: Kriegsheimkehrer in Ost- und Westdeutschland," in Hagemann and Schüler-Springorum, *Heimat-Front*, pp. 345–365, pp. 352f.

78. Two examples: Franz Petrasch, "Lebenskonflikt und Krankheit," *Frankfurter Hefte* 8 (1953), pp. 681–687; "Die Renten-Neurose: Das Recht auf Krankheit und die Pflicht zur Gesundheit," *Die Zeit*, May 6, 1954, p. 1.

79. Petrasch, "Lebenskonflikt und Krankheit," p. 683. Also for following citations.

80. Petrasch, "Lebenskonflikt und Krankheit," p. 684.

81. "Die Renten-Neurose: Das Recht auf Krankheit und die Pflicht zur Gesundheit," *Die Zeit*, May 6, 1954, p. 1. The Reichsbund der Kriegs- und Zivilbeschädigten, Sozialrentner und Hinterbliebenen protested sharply against Dehler's remark. At that, the minister of justice disputed the right of the Reichsbund to "speak on behalf of the victims of the war and of work" and made it clear that "what society owes them, the state provides of its own accord. It does not need to be admonished." See the correspondence in BA Koblenz, B 149, 1919, which also contains Dr. Thomas Dehler to the Reichsbund der Kriegs- und Zivilbeschädigten, Sozialrentner und Hinterbliebenen, December 24, 1951 (here the citation). As the correspondence indicates, the doctor involved was Karsten Jaspersen, head physician in the psychiatric department at Anstalt Sarepta, Bethel. On Dehler's political activity see Udo Wengst, *Thomas Dehler 1897–1967: Eine politische Biographie* (Munich, 1997).

82. In 1948, the number of unemployed in West Germany was 442,000; by January 1949 the figure had more than doubled to 937,000. In 1950, the figure was 1,868,505. The number did decline in the following years, but in the second half of 1955 it was still over one million. The rapid return to full employment would take place in the second half of the 1950s. The figures in Manfred Görtemaker, *Geschichte der Bundesrepublik Deutschland: Von der Gründung bis zur Gegenwart* (Munich, 1999), pp. 157f.; Bernhard Schäfers, *Gesellschaftlicher Wandel in Deutschland*, 6th ed. (Stuttgart, 1995), p. 227.

83. "Die Renten-Neurose," p. 1.

84. *Meines Vaters Pferde*, film 1953–1954, screenplay by Horst Budjuhn, directed by Gerhard Lamprecht.

85. See Biess, "Männer," p. 355.

86. On the debate over conservative family policies and gender relations of the 1950s, the simultaneous "remasculinization" and "civilization" of men occurring in this period, see, among others, Robert G. Moeller, "The 'Remasculinization' of Germany in the 1950s: Introduction," *Signs* 24 (1998), pp. 101–106; Moeller, "Last Soldiers"; Moeller, "The Homosexual Man Is a 'Man,' the Homosexual Woman Is a 'Woman': Sex, Society and the Law in Postwar West Germany," in Moeller, ed., *West Germany under Construction: Politics, Society, and Culture in the Adenauer Era* (Ann Arbor, MI, 1997), pp. 251–284; Dagmar Herzog, "Sex and Marriage in the Wake of the War," in Bessel and Schumann, *Life After Death*, pp. 161–192, esp. pp. 185ff.; Elizabeth Heineman, "Complete Families, Half Families, No Families at All: Female-Headed Households and the Reconstruction of the Family in the Early Federal Republic," *Central European History* 29 (1996), pp. 19–60; Kühne, *Kameradschaft*; Kühne, "Zwischen Vernichtungskrieg und Freizeitgesellschaft," pp. 108f.; Uta Poiger, "A New 'Western' Hero? Reconstructing German Masculinity in the 1950s," *Signs* 24 (1998), pp. 147–162.

87. For a differentiated look at the *Heimatfilm* (homeland film) see Fehrenbach, *Cinema in Democratizing Germany*, pp. 148ff.

88. For a summary of literature concerning the striking rise of the war as a theme in the media, which reached its apogee in the late 1950s, see Knoch, *Die Tat als Bild*, pp. 437ff.

89. *08/15*, film, 1954–1955, screenplay by Hans Hellmut Kirst, directed by Paul May. On the film and its reception in the press and politics, see esp. Reichel, *Erfundene Erinnerung*, pp. 101ff.; Knut Hickethier, "Militär und Krieg: 08/15 (1954)," in Werner Faulstich and Helmut Korte, eds., *Fischer Filmgeschichte*, vol. 3: *Auf der Suche nach Werten: 1945–1960* (Frankfurt am Main, 1990), pp. 222–251; Hickethier, "Der Zweite Weltkrieg und der Holocaust im Fernsehen der Bundesrepublik der fünfziger und frühen sechziger Jahre," in Greven and Wrochem, *Der Krieg in der Nachkriegszeit*, pp. 93–112. In the West German cinema of the 1950s, the character of the ideologically deluded officer is juxtaposed with that of the decent officer who distances himself from Hitler. In *Canaris*, 1954, directed by Alfred Weidenmann, as well as *Des Teufels General*, which was released a year later and directed by Helmut Käutner, officers are stylized into opponents of the Nazi system.

90. *Hunde, wollt ihr ewig leben?*, film, 1958, screenplay by Frank Wisbar and others, directed by Frank Wisbar. On this film see Robert G. Moeller, "'In a Thousand Years, Every German Will Speak of This Battle': Celluloid Memories of Stalingrad," in Omer Bartov et al., eds., *Crimes of War: Guilt and Denial in the Twentieth Century* (New York, 2002), pp. 161–190.

91. Reichel, *Erfundene Erinnerung*, p. 95.

92. This corresponded to the portrayal of the ordinary soldier in the glossy magazines of the day. See the summary in Knoch, *Die Tat als Bild*, pp. 451ff. Starting in the mid-1950s, "Stalingrad" becomes the representative locus of the war in countless stories—a development that influenced perception of the war in a basic way. Among the

many discussions of the topic, see Förster, *Stalingrad*; and in particular (with special relevance for the present context), Rolf Günter Renner, "Hirn und Her: Stalingrad als Gegenstand ideologischer und literarischer Diskurse," in Förster, *Stalingrad*, pp. 472–492; for a broader perspective see Peter Jahn, *Stalingrad erinnern: Stalingrad im deutschen und russischen Gedächtnis* (Berlin, 2003).

93. Knoch, *Die Tat als Bild*, p. 438; Etges, "Deutungswandel."

94. *Die Brücke*, film, 1959, screenplay by Bernhard Wicki, directed by Bernhard Wicki.

95. *Nacht fiel über Gotenhafen*, film, 1959, screenplay by Frank Wisbar, directed by Frank Wisbar.

96. *Der Arzt von Stalingrad*, film, 1957–1958, screenplay by Werner P. Zibaso, directed by Géza von Radvanyi.

CHAPTER 8

1. "Erinnerungen eines großen Arztes," *Die Zeit*, February 17, 1955, p. 8.

2. Hoimar von Ditfurth, "Was ist Krankheit?," *Die Zeit*, February 3, 1961, p. 10.

3. The psychiatrist and neurologist von Ditfurth insisted above all that psychoanalysis could stake no claim to being scientific: "The actual source of all psychoanalytic efforts," he argued, "is the innate human need to interpret the meaning of what he is experiencing." Ditfurth conceded that this need could not be satisfied by scientific medicine; people often found it unacceptable that illness could be caused by "blind fate." Yet although he did not champion academic medicine, he warned against hastily concluding that where healing proved impossible "the causal factor could only be discovered and influenced psychoanalytically."

4. Two eulogies for Ludwig Binswanger serve as examples: "Der Mensch in der Psychiatrie," *Süddeutsche Zeitung*, August 3–4, 1957, p. 44 (here also citation); "Ein Psychiater paktiert mit Heidegger: Selbst der Kranke hat noch die Freiheit der Entscheidung—meint Ludwig Binswanger," *Die Zeit*, May 15, 1958, p. 6.

5. See the discussion in the preceding chapter.

6. See, for example, "Wer krank ist, bestimmen die Krankenkassen: Die große Psychotherapie darf nicht länger als Luxus für reiche Privatpatienten betrachtet werden," *Die Zeit*, August 15, 1957, p. 4.

7. Frieder Naschold, *Kassenärzte und Krankenversicherungsreform: Zu einer Theorie der Statuspolitik* (Freiburg, 1967), pp. 103ff.

8. Alexander Mitscherlich, "Der 'genormte' Patient," *Die Zeit*, March 4, 1960.

9. The draft submitted under the aegis of federal minister of labor Theodor Blank (of the Christian Democratic Union party) was defeated in 1961. Above all, the proposed deductible for the insured—the grounds for which had been that a sense of entitlement was driving up the cost of medical care and personal responsibility needed to be strengthened—was severely criticized by the West Germany medical association, the unions, the Social Democratic Party, and the labor wing of the Christian Democratic Party. See "Ministerausschuß für die Sozialreform 1955–1960: Das Krankenversicherungs-Neuregelungsgesetz (KVNG)," in *Die Kabinettsprotokolle der*

382   Notes to Pages 260–62

Bundesregierung (http://www.bundesarchiv.de/kabinettsprotokolle/web/index.jsp); Ursula Reucher, *Reform und Reformversuche in der gesetzlichen Krankenversicherung (1956–1965)* (Düsseldorf, 1999).

10. Ditfurth, "Was ist Krankheit." Ditfurth, one of the few doctors to voice critical thoughts about the psychosomatic trend in the mass media since the war, commented: "It is no longer merely science, it is the fascination exerted by the Promethean audacity of such a concept that imbues the psychoanalytic physician and makes his missionary zeal comprehensible." The idea of a patient's extraordinary potential for self-healing was of course not entirely new to the period. It is expressed, for instance, in the rubble films in the form of an appeal for willpower and an evocation of the healing power of work. Here we find a blending of elements of psychiatric doctrine and reconstruction discourse rhetoric.

11. Mitscherlich, "Der 'genormte' Patient."

12. "Unsere Kinder brauchen ihre Mütter wieder," *Stern*, July 23, 1956, p. 8.

13. On the youth culture of the 1950s and the social reaction see esp. Uta G. Poiger, *Jazz, Rock, and Rebels: Cold War Politics and American Culture in a Divided Germany* (Berkeley, CA, 2000); Thomas Grotum, *Die Halbstarken: Zur Geschichte einer Jugendkultur der 50er Jahre* (Frankfurt am Main, 1994); Kaspar Maase, *Bravo Amerika: Erkundungen zur Jugendkultur der Bundesrepublik in den fünfziger Jahren* (Hamburg, 1992).

14. Andrea Riecken, *Migration und Gesundheitspolitik: Flüchtlinge und Vertriebene in Niedersachen 1945–1953* (Göttingen, 2006).

15. Both in England and in the United States, it appears that a very similar perspective was in vogue, spurred on by the psychoanalytic schools associated with the journal *Psychoanalytic Study of the Child* (founded in 1945 in London and New York). Starting in the late 1940s, increasingly frequent references to articles in this journal are seen when the danger posed to children by working mothers is thematized. Eli Zaretsky, *Freuds Jahrhundert: Die Geschichte der Psychoanalyse* (Vienna, 2006), pp. 380ff., pp. 384f., even sees psychoanalytic culture of the postwar years as serving the important function of "establishing the image of the full-time mother and housewife . . . as the ideal for the emerging welfare state" (citation p. 385).

16. See Elisabeth Pfeil, *Die Berufstätigkeit von Müttern: Eine empirisch-soziologische Erhebung an 900 Müttern* (Tübingen, 1961), pp. 324ff.

17. "Unsere Kinder brauchen ihre Mütter wieder," *Stern*, July 23, 1956, p. 9.

18. "Wer krank ist, bestimmen die Krankenkassen," *Die Zeit*, August 15, 1957, p. 4 (paradigmatic for this view).

19. Exemplary for this is "Wer krank ist, bestimmen die Krankenkassen," which is also the source of the previous quotation.

20. "Wer krank ist, bestimmen die Krankenkassen."

21. See the discussion in chapter 4, the section "The Psychiatric Treatment of Repatriated German Soldiers, 1945–1953," and in chapter 5, the sections "Pension Claims under Suspicion" and "The Dispute about Hereditability."

22. Willibald Steinmetz, "Ungewollte Politisierung durch die Medien? Die Contergan-Affäre," in Bernd Weisbrod, ed., *Die Politik der Öffentlichkeit—Die Öffentlichkeit der Politik: Politische Medialisierung in der Geschichte der Bundesrepublik* (Göttingen, 2003), pp. 195–228, p. 197.

23. Many facets of this development in Knoch, *Die Tat als Bild*, pp. 468ff.

24. Knoch, *Die Tat als Bild*, pp. 585ff.

25. One example: Bernhard Schnabel, *Macht ohne Moral: Eine Dokumentation über die SS* (Frankfurt am Main, 1956). *Die Tat*, the publication of the Society of People Persecuted by the Nazi Regime—a Communist federation of antifascists—played a pioneering role in shaking West Germany's integrative consensus through visual breaches of taboo. One of the most well-known illustrated volumes is Gerhard Schönberner, *Der gelbe Stern: Die Judenverfolgung in Europa 1933–1945* (Hamburg, 1960). See Knoch, *Die Tat als Bild*; Brink, *Ikonen der Vernichtung*; Brink, *"Auschwitz in der Paulskirche": Erinnerungspolitik in Fotoausstellungen der sechziger Jahre* (Marburg, 2000). Until the early 1960s, TV played a subordinate role; the few fictional films revolved around the problem of silencing the crime and complicity, the nonfictional films around the structure of the terror apparatus. See Christoph Classen, *Bilder der Vergangenheit: Die Zeit des Nationalsozialismus im Fernsehen der Bundesrepublik Deutschland 1955–1965* (Cologne, 1999), pp. 86ff.

26. Decisive in this respect was the establishment in 1958 of the Central Office of the State Justice Administrations for the Investigation of National Socialist Crimes in Ludwigsburg. The number of those accused had risen significantly by the following year. For a concise overview, see Bernd Weisbrod, "Die 'Vergangenheitsbewältigung' der NS-Prozesse: Gerichtskultur und Öffentlichkeit," in Eva Schumann, ed., *Kontinuität und Zäsuren—Rechtswissenschaft und Justiz im "Dritten Reich" und in der Nachkriegszeit* (Göttingen, 2008), pp. 247–270.

27. See, among others, Marc von Miquel, *Ahnden oder amnestieren? Westdeutsche Justiz und Vergangenheitspolitik in den 60er Jahren* (Göttingen, 2004); Annette Weinke, *Die Verfolgung von NS-Tätern im geteilten Deutschland: Vergangenheitsbewältigung 1949–1969 oder: Eine deutsch-deutsche Beziehungsgeschichte im Kalten Krieg* (Paderborn, 2002).

28. See, for example, "Denn sie mußten wissen, was sie tun: Im Arnsberger Schwurgerichtssaal wird eine schreckliche Vergangenheit lebendig," *Stern*, February 8, 1958, p. 14; "Hände, die töteten, statt zu heilen: Sollen ehemalige KZ-Ärzte wieder praktizieren dürfen?," *Die Zeit*, February 27, 1958, p. 2; "'Schweigen wird bei uns Psychiatern sehr groß geschrieben,' Kollegen Heydes vor dem Kieler Untersuchungsausschuß," *Frankfurter Allgemeine Zeitung*, May 1–2, 1961, p. 6.

29. Brochhagen, *Nach Nürnberg*, p. 293.

30. In 1958, *Stern* magazine used the headline "Starting in 1945 the 'Murderers' Were People Like You and Me" to highlight its reporting of the trial in Arnsberg, where a number of SS and Wehrmacht members stood accused of murdering 129 Russian forced laborers, seventy-seen women, and two children on the order of an SS general.

31. See Annette Wieviorka, *The Era of the Witness* (Ithaca, NY, 2006).

32. Gideon Hausner, *Gerechtigkeit in Jerusalem* (Munich, 1967), pp. 444 and 445f., cited from Annette Wieviorka, "Die Entstehung des Zeugen," in Smith, *Hannah Arendt Revisited*, pp. 136–159, pp. 142 and 143. The indication of number of witnesses: Wieviorka, p. 150.

33. Wieviorka, "Die Entstehung des Zeugen," pp. 148f. West German television regularly reported on the trial in its news broadcasts. In addition, while the trial was in progress it broadcast twenty-minute segments twice a week following the news. Alleg-

edly, these reports were followed by first 60 percent, and then 50 percent of the television audience. Furthermore, all West German radio stations reported daily on the trial from the first day. See Peter Krause, *Der Eichmann-Prozess in der deutschen Presse* (Frankfurt am Main, 2002), p. 91.

34. The number of survivors appearing as witnesses in the Auschwitz trial (211) was nearly twice as many as in the Eichmann trial. Annette Weinke, "Überreste eines 'unerwünschten Prozesses': Die Edition der Tonbandmitschnitte zum ersten Frankfurter Auschwitz-Prozess (1963–1965)," *Zeithistorische Forschungen/Studies in Contemporary History*, online edition, 2 (2005), http://www.zeithistorische-forschungen. de/16126041–Weinke-2-2005, p. 1, indicates that this fact alone guaranteed the trials worldwide media attention.

35. We find such a readiness for empathy in, for example, "Neurosen," *Frankfurter Hefte* 16 (1961), pp. 868–869, a review of Hans March, ed., *Verfolgung und Angst in ihren leib-seelischen Auswirkungen* (Stuttgart, 1960), which basically is a collection of assessments from compensation proceedings. While the volume was generally received very positively, the reviewer did criticize the fact that the material was presented "in its original scientific and official form," rendering it difficult for most readers to penetrate the "armor of specialized language." For this reason, it was urgent that the material be republished "as a living sourcebook."

36. Peter Weiss, *Die Ermittlung: Oratorium in 11 Gesängen* (Frankfurt am Main, 1965). On the contemporary debate about the play, see, among others, Reichel, *Erfundene Erinnerung*, pp. 228ff., p. 237; Stephan Braese, "'In einer deutschen Angelegenheit'—Der Frankfurter Auschwitz-Prozess in der westdeutschen Nachkriegsliteratur," in Fritz Bauer Institut, ed., *"Gerichtstag halten über uns selbst . . ." Geschichte und Wirkung des ersten Frankfurter Auschwitz-Prozesses* (Frankfurt am Main, 2001), pp. 217–244. For a concise overview of the Auschwitz trial see Reichel, *Vergangenheitsbewältigung in Deutschland*, pp. 158–181.

37. See, for example, "Angeklagt ist die Gesellschaft," *Süddeutsche Zeitung*, May 30–June 1, 1961, p. 19; "Das Dilemma der Seelenärzte: Ein Kongreß wie alle anderen wurde in die Wirklichkeit zurückgestoßen," *Die Zeit*, June 2, 1961, p. 12; "Im tiefsten Schatten der Vergangenheit," *Die Zeit*, August 11, 1961, p. 29.

38. See the discussion in chapter 6, "The Moral Challenge, 1956–1970." Psychiatrist Ulrich Venzlaff, who in 1958 proposed a diagnosis of "experientially determined personality change" in his academic qualification thesis, reacted to an article in *Die Zeit* that evidently had taken entire passages from the book without permission. In a letter to the editor, he remarked that in 1957 "a major medical publisher" had declined to publish his manuscript on the grounds "that there was no need to publish such studies" and his "findings did not correspond to prevailing psychiatric doctrine." *Die Zeit*, August 25, 1961, p. 15.

39. "Angeklagt ist die Gesellschaft," p. 19.

40. "Im tiefsten Schatten der Vergangenheit."

41. "KZ-Syndrom. Quälende Träume," *Der Spiegel* 18 (1964), pp. 96–98.

42. "Im tiefsten Schatten der Vergangenheit."

43. "KZ-Syndrom. Quälende Träume," p. 96 is a good example.

44. "Im tiefsten Schatten der Vergangenheit."

45. "Angeklagt ist die Gesellschaft."

46. "Im tiefsten Schatten der Vergangenheit."

47. "Das Dilemma der Seelenärzte."

48. "Im tiefsten Schatten der Vergangenheit."

49. Examples in Knoch, *Die Tat als Bild*, pp. 656f., citation p. 656.

50. "Mörder aus Ordnungssinn: Warum viele NS-Verbrecher so schnell zu braven Kleinbürgern wurden," *Die Zeit*, July 19, 1963, p. 3.

51. "'Weil ich Treue geschworen hatte . . . ,'" *Die Zeit*, July 21, 1961 (a good example in this respect); see also "Wir könnten alle Mörder sein," *Stern*, February 9, 1964, pp. 56–60, and the entire series "Die Mörder sind wie Du und ich," *Stern* July 2, 1965, pp. 58–66 and following editions.

52. Examples in Knoch, *Die Tat als Bild*, pp. 297ff. Inge Marszolek, "The Coverage of the Bergen-Belsen Trial and the Auschwitz Trial in the NWDR/NDR: The Reports of Axel Eggebrecht," unpublished manuscript, pp. 9ff., shows that the early perpetrators' profile in the media was not uniform.

53. This receives greater weight in Marc von Miquel, "NS-Prozesse und politische Öffentlichkeit in den 60er Jahren," in Fritz Bauer Institut, ed., *Gerichtstag halten über uns selbst*, pp. 97–116.

54. For a different argument see Rebecca Wittmann, *Beyond Justice: The Auschwitz Trial* (Cambridge, 2005), p. 247, who does not see this connection. More balanced in his assessment: Devin O. Pendas, *The Frankfurt Auschwitz Trial, 1963–65: Genocide, History and the Limits of the Law* (New York, 2006).

55. "Wir könnten alle Mörder sein," p. 56.

56. Between July 1961 and the end of 1964, the "Panorama" reported ten times on the subject of the integration into West German society of Nazi perpetrators; an equal number of programs were devoted to "hidden National Socialist attitudes" among West German citizens. Thus, the Nazi past emerged as one of the program's major concerns. See von Hodenberg, *Konsens und Krise*, pp. 306f.

57. "Die Mörder sind wie Du und ich," citations pp. 58 and 61. On Capesius's activities in Auschwitz, the evidence presented, and the verdict, see Irmtrud Wojak, ed., *Auschwitz-Prozess 4 Ks 2/63* (Frankfurt am Main, 2004), pp. 338ff.

58. Norbert Frei, "Die Wiederkehr des Rechts," in Frei, *1945 und wir*, pp. 63–82, pp. 77f.

59. See, among others, Martin Walser, "Unser Auschwitz," *Kursbuch* 1 (1965), pp. 189–200; Horst Krüger, "Im Labyrinth der Schuld," *Der Monat* 16 (1964), pp. 19–29.

60. Krüger's "Im Labyrinth der Schuld" was also broadcast on the radio on April 29, 1964. An expanded version of the original text was published in the autobiographical account, Horst Krüger, *Das zerbrochene Haus: Eine Jugend in Deutschland* (1966), 3rd ed. (Munich, 1988), pp. 148–179. The following citations of the text are from the above-cited version in *Der Monat*. For a more detailed description of West Germany's radio reporting on the Auschwitz trial, see René Wolf, "'Mass Deception without Deceivers'? The Holocaust on East and West German Radio in the 1960s," *Journal of Contemporary History* 41 (2006), pp. 741–755.

61. Krüger, "Im Labyrinth der Schuld," p. 23.

62. Krüger, *Das zerbrochene Haus*, p. 182.

63. Krüger, "Im Labyrinth der Schuld," p. 24.

64. In the afterword to *Das zerbrochene Haus*, p. 183, where Krüger explains the development of the book's individual chapters during the different phases of his life, he conceded the following: "An additional chapter meant to describe my war experiences as a German lance corporal between 1941 and 1945, and which accordingly belonged between "The Arrest" and "'45, the Zero Hour," repeatedly failed to materialize. In a way, service in the military and the war took place outside of my experience as a person. At least until now, I have not been able to really make them my own. For the critical reader a gap opens here that I acknowledge."

65. Among the many studies of the subject see esp. Saul Friedländer, *The Years of Extermination: Nazi Germany and the Jews, 1939–1945* (New York, 2007); Christian Hartmann et al., eds., *Verbrechen der Wehrmacht—Bilanz einer Debatte* (Munich, 2005); Arnold, *Die Wehrmacht*; Christian Gerlach, *Kalkulierte Morde: Die deutsche Wirtschafts- und Vernichtungspolitik in Weißrussland 1941–1944* (Hamburg, 2000); Christopher Browning, *Ordinary Men: Reserve Police Battalion 101 and the Final Solution in Poland* (New York, 1992); Hannes Heer and Klaus Naumann, eds., *Vernichtungskrieg: Verbrechen der Wehrmacht 1941–1944* (Hamburg, 1995).

66. Krüger, "Im Labyrinth der Schuld," p. 21.

67. Krüger, "Im Labyrinth der Schuld," p. 24.

68. Krüger, "Im Labyrinth der Schuld," pp. 25 and 26.

69. "Wir könnten alle Mörder sein," pp. 56 and 57.

70. "Wir könnten alle Mörder sein," p. 57.

71. For greater detail, see Part II of this book.

72. "Wir könnten alle Mörder sein," p. 72.

73. "Im tiefsten Schatten der Vergangenheit." For greater detail, see chapter 6, "The Moral Challenge, 1956–1970."

74. *Die Zeit* here quoted from a long passage in Venzlaff's 1958 qualifying thesis, in which he wrote about elderly women refugees. However, this was not obvious from the article in *Die Zeit*. The article was structured in such a way that it transitioned directly to the case of the Polish writer Tadeusz Nowakowski, who spent a number of years in various concentration camps. See Venzlaff, *Die psychoreaktiven Störungen*, p. 76 and "Im tiefsten Schatten der Vergangenheit."

75. For a more detailed discussion, see Part II, above all chapter 6, "The Moral Challenge, 1956–1970."

76. "Neurosen der Ächtung," *Frankfurter Allgemeine Zeitung*, December 3, 1963, p. 6.

77. "Billiger Dank," *Süddeutsche Zeitung*, December 3, 1963, p. 1; "Hat man die Kriegsopfer vergessen?," *Süddeutsche Zeitung*, November 30–December 1, 1963, p. 4. Since care of disabled veterans in the Saarland was only transferred to West Germany in 1959, France was seen as offering a reliable comparison. It seems that this resulted in officially recognized disabled veterans receiving smaller pensions.

78. See "Wir bleiben uns treu: Rechenschaftsbericht des Verbandes der Heimkehrer, Kriegsgefangenen und Vermisstenangehörigen Deutschlands e. V. für die Zeit vom Juli 1962 bis Juni 1964, gegeben aus Anlaß des 8. ordentlichen Verbandstages vom 23. bis 25. Oktober 1964 in Bad Godesberg," pp. 28f.; "Rechenschaftsbericht des Verbandes

der Heimkehrer, Kriegsgefangenen und Vermißtenangehörigen Deutschlands e. V. für die Zeit von Juli 1964 bis Juni 1966" (VdH-Sammelinformationen, 71, January–September 1966), p. 38; both texts in the archives of the Association of Returnees in Bonn.

79. Once again, see Part II of this book in its entirety.

80. "Wir bleiben uns treu: Rechenschaftsbericht," p. 29; "Wir bleiben uns treu. Ergebnisbericht," p. 10. In 1933, Auerbach had been arrested on account of his union activities and work for the Social Democratic Party. The same year, he emigrated to Amsterdam and six years later to England, where he remained during the war. On Auerbach's activities in exile, see Stefanie Averbeck, "The Post-1933 Emigration of Communication Researchers from Germany: The Lost Works of the Weimar Generation," *European Journal of Communication* 16 (2001), pp. 451–475.

81. "Wir bleiben uns treu: Ergebnisbericht," p. 10.

82. In the German Bundestag, the proposal to transfer the burden of proof to the state in cases of close temporal proximity between illness and military service in the war had been negotiated once before in 1960. (The Free Democratic Party delegate Rutschke had spoken up vehemently for this.) At the time, the Social Democratic delegate Pohle explained that his party had formulated the same idea in its own motion, but had decided against it after detailed discussions in the disabled-veterans committee. After listening to many specialists, he continued, it became clear "that perhaps we were not completely on track and would be opening the gates to a flood we did not intend." The motion was then rejected by the delegates present. *Verhandlungen des deutschen Bundestages, 3. Wahlperiode, Stenographische Berichte*, vol. 46 (Bonn, 1960), pp. 6492f.

83. "Wir bleiben uns treu. Ergebnisbericht," p. 11; partly identical in "Wir bleiben uns treu. Rechenschaftsbericht," pp. 37f., but the latter text includes the indication that there were "differences in the numerical distribution of physical and mental consequences," and, likewise, "differences of degree" that could be "classified according to the type and duration of the triggering cause." But in total, readers were informed, the mental and neurological changes presented the same picture.

84. See, among others, "Die Angstträume bleiben," *Stern*, December 11, 1966, pp. 112–117; "Mama, ich werde nie mehr derselbe sein: Feldpostbriefe amerikanischer Soldaten in Vietnam," *Stern*, April 30, 1967, pp. 194–199. In later research on trauma as well, the ascription of traumata involves a simultaneous acceptance of victim status. One example is Judith Herman's notion of "mental trauma" as "the suffering of the impotent." "Trauma," Herman observes, "emerges at a moment where the victim is rendered helpless by its overpowering force." In this formulation, "trauma" not only contains a statement about power relations but also portrays the participants in a highly specific way. Judith Herman, *Die Narben der Gewalt* (Munich, 1993), p. 54.

85. See esp. Young, *Harmony of Illusions*; and McNally, *Remembering Trauma*.

86. The complete broadcast ms. in BA Koblenz, B 126, 61073.

87. This was Paul and Herberg, eds., *Psychische Spätschäden*.

88. Handwritten note in the margin of a letter from the West German finance minister to the Foreign Office, March 17, 1964, in BA Koblenz, B 126, 61073. Here also the ms. of an anonymous presentation discussing the anthology; as becomes clear from the

files, this text was added as an appendix to the transcript of the eighth main medical conference for state delegates. The discussion of the book was then published in *Recht-sprechung zur Wiedergutmachung* 15 (1964), pp. 349–351, with *Oberregierungsmediz-inalrat* Helmuth Lotz specified as the author. The West German health ministry inter-vened in the campaign of its colleagues in the finance ministry and took the side of the doctors under attack. The intervention clearly points to a sense that West Germany was under pressure that had to be handled appropriately. As a result, the health ministry advised against publishing the anonymous presentation, not only because the substan-tive contents of the book had been assessed differently by other experts, but also be-cause publication would "internationally create a very unfavorable impression in re-spect to the government's attitude in the compensation question." The entire exchange in BA Koblenz, B 126, 61073.

89. "Späte Schäden der Psyche nach politischer Verfolgung," part 1, citation p. 2, in BA Koblenz, B 126, 61073.

90. "Späte Schäden der Psyche nach politischer Verfolgung," part 2, p. 22.

91. "Späte Schäden der Psyche nach politischer Verfolgung," part 2, pp. 7f. and 12, there also the citation of Eissler from his like-named essay in *Psyche* 17 (1963), pp. 241–291.

92. "Späte Schäden der Psyche nach politischer Verfolgung," part 1, p. 3.

93. "Späte Schäden der Psyche nach politischer Verfolgung," part 1, pp. 21f.

94. "Späte Schäden der Psyche nach politischer Verfolgung," part 1, p. 2, and part 2, p. 26.

95. "Späte Schäden der Psyche nach politischer Verfolgung," part 1, p. 37, and re-peated in part 2, p. 1.

96. "Kriegsgefangene. Skoro domoi," *Der Spiegel* 23 (1969), p. 84. Here *Der Spie-gel* cited Heidelberg historian Erich Maschke, head of the Commission for the History of German War Prisoners. Since 1957, the commission had been working on a complete history of the German POWs on behalf of the Federal Ministry for Expellees, Refugees, and Disabled Veterans, which backed the project with three million marks. When in the early 1960s it became clear that the first volumes would soon be ready, the ministry considered publication potentially harmful in view of the ongoing trials of Nazis. The feeling was that a documentation of the suffering the Germans had endured in connec-tion with the war ran the danger of being misunderstood. Presumably, the shift in poli-cies toward the East under Willy Brandt strengthened the reservations. Nevertheless, in the late 1960s the ministry decided to publish all twenty-two volumes in an extremely limited printing in order to make the material accessible to university libraries but not to the general public. See Erich Maschke [ed.], *Zur Geschichte der deutschen Kriegs-heimkehrer nach dem Zweiten Weltkrieg*, 22 vols. (Munich, 1962–1974). See Moeller, *War Stories*, pp. 179f.

97. Knoch, *Die Tat als Bild*, p. 921.

98. See "Kriegsgefangene: Skoro domoi" and "KZ-Schäden. Etiketten verteilt," *Der Spiegel* 23 (1969), p. 162.

99. On cinematic representation of the Holocaust see Frank Bösch, "Film, NS-Vergangenheit und Geschichtswissenschaft: Von 'Holocaust' zu 'Der Untergang,'" *Vi-erteljahreshefte für Zeitgeschichte* 55 (2007), pp. 1–32; Wulf Kansteiner, "Ein Völker-

mord ohne Täter? Die Darstellung der 'Endlösung' in den Sendungen des Zweiten Deutschen Fernsehens," in Moshe Zuckermann, ed., *Medien—Politik—Geschichte* (Göttingen, 2003), pp. 253–286.

100. *Mendel Schainfelds zweite Reise nach Deutschland*, directed by Hans-Dieter Grabe, produced in 1971.

CONCLUSION

1. Eva Hoffman, *After Such Knowledge: Memory, History, and the Legacy of the Holocaust* (New York, 2004), p. 34.

2. Hoffman, *After Such Knowledge*, pp. 34f.

3. In this respect, see also the account of Ruth Klüger, *Weiter leben: Eine Jugend*, 7th ed. (Munich, 1998), pp. 240ff., who describes her encounter as an adolescent with a psychoanalyst from Vienna now living in the States.

4. Klüger, *Weiter leben*, pp. 51f.

5. Klüger, *Weiter leben*, pp. 55ff.

6. Klüger, *Weiter leben*, p. 57.

7. Novick, *Nach dem Holocaust*, pp. 12f. and pp. 113ff., citation p. 114. Novick presents examples from the United States and Israel. See also Klüger, *Weiter leben*, pp. 225ff., here esp. pp. 229f.

8. Novick, *Nach dem Holocaust*, p. 14.

9. See esp. Lawrence Langer, *Holocaust Testimonies: The Ruins of Memory* (New Haven, 1991), which is one of the most innovative and interpretively deep works in the field, notwithstanding the fact that the concept of "deep memory" has been criticized for being overly static. For a critique, see the text (also thought-provoking) of Steven T. Ostovich, "Epilogue: Dangerous Memories," in Confino and Fritzsche, *The Work of Memory*, pp. 239–256, esp. pp. 246ff.

10. Klaus Dörner, "Posttraumatische Belastungsstörungen—Neues Fass im Gesundheitsmarkt," *Trauma und Berufskrankheit* 6, Supplement 3 (2004), pp. 327–328.

11. See, for instance, the evaluation of June 10, 1985, in the context of a multiple-year legal proceeding on the question of whether a plaintiff who had been raped repeatedly after Soviet troops marched into East Prussia was to be recognized as having war-related mental illness. Versorgungsamt Bielefeld, 16234, vol. 1, and Handakte I, Ia and Ib.

12. Dörner, "Posttraumatische Belastungsstörungen," pp. 327f., here citing psychotherapist Bert Hellinger in *Die Zeit*, November 2000.

13. See Lorraine Daston, ed., *Biographies of Scientific Objects* (Chicago, 2000), where the emergence and vanishing of scientific objects is presented through a range of examples.

14. See Wienand, *Returning Memories*.

Bibliography

SOURCES

Library Archives

Archiv des Verbandes der Heimkehrer, Bonn
Bibliothek für Zeitgeschichte, Stuttgart
  Sammlung Sterz, Nachkriegszeit 1945–1953
Bundesarchiv Koblenz
  B 126, 9838; 9856; 9860; 9903; 42530; 42531; 42511; 47169; 61073
  B 149, 1919; 1920; 1954; 1955; 2350; 2353; 2354; 7190; 11859
  B 150, 357, 339
Bundesarchiv-Militärarchiv Freiburg
  B 205 v. 1368
Hauptarchiv der von Bodelschwinghschen Anstalten Bethel
  Bestand Morija (Aufn. 1945–1960)
  Bethelkanzlei, Patientenakten (Aufn. 1945–1956)
  2/33–470; 2/33–670; 2/12–197; 2/12–202
Hauptstaatsarchiv Stuttgart
  Arbeitsministerium Baden-Württemberg, EA/8002, Bu 13; EA/8002, Bu 14.
Historisches Archiv der Stadt Köln
  Acc 627, Nr. 2; Acc 627, Nr. 3; Acc 627, Nr. 4; Acc 627, Nr. 5; Acc 627, Nr. 6;
  Acc 627, Nr. 7; Acc 627, Nr. 9; Acc 627, Nr. 10; Acc 627, Nr. 11.
Landeskirchliches Archiv Bielefeld
  C 11–04, Bd. 1–5
Psychiatrische und Neurologische Klinik Heidelberg
  Patientenakten (Aufn. 1945–1949)
Sarepta Archiv
  1676: Lazarette, Seelsorge, 1939–45; Sar1/545a
Universitätsarchiv Heidelberg
  Re. 63 Nachlass Walter Ritter von Baeyer
Versorgungsamt Bielefeld
  Ausgewöhlte Akten der Kriegsopferversorgung (Laufzeit bis ins Jahr 2000)
Wiener Library, London

Newspapers, Journals, and Periodicals

AJR Information
Allgemeine Zeitschrift für Psychiatrie und ihre Grenzgebiete (1949)
Aufbau
Bundesgesetzblatt
Bundesversorgungsblatt
Der Medizinische Sachverständige (1954–1974)
Der Nervenarzt (1939–1944) (1947–1970)
*Der Versorgungsbeamte. Fachzeitschrift für die Kriegsopferversorgung und
die angrenzenden Fachgebiete* (1952–1970)
Deutsche Medizinische Wochenschrift (1946–1958)
Die Zeit (1946–1963)
Fortschritte der Neurologie, Psychiatrie und ihrer Grenzgebiete (1949–1960)
Frankfurter Allgemeine Zeitung (1949–1956) (1961–1964)
Frankfurter Hefte (1946–1970)
Münchener Medizinische Wochenschrift (1939–1944) (1950–1970)
Psyche
Psychiatrie, Neurologie und medizinische Psychologie (1949–1958)
Rechtsprechung zum Wiedergutmachungsrecht (1950–1970)
*Sammlung von Entscheidungen aus dem Gebiete der Sozialversicherung und
Versorgung*
*Sammlung von Entscheidungen der Sozialversicherung, Versorgung und
Arbeitslosenversicherung*
Stern (1948–1970)
Stuttgarter Zeitung (1945–1947)
Süddeutsche Zeitung (1945–1953) (1956–1964)
Weser-Kurier (1945–1949)

Primary Sources

Adelsberger, Lucie. Psychologische Beobachtungen im Konzentrationslager Au-
schwitz. *Schweizerische Zeitschrift für Psychologie* 6 (1947), pp. 124–131.
Ammermüller, Hermann, and Hans Wilden. *Gesundheitliche Schäden in der Wiedergut-
machung: ärztliche und rechtliche Beurteilung.* Stuttgart, 1953.
Anders, Gunther. *Hiroshima ist überall.* München, 1982. pp. 191–360.
Andreas-Friedrich, Ruth. *Der Schattenmann. Tagebuchaufzeichnungen, 1938–1948.*
Frankfurt a. M., 2000.
Anhaltspunkte für die ärztliche Gutachtertätigkeit im Versorgungswesen. Bonn, 1958.
Anhaltspunkte für die ärztliche Gutachtertätigkeit im Versorgungswesen. Bonn, 1965.
Anhaltspunkte für die ärztliche Gutachtertätigkeit. Bonn, 1952.
Anonyma. Eine Frau in Berlin. *Tagebuchaufzeichnungen* vom 20. April bis 22. Juni
1945, Frankfurt a. M. 2003.
Arendt, Hannah. Die Nachwirkungen des Naziregimes—Bericht aus Deutschland. In
Hannah Arendt, *In der Gegenwart. Übungen im politischen Denken II.* München,
2000, pp. 38–63.

Atio-Pathogenese und Therapie der Erschöpfung und Vorzeitigen Vergreisung (IV. Internationaler Medizinischer Kongres, Bukarest, 22.–27. Juni 1964), 2 Bde.

Baldermann, Manfred. Die psychischen Grundlagen der Heimkehrerdystrophien und ihre Behandlung. *Münchener Medizinische Wochenschrift* 93 (1951), pp. 1285–1290.

Baldermann, Manfred. Wesen und Beurteilung der Heimkehrerdystrophien. *Münchner Medizinische Wochenschrift* 93 (1951), pp. 118–123.

Bally, Gustav. Zur Anthropologie der Kriegszeit. *Schweizer Archiv für Neurologie und Psychiatrie,* 61 (1948), pp. 22–40.

Bansi, H. W. *Das Hungerodem.* Stuttgart, 1949.

Beeck, Manfred in der. Psychische und charakterliche Veranderungen bei Hungerzuständen (Beobachtungen in Gefangenschaft 1945/46 und Heimat 1947/48). *Hippokrates* 20 (1949), pp. 44–47.

Bericht über die 3. Arbeitstagung Ost der Beratenden Fachärzte vom 24.–26. Mai 1943 in der Militärärztlichen Akademie Berlin. Berlin, 1943.

Beringer, Kurt. Über hysterische Reaktionen bei Fliegerangriff en. In Heinrich Kranz, ed., *Arbeiten zur Psychiatrie, Neurologie und ihre Grenzgebieten.* FS für Kurt Schneider. Heidelberg, 1947, pp. 131–138.

Berlin, Irving N. Guilt as an etiologic factor in war neuroses. *The Journal of Nervous and Mental Disease* 111 (1950), pp. 239–245.

Bláha, František. Die Folgen des Krieges für die menschliche Gesundheit nach 20 Jahren. In *Atio-Pathogenese,* pp. 241–244.

Bláha, František. Folgen des Krieges für die menschliche Gesundheit (Schlussbericht über das Forschungsproblem des Gesundheitsministeriums für die Jahre 1960–1963). In *Atio-Pathogenese und Therapie der Erschopfung und Vorzeitigen Vergreisung* (IV. Internationaler Medizinischer Kongres, Bukarest, 22.–27. Juni 1964), 2 Bde., pp. 121–198.

Bleuler, Manfred. Forschungen und Begriffswandlungen in der Schizophrenielehre 1941–1950. *Fortschritte der Neurologie, Psychiatrie und ihrer Grenzgebiete* 19 (1951), pp. 385–452.

Böll, Heinrich. *Der Engel schwieg.* München, 1997.

Bonhoeffer, Karl. Erfahrungen aus dem Kriege über die Atiologie psychopathologischer Zustände mit besonderer Berücksichtigung der Erschöpfung und Emotion. *Allgemeine Zeitschrift für Psychiatrie und psychischgerichtliche Medizin* 73 (1917), pp. 76–95.

Bonhoeffer, Karl. Psychopathologische Erfahrungen und Lehren des Weltkriegs. *Münchener Medizinische Wochenschrift* 81 (1934), pp. 1212–1215.

Bonhoeffer, Karl, Vergleichende psychopathologische Erfahrungen aus den beiden Weltkriegen. *Der Nervenarzt* 18 (1947), pp. 1–4.

Borchert, Wolfgang. *Drausen vor der Tür* (1947). Reinbek, 1983.

Böttcher, Karl Wilhelm. Menschen unter falschem Namen. *Frankfurter Hefte* 4 (1949), pp. 492–511.

Boveri, Margret. *Tage des Überlebens.* Berlin 1945, München, 1970.

Brunn, W. Die entschädigungsrechtliche Problematik psychischer Störungen. *Rechtsprechung zum Wiedergutmachungsrecht* 11 (1960), pp. 481–484.

Bumke, Oswald. Hysterische Reaktionen im Ersatzheer. In *Bericht über die Arbeitsta-*

gung Ost der beratenden Fachärzte in der Militärärztlichen Akademie Berlin. Berlin, 1942/1943, pp. 141.

Bumke, Oswald. Kriegsneurosen. Allgemeine Ergebnisse. In Oswald Bumke and Otfried Foerster, eds., *Handbuch der Neurologie.* Berlin, 1924. pp. 54–71.

Bundesentschädigungsgesetz, München, 196614, p. 23.

Bundesentschädigungsgesetze. Kommentar von Georg Blessin u. a. München, 1957. 2nd ed. pp. 5–76.

Bundesversorgungsgesetz in der Fassung des Dritten Gesetzes zur Änderung und Erganzung des Kriegsopferrechts, hg. v. Reichsbund der Kriegs- und Zivilbeschädigten, Sozialrentner und Hinterbliebenen e.V. Bonn, 1967.

Bures, R.. Beurteilung der Folgen des Krieges und der faschistischen Verfolgung. In *Atio-Pathogenese,* pp. 199–240.

BVG. Gesetz über die Versorgung der Opfer des Krieges (Bundesversorgungsgesetz). München, 1965.

Deveen, W. Fachgutachten und Pensionen. In *Atio-Pathogense,* pp. 579–581.

Die Kabinettsprotokolle der Bundesregierung. http://www.bundesarchiv.de.

Die "Neurose." Ihre Versorgungs- und Sozialmedizinische Beurteilung, hg. v. Bundesminister für Arbeit und Sozialordnung. In *Schriftenreihe des Bundesversorgungsblatts,* Heft 1. Bonn, 1960.

Eissler, Kurt. Die Ermordung von wie vielen seiner Kinder muss ein Mensch symptomfrei ertragen konnen, um eine normale Konstitution zu haben? *Psyche* 17 (1963), pp. 241–291.

Elsasser, Gunter. Erfahrungen an 1400 Kriegsneurosen (Aus einem neurologisch-psychiatrischen Reserve-Lazarett des 2. Weltkriegs). In *Psychiatrie der Gegenwart,* pp. 623–630.

Extreme Lebensverhältnisse und ihre Folgen (Schriftenreihe des Ärztlich-wissenschaftlichen Beirates des Verbandes der Heimkehrer Deutschlands e. V., B. 7) hg. v. Verband der Heimkehrer, Kriegsgefangenen und Vermisstenangehörigen Deutschlands. Bad Godesberg, 1959.

Extreme Lebensverhältnisse und ihre Folgen. Handbuch der ärztlichen Erfahrungen aus der Gefangenschaft, bearb. v. Ernst G. Schenck u. Wolfgang von Nathusius. Bad Godesberg, 1958 ff.

Faust, Clemens. Organische Hirnschäden nach Hungerdystrophie. *Fortschritte der Medizin* 21 (1953), pp. 71–72.

Fleischhacker, H. H. Healing the Wounds. *AJR Information* 11 (1956), p. 6.

Forte, Dieter. *In der Erinnerung.* Frankfurt a. M., 2001.

Franke, K. Katamnese der Heimkehrer. *Deutsche medizinische Rundschau* 3 (1949), p. 1278.

Frankl, Viktor E. Psychologie und Psychiatrie des Konzentrationslagers. In *Psychiatrie der Gegenwart,* Bd. 3, pp. 743–759.

Friedman, Paul. Some aspects of concentration camp psychology. *American Journal of Psychiatry* 105 (1949), pp. 601–605.

Gauger, Kurt. Die Dystrophie als psychosomatisches Krankheitsbild. München, 1952.

Gaupp, Robert. Die psychischen und nervosen Erkrankungen des Heeres im Weltkrieg. *Der Deutsche Militärarzt* 5 (1940), pp. 358–368.

Gerstacker, Wilhelm. Vorüberlegungen zur allgemeinen Psychologie und Psychopathologie des Krieges. *Archiv für Psychiatrie und Nervenkrankheiten* 182 (1949), pp. 32–50.

Gesetz über die Versorgung der Opfer des Krieges (Bundesversorgungsgesetz) in der Fassung vom 6. Juni 1956. In *Bundesgesetzblatt*, Teil 1, Jg. 1956, p. 475.

Gesetz zur Änderung und Erganzung des Kriegsopferrechts (Erstes Neuordnungsgesetz) vom 27. Juni 1960. In *Bundesgesetzblatt*; Nr. 32, 1960, pp. 453 ff.

Goetz, Ernst. Das anlagebedingte Leiden im Recht der Entschädigung für Opfer nationalsozialistischer Verfolgung. *Rechtsprechung zum Wiedergutmachungsrecht* 12 (1961), pp. 246–248.

Golovchansky, Anatoly u. a., ed. Ich will raus aus diesem Wahnsinn. Deutsche Briefe von der Ostfront 1941–1945. Aus sowjetischen Archiven. Reinbek, 1993.

Gottschick, Johann. Kriegsgefangenschaft und Psychosen. *Der Nervenarzt* 21 (1950), pp. 129–132.

Gottschick, Johann. Neuropsychiatrische Erkrankungen bei deutschen Kriegsgefangenen in den USA im Lichte statistischer Betrachtungen. *Archiv für Psychiatrie und Nervenkrankheiten* 185 (1950), pp. 491–510.

Grass, Gunter. *Im Krebsgang*. Göttingen, 2002.

Haag, Hilmar. Gefangenschaftsschäden. *Kriegsopferversorgung* 3 (1954), pp. 75–78.

Hampel, Bruno. Das mit dem Mais. In Thomas Friedrich, ed., *Aufräumungsarbeiten. Erzählungen aus Deutschland 1945–1948*. Berlin, 1983, pp. 10–15.

Hand, G. Zu den Begriffen: Anlage, wesentliche Mitverursachung, Manifestation und Krankheit. *Rechtsprechung zum Wiedergutmachungsrecht* 14 (1963), pp. 154–156.

Hand, G. Zur Definition der anlagebedingten Leiden im Sinne des § 4 der 2. DV-BEG. *Rechtsprechung zum Wiedergutmachungsrecht* 12 (1961), pp. 103–105.

Handbuch der ärztlichen Erfahrungen im Weltkriege 1914/1918, hg. v. Otto Schjerning. Bd. 4: Geistes- und Nervenkrankheiten, hg. v. Karl Bonhoeff er. Leipzig, 1922.

Hansen, Fritz. Kriegsgefangenschaft als ärztliches Erlebnis. *Münchener Medizinische Wochenschrift* 93 (1951), pp. 538–541.

Heidenhain, Adolf. *Die Psychiatrie im Dienste der Wehrmacht*. Leipzig, 1938.

Helweg-Larsen. Per, u. a., Die Hungerkrankheit in den deutschen Konzentrationslagern. In Max Michel, ed., pp. 148–171.

Helweg-Larsen. Per, u. a., Die sozialen Folgeerscheinungen der Deportation. In Max Michel, ed., pp. 256–267.

Hemsing, Walter. Die seelische Situation des Kriegsgefangenen und die innere Gesundung des Heimkehrers. *Bremer Ärzteblatt* 1 (1948), pp. 48–53.

Hemsing, Walter. Seelische Not hinter Stacheldraht. *Caritas* 49 (1948), pp. 6–10.

Hennies, Günter. Kriegsopferversorgung. *Der Medizinische Sachverständige* 60 (1964), pp. 71–72.

Hennies, Günter. Neurose und Leistungen aus der Rentenversicherung. *Der Medizinische Sachverständige* 55 (1964), pp. 169–175.

Hennies, Günter. Zum Neurose-Problem. BGH-Beschluss vom 13. Juli 1963. *der Medizinische Sachverständige* 60 (1964), pp. 119–120.

Hensge, E. Reaktive psychische Erkrankungen der Nachkriegszeit. *Psychiatrie, Neurologie und Medizinische Psychologie* 1 (1949), pp. 133–137.

Hermann, Knud. Das Syndrom der Konzentrationslager. Zehn Jahre nach der Befreiung. In Max Michel, pp. 59–72.

Hermann, Knud. Die psychischen Symptome des KZ-Syndroms. In Max Michel, pp.
40–47.

Heuer, Karl Heinz. Mitwirkendes Verschulden bei Neurose-Schäden? *Rechtsprechung
zum Wiedergutmachungsrecht* 15 (1964), pp. 429–432.

Hirschfeld, Gerhard, and Irina Renz, eds. *Vormittags die ersten Amerikaner: Stimmen
und Bilder vom Kriegsende 1945.* Stuttgart, 2005.

Hochrein, Max. Diagnostik und Therapie der vegetativen Dystonie. In *Extreme Lebensverhältnisse und ihre Folgen,* Bd. 7, pp. 125–159.

Hosenfeld, Wilm. *Ich versuche jeden zu retten. Das Leben eines deutschen Offiziers in
Briefen und Tagebüchern.* München, 2005.

Jacob, Wolfgang. Gesellschaftliche Voraussetzungen zur Überwindung der KZ-
Schäden. *Der Nervenarzt* 32 (1961), pp. 542–545.

Kalinowski, Lothar B. Problems of War Neuroses in the Light of Experiences in Other
Countries. *American Journal of Psychiatry* 107 (1950), pp. 340–346.

Kalinowski, Lothar B. In Ludwig J. Pongratz, ed., *Psychiatrie in Selbstdarstellungen.*
Bern, 1977.

Kaufman, M. R. Ill Health as an Expression of Anxiety in a Combat Unit. *Psychosomatic medicine* 9 (1947), p. 108.

Kempowski, Walter. *Das Echolot. Abgesang '45. Ein kollektives Tagebuch.* München,
2005.

Kerschbaumer, Max. Die Neurose in der Unfallversicherung und Kriegsopferversorgung. *Der Medizinische Sachverständige* 61 (1965), pp. 134–142.

Kessler, U. Kritisches zur Praxis der Entschädigungsverfahren. In *Spätschäden nach
Extrembelastungen.* Referate der II. Internationalen Medizinisch-Juristischen Konferenz in Düsseldorf 1969, hg. v. Hans-Joachim Herberg. Herford 1971, pp. 322–
325.

Kilian, Hans. Zur Psychopathologie der Heimkehrer. *Deutsche medizinische Rundschau* 3 (1949), p. 1278.

Klinisches Wörterbuch. *Die Kunstausdrucke der Medizin, begründet von Otto Dorn-
bluth, neubearbeitet von Willibald Pschyrembel.* Berlin, 1937.

Kluge, Erich. Über die Folgen schwerer Haftzeiten. *Der Nervenarzt* 29 (1958), pp.
462–465.

Kohler, A. Die Neurose. Ihr Wesen und ihre Bedeutung in der Sozialversicherung. *Der
Medizinische Sachverständige* 60 (1964), p. 165.

Kolle, Kurt. Die Opfer der nationalsozialistischen Verfolgung in psychiatrischer Sicht.
In ebd. 29 (1958), pp. 148–158.

Kornhuber, Hans H. Psychologie und Psychiatrie der Kriegsgefangenschaft. In *Psychiatrie der Gegenwart. Forschung und Praxis,* Bd. 3: Soziale und angewandte Psychiatrie. Berlin 1961, pp. 631–742.

Kranz, Heinrich. Zeitbedingte abnorme Erlebnisreaktionen. Versuch einer Übersicht.
Allgemeine Zeitschrift für Psychiatrie und ihre Grenzgebiete 124 (1949), pp. 336–
357.

Krober, Ernst. Über Haftpsychosen (Anlage- und exogene Faktoren bei der Entstehung von Haftreaktionen. Erfahrungen an Internierten). *Der Nervenarzt* 19 (1948), pp. 408–413.

Krüger, Horst. Das zerbrochene Haus. Eine Jugend in Deutschland [1966]. 3rd ed. München, 1988.

Krüger, Horst. Im Labyrinth der Schuld. *Der Monat* 16 (1964), pp. 19–29.

Krystal, Henry, ed. *Massive Psychic Trauma.* New York, 1968.

Ledig, Gert. *Vergeltung.* Frankfurt a. M., 1956.

Leonhard, Karl. Lassen sich in der Begutachtung von Neurosen keine scharferen Gesichtspunkte gewinnen? *Der Medizinische Sachverständige* 62 (1966), pp. 201–210.

Lewin, Bruno. Neurologisch-psychiatrische Untersuchungen und Beobachtungen an deutschen Kriegsgefangenen in Ägypten 1941–1947. *Psychiatrie, Neurologie und Medizinische Psychologie* 1 (1949), pp. 230–236.

Lifton, Robert Jay. *Thought Reform and the Psychology of Totalitarianism: A Study of Brainwashing in China.* New York, 1961.

Lipscomb, F. M. Medical Aspects of Belsen Concentration Camp. *The Lancet* 8 (Sept. 1945), pp. 313–315.

Lungershausen, Eberhard, and H. Matiar-Vahar. Erlebnisreaktive psychische Dauerschädigungen nach Kriegsgefangenschaft und Deportation. *Der Nervenarzt* 39 (1968), pp. 123–126.

Malten, Hans, Heimkehrer. *Medizinische Klinik* 41 (1946), pp. 593–600.

March, Hans, ed. *Verfolgung und Angst in ihren leib-seelischen Auswirkungen.* Stuttgart, 1960.

Marx, W. Über Dystrophie-Dauerschäden. *Deutsche medizinische Rundschau* 3 (1949), pp. 1272–1274.

Matussek, Paul. Die Konzentrationslagerhaft als Belastungssituation. *Der Nervenarzt* 32 (1961), pp. 538–542.

Max Mikorey. Hysterische Reaktionen im Feldheer. In *Bericht über die 2. Arbeitsgung Ost der beratenden Fachärzte in der Militärärztlichen Akademie Berlin.* Berlin, 1942/1943. p. 141.

Mende, Walter. Gutachterliche Probleme bei der Beurteilung erlebnisreaktiver Schädigungen. In Helmut Paul and Hans-Joachim Herberg, eds., *Psychische Spätschäden*, pp. 281–292.

Meyer, Joachim Ernst. Die abnormen Erlebnisreaktionen im Kriege bei Truppe und Zivilbevolkerung. In *Psychiatrie der Gegenwart*, Bd. 3: Soziale und angewandte Psychiatrie. Berlin, 1961, pp. 574–619.

Meyeringh, Heinz. Über Folgeerscheinungen der Dystrophie. *Ärztliche Wochenschrift* 5 (1950), pp. 889–893.

Michel, Max, ed. *Gesundheitsschäden durch Verfolgung und Gefangenschaft und ihre Spätfolgen.* Frankfurt a. M., 1955.

Michel, Max. Spätschäden und Summationsschäden. In Max Michel, ed., *Gesundheitsschäden durch Verfolgung und Gefangenschaft und ihre Spätfolgen.* Frankfurt a. M., 1955, pp. 48–51.

Mitscherlich, Alexander. *Ein Leben für die Psychoanalyse. Anmerkungen zu meiner Zeit.* Frankfurt a. M., 1984.

Mitscherlich, Alexander, and Fred Mielke. *Das Diktat der Menschenverachtung. Der Nürnberger Ärzteprozess und seine Quellen.* Heidelberg, 1947.

Mitscherlich, Alexander, and Margarete Mitscherlich. *Die Unfähigkeit zu trauern. Grundlagen kollektiven Verhaltens.* München, 1998 (1. Aufl . 1967).

Müller-Suur, Hemmo. Abgrenzung neurotischer Erkrankungen gegenüber der Norm. In *Handbuch für Neurosenlehre und Psychotherapie*, Bd. 1, Berlin 1959, pp. 250–262.

Niederland, William. *Folgen der Verfolgung: Das Überlebenden-Syndrom Seelenmord.* Frankfurt a. M., 1980.

Nonne, Max. Therapeutische Erfahrungen an den Kriegsneurosen. In Karl Bonhoeffer, ed., *Handbuch der ärztlichen Erfahrungen im Weltkriege 1914/1918*, Bd. 4: Geistes- und Nervenkrankheiten. Leipzig, 1922, pp. 102–121.

Panse, Friedrich. *Angst und Schreck in klinisch-psychologischer und sozialmedizinischer Sicht. Dargestellt an Hand von Erlebnisberichten aus dem Luftkrieg.* Stuttgart, 1952.

Panse, Friedrich. Der Krankheitswert der Neurose. *Der Medizinische Sachverständige* 61 (1965), pp. 114–120.

Panse, Friedrich. Hysterie, Simulation, unter besonderer Berucksichtigung der psychogenen Überlagerung bei organischen Schädigungen. In *Bericht über die 3. Arbeitstagung Ost der Beratenden Fachärzte vom 24.–26. Mai 1943 in der Militärärztlichen Akademie Berlin.* Berlin, 1943, pp. 217–218.

Paul, Helmut. Die Psyche des Hungernden und des Dystrophikers. In *Extreme Lebensverhältnisse und ihre Folgen*, Bd. 5. Bad Godesberg, 1961, pp. 5–127.

Paul, Helmut. *Einflüsse extremer Belastungen auf die psychischen und psychosozialen Verhältnisse ehemaliger Kriegsgefangener (Extreme Lebensverhältnisse als Risikofaktoren, Bd. 8).* Stuttgart, 1986.

Paul, Helmut. Erforschung der Spätfolgen von Gefangenschaft und Deportierung. *Ärztliche Praxis* 13 (1961), pp. 1565–1566.

Paul, Helmut. Internationale Erfahrungen mit psychischen Spätschäden. In Paul Helmut and Hans-Joachim Herberg, eds., *Psychische Spätschäden*, pp. 37–84.

Paul, Helmut, and Hans-Joachim Herberg, eds. *Psychische Spätschäden nach politischer Verfolgung.* Basel, 1963.

Pentz, Adolf. Richter und Sachverständiger auf dem Gebiet der Neurosen. *Rechtsprechung zum Wiedergutmachungsrecht* 17 (1966), pp. 49–54.

Peter, Cuno. Psychologische und psychiatrisch-neurologische Beobachtungen und Erfahrungen aus 29monatiger Gefangenschaft. *Der Nervenarzt* 20 (1949), pp. 202–206.

Picard, Max. *Hitler in uns selbst.* Erlenbach-Zürich, 1946.

Pongratz, Ludwig J., ed. *Psychiatrie in Selbstdarstellungen.* Bern, 1977.

Popper, Ludwig. Ärztliche Erfahrungen bei Untersuchungen nach dem Österreichischen Opferfürsorgegesetz. In Max Michel, ed., pp. 281–287.

Proske, Rüdiger, and Walter Weymann-Weyhe. Wir aus dem Kriege. Der Weg der jüngeren Generation. *Frankfurter Hefte* 3 (1948), pp. 792–803.

Psychiatrie der Gegenwart. *Forschung und Praxis, Bd. 3: Soziale und angewandte Psychiatrie.* Berlin, 1961.

Rauschelbach, Heinz-Harro. Unterschiede und Gemeinsamkeiten in der Begutachtung nach dem Bundesentschädigungs- und Bundesversorgungsgesetz. *Der Medizinische Sachverständige* 65 (1969), pp. 248–251.

Rauschelbach, Heinz-Harro. Zur Klinik der Spätfolgezustände nach Hungerdystrophie. *Forschritte der Neurologie, Psychiatrie und ihrer Grenzgebiete* 22 (1954), pp. 214–226.

Reese, Willy Peter. *Mir selber seltsam fremd. Die Unmenschlichkeit des Krieges, Russland 1941–1944*, hg. v. Stefan Schmitz. München, 2003.

Schellworth, Walter. *Neurosenfrage, Ursachenbegriff und Rechtssprechung.* Stuttgart, 1953.

Schelsky, Helmut. *Wandlungen der deutschen Familie in der Gegenwart. Darstellung und Deutung einer empirisch-soziologischen Tatbestandsaufnahme.* Dortmund, 1953.

Schmidt, Gerhard. Gestaltwandel von Massenreaktionen auf Kriegs- und Nachkriegsüberlastung. *Fortschritte der Neurologie, Psychiatrie und ihrer Grenzgebiete* 22 (1954), pp. 125–129.

Schmitz, Willi. Kriegsgefangenschaft und Heimkehr in ihren Beziehungen zu psychischen Krankheitsbildern. *Der Nervenarzt* 20 (1949), pp. 303–310.

Schnabel, Bernhard. *Macht ohne Moral. Eine Dokumentation über die SS.* Frankfurt a. M., 1956.

Schneider, Carl. Die strafrechtliche Verfolgung der Neurotiker. In *Bericht über die 4. Arbeitstagung der Beratenden Ärzte vom 16. bis 18. Mai 1944 im SS-Lazarett Hohenlychen,* o. O., o. J., pp. 273–274.

Schneider, Kurt. Der Psychopath in heutiger Sicht. *Fortschritte der Neurologie, Psychiatrie und ihrer Grenzgebiete* 26 (1958), pp. 1–9.

Schneider, Kurt. Die Psychopathenfrage beim Feldheer. In *Bericht über die 1. Arbeitstagung Ost der beratenden Fachärzte am 18. und 19. Mai 1942 in der Militärärztlichen Akademie Berlin.* o. O., o. J., pp. 158–167.

Schneider, Kurt. Einige psychiatrische Erfahrungen als Truppenarzt. *Zeitschrift für die gesamte Neurologie und Psychiatrie* 39 (1918), pp. 307–314.

Schneider, Kurt. Kraepelin und die gegenwartige Psychiatrie. *Fortschritte der Neurologie, Psychiatrie und ihrer Grenzgebiete* 24 (1956), pp. 1–7.

Schneider, Kurt. Neurosen vom Standpunkt der klinischen Psychiatrie. In *Bericht über die 4. Arbeitstagung,* pp. 270–271.

Schneider, Kurt. Selbstmord als Dienstbeschädigung—Schizophrenie als Dienstbeschädigung. *Der Nervenarzt* 21 (1950), pp. 480–483.

Schneider, Kurt. Zum Krankheitsbegriff in der Psychiatrie. *Deutsche Medizinische Wochenschrift* 17 (1946), pp. 306–307.

Schönberner, Gerhard. *Der gelbe Stern. Die Judenverfolgung in Europa 1933–1945.* Hamburg, 1960.

Schöneberg, Georg, ed. *Die ärztliche Beurteilung Beschädigter.* 2nd ed. Darmstadt, 1955.

Schubert, Eberhard. Die derzeitige höchstrichterliche Rechtsprechung zum Neurosen-Problem im Wiedergutmachungsrecht, im Versorgungsrecht und in der gesetzlichen Unfallversicherung. *Rechtsprechung zum Wiedergutmachungsrecht* 19 (1968), pp. 481–490.

Schubert, Eberhard. Die Neurose. Ihr Wesen und ihre Bedeutung in der Sozialversicherung. *Die Sozialgerichtsbarkeit* 10 (1963), pp. 321–327.

Schuddekopf, Carl. Im Kessel. Erzählungen von Stalingrad, München 2002. Schulte, Walter, Ausere Einflüsse auf neurologisch-psychiatrische Krankheiten, ein Vergleich mit den ersten Weltkriegserfahrungen. *Ärztliche Wochenschrift* 1 (1947), pp. 550–563.

Schulte, Walter. Cerebrale Defektsyndrome nach schwerer Hungerdystrophie und Möglichkeiten ihrer Kompensierung mit dem Blick auf Heimkehrerdepression und forensische Komplikationen. *Der Nervenarzt* 24 (1953), pp. 415–419.

Schulte, Walter, Gibt es eine Hirnversehrtheit infolge schwerer Dystrophien? *Ärztliche Wochenschrift* 8 (1953), pp. 233–236.

Schulte, Walter. Hirnorganische Dauerschäden nach Dystrophie: Wesens änderungen, Epilepsien und Apoplexien. *Medizinische Klinik* 46 (1951), pp. 1356–1359.

Schulte, Walter. *Über das Problem der seelischen Entstehungsbedingungen von Krankheiten.* Stuttgart, 1966.

Sebald, Winfried G.. *Luftkrieg und Literatur.* 5th ed. Frankfurt a. M., 2005.

Sedlmayr, Gert. Wandlungen im Krankheitsbild der Ostheimkehrer. *Medizinische Klinik* 44 (1949), pp. 1223–1225.

Störring, Gustav. Die Verschiedenheiten der psycho-pathologischen Erfahrungen im Weltkriege und im jetzigen Krieg und ihre Ursachen. *Münchener Medizinische Wochenschrift* 89 (1942), pp. 25–30.

Targowla, Rene. Die neuropsychischen Folgen der Deportation in den deutschen Konzentrationslagern. Syndrom der Asthenie der Deportierten. In Max Michel, pp. 30–40.

Targowla, Rene. Bericht zur Ausarbeitung einer neuen Rententabelle für ehemalige Verfolgte, Internierte und Deportierte. In Max Michel, ed., pp. 274–280.

Tas, Jacques, Psychical Disorders among Inmates of Concentration Camps and Repatriates. *Psychiatric Quarterly* 25 (1951), pp. 679–690.

Tuurnwald, Hilde. *Gegenwartsprobleme Berliner Familien. Eine soziologische Untersuchung an 498 Familien.* Berlin, 1948, pp. 172–180.

Thygesen, Paul, u. a. Die psychischen Symptome der Heimkehrer. In Max Michel, ed., pp. 52–58.

Thygesen, Paul. Allgemeines über die Spätfolgen. In Max Michel, ed., *Gesundheitsschäden durch Verfolgung und Gefangenschaft und ihre Spätfolgen.* Frankfurt a. M., 1955, pp. 21–29

Thysen, Eigel Hess, and Jorn Hess Thaysen. Medizinische Probleme bei früheren, in deutsche Konzentrationslager Deportierten. In Max Michel, ed., pp. 172–180.

Venzlaff, Ulrich. Das Problem des mitwirkenden Verschuldens (BGB § 254) in der Neurosenbeurteilung. *Rechtsprechung zum Wiedergutmachungsrecht* 14 (1963), pp. 193–198.

Venzlaff, Ulrich. Die Begutachtung psychischer Störungen Verfolgter. *Rechtsprechung zum Wiedergutmachungsrecht* 17 (1966), pp. 196–200.

Venzlaff, Ulrich. *Die psychoreaktiven Störungen nach entschädigungspflichtigen Ereignissen (die sogenannten Unfallneurosen).* Berlin, 1958.

Venzlaff,, Ulrich. Erlebnishintergrund und Dynamik seelischer Verfolgungsschäden. In Helmut Paul and Hans-Joachim Herberg, eds., *Psychische Spätschäden*, pp. 95–109.

Venzlaff, Ulrich. Grundsatzliche Betrachtungen über die Begutachtung erlebnisbedingter seelischer Störungen nach rassischer und politischer Verfolgung. *Rechtsprechung zum Wiedergutmachungsrecht* 10 (1959), pp. 289–292.

Venzlaff, Ulrich. Gutachten zur Frage des Zusammenwirkens erlebnisreaktiver, vegetativer und hormonaler Faktoren bei Verfolgungsschäden. In Helmut Paul and Hans-Joachim Herberg, eds., *Psychische Spätschäden nach politischer Verfolgung*, Basel 1963, pp. 111–124.

Venzlaff, Ulrich. Das Problem des mitwirkenden Verschuldens (BGB § 254) in der Neurosenbeurteilung. *Rechtsprechung zum Wiedergutmachungsrecht* 14 (1963), pp. 193–198.

Venzlaff, Ulrich. Schizophrenie und Verfolgung. *Rechtsprechung zur Wiedergutmachung* 12 (1961), pp. 193–196.

Verhandlungen des deutschen Bundestages 3. Wahlperiode, Stenographische Berichte, Bd. 44–46. Bonn. 1960.

Villinger, Werner. Psychiatrie und Wehrmacht. In *Münchener Medizinische Wochenschrift* 88 (1941), pp. 432–443.

von Baeyer, Walter. Der Begriff der Begegnung in der Psychiatrie. *Der Nervenarzt* 26 (1955), pp. 369–376.

von Baeyer, Walter. Die Freiheitsfrage in der forensischen Psychiatrie mit besonderer Berücksichtigung der Entschädigungsneurosen. *Der Nervenarzt* 28 (1957), pp. 337–343.

von Baeyer, Walter. Erlebnisbedingte Verfolgungsschäden. *Der Nervenarzt* 32 (1961), pp. 534–538.

von Baeyer, Walter. Erlebnisreaktive Störungen und ihre Bedeutung für die Begutachtung. *Deutsche Medizinische Wochenschrift* 83 (1958), pp. 2317–2122.

von Baeyer, Walter. Gegenwärtige Psychiatrie in den Vereinigten Staaten. *der Nervenarzt* 21 (1950), pp. 2–9.

von Baeyer, Walter. Walter Ritter von Baeyer. In Pongratz, ed., pp. 9–34.

von Baeyer, Walter. Zur Statistik und Form der abnormen Erlebnisreaktionen in der Gegenwart. *Der Nervenarzt* 19 (1948), pp. 402–408.

von Baeyer, Walter. In Pongratz, ed., pp. 9–34.

von Baeyer, Walter, Heinz Hafner, and Karl-Peter Kisker. Wissenschaftliche Erkenntnis oder menschliche Wertung der erlebnisreaktiven Schäden Verfolgter? *Der Nervenarzt* 34 (1963), pp. 120–123.

von Baeyer, Walter, H. Hafner, and K. P. Kisker. *Psychiatrie der Verfolgten. Psychopathologische und gutachtliche Erfahrungen an Opfern der nationalsozialistischen Verfolgung und vergleichbarer Extrembelastungen.* Berlin, 1964.

von Baeyer, Walter, Heinz Hafner, and Karl-Peter Kisker. Zur Frage des "symptomfreien Intervalles" bei erlebnisreaktiven Störungen Verfolgter. In Helmut Paul and Hans-Joachim Herberg, eds., *Psychische Spätschäden*, pp. 125–153.

Walser, Martin. Unser Auschwitz. In *Kursbuch* 1 (1965), pp. 189–200.

Weber, F. W. A.. Wie sollen wir uns in einem zukünftigen Kriege den Kriegsneurotikern stellen? in: Münchener Medizinische Wochenschrift 86 (1939), pp. 1305–1306.

Wilke, G. Zur Frage der Hirnödeme bei Unterernährung. In *Deutsche Medizinische Wochenschrift*, 1950, pp. 172–176.

Witter, Hermann. Erlebnisbedingte Schädigung durch Verfolgung. *Der Nervenarzt* 33 (1962), pp. 509–510.

Witter, Hermann. Zur Kausalitat bei sogenannten Neurosen. *Der Medizinische Sachverständige* 61 (1965), pp. 143–148.

Zum politischen Bewusstsein ehemaliger Kriegsgefangener. Frankfurt a. M., 1957.

Zutt, Jürg. Über den seelischen Gesundheitszustand der Berliner Bevölkerung in den vergangenen Jahren und heute. *Ärztliche Wochenschrift* 1 (1946), pp. 248–250.

Zweite Verordnung zur Durchführung des Bundesentschädigungsgesetzes (2. DV-BEG). In *Bundesentschädigungsgesetze*, pp. 1239–1245.

SECONDARY SOURCES

Abelshauser, Werner. *Deutsche Wirtschaftsgeschichte seit 1945.* München, 2004.

Ackermann, Volker. Das Schweigen der Flüchtlingskinder—Psychische Folgen von Krieg, Flucht und Vertreibung bei den Deutschen nach 1945. *Geschichte und Gesellschaft* 30 (2004), pp. 434–464.

Ahonen, Pertti. *After the Expulsion. West Germany and Eastern Europe 1945–1990.* Oxford, 2003.

Allport, Alan. *Demobbed: Coming Home After the Second World War.* New Haven, 2010.

Aly, Götz, ed. *Volkes Stimme. Skepsis und Führervertrauen im Nationalsozialismus.* Frankfurt a. M., 2006.

Arnold, Klaus Jochen. Die Wehrmacht und die Besatzungspolitik in den besetzten Gebieten der Sowjetunion. Kriegführung und Radikalisierung im "Unternehmen Barbarossa." Berlin, 2004.

Ash, Mitchell G. Verordnete Umbrüche—Konstruierte Kontinuitäten: Zur Entnazifizierung von Wissenschaftlern und Wissenschaften nach 1945. *Zeitschrift für Geschichtswissenschaft* 43 (1995), pp. 903–923.

Assmann, Aleida. Erinnerungsräume. *Formen und Wandlungen des kulturellen Gedächtnisses.* München, 1999.

Assmann, Aleida. Funktionsgedächtnis und Speichergedächtnis—Zwei Modi der Erinnerung. In Kristin Platt and Mihran Dabag, eds., *Generation und. Erinnerungen und kollektive Identitäten.* Opladen 1995, pp. 169–185.

Assmann, Jan. *Das kulturelle Gedächtnis. Schrift, Erinnerung und politische Identität in frühen Hochkulturen.* München, 1999.

Averbeck, Stefanie. The post-1933 emigration of communication researchers from Germany. The lost works of the Weimar Generation. *European Journal of Communication* 16 (2001), pp. 451–475.

Bacque, James. *Der geplante Tod. Deutsche Kriegsgefangene in amerikanischen und französischen Lagern 1945–1946.* Frankfurt a. M., 1989.

Bade, Klaus J. *Europa in Bewegung. Migration vom späten 18. Jh. bis in die Gegenwart.* München, 2000.

Bajohr, Frank. Hamburg—der Zerfall der "Volksgemeinschaft." In Herbert and Schildt, eds., pp. 318–336.

Bajohr, Frank, and Dieter Pohl. *Der Holocaust als offenes Geheimnis. Die Deutschen, die NS-Führung und die Alliierten.* München, 2006.

Barnouw, Dagmar. *Ansichten von Deutschland (1945): Krieg und Gewalt in der zeitgenössischen Photographie.* Basel, 1997.

Bartov, Omar. *Hitlers Wehrmacht. Soldaten, Fanatismus und die Brutalisierung des Krieges.* Reinbek, 1995.

Baumann, Imanuel. *Dem Verbrechen auf der Spur. Eine Geschichte der Kriminologie und Kriminalpolitik in Deutschland, 1880 bis 1980.* Göttingen, 2006.

Baumann, Stefanie. Opfer von Menschenversuchen als Sonderfall der Wiedergutmachung. In Hockerts et al, eds., Grenzen, pp. 147–194.

Baumann, Ursula. *Vom Recht auf den eigenen Tod. Die Geschichte des Suizids vom 18. bis zum 20. Jahrhundert.* Weimar, 2001.

Behrenbeck, Sabine. Between Pain and Silence. Remembering the Victims of Violence in Germany after 1949. In Bessel and Schumann, eds., pp. 37–64.

Behrends, Jan C. Freundschaft, Fremdheit, Gewalt. Ostdeutsche Sowjetunionbilder zwischen Propaganda und Erfahrung. In Gregor Thum, ed., *Traumland Osten. Deutsche Bilder vom östlichen Europa im 20. Jahrhundert.* Göttingen 2006, pp. 157–177.

Benz, Wolfgang. Postwar Society and National Socialism: Remembrance, Amnesia, Rejection. *Tel Aviver Jahrbuch für deutsche Geschichte* 19 (1990), pp. 1–12.

Beradt, Charlotte. *Das Dritte Reich im Traum.* Frankfurt a. M., 1994.

Bergen, Doris L. The Volksdeutschen of Eastern Europe, World War II, and the Holocaust: Constructed Ethnicity, Real Genocide. In Keith Bullivant et al, eds., *Germany and Eastern Europe: Cultural Identities and Cultural Differences*, Amsterdam 1999, pp. 70–93.

Berger, Georg. *Die Beratenden Psychiater des deutschen Heeres 1939 bis 1945.* Frankfurt a. M., 1998.

Berghoff, Hartmut, and Cornelia Rauh-Kühne. *Fritz K. Ein deutsches Leben im 20. Jahrhundert.* München, 2000.

Bessel, Richard. Leben nach dem Tod. Vom Zweiten Weltkrieg zur zweiten Nachkriegszeit. In Bernd Wegner, ed., *Wie Kriege enden. Wege zum Frieden von der Antike bis zur Gegenwart*, Paderborn 2002, pp. 239–258.

Bessel, Richard. The War to End all Wars. The Shock of Violence in 1945 and Its Aftermath in Germany. In Lüdtke and Weisbrod, eds., pp. 69–99.

Bessel, Richard, and Dirk Schumann. Introduction: Violence, Normality, and the Construction of Postwar Europe. In Bessel and Schumann, eds., pp. 1–13.

Bessel, Richard, and Dirk Schumann, eds. *Life After Death. Approaches to a Cultural and Social History of Europe During the 1940s and 1950s.* New York, 2003.

Bianchi, Bruna. Psychiatrists, Soldiers, and Officers in Italy during the Great War. In Micale and Lerner, eds., pp. 222–252.

Biess, Frank. *Homecomings. Returning POWs and the Legacies of Defeat in Postwar Germany.* Princeton, 2006.

Biess, Frank. Pioneers of a New Germany: Returning POWs from the Soviet Union and the Making of East German Citizens, 1945–1950. *Central European History* 32 (1999), pp. 143–180.

Biess, Frank. Vom Opfer zum Überlebenden des Totalitarismus: Westdeutsche Reaktionen auf die Rückkehr der Kriegsgefangenen aus der Sowjetunion, 1945–1955. In Bischof and Overmans, eds., pp. 365–389.

Birbaumer, Niels, and Dieter Langewiesche. Neuropsychologie und Historie—Versuch einer empirischen Annäherung. Posttraumatische Belastungsstörung (PTSD) und Soziopathie in Österreich nach 1945. *Geschichte und Gesellschaft* 32 (2006), pp. 153–175.

Bischof, Gunter, and Rüdiger Overmans, eds., *Kriegsgefangenschaft im Zweiten Weltkrieg. Eine vergleichende Perspektive.* Ternitz-Pottschach, 1999.

Black, Monica. *The Meaning of Death and the Making of Three Berlins: A History, 1933–1961.* (Diss., University of Virginia, MS).

Boelcke, Willi A. *Der Schwarzmarkt 1945–1948. Vom Überleben nach dem Kriege.* Braunschweig, 1986.

Bösch, Frank. Film, NS-Vergangenheit und Geschichtswissenschaft: Von "Holocaust" zu "Der Untergang." *Vierteljahreshefte für Zeitgeschichte* 55 (2007), pp. 1–32.

Borchard, Michael. *Die deutschen Kriegsgefangenen in der Sowjetunion. Zur politischen Bedeutung der Kriegsgefangenenfrage 1949–1955.* Düsseldorf, 2000.

Bourke, Joanna. The Emotions in War: Fear and the British and American Military, 1914–1945. *Historical Research* 74 (2001), pp. 314–330.

Bourke, Joanna. Postwar Adjustment of British and American Servicemen after the War. In Bessel and Schumann, eds., pp. 149–160.

Braese, Stephan. In einer deutschen Angelegenheit—Der Frankfurter Auschwitz-Prozess in der westdeutschen Nachkriegsliteratur. In Fritz Bauer Institut, ed., pp. 217–244.

Brandlmeier, Thomas. Von Hitler zu Adenauer: Deutsche Trummerfilme. In Hilmar Hoffmann and Walter Schobert, eds., *Zwischen Gestern und Morgen: Westdeutscher Nachkriegsfilm 1946–1962.* Frankfurt a. M., 1989. pp. 33–59.

Briesen Detlef, and Klaus Weinhauer, eds. *Jugend, Delinquenz und gesellschaftlicher Wandel. Bundesrepublik Deutschland und USA nach dem Zweiten Weltkrieg.* Essen, 2006.

Brink, Cornelia. *"Auschwitz in der Paulskirche." Erinnerungspolitik in Fotoausstellungen der sechziger Jahre.* Marburg, 2000.

Brink, Cornelia. *Ikonen der Vernichtung. Öffentlicher Gebrauch von Fotografien aus nationalsozialistischen Konzentrationslagern nach 1945.* Berlin, 1998.

Brink, Cornelia. "Keine Angst vor dem Psychiater." Psychiatrie, Psychiatriekritik und Öffentlichkeit in der Bundesrepublik Deutschland (1960–1980). In Fangerau and Nolte, eds., pp. 341–360.

Brink, Cornelia. Zwangseinweisungen in die Psychiatrie. In Herbert, ed., *Wandlungsprozesse*, pp. 467–507.

Brochhagen, Ulrich. *Nach Nürnberg. Vergangenheitsbewältigung und Westintegration in der Ära Adenauer.* Berlin, 1999.

Browning, Christopher. Ganz normale Männer. Das Reserve-Polizeibataillon 101 und die Endlösung. 3rd ed. In Krzeminski, *Polen.* Reinbek, 1999.

Burke, Peter. Die Kulturgeschichte der Träume. In Peter Burke, *Eleganz und Haltung.* Berlin, 1998, pp. 37–62.

Burgdorff, Stephan, and Christian Habbe, eds. *Als Feuer vom Himmel fiel. Der Bomb-enkrieg in Deutschland.* München, 2003.

Buruma, Ian. *Year Zero: A History of 1945.* New York, 2013.

Buske, Sybille. "Fraulein Mutter" vor den Richterstuhl. Der Wandel der öffentlichen Wahrnehmung und rechtlichen Stellung lediger Mütter in der Bundesrepublik 1948 bis 1970. *WerkstattGeschichte* 27 (2000), pp. 48–68.

Chiari, Bernhard. *Krieg und Militär im Film des 20. Jahrhundert.* München, 2003.

Ciompi, Luc. *Die emotionalen Grundlagen des Denkens. Entwurf einer fraktalen Affektlogik.* Göttingen, 1997.

Classen, Christoph. *Bilder der Vergangenheit. Die Zeit des Nationalsozialismus im Fernsehen der Bundesrepublik Deutschland 1955–1965.* Köln, 1999.

Cocks, Geoffrey. *Psychotherapy in the Third Reich. The Göring Institute.* 2nd ed. New Brunswick, 1997.

Cohen, Deborah. *The War Come Home. Disabled Veterans in Britain and Germany, 1914–1939.* Berkeley, 2001.

Confino, Alon. Narratives of Memory and Culture. In Confino, *Germany as a Culture of Remembrance. Promises and Limits of Writing History.* Chapel Hill, 2006. pp. 188–213.

Confino, Alon. Remembering the Second World War, 1945–1965: Narratives of Victimhood and Genocide. *Cultural Analysis: An Interdisciplinary Forum on Folklore and Popular Culture* 4 (2005), pp. 47–65.

Confino, Alon, and Peter Fritzsche. Introduction: Noises of the Past. In Confino and Fritzsche, eds., *The Work of Memory. New Directions in the Study of German Society and Culture*, Urbana 2002, pp. 1–21.

Crouthamel, Jason. *The Great War and German Memory: Society, Politics and Psychological Trauma, 1914–1945.* Exeter, 2009.

Daston, Lorraine, ed. *Biographies of Scientific Objects.* Chicago, 2000.

de Haan, Ido. Paths of Normalization after the Persecution of the Jews. The Netherlands, France, and West Germany in the 1950s. In Bessel and Schumann, eds., pp. 65–92.

Dehli, Martin. *Leben als Konflikt. Zur Biographie Alexander Mitscherlichs.* Göttingen, 2007.

Diamant, Neil J. *Embattled Glory: Veterans, Military Families, and the Politics of Patriotism, 1949–2007.* Lanham, MD, 2009.

Diehl, James M. *The Thanks of the Fatherland. German Veterans After the Second World War.* Chapel Hill, 1993.

Dörner, Klaus. Posttraumatische Belastungsstörungen—Neues Fass im Gesundheitsmarkt. *Trauma und Berufskrankheit* 6, Supplement 3 (2004), pp. 327–328.

Douglas, Lawrence. *The Memory of Judgement. Making Law and History in the Trials of the Holocaust.* New Haven, 2001.

Durth, Werner. Architektur und Stadtplanung im Dritten Reich. In Prinz and Zitelmann, eds., *Nationalsozialismus und Modernisierung.* Darmstadt, 1994. pp. 139–171.

Durth, Werner. Kontraste und Parallelen: Architektur und Stadtbau in West- und Ostdeutschland. In Schildt and Sywottek, eds., pp. 596–611.

Durth, Werner, and Niels Gutschow, eds. *Träume in Trümmern. Planungen zum Wieder-*

aufbau zerstörter Städte im Westen Deutschlands 1940–1950, Bd. 1: Konzepte; Bd. 2: Städte. Braunschweig, 1988.

Ebbinghaus, Angelika. Soldatenselbstmord im Urteil des Psychiaters Hans Bürger-Prinz. In Ebbinghaus and Linne, eds., *Kein abgeschlossenes Kapitel: Hamburg im Dritten Reich,* Hamburg 1997, pp. 487–531.

Ebbinghaus, Angelika, and Klaus Dörner, eds. *Vernichten und Heilen. Der Nürnberger Ärzteprozes und seine Folgen.* Berlin, 2001

Echternkamp, Jörg. Arbeit am Mythos: Soldatengenerationen der Wehrmacht im Urteil der west- und ostdeutschen Nachkriegsgesellschaft. In Naumann, ed., pp. 421–443.

Echternkamp, Jörg. Wut auf die Wehrmacht? Vom Bild der deutschen Soldaten in der unmittelbaren Nachkriegszeit. In Müller and Volkmann, eds., pp. 1058–1080.

Eghigian, Greg. Der Kalte Krieg im Kopf. Ein Fall von Schizophrenie und die Geschichte des Selbst in der sowjetischen Besatzungszone. *Historische Anthropologie* 11 (2003), pp. 101–122.

Eghigian, Greg. The German Welfare State as a Discourse of Trauma. In Micale and Lerner eds., pp. 92–112.

Etges, Andreas. The Best War Ever? Der Deutungswandel des Zweiten Weltkriegs in US-amerikanischen Filmen am Beispiel von "The Best Years of Our Lives" und "Saving Private Ryan." In Chiari, Rogg, and Schmidt, eds., pp. 163–178.

Fangerau, Heiner, and Karen Nolte, eds. *Moderne Anstaltspsychiatrie im 19. und 20. Jahrhundert. Legitimation und Kritik.* Stuttgart, 2006.

Fassin, Didier, and Richard Rechtman. *The Empire of Trauma: An Inquiry into the Condition of Victimhood.* Princeton, 2009.

Fehrenbach, Heide. *Cinema in Democratizing Germany. Reconstructing National Identity after Hitler.* Chapel Hill, 1995.

Fieseler, Beate. Der Kriegsinvalide in sowjetischen Spielfilmen der Kriegsund Nachkriegszeit (1944 bis 1964). In Chiari, Rogg, and Schmidt, eds.,, pp. 199–222.

Focke, Wenda. *William G. Niederland. Psychiater der Verfolgten. Seine Zeit—sein Leben—sein Werk. Ein Portrat.* Würzburg, 1992.

Förster, Alice, and Birgit Beck. Post-Traumatic Stress Disorder and World War II: Can a Psychiatric Concept Help Us Understand Postwar Society? In Bessel and Schumann, eds., pp. 15–38.

Förster, Jürgen, ed. *Stalingrad. Ereignis, Wirkung, Symbol.* 2nd ed. München, 1993.

Frei, Norbert. Von deutscher Erfindungskraft oder: Die Kollektivschuldthese in der Nachkriegszeit. In Smith, ed., 163–176.

Frei, Norbert. Hitlers Eliten nach 1945—eine Bilanz. In Frei, ed., *Hitlers Eliten,* pp. 269–299.

Frei, Norbert. Identitättätswechsel. Die "Illegalen" in der Nachkriegszeit. In König, Kuhlmann, and Schwabe, eds., *Vertuschte Vergangenheit. Der Fall Schwerte und die NS-Vergangenheit der deutschen Hochschulen.* München 1997, pp. 207–222.

Frei, Norbert. *Vergangenheitspolitik. Die Anfänge der Bundesrepublik und die NS-Vergangenheit.* 2nd ed. München, 1997.

Frei, Norbert. Die Wiederkehr des Rechts. In Frei, ed., *1945 und wir. Das Dritte Reich im Bewusstsein der Deutschen.* München, 2005. pp. 63–82.

Frei, Norbert, ed. *Hitlers Eliten nach 1945.* München, 2003.

Frei, Norbert, and Volkhard Knigge, eds. *Verbrechen erinnern. Die Auseinandersetzung mit Holocaust und Volkermord*. München, 2002.

Freimüller, Tobias. Mediziner: Operation Volkskörper. In Frei, ed., *Hitlers Eliten*, pp. 13–65.

Freimüller, Tobias. Der Umgang mit der NS-Vergangenheit in der Bundesrepublik Deutschland und die .Unfahigkeit zu trauern. In Francoise Lartillot, ed., *Die Unfähigkeit zu trauern*, Nantes 2004. pp. 11–26.

Freimüller, Tobias. Alexander Mitscherlich. Biographie und Wirkungsgeschichte eines kritischen Intellektuellen (Diss. Jena, 2006).

Frevert, Ute. Angst vor Gefühlen? Die Geschichtsmächtigkeit von Gefühlen im 20. Jahrhundert. In Paul Nolte et al., eds., *Perspektiven der Gesellschaftsgeschichte*. München, 2000. pp. 95–111.

Frevert, Ute. Frauen-Geschichte. Zwischen bürgerlicher Verbesserung und neuer Weiblichkeit. Frankfurt a. M., 1986.

Fried, Johannes. *Der Schleier der Erinnerung. Grundzuge einer historischen Memorik*. München, 2004.

Friedlander, Saul. *Das Dritte Reich und die Juden 2: Die Jahre der Vernichtung 1939–1945*. München, 2006.

Friedmann, Jan, and Jörg Später. Britische und deutsche Kollektivschuld-Debatte. In Herbert, ed., *Wandlungsprozesse*, pp. 53–90.

Friedrich, Jörg. *Der Brand. Deutschland im Bombenkrieg 1940–1945*. 4th ed. Berlin, 2002.

Fritz Bauer Institut, editor. *Gerichtstag halten wir über uns selbst . . . . Geschichte und Wirkung des ersten Frankfurter Auschwitz-Prozesses*. Frankfurt a. M., 2001.

Fritzsche, Peter. Volkstümliche Erinnerung und deutsche Identität nach dem Zweiten Weltkrieg. In Jarausch and Sabrow, eds., pp. 75–97.

Gausemeier, Bernd. *Natürliche Ordnungen und politische Allianzen. Biologische und biochemische Forschung an Kaiser-Wilhelm-Instituten 1933–1945*. Göttingen, 2005.

Gerhardt, Uta. *Denken der Demokratie. Die Soziologie im atlantischen Transfer des Besatzungsregimes. Vier Abhandlungen*. Stuttgart, 2007.

Gerlach, Christian. *Kalkulierte Morde. Die deutsche Wirtschafts- und Vernichtungspolitik in Weisrussland 1941–1944*. Hamburg, 2000.

Geyer, Michael. Das Stigma der Gewalt und das Problem der nationalen Identität. In Christian Jansen et al., eds., *Von der Aufgabe der Freiheit. Politische Verantwortung und bürgerliche Gesellschaft im 19. u. 20. Jahrhundert*, Berlin 1995. pp. 673–698.

Geyer, Michael. Der Kalte Krieg, die Deutschen und die Angst. Die westdeutsche Opposition gegen Wiederbewaffnung und Kernwaffen. In Naumann, ed., pp. 267–318.

Geyer, Michael. Endkampf 1918 and 1945. German Nationalism, Annihilation, and Self-Destruction. In Lüdtke and Weisbrod, eds., pp. 35–67.

Giordano, Ralph. *Die zweite Schuld oder Von der Last ein Deutscher zu sein*. Hamburg, 1987.

Goeschel, Christian. Suicide at the end of the Third Reich. *Journal of Contemporary History* 41 (2006), pp. 152–173.

Goltermann, Svenja. Angst in der Nachkriegszeit. Entnazifizierung und persönliche

Desorientierung. In Martin Sabrow, ed., *Zeiträume. Potsdamer Almanach.* 2006. Berlin, 2007. pp. 29–37.

Goltermann, Svenja. Languages of Memory. German POWs and their Violent Pasts in Postwar West Germany. In Moore and Hately-Broad, eds., pp. 165–173.

Goltermann, Svenja. Negotiating Victimhood in East and West Germany. In Jolande Withuis et al., eds., pp. 107–140.

Gortemaker, Manfred. *Geschichte der Bundesrepublik Deutschland. Von der Gründung bis zur Gegenwart.* München, 1999.

Goschler, Constantin. *Schuld und Schulden. Die Politik der Wiedergutmachung für NS-Verfolgte seit 1945.* Göttingen, 2005.

Goschler, Constantin. *Wiedergutmachung. Westdeutschland und die Verfolgten des Nationalsozialismus (1945–1954).* München, 1992.

Goschler, Constantin. Zwei Wege der Wiedergutmachung? Der Umgang mit NS-Verfolgten in West- und Ostdeutschland im Vergleich. In Hockerts and Kuller, eds., pp. 115–137.

Gray, Peter, and Kendrick Oliver. Introduction. In Gray and Oliver, eds., *The Memory of Catastrophe.* Manchester, 2004. pp. 1–18.

Gregor, Neil. "Is he still alive, or long since dead?": Loss, Absence and Remembrance in Nuremberg, 1945–1956. *German History* 21 (2003), pp. 183–203.

Greven, Michael Th., and Oliver Wrochem, eds. *Der Krieg in der Nachkriegszeit. Der Zweite Weltkrieg in Politik und Gesellschaft der Bundesrepublik.* Opladen, 2000.

Gries, Rainer. *Die Rationen-Gesellschaft. Versorgungskampf und Vergleichsmentalität: Leipzig, München und Köln nach dem Kriege.* Münster, 1990.

Grimm, Marion. *Alfred Storch (1888–1962), Daseinsanalyse und anthropologische Psychiatrie.* Giesen, 2004.

Groebner, Valentin. *Der Schein der Person.* München, 2004.

Gross, Jan T. *Fear: Anti-Semitism in Poland after Auschwitz.* Princeton, 2006.

Grossmann, Atina. A Question of Silence: The Rape of German Women by Occupation Soldiers. In Moeller, ed., pp. 33–52.

Grotum, Thomas. *Die Halbstarken: zur Geschichte einer Jugendkultur der 50er Jahre.* Frankfurt a. M., 1994.

Hacking, Ian. Memoro-politics, Trauma and the Soul. *History of the Human Sciences* 7 (1994), pp. 29–52.

Hacking, Ian. *Multiple Persönlichkeit. Zur Geschichte der Seele in der Moderne.* München, 1996.

Halbwachs, Maurice. Der Traum und die Erinnerungsbilder. In Halbwachs, *Das Gedächtnis und seine sozialen Bedingungen.* Frankfurt a. M., 1985. pp. 25–72.

Hanrath, Sabine. *Zwischen 'Euthanasie'. und Psychiatriereform. Anstaltspsychiatrie in Westfalen und Bandenburg. Ein deutsch-deutscher Vergleich (1945–1964).* Paderborn, 2002.

Harrington, Anne. *Die Suche nach Ganzheit. Die Geschichte biologisch-psychologischer Ganzheitslehren: Vom Kaiserreich bis zur New-Age-Bewegung.* Reinbek bei Hamburg, 2002.

Harrington, Ralph. On the Tracks of Trauma: Railway Spine Reconsidered. *Journal of the Society for the Social History of Medicine* 16 (2003), pp. 209–223.

Harrington, Ralph. The Railway Accident: Trains, Trauma, and Technological Crises in Nineteenth Century Britain. In Micale and Lerner, pp. 31–56.

Hartmann, Christian, Johannes Hurter, Ulrike Jureit, Jan Philipp Reemtsma, and Horst Möller, eds. *Verbrechen der Wehrmacht—Bilanz einer Debatte*. München, 2005.

Heer, Hannes, and Klaus Naumann, eds. *Vernichtungskrieg. Verbrechen der Wehrmacht 1941–1944*. Hamburg, 1995.

Heineman, Elizabeth. Complete Families, Half Families, No Families at All: Female-Headed Househoulds and the Reconstruction of the Familiy in the Early Federal Republic. *Central European History* 29 (1996), pp. 19–60.

Heineman, Elizabeth. *What Difference does a Husband Make? Women and Marital Status in Nazi and Postwar Germany*. Berkeley, 1999.

Herbert, Ulrich. *Best. Biographische Studien über Radikalismus, Weltanschauung und Vernunft 1903–1989*. 2nd ed. Bonn, 2006.

Herbert, Ulrich. Nicht entschädigungsfähig? Die Wiedergutmachungsansprüche der Ausländer. In Ludolf Herbst and Constantin Goschler, eds., *Wiedergutmachung in der Bundesrepublik Deutschland*. München, 1989. pp. 273–302.

Herbert, Ulrich. Rückkehr in die Bürgerlichkeit? NS-Eliten in der Bundesrepublik. In Bernd Weisbrod, ed., *Rechtsradikalismus in der politischen Kultur der Bundesrepublik*. Hannover, 1995. pp. 157–173.

Herbert, Ulrich, ed. *Wandlungsprozesse in Westdeutschland. Belastung, Integration, Liberalisierung 1945–1980*. Göttingen, 2002.

Herbert, Ulrich, and Axel Schildt, eds. *Kriegsende in Europa. Vom Beginn des deutschen Machtszerfalls bis zur Stabilisierung der Nachkriegsordnung 1944–1948*. Essen, 1998.

Herman, Judith. *Die Narben der Gewalt*. München, 1993.

Herzog, Dagmar. *Die Politisierung der Lust. Sexualität in der deutschen Geschichte des zwanzigsten Jahrhunderts*. München, 2005.

Herzog, Dagmar. *Sex after Fascism: Memory and Morality in Twentieth-Century Europe*. Princeton, 2007.

Herzog, Dagmar. Sex and Marriage in the Wake of the War. In Bessel and Schumann, eds., pp. 161–192.

Heyll, Uwe. Friedrich Panse und die psychiatrische Erbforschung. In *Die Medizinische Akademie Düsseldorf im Nationalsozialismus*. Essen, 1997. pp. 318–340.

Hickethier, Knut. Der Zweite Weltkrieg und der Holocaust im Fernsehen der Bundesrepublik der fünfziger und frühen sechziger Jahre. In Greven and Wrochem, eds., pp. 93–112.

Hickethier, Knut. Militär und Krieg: 08/15 (1954). In Werner Faulstich and Helmut Korte, eds., *Fischer Filmgeschichte, Bd. 3: Auf der Suche nach Werten. 1945–1960*. Frankfurt a. M., 1990. pp. 222–251.

Hilger, Andreas. *Deutsche Kriegsgefangene in der Sowjetunion 1941–1956. Kriegsgefangenschaft, Lageralltag und Erinnerung*. Essen, 2000.

Hillmann, Jörg, and John Zimmermann, eds. *Kriegsende 1945 in Deutschland*. München, 2002.

Hockerts, Hans Gunter. Wiedergutmachung. Ein umstrittener Begriff und ein weites Feld. In Hockerts and Kuller, pp. 7–33.

Hockerts, Hans Günter. Wiedergutmachung in Deutschland: eine historische Bilanz 1945–2000. *Vierteljahreshefte für Zeitgeschichte* 49 (2001), pp. 167–214.

Hockerts, Hans Günter. Zugange zur Zeitgeschichte. In Jarausch and Sabrow, ed., *Primärerfahrung, Erinnerungskultur, Geschichtswissenschaft*, pp. 39–73.

Hockerts, Hans Günter, et al, eds. *Grenzen der Wiedergutmachung. Die Entschädigung für NS-Verfolgte in West- und Osteuropa 1945–2000.* Göttingen, 2006.

Hockerts, Hans Günter, and Christiane Kuller, eds. *Nach der Verfolgung. Wiedergutmachung nationalsozialistischen Unrechts in Deutschland?* Göttingen, 2003.

Hofer, Hans-Georg. *Nervenschwäche und Krieg. Modernitätskritik und Krisenbewältigung in der österreichischen Psychiatrie (1880–1920).* Wien, 2004.

Hoff, Paul. *Emil Kraepelin und die Psychiatrie als klinische Wissenschaft.* Berlin, 1994.

Hoffman, Eva. *After Such Knowledge. Memory, History, and the Legacy of the Holocaust.* New York, 2004.

Hoffmann, Stefan-Ludwig. Besiegte, Besatzer, Beobachter. Das Kriegsende im Tagebuch. In Daniel Fulda et al., eds., *Demokratie im Schatten der Gewalt. Geschichten des Privaten im deutschen Nachkrieg.* Göttingen, 2009.

Hoffmann-Richter. Ulrike, Das Verschwinden der Biographie in der Krankengeschichte. Eine biographische Skizze. *BIOS. Zeitschrift für Biographieforschung und Oral History* 8 (1995), pp. 204–221.

Huyssen, Andreas. Trauma and Memory: A New Imaginary of Temporality. In Jill Bennett and Rosanne Kennedy, eds., *World Memory. Personal Trajectories in Global Time.* New York, 2003, pp. 16–29.

Jäger, Ludwig. Germanistik—eine deutsche Wissenschaft. Das Kapitel Hans Ernst Schneider. In König et al., eds., pp. 31–45.

Jahn, Peter. *Stalingrad erinnern. Stalingrad im deutschen und russischen Gedächtnis.* Berlin, 2003.

Jarausch, Konrad. *Die Umkehr. Deutsche Wandlungen 1945–1995.* Bonn, 2004.

Jarausch, Konrad, and Michael Geyer. *Zerbrochener Spiegel. Deutsche Geschichte im 20. Jahrhundert.* München, 2003.

Jarausch, Konrad, and Martin Sabrow, eds. *Verletztes Gedächtnis. Erinnerungskultur und Zeitgeschichte im Konflikt.* Frankfurt a. M., 2002.

Judt, Tony. *Geschichte Europas von 1945 bis zur Gegenwart.* München, 2006.

Jureit, Ulrike. Ein Traum in Braun. Über die Erfindung des Unpolitischen. In Christian Geulen and Karoline Tschuggnall, eds., *Aus einem deutschen Leben. Lesarten eines biographischen Interviews.* Tübingen, 2000. pp. 17–36.

Jureit, Ulrike. Zwischen Ehe und Männerbund. Emotionale und sexuelle Beziehungsmuster im Zweiten Weltkrieg. *WerkstattGeschichte* 22 (1999), pp. 61–74.

Kaes, Anton. *From Hitler to Heimat: The Return of History as Film.* Cambridge, MA, 1992.

Kaminsky, Anette, ed. *Heimkehr 1948. Geschichte und Schicksale deutscher Kriegsgefangener.* München, 1998.

Kansteiner, Wulf. Menschheitstrauma, Holocausttrauma, kulturelles Trauma. Eine kritische Genealogie der philosophischen, psychologischen und kulturwissenschaftlichen Traumaforschung seit 1945. In Friedrich Jaeger and Jorn Rüsen, eds., *Handbuch der Kulturwissenschaft en, Bd. 3: Themen und Tendenzen.* Stuttgart, 2004. pp. 109–138.

Kansteiner, Wulf. *In Pursuit of German Memory: History, Television, and Politics After Auschwitz*. Athens, 2006.

Kansteiner, Wulf. Ein Volkermord ohne Täter? Die Darstellung der Endlosung in den Sendungen des Zweiten Deutschen Fernesehens. In Zuckermann, ed., pp. 253–286.

Karner, Stefan. *Im Archipel GUPVI. Kriegsgefangenschaft und Internierung in der Sowjetunion 1941–1956*. München, 1995.

Kaufmann, Doris. Eugenik—Rassenhygiene—Humangenetik. Zur lebenswissenschaftlichen Neuordnung der Wirklichkeit in der ersten Hälfte des 20. Jahrhunderts. In Richard van Dülmen, ed., *Die Erfindung des Menschen. Schöpfungsträume und Körperbilder 1500–2000*. Wien, 2000. pp. 347–365.

Kaufmann, Doris. Eugenische Utopie und wissenschaftliche Praxis im Nationalsozialismus. Zur Wissenschaftsgeschichte der Schizophrenieforschung. In Wolfgang Hardtwig, ed., *Utopie und politische Herrschaft im Europa der Zwischenkriegszeit*. München, 2003. pp. 309–325.

Kaufmann, Doris. Science as Cultural Practice: Psychiatry in the First World War and Weimar Germany. *Journal of Contemporary History* 34 (1999), pp. 125–144.

Kaufmann, Doris. "Widerstandsfähige Gehirne" und "kampfunlustige Seelen." Zur Mentalitäts-und Wissenschaftsgeschichte des Ersten Weltkriegs. In Michael Hagner, ed., *Ecce Cortex. Beiträge zur Geschichte des Modernen Gehirns*. Göttingen, 1999. pp. 206–223.

Kershaw, Ian. *Hitlers Macht. Das Profil der NS-Herrschaft*. München, 1992.

Kershaw, Ian. *Popular Opinion and Political Dissent in the Third Reich: Bavaria, 1933–1945*. Oxford, 1983.

Kersting, Franz-Werner. *Anstaltsärzte zwischen Kaiserreich und Bundesrepublik. Das Beispiel Westfalen*. Paderborn, 1996.

Kersting, Franz-Werner. Vor Ernst Klee. Die Hypothek der NS-Medizinverbrechen als Reformimpuls. In Kersting, ed., *Psychiatriereform als Gesellschaftsreform. Die Hypothek des Nationalsozialismus und der Aufbruch der 60er Jahre*. Paderborn, 2003. pp. 63–80.

Kettenacker, Lothar, ed. *Ein Volk von Opfern? Die neue Debatte um den Bombenkrieg 1940–1945*. Reinbek, 2003.

Kienitz, Sabine, Körper-Beschädigungen. Kriegsinvaliditat und Männlichkeitskonstruktionen in der Weimarer Republik. In Karen Hagemann and Stefanie Schuler-Springorum, eds., *Heimat-Front. Militär und Geschlechterverhältnisse im Zeitalter der Weltkriege*. Frankfurt a. M., 2002. pp. 188–207.

Kittel, Sabine. *Places for the Displaced. Biographische Bewältigungsmuster von weiblichen judischen Konzentrationslager-Überlebenden in den USA*. Hildesheim, 2006.

Kivimäki, Ville. "Battled Nerves: Finnish Soldiers' War Experience, Trauma, and Military Psychiatry, 1941–44." PhD diss., University of Tampere, 2013.

Klee, Ernst. *Was sie taten—was sie wurden. Ärzte, Juristen und andere Beteiligte am Kranken- oder Judenmord*. Frankfurt a. M., 1998.

Kloocke, Ruth, Heinz-Peter Schmiedebach, and Stefan Priebe, eds. Psychisches Trauma in deutschsprachigen Lehrbüchern der Nachkriegszeit—die psychiatrische "Lehrmeinung" zwischen 1945 und 2002. *Psychiatrische Praxis* 32 (2005), pp. 1–15.

Kloocke, Ruth, Hans Peter Schmiedebach, and Stefan Priebe. Psychological Injury in the Two World Wars: Changing Concepts and Terms in German Psychiatry. *History of Psychiatry* 16 (2005), pp. 43–60.

Knoch, Habbo. *Die Tat als Bild. Fotografien des Holocaust in der deutschen Erinnerungskultur.* Hamburg, 2001.

Knoch, Habbo, and Daniel Morat, eds. *Kommunikation als Beobachtung. Medienwandel und Gesellschaftsbilder 1880–1960.* Paderborn, 2003.

Kohut, Thomas A., and Jürgen Reulecke. Sterben wie eine Ratte, die der Bauer ertappt. Letzte Briefe aus Stalingrad. In Jürgen Förster, ed., *Stalingrad. Ereignis—Wirkung—Symbol.* 2nd ed. München, 1993. pp. 456–471.

König, Helmut, Wolfgang Kuhlmann, and Klaus Schwabe, eds. *Vertuschte Vergangenheit. Der Fall Schwerte und die NS-Vergangenheit der deutschen Hochschulen.* München, 1997.

Koonz, Claudia. *The Nazi Conscience.* Harvard, 2003.

Koselleck, Reinhart. Der Einfluß der beiden Weltkriege auf das soziale Bewusstsein. In Wolfram Wette, ed., *Der Krieg des kleinen Mannes. Eine Militärgeschichte von unten.* 2nd ed. München, 1995. pp. 324–343.

Koselleck, Reinhart. "Erfahrungsraum" und "Erwartungshorizont"—zwei historische Kategorien. In Koselleck, ed., *Vergangene Zukunft. Zur Semantik geschichtlicher Zeiten.* 2nd ed. Frankfurt a. M., 1992. pp. 349–375.

Koselleck, Reinhart. Terror und Traum. Methodologische Anmerkungen zu Zeiterfahrungen im Dritten Reich. In Koselleck, ed., *Vergangene Zukunft. Zur Semantik geschichtlicher Zeiten,* Frankfurt a. M., 1992. pp. 278–299.

Krause, Peter. *Der Eichmann-Prozess in der deutschen Presse.* Frankfurt a. M., 2002.

Krukowska, Uta. *Kriegsversehrte. Allgemeine Lebensbedingungen und medizinische Versorgung deutscher Versehrter nach dem Zweiten Weltkrieg in der Britischen Besatzungszone Deutschlands—dargestellt am Beispiel der Stadt Hamburg.* Hamburg, 2006.

Krzeminski, Adam. Polen. In Frei and Knigge, eds., pp. 262–271.

Kühne, Thomas. Der Soldat. In Ute Frevert and Heinz Gerhard Haupt, eds., *Der Mensch im 20. Jahrhundert.* Frankfurt a. M., 1999. pp. 344–372.

Kühne, Thomas. Die Viktimisierungsfalle. Wehrmachtsverbrechen, Geschichtswissenschaft und symbolische Ordnung des Militärs. In Greven and von Wrochem, eds., pp. 183–196.

Kühne, Thomas. Gruppenkohäsion und Kameradschaftsmythos in der Wehrmacht. In Müller and Volkmann, eds., pp. 534–549.

Kühne, Thomas. Kameradschaft—"das Beste im Leben eines Mannes." Die deutschen Soldaten des Zweiten Weltkriegs in erfahrungs- und geschlechtergeschichtlicher Perspektive. *Geschichte und Gesellschaft* 22 (1996), pp. 504–529.

Kühne, Thomas. *Kameradschaft. Die deutschen Soldaten des nationalsozialistischen Krieges und das 20. Jahrhundert.* Göttingen, 2006.

Kühne, Thomas. Zwischen Vernichtungskrieg und Freizeitgesellschaft . Die Veteranenkultur der Bundesrepublik (1943–1995). In Naumann, ed., pp. 90–113.

Kühne, Thomas, and Benjamin Ziemann. Militärgeschichte in der Erweiterung. Konjunkturen, Interpretationen, Konzepte. In Kühne and Ziemann, eds., *Was ist Militärgeschichte?* Paderborn, 2000. pp. 9–48.

Kulka, Otto. Public Opinion in Nazi Germany: The Final Solution. In Michael R. Marrus, ed., *The Nazi Holocaust. Historical Articles on the Destruction of European Jews, Bd. 5, 1: Public Opinion and Relations to the Jews in Nazi Europe*, London 1989, pp. 139–150.

Kulka, Otto, and Eberhard Jackel, eds. *Die Juden in den geheimen NS-Stimmungsberichten 1933–1945*. Düsseldorf, 2004.

Laak, Dirk van. *Gespräche in der Sicherheit des Schweigens. Carl Schmitt in der politischen Geistesgeschichte der frühen Bundesrepublik*. 2nd ed. Berlin, 2002.

Lagrou, Pieter. *The legacy of Nazi occupation: patriotic memory and national recovery in Western Europe, 1945–1965*. Cambridge, 2000.

Langer, Lawrence. *Holocaust Testimonies: The Ruins of Memory*. New Haven, 1991.

LaRossa, Ralph. *Of War and Men: World War II and the Lives of Fathers and Their Families*. Chicago, 2011.

Latzel, Klaus. Töten und Schweigen—Wehrmachtssoldaten, Opferdiskurs und die Perspektive des Leidens. In Peter Gleichmann and Thomas Kühne, eds., *Massenhaftes Töten. Kriege und Genozide im 20. Jh*. Essen, 2004. pp. 320–338.

Leese, Peter. *Shell Shock: Traumatic Neurosis and the British Soldiers of the First World War*. London, 2002.

Lehmann, Albrecht. *Gefangenschaft und Heimkehr. Deutsche Kriegsgefangene in der Sowjetunion*. München, 1986.

Lengwiler, Martin. *Zwischen Klinik und Kaserne. Die Geschichte der Militärpsychiatrie in Deutschland und in der Schweiz 1870–1914*. Zürich, 2000.

Lerner, Paul. "Ein Sieg deutschen Willens." Wille und Gemeinschaft in der deutschen Kriegspsychiatrie. In Wolfgang U. Eckardt and Christoph Gradmann, ed., *Die Medizin und der Erste Weltkrieg*. Pfaffenweiler, 1996. pp. 85–107.

Lerner, Paul. From Traumatic Neurosis to Male Hysteria: The Decline and Fall of Hermann Oppenheim, 1889–1919. In Micale and Lerner, eds., pp. 140–171.

Lerner, Paul. *Hysterical Men. War, Psychiatry, and the Politics of Trauma in Germany, 1890–1930*. Ithaca, 2003.

Lerner, Paul, and Mark S. Micale. Trauma, Psychiatry, and History: A Conceptual and Historiographical Introduction. In Micale and Lerner, eds., pp. 1–27.

Leys, Ruth. *Trauma. A Genealogy*. Chicago 2000.

Lockenour, Jay. *Soldiers as Citizens: Former Wehrmacht Officers in the Federal Republic of Germany, 1945–1955*. Lincoln, NE, 2001.

Longerich, Peter. *Davon haben wir nichts gewusst! Die Deutschen und die Judenverfolgung 1933–1945*. München, 2006.

Loth, Wilfried, and Bernd-A. Rusinek, eds. *Verwandlungspolitik. NS-Eliten in der westdeutschen Nachkriegsgesellschaft*. Frankfurt, 1998.

Lowe, Keith. *Europe in the Aftermath of World War II*. London, 2012.

Lüdtke, Alf, and Bernd Weisbrod, eds. *No Man's Land of Violence. Extreme Wars in the 20th Century*. Göttingen, 2006.

Maase, Kaspar. *Bravo Amerika: Erkundungen zur Jugendkultur der Bundesrepublik in den fünfziger Jahren*. Hamburg, 1992.

Maier, Charles S. Consigning the Twentieth Century to History: Alternative Narratives for the Modern Era. In *The American Historical Review* 105 (2002), pp. 807–831.

Mallmann, Klaus-Michael, and Gerhard Paul, eds. *Karrieren der Gewalt. Nationalsozialistische Täterbiographien.* Darmstadt, 2004.

Manig, Bert-Oliver. *Die Politik der Ehre: die Rehabilitierung der Berufssoldaten in der frühen Bundesrepublik.* Göttingen, 2004.

Marszolek, Inge. The Coverage of the Bergen-Belsen Trial and the Auschwitz Trial in the NWDR/NDR. The Reports of Axel Eggebrecht. In David Bankier and Dan Michman, eds., *Holocaust and Justice: Representation and Historiography of the Holocaust in Post-War Trials.* New York, 2010. 131–157.

Maschke, Erich, ed. *Zur Geschichte der deutschen Kriegsheimkehrer nach dem Zweiten Weltkrieg, 22 Bde.* München, 1962–1974.

Mazower, Mark. *Der dunkle Kontinent. Europa im 20. Jahrhundert.* Berlin, 2000.

Mazower, Mark. Violence and the State in the Twentieth Century. *American Historical Review* 107 (2002), pp. 1158–1178.

McNally, Richard J. *Remembering Trauma.* Cambridge, 2003.

Meier, Marietta, et al. *Zwang zur Ordnung. Psychiatrie im Kanton Zürich, 1870–1970.* Zürich, 2007.

Merridale, Catherine. *Night of Stone. Death and Memory in Twentieth-Century Russia.* New York, 2000.

Merritt, Anna J., and Richard L. Merritt, eds. *Public Opinion in Occupied Germany: The OMGUS Surveys, 1945–1949.* Urbana, IL, 1970.

Meyer, Sibylle, and Eva Schulze. Als wir wieder zusammen waren, ging der Krieg im Kleinen weiter. Frauen, Männer und Familien im Berlin der 40er Jahre. In Niethammer and von Plato, eds., *Wir kriegen jetzt andere Zeiten,* pp. 305–326.

Meyer, Sibylle, and Eva Schulze. Von Liebe sprach damals keiner. Familienalltag in der Nachkriegszeit, München, 1985.

Micale, Mark. On the Disappearance of Hysteria: The Clinical Deconstruction of a Diagnosis. *Isis* 84 (1993), pp. 496–526.

Micale, Mark, and Paul Lerner, eds. *Traumatic Pasts. History, Psychiatry, and Trauma in the Modern Age, 1970–1980.* Cambridge, 2001.

Moeller, Robert G. Deutsche Opfer, Opfer der Deutschen. Kriegsgefangene, Vertriebene, NS-Verfolgte: Opferausgleich als Identitättätspolitik. In Naumann, ed., pp. 29–58.

Moeller, Robert G. Germans as Victims? Thoughts on a Post-Cold War History of World War II's Legacies. *History & Memory* 17 (2005), pp. 147–194.

Moeller, Robert G. *Geschützte Mutter. Frauen und Familien in der westdeutschen Nachkriegspolitik.* München, 1997.

Moeller, Robert G. In a Thousand Years, Every German Will Speak of This Battle. Celluloid Memories of Stalingrad. In Omer Bartov et al., eds., *Crimes of War. Guilt and Denial in the Twentieth Century.* New York, 2002. pp. 161–190.

Moeller, Robert G. Sinking Ships, the Lost Heimat and Broken Taboos: Günter Grass and the Politics of Memory in Contemporary Germany. *Contemporary European History* 12 (2003), pp. 1–35.

Moeller, Robert G. The Homosexual Man is a Man, the Homosexual Womas is a Woman.: Sex, Society and the Law, in Postwar West Germany. In Moeller, ed., *West Germany under Construction. Politics, Society, and Culture in the Adenauer Era.* Ann Arbor, 1997. pp. 251–284.

Moeller, Robert G. The Last Soldiers of the Great War and Tales of Family Reunions in the Federal Republic of Germany. *Signs* 24 (1998), pp. 126–146.

Moeller, Robert G. The Remasculinization of Germany in the 1950s: Introduction. *Signs* 24 (1998), pp. 101–106.

Moeller, Robert G. *War Stories. The Search for a Usable Past in the Federal Republic of Germany.* Berkeley, 2001.

Moeller, Robert G., ed. *Germany under Construction. Politics, Society, and Culture in the Adenauer Era.* Ann Arbor, 1997.

Mommsen, Hans. Wie die Bomber Hitler halfen. In Stefan Burgdorff and Christian Habbe, eds., *Als Feuer vom Himmel fiel. Der Bombenkrieg in Deutschland.* München, 2003. pp. 115–121.

Mommsen, Wolfgang J., ed. *Kultur und Krieg. Die Rolle der Intellektuellen, Künstler und Schriftsteller im Ersten Weltkrieg.* München, 1996.

Moore, Bob, and Barbara Hately-Broad, eds. *Prisoners of War, Prisoners of Peace: Captivity, Homecoming and Memory in World War II.* Oxford, 2005.

Morina, Christina. *Instructed Silence, Constructed Memory: The SED and the Return of German Prisoners of War as "War Criminals" from the Soviet Union to East Germany, 1950–1956.* Contemporary European History 13 (2004), pp. 323–343.

Morina, Christina. *Legacies of Stalingrad: Remembering the Eastern Front in Germany since 1945.* Cambridge, 2011.

Muhlhauser, Regina. Vergewaltigungen in Deutschland 1945. Nationaler Opferdiskurs und individuellen Erinnern betroffener Frauen. In Naumann, ed., pp. 384–408.

Müller, Rolf-Dieter, and Hans-Erich Volkmann, eds. *Die Wehrmacht. Mythos und Realitat.* München, 1999.

Müller, Sven-Oliver. *Die deutschen Soldaten und ihre Feinde. Nationalismus in der kriegführenden Wehrmacht, 1941–1944.* Frankfurt a. M., 2007.

Müller, Thomas. Zur Etablierung der Psychoanalyse in Berlin. In Thomas Müller, ed., *Psychotherapie und Körperarbeit. Praktiken der Etablierung—das Beispiel Berlin.* Husum, 2004, pp. 53–95.

Naimark, Norman M. *Die Russen in Deutschland: die sowjetische Besatzungszone 1945 bis 1949.* Berlin, 1999.

Naimark, Norman M. *Fires of Hatred. Ethnic Cleansing in Twentieth-Century Europe.* Cambridge, 2001.

Ned Lebow, Richard, et al. *The Politics of Memory in Postwar Europe.* Durham, 2006.

Naumann, Klaus. Einleitung. In Klaus Neumann, ed., pp. 9–26.

Naumann, Klaus, ed. *Nachkrieg in Deutschland.* Hamburg, 2001.

Neumann, Vera. Kampf um Anerkennung. Die westdeutsche Kriegsfolgengesellschaft im Spiegel der Versorgungsämter. In Vera Naumann, ed., pp. 364–383.

Neumann, Vera. *Nicht der Rede wert. Die Privatisierung der Kriegsfolgen in der frühen Bundesrepublik.* Münster, 1999.

Neumarker, Klaus-Jürgen. *Karl Bonhoeffer: Leben und Werk eines deutschen Psychiaters und Neurologen in seiner Zeit.* Berlin, 1990.

Neuner, Stephanie. *Politik und Psychiatrie: Die staatliche Versorgung psychisch Kriegsbeschädigter nach dem Ersten Weltkrieg in Deutschland, 1920–1939.* Göttingen, 2011.

Niehuss, Merith. Kontinuität und Wandel der Familie in den 50er Jahren. In Schildt and Sywottek, eds., pp. 316–334.

Niethammer, Lutz. Fragen—Antworten—Fragen. Methodische Erfahrungen und Erwägungen zur Oral History. In Niethammer and Plato, eds., *Wir kriegen jetzt andere Zeiten*, pp. 392–445.

Niethammer, Lutz. Privat-Wirtschaft. Erinnerungsfragmente einer anderen Umerziehung. In Lutz Niethammer, ed., *Hinterher merkt man, daß es richtig war, das es schiefgegangen ist. Nachkriegserfahrungen im Ruhrgebiet (Lebensgeschichte und Sozialkultur im Ruhrgebiet 1930 bis 1960, Bd. 2)*. Berlin, 1983. pp. 17–105.

Niethammer, Lutz, and Alexander v. Plato, eds. *Wir kriegen jetzt andere Zeiten. Auf der Suche nach der Erfahrung des Volkes in nachfaschistischen Landern (Lebensgeschichte und Sozialkultur im Ruhrgebiet 1930 bis 1960, Bd. 3)*. Berlin, 1985.

Niven, Bill. Introduction: German Victimhood at the Turn of the Millenium. In Niven, ed., pp. 1–25.

Niven, Bill, ed. *Germans as Victims. Remembering the Past in Contemporary Germany*. New York, 2006.

Noack, Thorsten. Über Kaninchen und Gift schlangen—Psychiatrie und Öffentlichkeit in der frühen Bundesrepublik. In Fangerau and Nolte, eds., pp. 311–340.

Nolte, Karen. *Gelebte Hysterie: Erfahrung, Eigensinn und psychiatrische Diskurse im Anstaltsalltag um 1900*. Frankfurt a. M., 2003.

Nolte, Paul. *Die Ordnung der deutschen Gesellschaft. Selbstentwurf und Selbstbeschreibung im 20. Jahrhundert*. München, 2000.

Novick, Peter. *Nach dem Holocaust. Der Umgang mit dem Massenmord*. München, 2003.

Olick, Jeffrey K. *In the House of the Hangman. The Agonies of German Defeat, 1943–1949*. Chicago, 2005.

Orth, Karin. *Das System der nationalsozialistischen Konzentrationslager. Eine politische Organisationsgeschichte*. Hamburg, 1999.

Ostovich, Steven T. Epilogue: Dangerous Memories. In *Confino and. Fritzsche, eds.*, pp. 239–256.

Overmans, Rüdiger. Die Rheinwiesenlager 1945: Ein untergeordneter Eintrag im Leidensbuch der jungeren Geschichte? In Bischof and Overmans, eds., pp. 233–264.

Overmans, Rüdiger. The Repatriation of Prisoners of War once Hostilities are Over: A Matter of Course? In Moore and Hately-Broad, eds., pp. 11–22.

Paul, Gerhard, ed. *Visual History. Ein Studienbuch*. Göttingen, 2006.

Pendas, Devin O. *The Frankfurt Auschwitz Trial 1963–65: Genocide, History and the Limits of the Law*. New York, 2006.

Perinelli, Massimo. *Liebe 47—Gesellschaft 49. Geschlechterverhältnisse in der deutschen Nachkriegszeit. Eine Analyse des Films Liebe 47*. Münster, 1999.

Peter, Jürgen. Unmittelbare Reaktionen auf den Prozess. In Ebbinghaus and Dörner, eds., pp. 452–475.

Pick, Daniel. *Faces of Degeneration: A European Disorder, 1848–1918*. Cambridge, 1993.

Poiger, Uta. A New Western Hero? Reconstructing German Masculinity in the 1950s. *Signs* 24 (1998), pp. 147–162.

Poiger, Uta. *Jazz, Rock, and Rebels: Cold War Politics and American Culture in a Divided Germany.* Berkeley, 2000.

Poiger, Uta. Krise der Männlichkeit. Remaskulinisierung in beiden deutschen Staaten. In Naumann, ed., pp. 227–263.

Porter, Roy. The Patient's View: Doing Medical History from Below. In *Theory and Society* 14 (1985), pp. 175–198.

Pross, Christian. *Wiedergutmachung. Der Kleinkrieg gegen die Opfer.* Berlin, 2001.

Raphael, Lutz. Die Verwissenschaftlichung des Sozialen als methodische und konzeptionelle Herausforderung für eine Sozialgeschichte des 20. Jahrhunderts. *Geschichte und Gesellschaft* 22 (1996), pp. 165–193.

Rauh-Kühne, Cornelia. Die Entnazifizierung und die deutsche Gesellschaft. *Archiv für Sozialgeschichte* 35 (1995), pp. 35–70.

Reichel, Peter. *Erfundene Erinnerung. Weltkrieg und Judenmord in Film und Theater.* Wien, 2004.

Reichel, Peter. *Vergangenheitsbewältigung in Deutschland. Die Auseinandersetzung mit der NS-Diktatur von 1945 bis heute.* München, 2001.

Reis, Matthias. *Die Schwarzen waren unsere Freunde. Deutsche Kriegsgefangene in der amerikanischen Gesellschaft 1942–1946.* Paderborn, 2002.

Renner, Rolf Günter. Hirn und Herz. Stalingrad als Gegenstand ideologischer und literarischer Diskurse. In Förster, ed., pp. 472–492.

Reucher, Ursula. *Reform und Reformversuche in der gesetzlichen Krankenversicherung (1956–1965).* Düsseldorf,1999.

Riedesser, Peter, and Axel Verderber, eds. *Maschinengewehre hinter der Front. Zur Geschichte der deutschen Militärpsychiatrie.* Frankfurt a. M., 1996.

Rodebush, Marc. A Battle of Nerves: Hysteria and Its Treatment in France During World War I. In Micale and Lerner, eds., pp. 253–279.

Roelcke, Volker. *Krankheit und Kulturkritik. Psychiatrische Gesellschaftsdeutungen im bürgerlichen Zeitalter (1790–1914).* Frankfurt a. M., 1999.

Roelcke, Volker. Psychiatrische Wissenschaft im Kontext nationalsozialistischer Politik und 'Euthanasie' In Doris Kaufmann, ed., *Geschichte der Kaiser- Wilhelm-Gesellschaft im Nationalsozialismus. Bestandsaufnahme und Perspektiven der Forschung.* Göttingen 2000. Bd. 1, pp. 112–150.

Roelcke, Volker. Psychotherapy between Medicine, Psychoanalysis, and Politics: Concepts, Practices, and Institutions in Germany, c. 1945–1992. *Medical History* 48 (2004), pp. 473–492.

Roelcke, Volker, G. Hohendorf, and M. Rotzoll. Psychiatrische Wissenschaft, Euthanasie und der Neue Mensch. Zur Diskussion um anthropologische Prämissen und Wertsetzungen der Medizin im Nationalsozialismus. In Andreas Frewer and Clemens Eickhoff, eds., *Euthanasie und die aktuelle Sterbehilfe-Debatte. Die historischen Hintergründe medizinischer Ethik.* Frankfurt a. M., 2002. pp. 193–217.

Roth, Karl-Heinz. Die Modernisierung der Folter in beiden Weltkriegen: Der Konflikt der Psychotherapeuten und Schulpsychiater um die deutschen "Kriegsneurotiker" 1915–1945. 1999. Zeitschrift für Sozialgeschichte des 20. und 21. *Jahrhunderts* 2 (1987), pp. 8–75.

Rousso, Henry. *The Vichy–Syndrome. History and Memory in France since 1944*. Harvard, 1991.

Rusinek, Bernd–A., ed. *Kriegsende 1945. Verbrechen, Katastrophen, Befreiungen in nationaler und internationaler Perspektive*. Göttingen, 2004.

Sachse, Carola. Persilscheinkultur. Zum Umgang mit der NS–Vergangenheit in der Kaiser–Wilhelm/Max–Planck–Gesellschaft . In Bernd Weisbrod, ed., *Akademische Vergangenheitspolitik. Beitrage zur Wissenschaftskultur der Nachkriegszeit*. Göttingen, 2002. pp. 217–246.

Schäfers, Bernhard. *Gesellschaftlicher Wandel in Deutschland*. Stuttgart, 1995[6].

Schanetzky, Tim. Unternehmer: Profiteure des Unrechts. In Frei, ed., *Hitlers Eliten*, pp. 69–113.

Scharffenberg, Heiko. *Sieg der Sparsamkeit. Die Wiedergutmachung nationalsozialistischen Unrechts in Schleswig–Holstein*. Bielefeld, 2004.

Schildt, Axel, and Arnold Sywottek, eds. *Modernisierung im Wiederaufbau. Die westdeutsche Gesellschaft der 50er Jahre*. Bonn, 1998.

Schissler, Hanna, ed. *The Miracle Years. A Cultural History in West Germany, 1949–1968*. Princeton, 2001.

Schissler, Hanna. Normalization as Project: Some Thoughts on Gender Relations in West Germany During the 1950s. In Schissler, ed., pp. 359–375.

Schlant, Ernestine. *The Language of Silence. West German Literature and the Holocaust*. New York, 1999.

Schmuhl, Hans-Walter. *Rassenhygiene, Nationalsozialismus, Euthanasie. Von der Verhütung zur Vernichtung lebensunwerten Lebens*. 2nd ed. Göttingen, 1992.

Schmuhl, Hans-Walter. Hirnforschung und Krankenmord. Das Kaiser-Wilhelm-Institut für Hirn forschung 1937–1945. *Vierteljahreshefte für Zeitgeschichte* 50 (2002), pp. 559–609.

Schmuhl, Hans-Walter. Die Patientenmorde. In Ebbinghaus and Dörner, eds., pp. 295–328.

Schmuhl, Hans-Walter. *Grenzüberschreitungen. Das Kaiser-Wilhelm-Institut für Anthropologie, menschliche Erblehre und Eugenik 1927–1945*. Göttingen, 2005.

Schmuhl, Hans-Walter, ed. *Rassenforschung an Kaiser-Wilhelm-Instituten vor und nach 1933*. Göttingen, 2003.

Schneider, Franka. Einigkeit im Unglück? Berliner Eheberatungsstellen zwischen Ehekrise und Wiederaufbau. In Naumann, ed., pp. 206–226.

Schörken, Rolf. *Jugend 1945. Politisches Denken und Lebensgeschichte*. Frankfurt a. M., 1995.

Schröder, Hans Joachim. *Die gestohlenen Jahre. Erzählgeschichten und Geschichtserzählung im Interview: Der Zweite Weltkrieg aus der Sicht ehemaliger Mannschaftssoldaten*. Tübingen, 1992.

Schröder, Hans Joachim. Töten und Todesangst im Krieg. In Alf Lüdtke and Thomas Lindenberger, eds., *Physische Gewalt. Studien zur Geschichte der Neuzeit*. Frankfurt a. M., 1995. pp. 106–135.

Schulze, Rainer, ed. *Unruhige Zeiten: Erlebnisberichte aus dem Landkreis Celle 1945–1949*. Second ed. München, 1991.

Schütz, Erhard. Von Lageropfern und Helden der Flucht. Kriegsgefangenschaft

Deutscher—Popularisierungsmuster in der Bundesrepublik. In Wolfgang Hardtwig and Erhard Schütz, eds., *Geschichte für Leser: Populäre Geschichtsschreibung in Deutschland im 20. Jahrhundert.* Stuttgart, 2005. pp. 181–204.

Schwelling, Birgit. *Heimkehr—Erinnerung—Integration: Der Verband der Heimkehrer, die ehemaligen Kriegsgefangenen und die westdeutsche Nachkriegsgesellschaft.* Paderborn, 2010.

Shandley, Robert R. *Rubble Films: German Cinema in the Shadow of the Third Reich.* Philadelphia, 2001.

Shephard, Ben. *A War of Nerves. Soldiers and Psychiatrists 1914–1994.* London, 2000.

Shorter, Edward. *Geschichte der Psychiatrie.* Berlin, 1999.

Smith, Arthur L. *Die vermisste Million. Zum Schicksal deutscher Kriegsgefangener nach dem Zweiten Weltkrieg.* München, 1992.

Smith, Arthur L. *Heimkehr aus dem Zweiten Weltkrieg. Die Entlassung der deutschen Kriegsgefangenen.* Stuttgart, 1985.

Smith, Gary, ed. *Hannah Arendt Revisited: 'Eichmann in Jerusalem'und die Folgen.* Frankfurt, 2000.

Sofsky, Wolfgang. *Traktat über die Gewalt.* 2nd ed. Frankfurt a. M., 1996.

Steege, Paul. *Black Market, Cold War: Everyday Life in Berlin 1946–1949.* Cambridge, 2007.

Steinbacher, Sybille. *Wie der Sex nach Deutschland kam: Der Kampf um Sittlichkeit und Anstand in der frühen Bundesrepublik.* Munich, 2011.

Steinmetz, Willibald. *Träumen im Zeitalter der Extreme. Für eine historische Analyse von Traumprotokollen* (unveröffentlichter Vortrag, Bochum 2000).

Steinmetz, Willibald. Ungewollte Politisierung durch die Medien? Die Contergan-Affäre. In Bernd Weisbrod, ed., *Politik,* pp. 195–228.

Stern, Frank. Film in the 1950s. Passing Images of Guilt and Responsibility. In Schissler, ed., pp. 266–280.

Stöver, Bernd. *Der Kalte Krieg.* München, 2007.

Süß, Winfried. *Der Volkskörper. im Krieg. Gesundheitspolitik, Gesundheitsverhältnisse und Krankenmord im nationalsozialistischen Deutschland, 1939–1945.* München, 2003.

Szodrzynski, Joachim. Das Ende der Volksgemeinschaft ? Die Hamburger Bevölkerung in der 'Trummergesellschaft' ab 1943. In Frank Bajohr and Joachim Szodrzynski, eds., *Hamburg in der NS-Zeit. Ergebnisse neuerer Forschungen.* Hamburg, 1995. pp. 281–305.

Tavris, Carol. Just Deal with It. *Times Literary Supplement* (August 15, 2003), pp. 10–11.

Ther, Philipp. *Deutsche und polnische Vertriebene. Gesellschaft und Vertriebenenpolitik in der SBZ/DDR und in Polen 1945–1956.* Göttingen, 1998.

Thomas, Gregory M. *Treating the Trauma of the Great War: Soldiers, Civilians, and Psychiatry in France, 1918–1940.* Baton Rouge, LA, 2009.

Thoms, Ulrike. Die ,Hunger-Generation' als Ernährungswissenschaftler 1933–1964 zwischen soziokulturellen Gemeinsamkeiten und der Instrumentalisierung von Erfahrung. In Matthias Middell et al., eds., *Verräumlichung, Vergleich, Generationalität. Dimensionen der Wissenschaftsgeschichte.* Leipzig, 2004. pp. 133–153.

Thum, Gregor. *Die fremde Stadt. Breslau 1945.* Berlin, 2003.

Trittel, Günter J. *Hunger und Politik. Die Ernährungskrise in der Bizone (1945–1949).* Frankfurt a. M., 1990.

Ulrich, Bernd. *Die Augenzeugen. Deutsche Feldpostbriefe in Kriegs- und Nachkriegszeit 1914–1933.* Essen, 1997.

van Laak, Dirk. *Gespräche in der Sicherheit des Schweigens. Carl Schmitt in der politischen Geistesgeschichte der frühen Bundesrepublik.* 2nd ed. Berlin, 2002.

Verhey, Jeffrey. *The Spirit of 1914. Militarism, Myth, and Mobilization in Germany.* Cambridge, 2000.

von Beyme, Klaus, ed. *Neue Städte aus Ruinen. Städtebau der Nachkriegszeit.* München, 1992.

von Hodenberg, Christina. *Konsens und Krise. Eine Geschichte der westdeutschen Medienöffentlichkeit 1945–1973.* Göttingen, 2006.

von Miquel, Marc. *Ahnden oder amnestieren? Westdeutsche Justiz und Vergangenheitspolitik in den 60er Jahren.* Göttingen, 2004.

von Miquel, Marc. Wir mussen mit den Mördern zusammenleben! NS-Prozesse und politische Öffentlichkeit in den 60er Jahren. In Fritz Bauer Institut, ed., pp. 97–116.

von Plato, Alexander. Wo sind die ungläubigen Kinder geblieben? Kritik einiger Thesen des Projekts. Tradierung von Geschichtsbewusstsein. *WerkstattGeschichte* 30 (2001), pp. 64–72.

von Plato, Alexander, and Almut Leh. *Ein unglaublicher Frühling. Erfahrene Geschichte im Nachkriegsdeutschland 1945–1948.* Bonn, 1997.

Wanke, Paul *Russian/Soviet Military Psychiatry, 1904–1945.* New York, 2004.

Weckel, Ulrike. Die Mörder sind unter uns oder: Vom Verschwinden der Opfer. *WerkstattGeschichte* 25 (2000), pp. 105–115.

Weckel, Ulrike. The *Mitläufer* in Two German Postwar Films. *History & Memory* 15 (2003), pp. 64–93.

Weckel, Ulrike. Spielarten der Vergangenheitsbewältigung—Wolfgang Borcherts Heimkehrer und sein langer Weg durch die westdeutschen Medien. In Moshe Zuckermann, ed., pp. 125–161.

Wehler, Hans-Ulrich. *Deutsche Gesellschaftsgeschichte, Bd. 4: Vom Beginn des Ersten Weltkriegs bis zur Gründung der beiden deutschen Staaten 1914–1949.* 2nd ed. München, 2003.

Weimar, Klaus. Der Germanist Hans Schwerte. In König et al., eds., pp. 46–59.

Weindling, Paul. From Medical War Crimes to Compensation: the Plight of the Victims of Human Experiments. In Wolfgang U. Eckardt, ed., *Man, Medicine and the State.* Stuttgart, 2006. pp. 237–249.

Weindling, Paul. *Health, Race and German Politics between National Unification and Nazism, 1970–1935.* Cambridge, 1993.

Weingart, Peter. *Die Wissenschaft der Öffentlichkeit. Essays zum Verhältnis von Wissenschaft, Medien und Öffentlichkeit.* Weilerswist, 2005.

Weinke, Annette. *Die Verfolgung von NS-Tätern im geteilten Deutschland: Vergangenheitsbewältigung 1949–1969 oder: eine deutsch–deutsche Beziehungsgeschichte im Kalten Krieg.* Paderborn, 2002.

Weinke, Annette. Überreste eines "unerwünschten Prozesses": Die Edition der Tonbandmitschnitte zum ersten Frankfurter Auschwitz Prozess (1963–1965). In *Zeithistorische Forschungen/Studies in Contemporary History*, Online-Ausgabe, 2 (2005), H. 2. <http://www.zeithistorische-forschungen. de/16126041–Weinke-2–2005>.

Weisbrod, Bernd. Der 8. Mai in der deutschen Erinnerung. *Werkstatt-Geschichte* 13 (1996), pp. 72–81.

Weisbrod, Bernd. Nachkriegsprozesse und 'Vergangenheitsbewältigung'. Gerichtskultur und Medienwirkung. In Eva Schumann, ed., *Kontinuitat und Zäsuren— Rechtswissenschaft und Justiz im ,Dritten Reich' und in der Nachkriegszeit.* Göttingen 2007.

Weisbrod, Bernd, ed. *Die Politik der Öffentlichkeit—Die Öffentlichkeit der Politik. Politische Medialisierung in der Geschichte der Bundesrepublik.* Göttingen, 2003.

Weiß, Hermann. *Biographisches Lexikon zum Dritten Reich.* Frankfurt, 2002.

Welzer, Harald. *Das kommunikative Gedächtnis. Eine Theorie der Erinnerung.* München, 2002.

Welzer, Harald. Familiengedächtnis. Über die Weitergabe der deutschen Vergangenheit im intergenerationellen Gespräch. *WerkstattGeschichte* 30 (2001), pp. 61–64.

Welzer, Harald. u. a. *Opa war kein Nazi. Nationalsozialismus und Holocaust im Familiengedächtnis.* Frankfurt a. M., 2002.

Wengst, Udo. *Thomas Dehler 1897–1967. Eine politische Biographie.* München, 1997.

Wienand, Christiane. *Returning Memories: Former Prisoners of War in Divided and Reunited Germany.* New York, 2015.

Wierling, Dorothee. Erzählungen im Widerspruch? Der Nationalsozialismus und die erste Nachkriegsgeneration der DDR. *WerkstattGeschichte* 30 (2001), pp. 17–31.

Wierling, Dorothee. *Geboren im Jahr eins. Der Jahrgang 1949 in der DDR. Versuch einer Kollektivbiographie.* Berlin, 2002.

Wierling, Dorothee. Nationalsozialismus und Krieg in den Lebensgeschichten der ersten Nachkriegsgeneration der DDR. In Elisabeth Domansky and Harald Welzer, eds., *Eine offene Geschichte. Zur kommunikativen Tradierung der nationalsozialistischen Vergangenheit.* Tübingen, 1999. pp. 35–56.

Wieviorka, Anette. Die Entstehung des Zeugen. In Smith, ed., pp. 136–159.

Wieviorka, Anette. *The Era of the Witness.* Ithaca, 2006.

Wildt, Michael. *Generation des Unbedingten. Das Führungskorps des Reichssicherheitshauptamtes.* Hamburg, 2003.

Wildt, Michael. *Vom kleinen Wohlstand. Eine Konsumgeschichte der fünfziger Jahre.* Frankfurt a. M., 1996.

Wilharm, Irmgard. *Bewegte Spuren. Studien zur Zeitgeschichte im Film.* Hannover, 2006.

Winkler, Christiane. Männlichkeit und Gesundheit der deutschen Kriegsheimkehrer im Spiegel der Ärztekongresse des "Verbands der Heimkehrer." In Martin Dinges, ed., *Männlichkeit und Gesundheit im historischen Wandel ca.1800—ca. 2000.* Stuttgart, 2007.

Winter, Jay. Shell-shock and the Cultural History of the Great War. *Journal of Contemporary History* 35 (2000), pp. 7–11.

Withuis, Jolande, et al. *The Politics of War Trauma. A Comparative European Approach.* Amsterdam, 2009.

Wittmann, Rebecca. *Beyond Justice: The Auschwitz Trial, Cambridge 2005.*

Wojak, Irmtrud, Eichmanns Memoiren. Ein kritischer Essay. Frankfurt a. M., 2001.

Wittmann, Rebecca, ed. *Auschwitz-Prozess 4 Ks 2/63.* Frankfurt a. M., 2004.

Wolf, René. Mass Deception without Deceivers? The Holocaust on East and West German Radio in the 1960s. *Journal of Contemporary History* 41 (2006), pp. 741–755.

Young, Allan. *The Harmony of Illusions. Inventing Post-Traumatic Stress Disorder.* Princeton, 1995.

Young, Allan. Suffering and the Origins of Traumatic Memory. *Daedalus* 125 (1996), pp. 245–260.

Zaretsky, Eli. *Freuds Jahrhundert. Die Geschichte der Psychoanalyse.* Wien, 2006.

Zertal, Idith. *Nation und Tod. Der Holocaust in der israelischen Öffentlichkeit.* Göttingen, 2003.

Zierenberg, Malte. *Von Schiebern und Schwarzen Märkten. Zur Geschichte des Berliner Schwarzhandels im Übergang vom Zweiten Weltkrieg zur Nachkriegszeit.* Göttingen, 2008.

Zondergeld, Gjalt R. Hans Ernst Schneider und seine Bedeutung für das SS-Ahnenerbe. In Helmut König, et al., eds., pp. 14–30.

Zuckermann, Moshe, ed. *Medien—Politik—Geschichte (Tel Aviver Jahrbuch für deutsche Geschichte, Bd. 31).* Göttingen, 2003.

Index

Academy of Military Medicine in Berlin, 115
acute fright reaction (*akute Schrecken-reaktion*), 121
Allies, 36–37, 43–44, 48, 50, 61, 74, 78; denazification policy of, 62; pension policy of, 142, 185; presence of, in fears of Germans, 43, 74
Andreas-Friedrich, Ruth, 50, 62
anxiety, 13, 38–47, 52, 59, 63–64, 67, 83, 91, 103, 121, 128–33, 137, 151–52, 196, 264–67, 272, 285–86; concerning future, 37, 103–4, 286; concerning punishment among soldiers in postwar Germany, 45–47, 69–80, 84, 286; as conservatory of memory, 38–39; dreams, 32, 264, 275–76, 279; in historiography, 37; spiral of, as Nazi propaganda, 37–38; syndrome (fear of life), 196
Arendt, Hannah, 28–29, 36, 126
army medical inspector's office (*Heeres-sanitätsinspekteur*), 117–18
Association of Returnees (Verband der Heimkehrer), 22, 170–71, 217, 224, 274
Auerbach, Walter, 274
Auschwitz trials, 228, 264–76
autogenic training, 117

Baeyer, Walter von, 125–30, 144, 158–59, 198, 207–25, 272–73
Baky, Josef, 235
Bansi, Hans Wilhelm, 139, 175–76, 183
Beeck, Manfred in der, 130
Beringer, Kurt, 129
Berlin, Irving N., 57

Bodelschwingh Clinics (von Bodel-schwinghsche Anstalten), 20, 161, 166
Bonhoeffer, Karl, 107–13, 117, 129, 211
Borchert, Wolfgang, 138
brain atrophies, 140, 184
Brunn, W., 214–15
Bumke, Oswald, 111
Bürger-Prinz, Hans, 178–79, 267, 271–72

case histories: Adolf W., 52–53, 67–68, 161–62; Alfred J., 56; Dietmar B., 40; Dietmar F., 35–36, 93–94; Eberhard L., 94–96; Eduard S., 163; Egon M., 91; Franz F., 75; Friedrich H., 166–67; Friedrich M., 151–53; Gerd M., 53–54, 86; Gerhard K., 39–40; Günter B., 43; Gustav B., 50–52; Gustav K. 154–59; Gustav N., 45–47, 73; Hans H., 7–10, 89, 92–93; Hans S., 34–35; Helmut G., 56–57, 97–99; Herbert I., 44–45; Herbert L., 86–89; Hermann H., 160–61; Hermann M., 42–43, 163–64; Hubert B., 86; Karl D., 92; Karl W., 163; Kurt A., 84–86; Kurt T., 75–78; Leopold F., 167–69; Ludwig D., 54–55, 74, 94, 148–51; Martin B. 145–47; Martin M., 165; Reinhard G., 58–59, 78–80; Reinhard K., 31–32; Rolf S., 36–37, 43, 65; Rudolf B., 32–34, 66; Rudolf R., 89; Theodor M., 66; Walter M., 70–72; Walter W., 100–102; Werner F., 63–65; Werner P., 41; Werner Z., 90–91; Wilfried M., 58, 73; Wilhelm S., 162; Willi M., 40